Handbook of Social Media and the Law

Handbook of Social Media and the Law

Laura Scaife

informa law
from Routledge

First published 2015
by Informa Law from Routledge
2 Park Square, Milton Park, Abingdon, Oxon OX14 4RN

and by Informa Law from Routledge
711 Third Avenue, New York, NY 10017

Informa Law from Routledge is an imprint of the Taylor & Francis Group, an Informa business

© Laura Scaife 2015

The right of Laura Scaife to be identified as the author of this work has been asserted in accordance with sections 77 and 78 of the Copyright, Designs and Patents Act 1988.

All rights reserved. No part of this book may be reprinted or reproduced or utilized in any form or by any electronic, mechanical, or other means, now known or hereafter invented, including photocopying and recording, or in any information storage or retrieval system, without permission in writing from the publishers.

Trademark notice: Product or corporate names may be trademarks or registered trademarks, and are used only for identification and explanation without intent to infringe.

Every attempt has been made to obtain permission to reproduce copyright material. If any proper acknowledgement has not been made, we would invite copyright holders to inform us of the oversight.

British Library Cataloguing in Publication Data
A catalogue record for this book is available from the British Library

Library of Congress Cataloging-in-Publication Data
Scaife, Laura.
 Handbook of social media and the law / Laura Scaife.
   pages cm
 Includes bibliographical references and index.
 ISBN 978-0-415-74548-2 (hardback) — ISBN 978-1-315-79785-4 (ebook) 1. Social media—Law and legislation—Great Britain. I. Title.
 KD667.C65S27 2014
 343.4109'944—dc23
                                                            2014018176

ISBN 978-0-415-74548-2
eISBN 978-1-31579-785-4

Typeset in Plantin by RefineCatch Limited, Bungay, Suffolk

Printed and bound by CPI Group (UK) Ltd, Croydon, CR0 4YY

This book is dedicated to the memory of my late brother Robert Scaife

Contents

Preface	xxv
Foreword	xxxii
Acknowledgements	xxxv
List of Cases	xxxvi
List of Legislation	xliv

PART 1
Background

1

1 Introduction to social media and the law	3
2 Human rights	21

PART 2
Civil claims

51

3 Defamation	53

PART 3
Criminal liability

125

Part 3.1: Communications-based offences

127

4 Communications Act 2003	129
5 Malicious Communications Act 1988	165
6 Serious Crime Act 2007	167
7 Crime and Disorder Act 1998	175
8 Public Order Act 1986	177
9 Protection from Harassment Act 1997	180

viii *Contents*

10 Computer Misuse Act 1990   183

Part 3.2: Criminal law: procedure   189

11 Contempt of Court Act 1981   191

12 Evidence and procedure   212

PART 4
Commercial law   233

13 Data protection and privacy   235

14 Trading and advertising standards   342

15 FCA regulated bodies   360

16 Insurance   368

Bibliography   372
Index   381

Detailed contents

Preface	xxv
Foreword	xxxii
Acknowledgements	xxxv
List of Cases	xxxvi
List of Legislation	xliv

PART 1

Background   **1**

1 Introduction to social media and the law   **3**

1.1	Introduction	3
	1.1.1 Utility of social media	3
	1.1.2 Background to the development of social media	3
1.2	What is 'social media' and a 'social network'	4
	1.2.1 History	4
	1.2.2 Social interaction	5
	1.2.3 Diagram of social connectivity for users	6
1.3	How social networking sites operate	6
	1.3.1 Nature of information sharing	6
	1.3.2 Nature of information storing	7
1.4	Taxonomy of social networking data	7
	1.4.1 Types of data processed	7
	1.4.2 Summary diagram of monitoring and engagement	8
1.5	Categories of social media	8
	1.5.1 Types of sites	8
	1.5.2 Specific social media platforms explained	9
	1.5.3 Foreign language social networks	12
	1.5.3.1 Belgium	12
	1.5.3.2 Brazil	12
	1.5.3.3 China	12
	1.5.3.4 Greece	13
	1.5.3.5 Hungary	13
	1.5.3.6 Iran	13
	1.5.3.7 Japan	14
	1.5.3.8 Netherlands	14

x *Detailed contents*

		1.5.3.9	Poland	14
		1.5.3.10	Russia	14
		1.5.3.11	Spain	14
		1.5.3.12	Sweden	15
	1.5.4	Vertically organized communities gathered around a specific topic		15
	1.5.5	Mobile-only social networks		16
1.6	Legal classification of SNSs			16
	1.6.1	Locating an SNS within existing statutory frameworks		16
	1.6.2	Information society service provider		16
	1.6.3	Electronic communications service		17
	1.6.4	Intelligence and Security Committee: access to communications data by the intelligence and security agencies		19
1.7	Summary chart			19

2 Human rights   **21**

2.1	Introduction			21
2.2	The European Convention of Human Rights			21
	2.2.1	Nature of rights contained within the European Convention of Human Rights		21
	2.2.2	Convention applicants		22
	2.2.3	Convention respondents		22
2.3	The Human Rights Act 1998			23
	2.3.1	Background		23
	2.3.2	The interpretative obligation		23
	2.3.3	Public authorities		25
		2.3.3.1	Section 6 HRA 1998	25
		2.3.3.2	Locus standi	25
		2.3.3.3	Limitation	26
2.4	Convention rights			26
	2.4.1	Rights of particular application to social networking sites		26
	2.4.2	Article 6: The right to a fair trial		26
	2.4.3	Article 8: The right to privacy		27
		2.4.3.1	Correspondence	28
		2.4.3.2	The concept of a reasonable expectation of privacy	29
	2.4.4	Article 10: Freedom of expression		30
		2.4.4.1	The margin of appreciation and justifying interference	31
	2.4.5	Balancing Article 8 and Article 10		32
		2.4.5.1	Why the rights must be balanced	32
		2.4.5.2	The correct approach towards balancing competing Convention rights	33
2.5	Freedom of expression and human rights in European and international jurisprudence and opinion			35
	2.5.1	International Covenant on Civil and Political Rights 1966		35
	2.5.2	Approach to restrictions and censorship		36

Detailed contents xi

	2.5.3	Special Rapporteur's Joint Declaration on Freedom of Expression	36
		2.5.3.1 Censorship and blocking	37
		2.5.3.2 Role of intermediaries	37
	2.5.4	The United Nations Comprehensive Study on Cybercrime Paper	38
		2.5.4.1 The Committee's reasons for drafting the White Paper	38
		2.5.4.2 The role of national guidelines	38
		2.5.4.3 The Draft Reports analysis of ICCPR and its application to social media	41
2.6	Terrorism		42
	2.6.1	Introduction	42
	2.6.2	Social media and terrorism	43
	2.6.3	Terror groups using social media	43
	2.6.4	US Committee on Homeland Security's Subcommittee on Counterterrorism and Intelligence	44
	2.6.5	Platform providers' response to terrorism	45
		2.6.5.1 Twitter	45
		2.6.5.2 YouTube	47
		2.6.5.3 Facebook	47
	2.6.6	Case law	48
		2.6.6.1 _U.S. v LaRose_ 'Jihad Jane'	49
		2.6.6.2 _State of New York v Jose Pimentel_	49
		2.6.6.3 @Anonymous – Arab Spring	49

PART 2
Civil claims   51

3 Defamation   53

3.1	Application to social media	53
3.2	Sources of defamation law	54
3.3	The Defamation Act 2013	54
	3.3.1 Background to reform	54
	3.3.2 Technology outstripping the law	55
	3.3.3 Meeting of the Culture, Media and Sport Committee of the House of Commons	55
	3.3.4 The journey to the Bill	55
		3.3.4.1 Joint Committee on the Draft Defamation Bill	56
		3.3.4.2 The Bill in Parliament	56
		3.3.4.3 Suggestions that did not make the final cut	57
3.4	A defamation claim: what is defamation and what is needed to bring a claim?	57
	3.4.1 Who can sue?	57
	3.4.2 What is defamation?	58
	3.4.3 The 'essential ingredients' of an action	58
3.5	The distinction between libel and slander	59

xii *Detailed contents*

3.6	A defamatory statement	60
	3.6.1 Does the statement convey a defamatory meaning?	60
	3.6.2 Determining the meaning of words	61
	3.6.2.1 Social media: specific considerations	61
3.7	The Test of Substantial Harm	64
	3.7.1 Position prior to the Defamation Act 2013	64
	3.7.2 Joint Committee's Report on the Draft Defamation Bill	64
	3.7.2.1 Nature of the publication	65
	3.7.3 The Government's response to the Joint Committee's Report on the Draft Defamation Bill	65
	3.7.4 Summary	66
	3.7.4.1 Summary of substantial harm and key considerations	66
	3.7.4.2 Summary chart	67
	3.7.5 The test of substantial harm in relation to 'entities that trade for a profit'	67
3.8	Publication	69
	3.8.1 Introduction	69
	3.8.2 Primary and secondary publishers	69
	3.8.2.1 Hyperlinks	70
	3.8.2.2 Search engines	72
	3.8.2.3 'Facebook rape'	72
	3.8.3 Size of audience	73
3.9	The single publication rule	73
	3.9.1 Limitation period	73
	3.9.2 Background to section 8 of the Defamation Act 2013	73
	3.9.3 Section 8 of the Defamation Act 2013	74
	3.9.4 Archiving and re-tweets	75
	3.9.5 Republication: re-tweets	76
	3.9.6 Comparison with United States	77
3.10	Section 10 actions against secondary publishers	78
	3.10.1 Introduction	78
	3.10.2 Common law position	78
	3.10.3 Interrelationship with section 5 of the Defamation Act 2013	79
3.11	Jurisdiction	80
	3.11.1 Introduction	80
	3.11.2 The approach of the Defamation Act 2013 to actions against persons not domiciled in the UK or a Member State, etc.	81
3.12	Self-regulation by social media sites	82
	3.12.1 Site terms	82
	3.12.2 Facebook	83
	3.12.2.1 Groups	83
	3.12.3 Twitter	83
	3.12.4 Practical considerations for businesses and organizations	84
	3.12.5 Self-help measures for ISPs	85

3.13	Defences	86
	3.13.1 Truth	86
	3.13.1.1 A new statutory defence of truth	86
	3.13.1.2 The 'repetition rule'	86
	3.13.2 Honest opinion	87
	3.13.2.1 New statutory defence of honest opinion	87
	3.13.2.2 Conditions for defence to apply	87
	3.13.2.3 Defeating the defence	89
	3.13.2.4 Repeal of Section 6	89
	3.13.3 Publication on matters of public interest	89
	3.13.3.1 Creation of a new defence for matters of public interest	89
	3.13.3.2 Reportage	90
	3.13.3.3 Role of editorial judgment	90
	3.13.4 The new defence for website operators	90
	3.13.4.1 Section 5 of the Defamation Act 2013	90
	3.13.4.2 Defeating the defence	92
	3.13.4.3 Service of a claim via a social networking site	92
3.14	The Defamation (Operators of Websites) Regulations 2013	95
	3.14.1 Defamation (Operators of Websites) Regulations 2013	95
	3.14.2 Procedure	96
	3.14.3 Editorial control	96
	3.14.4 Moderated sites	97
3.15	Other defences	97
	3.15.1 Introduction	97
	3.15.2 Section 1 of the Defamation Act 1996	97
	3.15.3 Regulation 19 of the Electronic Commerce (EC Directive) Regulations 2002	98
3.16	Offers of Amends	98
	3.16.1 Background to the Defamation Act 1996 reforms	98
	3.16.1.1 General	98
	3.16.1.2 The offer	100
	3.16.1.3 Timing of the offer	102
	3.16.1.4 Qualified offers	102
	3.16.1.5 Disagreements as to meaning and interpretation	102
	3.16.1.6 Consecutive or multiple allegations – part offers	103
	3.16.1.7 Withdrawal or substitution of the Offer of Amends	104
	3.16.1.8 Acceptance of the offer	104
	3.16.2 Multiple defendants – publication by more than one party	105
	3.16.3 Effective offers: practical considerations	106
	3.16.3.1 A suitable correction and sufficient apology	106
	3.16.4 Apologies	108
	3.16.5 Publication problems presented by social media	108
	3.16.5.1 Re-tweets	108
	3.16.5.2 @replies: other users	109

xiv *Detailed contents*

3.16.6 Additional incentives to accept the offer	110
3.16.6.1 Proof of deletion	110
3.16.6.2 Undertakings	111
3.16.6.3 Hiring a social media expert	111
3.16.6.4 Facebook wall posts and statuses	111
3.16.7 Damages	111
3.16.7.1 Introduction	111
3.16.7.2 Stalemate situations: disagreement as to damages and apologies	113
3.16.7.3 The court's case management powers	114
3.16.7.4 Qualified offers	115
3.16.7.5 Costs and damages in lieu of a specific agreement	115
3.16.8 Non-acceptance	116
3.16.9 Disqualification	116
3.16.9.1 When offers will be disqualified	116
3.16.9.2 Knowledge	117
3.16.9.3 Reason to believe	117
3.16.9.4 The interrelationship with other defences	119
3.16.9.5 Claimant refuses to accept a qualified offer	119
3.16.10 Rejection of the offer by the claimant	120
3.16.11 Considerations for claimants	121
3.16.12 Considerations for defendants	122
3.17 Part 36 offer	123
3.18 Summary judgment	123

PART 3
Criminal liability   125

Part 3.1: Communications-based offences   127

4 Communications Act 2003   **129**

4.1 Introduction	129
4.2 Section 127 Communications Act 2003	130
4.2.1 Background to the Communications Act 2003	130
4.2.2 The meaning of 'gross offence'	131
4.2.2.1 *Actus reus*	132
4.2.2.2 *Mens rea*	132
4.2.2.3 *DPP v Chambers*	134
4.2.2.4 *Woods*	135
4.2.2.5 Tom Daley	138
4.3 CPS interim guidance	139
4.3.1 The Interim Guidelines	139
4.3.2 The General Principles	139
4.3.3 Cases that fall within paragraphs 12(1), 12(2) or 12(3)	141
4.3.3.1 Credible threats	141
4.3.3.2 Aggravating factors	141

		4.3.3.3 Communications targeting specific individuals	141
		4.3.3.4 Breach of court orders	142
		4.3.3.5 Cases that fall within paragraph 12(4)	142
		4.3.3.6 The high threshold	143
		4.3.3.7 Summary	143
		4.3.3.8 Children and young people	144
	4.3.4	Interrelationship with the Human Rights Act and speech value	145
		4.3.4.1 Introduction	145
		4.3.4.2 Speech value and the European Court of Human Rights	145
		4.3.4.3 Context and intent	146
	4.3.5	Cases decided after the implementation of the Guidelines	147
		4.3.5.1 Isabella Sorley and John Nimmo	147
		4.3.5.2 Issues of anonymity	148
		4.3.5.3 Private entrapment	149
	4.3.6	Summary diagrams of CPS Guidelines	152
	4.3.7	Refining the CPS model	153
		4.3.7.1 A two-tier approach	153
		4.3.7.2 The Theft Act 1988	153
	4.3.8	The role of platform providers	155
		4.3.8.1 Leveson	155
		4.2.8.2 Public electronic communications network	155
		4.3.8.3 France: #unbonjuif	157
		4.3.8.4 Germany: Besseres-Hannover-@hannoverticker	159
		4.3.8.5 Facebook Community Standards	159
	4.3.9	Censorship and monitoring	160
		4.3.9.1 Interrelationship with human rights	160
		4.3.9.2 China	160
		4.3.9.3 Real-name requirement	161
		4.3.9.4 South Korea	162
	4.3.10 Summary		163

5 Malicious Communications Act 1988 — 165

	5.1	Background	165
	5.2	Section 1 of the Malicious Communications Act 1988	165
	5.3	Distinguishing the Malicious Communications Act 1988 from the Communications Act 2003 – 'sent to another person'	166
		5.3.1 Comparison with the Communications Act 2003	166
		5.3.2 Tagging and open posts/tweets	166

6 Serious Crime Act 2007 — 167

	6.1	Background	167
	6.2	House of Commons Justice Committee White Paper	167
	6.3	Sections 44 and 46 of the Serious Crime Act 2007	168

xvi *Detailed contents*

		6.3.1	Section 44: Intentionally encouraging or assisting an offence	168
		6.3.2	Section 46: Encouraging or assisting offences believing one or more will be committed	168
		6.3.3	Section 19: Serious Crime Prevention Orders	168
	6.4	Case Law		169
		6.4.1	Recent development of a body of case law	169
		6.4.2	*R v Blackshaw*	169
		6.4.3	*R v Perry John Sutcliffe-Keenan*	171
			6.4.3.1 Attempts by the defendant to mitigate actions	171
		6.4.4	*R v Pelle*	172
			6.4.4.1 Intent	173
		6.4.5	*R v Bentley*	174

7 Crime and Disorder Act 1998 — **175**
- 7.1 Background — 175
- 7.2 Section 31 Crime and Disorder Act 1998 — 175
- 7.3 Case law — 175
  - 7.3.1 *R v Cryer* — 175
    - 7.3.1.1 Aggravating factors — 175
    - 7.3.1.2 Mitigation — 176
    - 7.3.1.3 Sentencing — 176

8 Public Order Act 1986 — **177**
- 8.1 Introduction — 177
- 8.2 Case law — 177
  - 8.2.1 *R v Stacey* — 177
    - 8.2.1.1 Continuing availability of the posts — 178
    - 8.2.1.2 Role of remorse — 178
    - 8.2.1.3 Factors put forward in mitigation — 178
    - 8.2.1.4 Effect of Alcohol — 179
- 8.3 The CPS Interim Guidelines on cases involving social media — 179
- 8.4 Role of Part III of the Act — 179

9 Protection from Harassment Act 1997 — **180**
- 9.1 Introduction — 180
- 9.2 Sections 1 and 4 of the Protection from Harassment Act 1997 — 180
  - 9.2.1 Conduct amounting to harassment — 180
  - 9.2.2 Sentencing — 180
- 9.3 Section 4 — 181
- 9.4 Restraining orders — 181
- 9.5 Home Office Review of 'The Protection from Harassment Act 1997: Improving Protection for Victims of Stalking' — 182

10 Computer Misuse Act 1990 — **183**
- 10.1 Introduction — 183
- 10.2 Section 1 of the Computer Misuse Act 1990 — 183
  - 10.2.1 Sentencing — 183

Detailed contents   xvii

10.3	Section 3 of the Computer Misuse Act 1990	184
	10.3.1 Sentencing	184
10.4	Case law	185
	10.4.1 *R v Gareth Crosskey*	185
	10.4.2 *R v Glenn Mangham*	185
	10.4.2.1 Accessing servers and restricted areas on SNS servers	185
	10.4.2.2 Mitigating factors	186
	10.4.2.3 Aggravating factors	186
	10.4.2.4 Challenges presented by sentencing	187

Part 3.2: Criminal law: procedure   189

11   Contempt of Court Act 1981   191

11.1	Introduction	191
11.2	Challenges presented by social media	191
11.3	What is contempt of court?	192
11.4	The meaning of 'communication'	193
11.5	The meaning of a publication	193
11.6	Requirement to be 'addressed to the public'	194
11.7	Section 8 Contempt of Court Act 1981: contempt by jurors	194
	11.7.1 Law Commission's White Paper	194
	11.7.2 Section 8 of the Contempt of Court Act 1981	194
	11.7.3 Impact of social media upon juror deliberations	195
	11.7.4 Jurors conducting their own research on the internet and deliberate disobedience of jury directions	196
11.8	Law Commission's Report and *Your Guide to the Jury Service*	196
11.9	Video: the role of a juror	196
11.10	Court staff warning	197
11.11	The courts' approach to dealing with technology	197
11.12	Jurors' ability to recall directions	198
	11.12.1 Role of jurors, their duties, their intention, and their ability to recall directions for the court	198
	11.12.2 Submissions in defence	199
	11.12.3 Submissions in relation to creating a real risk of interference or prejudice to the administration of justice	199
	11.12.4 Role of jury booklet, the video, the speech by the jury manager, and the warning signs as directions which jurors must follow	200
11.13	Injunctions and protected proceedings	201
	11.13.1 *Attorney General v Harkins and Liddle*	201
	11.13.1.1 Sentencing	204
	11.13.1.2 Aggravating factors	204
	11.13.1.3 Mitigating factors	205
	11.13.2 *Attorney General v Baines*	205
	11.13.2.1 Aggravating factors	206
	11.13.2.2 Mitigating factors	206

xviii *Detailed contents*

11.14 Protected proceedings	208
11.14.1 Children and Young Persons Act 1933	208
11.14.2 Publications by private individuals	208
11.15 Injunctions granted in relation to social media specifically	209
11.15.1 *W v M*	209
11.15.2 Court of Protection Rules 2007	209
11.15.2.1 Rule 92(2) Court of Protection Rules 2007	209
11.15.2.2 Legal basis for reporting restrictions	210
11.16 Future advisory notes from the Attorney General	211
11.17 Incorporated Council of Law Reporting (ICLR) blog post on 'The internet, social media and contempt of court: some recent developments'	211

12 Evidence and procedure **212**

12.1 Introduction	212
12.2 The use of evidence from social networking sites in criminal proceedings	212
12.2.1 Types of proceedings to which SNS evidence has had application	212
12.2.2 Types of data exhibited	213
12.2.3 Activity on social networking sites that may amount to criminal activity	213
12.2.4 Interrelationship with Article 6 of the Human Rights Act 1998	213
12.2.5 Comparison with United States	214
12.2.5.1 Federal Rule of Evidence 401	214
12.2.5.2 Establishing admissibility	214
12.3 Investigating known suspects	214
12.4 Identifying suspects	215
12.4.1 Use of SNS data	215
12.4.2 Safeguards for authorities seeking to adduce such evidence	216
12.4.3 Risk of vigilantism	216
12.5 Bad character	217
12.5.1 Defendants	217
12.5.1.1 Admissibility of bad character evidence	217
12.5.1.2 Definition of bad character	218
12.5.1.3 Admissibility	218
12.5.1.4 Exclusion of bad character evidence	219
12.5.1.5 Powers of the court	220
12.5.1.6 Defendants: SNS activity as bad character	221
12.5.2 Co-defendants	222
12.5.2.1 Adducing evidence under section 101(1)(e)	222
12.5.2.2 Publically available information	222
12.5.2.3 Fabrications, spiteful postings, and exaggeration	222
12.5.3 Confessions	222

12.5.4	Bad character of non-defendants		223
	12.5.4.1	Definition of non-defendants	223
	12.5.4.2	Protection of feelings and reputation	223
	12.5.4.3	Admissibility	223
	12.5.4.4	Malicious motives or willingness to give false evidence	224
12.5.5	Witness testimony		224
	12.5.5.1	Witness's previous statements	224
	12.5.5.2	Previous inconsistent statements	225
12.5.6	Compelling a suspect to reveal his SNS password		225
12.5.7	Authentication issues		226
	12.5.7.1	Definition of a document	226
	12.5.7.2	Guidance on authentication for judges	226
	12.5.7.3	Proof of authorship	226
12.5.8	Excluding social media evidence		229
	12.5.8.1	Introduction	229
	12.5.8.2	Hearsay	229

PART 4
Commercial law 233

13 Data protection and privacy 235

13.1	Application to social media		235
	13.1.1	General	235
	13.1.2	Issues raised by social media	236
	13.1.3	Committee of Ministers for the Council of Europe	237
	13.1.4	Application to businesses	237
13.2	What is privacy and why is it protected?		238
	13.2.1	Social media and data protection in the context of privacy	238
	13.2.2	Application of privacy and individuals' right of protection	238
	13.2.3	Defining 'privacy': a brief history	238
	13.2.4	Defining 'privacy' in the modern sphere	240
	13.2.5	Interrelationship with data security	240
13.3	History of data protection legislation		241
	13.3.1	Introduction	241
	13.3.2	The Younger Committee Report	242
	13.3.3	The Lindop Report	242
	13.3.4	The OECD Guidelines	242
	13.3.5	The Data Protection Act 1984	243
	13.3.6	The 1995 EU Directive	243
	13.3.7	Article 29 Working Party and Europe	243
	13.3.8	The Rome Memorandum	245
		13.3.8.1 Children and minors	246
	13.3.9	Facebook's audit	246
	13.3.10	The Data Protection Act 1998	248

xx   *Detailed contents*

13.3.11	Draft European General Data Protection Regulation	248
13.3.12	Leveson	250

13.4 The Data Protection Act 1998 250

13.4.1	Framework created by the Data Protection Act 1998	250
13.4.2	Application to social networking sites	251
13.4.3	The Rome Memorandum 2008	251
13.4.4	Scope of DPA 1998 and definitions	253
	13.4.4.1 Data controllers and data processors	253
	13.4.4.2 Data controller	253
	13.4.4.3 Processors	256
	13.4.4.4 ICO guidance on identifying data controllers and data processors	256
	13.4.4.5 Contracts	256
	13.4.4.6 Data Protection Directive	257
	13.4.4.7 Article 29 Working Party standard clauses	257
13.4.5	The eight principles of data protection	257
13.4.6	The meaning of processing	258
13.4.7	The meaning of a data subject	258
13.4.8	The meaning of personal data	259
	13.4.8.1 Sensitive personal data: additional rules	262
	13.4.8.2 IP addresses	262
13.4.9	Conditions for processing	263
	13.4.9.1 General rules for conditions for processing	263
	13.4.9.2 Additional rules for sensitive personal data	264
13.4.10	The rights of data subjects	264
13.4.11	Consent	265
	13.4.11.1 Meaning of consent	265
	13.4.11.2 Further consents for new processing activities	266
	13.4.11.3 Cookies	267
13.4.12	Accuracy of data	268
	13.4.12.1 Principle 4 of the DPA 1998	268
	13.4.12.2 Online forums	269
	13.4.12.3 The right to prevent processing likely to cause damage or distress	276
	13.4.12.4 Rectification, erasure blocking, and destruction	277
	13.4.12.5 Erasure and the right to be forgotten	278
	13.4.12.6 Steps for seeking the removal of data online	284
	13.4.12.7 Retention of personal data	285
	13.4.12.8 Data transfers by third parties	287
	13.4.12.9 Mobility and geolocation	291
13.4.13	Direct marketing	294
	13.4.13.1 Value of social media	294
	13.4.13.2 Types of marketing conducted via social media	294
	13.4.13.3 Section 11(3) DPA 1998	295
13.4.14	Fair processing and consent	295

13.4.14.1	Information that must be provided to data subjects	295
13.4.14.2	European data regulators place spotlight on using legitimate interests as a ground for data processing	296
13.4.14.3	Privacy and Electronic Communications Regulations	297
13.4.14.4	The Data Protection Directive	299
13.4.14.5	Personal messages	299
13.4.15	Compensation	299
13.4.15.1	Section 13 DPA 1998	299
13.4.15.2	Recital 118 and Article 79 DPR	301
13.4.16	The right to object to profiling	301
13.4.16.1	Social media sites' use of profiling	301
13.4.16.2	Data Protection Directive's approach to profiling under DPR	303
13.4.16.3	Practical tips in relation to marketing	304
13.4.16.4	Interrelationship with the criminal law	304
13.4.17	The right to access data	305
13.4.17.1	Sections 7 and 8 of the DPA 1998	305
13.4.17.2	Opinion of the Article 29 Working Party	306
13.4.17.3	The ICO's Code on Subject Access Requests	307
13.4.17.4	Subject access requests made via social networking sites	308
13.4.17.5	Exemptions	309
13.4.17.6	Disproportionate effort	310
13.4.17.7	Dealing with repeated or unreasonable requests	310
13.4.17.8	DPR	311
13.4.18	Jurisdiction	312
13.4.18.1	Applicability of DPA 1998 to establishments located overseas	312
13.4.18.2	DPR	313
13.4.18.3	Overseas transfers of data	315
13.4.18.4	Ensuring adequacy via other means	319
13.4.19	Breach notification	322
13.4.19.1	Reporting a breach	322
13.4.19.2	ICO PECR security breach guidance	322
13.4.19.3	When and how to notify customers	323
13.4.19.4	Notifying breaches to subscribers	323
13.4.19.5	Risks of using automated systems – reputation management	324
13.5	Terms and conditions and privacy policies	325
13.5.1	Introduction	325
13.5.2	What is a privacy statement?	325
13.5.3	Incorporation issues	325
13.5.4	Unfair Terms in Consumer Contract Regulations 1999 (Regulations)	326

xxii *Detailed contents*

	13.5.5 Terms of use (terms and conditions)	326
	13.5.5.1 Being bound by the terms of use	326
	13.5.5.2 Unilateral right to vary the terms	326
	13.5.5.3 Reserving wide discretion	326
	13.5.5.4 Technical jargon	327
	13.5.5.5 Assessing what data an organization is gathering	327
	13.5.5.6 Making sure that individuals understand	328
	13.5.5.7 Data utilization and monetization	328
	13.5.5.8 Aggregate data	330
	13.5.5.9 Use of 'Like' buttons, 'plug-ins' and 'analytics' by social media sites	330
	13.5.5.10 Facebook Beacon	332
13.6	Guidance for social networking providers	335
	13.6.1 General recommendations	335
	13.6.2 List of recommendations	336
	13.6.2.1 Privacy policy/data use policy	336
	13.6.2.2 Advertising	336
	13.6.2.3 Access requests	337
	13.6.2.4 Retention	337
	13.6.2.5 Cookies/social plug-ins	337
	13.6.2.6 Third party apps	338
	13.6.2.7 Disclosures to third parties	339
	13.6.2.8 Facial recognition/tag suggestion	339
	13.6.2.9 Data security	339
	13.6.2.10 Deletion of accounts	340
	13.6.2.11 Friend finder	340
	13.6.2.12 Tagging	340
	13.6.2.13 Posting on other profiles	340
	13.6.2.14 Pseudonymous profiles	341
	13.6.2.15 Abuse reporting	341
	13.6.2.16 Compliance management/governance	341
13.7	Practical guidance for individuals	341

14 Trading and advertising standards   **342**

14.1	Introduction	342
14.2	Application to social media context	342
14.3	Regulatory bodies	343
14.4	The Committee of Advertising Practice Code (CAP)	344
	14.4.1 Application of the Code	344
	14.4.2 Extension of the remit of the Code to the social media context	344
	14.4.3 Exceptions	345
	14.4.3.1 Editorials and press releases	345
	14.4.4 Heritage advertising	345
	14.4.5 Sanctions	345
14.5	Consumer Protection from Unfair Trading Regulations 2008	345
	14.5.1 Application in social media context	345

	14.5.2 Enforcement	347
	14.5.3 Legislative and Regulatory Reform Act 2006	347
	14.5.4 Site terms and conditions	347
14.6	Indirect marketing and falsely holding out as a consumer	347
14.7	Paid promotions	348
14.8	United States of America	350
	14.8.1 The Federal Trade Commission	350
	14.8.2 The Word of Mouth Marketing Association	350
	14.8.3 Space-constrained tweets	351
	14.8.4 #spon	351
	14.8.5 bit.ly	352
	14.8.6 Series of related tweets	352
14.9	Contractual obligation to promote the company even if the form of the message is not determined by the advertiser	353
14.10	Links to paid subscriptions	354
14.11	Clarity of adverts' content	355
14.12	Endorsements and testimonials by bloggers	355
	14.12.1 Blurring advertising and blogs – why it pays to know the Ad Rules	355
	14.12.2 Companies and PR agencies looking to enter into commercial relationships with bloggers	356
	14.12.3 Commercial considerations and reputation management	357
	14.12.4 Approach taken in US by the Federal Trade Commission	357
14.13	Summary chart	358
14.14	Advergames	359
15	**FCA regulated bodies**	**360**
15.1	Introduction	360
15.2	Financial promotions using new media	360
	15.2.1 Background	360
	15.2.2 What is a financial promotion?	361
	15.2.3 Relationship with the Financial Promotion Rules	361
	15.2.3.1 COBS 4: Communicating with clients, including financial promotions	361
	15.2.3.2 BCOBS 2: Communications with banking customers and financial promotions	362
	15.2.3.3 ICOBS 2: General matters	362
	15.2.3.4 MCOB3: Financial promotion of qualifying credit, home reversion plans and regulated sale and rent back agreements	362
15.3	The FSA's 2010 review	362
	15.3.1 FSA's research of social media sites	362
	15.3.2 Findings	363
15.4	Non-promotional communications	363
15.5	Image advertisements	363
15.6	Stand-alone compliance	364

xxiv *Detailed contents*

15.7	Requirements for social media postings	364
15.8	2014 Guidance?	365
15.9	Penalties for breaching the financial promotions regime	365
	15.9.1 Disciplinary action	365
	15.9.2 Other penalties	366
15.10	What should firms consider before using new media?	366
	15.10.1 Checklist of social media issues	366
	15.10.2 Use of checklists	367

16 Insurance   **368**

16.1	Purchasing insurance against social media claims	368
16.2	Common areas of exposure to risk	368
16.3	ABI report	368
16.4	Coverage	369
	16.4.1 Areas to consider	369
	16.4.2 Publicity coverage	370
	16.4.3 Third-party loss	370
16.5	Key coverage enhancements to seek	370

Bibliography	372
Index	381

Preface

What is the argument on the other side? Only this that no case has been found in which it has been done before. That argument does not appeal to me in the least. If we never do anything which has not been done before, we shall never get anywhere. The law will stand still whilst the rest of the world goes on; and that will be bad for both.[1]

Lord Denning, *Packer v Packer*

The explosion of the digital age has revolutionized the way that individuals engage with mass media, putting knowledge at their fingertips. In 2014, the number of active mobile phones will exceed 7 billion. It is in mobile where IT growth is mainly happening. The unique combination of mobile's features, such as 24/7 access and internet connectivity, fuels consumer desire for the deployment of new and innovative applications. In particular, social networking sites have changed the way in which individuals socialise with one another, acting as a giant digital coffee shop for the exchange of ideas and connection of individuals regardless of geographical borders. The incredible reach of social media brings with it many positive benefits but also risks for consumers and businesses alike. Inevitably, where technology leads, the law eventually follows. One of the most fascinating aspects of the law in this area is its dynamic quality. Once this book goes to print, new cases, guidelines, and views will occur that will lead to further developments in the law. Thankfully, the advent of the internet also allows for case updates which will be issued at intervals in conjunction with this text so that readers can benefit from the most up-to-date analysis of the law.

I hope that you enjoy reading this text, challenging the views presented, and considering your own analysis of the law as much as I did during the writing of the book.

The Handbook: a fresh approach to understanding the law

This Handbook explores a range of areas of law upon which social media has had an impact or resulted in changes to the law. While there is no 'stand alone' concept of 'social media law', this Handbook seeks to provoke discussion on the topic as is applicable to modern business and media courses that involve aspects of social media. The range of law that social media has impacted upon is significant and diverse, including everything from the criminal law to how advertisers market to consumers.

---

1   The Right Honourable Lord Denning, OM, PC, DL, *Packer v Packer* [1954] P. 15 at 22.

xxvi *Preface*

To date, there is no text that covers the specific issues highlighted by social media and presents them in a practical, easily accessible manner by reference to contemporaneous examples and looks at how to resolve the issues that social media presents. This Handbook is designed to familiarize you with issues surrounding social media and its interrelationship with the law and introduce you to key cases, statutes, and guidance notes surrounding its regulation.

In addition to an exploration of the 'black letter law' in order to aid learning, the Handbook will include the following study aids:

- Flowcharts
- Checklists
- Tables of Key Cases
- Case Studies

It is hoped that organizing the law in this way will assist in bringing issues alive and encourage businesses and academics alike to consider the real impact of social media on the law and upon everyday business and expressive activity.

Practitioners

The Handbook takes a new approach to the law, including practical tips for claimants and defendants, looking at innovative ways to handle claims using the existing law, and working within the rules of the platform providers themselves. The Handbook offers a grounding of the basic legal landscape in the law and then goes on to explore tactical considerations (from a claimant and defendant perspective) which practitioners need to be alive to, and includes explanatory tables and practical drafting tips. It is fully acknowledged that books exist which seek to present the law in a compendious manner, and the intention of this Handbook is not to compete with these eminent and respected texts. Rather, the aim of this Handbook is to look at social media in depth, placing the law within the legal framework in which social networks operate and considering how different areas of law interact in relation to social media (e.g. marketing and privacy).

The text therefore offers the opportunity to look at areas in which the law crosses over and identifies where aspects of the law may intersect and the effect that this may have in terms of case management and case analysis. It is also envisaged that through considering key concerns for businesses (e.g. reputation management), practitioners will be able to look at how the law affects their clients' day-to-day business operations and offer practical advice that addresses their key concerns and business objectives. It is suggested that this fresh approach to legal resources and knowledge development will allow practitioners to address their clients' commercial challenges and added value to their legal offerings by looking at how to obey the law, rather than solely address the results arising from a lack of compliance.

Students and academics

For the academic community, the exploration of social media and the law has begun to grow significantly in the past few years. However, there are few texts that seek to draw together different areas of the law and consider them in a holistic way. This

Preface xxvii

Handbook has been designed to offer students grounding in the basis of the law, which will allow them to learn about the key issues social media presents to the application and development of the law. The text can be used as a course book for legal, journalism, business, and marketing courses, acting as a discussion point and learning tool for understanding this evolving body of law, which is, at times, complex.

Businesses

For stakeholders in the law, such as in-house counsel and those charged with dealing with business management (e.g. HR, IT, and Marketing departments), the departure away from the traditional legal textbook model towards a commercial handbook will allow them to explore the law and assist them with locating and understanding the latest legal developments that directly affect their businesses. It will also allow them to consider not only how to deal with claims, but also to explore the risks which social media may present in a manner that allows them to determine what procedures, policies, specifications, and standards must be adopted in terms of a given organization's internal governance and how to build regulatory frameworks around how to achieve compliance.

In order to assist businesses, the Handbook includes throughout its chapters compliance and risk 'points to note', which will assist in the identification, assessment, and prioritization of risks presented by that particular aspect of the law, followed by coordinated and economical application of resources to minimize, monitor, and control the probability and/or impact of unfortunate events or to maximise the realization of opportunities.

The Handbook will offer these stakeholders ideas as to how to work towards ensuring that personnel are aware of, and take steps to comply with, relevant laws and regulations in a pro active rather than reactionary manner. The book will also allow businesses to consider who should be dealing with social media issues within organizations and address the key concerns raised by businesses and individuals. The types of issues that will be considered include:

- How social media can assist a business's customer service function, marketing, distribution of information, brand monitoring, and research and development.
- Current trends in how businesses are using social media to move away from traditional 'push' marketing and encourage greater engagement with their customers and employees.
- Who should represent a brand on social media channels; should it be managed in-house or outsourced to an agency?
- Examining the potential risk areas associated with social media and how to manage those risks in order to avoid future problems.

How this book is organized

This book comprises 16 chapters, each focusing on a different area of the law that has seen significant developments as a result of the growth in social media and the special measures and issues that practitioners and businesses need to consider in order to minimize their exposure to risk. It is recommended that the book is read from cover xxviii *Preface*

to cover so that the reader gets an understanding of how the different areas of law interact and to understand the risks social media presents. The chapters also stand on their own, offering a useful and comprehensive guide to a specific area of law that readers can focus on, and to consider a specific area that may be of paramount concern, offering readers the flexibility they need when exploring these wide and often complex and overlapping areas of law.

Chapter summaries

The first two chapters of this book are introductory in nature and are designed to give the reader a grounding in the ways in which social media sites are defined in law, how they are organized technically, and the principles of human rights law that underlie the application of the law to social media. It is recommended that you look at these chapters before focusing on a particular area of interest, as they will help you to understand the rationale for the ways in which the courts and policy-makers have developed the law.

Chapter 1: Introduction to social media and the law

This chapter considers what is meant by a 'social network', and looks at some of the main sites through which social media operates. The chapter looks at sites that are popular in the UK and the USA, and sites that are popular internationally, which have large followings but which many not be familiar to western audiences. The chapter goes on to consider how social media websites work at a technical level and the ways in which the law has sought to locate sites within the existing legal landscape.

Chapter 2: Human rights

Social media has raised many questions in relation to the conflicting rights of privacy and freedom of expression. This chapter considers some of the basic principles of social media law and looks at some of the key cases that have developed privacy law at a UK and European level. The chapter also considers the way in which international instruments such as the International Covenant on Civil and Political Rights 1966 have informed the development of the application of civil and human rights law to the arena of social media.

Chapter 3: Defamation

Chapter 3 considers how defamation law has altered as a result of the explosion of internet communication and the ways in which comments made in haste or poor taste can become the subject matter of defamation proceedings. The chapter looks at the role of the post itself, re-publication, re-tweets, tweets taken out of context, and what if any role emoticons play when determining if a comment is defamatory and the extent of the reputational harm or distress it has caused the claimant and what this may mean in terms of damages.

The chapter considers the challenges that this has presented for the courts and the background to the introduction of the Defamation Act 2013. Much of the chapter concentrates on defamation proceedings in practice and looks at how those who have been accused of posting defamatory content online may wish to defend a claim or indeed apologize for the content of the postings made. For those faced with libellous comments made about themselves or their business, the chapter looks at reputation management and the ways in which 'anonymous posters' can be tracked down to serve them with proceedings.

Chapters 4–9: Communications-based offences

Chapter 4: Communications Act 2003; Chapter 5: Malicious Communications Act 1988; Chapter 6: Serious Crime Act 2007; Chapter 7: Crime and Disorder Act 1998; Chapter 8: Public Order Act 1986; Chapter 9: Protection from Harassment Act 1997.

Chapters 4–9 consider the potential for the criminalization of postings online and the issues this presents in terms of protecting individuals' rights to freedom of expression. The chapters look at each of the key statutes under which prosecutions can be pursued and the case law that has come before the courts to date.

The chapter looks at the aggravating and mitigating factors in relation to various types of postings such as those inciting terrorism, those which contain distasteful content, and cases which are jokes which have got out of control.

Each chapter considers the key elements that must be considered in order to pursue a prosecution and looks at some of the key issues that could be raised in defence.

Chapter 10: Computer Misuse Act 1990

The chapter on computer misuse focuses on offences where users have interfered with the infrastructure of the social networking sites themselves, often accessing their servers and the risks this has presented in terms of data security. The key elements of each offence under the Communications Act 2003, so far as applicable to social media are considered, together with the sentences that may be delivered and the sorts of issues that may aggravate or mitigate a crime based on its particular facts.

Chapter 10 may usefully be compared with Chapter 13, on data protection and security, for those looking to understand what assurances sites can give in terms of the security of user data and the vulnerability of the systems which 'hackers' have brought to light in these criminal cases.

Chapters 11–12: Criminal law: procedure

Chapter 11: Contempt of Court Act 1981; Chapter 12: Evidence and Procedure.

Chapters 11 and 12 have been sectioned together so that readers can gain an understanding of the impact that social media has had in terms of the management of cases, the ways in which social media evidence can be presented at court, as well as the procedural hurdles that must be overcome in order to adduce social media postings as evidence.

Chapter 11 looks at the dangers that jurors posting about trials can have on the administration of justice and how injunctions can become meaningless when stories go 'viral'. Chapter 12 looks at the problems of presenting social media evidence where it cannot be shown that the person about whom it is adduced was telling the truth or merely being boastful.

xxx   *Preface*

Chapter 13: Data protection and privacy

The Data Protection Act 1998, which presently governs the regulation of data in the UK, is a difficult piece of legislation, but data protection is simple in concept and does not need to be complicated or difficult in practice or when considering how it applies to social media.

This chapter will take you through the main compliance issues and alerts you to the possible pitfalls without wasting your time on aspects that are unlikely to be relevant to social media, and also considers how the law may change in the future as a result of draft regulations and directives that are being considered and refined at an EU-wide level.

The chapter also looks at data monetization and how to increase data utilization in a legally compliant way. The chapter also looks at conducting online campaigns via websites, apps, and the risks presented when linking your service to that of a social networking site. The chapter considers the importance of privacy policies and what must be contained within them and how to validly incorporate these terms into the contracts that you have with customers. The chapter will help businesses to understand what they can do, rather than focusing on what they cannot do, and takes a pragmatic and commercially driven approach to data protection.

Chapter 14: Trading and advertising standards

Social networking sites are essentially self-promoting, in that users spread the word for the sites. In a world where instant communication prevails, tweets, re-tweets, and viral messages, not to mention video clips, projected via an array of digital platforms are the quickest means of spreading a marketing message. The more quickly social networking sites grow, the more quickly the content uploaded to them spreads. This viral quality is therefore an appealing way for businesses to market their products and services. Social media platforms are sophisticated enough to enable specific targeted advertisement (e.g. on Facebook) or to enable companies to provide adverts and links to existing offerings such as online shops on their website. A tweet, for example, could have the direct link imbedded along with an advert highlighting the arrival of the company's latest products or services. It is for these reason that many advertisers have chosen to conduct consumer promotions involving social media to generate attention to and participation in their promotions. Public image for celebrities, in particular, is a potentially lucrative source of revenue, allowing celebrities to engage directly with their fan base. Getting a re-tweet or a favourite from a celebrity is a modern-day equivalent of an autograph.

This chapter will consider the pitfalls to avoid when using social media for marketing purposes. The chapter will look at how to run a successful social media marketing campaign that is legally compliant and the risks that advertisers, celebrities, businesses, and PR agencies need to be aware of when conducting online promotions.

Chapter 15: FCA regulated bodies

The Financial Conduct Authority (FCA) is the regulator the financial services industry in the UK. Its aims are to protect consumers, ensure the financial services industry remains stable, and promote healthy competition between financial services providers. The FCA has rule-making, investigative, and enforcement powers that they use to protect and regulate the financial services industry. Regulated firms need to be aware of the rules that govern the marketing of their services via social networking accounts (which may include YouTube, Facebook, Twitter, etc.).

The law in relation to advertising promotions is dealt with in Chapter 14, but in relation to bodies regulated by the FCA there are special rules in relation to financial promotion. Chapter 15 considers these special rules by reference to the FSA handbook and offers checklists that FCA-regulated bodies can use when conducting social media campaigns.

Chapter 16: Insurance

Social media claims or potential claims may arise in almost any context, from branding and advertising issues to defamation and privacy claims, consumer class actions and securities claims. This chapter will look at what you need to consider when purchasing or renewing insurance coverage, exploring risk, and key areas of coverage (or indeed coverage that you may need to seek which you do not already have).

Foreword

In 1964, the media was famously described as an 'extension of man'.[1] In today's world, where technology has given us the means to be able to transmit and receive communications, almost constantly, anywhere in the world, with a click of a mouse or a flick of a finger, never has a description seemed so prophetic and apt. Social media platforms have become this 'extension'. They are used as a way of not only receiving news,[2] but of instantaneously, and without filter, expressing opinions and venting and sharing emotions, thoughts and feelings in real-time.

The international media landscape is undergoing profound change, and at the forefront of the reformulation of this vista[3] is social media. For instance, on United Nations World Press Day in 2012, Abdulaziz Al-Nasser, President of the UN General Assembly, stated: 'Governments that try to suppress or shut-down new media platforms should rather embrace new media for the beneficial transformation of their societies.'[4] In early 2014, the House of Lords Select Committee on Communications Report on Media Plurality recognized the increasingly important role that new media is playing within society.[5] This view has been mirrored in the United States, where the influence of social media was summed up by the Criminal Court of the City of New York in *New York v Harris*: 'The reality of today's world is that social media, whether it be Twitter, Facebook, Pinterest, Google+ or any other site, is the way people communicate.'[6]

---

1 M. McLuhan, 1964, *Understanding Media: The Extensions of Man*. Cambridge, MA: MIT Press.
2 According to Ofcom's report, The Communications Market 2013 (at para 1.9.7), 23% of people use social media platforms, such as Facebook and Twitter, for news [http://stakeholders.ofcom.org.uk/binaries/research/cmr/cmr13/UK_1.pdf; accessed 19 March 2014].
3 The Report of the High Level Group on Media Freedom and Pluralism, 'A Free and Pluralistic Media to Sustain European Democracy', January 2013, pp. 26–27.
4 'UN highlights role of press freedom as catalyst for social and political change', UN News Centre [http://www.un.org/apps/news/story.asp?NewsID=41911&Cr=journalist&Cr1; accessed 28 April 2014].
5 House of Lords Select Committee on Communications, First Report of Session 2013–14, Media Plurality, 4 February 2014 at [46]–[52].
6 *New York v Harris*, 2012 NY Misc LEXIS 1871 *3, note 3 (Crim Ct City of NY, NY County, 2012).

Foreword xxxiii

Thus, whether it be large-scale social 'events', such as the 2011 UK riots[7] or the Arab Spring,[8] football players' use of platforms such as Twitter and Instagram,[9] or issues affecting society generally, such as the 'revenge porn' phenomenon,[10] not a day seems to go by without social media, and its interaction with the law, being in the news. For many people, social media has not just replaced the written word, it has become a substitute for the spoken word, as illustrated and contextualized by the following statistics. Twitter states that it normally 'takes in' approximately 500 million tweets per day, equating to an average of 5,700 tweets per second.[11] According to Facebook, as of 31 December 2013, it had 1.23 billion monthly active users, 945 million of whom use their mobile products.[12] Late 2013 saw Instagram's global usage expand by 15%, in just two months, to 150 million people.[13] LinkedIn's current membership is 277 million.[14] These established platforms are only the tip of the social media iceberg. Pinterest continues to grow rapidly,[15] as do emerging platforms, such as Snapchat and WhatsApp.[16]

However, unlike the transitory nature of things said in passing, or in elation, or anger, or frustration, a 140-character tweet, a Facebook post, or a picture on Instagram are, to a large extent, permanent. In a legal terrain that remains largely uncharted, and is constantly shifting, the exponential growth of social media platforms demonstrates our obsession with them, and the increasing power they wield. Consequently, the permanency of this intersection between communication and technology creates complex challenges for the law, lawyers, and media professionals.

This book is an important and welcome step towards effectively charting this terrain. It takes the reader on a journey through this dynamic area, plotting a course that provides indispensable clarity for the multitude of stakeholders engaged with social media and the law.

---

7 See *R v Blackshaw* [2011] EWCA Crim 2312 per Lord Judge LCJ at [73]. Evidence suggested that social media was used to coordinate riots and public disorder across the UK.

8 D. McGoldrick, 'The Limits of Freedom of Expression on Facebook and Social Networking Sites: A UK Perspective', HRLR 13 (2013), 125–151, 130.

9 For example, see 'Sagbo fined for tweet', *The Times*, 23 April 2014; M. Drake, 2014, 'Sunderland star Steven Fletcher SPITS on rickshaw driver – then posts pic on Instagram calling him a c★★★', *The Mirror*, 19 January [http://www.mirror.co.uk/news/uk-news/sunderland-star-steven-fletcher-spits-3036626; accessed 28 April 2014]; 'Michael Chopra: Blackpool fine striker for derogatory tweet', *BBC Sport*, 7 January [http://www.bbc.co.uk/sport/0/football/25637583; accessed 28 April 2014].

10 '"Revenge porn": campaigners call for change in the law', *BBC News*, 10 April 2014 [http://www.bbc.co.uk/news/uk-26961279]; G. Dawson, 2014, '"Revenge porn" is increasing in the UK, say charities', *BBC News*, 3 April 2014 [http://www.bbc.co.uk/newsbeat/26851276]; '"Revenge porn" law considered by California', *BBC News*, 28 August 2013 [http://www.bbc.co.uk/news/technology-23863501], all accessed 28 April 2014.

11 https://blog.twitter.com/2013/new-tweets-per-second-record-and-how [accessed 14 March 2014].

12 https://newsroom.fb.com/key-Facts [accessed 14 March 2014].

13 http://instagram.com/press/#; UK Social Media Statistics for 2014 [http://socialmediatoday.com/kate-rose-mcgrory/2040906/uk-social-media-statistics-2014; accessed 12 March 2014].

14 http://press.linkedin.com/about [accessed 14 March 2014].

15 In 2011–12, Pinterest had around 200,000 users in the UK. In the summer of 2013, this had grown to over 2 million. UK Social Media Statistics for 2014 [http://socialmediatoday.com/kate-rose-mcgrory/2040906/uk-social-media-statistics-2014; accessed 12 March 2014].

16 Ibid.

xxxiv *Foreword*

Part 1 informs the rest of this text by providing a review of the development of the social media phenomenon, and a clear explanation of different platforms from around the world. How these platforms operate, and the part they now play in the way we, as members of society, communicate and interact, is dealt with, in addition to the impact of the European Convention on Human Rights and associated Strasbourg jurisprudence.

Part 2 provides commentary on the law of defamation, in the context of allegedly defamatory postings made via social media platforms. The potential practical implications of the Defamation Act 2013 are given in-depth consideration, as are remedies, damages, and Part 36 offers.

In successive chapters, Part 3 deals with a multitude of criminal offences that have arisen, or could arise, as a result of the use of social media. Criminal liability is explored in the context of its interrelationship with human rights and the value of speech, and is discussed practically, in light of evidential and procedural issues.

This comprehensive Handbook is rounded off by Part 4, which looks at social media from a commercial law perspective. In particular, it provides insight into the operation of laws relating to data protection and privacy, trading and advertising standards, Financial Conduct Authority regulated bodies and, finally, insurance.

A constant theme throughout this text is accessible analytical commentary coupled with incisive practical guidance. It offers both a domestic and international perspective that will be of interest and benefit to not only practising lawyers, legal scholars, and law students, but also media professionals and businesses.

Peter Coe

Acknowledgements

It is not possible to mention everyone who has made this book possible, but special appreciation and acknowledgement goes to everyone who was involved in the editing, marketing, and production of this volume.

In relation to the drafting of the Handbook, special thanks goes to Peter Coe, for his valuable insights, contributions to this volume, and academic support. I would also like to thank Alexia Sutton and David Cummings for getting the book to final form, which is no small task and therefore cannot go unaccredited. I also thank Rebecca Brennan, for considering the book proposal and assisting me with securing its publication.

There are of course a few special people who this book would never have occurred without. First, I would like to thank my parents for their continuous support, all the way from nursery school to private practice, with no sign of their love, support or kindness waning. Secondly (but equally), I would like to thank Peter Stapleton, for being with me through the highs and lows of the drafting and for his continual and unswerving belief in me. It is an extraordinary gift when someone can give their time so selflessly to support someone else's dreams, and I am eternally grateful for having Peter in my life. Thanks too go to Sean Corbett of Formula One Management, for many a fine legal debate over a pint – your feedback and support has been of immeasurable benefit.

Finally, I would like to make a special mention of my most valued legal mentor and former training principal Bruce Jones. Bruce is a solicitor, patent attorney, and qualified barrister of extraordinary ability, with a quick wit and sense of humour to match. It was a pleasure and a privilege to be trained by him.

List of Cases

A [2009] EWCA Crim 513 . . . . 221, 231
A v B plc [2003] QB 195 . . . . 29, 33
AA [2007] EWCA Crim 1779 224
Abu v MGN Limited [2003] EMLR 432; [2002] EWHC 2345 (QB); [2013]
   EWHC 515 (QB); 2013 WL 617648 . . . . 99, 100, 113, 115, 121
Ahma (Bilal Zaheer) 2012 WL 5995906 286
Ahmed (Azhar), 9 October 2012, (Unreported), Huddersfield Magistrates
   Court 42
AKO Capital LLP & Another v TSF Derivatives & Others (February 2012) 93
Alfacs Vacances SL v Google Spain SL, 23 February 2012 314
Al-Fagih [2001] EWCA Civ 1634 90
Ali [2008] EWCA Crim 1522 217
Altajir SC 18706 (Conn. Supreme Court 2012) 226
Angel (Norman) v Stainton & Repaircraft [2006] EWHC 637 (QB) 114
Applause Store Productions Ltd v Raphael [2008] EWHC
   1781 (QB) 7, 73, 94, 228
Athwal [2009] EWCA Crim 789 224
Attorney General v Baines [2013] EWHC 4326 (Admin) 205–8
Attorney General v Dallas [2012] 1 WLR 991 196
Attorney General v Davey (Kasim) and Joseph Beard [2012]
   1 WLR 991 . . . . 193, 196, 197, 198–200, 201
Attorney General v Fraill (Joanne) and Jamie Stewart [2011] EWCA
   Crim 1570 . . . . 195, 200–1
Attorney General v Guardian Newspapers Ltd ('Spycatcher') [1990]
   1 AC 109 201
Attorney General v Harkins and Liddle [2013] EWHC 1455 (Admin) 201–5
Attorney General's Reference (No. 2 of 2002) [2003] 1 Cr App R 21 217
Attorney General's Reference (No. 3 of 2000) [2001] UKHL 53 . . . . 150, 151
Autronic AG judgment of 22 May 1990, Series A No. 178 31
Axe Market Gardens v Craig Axe, claim number CIV: 2008-485-2676 . . . . . 93, 94

Bailey [2008] EWCA Crim 817 . . . . 222, 226
Barrett v Rosenthal, 40 Cal. 4th 33 (2006) 77
Bartlett v Crittenden, 5 McLean 32, 4I (1849) 239
Batcherlor [2010] EWCA Crim 1025 169
Belfast City Council v Miss Behavin' Ltd [2007] UKHL 19 145

List of Cases xxxvii

Bentley, Leeds Crown Court, 29 November 2011 (unreported) 174
Best v Charter Medical of England Limited [2001] EWCA Civ 1588 71
Billingham [2009] Crim LR 529. 225
Blackshaw [2011] EWCA Crim 2312 . . . . . . 166, 169–71, 173, 174, 176, 177, 178
Blaney's Blarney, unreported 2009 94
Bloom v National Federation [1918] 35 TLR 50 CA 58
Boyle [1914] 3 KB 339, CCA. 154
Braithwaite [2010] EWCA Crim 1082 . . . . 223, 224
Brewster [2010] EWCA Crim 1194 223
Brunswick (Duke of) v Harmer (1849) 14 QB 185 74
Bryce v Barber, unreported July 26 [2010] (HC) 73
Bucknor [2010] EWCA Crim 1152 . . . . .213, 226, 229
Budu (Samuel Kingsford) v BBC [2010] EWHC 616 (QB) 72
Bunt v Tilley [2006] EWHC 407 (QB). 70
Burstein v Times Newspapers [2001] 1 WLR 579 115

Cairns v Modi [2012] EWCA Civ 1382; [2012] WLR(D) 302; [2012]
   EWHC 756 (QB) 53, 81, 87, 107, 112, 114
Calderbank v Calderbank [1976] 3 All ER 333. 116
Cammish v Hughes [2012] EWCA Civ 1655; [2013] EMLR 13. . . . . . . 60, 66, 67
Campbell v MGN Ltd [2004] AC 457; [2004] UKHL 22 . . . . .29, 31, 32, 42, 145
Campbell v United Kingdom [1992] ECHR 13590/88 29
Campbell-James v Guardian Media Group [2005] EMLR 24 114
Carr [2008] EWCA Crim 1283 223
Chase v News Group Newspapers Ltd [2002] EWCA Civ 1772 86
Cheng v Tse Wai Chun Paul (2000) 10 BHRC 525 88
Chinn [2012] EWCA Crim 501 224
Church v MGN Ltd [2012] EWHC 693 (QB); [2012] EMLR 28 (QB) 67
Clear [1968] 1 QB 670; 52 Cr App Rep 58, CA 153
Cleese v Clark & Associated Newspapers Limited [2003] EWHC 137 (QB); [2004]
   EMLR 37 . . . . .99, 100, 106, 114
Club La Costa (UK) Ltd v Gebhard [2008] EWHC 2552 (QB); The Times, 10
   December 2008 104
Connolly v DPP [2007] EWHC 237 (Admin); [2008] 1 WLR 276. . . . . . 134, 136
Crosskey, Southwark Crown Court, 16 May 2012 (unreported) 185
Cryer, Newcastle Magistrates' Court, 21 March 2012 (unreported) 175–6
CTB v News Group Newspapers [2011] EWHC 1232 208

Daniels v BBC [2010] EWHC 3057 (QB) 67
Dehal v CPS [2005] EWHC 2154 (Admin) 180
Delaney [2010] EWCA Crim 105. . . . . 213, 222
Dell'Olio v Associated Newspapers [2011] EWHC 3472 (QB) 60, 66, 67
Derbyshire County Council v Times Newspapers [1993] AC 534. . . . . 22, 58
DFT v TFD. 29
Digital Rights Ireland and Seitlinger and Others (Joined Cases C-29312 and
   C-594/12). 19
Doe II v Myspace, Inc., 175 Cal. App. 4th 561 (2009) 77
Douglas v Hello! Ltd [2001] QB 967 32

xxxviii   *List of Cases*

DPP v Chambers [2012] EWHC 2157; 2012 WL 2923016 . . 34, 131, 134–5, 136, 137, 141, 143, 144, 146, 153, 156
DPP v Collins [2006] UKHL 40 . . . . 129, 131, 132, 133, 134, 137, 146, 154, 166
DPP v Sutcliffe-Keenan; DPP v Blackshaw [2011] EWCA Crim 2312 129
Dubai Bank Ltd v Galadari (No. 3) [1990] 1 WLR 731 120
Durant v Financial Services Authority [2003] EWCA Civ 1746 259–60

Ecclestone v Telegraph Media Group [2009] EWHC 2779 (QB) 67
Edem v The Information Commissioner & Anor [2014] EWCA Civ 92 260
Eleck 130 Conn. App. 632, 32 A. 3d 818 (2011) 227
Elsbury (Colin) v Eddie Talbot, June 2009 (unreported) 53
English & Scottish Cooperative Investment Mortgage and Investment Society
   Limited v Odhams Press Limited [1941] KB 440 102–3
ETK v News Group Newspapers Ltd 29
Evans and McDonald (unreported) 20 April 2012 142

Fair Housing Council v Roommates, Inc., 521 F.3d 1157 (9th Cir. 2008) 78
Ferguson v Associated Newspapers, Gray J, 15/3/02 Westlaw 1654855 115
Flexman v BG Group, (unreported) 260–1
Flood v Times Newspapers Ltd [2013] EWHC 2182 (QB) 63–4, 74
F.P. 878 A. 2d 91 (Pa. Super, 2005). 226
Fuentes Bobo v Spain (2001) 31 EHRR 50 145

Glimmerveen and Hagenbeek v Netherlands (1982) 4 EHRR 260 137
Golders v United Kingdom [1975] 1 EHRR 524 28
Goldsmith v Bhoyrul [1998] 2 WLR 435 58
Goodwin (Fred) v News Group Newspapers Ltd and VBN [2011]
   EWHC 1437. 29
Google joined cases (C–236/08, C–237/08 & C–238/08). 17
Google v Spain (Google Spain SL (1) and Google Inc (2) v Agencia
   Española de Protección de Datos (AEPD) (1) and Costeja González (2)
   (Case C–131/12)) 72, 110, 157, 280–4, 312–13
Gorelishvili v Georgia (2009) 48 EHRR 36. 145
Greater Manchester Police v Andrews [2011] EWHC 1966 225
Green v Times Newspapers, unreported, 17 January 2001 108
Griffin v State of Maryland 419 Md. 343, 19 A. 3d 415 (2011) 227, 229

H [1995] 2 AC 596 220
H [2009] EWCA Crim 1453 215
H [2011] EWCA Crim 2344 224
H (Buick Wildcat) [2008] EWCA Crim 3321. 213
Haji Ioannu v Mark Dixon, Regus Group Plc [2009] EWHC 178 (QB) 66
Halford v United Kingdom [1997] 14 24 EHRR 523 28
Halliday v Creation Consumer Finance Ltd [2013] EWCA Civ 333 299–300
Hancox [2010] EWCA Crim 1025 169
Handyside v United Kingdom (1976) 1 EHRR 734 . . . . 30, 34, 138
Haque and Nuth [2009] EWCA Crim 1453 . . . . 212, 213
Hashman and Harrup judgment of 25 November 1999, Reports 1999-VIII 31

List of Cases xxxix

Heath v Tang [1993] 1 WLR 1421 CA. 57
Hebditch v Macllwaine [1984] 2 QB 54 CA 69
Herczegfalvy judgment of 24 September 1992, Series A No. 244 31
Hird v Wood [1894] 38 SJ 234 70–1
Holland (John) Group Pty Ltd v John Fairfax Publications PTY Limited [2006]
    ACTSC 34 58
Horncastle [2009] UKSC 14 23
Horrocks v Lowe [1975] AC 135 . . . . .116, 117, 118
Hothi [2011] EWCA 1039 213
Hutcheson (Christopher) (previously known as KGM) v News Group
    Newspapers and ors 29

Jabar [2010] EWCA Crim 130 217
Jameel v Dow Jones [2005] EWCA Civ 75; [2005] QB 946 64
Jameel v Wall Street Journal Europe SPRL (No.3) [2006] UKHL 44; [2007] 1 AC
    359; [2007] Bus LR 291; [2006] 3 WLR 642; [2006] 4 All ER 1279; [2007]
    EMLR 2; [2006] HRLR 41; 21 BHRC 471; (2006) 103(41) LSG 36; (2006)
    156 NLJ 1612; (2006) 150 SJLB 1392; The Times, 12 October 2006; The
    Independent, 17 October 2006; Offi cial Transcript, HL 2006–10–11. 69
Jenkins [2011] HCJAC 86 216
Jeynes v News Magazines Limited [2008] EWCA Civ 130 61
John v MGN Ltd [1997] QB 586 111–12
Jones v Associated Newspapers Limited [2007] EWHC 1489 (QB); [2008] 1 All
    ER 240; [2008] EMLR 6 123
Jones v Pollard [1997] EMLR 233 103
Jones v Skelton [1963] 1 WLR 1362 61

Kaim v Neill [1996] EMLR 493 . . . . 113, 122
Kearley [1992] 2 AC 228 231
Khan [1997] AC 558 23
Krinsky v Doe 159 Cal. App. 4th 1154, 1172 (2008) 94–5

Landgericht Berlin Im Namen des Volkes Geschäftsnummer: 16 O 551/10 Urteil
    verkündet am: 06.03.2012. 248
Lane v Facebook, Inc., 696 F. 3d 811 (2012); Civ. No. C 08–3845, 2010 WL
    9013059 (ND Cal., Mar. 17, 2010); 709 F. 3d 791 (2013) 332–3
Law Society and Others v Rick Kordowski (Solicitors from Hell) [2011] EWHC
    3185 (QB) 254
Lawrence & Pomroy (1971) 57 Cr App Rep 64, CA. 153
Lehideux and Isornia v France (1998) 5 BHRC 540. 145
Ley v Hamilton (1935) 153 LT 384 108
Lindqvist (Bodil) v Kammaraklagaren Case C–101/01 [2003]
    ECR I–12971 . . . . 256, 259
Lister v Forth Dry Dock & Engineering Co Limited [1990] 1 AC 546 24
Locke v Stuart & AXA [2011] EWHC 399 (QB) 213, 236
London Association for the Protection of Trade v Greenlands Ltd [1913]
    3 KB 507 105
London Association v Greenlands [1916] 1 AC 58

xl *List of Cases*

Loosley [2001] UKHL 53 . . . . 150, 151
L'Oreal SA v eBay International AG [2012] All E.R. (EC) 501. . . . . 17, 214
Loutchansky v Times Newspapers Ltd & Others [2001] EWCA Civ 1805; [2002]
    1 All ER 652. . . . . 66, 74, 75
Lysko v Bradley [2006] 79 O.R. (3d) 721 ont. CA 69

McAlpine v Bercow [2013] EWHC 1342 (QB). 61–3, 71, 76, 109, 112, 113
McCallum v United Kingdom [1990] 13 EHRR 596 29
McCullough [2011] EWCA Crim 1413 . . . . .213, 215, 216
McGrath and another v Dawkins and others [2012] EWHC B3 (QB). 71
Mach, Southwark CC, September 2009 (unreported). 215
Malone v United Kingdom [1984] 7 EHRR 28
Mama Group Limited & Lovebox Festivals Limited v Sinclair & Joseph [2013]
    EWHC 2374 (QB) 67, 69
Mangham (Glenn), Southwark Crown Court, 17 February 2012 (unreported);
    [2012] EWCA Crim 973. 185–7
Mansfield v John Lewis, unreported May 2014. 298
Manuel II No. 12–09–00454-CR, WL 3837561 (2011) 226
Marek v Sean Lane, 571 U S (2013). 332
Markt Intern v Germany (1989) 12 EHRR 161 145
Mateza [2011] EWCA Crim 2587 . . . . 224, 231
Merchant [1914] 3 KB 339, CCA 154
Metropolitan International Schools Ltd v Designtechnica Corporation and others
    [2009] EWHC 1765 (QB) 72
Miles v Raycom Media Inc 2010 U.S. Dist. LEXIS 122712 231
Miller [2010] EWCA Crim 1153 . . . . 223, 224
Milne v Express Newspapers [2004] EWCA Civ 664; [2005]
    1 All ER 1021. . . . . .100, 116, 117
MKM Capital Property Limited v Carmela Rita Corbo and Gordon Kinsley
    Maxwell Poyser (a bankrupt) case (No. SC 608 of 2008) 93, 94
MNB v News Group Newspapers. 29
Muller v Switzerland (1991) 13 EHRR 212 145
Murphy [1990] NI 306. 228
Murray v Big Pictures Ltd [2008] 3 WLR 1360 33
Musone [2007] EWCA Crim 1237. 219

Nail v News Group Newspapers Limited, Rebekah Wade, Jules Stenson,
    Geraint Jones, Harper Collins Publications Ltd [2004] EWCA Civ 1708;
    [2005] 1 All ER 1040 . . . . 99, 106, 114
Nimmo, unreported, Westminster Magistrates Court 24 January 2014 . .147–8, 223
NMC v Persons Unknown 29
Norwich Pharmacal Co. & Others v Customs and Excise Commissioners [1974]
    AC 133. 79
Norwood v United Kingdom (2004) 40 EHRR SE 111 . . . . 137, 145
Novartis Pharmaceuticals UK Ltd v Stop Huntingdon Animal Cruelty [2009]
    EWHC 2716 (QB); [2010] HRLR 8. 136
Ntuli v Donald 29
NUGMW v Gillan [1946] KB 81 58

List of Cases xli

Peck v United Kingdom (2003) 36 EHRR 41; [2003] EMLR 287 239
Pelle (Ahmad), Nottingham Crown Court, 25 August 2011 (unreported). . . 172–3, 175, 177
People v Clevenstine 68 A.D. 3d 1448, 891 N.Y.S. 2d 511 (2009) 227
People v Oyerinde 2011 Mich. App. LEXIS 2104. 231
People v Valdez, (16 December 2011) Case No. G041904 (California Court of Appeals) WL 6275691; 201 Cal. App. 4th 1429 (2011) 222, 229
Percy v DPP [2001] EWHC Admin 1125; [2002] ACD 24 136
Phillips [2010] EWCA Crim 378 230
Preminger (Otto) v Austria (1995) 19 EHRR 34. 145
Productores de Musica de España (Promusicae) v Telefónica de España SAU (C–275/06) [2006] ECR I–271; [2008] 2 CMLR 17 304

Quagliarello v Dewees 2011 U.S. Dist. LEXIS 86914. 214
Queensberry (Duke of) v Shebbeare, 2 Eden 3 329 (1758) 239
Quilter v Heatly (1883) 23 Ch. D 120
Quinn [2011] NICA 19 228

R (Gaunt) v Office of Communications [2011] EWCA Civ 692 147
R (Kelway) v The Upper Tribunal (Administrative Appeals Chamber) and Northumbria Police and R (Kelway) v Independent Police Complaints Commission [2013] EWHC 2575 (Admin). 260
R (NTL Group Ltd) v Ipswich Crown Court [2002] EWHC 1585 (Admin); [2003] Q.B. 131 18
Redmond-Bate v DPP, Divisional Court, 23 July 1999 179
Reynolds v Times Newspapers [2001] 2 AC 127 88
Rice v Reliastar Life Insurance Co 2011 U.S. Dist. LEXIS 32831 (M.D. La. Mar. 29, 2011). 224, 231
Riches v Newspapers Limited [1986] QB 256. 57
Rigg v Associated Newspapers [2003] EWHC 710 120
Rizwan [2003] EWCA Crim 3067 213
RJW & SJW v The Guardian newspaper & Person or Persons Unknown 29
Roache v News Group Newspapers [1998] EMLR 161 . . . . 59, 121
Robson [1972] 1 WLR 651 228

S, Re [2005] 1 AC 593 33
S (A Child) (Identification: Restriction on Publication), Re [2004] UKHL 47 210
Sang [1980] AC 402. 150
Saward [2005] EWCA Crim 3183 226
Schrems (Max) v Data Protection Commissioner JR No 765 JR 2013. 319
SD Marine Ltd v Powell [2006] EWHC 3095 (QB) 101
Shannon [2001] 1 WLR 51 151
Shayler [2003] 1 AC 247 34
Shevill v Presse Alliance SA [1995] ECR i–415 ECJ 80, 81
Sim v Stretch [1936] 2 All ER 1237 . . . . 60, 63
Slipper v BBC [1991] 1 QB 283 108

xlii   *List of Cases*

Smith (Nigel) v ADVFN Plc and others [2008] EWHC
  1797 (QB) 59, 60, 65, 146
Smurthwaite [1994] 1 All ER 898. . . . . 150, 151
Sorley and Nimmo, unreported, Westminster Magistrates Court
  24 January 2014 . . . . .147–8, 223
South Hetton Coal Co. v N.E News [1894] 1 QB. 58
Southam [2009] EWCA Crim 2335 212
Spiller v Joseph [2010] UKSC 53 . . . . 87, 88
Stacey, Swansea Crown Court (unreported); Appeal No: A20120033
  30 March 2011 177–79
Standard Verlags GmbH v Austria (No. 2) Application No. 21277/05 31
State of New York v Pimentel (Jose), Criminal Court, 20 November 2011 49
State v Bell, 2009-Ohio–2335 (18 May 2009). 226
Steel & Morris v United Kingdom [2005] EMLR 15 67
Sunday Times v United Kingdom (1979) 2 EHRR 245 34
Sunday Times v United Kingdom (No 2) [1992] 14 EHRR 123. . . . . 143, 153
Sutcliffe-Keenan (Perry John) [2011] EWCA Crim 2312 . . . . 171–2, 173, 174,
                                                                           176, 177, 178
Sweet v Parsley [1970] AC 132. 133

Taylor v Chief Constable of Cheshire [1986] 1 WLR 1479. 230
Terry (John) (previously 'LNS') v Persons Unknown 29
Tesco Stores Ltd v Guardian News & Media Ltd [2009] EMLR 5 102
Thompson (Jacqueline) v Mark James, Carmarthenshire County Council [2013]
  EWHC 515 (QB), 2013 WL 617648 60
Thorne v Motor Trade Association [1937] AC 797 153
Thornton (Sarah) v Telegraph Media Group [2010] EWHC 1414; [2011]
  1 WLR 1985; [2010] EMLR 25; [2010] EMLR 25; [2010] EWHC 1414
  (QB); [2011] EWHC 1884 (QB); 2011 WL 2747828 . . . . .60, 64, 67, 117
Tienda No. PD–0312–11 (2012) 226
Times Newspapers Limited v UK [2009] ECHR 451 74
Toissant-Collins [2009] EWCA Crim 316 230
Tomlinson [1895] 1 QB 706 154
Trantum v McDowell [2007] NSWC 138 69
Treacy v DPP [1971] AC 537; 55 Cr App Rep 113 153
Turner v News Group Newspapers Ltd [2006] 1 WLR 3469 115
Twist [2011] EWCA Crim 1143. . . . . 230, 231

United States v O'Keefe 537 F. Supp. 2d 14, 20 (D.D.C. 2008) 228
US v LaRose, U.S. District Court for the Eastern District of Pennsylvania,
  4 March 2010 49

Veliu (Muhamed) v Xhevdet Mazrekaj, Skender Bucpapaj [2006] EWHC 1710
  (QB); 2006 WL 1981690 . . . . .105, 106, 112, 113
Venables, Thompson v News Group Newspapers Ltd 2001 WL 14890; [2001]
  2 WLR 1038. . . . . .201, 206, 207
Von Hannover v Germany 40 EHRR 1. 31

List of Cases   xliii

W v M [2011] EWHC 1197 (COP) 209, 211
Walker [2011] EWCA Crim 141 213
Warren v Random House Group Limited [2007] EWCH 2856 (QB); [2009]
    QB 600; [2008] 2 WLR 1033 103–4
WER v REW 29
Williams, 456 Mass. 857; 926 N.E. 2d 1162 (2010) 227
Wissa v Associated Newspapers Limited [2014] EWHC 1518 (QB) 71
Worm v Austria (1997) 25 EHRR 454 31

Yildirim (Ahmet) v Turkey Application No. 3111/10, 18 December 2012. 31

Z [2000] 2 AC 483. 218

List of Legislation

Anti-Terrorism, Crime and Security Act 2001 279

British Telecommunications Act 1981
  s 49(1)(a) 130

Children and Young Persons Act 1933 . . . . 208, 209
  s 33(1)(b) 208
  s 39 208
Civil Liability (Contribution) Act 1978
  s 1(4) 105
Communications Act 2003 . . . . 29, 30, 42, 45, 85, 129, 130, 131, 133,
                             134, 135, 136, 146, 165, 166, 173, 176, 208, 215
  s 5 176
  s 32 18
  s 127 . . . . 129, 130, 131, 138, 141, 142, 143, 148, 152, 163
  s 127(1) 130, 137, 153, 176
  s 127(1)(a) 130, 131, 132, 133, 134, 141, 147
  s 127(1)(b) 130
  s 127(2) 130, 153
  s 127(2)(a)–(c) 130
  s 127(3) 130, 176
  s 151 322
Computer Misuse Act 1990 . . . . 150, 183
  s 1 . . . . 183, 185, 186
  s 1(1)(a)–(c) 183
  s 1(2) 183
  s 1(3)(a) 183
  s 1(3)(b)–(c) 184
  s 2(a)–(c) 183
  s 3 . . . . 183, 184, 185, 186
  s 3(1)(a)–(b) 184
  s 3(2) 184
  s 3(2)(a)–(d) 184
  s 3(3) 184
  s 3(4)(a)–(c) 184
  s 3(5)(a)–(c) 184

List of Legislation xlv

s 3(6)(a) 184
s 3A 186
Contempt of Court Act 1981 .... 21, 29, 140, 142, 148, 191, 192, 211
  s 1...192, 193, 208
  s 2... 192
  s 2(2) 192
  s 4... 193
  s 4(2) 192
  s 5... 193
  s 8.. 192, 194
  s 14(1) 194
Copyright, Designs and Patents Act 1988
  s 1(3)(a)–(e) 79
Crime and Disorder Act 1998............................. 42, 175, 176
  s 28.. 141, 142
  s 28(1)(b) 137
  s 29-s 30.. 141, 142
  s 31..141, 142, 175
  s 31(1)(c) 137, 175, 176
  s 31(5) 175
  s 32.. 141, 142
Criminal Appeal Act 1968
  s 23.. 171
Criminal Justice Act 2003.................................... 223, 229
  s 9(2) 217
  s 98... 217
  s 99.. 217, 218
  s 99(1) 217
  s 100.. 217, 223
  s 100(2) 223
  s 101.. 217, 218
  s 101(1)(a)–(d) 219, 220
  s 101(1)(e)–(f) 219, 220, 222
  s 101(1)(g) 219, 220
  s 101(3) 219
  s 102.. 217
  s 102(1)(b) 218
  s 103.. 217
  s 103(1)(a) 218
  s 104-s 106 217
  s 107.. 217, 220
  s 107(1) 220
  s 107(1)(b) 220
  s 107(1)(b)(ii)... 220
  s 107(2) 221
  s 108-s 111 217
  s 112.. 217, 218
  s 112(3) 220

xlvi   *List of Legislation*

s 112(3)(b) 217
s 113. 217
s 114. 215
s 118(1) 217
s 119. 225
s 119(1)(a)–(b) 225
s 120. . . . . 224, 225
s 120(2) 224
s 120(4) 224
s 120(6)–(7) 224
s 128(2) 222
s 133. 226
s 134(1) 226
s 141. 217
s 145-s 146 . . . . 141, 142
Criminal Justice and Police Act 2001 165
Criminal Procedure Act 1865
s 3-s 5 225
Criminal Procedure (Insanity) Act 1964
s 4A 220

Data Protection Act 1984 . . . . 243, 248
Data Protection Act 1998 . . . . 28, 237, 238, 243, 248, 250–1, 253, 254, 257,
258, 259, 261, 263, 270, 271, 272, 276, 288,
290, 293, 294, 295, 296, 297, 300, 305, 307,
309, 311, 314, 315, 320, 321, 323,
328, 329, 335
s 1. 253
s 1(1) 258, 259
s 2. 262
s 3. 278
s 4(4) 255
s 5. 251
s 7. . . . . .265, 304, 305, 308
s 7(1)(a) 265
s 7(1)(d) 265
s 8. . . . . .304, 305, 308
s 8(2) 309
s 8(6) 310
s 10. . . . . 276, 277
s 10(1) 276, 277
s 10(1)(a)–(b) 276, 278
s 10(2) 276
s 10(3)–(5) 277
s 11. . . . . .265, 287, 294
s 11(1) 295
s 11(3) 295
s 12. 265

List of Legislation   xlvii

s 13 . . . . .265, 278, 299
s 13(1) 299
s 13(3) 299
s 14 . . . . 265, 277
s 14(1) 278
s 14(3)–(4) 278
s 15 265
s 16 278
s 17 . . . . 256, 278
s 17(1) 255
s 18 265
s 19 255
s 27(1) 255
s 29(3) 308
s 32 . . . . .270, 274, 308
s 34 309
s 35 308
s 36 . . . . .270, 271, 272, 274, 275
s 70 311
Sched 1 . . . . .257, 258, 295
    para 7 . . . . 268, 278
    para 13 315
    para 70(2) 268
Sched 2 264
    para 1 266
Sched 3 264
    para 1 266
Sched 4
    para 1 266
    para 4 317
Defamation Act 1952 . . . . 54, 55, 87
s 4 98
s 6 89
Defamation Act 1996 . . . . 54, 55, 86, 98, 99, 103, 105, 121, 123
s 1 . . . . .78, 79, 80, 91, 97
s 1(3) 97, 98
s 1(3)(c) 98
s 1(3)(e) 98
s 2 . . . . .65, 99, 101, 103, 119
s 2(2) 102, 103, 104
s 2(4) 101, 107, 111
s 2(4)(a) 101, 107
s 2(4)(b) 101, 107, 108
s 2(4)(c) 101, 112
s 2(5) 102, 103, 113
s 2(6) 102, 104
s 3 . . . . .99, 103, 112, 113, 120
s 3(1) 105, 107, 112

xlviii *List of Legislation*

s 3(2)–(4) 105, 107
s 3(5) 99, 105, 107, 112, 118
s 3(6)–(7) 105
s 3(8) 105
s 3(8)(b) 105
s 4. . . . . 99, 103, 120
s 4(2) 99, 119, 120
s 4(3) 116, 117, 118
s 4(3)(a)–(b) 116
s 4(4) 99, 119
s 8-s 10 100
s 14-s 15 88
Defamation Act 2013 . . . . 37, 54, 55, 64, 69, 70, 79, 81, 98, 108
s 1. . . . . 64, 78, 87
s 1(1) 64, 68
s 1(2) 67, 68, 69, 73
s 1(3) 69, 78
s 1(3)(a) 78
s 2. 86
s 2(1) 86
s 2(2)–(3) 87
s 2(4) 86
s 3. 87
s 3(2)–(3) 87, 88, 90
s 3(4) 88, 89, 90
s 3(4)(a)–(b) 87
s 3(5) 89, 90
s 3(6) 89
s 3(7) 88
s 3(8) 89
s 4. . . . . 88, 89
s 4(1) 89
s 4(1)(a)–(b) 89
s 5. . . . . 37, 78, 79, 80, 87, 90, 91, 94, 95, 96, 97
s 5(2) 91, 97
s 5(3) 92, 96
s 5(3)(a)–(c) 92
s 5(4) 92
s 5(6) 80, 95
s 5(11) 96
s 5(12) 96, 97
s 6. 88
s 8. . . . . 73, 74, 75
s 8(1)(a)–(b) 75
s 8(2) 75
s 8(5) 75
s 8(5)(a)–(b) 75
s 9. 81

s 9(1)	81
s 9(2)	81, 82
s 9(3)	82
s 10	78
s 10(1)	70, 78, 79
s 10(2)	78
s 12	123
s 13	78, 79
s 13(1)	78
s 13(1)(b)	78
Data Retention and Investigatory Powers Act 2014	19
Disability Discrimination Act 1995	305
Equality Act 2010	305
European Communities Act 1972	21
Financial Services Act 2012	343
s 89	366
Financial Services and Markets Act 2000	361
s 21	361, 365
s 25	365
s 30	365
s 31	361
s 380	365
s 382(1)	365
Football Supporters Act 1989	177
Freedom of Information Act 2000	309
Gambling Act 2005	
s 42	213
Human Rights Act 1998	21, 23, 24, 26, 29, 104, 134, 213
s 2	23
s 3	23, 24, 135, 136
s 3(1)	24
s 3(2)(a)–(c)	24
s 4	24
s 6	25, 33
s 6(1)	25
s 6(2)(a)–(b)	25
s 6(3)	25
s 7(1)	25
s 7(5)	26
s 10	24
Sched 1	23
Law of Libel Amendment Act 1888	98
Legislative and Regulatory Reform Act 2006	
s 22-s 23	347

l *List of Legislation*

Limitation Act 1980
  s 4(a) 73
Limited Liability Partnerships Act 2000 57

Malicious Communications Act 1988. . . . . .134, 146, 165, 166, 173
  s 1. . . . . .142, 143, 165
  s 1(1) 134, 166
  s 1(1)(b) 134
  s 1(2A) 165
  s 1(4) 134

Offences Against the Person Act 1861
  s 16. 141

Police and Criminal Evidence Act 1984
  s 9. 18
  s 76. 222
  s 76(2)(b) 223
  s 76A 222
  s 78. . . . . .150, 151, 219, 220
  s 78(1)–(2) 150
Post Office Act 1953
  s 11(1)(b) 131
  s 66(a) 130
Post Office Act 1969
  s 78. 130
Post Office (Amendment) Act 1935
  s 10(2)(a) 130
Postal Services Act 2000
  s 85(3) 131
Protection from Harassment Act 1997 .140, 141, 166, 180
  s 1. 180
  s 1(1) 180
  s 1(1)(a)–(b) 180
  s 1(2) 180
  s 1(3)(a)–(c) 180
  s 2. . . . . 180, 181
  s 4. . . . . .141, 180, 181
  s 4(1) 181
  s 4(3) 181
  s 4(3)(a)–(c) 181
  s 4(4)(a)–(b) 181
  s 4(5) 181
  s 7. 141
Public Order Act 1986 . . . . 45, 177, 179
  Part I 179
  Part III 179
  s 5. 137

List of Legislation   li

s 6(4) 132
s 18... 137
s 30... 177
s 31... 177
s 31(1)(b) 177
s 32-s 37 177

Regulation of Investigatory Powers Act 2000 .... 16, 18, 28, 29, 150, 279, 304
s 2(1) 18
s 12.. 18
s 22(4) 18
s 25(1) 18
s 49... 225
s 56... 225

Serious Crimes Act 2007 .... 42, 45, 168, 173, 174, 186
Part 2 167
s 1.. 168
s 2(2) 168
s 6-s 15 168
s 19... 168
s 19(2) 169
s 44... 168, 173
s 44(1)(a)–(b) 168
s 44(2) 168
s 46... 168, 173
s 46(1)(a) 168
s 46(1)(b)(i)–(ii) 168
Sched 1.. 168
Sexual Offences (Amendment) Act 1992
s 5...140, 142, 152
Supreme Court Act 1981
s 37... 102

Telecommunications Act 1984..................................... 131
s 43... 131
s 43(1)(a) 130
Theft Act 1968... 366
s 21(1) 153
Trade Description Act 1986
s 29... 347

Unfair Contract Terms Act 1977 85
Guidelines
CPS Legal Guidance on Stalking and Harassment. 142, 181, 182
Interim Guidelines on Prosecuting Cases Involving Communications
Sent via Social Media 139–53
Magistrates' Court Sentencing Guidelines.......................... 154

lii *List of Legislation*

OECD Guidelines on Data Protection 242–3
Secondary legislation
Civil Procedure Rules 92
    Part 21 57
    Part 23 78
    Part 31 120
    Part 33 86
    Part 36 . . . . 122, 123
    Part 54 26
    PD3 . . . . 105, 114
    PD7 58
    PD53 112
    rule 1.1 102
    rule 3.1 120
    rule 6.15 92
    rule 6.27 92
    rule 31.12 120
    rule 31.14 120
    rule 36.14 123
Consumer Protection from Unfair Trading Regulations 2008
    (SI 2008/1277) 366
    reg 2(1) 345
    reg 3(4) 346
    reg 3(4)(b) 346
    reg 6 346
    reg 19 347
    reg 19(4) 347
    Sched 1
        para 11 346
        para 22 346
        para 26 346
Court of Protection Rules 2007
    rule 92(2) 209, 210
Data Retention (EC Directive) Regulations 2009 . . . . 18, 279
Defamation Act (Commencement) (England and Wales) Order 2013
    (SI 2013/3027) 54, 55
Defamation (Operators of Websites) Regulations 2013 . . . . 95, 96, 97
    reg 2–reg 4 95
    Schedule 95
Electronic Commerce (EC Directive) Regulations 2002 (SI 2002/2013) 54
    reg 19 . . . . 80, 91, 98
Privacy and Electronic Communications (EC Directive)
    (Amendment) Regulations 2011 (SI 2011/1208) 267, 297
Privacy and Electronic Communications (EC Directive)
    Regulations 2003 (SI 2003/2426) 267, 279, 287, 294, 296, 298
    reg 2 322
    reg 4 297
    reg 5(1) 322

List of Legislation liii

reg 5A 322
reg 6(1)–(2). 267
reg 14(4)(b). 293, 294
reg 22 297
Regulation of Investigatory Powers (Acquisition and Disclosure of
   Communications Data: Code of Practice) Order 2007
   (SI 2007/2197) 279
Serious Crimes Act 2007: Appeals under Section 24 Order 2008,
   SI 2008/1863. 188
Unfair Terms in Consumer Contract Regulations 1999. . . . . 325, 326
   reg 5 326
   reg 5(1) 325
   reg 7 326
Unfair Terms in Consumer Contracts Regulations 1994 (SI 1994/3159). 85

EU legislation

Commission Decisions

Commission Decision 2001/497/EC, 15 June 2001 317
Commission Decision 2002/16/EC, December 2001 317
Commission Decision 2004/915/EC, dated 2004. 317
Commission Decision 2010/87/EU, 5 February 2010 318

Directives

Directive 95/46/EC (Data Protection Directive 1995) 72, 243, 248, 249,
                                                        251, 279, 283, 319
   Art 1 251
   Art 2(h) 265
   Art 3(1) 256
   Art 3(2) 255, 256
   Art 4(1)(a) 311, 312, 313
   Art 4(1)(c) 311
   Art 7 296
   Art 7(a) 266
   Art 8 266
   Art 8(2)(a) 262
   Art 8(4) 262
   Art 10-Art 11 262
   Art 12 . . . . 262, 305
   Art 13 262
   Art 13(1) 304
   Art 14 . . . . 262, 305
   Art 24 257
   Art 26(1)(a) 266
   Art 26(2) 317
   Art 73 257
Directive 97/66 concerning the processing of personal data and the protection
   of privacy in the telecommunications sector [1997] OJ L24/1 18
   Art 5 18
Directive 98/34/EC on the legal protection of services based on, or consisting
   of, conditional access 17

liv *List of Legislation*

Art 1(2) 251
Directive 98/48/EC (OJ L 217, 5 August 1998) 17, 251
Directive 2000/31 on electronic commerce [2000] OJ L178/1 . . . . 16, 17,
54, 98
Directive 2002/21 on a common regulatory framework for electronic
communications networks and services (Framework Directive)
Art 2(c) 16, 285
Directive 2002/22/EC on universal service and users' rights relating to
electronic communications networks and services. 267
Directive 2002/58 on privacy and electronic communications [2002]
OJ L201/37 . . . . 18, 279, 293
Art 5(1) 18
Directive 2002/58/EC concerning the processing of personal data and
the protection of privacy in the electronic communications sector. 267
Art 5(3) 267
Art 15(1) 304
Directive 2005/29 (Unfair Commercial Practices Directive
(UCPD)). 345
Directive 2006/24 on data retention [2006] OJ L105/54 . . . . 18, 285, 286
Directive 2009/136/EC (Citizen's Rights Directive) 267

Regulations

Brussels Regulation 44/2001 . . . . 80, 81
Art 2 80
Art 5(3) 80
General Data Protection Regulation (Draft) 249, 298, 300, 313, 314
Art 3 249
Art 3(2) 312
Art 6(1)(a) 279
Art 6(1)(e) 279
Art 7 . . . . 266, 303
Art 9 303
Art 14 303
Art 15 310
Art 15(1) 310
Art 15(2) 311
Art 17(1) 279
Art 17(1)(a)–(d). 279
Art 17(2) 279
Art 17(3) 279
Art 17(3)(d). 285, 286
Art 17(4) 280
Art 18(2) 280
Art 19(2) 298
Art 20 . . . . 302, 310
Art 20(1) 302
Art 20(3) 303
Art 79 300
Art 80-Art 81 279

Art 83 279
Regulation No. 2006/2004 on cooperation between national authorities
  responsible for the enforcement of consumer protection laws 267
Treaties
Treaty of Rome 1957. 21
German legislation
Data Protection Act 319
Unfair Competition Act 2004 248
Indian legislation
Information Technology Act 2000
  s 66A(a) 130
South Korean legislation
Act on Promotion of Information and Communications Network Utilization and
  Data Protection, etc
  Art 44–5 162
Personal Information Protection Act of 2011. 163
US legislation
Communications Decency Act 1996
  s 230 . . . . 77, 78
Federal Rules of Evidence
  rule 401. 214
  rule 801. 231
  rule 901. . . . . 226, 228
International treaties and conventions
Convention Against Torture
  Art 4 40
Convention on the Elimination of all Forms of Racial Discrimination
  Art 4 137
Council of Europe Convention for the Protection of Individuals with regard to
  Automatic Processing of Personal Data 1981 . . . . .242–3, 316
European Convention on Human Rights and Fundamental
  Freedoms 21, 23, 26, 135
  Art 1 22
  Art 2(1). 40
  Art 6 . . . . 26, 27, 35, 104, 148, 211, 213, 214, 225
  Art 7 26
  Art 8 . . . . 26, 27, 28, 29, 32, 33, 34, 169, 200, 208, 210
  Art 8(1). 27
  Art 8(2). 28, 34, 200
  Art 10 . . . . .26, 30, 31, 32, 33, 34, 60, 66, 74, 97, 104, 134, 137,
                          143, 145, 146, 152, 153, 200, 208, 210, 270
  Art 10(1). 31
  Art 10(2). 30, 32, 34, 134, 200
  Art 13 22
  Art 17 137
  Art 24-Art 25. 22
International Covenant on Civil and Political Rights 30, 35, 41, 45
  Art 15(1). 40

lvi   *List of Legislation*

Art 17-Art 18 41
Art 19 . . . . 30, 42

Art 19(2)–(3) 35, 36
Art 20 . . . . 41, 42
Art 20(2) 137
Art 21 41
Lugano Convention 81
Universal Declaration of Human Rights 30
Art 19 30

Part 1
Background

1 Introduction to social media and the law

1.1 Introduction

1.1.1 *Utility of social media*

As an emerging technology with nearly limitless boundaries and possibilities, social media has given users unprecedented engagement with brands, companies, and other users. It is possible – common even – to reach an unlimited audience with the click of a mouse or the use of a Smartphone. However, although most users will have an idea of what social media means to them (e.g. the ability to contact friends or make new connections), in order to locate social media within the law it is necessary in this first chapter to consider the types of social media that individuals use every day and how it is defined by the law. Without doing so it would be impossible to go on and apply the areas of law that social media affects in a meaningful way, or understand why the law has developed or the deficiencies in the law that have been presented due to a misunderstanding as to what the law is seeking to achieve.

1.1.2 *Background to the development of social media*

The potential for computer networking to facilitate newly improved forms of computer-mediated social interaction was initially suggested during the infancy of the internet.[1] Efforts to support social networks via computer-mediated communication were made in many early online services, including Usenet,[2] ARPANET, LISTSERV, and bulletin board services. Many prototypical features of social networking sites (SNSs) were also present in online services such as America Online, Prodigy, CompuServe, ChatNet, and The WELL.[3] Early social networking on the World Wide Web began in the form of generalized online communities such as Theglobe. com (1995),[4] Geocities (1994), and Tripod.com (1995).

---

1 Starr Roxanne Hiltz and Murray Turoff (1978) *The Network Nation: Human Communication via Computer*. New York: Addison-Wesley (Revised edition, 1993. Cambridge, MA: MIT Press).
2 Michael Hauben and Ronda Hauben (1997) *Netizens: On the History and Impact of Usenet and the Internet*. Los Alamitos, CA: IEEE Computer Society Press.
3 Katie Hafner (2001) *The Well: A Story of Love, Death and Real Life in the Seminal Online Community*. New York: Carroll & Graf.
4 David Cotriss (2008) 'Where are they now: TheGlobe.com', *The Industry Standard*, 29 May.

4   *Background*

The early communities focused on 'bringing people together' to interact with each other through chat rooms, and encouraged users to share personal information and ideas via personal web pages by providing easy-to-use publishing tools and free or inexpensive web space. However, other communities, such as www.classmates.com, took a different approach by simply having people link to each other via email addresses.

By the late 1990s, the nature of the sites began to change. User profiles became increasingly important as user demand for the ability to compile lists of connections, often referred to as 'friends', increased. The use of profiles with user data allowed users to search for and connect with other users with similar interests or shared connections. As user demand for such features increased, sites developed increasingly sophisticated offerings that allowed users to find and manage friends.[5] In 1997, the 'next generation' social networking sites began to flourish with the introduction of sites such as SixDegrees.com.

The third generation of networking sites began in the early 2000s. Makeoutclub was introduced in 2000, with Hub Culture and Friendster following in 2002.[6] Facebook was first introduced (in 2004) as a Harvard social networking site.[7]

Such sites soon became part of users' internet consumption, and by 2005, it was reported that MySpace was getting more page views than Google. Facebook[8] became the largest social networking site in the world[9] in early 2009.[10]

1.2 What is 'social media' and a 'social network'

1.2.1 *History*

Owing to the explosion of Web 2.0 and the increasing sophistication of technologies that can be used to access web content, users both produce and consume significant quantities of multimedia content. Moreover, this behaviour when combined with social networking (i.e. communication between users through online communities) has formed a new internet era where multimedia content sharing through social networking sites is an everyday practice. More than 200 social networking sites of worldwide impact are known today and this number is growing fast. Many of the existing top websites are either pure social networking sites or offer some social networking capabilities.[11]

A social networking service is a platform to build social networks or social relations among people who, for example, share interests, activities, backgrounds or real-life connections. A social network service consists of a representation of each user (often

---

5 C. Romm-Livermore and K. Setzekorn (eds) (2008) *Social Networking Communities and E-Dating Services: Concepts and Implications*. New York: IGI Global, p. 271.

6 E. Knapp (2005) *A Parent's Guide to MySpace*. DayDream Publishers.

7 D.M. Boyd and N.B. Ellison (2007) 'Social network sites: definition, history and scholarship', *Journal of Computer-Mediated Communication*, 13(1): 210–230.

8 Steve Rosenbush (2005) 'News Corp's place in MySpace', *Business Week*, 19 July (MySpace page views figures).

9 'Social graph-iti: there's less to Facebook and other social networks than meets the eye,' *The Economist* [http://www.economist.com/node/9990635; retrieved 19 January 2008].

10 Andy Kazeniac (2009) 'Social networks: Facebook takes over top spot, Twitter climbs', Blog.compete. com, 9 February [https://blog.compete.com/2009/02/09/facebook-myspace-twitter-social-network/; retrieved 7 August 2013].

11 http://www.alexa.com [accessed November 2010].

Introduction to social media and the law 5

a profile), his or her social links, and a variety of additional services. Most social network services are web-based and provide means for users to interact over the internet, such as email and messaging. The service usually allows individuals to create a public profile, to create a list of users with whom to share connection, and view and cross the connections within the system.[12] In recent years, social networking sites have become increasingly varied and they now commonly incorporate new information and communication tools, such as mobile connectivity, photo/video/sharing, and blogging.[13] Online community services are sometimes considered to be social networking sites, though in a broader sense, social networking site usually means an individual-centred service, whereas online community services are group-centred. Social networking sites allow users to share ideas, pictures, posts, activities, events, and interests with people in their network.

1.2.2 *Social interaction*

Social media has arguably changed the way in which we entertain ourselves and as a result the way in which individuals conduct their daily lives. Social networking is one of the primary reasons that many people have become avid internet users. In 2014, the number of active mobile phones will exceed 7 billion. However, as noted by the US Subcommittee on Counterterrorism and Intelligence in 2011, 'though the term "social networking" tends to conjure up immediate visions of Facebook and Twitter, the origins of the term are far less humble. In the era before the existence of the internet, social networking was the process of conventional human interaction that took place in key locations like schools, marketplaces, religious centres, and sports events.'[14]

It has been suggested by research conducted by Ellison, Steinfield, and Lampe that online social networking sites support both the maintenance of existing social ties and the formation of new connections.[15] Much of the early research on online communities assumed that individuals using these systems would be connecting with others outside their pre-existing social group or location, liberating them to form communities around shared interests, as opposed to shared geography.[16] The early research was predicated on an assumption that when online and offline social networks overlapped, the directionality was *online to offline* – online connections resulted in face-to-face meetings. Parks and Floyd (1996) report that one-third of their respondents later met their online correspondents face-to-face and that this implied that online relationships rarely stayed there.[17]

---

12 D.M. Boyd and N.B. Ellison (2007) 'Social network sites: definition, history and scholarship', *Journal of Computer-Mediated Communication*, 13(1): 210–230.

13 Ibid.

14 Testimony of Evan F. Kohlmann with Josh Lefkowitz and Laith Alkhouri to the UN Congress for Data Security, 6 December 2011.

15 N.B. Ellison, C. Steinfield and C. Lampe (2007) 'The benefits of Facebook "Friends": social capital and college students' use of online social network sites', *Journal of Computer-Mediated Communication*, 12(4): 1143–1168.

16 B. Wellman, J. Salaff, D. Dimitrova, L. Garton, M. Gulia and C. Haythornthwaite (1996) 'Computer networks as social networks: collaborative work, telework, and virtual community', *Annual Review of Sociology*, 22: 213–238.

17 M.R. Parks and K. Floyd (1996) 'Making friends in cyberspace', *Journal of Computer-Mediated Communication*, 1(4) [http://jcmc.indiana.edu/vol1/issue4/parks.html; retrieved 14 July 2006].

6 *Background*

It is suggested that next-generation social networking sites have significantly changed the way in which individuals communicate with other and that the shift from online to offline as suggested by early research does not necessarily correlate with how modern social networking occurs. Although this early work acknowledged the ways in which offline and online networks bled into one another, the assumed online-to-offline directionality may not apply to today's social networking sites, which are, according to Ellison and colleagues, 'structured both to articulate existing connections and enable the creation of new ones'.[18] Limited empirical research has addressed whether members use social networking sites to maintain existing ties or to form new ones.

1.2.3 *Diagram of social connectivity for users*

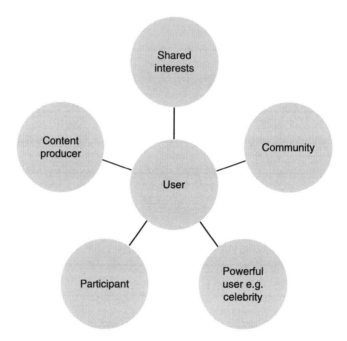

1.3 How social networking sites operate

1.3.1 *Nature of information sharing*

When a communication is sent via a social networking site, be it via a Smartphone, tablet or web browser, the content is normally only saved on the social networking site server. This type of cloud computing is a common way in which the majority of social networking sites operate.[19]

---

18 N.B. Ellison, C. Steinfield and C. Lampe (2007) 'The benefits of Facebook "Friends": social capital and college students' use of online social network sites', *Journal of Computer-Mediated Communication*, 12(4): 1143–1168.
19 The focus of this article will be social networking sites that host users' profiles on SNS servers, although we acknowledge that many different legal issues would arise if open source social networking sites (whereby users control their own servers) such as Diaspora were to become popular.

Although different hardware may be used to access the site, the way in which the social networking site server stores the information is the same. The use of the site will involve the storage of a number of pieces of data about a user, such as the user's IP address (location, etc.).[20] If a user accesses their account from a different computer or device, then this will also be recorded and assigned to that user. In this way, the activity logs of that user and their movement can be recorded such as their communications and their geographic migration.[21]

1.3.2 *Nature of information storing*

The way in which this activity log occurs is best illustrated by way of a simple example where 'A' posts on 'B's' wall. This posting will be saved on B's profile and on the SNS server. The information may also be stored on A's computer if he or she used the World Wide Web to make the posting. Analysis of a computer's hard-drive may sometimes reveal the contents of social networking site communications, but normally that information would have to be acquired by either accessing the profile itself online, or seeking the information from the relevant social networking sites that store it on their server.

1.4 Taxonomy of social networking data

1.4.1 *Types of data processed*

Several types of data may be shared via social networking sites. The table below shows the types of data that may be uploaded via a social networking site and the groups of users with which other users may wish to share their data.

Type of data	Description
Service data	Data a user may provide to a social networking site in order to set up an account. Such data might include a user's legal name, age, home address, gender, and email address.
Disclosed data	Data which the user posts on their own page, e.g. status updates, tweets, blog entries, photographs, messages, comments, and so on.
Entrusted data	Data posted on other account holders' pages, often similar in content to disclosed data, expect that the user relinquishes a degree of control over the data once it has been posted. Although such data may be deleted, the replication or re-sharing of the data, who views it, or the comments which are posted next to it may not be so easy to control.
Incidental data	Data posted by other users, e.g. comments, photographs taken by others that a user is tagged in. The user does not control this data and it is not created by the user who is the subject matter of the posting.
Behavioural data	Data collected by the social networking site which concerns a user's habits and preferences. The data is gathered by recording user activity and interactions with other users. It might include games played, topics the user writes about, news articles accessed, etc.
Derived data	Data about a user that is derived from all other sources of data.

20 *Applause Store Productions Ltd v Raphael* [2008] EWHC 1781 (QB).
21 Ibid. at [11].

8 Background

1.4.2 *Summary diagram of monitoring and engagement*

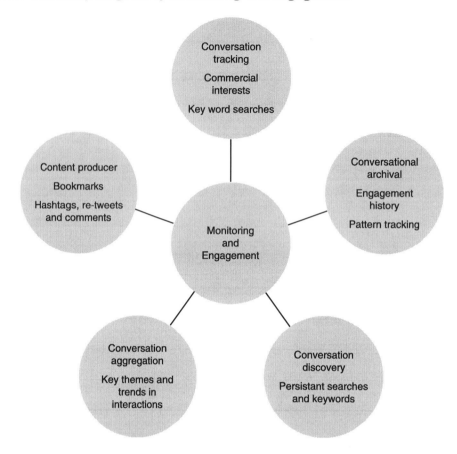

1.5 Categories of social media

1.5.1 *Types of sites*

Social media sites, applications, and services fall into one or more of several fundamental categories. Because of constantly evolving technology and the growing mainstream use of social media, certain websites, web services, and applications fit into more than one category, and may evolve over time to fall into different categories. It is useful to understand the characteristics of each category when examining the legal issues explored in this Handbook.

Type of media	Description
Blog	A 'web log' or website listing posted information and other content dated in reverse chronological order, self-published by authors (known as bloggers) on sites such as Blogspot, WordPress, Tumblr and Blogger.
Social and business networking site	A website where individual, corporate, and organizational users can connect to other users and display online their networks of friends and contacts for other users to see and form connections with. Prominent examples include Facebook and LinkedIn.

Introduction to social media and the law 9

Digital media sharing site	A website where users can upload and share videos, photos, and accompanying text. YouTube and Flickr are the main sites in this category.
MMPORG (Massively Multiplayer Online Role-Playing Game) site	MMORPG is a genre of video games that can be played by several users simultaneously regardless of physical location, over the Internet. Players adopt avatars to represent themselves in the virtual world online and interact with each other. SecondLife is the most popular example of this category. An avatar is a customized character in digital form created by an online user to personify his presence on a website and interact with other users, such as in online gaming communities, virtual worlds or forums.
Virtual world	A computer-based environment, such as a MMORPG, created to simulate a real or fictitious environment, often containing elements of both. Users of online virtual worlds interact through their avatars. Popular examples include ActiveWorlds, Kaneva, and SecondLife.

1.5.2 *Specific social media platforms explained*

Social media platform	*Description*
A Small World	An invitation-only social networking service that includes private messaging, forums, and event calendars.
Badoo	Badoo is a dating-focused social networking service, founded in 2006. It has in excess of 70 million users according to Alexa.com. It is managed out of its Soho, London headquarters but owned by a company based in Cyprus. The site operates in 180 countries and is most popular in Latin America, Spain, Italy, and France.
Delicious (formerly del.icio.us)	A social bookmarking site where members can save their website bookmarks in a central online location for future retrieval from any Internet browser at any time, and share those bookmarks with friends.
Digg	An online community where users discover, vote for, share, and comment on content from the Internet, including news, video, and images.
Doostang	A career-focused social networking site that enables members to post and apply for job openings, network with friends and friends of friends online, and conduct job searches according to industry, geography, and other criteria.
Facebook	Facebook operates as a social networking site based on interconnection with other users to generate content. Users must register before using the site, after which they may create a personal profile, add other users as friends, and exchange messages, including automatic notifications when they update their profile. Additionally, users may join common-interest user groups, organized by workplace, school or college, or other characteristics. Facebook also operates bespoke Privacy settings that allow users to categorize their friends into lists such as 'People From Work' or 'Close Friends' and grant them access to content accordingly. Individuals within these networks can 'Like' or 'Comment' on the posts of the users within their shared networks.
Flickr	An online photo management and sharing application that enables members to make the photo and video content they upload available on the web for viewing and commenting (public and private). Flickr is for personal (non-commercial) use only.

(continued)

10 Background

Social media platform	Description
Foursquare	A location-based social networking service generally logged into using a mobile device where users share their location with friends, check in to businesses to collect points and badges, and post information about nearby businesses or venues.
Friendster	Originally a social networking site that was re-launched in 2011 as a social gaming site. Also has a micropayments component called Friendster Wallet, enabling pre-paid payments between members on their sites for virtual gifts and games.
Geni	A website for families to privately connect with relatives, post pictures and send messages to other members in their online family tree. Members build their family tree by connecting with other relatives who are members of the website and posting personal family data.
Google +	A social network launched by Google in 2011 where members can connect with friends and other people in their 'circle' and see what other people are posting through their 'stream'. Members can also 'hang out' and video chat.
Instagram	A photo-sharing service where users can share photos that have had digital filters added to them onto social networks like Facebook or Twitter. The site is owned by Facebook.
Kaneva	A platform that hosts a free, 3D virtual world for users to gain an interactive experience through chatting, playing games, shopping, and hanging out.
Kickstarter	A crowd funding website that allows members to invest in projects for non-commercial gain.
LinkedIn	A professional networking website where members can maintain connections with other members, establish connections to contacts of members in their network, and be introduced to other members for help in job searches and other career-related goals.
Meetup	A social networking website that allows users to organize into groups and plan face-to-face meetings.
MySpace	A social networking website where members can personalize their profile pages, and to which they can post text, pictures, video, and audio. Members can share all of the content they post with member friends connected to their profile, as well as with the public, and can make their pages private so that they are not accessible to unconfirmed friends.
Newsvine	An online news website where members can post news articles and comments, and vote for published articles to appear at the top of Newsvine's popularity list of news stories. Newsvine is a subsidiary of NBCNews.com.
Orkut	A social networking website that is owned and operated by Google. The service is designed to help users meet new and old friends and maintain existing relationships. The website is named after its creator, Google employee Orkut Büyükkökten. Most frequently visited by users from India and Brazil. Originally hosted in California, in August 2008 Google announced that Orkut would be fully managed and operated in Brazil, by Google Brazil, in the city of Belo Horizonte. This was decided due to the large Brazilian user base and growth of legal issues.
Pinterest	A pin-board style social sharing site where users can create and manage image collections based on themes such as events, interests, and hobbies. Users can 're-pin' other people's images to their own board, like images or search through categories that interest them.

Posterous	A unique way to post small messages to various destinations. Posterous enables a user to connect his or her social networking accounts to the Posterous platform and to deliver the posts also to other social networking sites or email addresses of choice.
Reddit	A social news website that allows users to submit content that other users vote on, which ranks the posts and determines their position on the site's pages.
Second Life	A user-created, three-dimensional virtual world community, where members can create and customize an online 3D persona known as an avatar and conduct purchases using virtual currency known as Linden dollars (L$). Second Life provides the capability for businesses to develop and maintain a virtual presence, as well as a web-based marketplace where members can buy and sell products for avatars' use on the site.
Snapchat	A photo messaging application that allows users to take photos, record videos, add text and drawings referred to as 'Snaps'. Snaps can be sent to a controlled list of recipients, and users set a time limit for how long recipients can view their Snaps, after which they will be hidden from the recipient's device and deleted from Snapchat's servers.
StumbleUpon	A discovery engine (a form of search engine) that finds and recommends content that is relevant to its users.
Twoo	A site that allows users to chat, search, share photos, and play fun introductory games.
Viadeo	A professional networking site that is similar to LinkedIn. The site is available in English, French, German, Italian, Portuguese, Spanish. and Russian.
Wordpress	An open-source software program that allows users to publish websites or blogs.
Xing (called open BC/*Open Business Club* until 17 November 2006)	A social software platform for enabling a small-world network for professionals. Available languages include Dutch, English, Finnish, French, German, Hungarian, Italian, Japanese, Korean, Spanish, Polish, Portuguese, Russian, Simplified Chinese, Swedish, and Turkish. The platform offers personal profiles, groups, discussion forums, event coordination, and other common social community features. Basic membership is free. Many core functions, however, such as searching for people with specific qualifications or messaging people to whom one is not already connected, can only be accessed by premium members. Xing has a special 'Ambassador' program for each city or region around the world with a substantial constituency. The Ambassadors hold local events that promote the use of social networking as a business tool, letting members introduce business ideas to one another, and get to know each other on a personal level.
Yammer	A micro blogging site similar to Twitter aimed at streamlining internal workplace communications. Although it is free for employees to use, companies who want to get control of and manage their corporate Yammer networks must pay a fee. Yammer is owned by Microsoft.
YouTube	An online video community that allows users to publicly post, share, and view original videos, with a forum for user comments and a platform for creating individual channels. YouTube provides for video embedding, allowing users to link video posted on YouTube to their profiles on Facebook. Many businesses also send samples of their products to respected bloggers, e.g. in fashion and beauty to review or promote their products. (The advertising and marketing implications of such activities are considered in Chapter 14: Trading and Advertising Standards.)

12   *Background*

1.5.3 *Foreign language social networks*

In addition to English-speaking sites, there are a number of foreign language sites that are popular in different countries. Some have emerged to offer a tailored site based on cultural and social preferences, while others are worth a mention as censorship and privacy laws have meant that some of the sites detailed above are not accessible within that country.

1.5.3.1 *Belgium*

Netlog	Netlog (formerly known as Facebox and Bingbox) is a Belgian social networking website specifically targeted at the global youth demographic. On Netlog, members can create their own web page, extend their social network, publish their music playlists, share videos, and post blogs.
	The site was founded in July 2003 in Ghent, Belgium, by Lorenz Bogaert and Toon Coppens, and by 2007 had attracted 28 million members. The site now claims to have over 94 million registered users across 40 languages.
	In January 2011, Netlog announced that the site would become part of Massive Media, a global media group, focusing mainly on social media, and allowing product portfolio to expand into new markets.

1.5.3.2 *Brazil*

Orkut	A social networking website that is owned and operated by Google. The service is designed to help users meet new and old friends and maintain existing relationships. The website is named after its creator, Google employee Orkut Büyükkökten.

1.5.3.3 *China*

China is worth a special mention as neither Facebook nor Twitter are permitted there, and so a vast number of Chinese social networks take their place.

Sina Weibo	'Weibo', meaning micro blog, is the Chinese equivalent of Twitter and used by 22% of Chinese Internet users (there are 540 million Internet users in China).
Tencent Weibo	Tencent Weibo is very similar to its competitor Sina Weibo, but incorporates elements of Facebook by connecting people like a social network. It has 200–250 million users.
RenRen	The Chinese equivalent of Facebook. It started as a school reunion network and has around 31 million active users a month.
PengYou	A real-name social network owned by Tencent.
QZone	A social network that also allows people to blog; it is the most popular social network in China with 712 million registered users.

1.5.3.4 *Greece*

Zoo	The site gives users an in-site application to exchange mails with each other, join the chat, read news through FanClubs, an internal site application that reproduces news items from various websites, or play games, either single-player or multi-player.

Introduction to social media and the law 13

All games are programmed in Flash and include very simple and common games like chess, crosswords, backgammon, pool table, poker, and blackjack.

1.5.3.5 *Hungary*

IWIW (abbreviation for *International Who is Who*) — Hungarian social networking web service started on 14 April 2002 as *WiW* (*Who Is Who*). As of 2007 August, it has 2.6 million registered users with real names.

Every user can provide personal information such as the place they live, date of birth, schools and universities they attended, workplaces, interests, and pets. One can find friends by a search tool or looking through one's acquaintances' acquaintances.

1.5.3.6 *Iran*

Cloob — A Persian-language social networking website, mainly popular in Iran. After the locally (and internationally) popular social networking website Orkut was blocked by the Iranian Government, a series of local sites and networks, including Cloob, emerged to fill the gap.

Users have access to features like: internal email (for individual friends, groups of friends, and community members), communities and community discussions (clubs), personal and community photo albums, article archive for communities, live messaging and chat rooms for communities, weblog, job and resumé database, virtual money (called coroob), income/expense bookkeeping for individual members, online shops for offering goods and services, classifieds, questions and answers, link and content sharing, news, member updates, and extensive permission setting capabilities.

The Iranian Government censored Cloob on 7 March 2008 (the period of the Parliamentary elections). However, after what the Cloob management called 'removal of illegal and controversial content', access was restored to Iranian Internet users on 29 April 2008. On 25 December 2009, the site was censored and remained so for some time. As of 2011, Cloob appears to be in working order once again.

1.5.3.7 *Japan*

Mixi — Mixi is a community used for meeting new people based on common interests. Users can send and receive messages, write in a diary, read and comment on others' diaries, organize and join communities, and invite their friends.

Registration requires a valid Japanese cell phone number, which bars anyone who is not or has not been a resident of Japan. Since 2012, both Android and iPhone users can apply for a new Mixi account via specific apps made for their devices.

14 *Background*

1.5.3.8 *Netherlands*

Hyves	A social networking site used by two-thirds of the Dutch population where it competes with sites such as Facebook and MySpace. The name refers to beehives and the fact that social networks are built the same way. In May 2006, it became public that the Dutch police were using Hyves as a tool to investigate possible suspects. Only information that is uploaded by suspects is being checked. Hyves' users had the option to make their profiles only available (to a degree chosen by the user) to friends or friends of friends (the so-called 'connections'). Users could also protect their messages by making them visible only to friends or connections.
Partyflock	Dutch virtual community for people interested in house music and other electronic dance music.

1.5.3.9 *Poland*

Nasza Klasa	Polish social networking service that brings together students and alumni. The users are able to keep and maintain a personal page containing information such as their name, age, photos, interests, and the history of schools and classes attended. Nasza Klasa does not require an invitation to join; however, registration is necessary to browse the service.

1.5.3.10 *Russia*

VKonakte	Founded in 2006 by Pavel Durov, it has around 300 million visitors a month. In addition to its Facebook-like features, users can also stream video on the site.
Odnoklassniki	Russia's class reunion social network.

1.5.3.11 *Spain*

Tuenti	Tuenti is a Spanish, social networking service that has been referred to as the 'Spanish Facebook'. Although the name sounds similar to the English word *twenty*, it actually comes from *tu[id]enti[dad]*, meaning 'your identity'. The service was targeted at the Spanish market, but since 2012 is growing globally. Tuenti features many tools common to social networking sites. It allows users to set up a profile, upload photos, link videos, and connect with friends; recently, a chat application has been added. Many other utilities, such as the ability to create events, are also offered. Unlike similar social networking sites, which feature banner advertisements, Tuenti has opted out of these traditional forms of 'noisy' and obstructive advertising.

1.5.3.12 *Sweden*

LunarStorm	A social networking site that is similar to Facebook/MySpace but published in Swedish. Users can upload content, link shared interests to form groups, and post on each other's walls.

Introduction to social media and the law 15

1.5.4 *Vertically organized communities gathered around a specific topic*

Although these may not be considered as pure social networks, special attention should be given to the social sites that are dedicated to vertical markets such as the travellers' community (for example, tripadvisor[22] and travbuddy[23]), films or music. These sites offer service opinion-sharing by the users and they compute rankings. For example, dopplr allows its members to register their personal and business travel plans and get alerts from friends in the same places, travel overlaps, or get travel advice from other travellers. One of the open issues is to establish methodologies and tools to distinguish between real and fake opinions on those social sites, which is applicable to social networks in general.

Last.fm	Using a music recommender system called 'Audioscrobbler', Last.fm builds a detailed profile of each user's musical taste by recording details of the tracks the user listens to, either from Internet radio stations, or the user's computer or many portable music devices. This information is transferred ('scrobbled') to Last.fm's database either via the music player itself (Radio, Spotify, Clementine, Amarok) or via a plugin installed into the user's music player. The data is then displayed on the user's profile page and also compiled to create reference pages for individual artists.
Goodreads	A website that allows individuals to freely search Goodreads' extensive user-populated database of books, annotations, and reviews. Users can sign up and register books to generate library catalogues and reading lists. They can also create their own groups of book suggestions and discussions.
PatientsLikeMe	Online community for patients with life-changing illnesses to find other patients like them, allowing them to share their data with others, and learn more about their condition to improve their outcome. (See Chapter 13: 'Data Protection' for an exploration of privacy concerns into sensitive personal data concerning health.)
Wiser.org	Online community space for the social justice and environmental movement.
Zooppa	Online community for creative talent (host of brand-sponsored advertising contests).

1.5.5 *Mobile-only social networks*

Some sites work only via mobile phones or tablets.

Itsmy	Itsmy is a pure mobile social gaming network that combines open mobile games and mobile communication between gamers. In addition to mobile phones, games can also be played on almost all devices with Internet access.

There were a number of other mobile-only sites such as *Mobiluck* and *Brightkite* but these are no longer available for user subscription.

---

22 www.tripadvisor.co.uk.
23 www.travbuddy.com (also available through a Facebook app: https://apps.facebook.com/mytravelmap).

16   *Background*

1.6 Legal classification of SNSs

1.6.1 *Locating an SNS within existing statutory frameworks*

Many of the legislative provisions in this Handbook apply to social media, but they are not social media specific. For example, defamation can be committed in a number of ways, including publication in a newspaper, and public order offences can be committed in relation to rioting or violence, which is far removed from online activities. In order to put social media into a legal context and understand how the law is applied to it, it is therefore necessary to consider the various ways in which social networking is defined by the law, if indeed it is defined in a definitive way at all.

The way in which social networking sites operate is highly technical and therefore attempting to situate such sites within the existing law is a difficult task indeed. There is a suite of existing legal and regulatory frameworks such as the Regulation of Investigatory Powers Act 2000 (RIPA 2000), EU classifications of 'information society service' (ISS),[24] and 'electronic communications service' (ECS)[25] into which social networking sites may be categorised.

1.6.2 *Information society service provider*

An information society service (ISS) provider is defined in the Directive for Electronic Commerce[26] as, 'any service normally provided for remuneration at a distance, by means of electronic equipment for the processing (including digital compression) and storage of data, at the individual request of a recipient of the service'.[27]

It is important to note that social networking sites are accepted by the Section 29 Working Party (the Working Party)[28] to fall within the terms of an ISS.[29] The Working Party note that the definition of information society services already exists in Community law in Directive 98/34/EC of the European Parliament and of the Council of 22 June 1998. It also lays down a procedure for the provision of information in the field of technical standards and regulations and of rules on information society services.[30] Directive 98/84/EC of the European Parliament and of the Council of 20 November 1998 on the legal protection of services based on, or consisting of, conditional access states this is any service normally provided for remuneration, at a distance, by means of electronic equipment for the processing (including digital compression) and storage of data, and at the individual's request.

---

24 Directive 2000/31 on electronic commerce [2000] OJ L178/1. See Recital 17 for paraphrasing of the definition of an ISS.

25 Directive 2002/21 on a common regulatory framework for electronic communications networks and services (Framework Directive) Article 2(c) [2002] IJ L108/33.

26 Directive 2000/31/EC of the European Parliament and of the Council of 8 June 2000 on certain legal aspects of information society services, in particular electronic commerce, in the Internal Market ('Directive on electronic commerce') (Framework Directive) Article 2(c) [2002] IJ L108/33.

27 Ibid. at Recital [17].

28 EU Article 29, Data Protection Working Party (DPWP), Published Opinion 5/2009 on online social networking (12 June 2009), p. 4.

29 Directive 2000/31 on electronic commerce [2000] OJ L178/1. See Recital 17 for paraphrasing of the definition of an ISS.

30 OJ L 204, 21 July 1998, p. 37. Directive as amended by Directive 98/48/EC (OJ L 217, 5 August 1998, p. 18).

Introduction to social media and the law   17

According to *L'Oreal SA v eBay International AG*,[31] the key to establishing if a provider falls within the definition of an ISS is that the service must be provided neutrally by technical or automatic means such that the intermediary does not assume responsibility for the content that it hosts.[32] The types of providers who may fall within these categories include:

- Search engines
- Hosting companies
- Internet access providers
- Website operators.

It is important to remember that when determining if a provider falls within the definition of an ISS, the function that the site is performing must always be a key consideration. According to the Court in *L'Oreal*,[33] such factors will include a consideration of whether the operator plays such a role when it provides assistance that entails, in particular, optimizing the presentation of the offers for sale in question or promoting them.

1.6.3 *Electronic communications service*

An electronic communications service (ECS) is defined in the Communications Act 2003 as 'a service consisting of, or having as its principal feature, the conveyance by means of an electronic communications network of signals, except in so far as it is a content service'.[34] The Information Commissioners Office, who oversee data protection rights in the UK, has stated that an electronic communications service is any such service that is provided so as to be available for use by members of the public.[35]

In terms of the application of ECS to social networking, having regard to the above, it has been suggested by some commentators[36] that social networking sites constitute ISSs, but not ECSs. This is supported by the fact that retention obligations in the Data Retention (EC Directive) Regulations 2009 do not currently extend to any SNS communications.[37]

---

31 [2012] All ER (EC) 501.
32 See *L'Oreal SA v eBay International AG* [2012] All ER (EC) 501 and the Google joined cases C-236/08, C-237/08, and C-238/08.
33 At paras 6 and 7.
34 Section 32 Communications Act 2003.
35 http://ico.org.uk/for_organizations/privacy_and_electronic_communications/the_guide/security_of_services?hidecookiesbanner=true.
36 D. Ormerod and M. O'Floinn, Social networking sites, RIPA and criminal investigations [2011] Crim LR, Issue 10 2011.
37 Directive 2006/24 on data retention [2006] OJ L105/54. See further, responses of Mr. Vernon Coaker to questions posed during the discussion of the Draft Data Retention (EC Directive) Regulations 2009 (Fourth Delegated Legislation Committee, 16 March 2009), and Data Retention Expert Group (Commission Decision 2008/324/EC) on webmail and web-based messaging: DATRET/EXPGRP (2009) 2 – FINAL – ANNEX – 12 March 2009. For a critique of the Directive, see Feiler above and I. Brown, 'Communications data retention in an evolving Internet' (2011) IJL & IT 19(2), 95–109. Many countries have expressed concern over the directive and the ECJ is soon due to rule on its legality following a referral from Ireland. See further opinion of the European Data Protection Supervisor [http://www.edps.europa.eu/EDPSWEB/webdav/site/mySite/shared/Documents/EDPS/PressNews/Press/2011/EDPS-2011-06_DataRetentionReport_EN.pdf; accessed 2 August 2011].

18 Background

Locating the definition of a social networking site within the law is important, as the classification of an SNS affects the application of other legislation such as RIPA 2000. Ormerod[38] suggests that if an SNS does not fall into the definition of an ECS, it will not fall within the scope of the broad definition of a 'telecommunication service', contained in section 2(1) of RIPA 2000. Article 5(1) of the E-Privacy Directive[39] would also not apply. Furthermore, one of the stated purposes[40] behind RIPA 2000 was to implement Article 5 of the Telecommunications Data Protection Directive,[41] the precursor to the E-privacy Directive. Since social networking sites are not a 'telecommunication service', section 12 of RIPA 2000 is inapplicable to UK-based SNSs and they cannot (legally) be required to provide communications data under RIPA 2000.[42] However, the Intelligence and Security Commissions report on access to communications data suggests that such data will be accessible to intelligence and security agencies.

1.6.4 Intelligence and Security Committee: access to communications data by the intelligence and security agencies

In June 2012, the UK Government published its Communications Data draft Bill.[43] The intention of the Bill is to ensure that the police and other public bodies continue to be able to access communications data.

The Intelligence and Security Committee draft Bill states that 'communications data' is information about a communication. It applies to telephones (both landline and mobile) and to internet-based communications (including email, instant messaging, web browsing, and social media).[44] In relation to social media, the online username, login name or account name from which a message is sent or received; the date/time the message is sent; and the IP addresses of the computers used. The report offers sites such as Facebook and Twitter, online mail services such as Hotmail and Yahoo!Mail, and instant messaging services such as MSN Instant Messenger and Google Chat as examples of the types of social media that fall within the ambit of communications data.

---

38 D. Ormerod and M. O'Floinn, Social networking sites, RIPA and criminal investigations [2011] Crim LR, Issue 10 2011 at [669–770].

39 Directive 2002/58 on privacy and electronic communications [2002] OJ L201/37.

40 RIPA 2000, Explanatory Notes, para 9.

41 Directive 97/66 concerning the processing of personal data and the protection of privacy in the telecommunications sector [1997] OJ L24/1. Note the definition of 'telecommunication service' under this Directive was much broader than the new definition of ECS.

42 Section 22(4) RIPA 2000 and see s 25(1) for definition of 'telecommunications operator'. RIPA 2000 is not the only regulatory scheme applicable to information gathering from SNS providers. If communications data or content is stored, the information could potentially be requested under s 9 PACE 1984. See *R (on the application of NTL Group Ltd) v Ipswich Crown Court* [2002] EWHC 1585 (Admin); [2003] QB 131, which controversially sanctioned non-RIPA authorised interceptions of communications. However, the evidence is often based abroad, as is the provider, thereby hampering investigations. See I. Walden (2011). *Law Enforcement Access in a Cloud Environment*. London: Queen Mary School of Law, March, p. 12.

43 Draft Communications Data Bill, June 2012 Cm 8359.

44 Intelligence and Security Committee: Access to communications data by the intelligence and security Agencies at para [6].

The draft notes that there is an important distinction to be made between content and data. Communications data does not include the content of the communication, i.e. what is said in a telephone call; the subject, body and attachment(s) of an email; what is typed in an instant message; and postings on social media sites.[45]

1.6.5 Data Retention and Investigatory Powers Act 2014

The Data Retention and Investigatory Powers Act 2014 received Royal Assent on 17 July 2014. The purpose of the legislation is to allow security services to continue to have access to phone and internet records of individuals. The DRIP Act replaces previous UK regulations on data retention that had implemented an EU law which earlier this year was ruled to be invalid the Court of Justice of the EU (CJEU) in *Digital Rights Ireland and Seitlinger and Others* (Joined Cases C-293/12 and C-594/12).

The main provisions of the act are to allow the security services through the Secretary of State to retain the powers to require a public telecommunications operator to retain communications data in line with the purposes of the Regulation of Investigatory Powers Act 2000. The relevance of the Regulation of Investigatory Powers Act 2000 will be reviewed on a bi-annual basis. The type of communications data that can be accessed varies with the reason for its use, and cannot be adequately explained here, readers should refer to the legislation for more specific information.

In order to ensure that privacy aspects are afforded adequate consideration the Act contains provisions relating to the annual publication of a report of the amount of data intercepted under the regulations and will create a privacy and civil liberties board to act as an independent watchdog overseeing the security services' use of these powers.

The Act also acknowledges data protection issues which arise from compliance with the data protection principles (see Chapter 13). The Act requires a reduction in the number of public bodies that can access the data collected under the legislation and to limit the data which can be accessed under the regulations to only data that is relevant. To restrict the length of time such data can be held to 12 months. In terms of overseas transfers and collaboration with the USA, a diplomat to negotiate data transfers of such information with the United States will be appointed.

1.7 Summary Chart

See overleaf.

45 Ibid. at para [7].

Summary chart

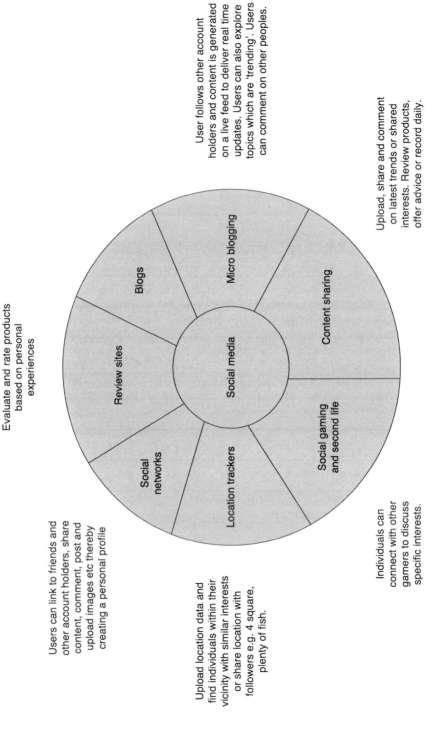

2 Human rights

2.1 Introduction

No volume discussing the interaction between social media and the law would be complete without considering the impact of the European Convention of Human Rights (ECHR)[1] and associated Strasbourg jurisprudence. The reason for this is that it has informed the development of all of the areas of law explored in this Handbook.

This chapter has been included not as a compendious exploration of the large breadth of case law effected by the ECHR, which is covered admirably in several other eminent texts. Rather, it is to provide background as to the interpretation given by the Courts to cases through the Human Rights Act 1998 and inform readers' understanding of the rest of the Handbook.

2.2 The European Convention of Human Rights

2.2.1 *Nature of rights contained within the European Convention of Human Rights*

The European Convention on Human Rights and Fundamental Freedoms (the ECHR, the Convention) treaty was signed in 1950 by the then members of the Council of Europe. As an instrument of international law, the ECHR was not directly part of UK law *per se*. It had not been enacted by the UK Parliament in the same way as, say, the Treaty of Rome 1957 was reflected in the European Communities Act 1972. Nevertheless, even before the Human Rights Bill, the Convention affected UK law in a number of ways. First, it provided a spur to legislation. To comply with its international obligations, the UK Government is obliged to attempt to secure legislative reform whenever it is found to be in breach. Legislation prompted by the European Convention, at least in part, includes, for example, the Contempt of Court Act 1981.[2]

The ECHR contains a number of rights such as the right to freedom of expression, the right to life, the right to privacy, and the right to a fair trial (this is not an exhaustive list, but is provided to illustrate the range of rights covered by the Convention to which social media has had the most profound application).

---

1 Convention for the Protection of Human Rights and Fundamental Freedoms: Rome, 4.XI.1950.
2 Considered in depth in Chapter 11.

22 Background

2.2.2 Convention applicants

It is a requirement of Article 1 of the Convention that Contracting Parties shall secure enjoyment of the rights and freedoms. Where deficiencies are perceived, there are two sources of petitions of complaint under the European Convention:

- The first source is inter-state applications. Governments are the traditional parties in international human rights law, and the idea of an inter-state application under Article 24 is to raise repeated and widespread, almost endemic, state-sponsored abuses of rights.
- The second involves petitions by individual persons under Article 25. This route has produced a far greater volume of case-law and has achieved for the Convention a degree of immediacy and relevance not rivalled by the vast bulk of other international laws. As far as the UK is concerned, individual petition has been recognised since 1966 and is renewed every five years (the current recognition period commenced in January 1996). Applicants may be natural persons (whether citizens or not), corporations, organizations or interest groups, but in all cases the applicant must be a 'victim', so actions cannot be brought *in abstracto* or on behalf of others.

2.2.3 Convention respondents

The application must be brought against a 'Contracting Party', in other words, a national government. State responsibility extends to agencies, bodies or persons acting with the authority of the state (such as the police). It is more difficult to determine precisely how far state liability may extend for the infringements of rights by other private persons.

By reference to Articles 1 and 13 (which requires Contracting Parties to provide an 'effective remedy' under national law for claims under the Convention), it is established that the national state must provide a satisfactory legal framework; in other words, one which allows Convention rights to be secured but in a way that is proportionate and consistent with other Convention rights. For example, states have been held to be in breach where laws did not allow for the prosecution of a sexual assault on a mental patient, or where in practice the free speech of demonstrators and policing action against disruptive and violent counter-demonstrators were inadequate.

With regard to statutes, the English courts, adopting the rule of construction that Parliament does not intend to legislate contrary to UK international law, have stated that the requirements of the Convention ought to be considered by them, though this applies only where English statute law is unsettled or ambiguous or is directly seeking to implement Convention requirements.

The application of the ECHR to the common law has been more problematic and has resulted in differing approaches depending on its application by the judiciary. In *Derbyshire County Council v Times Newspapers*[3] (a case concerning a defamatory publication), the House of Lords concluded that the ECHR had no relevance to the interpretation of the common law libel rules as to whether local corporations could

---

3 [1993] AC 534.

bring an action, although the reverse position was taken in the same case when it was heard before the Court of Appeal.

2.3 The Human Rights Act 1998

2.3.1 *Background*

The Labour government's manifesto for the May 1997 election campaign gave a firm commitment to incorporate by statute the ECHR into UK law. The commitment reflected the New Labour consultation paper, *Bringing Rights Home*, which had been issued in December 1996.[4] Subsequently, the provisions of the European Convention on Human Rights were to a large extent incorporated into domestic law by the Human Rights Act 1998 (HRA 1998). In brief, the effect of the HRA 1998 is to make it possible for litigants in the UK to rely on the Convention rights (the relevant Convention rights in the UK domestic courts without having to take the case to the European Court of Human Rights in Strasbourg, which was an expensive and time-consuming process).

The concept of Convention rights is central to the HRA 1998. There are certain rights from the ECtHR that are listed in Schedule 1 to the HRA 1998. Section 2 of the Act requires that any court or tribunal determining a Convention right must take into account any decision of the Strasbourg institutions, in particular judgments of the ECtHR. These decisions are not binding in the same way that decisions of higher courts within the UK are, or even decisions of the European Court of Justice (ECJ) in the context of European Community Law (EC Law), they must only be taken into account. Clearly, they will be highly persuasive, but should a court feel the need to decide the matter differently, then it is free to do so.[5]

It should be borne in mind throughout this book that social media, as an emerging technology, means that to an extent there is an uncertainty as to how to interpret the law. For this reason, when considering any legal or compliance issue, decisions given on Convention rights may also require looking further afield than Strasbourg. In *R v Khan*,[6] the Supreme Court accepted that it is appropriate to look to case law from other jurisdictions in determining such matters.

2.3.2 *The interpretative obligation*

Section 3 (Interpretation of Legislation) of the HRA 1998 states that:

> so far as it is possible to do so, primary legislation and subordinate legislation must be read and given effect in a way which is compatible with the Convention rights. This section –

---

4 See also the House of Commons, Library Research Papers, The Human Rights Bill [HL], Bill 119 of 1997/98, No 98/24, February 1998.
5 *R v Horncastle* [2009] UKSC 14.
6 [1997] AC 558.

- applies to primary legislation and subordinate legislation whenever enacted (s 3(2)(a) HRA 1998);
- does not affect the validity, continuing operation or enforcement of any incompatible primary legislation (s 3(2)(b) HRA 1998); and
- does not affect the validity, continuing operation or enforcement of any incompatible subordinate legislation if (disregarding any possibility of revocation) primary legislation prevents removal of the incompatibility (s 3(2)(c) HRA 1998).

The interpretative obligation applies to enactments prior to the HRA 1998 and after, and all legislation must be read in a way that is compatible with Convention rights, even if it is unambiguous so long as the wording will bear such an interpretation. Cases that demonstrate the purposive approach to interpretation include *Lister v Forth Dry Dock & Engineering Co Limited*,[7] in which the House of Lords (now the Supreme Court) were prepared to read delegated legislation as if the word needed to give effect to the ECHR were there in order to comply. Section 3 extends this 'purposive' approach beyond those pieces of legislation that implement EC law to all legislation. The diagram below breaks down this process.

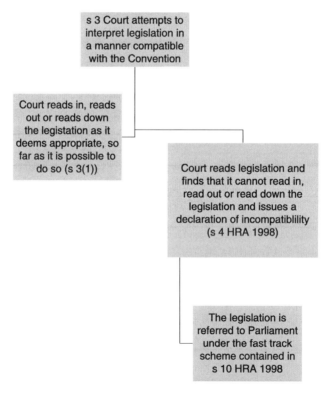

[7] [1990] 1 AC 546.

2.3.3 *Public authorities*

2.3.3.1 *Section 6 HRA 1998*

Even where there is no legislation in issue, *all* public authorities have an obligation to act in accordance with Convention rights. Under section 6(1) HRA 1998, 'It is unlawful for a public authority to act in a way which is incompatible with a Convention right.' However, section 6(1) does not apply to an act if:

- as the result of one or more provisions of primary legislation, the authority could not have acted differently (s 6(2)(a) HRA 1998); or
- in the case of one or more provisions of, or made under, primary legislation which cannot be read or given effect in a way which is compatible with the Convention rights, the authority was acting so as to give effect to or enforce those provisions (s 6(2)(b) HRA 1998).

Public authorities may find themselves challenged because the statutory framework within which they operate gives rise to the indirect application of Convention rights via the interpretive obligation. However, in addition, the Convention can be applied directly to their activities; it is not necessary for a litigant first to find a legal provision to interpret purposively.

Section 6 does not fully define a public authority, instead section 6(3) states that a '"public authority" includes – a court or tribunal, and any person certain of whose functions are functions of a public nature. It should be noted that this does not include either House of Parliament or a person exercising functions in connection with proceedings in Parliament.' The courts are still deciding exactly what this means. The following are definitely public authorities,[8] although the list is not exhaustive:

- central government
- local government
- local authorities
- police, prison, and immigration services
- NHS Trusts
- courts and tribunals
- planning inspectorate
- executive agencies
- statutory regulatory bodies.

2.3.3.2 *Locus standi*

There are special procedural rules when section 6 is invoked to challenge public authority. Section 7(1) introduces a locus standi test by which the claimant must prove that they are a victim of the unlawful act. Existing case law suggests that such

---

8   As confirmed by the Ministry of Justice, *Making Sense of Human Rights*, DCA 45/06, 2006 paper.

26 Background

persons must be actually and directly affected by the act or omission that is the subject of the complaint.[9] If, when interpreting the law, a body is unsure if the organization in question is a public authority, they should check this with a senior figure within the organization. In any event, following human rights standards will be good practice, even in matters not strictly covered by the ambit of the HRA 1998.

2.3.3.3 Limitation

Under section 7(5), section 6 challenges are subject to a one-year limitation period from the date when the offending act took place. However, it should be noted that this can be extended if the court determines that it would be equitable to do so in the circumstances. If judicial review is used, it must be done so promptly and in any event within three months.[10] Litigants should consider which route they wish to use to challenge the pubic authority. The section 3 interpretative obligation is not subject to these special provisions.

2.4 Convention rights

2.4.1 *Rights of particular application to social networking sites*

The substantive Convention rights that are of most importance for the purposes of this Handbook are:

- The right to a fair trial (Article 6 ECHR).
- The right to respect for private life and family life (Article 8 ECHR).
- The right to freedom of expression (Article 10 ECHR).

These Convention rights are explored in detail below.

2.4.2 *Article 6: The right to a fair trial*

Article 6 ECHR provides that everyone has the right to a fair trial in both civil and criminal cases. A party to legal proceedings has the right to be heard by an independent, impartial tribunal, in public, and within a reasonable amount of time. Article 6 is not subject to any exceptions, though the procedural requirements of a fair trial may differ according to the circumstances.

> ### Article 6: The right to a fair trial
>
> 1. In the determination of his civil rights and obligations or of any criminal charge against him, everyone is entitled to a fair and public hearing within

---

9 Note that this is a narrower test than judicial review, under which the complainant must demonstrate 'sufficient interest'.

10 Civil Procedure Rules Part 54.

a reasonable time by an independent and impartial tribunal established by law. Judgment shall be pronounced publicly but the press and public may be excluded from all or part of the trial in the interest of morals, public order or national security in a democratic society, where the interests of juveniles or the protection of the private life of the parties so require, or to the extent strictly necessary in the opinion of the court in special circumstances where publicity would prejudice the interests of justice.

2. Everyone charged with a criminal offence shall be presumed innocent until proved guilty according to law.

3. Everyone charged with a criminal offence has the following minimum rights:

(a) to be informed promptly, in a language which he understands and in detail, of the nature and cause of the accusation against him;

(b) to have adequate time and facilities for the preparation of his defence;

(c) to defend himself in person or through legal assistance of his own choosing or, if he has not sufficient means to pay for legal assistance, to be given it free when the interests of justice so require;

(d) to examine or have examined witnesses against him and to obtain the attendance and examination of witnesses on his behalf under the same conditions as witnesses against him;

(e) to have the free assistance of an interpreter if he cannot understand or speak the language used in court.

The state is obliged to establish courts that give all those accused a fair trial, and to ensure that nobody is punished without a fair trial. Article 6 ECHR imposes two different types of obligations on the state:

- a negative obligation not to punish anyone without a fair trial; and
- a positive obligation to establish a court system which upholds this right – for example, by providing interpreters or legal aid in criminal proceedings.

Article 6 ECHR specifies some additional aspects of the right to a fair trial that apply in criminal cases: the accused should be informed promptly about the charges against them in language they understand; they should have sufficient time and facilities to prepare a defence; they should be able to defend themselves in person or through a lawyer of their own choosing; and they should be given legal aid if they cannot afford representation and the interests of justice require it. They should also be able to call and question witnesses in the same way as the defence. The use of social networking in criminal proceedings is explored in Chapter 12: Evidence and Procedure.

2.4.3 *Article 8: The right to privacy*

Article 8(1) protects the private life of individuals against arbitrary interference by public authorities and private organizations such as the media. It covers four distinct areas:

- private life

28   *Background*

- family life
- home
- correspondence.

Article 8 is a qualified right, so in certain circumstances public authorities can interfere with the private and family life of an individual. These circumstances are set out in Article 8(2). Such interference must be proportionate, in accordance with law and necessary to protect national security, public safety or the economic well-being of the country; to prevent disorder or crime, protect health or morals, or to protect the rights and freedoms of others.

The concept of private life in UK law is based on the classic civil liberties notion that the state should not intrude into the private sphere without strict justification. In our modern system, aspects of this right are protected by several regulators and pieces of legislation, including the Data Protection Act 1998[11] and the Regulation of Investigatory Powers Act 2000.

Article 8: The right to respect for private and family life

1. Everyone has the right to respect for his private and family life, his home and his correspondence.
2. There shall be no interference by a public authority with the exercise of this right except such as is in accordance with the law and is necessary in a democratic society in the interests of national security, public safety or the economic well-being of the country, for the prevention of disorder or crime, for the protection of health or morals, or for the protection of the rights and freedoms of others.

Article 8 imposes two types of obligations on the state and public authorities:

- a negative obligation not to interfere with an individual's private life, family life, home and correspondence; and
- a positive obligation to take steps to ensure effective respect for private and family life, home and correspondence, between the state and the individual, the individual and private bodies, and between private individuals through law enforcement, legal and regulatory frameworks and the provision of resources.

2.4.3.1 *Correspondence*

Correspondence includes postal correspondence, telephone calls, emails, and text messages.[12] Examples of interference with correspondence include opening, reading,

---

11 See Chapter 13: Data Protection and Privacy, which focuses on information privacy, and concerns the collection, use, tracking, retention, and disclosure of personal information.

12 For interception of telephone calls, see *Malone v the United Kingdom* [1984] 7 EHRR; for emails, *Halford v the United Kingdom* [1997] 14 24 EHRR 523; and for post, *Golders v the United Kingdom* [1975] 1 EHRR 524.

Human rights 29

censoring or deleting correspondence.[13] It is interesting to note the categories of information that fall within correspondence, as presumably if email falls within the definition, then private messages communicated via social networking sites would also benefit from the same protection.

2.4.3.2 *The concept of a reasonable expectation of privacy*

It is important to understand that prior to the HRA 1998, there was no explicit right to privacy in English law. Instead, remedies for breaches of particular privacy interests have relied on certain aspects of the common law. For example, a person's reputation and confidential information were protected by the defamation and confidentiality laws; personal and property interests by the law of trespass.[14]

By incorporating Article 8 into UK law, the HRA 1998 changed how privacy was perceived and valued in the UK. It led to increased protection for the right to private and family life, and imposed obligations on the state to protect and promote Article 8; for example, the Regulation of Investigatory Powers Act 2000 provides protection from infringements of privacy relating to personal data and surveillance. The common law position in relation to privacy has had a great deal of application to social networking sites, with notable examples including the so-called 'Super Injunctions'[15] and revelation of the identity of John Venables on Twitter.[16] It is therefore necessary to consider the case law surrounding privacy law to locate social media within the development of this body of case law.

In *Campbell v MGN Ltd*,[17] Lord Nicholls stated 'essentially the touchstone of private life is whether in respect of the disclosed facts the person in question had a reasonable expectation of privacy'.[18] Lord Hope expressed that 'the underlying question in all cases where it is alleged that there has been a breach of the duty of confidence is whether the information that was disclosed was private and not public'.[19] Essentially, there must be some interest of a private nature that the claimant wishes to protect.[20] In some cases, the answer to the question whether the information is public or private will be obvious. Where it is not, the broad test is whether disclosure of the information about the individual ('A') would give substantial offence to A, assuming that A was placed in similar circumstances and was a person of ordinary sensibilities.[21]

---

13 *McCallum v the United Kingdom* [1990] 13 EHRR 596; *Campbell v the United Kingdom* [1992] ECHR 13590/88.

14 M. Amos (2006) *Human Rights Law*. Oxford: Hart Publishing, pp. 343–344.

15 *Christopher Hutcheson (previously known as KGM) v News Group Newspapers and ors* – injunction initially granted but later the courts refused to continue it; *John Terry (previously 'LNS') v Persons Unknown; WER v REW* – relates to an alleged extramarital relationship; *DFT v TFD; Ntuli v Donald; Fred Goodwin v News Group Newspapers Ltd and VBN* [2011] EWHC 1437 and *MNB v News Group Newspapers; NMC v Persons Unknown; ETK v News Group Newspapers Ltd; RJW & SJW v The Guardian newspaper & Person or Persons Unknown* – the Trafigura case.

16 These cases are considered in Chapter 4: Communications Act 2003 and Chapter 11: Contempt of Court Act 1981.

17 [2004] AC 457.

18 [2004] AC 457 at [21].

19 [2004] AC 457 at [91].

20 *A v B plc* [2003] QB 195, 206 para 11(vii).

21 [2004] AC 457 at [91].

30   *Background*

2.4.4 *Article 10: Freedom of expression*

Freedom of expression has been described as the cornerstone of a democratic society, enabling free decision-making through access to ideas and information imparted freely. The ECtHR describes it as 'one of the basic conditions for the progress of democratic societies and for the development of each individual'.[22]

> **Article 10: Freedom of expression**
>
> 1. Everyone has the right to freedom of expression. This right shall include freedom to hold opinions and to receive and impart information and ideas without interference by public authority and regardless of frontiers. This Article shall not prevent States from requiring the licensing of broadcasting, television or cinema enterprises.
> 2. The exercise of these freedoms, since it carries with it duties and responsibilities, may be subject to such formalities, conditions, restrictions or penalties as are prescribed by law and are necessary in a democratic society, in the interests of national security, territorial integrity or public safety, for the prevention of disorder or crime, for the protection of health or morals, for the protection of the reputation or rights of others, for preventing the disclosure of information received in confidence, or for maintaining the authority and impartiality of the judiciary.

Government has also ratified the Universal Declaration of Human Rights (UDHR)[23] and the International Covenant on Civil and Political Rights (ICCPR),[24] and Article 19 of both treaties protects freedom of expression.[25] The Press Complaints Commission administers self-regulation for the press and complaints about editorial content and journalists' conduct.

Article 10 is not an absolute right, it is qualified so that the state may validly interfere with such freedom (irrespective of the medium through which opinions, information, and ideas are expressed) if such interference can be justified under subsection 2 of Article 10. If the conditions laid down in the second paragraph are not fulfilled, a limitation on freedom of expression and information will amount to a violation of the Convention. The restrictions on the exercise of freedom of expression and information that are admissible according to Article 10, para 2, fall into three categories:

- those designed to protect the public interest (national security, territorial integrity, public safety, prevention of disorder or crime, protection of health or morals);

---

22 *Handyside* judgment of 7 December 1976, Series A No. 24, at para [49].
23 Declaration adopted by the United Nations General Assembly on 10 December 1948 at the Palais de Chaillot, Paris.
24 Multilateral treaty adopted by the United Nations General Assembly on 16 December 1966, and in force from 23 March 1976.
25 The ICCPR and its application to social media is discussed in depth in Chapter 4: Communications Act 2003.

Human rights 31

- those designed to protect other individual rights (protection of the reputation or rights of others, prevention of the disclosure of information received in confidence);
- those that are necessary for maintaining the authority and impartiality of the judiciary.

Cases of legitimate restrictions are to be specified in law[26] and can be accepted only when they are considered to be necessary in a democratic society.

2.4.4.1 *The margin of appreciation and justifying interference*

The Court has repeatedly stressed the importance of testing whether interference is necessary in the context of European supervision. The Court has consistently held that:

> contracting States enjoy a certain margin of appreciation in assessing the need for an interference, but this margin goes hand in hand with European supervision, whose extent will vary according to the case. Where there has been an interference with the exercise of the rights and freedoms guaranteed in paragraph 1 of Article 10, the supervision must be strict, because of the importance of the rights in question; the importance of these rights has been stressed by the Court many times. The necessity for restricting them must be convincingly established.[27]

In regard to the press, the Court held that 'the national margin of appreciation is circumscribed by the interest of democratic society in ensuring and maintaining a free press'.[28]

The European Court of Human Rights (ECtHR) has dealt with some aspects of internet communications,[29] but not issues arising from social networking sites. For contracting parties to the ECHR, even if the ECtHR might deem some SNS speech of little value,[30] SNS regulation will have to comply with the rigorous demands of

---

26 In the *Herczegfalvy* judgment, the Court found that Article 10 had been violated owing to the lack of a legal basis for the restrictions imposed on the applicant, who wanted access to reading matter, radio and television, and through interference in the exercise of his right to receive information during his psychiatric treatment and confinement. European Court of H.R., *Herczegfalvy* judgment of 24 September 1992, Series A No. 244. See also the *Hashman and Harrup* judgment of 25 November 1999, Reports 1999-VIII.

27 *Autronic AG* judgment of 22 May 1990, Series A No. 178, para 61.

28 *Worm v Austria* (1997) 25 EHRR 454, Reports 1997-V, para 47.

29 Nina Vajić and Panayotis Voyatis (2012) 'The internet and freedom of expression: a "brave new world" and the ECtHR's evolving case-law', in J. Casadevall, E. Myjer, M. O'Boyle and A. Austin (eds) *Freedom of Expression*. Oisterwijk: Wolf Legal Publishers, p. 391; and *Ahmet Yildirim v Turkey* Application No. 3111/10, 18 December 2012 (restriction of internet access without a strict legal framework regulating the scope of the ban and affording the guarantee of judicial review to prevent possible abuses violated Article 10 ECHR).

30 *Von Hannover v Germany* 40 EHRR 1; *Standard Verlags GmbH v Austria* (No. 2) Application No. 21277/05, Merits, 4 June 2009, at paras. 42–56. Cf. *Campbell v MGN* [2004] UKHL 22 at 149. See also Part 3: Communications-Based Offences, which deals with the 'tiers' of speech value, and L. Scaife (2013) 'The Communications Act 2003: a new approach coming out of the woods', *Communications Law Journal*, 18(1), 5–10.

32   Background

Article 10(2) of the ECHR.[31] However, the Commissioner for Human Rights in 2012, speaking in relation to social media, stated such networks 'host a vast and growing repository of personal data, all of it in digital form. It falls to our national and international authorities to ensure that our individual rights to privacy and data protection are not sacrificed to social networks, but rather reinforced to recognize and meet the range of new challenges these powerful new media present',[32] highlighting once again the importance of Convention rights in relation to online activity, specifically in the social media setting.

The courts have recognized that there is a hierarchy of speech value. On the Article 8 side, 'the more intimate the aspect of private life that is being interfered with, the more serious must be the reasons for interference before the latter can be legitimate'.[33] In *Campbell*,[34] Baroness Hale said of Article 10, that:

> there are undoubtedly different types of speech, just as there are different types of private information, some of which are more deserving of protection in a democratic society than others. Top of the list is political speech. The free exchange of information and ideas on matters relevant to the organization of the economic, social and political life of the country is crucial to any democracy. Without this, it can scarcely be called a democracy at all. This includes revealing information about public figures, especially those in elective office, which would otherwise be private but is relevant to their participation in public life. Intellectual and educational speech and expression are also important in a democracy, not least because they enable the development of individuals' potential to play a full part in society and in our democratic life. Artistic speech and expression is important for similar reasons, in fostering both individual originality and creativity and the free-thinking and dynamic society we so much value. No doubt there are other kinds of speech and expression for which similar claims can be made. But it is difficult to make such claims on behalf of the publication with which we are concerned here. The political and social life of the community, and the intellectual, artistic or personal development of individuals are not obviously assisted by pouring over the intimate details of a fashion model's private life.[35]

2.4.5 Balancing Article 8 and Article 10

2.4.5.1 Why the rights must be balanced

As noted above, freedom of expression is a qualified right and so must be carefully balanced against other rights. Article 10(2) explicitly states that the exercise of freedom of expression carries with it 'duties and responsibilities'. It can be restricted

---

31 See J. Rowbottom (2012) 'To rant, vent and converse: protecting low level digital speech', *Cambridge Law Review*, 71(2): 355–383, and L. Scaife (2013) 'The Communications Act 2003: a new approach coming out of the woods', *Communications Law Journal*, 18(1): 5–10.

32 Social Media and Human Rights, Strasbourg February 2012, CommDH (2012) 8.

33 *Douglas v Hello! Ltd* [2001] QB 967, Keene LJ at [168].

34 [2004] UKHL 22.

35 [2004] UKHL 22 per Baroness Hale at [158–159].

on several grounds, including national security, the prevention of disorder or crime, and the protection of the reputation or rights of others. Achieving this balance is not always an easy task. In *A v B Plc*,[36] Lord Woolf CJ explained that the court, as a public authority, was able to fulfil its duty under section 6 of the Human Rights Act 1998 'by absorbing the rights which articles 8 and 10 protect into the long-established action for breach of confidence'.[37] He went on to say:

> There is a tension between the two articles which requires the court to hold the balance between the conflicting interests they are designed to protect. This is not an easy task but it can be achieved by the courts if, when holding the balance, they attach proper weight to the important rights both articles are designed to protect. Each article is qualified expressly in a way which allows the interests under the other article to be taken into account.[38]

2.4.5.2 *The correct approach towards balancing competing Convention rights*

The Court must carry out the parallel analysis as suggested by the House of Lords in *Re S*[39] per Lord Steyn, which he described as the 'ultimate balancing test':[40]

- Firstly an acknowledgement, when conducting the exercise that neither article has as such precedence over the other.
- Where the values under the two articles are in conflict, conducting an intense focus on the comparative importance of the specific rights being claimed in the individual case is necessary.
- After undertaking stage two, considering carefully the justifications for interfering with or restricting each right must be taken into account; and
- Undertaking a proportionality impact assessment in relation to each right in question.[41]

Accordingly, there are two key questions that must be answered in a case where the complaint is of the wrongful publication of private information:

- Is the information private in the sense that it is in principle protected by Article 8 (i.e. such that Article 8 is in principle engaged)? And, if so:
- Whether in all the circumstances the interest of the owner of the information must yield to the right to freedom of expression conferred on the publisher by Article 10?[42]

---

36 [2003] QB 195.
37 [2003] QB 195 at [4].
38 [2003] QB 195 at [6].
39 [2005] 1 AC 593.
40 [2005] 1 AC 593 at [17].
41 Ibid.
42 *Murray v Big Pictures Ltd* [2008] 3 WLR 1360, Sir Anthony Clarke MR at [27].

34 Background

As the structure of Articles 8 and 10 of the Convention are the same, the like considerations apply to Article 8(2) as apply to Article 10(2). In this regard, the House of Lords in *R v Shayler*[43] noted that it:

> is plain from the language of Article 10 (2), and the European Court has repeatedly held, that any national restriction on freedom of expression can be consistent with Article 10 (2) only if it is prescribed by law, is directed at one or more of the objectives specified in the article and is shown by the state concerned to be necessary in a democratic society. The House of Lords stated that 'necessary' has been strongly interpreted in case law, but that it is not synonymous with 'indispensable'. It does not have the flexibility of such expressions as 'admissible, ordinary, useful, reasonable or desirable'.[44]

It was suggested in *Shayler* that Courts must consider:

- If the interference complained of corresponded to a pressing social need;
- Whether it is proportionate to the legitimate aim pursued; and
- Whether the reasons given by the national authority to justify it are relevant and sufficient under Article 10(2).[45]

Further, in *Shayler* Lord Hope said that the principle of legality requires the court to address itself to three distinct questions:

- Is there is a legal basis in domestic law for the restriction?
- Is the law or rule in question sufficiently accessible to the individual who is affected by the restriction, and sufficiently precise to enable him to understand its scope and foresee the consequences of his actions so that he can regulate his conduct without breaking the law?
- Assuming that the these two requirements are satisfied, it is nevertheless open to the criticism on the Convention ground that it was applied in a way that is arbitrary because, for example, has it been resorted to in bad faith or in a way that is not proportionate?[46]

Lord Hope elaborated on the meaning of proportionality in this context and concluded that the following three-stage test should be applied:

- Whether the objective to be achieved, that is to say, 'the pressing social need', is sufficiently important to justify limiting the fundamental right;
- Whether the means chosen to limit that right are rational, fair, and not arbitrary; and
- Whether the means used impair the right as minimally as possible.

---

43 [2003] 1 AC 247.
44 See *Handyside v United Kingdom* (1976) 1 EHRR 734, 754, at para 48.
45 [2003] 1 AC 247 per Lord Bingham at [23]; adopting the analysis of the Court in *The Sunday Times v United Kingdom* (1979) 2 EHRR 245, 277–278 at para [62].
46 [2003] 1 AC 247 at [56].

The same approach can be applied to conflicts with other rights, such as Article 6.

2.5 Freedom of expression and human rights in European and international jurisprudence and opinion

As affirmed in *DPP v Chambers*,[47] the ECtHR has long adopted the view in its significant body of jurisprudence, that an individual's freedom of expression includes the right to say things or express opinions 'that offend, shock or disturb the state or any sector of the population'.[48] The United Nations Special Rapporteur on Freedom of Expression has asserted the same approach.[49]

2.5.1 *International Covenant on Civil and Political Rights 1966*

The UK is also a party to the International Covenant on Civil and Political Rights 1966 (ICCPR 1966). Article 19(2) provides:

> Everyone shall have the right to freedom of expression; this right shall include freedom to seek, receive and impart information and ideas of all kinds, regardless of frontiers, either orally, in writing or in print, in the form of art, or through any other media of his choice.

From the body of jurisprudence evolving out of the Human Rights Committee (HRC), it is evident that the HRC has had no difficulty in applying that provision to freedom of expression on the internet.[50] In its General Comment in 2011, expression was deemed to include 'all forms of electronic and internet-based modes of expression'.[51] It has therefore been recommended by the HRC that states who are party to its provisions should ensure that there are legislative and administrative frameworks in place to accommodate and address the regulation of the mass media in a manner that is consistent with Article 19(3) of the ICCPR 1966, which provides:

---

47 [2012] EWHC 2157; 2012 WL 2923016 at [38].

48 *Handyside v United Kingdom* (1976) 1 EHRR 737, at para 49.

49 See Frank La Rue, 'Report of the Special Rapporteur on the promotion and protection of the right to freedom of opinion and expression', A/HRC/17/27, 16 May 2011, at para 2. The Report also acknowledges that the internet has created challenges to the right of all individuals to seek, receive, and impart information and ideas of all kinds through the internet and considers key trends (see para 37 of the Report).

50 See also 'General principles on the right to freedom of opinion and expression and the internet'; and Human Rights Council, Resolution 20/8, A/HRC/RES/20/8, 16 July 2012, at para 1.

51 GC 34, supra no. 4 at para 12. Human Rights Committee, General Comment No. 34: 'Freedoms of opinion and expression', CCPR/C/GC/34 (GC 34) 12 September 2011, at para 15 states: '[I]nternet and mobile based electronic information dissemination systems, have substantially changed communication practices around the world. There is now a global network for exchanging ideas and opinions that does not necessarily rely on the traditional mass media intermediaries.' See also Michael O'Flaherty (2012). 'Freedom of expression: Article 19 of the ICCPR and the Human Rights Committee's General Comment No. 34', *Human Rights Law Review*, 12(4): 627.

36 *Background*

The exercise of the rights provided for in para 2 of this Article carries with it special duties and responsibilities. It may therefore be subject to certain restrictions, but these shall only be such as are provided by law and are necessary: (a) For respect of the rights or reputations of others; (b) For the protection of national security or of public order (ordre public), or of public health or morals.

2.5.2 *Approach to restrictions and censorship*

In terms of ensuring that rights are respected, the HRC considers that any restrictions on the operation of websites, blogs or any other internet-based, electronic or other such information dissemination system, including systems to support such communication, such as internet service providers or search engines, are only permissible to the extent that they are compatible with Article 19(3). The HRC has considered that journalism is a function shared by a wide range of actors, including bloggers and others who engage in forms of self-publication on the internet or elsewhere. This is particularly interesting given that in ECtHR jurisprudence everyday speech has been afforded a low value in terms of its protection. However, this approach was not adopted in the case of *Woods* (see Chapter 4 'Communications Act 2003' for a discussion of *Woods*).

2.5.3 *Special Rapporteur's Joint Declaration on Freedom of Expression*

On 1 June 2011, the Special Rapporteur, together with the Special Rapporteur for Freedom of Expression of the Inter-American Commission on Human Rights of the Organization of American States, the Representative on Freedom of the Media of the Organization for Security and Cooperation in Europe, and the Special Rapporteur on Freedom of Expression of the African Commission on Human and Peoples' Rights, issued a Joint Declaration establishing guidelines to protect freedom of expression on the internet, reinforcing the need to protect freedom of expression even in the online context. It is suggested that the report's findings are of equal applicability to social media sites. The 2011 opinion provided useful further guidance for national regulators stating they should take into account the differences between the print and electronic media and how this impacts upon media coverage.[52]

In the Joint Declaration, the four Rapporteurs declared that states have the obligation to promote universal access to the internet, and cannot justify for any reason the interruption of that service to the public, not even for public safety or national security reasons. This means in practice that any measure that limits access to the network is unlawful, unless it meets the strict requirements established by international standards for such actions. It is especially noted in the report that the rights in relation to

---

52 Joint Declaration on Freedom of Expression and the internet, The United Nations (UN) Special Rapporteur on Freedom of Opinion and Expression, the Organization for Security and Cooperation in Europe (OSCE) Representative on Freedom of the Media, the Organization of American States (OAS) Special Rapporteur on Freedom of Expression and the African Commission on Human and Peoples' Rights (ACHPR) Special Rapporteur on Freedom of Expression and Access to Information, Press Release R50/11.

Human rights 37

freedom of expression must apply to the internet in the same way it applies to all other media. If restrictions are to be imposed, they must comply with the international standards in force, such as being expressly established by law, pursuing a legitimate aim recognised by international law, and being necessary to accomplish such aim as is consistent with the recommendations of other human rights bodies (explored throughout this chapter).

2.5.3.1 *Censorship and blocking*

On the issue of censorship, the mandatory blocking of websites are extreme actions that may only be justified in accordance with international standards. The Rapporteurs state that content-filtering systems that cannot be controlled by the users, imposed by governments or commercial providers, are also actions that are incompatible with freedom of expression. It is noted that in relation to the criminal law this has caused significant difficulties in the UK as to when filtering and content removal should occur (see Chapter 4: Communications Act 2003 for a discussion of the implications of censorship and monitoring).

2.5.3.2 *Role of intermediaries*

According to the Declaration, internet service intermediaries must not be held responsible for content generated by third parties nor may they be required to control user-generated content. The Rapporteurs noted an awareness on their part when drafting the Declaration that the vast range of actors who act as intermediaries for the internet – providing services such as access and interconnection to the internet, transmission, processing and routing of internet traffic, hosting and providing access to material posted by others, searching, referencing or finding materials on the internet, enabling financial transactions and facilitating social networking – has led to attempts by some states to deputise responsibility for harmful or illegal content to these actors.

The Rapporteurs suggest that intermediaries should only be held responsible for such content if they fail to exclude such content when directed to do so in a lawful court order, issued in accordance with due process, and provided that they have the technical capacity to do so. The intermediaries must in the view of the Rapporteurs be required to be transparent with respect to their practices for the management of traffic or information, and must not discriminate in any way in the treatment of data or traffic. Such transparency can be viewed, for instance, though Twitter's quarterly Reports for Information Requests, Content Removal Requests and Copyright Infringement.[53]

Interestingly, the Rapporteurs suggest that private individuals who feel adversely affected by certain content disseminated on the web should only be able to take legal action in the jurisdiction in which they can demonstrate having suffered a substantial harm. The interrelationship with the Defamation Act 2013 is most interesting in this regard, especially with the introduction of section 5 of the Defamation Act 2013, the website host and intermediaries defence.[54]

---

53 Reports for Information Requests, Content Removal Requests, and Copyright Infringement can all be accessed via the hub website: https://transparency.twitter.com/.
54 The defence and linked defences for hosts and intermediaries is explored in Chapter 3: Defamation.

38 Background

2.5.4 *The United Nations Comprehensive Study on Cybercrime Paper*

2.5.4.1 *The Committee's reasons for drafting the White Paper*

The United Nations Office on Drugs and Crime (UNODC) Comprehensive Study on Cybercrime Paper (the Cybercrime Paper)[55] notes that the increasing use of social media and user-generated internet content has resulted in regulatory responses from governments, including the use of criminal law, and calls for respect for rights to freedom of expression. The Cybercrime Paper states[56] that:

> online content has particular features – including the fact that the impact and longevity of information can be multiplied when placed on the internet, that content is easily accessible to minors, and that developments in social media and user-generated internet content have begun to challenge traditional monopolies over information.[57]

As a result, the interpretation of human rights provisions must take into account the specific nature of the internet as a means of imparting information.[58]

The UNODC report on cybercrime notes that social media (and the internet) have become increasingly important aspects of political activity and socio-cultural expression. Due to the increase in the use of social media to express such views, it has been suggested in the report that there is an emerging need for:

*   national clarifications regarding the criminal law applicable to forms of online expression; and
*   discussion concerning criminalization differences arising from jurisdictional issues and diverse legal traditions.

2.5.4.2 *The role of national guidelines*

The UN, like the Rapporteurs in their Joint Declaration, noted that faced with a large rise in social media 'crimes',[59] some countries have, for example, recently issued interim guidance on prosecuting cases involving communications sent via social media,[60]

---

55 Comprehensive Study on Cybercrime Paper, The United Nations Office on Drugs and Crime, Draft 2013.
56 Ibid.
57 United Nations Human Rights Council (2012) 'Summary of the Human Rights Council panel discussion on the promotion and protection of freedom of expression on the internet', Report of the Office of the United Nations High Commissioner for Human Rights, A/HRC/21/30, 2 July 2012.
58 ECtHR, Research Division (2011) *Internet: Case-Law of the European Court of Human Rights.*
59 In 2008 in England and Wales, for example, there were 556 reports of alleged social media crimes with 46 people charged. In 2012, there were 4,908 reports with 653 people charged; see http://www.bbc.co.uk/news/uk-20851797. In Western Asia, a number of recent criminal cases related to internet social media content have also been reported; see http://www.bbc.co.uk/news/worldmiddle-east-20587246.
60 Crown Prosecution Service (2012) 'Interim guidelines on prosecuting cases involving communications sent via social media', issued by the Director of Public Prosecutions, 19 December 2012. These guidelines are discussed in detail below.

including the UK. A common feature running throughout the guidelines is an emphasis that criminal provisions must be interpreted consistently with free speech principles and can assist in clarifying the extent of acceptable expression.

The human rights doctrine of the 'margin of appreciation' allows a certain amount of leeway to countries in determining the boundaries of acceptable expression in line with their own cultures and legal traditions.[61] The UNODC report acknowledges[62] that there are diverse national approaches to the criminalization of internet and social media content that can be accommodated by international human rights law, within certain boundaries. These include permissible criminal prohibitions on:

- Child pornography;
- Direct and public incitement to commit genocide;
- Advocacy of national, racial or religious hatred that constitutes incitement to discrimination, hostility or violence;
- Incitement to terrorism; and
- Propaganda for war.

However, this is not to suggest that criminalization may fall within the margin of appreciation in every case; the UN suggests that criminalization may not be justified if it concerns criminal offences relating to:

- Defamation;
- Obscene material; or
- Insult.

These types of activity will likely face a high threshold test, even within the margin of appreciation, in order to demonstrate that the measures conform to the principle of proportionality, are appropriate to achieve their protective function, and are the least intrusive instrument among those which might achieve protection.[63]

---

61 Where a particularly important right or value is at stake, the margin of appreciation accorded to a state will, in general, be restricted (ECtHR, Application No. 44362/04, 18 April 2006). In contrast, if the aim pursued does not enjoy universal consensus – such as the meaning of the 'protection of morals' – the margin of appreciation will be wide (ECtHR, Application No. 10737/84, 24 May 1988). The ECtHR employs, among other things, a common (European) consensus test in determining the margin available – when consensus on the meaning or need for limitations on particular rights is absent, the margin expands. Conversely, when consensus is present, it is taken to mean that the 'core' meaning of the right is narrowly defined and the margin to deviate contracts. The domestic margin of appreciation thus goes hand in hand with a 'European supervision' – concerning both the aim of interferences and their 'necessity'. The margin of appreciation doctrine is less developed in the work of the Inter-American Court of Human Rights and the United Nations Human Rights Committee. Nonetheless, commentators note that there is an increasing role for the margin of appreciation in the Inter-American system, and that ample evidence supports the proposition that the doctrine forms part of the United Nations Human Rights Committee's practice (A. Legg (2012) *The Margin of Appreciation in International Human Rights Law.* Oxford Monographs in International Law. Oxford: Oxford University Press).

62 Comprehensive Study on Cybercrime Paper, The United Nations Office on Drugs and Crime, Draft 2013, Chapter 4: *Criminalization* at p. 116.

63 United Nations Human Rights Committee (2011) General Comment No. 34, Article 19: 'Freedoms of opinion and expression', CCPR/C/GC/34, 12 September 2011 at para [34].

40 *Background*

The increasing use of social media and user-generated internet content has resulted in regulatory responses from government, including the use of criminal law, and calls for respect for rights to freedom of expression.[64] Over 30 years ago, the Chair of the then United Nations Committee on Crime Prevention and Control[65] stated that, 'crime is what is defined by law as such. On the other hand, the definition must take into account the existence of, and respect for human rights and not merely be the expression of arbitrary power.'[66] In other words, national criminal laws are not to be excluded from the oversight of international human rights law.[67]

With some notable exceptions (such as the obligation to make all acts of torture a criminal offence and the prohibition of retroactive criminal offences),[68] international human rights law has not traditionally specified directly what should, or should not, be a criminal offence in national law.[69] However, this is not to suggest that international human rights law jurisprudence does not increasingly face the question of whether the criminalization of certain conduct is compatible with, or even required by, individual human rights and in doing so can act both as a 'shield' and a 'sword', either neutralizing or triggering the criminal law.[70]

The report considered this issue in some depth, noting that while the state which is party to human rights treaties has an obligation to establish criminal law and systems sufficient to deter and respond to attacks on individuals,[71] it must not go so far as to deny individual rights by its criminalization of particular conduct.[72] In order to

64 Comprehensive Study on Cybercrime Paper, The United Nations Office on Drugs and Crime, Draft 2013, Chapter 4: *Criminalization* at p. 107.

65 The Committee was established by resolution of the United Nations Economic and Social Council in May 1971. See United Nations Economic and Social Council, Resolution 1548(L), 1971.

66 M. López-Rey (1978) 'Crime and human rights', *Federal Probation*, 43(1): 10–15, at p. 11.

67 The human rights contained in customary international law, the nine core international human rights treaties and their protocols, as well as the treaties of the three regional human rights mechanisms, and the authoritative interpretations of these instruments by mechanisms established thereunder, or otherwise for the purposes of their promotion and implementation, are taken as the principal expression of 'international human rights law'. Including: ICCPR, ICESCR, ICERD, CEDAW, CAT, CRC, ICRMW, CPED, and CRPD. In addition, Optional Protocols to ICESCR, ICCPR, CEDAW, CRC, CAT, and CRPD cover areas such as the abolition of the death penalty (ICCPR-OP2), the involvement of children in armed conflict (OP-CRC-AC), and the sale of children, child prostitution, and child pornography (OP-CRC-SC). At the regional level, including: EHCR and its 15 Protocols, including on protection of property and the right to education, freedom of movement, abolition of the death penalty, and a general prohibition on discrimination, the ACHR in the Americas, and in Africa, the ACHPR. At present, there is no Asia-wide convention on human rights.

68 CAT, Article 4 and ICCPR, Article 15(1).

69 It should be noted, however, that international human rights law does require redress for violations of human rights and that this may imply in turn the promulgation of appropriate criminal laws sufficient to deter and respond to certain violations.

70 F. Tulkens (2011) 'The paradoxical relationship between criminal law and human rights', *Journal of International Criminal Justice*, 9(3): 577–595.

71 See, for example, ECtHR, Application No. 23452/94, 28 October 1998, in which the court stated that the right to life (ECHR, Article 2(1)) included the obligation to put in place 'effective criminal law provisions to deter the commission of offences against the person backed up by law enforcement machinery for the prevention, suppression and sanctioning of breaches of such provisions'.

72 United Nations Commission on Narcotic Drugs, and Commission on Crime Prevention and Criminal Justice (2010) 'Drug control, crime prevention and criminal justice: a human rights perspective'. Note by the Executive Director, E/CN.7/2010/CRP.6 – E/CN.15/2010/CRP.1. 3 March 2010.

undertake an impact assessment, states must therefore assess criminal provisions on a 'right-by-right' basis.[73] By approaching an analysis of the provisions in this way, it is possible to test whether its contents infringe a range of individual rights – such as the right not to be subjected to arbitrary or unlawful interference with privacy, family, home or correspondence,[74] the right to freedom of thought, conscience, and religion,[75] or the right of peaceful assembly.[76]

2.5.4.3 *The Draft Reports analysis of ICCPR and its application to social media*[77]

As noted above, the UK is a signatory to the ICCPR. It is therefore useful to consider the analysis of the application of the ICCPR in the social media context and how the ICCPR may be interpreted in the future. This may give an indication as to the way in which the government, the courts, and other regulatory bodies may approach cases involving a social media aspect and how the law may be reformed in a way that is compatible with the demands of international law.

The report highlights several issues as of particular concern in the social media context. These include the increase in cases involving the internet that raise hate speech issues, including video containing anti-Islamic content and Twitter messages inciting racism.[78]

It is suggested by the UN that while Article 20 ICCPR is engaged as it imposes an obligation to combat such expression, it is important to recall that ICCPR Article 20 requires a high threshold. In order to meet the threshold, restrictions on such speech must meet the following three-part test:

* Legality;
* Proportionality; and
* Necessity.

The severity of the hate speech which may justify restricting freedom of expression must also be considered, which the UN indicate should include an assessment of:

* the context of the statement;
* the position or status of the speaker;
* the intent (negligence and recklessness should not suffice);
* the content or form of statement;
* the extent of the statement; and
* the degree of risk of resulting harm.[79]

---

73 Ibid.
74 ICCPR, Article 17.
75 ICCPR, Article 18.
76 ICCPR, Article 21.
77 Comprehensive Study on Cybercrime Paper, The United Nations Office on Drugs and Crime, Draft 2013, Chapter 4: *Criminalization* at p. 113.
78 Ibid.
79 United Nations Office of the High Commissioner for Human Rights (2012) 'Rabat Plan of Action on the prohibition of advocacy of national, racial or religious hatred that constitutes incitement to discrimination, hostility or violence'. Conclusions and recommendations emanating from the four regional expert workshops organized by OHCHR, in 2011, and adopted by experts in Rabat, Morocco on 5 October 2012.

42 Background

Non-binding principles further highlight that the terms 'hatred' and 'hostility' used in ICCPR Article 20 refer to 'intense and irrational emotions of opprobrium, enmity and detestation towards the target group'.[80] At the European level, the ECtHR emphasises the need for genuine and serious incitement to extremism, as opposed to ideas that simply offend, shock or disturb others.[81]

In the UK, such postings could be prosecuted via an umbrella of existing legislation such as the Serious Crimes Act 2007, Crime and Disorder Act 1998, and the Communications Act 2003. Although falling into the category of a grossly offensive tweet, the prosecution of *Azhar Ahmed*[82] for posting a message on Facebook about the deaths of six British soldiers in Afghanistan, which read 'All soldiers should die and go to hell', could be described as a category of posts which disapproves of measures to counteract terrorism. Ahmed was charged after the mother of one of the soldiers read the comments and was so upset she called the police. The police described the tweet as a 'racially aggravated public order offence'. However, applying the factors above, it is likely that such a post would fall short of racist activity, as the tweet itself did not refer to any racist content. In the case, Ahmed received 240 hours' community service. District Judge Jane Goodwin said the law should not stop legitimate political opinions being strongly voiced, but she said the test was whether what was written was 'beyond the pale of what's tolerable in our society'.

The case demonstrates the importance of considering the value of speech[83] and the right to freedom of expression and that this is a most careful balancing act which must be undertaken before an individual's speech is criminalised and when there may be a racially aggravating factor.[84]

2.6 Terrorism

2.6.1 *Introduction*

As noted above, the Cybercrime Paper also made observations of the use of social media to promote terrorism and terrorist activity.[85] The Cybercrime Paper noted that

---

80 Article 19, 2009. The Camden Principles on Freedom of Expression and Equality. Principle 12.
81 Council of Europe, July 2012. *Factsheet – Hate speech*, accessible via http://www.echr.coe.int/Documents/FS_Hate_speech_ENG.pdf.
82 9 October 2012, Unreported, Huddersfield Magistrates' Court, Before: District Judge (Magistrates' Court) Goodwin.
83 Note that political speech is at the pinnacle of the protection of speech in Strasbourg Jurisprudence, see Chapter 4: Communications Act 2003 (Interrelationship with the Human Rights Act and Speech Value) and *Campbell v MGN* at [158]–[159] and Chapter 2: Human Rights (Conducting the Balancing Exercise), which extracts the key passages of Baroness Hale in the *Campbell* judgment.
84 Interestingly, the Court made reference to the damage to commercial reputation of Mr Ahmed's previous employer, Fox's Biscuits, which was taken into account when determining the sentence to be delivered to Mr. Ahmed and the impact of his actions. In the sentencing remarks, the District Judge noted, 'Mr Oakland of Fox's Biscuits described how the company received numerous calls and e-mails regarding your involvement with the company. Fox's Biscuits have a strong local heritage in West Yorkshire and such was the impact that the matter had to be referred to the parent company and CEO to prevent serious damage to their reputation.' The sentencing remarks are accessible via https://www.judiciary.gov.uk/Resources/JCO/Documents/Judgments/azhar-ahmed-sentencing-remarks-09102012.pdf.
85 Comprehensive Study on Cybercrime Paper, The United Nations Office on Drugs and Crime, Draft 2013, Chapter 4: *Criminalization* at page [114].

Human rights   43

'as with forms of hate speech, the internet and social media create new, broad-reaching platforms for incitement to terrorism'.[86] It is therefore critical that when governments apply existing laws and develop new laws, they take a critical approach, as set out in the UNODC publication on *The Use of the Internet for Terrorist Purposes*,[87] that states must 'strike a sensible balance between the requirements of law enforcement and the protection of human rights and liberties' in this area.[88]

In terms of how states have approached this task, reports submitted by Member States to the United Nations Counter-Terrorism Committee on the implementation of UNSC Resolution 1624 (2005), demonstrated considerable diversity in the way in which incitement to terrorism is defined and prohibited in national legislation. In relation to social media, the Cybercrime report notes that national responses may include or exclude broader acts such as justifying or glorifying terrorist acts and that tweets, Facebook statuses, and posts that glorify terrorist acts may fall within a category justifying prosecution.

2.6.2 *Social media and terrorism*

In a study from the University of Haifa, Gabriel Weimann found that nearly 90% of organized terrorism on the internet takes place via social media.[89] According to Weimann, terror groups use social media platforms like Twitter, Facebook, YouTube, and internet forums to spread their messages, recruit members, and gather intelligence.

Terror groups take to social media because social media tools are cheap and accessible, facilitate quick, broad dissemination of messages, and allow for unfettered communication with an audience without the filter or 'selectivity' of mainstream news outlets.[90] Also, social media platforms allow terror groups to engage with their networks. Whereas previously terror groups would release messages via intermediaries, social media platforms allow terror groups to release messages directly to their intended audience and converse with their audience in real time.

2.6.3 *Terror groups using social media*

Al-Qaeda has been noted as being one of the terror groups that uses social media the most extensively.[91] The Taliban has been active on Twitter since May 2011, tweeting under the handle @alemarahweb. The Taliban tweets frequently, on some days nearly hourly[92] and has more than 8,000 followers.[93] In December 2011,

---

86 See, for example, http://www.justice.gov/opa/pr/2011/February/11-nsd-238.html and http://www.cps.gov.uk/news/press_releases/137_07/.

87 The Use of the Internet for Terrorist Purposes, The United Nations Office on Drugs and Crime, United Nations, September 2012.

88 Ibid. at p. 41.

89 Gabriel Weimann (2006) *Terror on the Internet: The New Arena, the New Challenges*. Washington, DC: US Institute of Peace Press.

90 Calvin Dark (2011) 'Social media and social menacing . . .', *Foreign Policy Association*, 20 December [http://foreignpolicyblogs.com/2011/12/20/social-media-and-social-menacing/].

91 Brian Jenkins (2011) 'Is Al Qaeda's internet strategy working?', CT-371, 6 December.

92 'Twitter page of the Taliban' [https://twitter.com/alemarahweb].

93 https://twitter.com/alemarahweb following size accurate when accessed on 6 March 2013.

44 Background

Somalia-based terror cell Al-Shabaab was using a Twitter account under the name *@HSMPress*[94] and amassed tens of thousands of followers due to its frequent tweets. In December 2011 in response to the news that Al-Shabaab was using Twitter, US officials called for the company to shut down the account. Twitter executives did not comply with the demands and declined to comment on the case,[95] although the account has since been shut down by Twitter.[96] Terrorist activity has not just occurred on Twitter. Shortly after a series of coordinated Christmas bombings in Kono, Nigeria in 2011, the Nigeria-based terror group Boko Haram released a video statement defending their actions to YouTube.[97]

2.6.4 *US Committee on Homeland Security's Subcommittee on Counterterrorism and Intelligence*

On 6 December 2011, the US Committee on Homeland Security's Subcommittee on Counterterrorism and Intelligence held a hearing entitled 'Jihadist Use of Social Media – How to Prevent Terrorism and Preserve Innovation'.[98]

A number of testimonies from leading researchers, experts, and practitioners were heard at the committee hearing, notably William McCants, Aaron Weisburd, Brian Jenkins, and Evan Kohlmann. It was suggested by McCants that while terrorist groups had an active social media presence, and were using such platforms to further their objectives, the research he had conducted did not conclude that the social media strategies adopted by organizations and cells were proving to be effective. He stated that he did not believe that closing online user accounts would be effective in stopping radicalization and stated that closing online accounts could even disadvantage US security and intelligence forces, as they would not be able to garner intelligence about the organizations by performing analytics on their accounts (e.g. post content, followers, geographic location of postings, location of followers, concentrations of activity, etc.).

While McCants' research had concluded that there was no direct link between successful campaigns and an active social media presence, Weisburd argued that social media lends an air of legitimacy to content produced by terror organizations and provides terrorist organizations an opportunity to brand their content. He stated: 'branding in terrorist media is a sign of authenticity, and terrorist media is readily identifiable as such due to the presence of trademarks known to be associated with particular organizations'.[99] He concluded that the goal of intelligence and security

---

94 This account is now suspended; notice of the suspension can be found at https://twitter.com/account/suspended.

95 Uri Friedman (2011) 'U.S. officials may take action again [*sic*] al-Shabab's Twitter account', *Foreign Policy*, 20 December [http://blog.foreignpolicy.com/posts/2011/12/20/us_officials_may_take_action_again_al_shababs_twitter_account; retrieved 5 April 2012].

96 Ibid.

97 'Boko Haram: Nigerian Islamist leader defends attacks', BBC News [http://www.bbc.co.uk/news/world-africa-16510929].

98 United States Subcommittee on Counterterrorism and Intelligence of the Committee on Homeland Security's Subcommittee on Counterterrorism and Intelligence, 'Jihadist Use of Social Media – How to Prevent Terrorism and Preserve Innovation', 112th Congress, First Session, 6 December 2011.

99 Ibid.

Human rights 45

forces should not be to drive all terrorist media offline, but rather to deprive terror groups from the branding power gleaned from social media.

From the UNODC report and the ICCPR 1966, it is not clear if moderation on the grounds of removing legitimacy would be enough to justify an interference with freedom of expression if the content in question did not engage the criminal law or incite individuals to engage in terrorist activity. In the UK, such content could however still be deemed as grossly offensive within the meaning of the Communications Act 2003, Public Order Act 1986 or Serious Crimes Act 2007, for example.[100] In his testimony, referring to the activities of Al-Qaeda, Jenkins acknowledged the inherent difficulties of policing social media sites and that the activities engaged in by terrorist organizations do not necessarily justify an attempt to impose controls on content distributors. He noted that in addition to the legal difficulties, there were practical matters that would be hard to overcome, such as the cost of monitoring and the lack of evidence.

2.6.5 *Platform providers' response to terrorism*

Social networking sites are private corporations that may allow anyone to use their platforms. There will be situations where like any organization or citizen they are required to comply with the law. However, social networking sites are not arbiters of the law and as such must ensure that they do not make inroads into individuals' ability to express themselves or assert their freedom of expression. Site moderation and censorship has caused conceptual difficulties for platform providers and in the context of terrorism has raised additional specific issues that have formed the subject matter of significant discussion in the US Congress.

2.6.5.1 *Twitter*

As referred to above, at the end of January, Twitter suspended the account of the Somali-based Al-Qaeda-linked terrorist group Al-Shabaab. The account was taken offline after the group posted a video on Twitter threatening to kill two Kenyan hostages unless the Kenyan Government met its demands. Twitter didn't comment on the account's deletion. However, it is suggested that Al-Shabaab's account was suspended and access to the postings on the pages wall removed as the account had violated Twitter's terms of service, which prohibit direct threats of violence. The relevant term states, 'you may not publish or post direct, specific threats of violence against others'.[101] When it comes to government demands, Twitter, for example, functions on a country-by-country basis. So if the government has a legally binding order and makes it clear that the content in question is against the law, then the service is obligated to take it down or block it. In October, Twitter blocked a neo-Nazi account *@Besseres_Hannover*[102] after a request from the German Government, which argued that the account violated its laws against hate speech.

---

100 Each of these statutes is considered in depth in the following chapters.
101 The relevant term is accessible via https://support.twitter.com/articles/20169997#.
102 Discussed in depth in Chapter 4: Communications Act 2003.

46 *Background*

2.6.5.1.1 TRANSPARENCY REPORTS[103]

Twitter began releasing transparency reports in 2012. In the first report,[104] Twitter noted that there had been a steady increase in government requests for content removal and copyright notices. Twitter stated in the first report that in the majority of cases it had not complied with the requests to take down the content. The report stated that on occasion requests are not complied with because the content that the entity sought to remove hadn't been sufficiently identified; however, it did not state why other content that has been identified is not removed.

2.6.5.1.2 TWITTER'S APPROACH TO CENSORSHIP

In January 2012, Twitter announced changes to their censorship policy, stating that they would now be censoring tweets in certain countries when the tweets risked breaking the local laws of that country.[105] The reason behind the move was stated on their website as follows:

> As we continue to grow internationally, we will enter countries that have different ideas about the contours of freedom of expression. Some differ so much from our ideas that we will not be able to exist there. Others are similar but, for historical or cultural reasons, restrict certain types of content, such as France or Germany, which ban pro-Nazi content. Until now, the only way we could take account of those countries' limits was to remove content globally. Starting today, we give ourselves the ability to reactively withhold content from users in a specific country – while keeping it available in the rest of the world. We have also built in a way to communicate transparently to users when content is withheld, and why.[106]

The move drew criticism from many Twitter users who said the move was an affront to free speech and open web practices.[107] Twitter produced an update on 27 January 2012 noting that they believed 'the new, more granular approach to withheld content is a good thing for freedom of expression, transparency, accountability – and for our users. Besides allowing us to keep tweets available in more places, it also allows users to see whether we are living up to our freedom of expression ideal.'[108] Twitter explained that they do not filter content due to the sheer volume of tweets posted every day and that they would be taking a reactive approach to post removal or

---

103 Reports for Information Requests, Content Removal Requests, and Copyright Infringement can all be accessed via the hub website: https://transparency.twitter.com/.

104 https://transparency.twitter.com/removal-requests/2012/jan-jun.

105 'Tweets still must flow', Thursday, 26 January 2012 | By Twitter (@twitter) [19:25 UTC] [https://blog.twitter.com/2012/tweets-still-must-flow].

106 Ibid.

107 Omar El Akkad (2012) 'Why Twitter's censorship plan is better than you think', *The Globe and Mail*, 31 January (updated 6 September) [http://www.theglobeandmail.com/technology/digital-culture/social-web/why-twitters-censorship-plan-is-better-than-you-think/article543062/].

108 'Tweets still must flow', Thursday, 26 January 2012 | By Twitter (@twitter) [19:25 UTC] [https://blog.twitter.com/2012/tweets-still-must-flow].

Human rights 47

moderation, only withholding specific content, when required to do so in response to what Twitter believe to be a valid and applicable legal request.[109]

2.6.5.2 *YouTube*

In December 2010, in response to growing demands that YouTube pull video content from terrorist groups from its servers, the company created a new category through which viewers could 'flag' offensive content. The category is called 'promotes terrorism', and now appears as an option under the 'violent or repulsive content' category.[110]

2.6.5.3 *Facebook*

2.6.5.3.1 EXAMPLES OF TERRORIST ACTIVITY CONDUCTED VIA FACEBOOK

In December 2012 in Pakistan, Facebook suspended the account of the Pakistani Taliban's media branch, Umar Media. The page was removed because it violated Facebook's rules on fan pages that promote terrorism. Just two weeks later a new Umar Media account appeared on Facebook, although it's unclear if it belongs to the same group.

The Electronic Frontier Foundation, a US-based internet activist organization, has also reported on a growing number of requests by US Government officials for Twitter to suspend accounts of alleged terrorist groups. According to Rebecca MacKinnon, 'Facebook is less transparent about how they are responding to government requests or what kinds of requests they are receiving from what governments, so it's kind of difficult to know'.[111]

2.6.5.3.2 PRIVACY SETTINGS

William F. McCants notes that the task of tackling terrorism online came with inherent difficulties, as social networking online becomes more private and confined to one's acquaintances. For legal and technological reasons, it is harder to access information on corporate-owned sites like Facebook compared with Al-Qaeda-owned forums. Although beyond the scope of his expertise, McCants emphasised that the first priority should be monitoring and not taking down content.[112] The issues presented by terrorism highlight that even law enforcement agencies must consider complex issues

---

109 'Tweets still must flow', Thursday, 26 January 2012 | By Twitter (@twitter) [19:25 UTC] [https://blog.twitter.com/2012/tweets-still-must-flow], update 27 January 2012 | By Twitter (@twitter) [14:20 UTC].
110 Craig Kanalley (2010) 'YouTube gives users ability to flag content that promotes terrorism', *The Huffington Post*, 13 December [http://www.huffingtonpost.com/2010/12/13/youtube-terrorism-flag_n_796128.html].
111 D. Kjuka (2013) 'How social networks are dealing with terrorists', 19 February [http://www.rferl.org/content/twitter-facebook-terrorists/24906583.html].
112 United States Subcommittee on Counterterrorism and Intelligence of the Committee on Homeland Security's Subcommittee on Counterterrorism and Intelligence, 'Jihadist Use of Social Media – How to Prevent Terrorism and Preserve Innovation', 112th Congress, First Session, 6 December 2011, Expert Testimony of William F. McCants.

48 *Background*

relating to privacy and freedom of expression. It also highlights the difficult balancing act that the platform providers themselves must undertake when determining if content should be blocked or deleted, and if indeed the platform providers should be censoring their sites at all. While for illegal content each site has its own provisions,[113] the task of moderating speech that falls short of incitement to terrorist activity such as glorification or political views requires very careful consideration indeed. It is suggested that governments and regulatory bodies undertake such a task to ensure that there is no chilling effect on freedom of expression.

The report of the congress states that if real progress is to be made towards cleansing online social networks of terrorists and their supporters, 'the U.S. Congress must bring pressure to bear on commercial providers who are themselves being victimised in the process to start acting more like aggrieved victims instead of nonchalant bystanders'.[114] The report authors suggest that pause for thought must be given to the curbing effect that this may have on freedom of expression, although they contend that it is unclear why official terrorist recruitment material is any less of an odious concern for YouTube or Facebook than pornography. Unfortunately, current US law gives few incentives for companies like YouTube for volunteering information on illicit activity, or even cooperating when requested by US law enforcement. Congress stated, 'if such companies are to be trusted to self-police their own professed commitments to fighting hate speech, then they must be held to a public standard which reflects the importance of that not unsubstantial responsibility'.[115]

Evan Kohlmann states US government officials must do more to pressure social media groups like YouTube, Facebook, and Twitter to remove content produced by terror groups.

However, China, which has devoted immense resources to controlling social media networks with far fewer concerns about freedom of speech, has been unable to block the micro blogs that flourish on the web.[116] 'Faced with the shutdown of one site, jihadist communicators merely change names and move to another, dragging authorities into a frustrating game of Whac-a-Mole and depriving them of intelligence while they look for the new site.'[117]

2.6.6 *Case law*

There have yet to be any prosecutions in the UK for the use of social media by terrorists. However, in the USA there are several examples worthy of mention so as to explore how the law in the UK may develop in the future.

---

113 See Chapter 4: Communications Act 2003, *Role of the Platform Providers* for a full discussion of the platform providers role in site moderation.

114 United States Subcommittee on Counterterrorism and Intelligence of the Committee on Homeland Security's Subcommittee on Counterterrorism and Intelligence, 'Jihadist Use of Social Media – How to Prevent Terrorism and Preserve Innovation', 112th Congress, First Session, 6 December 2011.

115 Ibid.

116 See Chapter 4: Communications Act 2003, *Censorship and Monitoring* (China).

117 Brian Jenkins (2011) 'Is Al Qaeda's internet strategy working?', CT-371, 6 December.

2.6.6.1 *U.S. v LaRose* 'Jihad Jane'[118]

Colleen LaRose was arrested on her return to the United States as part of a terror plot that targeted a Swedish cartoonist. She enthusiastically posted and commented on YouTube videos of supporting Al-Qaeda and their allies, but her enthusiasm for jihad went beyond watching videos and offered moral support as well. She made contacts online with other jihadis, solicited funding, and orchestrated an actual terror plot. LaRose was arraigned on 18 March 2010, and pleaded not guilty to all four counts. US magistrate judge Lynne Sitarski set her trial date for 3 May 2010; during the interim she remained in federal custody. LaRose later changed her plea to guilty and was sentenced to 10 years' imprisonment.

2.6.6.2 *State of New York v Jose Pimentel*[119]

Jose Pimentel was arrested for preparing bombs to use in attacking targets in New York City. Before his arrest, Mr Pimentel had been active online. He ran a blog, held two YouTube accounts, and operated a Facebook profile, all dedicated to jihadi propaganda. It was stated that the judge had taken into account 'internet postings from the defendant, both on a website maintained by him and on blogs, in which the defendant described his support of the terrorist organization Al Qaeda and his belief in violent jihad'.

2.6.6.3 *@Anonymous – Arab Spring*

As noted by William McCants, not all campaigns bear a direct correlation between success in inciting terrorist activity and social media campaigns. However, such campaigns may legitimise or add to the reputation of the organization.[120] When it comes to looking at the power of social media, the report of the sub-committee noted that it is useful to consider the case study of 'the Arab Spring'. As the Arab Spring ensued, social media spread messages to which the world subscribed, followed, tweeted, and re-tweeted. For instance, the week before Egyptian President Hosni Mubarak's resignation, the total rate of tweets about political change in Egypt ballooned ten-fold. The top 23 videos featuring protests and political commentary had nearly 5.5 million views. More than 75% of people that clicked on embedded Twitter links about the Arab Spring were from outside the Arab world. According to the report, 'Social media became a "megaphone" that disseminated information and excitement about the uprisings to the outside world. The users of social media in the Middle East caused the world to take notice and to witness a revolution. Social media enabled these revolutionaries, change agents in their own right, to spread their messages beyond national borders to all corners of the world.'[121]

---

118 Indictment, *U.S. v LaRose*, U.S. District Court for the Eastern District of Pennsylvania, 4 March 2010.

119 *State of New York v Pimentel, Jose*, Criminal Court, 20 November 2011.

120 United States Subcommittee on Counterterrorism and Intelligence of the Committee on Homeland Security's Subcommittee on Counterterrorism and Intelligence, 'Jihadist Use of Social Media – How to Prevent Terrorism and Preserve Innovation', 112th Congress, First Session, 6 December 2011, Expert Testimony of William F. McCants.

121 Statement of Ranking Member Jackie Speier (D-CA), 'Jihadist Use of Social Media – How to Prevent Terrorism and Preserve Innovation'.

Part 2

Civil claims

3 Defamation

3.1 Application to social media

> *If slander be a snake, it is a winged one – it flies as well as creeps.*
> Douglas W. Jerrold, *Specimens of Jerrold's Wit, Slander*

Though published in 1859, approximately 140 years before the advent of social media, the quotation of Jerrold concerning libel remains remarkably apt. As the Court of Appeal stated in *Cairns v Modi*:[1]

> as a consequence of modern technology and communications systems . . . stories will have the capacity to 'go viral' more widely and more quickly than ever before. Indeed, it is obvious that today, with the ready availability of the worldwide web and of social networking sites, the scale of this problem has been immeasurably enhanced, especially for libel claimants who are already, for whatever reason, in the public eye.[2]

Contrary to a general belief that expressive activities posted via social media are exempt from libel laws because they are fleeting, perhaps made as a joke and are transient, libel laws apply to the internet the same way they do to newspapers, magazines, books, films, and other similar publications. In *Colin Elsbury v Eddie Talbot*,[3] the defendant, Colin Elsbury, made remarks about a rival stating that the claimant, Eddie Talbot, had been removed from the polling station by the police at the time of the election. He remarked: 'It's not in our nature to deride our opponents however Eddie Talbot had to be removed by the Police from a polling station.' A man had been removed from the polling station that day but it was not the claimant and the High Court approved a settlement of £3,000 with the defendant also having to pay the claimant's legal costs. The case marked the first in the United Kingdom in which a libel claim was brought against another for defamatory remarks made online in which Twitter was used as the platform for such communication.

---

1 [2012] EWCA Civ 1382 [2012] WLR(D) 302.
2 Court of Appeal said in *Cairns v Modi* [2012] EWCA Civ 1382, [2012] WLR(D) 302 at [27].
3 A councillor is to pay £3,000 and costs to a political rival for posting a libellous comment on Twitter [http://www.bbc.co.uk/news/uk-wales-south-east-wales-12704955, June 2009 (unreported)].

54 *Civil claims*

In this chapter, we will focus on defamation in the context of allegedly defamatory postings made via social media sites and will consider the specific issues such sites raise. The chapter will:

- Explain how defamation can occur (specifically online and on social media sites).
- The sanctions that can be imposed if a statement is found to be defamatory.
- The basic procedural aspects of a claim in defamation.
- Identify the defences available.
- Consider the changes posed by the Defamation Act 2013.
- Explore the position in relation to social networking sites and the inherent difficulties that such mediums may raise.
- Consider practical measures for businesses seeking to manage their social media presence and negative or untruthful commentary posted on social networking sites, websites and blogs.
- Consider practical measures for internet service providers, social networking sites, and Blogs faced with claims that postings on their site are defamatory and what to do if asked to take down such content.

3.2 Sources of defamation law

The rules as to when a statement is defamatory, who may sue, when publication has occurred, and whether a defence applies are laid down in centuries of case law and are supplemented by:

- The Defamation Act 1952.
- The Defamation Act 1996.
- The EC Directive on electronic commerce (2000/31/EC) (E-Commerce Directive). This is given effect in the UK by the Electronic Commerce (EC Directive) Regulations 2002 (SI 2002/2013) (E-Commerce Regulations).
- The Defamation Act 2013, which was given Royal Assent on 25 April 2013, and came into force in England and Wales on 1 January 2014 by the Defamation Act (Commencement) (England and Wales) Order 2013 (SI 2013/3027).

3.3 The Defamation Act 2013

3.3.1 *Background to reform*

In recent years, there has been an increasing trend for individuals and companies who contend that they have been defamed to pursue the internet service provider (ISP) who published the content via their website URLs. However, while tactically this approach has usually been adopted to appeal to the individuals capable of removing the post, or who may have resources that make them a preferable party to pursue for damages, the risk exposure to search engines, website registrants, Usenet hosts (internet servers on which newsgroup bulletins are stored), website design companies, and companies who use the internet for sales or marketing purposes has been significant.

3.3.2 *Technology outstripping the law*

The vast scope of communication and methods by which defamatory content can be conveyed forms the background of how and why defamation law required reform. The law had become ill-adapted to meet the challenges presented by modern technology, which continue to develop at a phenomenal rate and was simply not envisaged at the time of the enactment of the 1952 Act and also the enactment of the 1996 Act when the internet and mobile technology was still very much in its infancy. Compare, for instance, the fact that mobile telephones, email, and SMS messaging were only just becoming used by businesses, in 1996, to the present position where Smartphones, laptops, and tablets pervade every aspect of our business and social lives. Under the new regime detailed in the Defamation Act 2013,[4] the law has been updated for the age of the internet and seeks to put the focus back on the poster of the allegedly defamatory content.

3.3.3 *Meeting of the Culture, Media and Sport Committee of the House of Commons*

During the 2009 meeting of the Culture, Media and Sport Committee of the House of Commons, the House took evidence from a wide variety of witnesses as part of its enquiry into press standards, privacy, and libel. Their report, published on 23 February 2010, recommended several reforms, namely in relation to the defence of trust (justification) and the issues presented by so-called 'libel tourism'. The Culture Committee was not the only governmental body to give attention to the increasing outmoded nature of libel law. The Lord Chancellor had also established a Working Group on libel and published a report on 23 March 2010 looking at areas such as libel tourism, public interest considerations when establishing defences to a libel action, the issues presented by the multiple publication rule (becoming a particular issue as each hit on a web page could count as a fresh publication, revealing the unsuitability of current defamation law for the digital age), and other procedural issues.

The age of the internet led to much debate about libel law and the impact of it upon freedom of expression in the digital age, with all three major political parties making commitments to reform the law in their 2010 election manifestos. On 26 May 2010, Lord Lester of Hearne Hill QC introduced to the Lords a Private Member's Bill, the Defamation Bill. In July that year a report was published by the Ministry of Justice outlining plans to reform the laws of defamation. The report noted that in order to effect such change, a great deal of consultation would be required with interested parties before a draft bill could be published.

3.3.4 *The journey to the Bill*

In March 2011, the Ministry published a consultation paper,[5] which included in Annexe A a draft bill to reform the law of defamation. However, describing the Bill as an amending piece of legislation could be considered misleading, as the intent of

---

4   Given Royal Assent on 25 April 2013, and came into force in England and Wales on 1 January 2014 by the Defamation Act (Commencement) (England and Wales) Order 2013 (SI 2013/3027).

5   Ministry of Justice *Draft Defamation Bill: Consultation*, Consultation Paper CP3/11, March 2011

56 *Civil claims*

the Bill was actually a mixture of codification of established principles of defamation and reform. The Bill recognized that many of the key issues in relation to defamation would require significant consultation and as such were not included in the draft bill. The task of gathering evidence and views in relation to the Bill was tasked to the Joint Parliamentary Committee on the Defamation Bill. The Joint Committee published extensive evidence from a range of individuals and bodies including, but not limited to, academics, lawyers, non-governmental organizations, ISPs, trade unions, judges, the Lord Chancellor, and the Ministry of Justice.

3.3.4.1 *Joint Committee on the Draft Defamation Bill*

The Joint Committee issued a report on the Defamation Bill on 19 October 2011.[6] The report noted that the draft bill did not necessarily always clarify the law and increase accessibility to the public. In particular, the challenge of balancing freedom of expression against the protection of reputation was considered, as well as the challenges faced in relation to policing the 'Wild West' of the internet.

The four key areas that influenced the report are as follows:

- The balance between freedom of expression and the protection of reputation.
- Reducing the costs associated with bringing and defending claims.
- Accessibility of the law.
- How to meet the challenges presented by the online environment, including: jurisdictional issues, anonymity and trolling, and wide dissemination of content.

3.3.4.2 *The Bill in Parliament*

On 10 May 2012, the Defamation Bill (the Bill) was introduced into the House of Commons. The aims of the Bill at the time of its introduction were to:

- Consider the balance between freedom of expression and an individual's right to protection of their reputation, and rebalance the law so that free speech is not unjustifiably interfered with.
- Ensure that scientific and academic debate is not unjustifiably interfered with.
- Encourage responsible journalism.
- Consider the problems raised by libel tourism and reduce its potential.

The Bill proceeded to the House of Lords with minor amendments on 8 October 2012. While in the Lords, concerns were expressed about the Bill and how it would be affected by the outcome of the Leveson Enquiry. The *Leveson Report on Culture, Practices and Ethics of the Press* was published on 29 November 2012.[7] Lord Leveson's report did deal with matters relating to defamation, harassment, and privacy. The report recommended not just tweaking the statutory frameworks governing such areas, but also made recommendations for procedural reform. Leveson recom-

---

6 HL Paper 203, HC 930-I, 19 October 2013.
7 Report into the Culture, Practices and Ethics of the Press was published on Thursday 29 November 2012 [http://www.official-documents.gov.uk/document/hc1213/hc07/0780/0780.asp].

mended the establishment of an arbitration body to allow individuals to resolve matters with publishers and to consider issues relating to costs, post-Jackson Reforms.

3.3.4.3 *Suggestions that did not make the final cut*

A group of Lords (Lord Puttnam, Lord MacKay of Clashfern, Baroness Boothroyd, and Baroness Scotland of Asthal) proposed amendments to the Bill that would have done the following:

- Established a statutory press regulation body.
- Established an arbitration service for defamation and associated civil claims against publishers.
- Made changes to the costs regime that would have allowed for exemplary damages and indemnity costs against publishers who did not sign up to the regulatory regime or make use of the proposed arbitration service.

While calls were made to incorporate elements of the report into the Bill, the Bill was a substantive consideration of the law of defamation and was not considered a suitable vehicle in which to incorporate some of the Leveson report's recommendations.

Although these measures were not adopted, the Bill still seeks to clarify the law relating to defamation, especially in relation to tackling defamation on the internet, which will be explored in this chapter, most especially in relation to defamatory content published on social networking sites.

3.4 A defamation claim: what is defamation and what is needed to bring a claim?

Before we begin considering the law in depth, it will be useful to explore some of the key questions that often are not explored in textbooks. Often individuals want to know if they have the standing to sue and what in essence they need to prove in order to start a claim. These 'frequently asked questions' will be dealt with in turn.

3.4.1 *Who can sue?*

The general rule with regard to bringing defamation claims is that any natural or juristic person may sue for defamation. Defamation claims can be brought by, among others:

- An individual
- A class of individuals, as long as it is not too large[8]
- A bankrupt[9]
- Minors and patients (as defined) through their litigation friend[10]

---

8 *Riches v Newspapers Limited* [1986] QB 256.
9 *Heath v Tang* [1993] 1 WLR 1421 CA.
10 Part 21, Civil Procedure Rules 1998.

58   *Civil claims*

- Limited companies,[11] foreign companies, and company directors[12]
- Trade unions (although this is not entirely settled law[13])
- Firms through their partners[14]
- Limited liability partnerships[15]
- Members of Parliament.

However, defamation claims cannot be brought by:

- The estate of the dead through trustees
- Governing bodies
- Political parties[16]
- Unincorporated associations[17]
- Local government corporations.[18]

3.4.2 *What is defamation?*

There are varying definitions of defamation to be found in leading textbooks; indeed, you may feel that you already have an idea of what a claim in defamation may encompass. However, to appreciate its application to social media, it is necessary to gain an understanding of the basic elements of a cause of action in defamation. In order to facilitate this process, it is helpful to break down the recipe of the offence into as many ingredients as possible, so as to appreciate the importance of each element.

3.4.3 *The 'essential ingredients' of an action*

To bring a successful action for defamation, the claimant must prove each of the following elements in order to substantiate a claim:

- There is a publication which: (i) the defendant has published or (ii) is responsible for publishing;
- Defamatory material;
- Which is reasonably understood:
  - To refer to the claimant:
  - By means of name or other identification.

---

11 *South Hetton Coal Co v NE News* [1894] 1 QB.

12 *John Holland Group Pty Ltd v John Fairfax Publications PTY Limited* [2006] ACTSC 34 (allegations against a senior employee, who was not a controlling mind of the company, did not defame the company, but the individual).

13 Compare *NUGMW v Gillan* [1946] KB 81 with P. Milmo and W.V.H. Rogers (eds) (2004) *Gatley on Libel and Slander* (10th edn). London: Sweet & Maxwell, para 8.23.

14 Partnerships, unlike incorporated bodies, are not separate from their partners; however, an action can be brought by a firm if the firm's name suffers damage, CPR PD7, para 5A.3.

15 Limited Liability Partnerships (LLPs) are incorporated entities under the Limited Liability Partnerships Act 2000 and are treated in the same manner as a company, that is, a separate legal entity for the purposes of defamation law.

16 *Goldsmith v Bhoyrul* [1998] 2 WLR 435.

17 *London Association v Greenlands* [1916] 1 AC at 20, 30, 39; *Bloom v National Federation* [1918] 35 TLR 50 CA.

18 *Derbyshire County Council v Times Newspapers* [1993] AC 534.

However, even if the elements of defamation are present, it may be that the individual accused of making the statement has a defence open to them. The main defences open to a defendant are:

- Truth (i.e. that the statement is true[19])
- Honest opinion
- Privilege

A claim may also fail because it is without merit, acting as a sage reminder for readers that an understanding of the basic ingredients of what the claimant must prove is essential when considering defamation.

Unless the ingredients of the offence and the lack of a defence is demonstrated in relation to the statement, then the material in question remains just that, a statement; it only takes on the label of libel or slander in the absence of a defence. This understanding is the grounding of the rest of the book and will inform reading for both claimants and defendants. In the event that the defendant cannot put forward a defence or the defence proves unsuccessful, then the claimant will be entitled to recover a sum of damages.[20]

3.5 The distinction between libel and slander

The terms of reference libel, defamation, and slander are often used interchangeably. Libel is an offence that concerns the publication of material in writing or some other permanent form. If it is spoken or in some sort of other transient form, it is a slander. In relation to statements made on the internet, it is now generally accepted that defamatory statements are to be regarded as libel. However, in *Nigel Smith v ADVFN Plc and others*,[21] the High Court classified chat on an internet bulletin board as more akin to slander than to libel as the posts are:

> like contributions to a casual conversation (the analogy sometimes being drawn with people chatting in a bar) which people simply note before moving on; they are often uninhibited, casual and ill thought out; those who participate know this and expect a certain amount of repartee or 'give and take'.[22]

In relation to social media sites, which arguably fall within the description above advanced by Eady J, given the volume with which micro sites generate content, especially micro blogging sites such as Twitter, it will be interesting to see if the courts interpret such publications as libel rather than slander and the matter must be considered carefully when starting a claim.

---

19 Note that the claimant does not need to prove that the allegation is false in order to bring a claim. Claimants should, however, consider any weaknesses in their case and anticipate arguments that the defendant may raise.
20 However, the sum awarded by the Court may be affected by the behaviour of the parties, *Roache v News Group Newspapers* [1998] EMLR 161.
21 [2008] EWHC 1797 (QB).
22 [2008] EWHC 1797 (QB) at [14].

60　*Civil claims*

This may lead to the question, what difference would this materially cause for defendants if faced with a claim? The difference is significant in one particular but important way – in the case of certain forms of slander, the claimant must prove some sort of financial loss. In *Jacqueline Thompson v Mark James, Carmarthenshire County Council*,[23] it was suggested that the ruling of Eady J in *Smith v ADVFN* would be important in determining the context in which the defamation was made and that 'words must always be interpreted in their context, and blogs or bulletin boards are a context which may give rise to a different interpretation'.[24]

3.6 A defamatory statement

3.6.1 *Does the statement convey a defamatory meaning?*

What constitutes a defamatory statement has been considered many times, yet there remains no one comprehensive answer; it is as fluid as the words complained of. There have, however, been cases that have sought to get close to providing a comprehensive analysis of the meaning of a defamatory statement. In *Sim v Stretch*,[25] a defamatory statement was framed as one which tends to lower the claimant in the estimation of right-thinking members of society generally. *Dell'Olio v Associated Newspapers*[26] further sought to clarify this. Tugenhadt LJ stated that 'the question is whether the words complained of are capable of substantially affecting (or tending to affect) in an adverse manner the attitude of other people towards *that Claimant*, whether in the meaning advanced by the Claimant, or in some other meaning' (emphasis added).[27] Considering the threshold of seriousness which must be passed before it can be said that words are defamatory, the formulation of the test in *Thornton v Telegraph Media Group*[28] is that 'it substantially affects in an adverse manner the attitude of other people towards him, or has a tendency so to do'.[29] However, the Court of Appeal has not yet considered directly whether defamatory statements at common law must satisfy a test of seriousness. In *Cammish v Hughes*,[30] the Court stated:

> The law does not provide remedies for inconsequential statements, that is, of trivial content or import. It is necessary that there should be some threshold test of seriousness to avoid normal social banter or discourtesy ending up in litigation and to avoid interfering with the right to freedom of expression conferred by article 10 of the European Convention on Human Rights.[31]

---

23 [2013] EWHC 515 (QB), 2013 WL 617648.
24 *Jacqueline Thompson v Mark James, Carmarthenshire County Council* [2013] EWHC 515 (QB), 2013 WL 617648 at [270].
25 [1936] 2 All ER 1237.
26 [2011] EWHC 3472 (QB).
27 [2011] EWHC 3472 (QB) at [27].
28 [2010] EMLR 25.
29 [2010] EMLR 25 at [95].
30 [2012] EWCA Civ 1655.
31 [2012] EWCA Civ 1655 at [38]

3.6.2 *Determining the meaning of words*

Determining the meaning of words, especially in space-constrained postings or tweets, can give rise to a great deal of uncertainty in a libel action. The reason for this is that it is not only the superficial meaning that may be defamatory, but also 'hidden' meaning that can be inferred. With throw-away tweets or spur-of-the-moment postings, this can be especially dangerous. It is important to be aware that words can also have an inference, that is, a meaning that can be read between the lines without any specialist knowledge and/or an innuendo meaning that can be attributed to the words by readers who have a specialist knowledge.

In terms of who must show that the words convey that meaning, the onus is on the claimant to prove the defamatory meaning they allege. In doing so, the words must be put in their full context, including headings and captions to any photographs and, as we will see below, emoticons when deciding whether words are defamatory. Social media users who may see their remarks as throw-away or tongue in cheek need to be aware that the intention of the author (i.e. poster) is irrelevant; all that matters is the impression that the words give to readers.

A 'natural and ordinary meaning' may include implication or inference which a reasonable reader not guided by any special knowledge would draw from the words (*Jones v Skelton* [1963] 1 WLR 1362 at 1370–1371, confirmed in the social media context in *McAlpine v Bercow* at [2013] EWHC 1342 (QB) at [48]). An 'innuendo meaning' is one implied on the basis of other 'extrinsic facts' known to the reader. The governing principle for meaning is 'reasonableness', some implication is permitted but the reasonable reader is not 'avid for scandal', the intention of the publisher is irrelevant (see generally *Jeynes v News Magazines Limited* [2008] EWCA Civ 130 at [14]–[15]).

3.6.2.1 *Social media: specific considerations*

Defamatory postings on social networking sites and micro-blogs such as Facebook and Twitter can present their own challenges. An example of the problems highlighted by social media involved a tweet posted by the editor of the London-based Bureau of Investigative Journalism, Iain Overton, with reference to 'Operation Yewtree', a police investigation into sexual abuse allegations, predominantly the abuse of children, against the British media personality Jimmy Savile and others. The investigation, led by the Metropolitan Police Service, started in October 2012. After a period of assessment it became a full criminal investigation, involving inquiries into living people as well as Savile. Mr Overton's tweet suggested that a senior political figure in the UK could be 'outed' as a paedophile. The tweet read 'if all goes well we've got a Newsnight out tonight about a very senior political figure who is a paedophile'. No individual was named in the tweet and it later transpired that the accuser had misidentified the person who had abused him. However, subsequent to the tweet, several posters outed Lord McAlpine online as the perpetrator of the alleged offences. Lord McAlpine is expected to sue at least 10,000 people over the malicious claims that appeared in the wake of a BBC *Newsnight* investigation into a paedophile ring at care homes in North Wales.

On Sunday 4 November 2012, Ms Bercow, the wife of the Speaker of the House of Commons, tweeted the following to her 56,000 followers:'Why is Lord McAlpine trending? *Innocent face*'.

62 Civil claims

Lord McAlpine subsequently issued libel proceedings. Upon hearing the matter, the court noted that in its opinion a substantial number of people had seen the *Newsnight* report and that, by 4 November 2012, a very large number of people had read the media reports about it. In relation to Ms Bercow's tweet, Tugenhadt J noted that a substantial number of readers of the tweet would also have read the reports and seen the broadcast and therefore been able to put the tweet into contemporary context (see para [30] of the judgment ([2013] EWHC 1342 (QB)). Therefore, a reasonable reader would have linked the claimant to the *Newsnight* report, essentially for two reasons:

- Ms Bercow's Twitter followers were interested in politics and current affairs;
- Even without prior knowledge of the claimant they would have known (from the use of the title 'Lord') that the individual was a prominent public figure, not otherwise in the public eye at the time and 'there was much speculation about the identity of an unnamed politician who had been prominent some 20 years ago' ([2013] EWHC 1342 (QB) at [83]).

Much of the judgment also considered the meaning to be attributed to the words 'innocent face'. Lord McApline submitted that the meaning was not literal, in fact it should be read as quite the contrary. The defendant argued that the words should be viewed in a neutral way, as she had noticed the claimant was trending on Twitter and was looking for someone to tell her why. The argument advanced by the defence was rejected by the court, as 'a reasonable reader would understand the words "innocent face" as being insincere and ironical. There is no sensible reason for including those words in the Tweet if they are to be taken as meaning that the Defendant simply wants to know the answer to a factual question' ([2013] EWHC 1342 (QB) at [84]).

3.6.2.1.1 'TRENDING'

The judgment is also interesting for considering the issue of discussing 'trending' topics. The court stated that as the defendant was telling her followers that the claimant was trending on Twitter, there was 'no alternative explanation for why this particular peer was being named in the tweets which produce the Trend, then it is reasonable to infer that he is trending because he fits the description of the unnamed abuser. I find the reader would infer that. The reader would reasonably infer that the Defendant had provided the last piece in the jigsaw' ([2013] EWHC 1342 (QB) at [85]).

As a result, taking *into* account the so-called 'repetition rule' (the rule that a defendant who repeats a defamatory allegation made by another is treated as if he had made the allegation himself ([2013] EWHC 1342 (QB) at [44])), the defendant was to be treated as if she had made, with the addition of the claimant's name, the allegation made on *Newsnight*. This was an allegation of actual guilt.

As a result, the judge concluded that 'the Tweet meant, in its natural and ordinary defamatory meaning, that the Claimant was a paedophile who was guilty of sexually abusing boys living in care' ([2013] EWHC 1342 (QB) at [90]). In the alternative, the tweet bore an 'innuendo meaning' to the same effect: one that was understood by the small number of readers who, before reading the tweet, either remembered or learnt that the claimant had been a prominent Conservative politician in the Thatcher years ([2013] EWHC 1342 (QB) at [91]).

3.6.2.1.2 EMOTICONS

In the context of postings made via social media sites, the advent of new technologies has meant that individuals can express themselves in different ways, such as by posting funny pictures or using emoticons in addition to the text that they post. Posters should be aware that the use of emoticons (a type of symbol commonly used in a text message or email, e.g. smiling face, embarrassed face) or similar graphics can be considered by courts when determining if a statement is defamatory.

In the preliminary decision on meaning in *McAlpine v Bercow*,[32] the court held that a tweet suffixed with an emoticon could be defamatory. In *McAlpine*, Sally Bercow, the wife of the Speaker of the House of Commons John Bercow, posted a tweet via the micro site Twitter, two days after the BBC's *Newsnight* wrongly linked a 'leading Conservative politician' to sex abuse claims. Amid widespread speculation about his identity, she wrote: 'Why is Lord McAlpine trending. *innocent face*.' In analysing the tweet by reference to the emotion contained within it, the court stated:

> It is common ground between the parties that the words 'innocent face' are to be read like a stage direction, or an emoticon. Readers are to imagine that they can see the defendant's face as she asks the question in the tweet. The words direct the reader to imagine that the expression on her face is one of innocence, that is an expression which purports to indicate (sincerely, on the Defendant's case, but insincerely or ironically on the Claimant's case) that she does not know the answer to her question.[33]

This decision highlights the risk of using an emoticon in a tweet, or on other such platforms that allow for the use of emoticons. Although an emoticon may be added thoughtlessly, the courts have indicated that they may be taken into account when determining the state of mind of the poster behind the tweet or publication. Emoticons may be especially relevant when considering if there has been an element of malice.

3.6.2.1.3 TIMING OF PUBLICATION – TEMPORAL MEANING

As noted in *Sim*,[34] a defamatory statement is one that tends to lower the claimant in the estimation of right-thinking members of society. In *Flood v Times Newspapers Ltd*,[35] the High Court ruled, as a preliminary issue, on the meaning of the newspaper article in a website publication, which the claimant alleged was defamatory when it was read after 5 September 2007, when the defendant knew that the comments were defamatory as the investigations giving rise to the speculation surrounding Mr Flood had been dropped.

---

32 *Lord McAlpine of West Green v Bercow* [2013] EWHC 1342 (QB).
33 [2013] EWHC 1342 (QB) at [7].
34 [1936] 2 All ER 1237.
35 [2013] EWHC 2182 (QB), 25 July 2013.

64 *Civil claims*

Tugendhat J agreed with the meaning put forward by Mr Flood that the words would be read by readers not only about events as they were on 2 June 2006, the date at the head of the article, but also about events up to the date at which it was being read. The judge dismissed the defendant's argument that the reasonable fair-minded reader would have understood that the allegations might, in the interim, have turned out to be ill-founded, when the update did not suggest that.

3.7 The Test of Substantial Harm

3.7.1 *Position prior to the Defamation Act 2013*

Prior to the Defamation Act 2013, the common law position was that the courts had power to throw out any claim that fails to meet a 'threshold of seriousness', including where no 'real and substantial' wrongdoing can be demonstrated.[36] However, in practice this is a potentially low hurdle, merely requiring prospective claimants to demonstrate that harm which is more than minimal has been suffered in relation to their reputation.[37] From 1 January 2014, section 1 of the Defamation Act 2013 introduced a requirement that a statement must have caused (or be likely to cause) 'serious harm' to the claimant's reputation in order for it to be defamatory.[38]

3.7.2 *Joint Committee's Report on the Draft Defamation Bill*[39]

In the Joint Committee's Report on the Draft Defamation Bill, it was recommended by the Joint Committee that the draft bill's test of 'substantial harm' to reputation be a stricter test, which would have the effect of requiring 'serious and substantial harm' to be established.[40] It was noted by the Joint Committee that a number of contributors to the report proposed that claims should be required to be 'serious' or 'serious and substantial' in order to proceed.[41]

The Joint Committee considered that a threshold test that focuses on the seriousness of the allegation would raise the bar in a meaningful way and give greater confidence to publishers that statements which do not cause significant harm, including jokes, parody, and irreverent criticism, do not put them at risk of losing a libel claim. In the context of social media sites and the content that is uploaded to them by account holders, such flexibility would be important given the low-level value of much of the speech, often spoken in jest and sent without real thought as to the consequences of the posting.[42] In the report, the Joint Committee noted that when

---

36 *Thornton v Telegraph Media Group Ltd* [2010] EWHC 1414 (QB); *Jameel v Dow Jones* [2005] EWCA Civ 75; [2005] QB 946.

37 *Jameel v Dow Jones* [2005] EWCA Civ 75; [2005] QB 946.

38 Section 1(1) Defamation Act 2013.

39 Session 2010–2012, HL 203, HC 930-I. The committee held oral evidence sessions between April and July 2011 and its final report was published on 19 October 2011.

40 The Joint Committee on the Draft Defamation Bill Report Session 2010–2012, HL 203, HC 930-I, paras 28 and 62.

41 See, for example, Q 303 (Mackay) and Libel Reform Campaign, Vol. II, p. 71.

42 For a discussion of speech value and the issues raised in relation to low-level speech, see Chapter 2: Human Rights and Chapter 4: Communications Act 2003.

people are harmed by a defamatory statement, it makes no difference to them whether it happened online or offline and defamation is defamation regardless of the medium through which it is published. However, the Joint Committee noted that many derogatory and mocking statements on blogs and social networking sites may be read casually, remain fleeting in their impact, and be given limited credence by readers when compared, for example, with material published by reputable media organizations.

This approach is reflected in the case of *Smith v ADVFN Plc*,[43] in which it was suggested that live online discussions should be treated more like slander, or spoken defamation. The Court in *Smith* noted that: 'people do not often take a "thread" and go through it as a whole like a newspaper article. They tend to read the remarks, make their own contributions if they feel inclined, and think no more about it.'[44]

Eady LJ went further in the judgment by also stating that from the context of casual conversations, one can often tell that a remark is not to be taken literally or seriously and is rather to be construed merely as abuse. Eady LJ was of the opinion that this is less common in the case of more permanent written communication, although it is by no means unknown. However, in the case of a bulletin board thread, he considered that it would be more obvious to the casual observer that individuals are posting the first thing that comes into their heads and reacting in the heat of the moment. In such a context, the remarks are often not intended, or to be taken, as serious.[45] If this approach is adopted, then this may mean that live online discussions should only be actionable where – in line with slander following the introduction of section 2 of the Defamation Act 1996 – the words suggest the commission of a criminal offence or are likely to disparage the subject in any office, profession, trade or business.

3.7.2.1 *Nature of the publication*

It was also noted by the Joint Committee that the threshold test should relate to harm to reputation and not to feelings, although the latter is an important aspect of damages if an action proceeds.[46] The Joint Committee felt that allowance should be made for such matters as the nature of the charge, prompt apologies, the width of publication, and any other relevant background. The approach that the courts will adopt in this regard is not yet known, due to the infancy of the application of the Act. In relation to postings on social media sites, however, it will be interesting to see how the precise meaning of 'serious and substantial' is interpreted as part of the threshold test, and how a balance will be struck between free speech and reputation.

3.7.3 *The Government's response to the Joint Committee's Report on the Draft Defamation Bill*

The Government's response to the Joint Committee's report was published on 29 February 2012[47] and set out the Government's conclusions, including on

---

43 *Smith v ADVFN Plc* [2008] EWHC 1797 (QB).
44 [2008] EWHC 1797 (QB) at [16].
45 [2008] EWHC 1797 (QB) at [17].
46 The Joint Committee on the Draft Defamation Bill Report Session 2010–2012, HL 203, HC 930-I, para 28.
47 The Government's Response to the Report of the Joint Committee on the Draft Defamation Bill Cm 8295.

66 *Civil claims*

certain matters raised in the public consultation but not specifically addressed in the Committee's report. The Government were concerned that the use of two separate terms alongside each other would be likely to cause uncertainty and litigation over what difference may exist between the two terms, which would add to disputes and costs. However, in light of the Committee's views and the balance of opinions received on consultation, the Government were persuaded that it is appropriate to raise the bar for bringing a claim. A test of 'serious harm' was thought to achieve this, while maintaining a balance that is not unduly restrictive on claimants' rights.

It is suggested that it is likely, following the recommendations of the Committee that the courts will need to consider postings in their context when deciding whether the harm test is satisfied. Moreover, the sting of a defamatory allegation is likely to be lessened or removed altogether where the publisher makes a rapid correction or apology, or where a notice is attached to material on the internet indicating that it has been challenged as libellous.[48] The Committee also suggested that the law must encourage attempts by publishers to correct false information in support of responsible free speech and the protection of reputation and that there should be recognition that prompt action can undo the risk of harm.

3.7.4 *Summary*

3.7.4.1 *Summary of substantial harm and key considerations*

The factual matrix surrounding the defamatory content will inform whether or not the threshold of serious harm has been met and must therefore be considered on a case-by-case basis.[49] Moreover, adequate consideration must be given to Article 8 and Article 10 of the ECHR.[50] Matters which the court may consider as part of this exercise may include:

- the nature of the allegation;
- the gravity of the allegation;
- the mode of publication, e.g. whether the publication was oral or written;
- the number of publishers;
- whether the allegations were believed;
- the status of the publisher and whether this makes it more likely that the allegation will be believed; and
- the transience of the publication.[51]

---

48 The Joint Committee on the Draft Defamation Bill Report Session 2010–2012, HL 203, HC 930-I, para 30; the courts offered support to this approach in *Loutchansky v Times Newspapers Ltd & Others* [2001] EWCA Civ 1805, [2002] 1 All ER 652.

49 *Cammish v Hughes* [2012] EWCA Civ 1655 CA; [2013] EMLR 13 at [40]. See also, per Sharp J in *Haji Ioannu v Mark Dixon, Regus Group Plc* [2009] EWHC 178 (QB) at [30].

50 See Chapter 2: Human Rights for a comprehensive discussion of the application of human rights law. See also *Dell'Olio v Associated Newspapers Ltd* [2011] EWHC 3472 (QB) per Tugendhat J at [13].

51 Significantly for social media sites, the Joint Committee recommended that the court must additionally take into account the nature of the setting in which the statement was made as part of considering its full context.

Defamation   67

3.7.4.2 *Summary chart*

Although defamation claims will revolve around their particular facts, several recent cases offer useful guidance as to how the courts may approach cases going forward.

3.7.4.2.1 BELOW THE NECESSARY THRESHOLD

Thornton v Telegraph Media Group[i]	Claimant author had engaged in copy approval – that is, giving interviewees the right to read what the author had said about them and to change it. The case therefore fell below the threshold required and was not defamatory of the claimant.
Ecclestone v Telegraph Media Group[ii]	Allegation that the claimant was dismissive of the views of several well-known vegetarians was not capable of being defamatory. At worst this was a breach of conventional etiquette but did not reach the level of seriousness required to be actionable.
Daniels v BBC[iii]	Minor criticisms of the claimant's performance at work would not be defamatory.
Dell'Olio v Associated Newspapers[iv]	An imputation that the claimant was a serial 'gold-digger' who cynically sought out relationships with older men because they were millionaires and not for any genuine reason did not meet the threshold of seriousness.

[i] [2010] EWHC 1414; [2011] 1 WLR 1985; [2010] EMLR 25.
[ii] [2009] EWHC 2779 (QB).
[iii] [2010] EWHC 3057 (QB) at [20].
[iv] [2011] EWHC 3472 (QB) at [32].

3.7.4.2.2 CASES WHERE THE THRESHOLD OF SERIOUSNESS WAS MET

Church v MGN Ltd[i]	Imputation that the claimant had made an embarrassingly drunken spectacle of herself as she proposed to her boyfriend while singing karaoke in a pub in the early hours of the morning met level of seriousness.
Cammish v Hughes[ii]	Allegation of serious incompetence against a businessman was sufficient to meet the necessary threshold, as it was capable of affecting his livelihood. The Court of Appeal noted that reputation is important to a businessman as he needs to persuade others to trust that he will competently perform commitments entered into in the course of business.

[i] [2012] EWHC 693 (QB); [2012] EMLR 28 (QB).
[ii] [2012] EWCA Civ 1655 CA; [2013] EMLR 13 at [41].

3.7.5 *The test of substantial harm in relation to 'entities that trade for a profit'*

In relation to businesses,[52] although the European Court of Human Rights has acknowledged that the reputation of a trading corporation is worthy of

---

52 Which is defined as a body that trades for profit, s 1(2) Defamation Act 2013.

68 Civil claims

protection,[53] section 1(2) of the Defamation Act 2013 requires that the entity must show that the statement has caused or is likely to cause it 'serious financial loss' before it can demonstrate that it has met the threshold of serious harm, as defined in section 1(1) of the Defamation Act 2013.

The Joint Committee considered that corporations might find it difficult to prove actual financial loss.[54] Such a narrow test would risk creating injustice for corporations that have suffered a serious libel without experiencing immediately identifiable financial harm. Adopting the approach of Lord Lester, the Joint Committee suggested that corporations be able to rely upon likely financial loss.

In considering how this approach may be interpreted by the courts, it may be that the test of 'substantial financial loss' will focus on whether there has been, or is likely to be, a substantial loss of custom directly caused by defamatory statements, such as a material reduction in customer numbers and turnover more generally. Moreover, where a trading corporation can prove a general downturn in business as a consequence of a libel, even if it cannot prove the loss of specific customers or contracts, this will suffice as a form of actual loss (albeit unquantified).

It was suggested by the Joint Committee, however, that a corporation should not be entitled to rely on the following factors when seeking to justify bringing a claim for libel:

- A fall in its share price, as the loss is suffered by its shareholders rather than the corporation itself.[55]
- Injury to goodwill, as in the Committee's opinion the concept is too vague.[56]
- Any expense incurred in mitigation of damage to reputation, as in the Committee's opinion any corporation can decide to create its own mitigation costs, for instance by spending money on advertising to counter the impact of an allegedly defamatory statement.[57]

In relation to goodwill, this may potentially cause problems with postings made on social media sites which are more akin to low-level grumblings about a company, such as by a dissatisfied customer or employee, which damage reputation and cause the company reputational management issues, but do not necessarily reach the legal threshold of serious harm but nevertheless are damaging to a company's reputation. In such circumstances, it is suggested that entities could appeal to the social networking site directly to seek the removal of the post.

Although the practical outcome of this provision is yet unclear, it seems likely that it will make it more difficult for profit-making bodies to sue for defamation. However, businesses should recall that in *Mama Group Limited & Lovebox Festivals Limited v Sinclair & Joseph*,[58] Dingemans J stated obiter that the balance to be weighed between

---

53 See the judgment of the European Court of Human Rights in *Steel & Morris v United Kingdom* [2005] EMLR 15 at [94].

54 Lord McNally, Vol. II, p. 438; Q 151 [Christie-Miller]; Law Society, Vol. III, p. 99.

55 The Joint Committee on the Draft Defamation Bill Report Session 2010–2012, HL 203, HC 930-I, para 115.

56 Ibid.

57 Ibid.

58 [2013] EWHC 2374 (QB) at [42].

the reputation of a trading corporation and freedom of expression is a matter for the judgment of national authorities.[59] The court suggested that the balance had been struck by Parliament by their making provision in the Defamation Act 2013 to leave pre-existing causes of action unaffected by the new provisions contained in the 2013 Act. Moreover, while the courts may have regard to the Joint Committee's report, the standards are illustrative only and it may be possible to successfully argue that there has been a financial loss based upon one of the above factors. What is clear is that in light of *Mama Group Limited* and the report, companies will need to think carefully about how to construct such an argument given the likelihood that the Joint Committee's report may be used as guidance by the courts when formulating judgments during the infancy of the case law coming out of section 1(2) of the Defamation Act 2013.

3.8 Publication

3.8.1 *Introduction*

In order to proceed with an action for libel or slander, the material in question must have been published. It is the publication, not the writing, of the material that is the material element of the cause of the action.[60] This inevitably raises the question, what constitutes a publication? To constitute publication, the material must be:

- published by the defendant;[61] and
- communicated to a third party, being at least one more person than the prospective claimant.[62]

3.8.2 *Primary and secondary publishers*

For liability to attach to a prospective defendant, they must be the publisher of that defamatory statement. The common law definition of a publisher is very wide, and includes anyone who participated in the publication of the statement (e.g. primary and secondary publishers). Secondary publishers do not take an active editorial role but still make the defamatory comments available to third parties. Examples of activities that can be undertaken without making the person a primary publisher are set out in section 1(3) of the Defamation Act 1996 (these include libraries, news-stands, bookshops, and ISPs). Secondary publishers can still be liable for defamatory material communicated to a third party, even in the absence of proof of fault.

The notion of who is a publisher has special significance in the context of the internet and social networking sites. The reason for this is that it can be difficult to

---

59 *Jameel v Wall Street Journal Europe SPRL (No.3)* [2006] UKHL 44; [2007] 1 AC 359; [2007] Bus LR 291; [2006] 3 WLR 642; [2006] 4 All ER 1279; [2007] EMLR 2; [2006] HRLR 41; 21 BHRC 471; (2006) 103(41) LSG 36; (2006) 156 NLJ 1612; (2006) 150 SJLB 1392; *The Times*, 12 October 2006; *The Independent*, 17 October 2006; *Official Transcript*, HL 2006-10-11 at [20].
60 See, for example, *Hebditch v Macllwaine* [1984] 2 QB 54 CA at 58 and 61 per Lord Escher MR.
61 In *Lysko v Bradley* [2006] 79 OR (3d) 721 ont CA, it was held that the publication must be one made by an identifiable defendant.
62 *Trantum v McDowell* [2007] NSWC 138.

70 *Civil claims*

identify with certainty the original poster of a defamatory statement on the internet; for example, @MrJones may be posting via an anonymous account '@Anonymous' as featured in the *Arab Springs* wikileaks case.[63] Moreover, even if the poster is identified as the primary publisher of the defamatory statement (e.g. @MrJones turns out to be Mr A. Jones of 123 Somewhere Road, A City), they may not be worth suing as they may lack financial means. For these reasons, a prospective claimant may instead choose to pursue a secondary publisher, such as the owner of the website (as the primary publisher) or the ISP (as a secondary publisher).

Prior to the coming into force of the Defamation Act 2013, ISPs were often the first port of call for claimants wishing to remove a defamatory statement from the internet. The Defamation Act 2013 sees a significant departure away from ISPs and social networking sites, putting liability for publication back on the original poster. Section 10(1) of the Defamation Act 2013, which came into force on 1 January 2014, provides that the court does not have jurisdiction to hear an action that is brought against a person who is not the author, editor or publisher of the statement complained of unless it is not reasonably practicable for an action to be brought against the author, editor or publisher.

However, there is a note of caution (as discussed below). If an ISP or social media platform can be considered to be a publisher, they may still be potentially liable for statements made by their users. This inevitably raises the question of when a social networking site or ISP will be a publisher and what they can do to demonstrate that they are not a publisher and/or did not know or have reason to believe they were implicated in the publication of a defamatory statement, and that it is 'reasonably practicable' to bring an action against the person actually responsible for posting the statement. The necessary evidence that would have to be presented by claimants remains to be seen. In relation to online publication, the distinction between primary and secondary publishers can become blurred. By way of example, if a newspaper also has an online website, and publishes its print articles on the internet too, it would be suggested that by merely providing the same content online they are acting as a secondary publisher. This view was supported in the case of *Bunt v Tilley*,[64] in which the High Court held that an ISP that merely passively facilitated postings on the internet could not be deemed to be a 'publisher' at all. However, if the company decides to exert some form of editorial control by editing the articles or providing summary extracts, it may become a primary publisher. Undoubtedly, the distinction between primary and secondary publishers will produce a great variety of case law that will inform the application of the reforms made by the Defamation Act 2013.

3.8.2.1 *Hyperlinks*

In relation to social media sites, there is also doubt as to whether providing hyperlinks to content falls within the definition of publisher. In considering if this may be a supportable view, the case of *Hird v Wood*[65] is worthy of analysis. In *Hird*, a man

---

63 For a discussion of *Arab Springs*, see Chapter 4: Communications Act 2003, Censorship and Monitoring.
64 [2006] EWHC 407 (QB).
65 [1894] 38 SJ 234.

sitting in a chair pointed out to passers-by a defamatory sign erected over the road. He was held to be a publisher as he had pointed out the sign and therefore contributed to its publication. In principle, a tweet or post that offers a link to a defamatory publication could therefore fall within the definition of a publication. Moreover, if the link were combined with an emoticon or additional text, then these factors could produce a stronger presumption that the poster is publishing defamatory content, although it is acknowledged that much will depend on the facts, such as whether automated tweet services such as Hootsuite, or marketing agencies, are being used to author tweets, etc.

Other factors may also relate to whether the poster of the hyperlink is a publisher, such as if the link is to a mini website rather than a specific article. However, confusion may arise here if for instance a link is provided to an online website and the 'banner' story is defamatory but actually the poster was linking to a much smaller article further down the page. In *McGrath and another v Dawkins and others*,[66] the High Court refused to strike out a claim that the operator of a website was liable for allegedly defamatory postings on a website that it linked to even though the originating website carried no defamatory postings itself. Again the role of emoticons, additional text, and the use of hashtags (e.g. #guilty) and a hyperlink about a high-profile figure and bribery may assist the court in determining if a publication has taken place. Unfortunately, there is no definitive answer in case law on the point. Even if a hyperlink provider is found to be a publisher of material that can be accessed by clicking the link provided by them, they may still be able to avail themselves of section 8 of the Defamation Act 2013, 'the single publication rule' (considered below).

It is also important to note that when pleading a defamation claim, claimants must reproduce the precise words complained of (including emoticons if they are considered to have bearing on the meaning; see above for the discussion of *McAlpine v Bercow* ([2013] EWHC 1342 (QB)) and it is not enough to refer to the source where they can be found (e.g. a particular user's Twitter account or a URL address). In the case of *Wissa v Associated Newspapers Limited* ([2014] EWHC 1518 (QB)), the claimant referred in his Particulars of Claim simply to the URL that was alleged to contain the words complained of. The defendant applied to strike out the claim on the basis that the words complained of had not been sufficiently identified. The court held that the URL did not of itself identify the words for the following reasons:

- on that day there were several different versions of the article which were published via the URL identified in the Particulars of Claim; and
- the article published on that URL contained large amounts of tec Claimant wanted to complain about.

The court also referred to the effect of CPR 16.4, PD 53 and the court's views in *Best v Charter Medical of England Limited* ([2001] EWCA Civ 1588), which states that it is necessary for a claimant to set out 'word for word' the alleged defamatory content, whether that is the whole of the text or an extract from a larger text.

---

66 [2012] EWHC B3 (QB), 30 March 2012.

72 *Civil claims*

This case highlights the importance of ensuring that defamatory content is sufficiently identified. Although in relation to an online newspaper story, it also identifies the importance on social media of identifying the words complained of if an initial wall-post or tweet has many comments made by other users. Claimants should set out why the initial tweet or subsequent tweets are defamatory and be careful to ensure that they identify why the words complained of in that user's comment or post are defamatory.

3.8.2.2 *Search engines*

Although individuals or companies who upload content may fall within the definition of a publisher, there is also the issue of whether a search engine such as Google can be considered a publisher. In *Metropolitan International Schools Ltd v Designtechnica Corporation and others*,[67] Google Inc was held not to be a publisher of a defamatory statement that could be located though a keyword search (for keywords relating to a defamatory statement) of its search engine. The High Court stated that Google had no control over deciding the search terms that were input by the search engine users or provided the content in any meaningful sense. Keywords had been input and those keywords had produced a result, and it had therefore merely facilitated a service by which content could be sourced. However, that was not the same as publishing in any meaningful sense. In addition, unlike a website host who would be easily able to locate and remove offending content, the search engine had no easy way to locate such publications and ensure that they did not appear in search results. Google has also taken steps to identify certain URLs that contain offending content and block access to them. However, if Google were to identify certain keywords that produced the result, and block them, it would also block a significant amount of other content that was not linked to the content that formed the subject matter of the defamation claim. As such, the claimant would have difficulty in establishing that Google had acquiesced in the publication of defamatory content.

The role of search engines was also considered in *Samuel Kingsford Budu v BBC*.[68] In this case, however, the point of view considered was that of the original material listed in the search engine results. In *Budu*, the court ruled that, where a Google keyword search against the claimant's name brought up a 'snippet' of a BBC article, which when reproduced in a Google search engine result for keyword terms, was divorced from its context, thereby rendering it libellous, the BBC could not be held responsible for the libel and the claim was struck out.

For a discussion of the *Google v Spain (Google Spain SL (1) and Google Inc (2) v Agencia Española de Protección de Datos (AEPD) (1) and Costeja González (2)* (Case C-131/12)) judgment, which classified Google as a data controller within the meaning of the Data Protection Directive 1995, see Chapter 14.

3.8.2.3 *'Facebook rape'*

Individuals who access the accounts of others to post mischievous postings, colloquially refereed to as 'Facebook rape' or 'Frape', need to be aware that this may

---

67 [2009] EWHC 1765 (QB).
68 [2010] EWHC 616 (QB).

also constitute a defamatory posting and can lead to the award of substantial damages.

In *Bryce v Barber*,[69] a university student was awarded £10,000 in damages for remarks made by another on his Facebook account in 2010. The defendant posted indecent images of children on the claimant's, Raymond Bryce's, Facebook profile along with the comment, 'Ray, you like kids and you are gay so I bet you love this picture, Ha ha'. It was suggested by the claimant that the material would be seen by more than 800 people (his Facebook friends and others within the network), defame his character, and even subject him to violence. The defendant also attached the names of eleven other individuals to the images, which meant that they may well have been seen by thousands. Tugendhat J agreed and awarded him damages for stress endured and any ensuring anxiety brought by knowing that those close to him would have seen the offensive image stating that, 'This was not only defamatory but a defamation which goes to a central aspect of Mr Bryce's . . . public reputation'.

3.8.3 *Size of audience*

In *Applause Store Productions Ltd v Raphael*,[70] the court accepted that a substantial publication had occurred despite a lack of evidence, as the potential one million publications was enough. It was also noted that the potential for searching the information that would lead to that profile or group meant that users of the micro site Facebook could find the 'offending material without difficulty'. Interestingly, although there was no evidence of actual financial loss, the court was willing to make a substantial award of damages, which can be seen as indicative of the potential damage that social media sites could cause. Under the new test contained in section 1(2) Defamation Act 2013, relating to entities that trade for a profit, it is unlikely that this finding would be reached again.

3.9 The single publication rule

3.9.1 *Limitation period*

Under section 4(a) of the Limitation Act 1980, a claimant has only one year from the date of publication of a defamatory statement to sue for defamation. Under the court's broad discretion it can however extend the limitation period if it believes there are circumstances where it is equitable to do so. In determining if it would be equitable to allow for issue after the expiry of the limitation period, the court will have regard to a number of factors such as the reason for the delay and the effect that the delay may have upon the reliability of the evidence in support of the claim.

3.9.2 *Background to section 8 of the Defamation Act 2013*

Prior to the coming into force of section 8 of the Defamation Act 2013, the common law position concerning publication was that a fresh cause of action in defamation

---

69 *Bryce v Barber Unreported July 26* [2010] (HC).
70 [2008] EWHC 1781 (QB).

74   *Civil claims*

occurred each time that a defamatory statement was published.[71] The practical effect of this was that the limitation period for bringing a claim was extended each time the defamatory statement was republished (as each time it would constitute a 'fresh publication'). Section 8 seeks to reform the law so that 'stale' defamation actions are not brought in respect of republished material that would otherwise have been barred by limitation but for the 'fresh' publication. In relation to the internet and specifically social media, the rule was particularly relevant as comments can be stored or republished.

Problematically for internet providers, in the context of websites to mean that, each new 'hit' on a web page constituted a fresh publication, such as in the case of *Loutchansky v Times Newspapers Ltd*.[72] The High Court of Australia also rejected arguments in favour of a 'single publication' rule in the case of *Dow Jones v Gutnick*,[73] holding that:

> Harm to reputation is done when a defamatory publication is comprehended by the reader, the listener, or the observer. Until then, no harm is done by it. This being so it would be wrong to treat publication as if it were a unilateral act on the part of the publisher alone. It is not. It is a bilateral act – in which the publisher makes it available and a third party has it available for his or her comprehension.[74]

While the case was held by the European Court of Human Rights in *Times Newspapers Limited v UK*[75] to be consistent with Article 10 of the ECHR, in terms of libel proceedings made in relation to 'stale' posts, the ECtHR did state that since a significant lapse of time was taken by claimants to bring proceedings, the court was of the view that such circumstances may give rise to a disproportionate curb on a publisher's freedom of expression. It is important to note that this judgment was given in relation to newspapers and it is not yet clear what speech value will be afforded to 'low-level speech' or 'everyday speech' in such circumstances (i.e. made on social media sites).[76]

The reform to the law is important in the context of ISPs, as it will arguably reduce the need to monitor archived content in light of cases such as *Flood v Times Newspapers Ltd*,[77] where a publisher was held liable after failing to add a warning notice to defamatory material knowingly held in its archive.

3.9.3 *Section 8 of the Defamation Act 2013*

The approach at common law has now been replaced by section 8 of the Defamation Act 2013. Section 8 introduces the 'single publication rule'. This 'rule' will mean that a cause of action in defamation accrues from the date of the first publication to the

---

71 *Duke of Brunswick v Harmer* (1849) 14 QB 185.
72 [2001] EWCA Civ 1805.
73 [2002] HCA 56.
74 [2002] HCA 56 at [26].
75 [2009] ECHR 451, 10 March 2009.
76 For a discussion of the problems raised by speech value, see Chapter 2: Human Rights.
77 [2010] EWCA Civ 804 and [2013] EWHC 2182 (QB).

Defamation 75

public,[78] or a section of the public,[79] and expires at the end of the one-year limitation period.

Publications published by the same publisher that are 'substantially the same' are covered by section 8(1)(b) of the Act. However, the section will not apply if the content of the subsequent publication is materially different from the first publication.[80] In determining this, the court will be entitled to give regard to:

- The level of prominence that the statement is given (s 8(5)(a)).
- The extent of the subsequent publication (s 8(5)(b)).

In relation to social media sites, this could prove significant. Consider, for example, a tweet or post made by an account holder who has 100 followers, compared with it being re-tweeted (forwarding another person's tweet) by a celebrity follower who has in excess of 2 million followers. Although the example may seem far removed, a recent example that shows the problems highlighted by social media involved a tweet posted by the editor of the London-based Bureau of Investigative Journalism, Iain Overton, suggesting that a senior political figure may be 'outed' as a paedophile: 'If all goes well we've got a Newsnight out tonight about a very senior political figure who is a paedophile.' Subsequent to the tweet, several posters outed Lord McAlpine online as the perpetrator of the alleged offences. Lord McAlpine is expected to sue at least 10,000 people over the malicious claims that appeared in the wake of a BBC *Newsnight* investigation into a paedophile ring at care homes in North Wales.

3.9.4 *Archiving and re-tweets*

Section 8 has been developed in particular to address the issues raised by the increasing trend for archiving published material. With regards to social media, this could have had important ramifications. In 2012, Dick Costolo (@dickc), chief executive of Twitter, during a talk at the University of Michigan in Ann Arbor stated that down-loadable Twitter archives were in the process of being made available to account holders.[81] Once an account holder has downloaded their Twitter archive, they can view their tweets by month, or search their archive to find tweets with certain words, phrases, hashtags or @usernames. Users can even engage with old tweets just as users can with current ones, which clearly may have ramifications in relation to libel.

Although the ability to store materials may have a social utility,[82] it has raised concerns that material which has long since been forgotten on the web may be accessed and retrieved much later than a year after the limitation period began. In relation to archived material, it is interesting to note that in *Loutchansky*,[83] the social utility of providing archives was not considered so great as to merit a change in the law, Lord Phillips MR stated:

---

78 Section 8(1)(a) Defamation Act 2013.
79 Section 8(2) Defamation Act 2013.
80 Section 8(5) Defamation Act 2013.
81 This technology became available on Wednesday, 19 December 2012.
82 *Loutchansky v Times Newspapers Ltd & Others* [2001] EWCA Civ 1805, [2002] 1 All ER 652.
83 [2001] EWCA Civ 1805.

76   *Civil claims*

> We do not accept that the rule . . . imposes a restriction on the readiness to main-
> tain and provide access to archives that amounts to a disproportionate restriction
> on freedom of expression. We accept that the maintenance of archives, whether
> in hard copy or on the internet, has a social utility, but consider that the mainten-
> ance of archives is a comparatively insignificant aspect of freedom of expression.
> Archive material is stale news and its publication cannot rank in importance with
> the dissemination of contemporary material. Nor do we believe that the law of
> defamation need inhibit the responsible maintenance of archives. Where it is
> known that archive material is or may be defamatory, the attachment of an appro-
> priate notice warning against treating it as the truth will normally remove any
> sting from the material.[84]

Although not impossible, it would have been much more difficult to pursue actions
for 'stale comments' in relation to traditional print media like newspapers and
magazines, which are more temporal in nature. While the changes are useful in terms
of website content, it is argued that not enough has happened to address the problems addressed by micro-blogs such as Twitter and micro-sites such as Facebook,
which generate content at a phenomenal pace. Recent data shared by Twitter indicate
that the number of tweets sent per day is in excess of 500 million.[85]

The single publication rule, however, does not actually address the issues around
the Web 2.0 environment of Twitter, which is predicated upon the real time prolifer-
ation of content. It is arguable that tweets are 'of the moment', commenting on a
particular topic or event at that time and the retrieval of archived content may not
reflect the context in which it is posted. Moreover, the re-tweeting period is likely to
be concentrated within a short time frame from when the initial post was made. The
amount of re-tweeting of the re-tweets will also be dependent upon the number of
followers who the re-tweeter has for their account.

The vast majority of re-tweets of the defamatory tweets published occurred within
a 24-hour period of the tweet being posted, as was exemplified by the Ryan Giggs
Super Injunction tweets and *McAlpine*. In *McAlpine*, Andrew Price, Lord McAlpine's
solicitor said: 'We already have all the information. We have found a couple of firms
of experts who have produced pre-tweets, post-tweets, the effect of the tweets and the
re-tweets. What starts as one ends up at 100,000 in some cases.'[86]

3.9.5 *Republication: re-tweets*

The single publication rule means that a tweet if re-tweeted, it is treated as a fresh
publication actionable within itself under the normal provisions of liability. In simple
terms, this means that a re-tweet is as actionable as the original tweet, as the 'point of
publication' is the point at which the material has been uploaded onto a server.

---

84 [2001] EWCA Civ 1805 at [74].
85 According to Twitter CEO Dick Costolo in October 2012 – up from the last official number of 400
   million in June 2012, so now likely to be a lot higher. But Twitter is still giving out the 400 million stat-
   istic [https://blog.twitter.com/2011/numbers].
86 'Pay up, twits: Lord McAlpine will also go after celebrities for untrue pervert accusations', *Daily Mirror*,
   19 November 2012.

Materials published by a publisher (tweeter) and a re-publisher (re-tweeter) are regarded as entirely distinct from one another, as the point of publication has changed; as the key point of publication is when the material is uploaded.

The Joint Committee on the Draft Defamation Bill initially wanted to have the single publication rule apply to all publications of the same content of the original publication regardless of whom they were made. The content would be covered by a single 12-month period that would have accrued from the point at which the original publication had been uploaded. The Government rejected the proposal stating:

> The Committee's recommendation would extend the scope of the single publication rule much more widely than the approach adopted in the draft Bill, and would prevent an action being brought against anyone who republishes the same material in a similar manner. The Government does not believe that this would provide adequate protection for claimants. For example, if the claimant were to bring an action in the one year period then they would be prevented from bringing any further action in relation to that material, irrespective of who might republish it. Whilst the claimant may have obtained a court injunction against the original publisher to prevent further publication of the defamatory material, any other publisher would still be free to republish it, and the claimant would have no recourse.[87]

3.9.6 *Comparison with United States*

In the United States, liability for republication of a defamatory statement is the same as for original publication, provided the defendant had knowledge of the contents of the statement, as well as had editorial control over the communications. Section 230 of the Communications Decency Act 1996, states that 'no provider or user of an interactive computer service shall be treated as the publisher or speaker of any information provided by another information content provider'. Simply put, this means you cannot be sued for something you re-tweet, even if the original tweet is libellous so long as the libellous content was created by a third party. In *Barrett v Rosenthal*,[88] an alternative medicine advocate named Ilena Rosenthal posted to her message board a defamatory article that had been published elsewhere about two 'quack' doctors who opposed her practices. Even though Rosenthal took an active role in selecting and disseminating the article on her board, she was provided section 230 immunity because she was found to be 'a mere distributor' of content. In *Doe II v Myspace, Inc*,[89] Myspace was held to be immune from liability for the sexual assault of teenage girls who had met their assailants through the social networking website. The court granted immunity to Myspace because under section 230, it could not be liable for the publication of third-party content. It should be noted that the Ninth Circuit has found that a website acting as a 'content provider' rather than a mere 're-publisher'

---

87 Ministry of Justice, 'Government's Response to the Report of the Joint Committee on the Draft Defamation Bill' (February 2012), paras 50–51.
88 *Barrett v Rosenthal*, 40 Cal 4th 33 (2006).
89 *Doe II v Myspace, Inc*, 175 Cal App 4th 561 (2009).

78   *Civil claims*

does not have immunity. In *Fair Housing Council v Roommates, Inc,*[90] Roommates. com 'filtered' the results displayed to users based on the preferences they selected. The court reasoned that such a 'collaborative effort' fell outside the protection offered under section 230. However, if the user does have control to modify or add to the content of the tweet before re-tweeting it, the user may be held responsible for all of the content of the re-tweet, or at a minimum, the portion of the re-tweet that has been added.

3.10 Section 10 actions against secondary publishers

3.10.1 *Introduction*

Section 10 of the Defamation Act 2013 applies to secondary publishers. Section 10(1) provides that a court does not have jurisdiction to hear and determine an action for defamation brought against a person who was not the author, editor or publisher of the statement complained of unless the court is satisfied that it is not practical against the author, editor or publisher.[91]

Section 10 should be considered in conjunction with section 13. Section 13(1) provides that where a court gives judgment for a claimant in an action for defamation, the court may order:

- That the operator of a website on which the defamatory statement is posted to remove the statement (s 13(1)(a)); or
- Any person who was not the author, editor or publisher of the defamatory statement to stop distributing, selling or exhibiting material containing the statement (s 13(1)(b)).

Section 10 could give rise to a potential problem in relation to section 5 of the Defamation Act 2013, where the claimant would be able to sue the author of the publication, but would be unable to pursue the removal or further dissemination of the comment. Section 13 was therefore introduced to remedy this potential lacuna. It is envisaged that orders made pursuant to section 13 will be done so shortly after the conclusion of proceedings against the primary publisher. An application could also be made under Part 23 of the Civil Procedure Rules 1998 (CPR).

3.10.2 *Common law position*

It is important, when considering the application of section 10 of the Defamation Act 2013, to be aware that section 1 of the Defamation Act 1996, which deals with responsibility for publication, remains in force. Subsection 1(3) provides that a person shall not be considered the author, editor or publisher if he is only involved:

- in printing, producing, distributing or selling printed material containing the statement (s 1(3)(a));

---

90 *Fair Housing Council v Roommates, Inc*, 521 F.3d 1157 (9th Cir 2008).
91 Section 10(2) provides that author, editor, and publisher have the same meaning as contained in s 1 Defamation Act 1996.

- in processing, making copies of, distributing, exhibiting or selling a film or sound recording (as defined in Part I of the Copyright, Designs and Patents Act 1988) containing the statement (s 1(3)(b));
- in processing, making copies of, distributing or selling any electronic medium in or on which the statement is recorded, or in operating or providing any equipment, system or service by means of which the statement is retrieved, copied, distributed or made available in electronic form (s 1(3)(c));
- as the broadcaster of a live programme containing the statement in circumstances in which he has no effective control over the maker of the statement (s 1(3)(d));
- as the operator of or provider of access to a communications system by means of which the statement is transmitted, or made available, by a person over whom he has no effective control (s 1(3)(e)).

When a case does not fall within subsections within paragraphs (a) to (e), the court may have regard to those provisions by way of analogy in deciding whether a person is to be considered the author, editor or publisher of a statement. It suggested that section 1(3)(e) will cover the internet, and by extension social networking sites. In the Public Bill Committee on the Bill for the Defamation Act 2013, in the House of Commons it was noted that when considering the interaction between clause 10 and section 1 of the Defamation Act 1996, 'the defence under section 1 will continue to be available alongside clause 10, so that in the event of an action against a secondary publisher being allowed, the section 1 defence will be available where appropriate'.[92] It is anticipated that although these avenues will remain open to secondary publishers, section 10 will gain in prevalence as the preferred way to rebut liability.

3.10.3 *Interrelationship with section 5 of the Defamation Act 2013*

Inevitably, where social media is concerned, questions arise as to when it may not be 'reasonably practicable' (s 10(1)) to bring an action against a primary publisher. In such an instance, the reader will recall that a claimant can, under section 5 and the Regulation request that the website operator provide to the prospective claimant sufficient details to allow them to pursue a claim. Defendants who operate websites may argue that claimants could obtain sufficient details though seeking a *Norwich Pharmacal Order*,[93] which would have the potential to make the section 5 procedure redundant. However, it is unlikely that such arguments would find good grace with the courts, which would be unlikely to see section 10 as a defence to avoid responding to a section 5 notice (a response to the notice is required by the regulations). It will be interesting to see, however, if alternate methods of service such as Facebook and Twitter private messaging find increasing favour with the courts.

Under section 13 of the Defamation Act 2013, a court that has given judgment for the claimant in an action for defamation will be able to order the operator of a website on which the defamatory statement is posted to remove the material in question. This

---

92 Public Bill Committee, Tuesday, 26 June 2012 (Morning), Session 2012–13, Publications on the Internet Defamation Bill, *Hansard*, Column no. 163.
93 *Norwich Pharmacal Co & Others v Customs and Excise Commissioners* [1974] AC 133.

80 *Civil claims*

provision is designed to give claimants a remedy in situations where the website operator has a defence under section 5 of the Defamation Act 2013 because it did not post the statement on its website itself.

The section 5 'website operators' defence' is a welcome protection for website operators against actions brought in respect of third-party content on their websites. It goes further than the previously available intermediaries' defences contained in section 1 of the Defamation Act 1996 and the E-Commerce Regulations (both discussed below). In particular, Regulation 19 of the E-Commerce Regulations only protects those who have no involvement in the content of the site (because they are merely hosting) and do not have 'actual knowledge' (that is, they are not on notice) or knowledge of facts or circumstances from which it is apparent that the activity or information is illegal (as opposed to defamatory). Equally, the defence under section 1 of the Defamation Act 1996 is defeated where the intermediary has knowledge, or reason to believe, that what it did caused or contributed to the publication of a defamatory statement. Section 5 of the Defamation Act 2013, on the other hand, applies to website operators who moderate content posted by users and who, arguably, are made aware of the offending nature of the content through receipt of a valid notice of complaint (section 5(6) of the Defamation Act 2013 contains the requirements for a notice to be valid), so long as they comply with its processes. However, these processes place a considerable administrative burden on website operators to ensure compliance and could give rise to situations where defamatory content remains online for up to 12 days after notification while regulatory time-frames are complied with, even where the poster of the content ultimately consents to its removal.

3.11 Jurisdiction

3.11.1 *Introduction*

In order to bring a claim for defamation, a prospective claimant must establish that the UK courts have jurisdiction to hear the matter. In the UK, this is determined by three separate areas of law depending upon where the claimant is domiciled. If the defendant is domiciled in an EU State (other than Denmark), then jurisdiction will be governed by the Brussels Regulation,[94] which came into effect in March 2002. The Brussels Regulation states at Article 2 that persons domiciled in an EU Member State other than Denmark may be sued in the courts of that Member State. UK courts will therefore have jurisdiction where the defendant is a person who lives in the UK or is a company who has its registered office based in the UK.

Article 5(3) of the Brussels Regulation states that such matters may relate to tort, delict in the place where the harmful event occurred or may occur. In *Shevill v Presse Alliance SA*,[95] a case concerning an article in a French newspaper which alleged that a UK resident from Yorkshire had been involved in a drug trafficking network, the ECJ held that the claimant could bring a claim:

---

94 Regulation on the recognition and enforcement of judgments in civil and commercial matters (44/2001/EC (Brussels regulation)).
95 [1995] ECR i-415 ECJ.

- where the publisher of the statement was established; or
- in the court of the contracting State where the statement was distributed and the damage to the reputation occurred.

In *Shevill*, the majority of the newspapers had been sold in France but five copies had been circulated in Yorkshire. This is significant, as the ECJ held that if the claimant chose to sue where the harm occurred, the State only had jurisdiction to rule in relation to the harm caused in that State, while the State of the claimant had the jurisdiction to award damages for the total harm in all countries. Clearly, with the cross-jurisdictional scope of social media publications, such damages may be significant and the issue of jurisdiction is brought into sharp focus on the question of damages, particularly if a large number of tweets are circulated outside of the poster's country of domicile.

In *Cairns v Modi*,[96] Mr Modi denied that any real or substantial tort had occurred in the United Kingdom and brought proceedings to have the claim set aside for abuse of process, as he argued that its effects on the claimant in the UK were trivial and speculative. Modi suggested that at the time of posting, he would have had about 90 followers on Twitter in the UK and of these many would not have read the tweet once it had been sent out, and suggested that in the jurisdiction proceedings only about 35 people would have actually seen the remarks. Tugendhat J took advice from two experts in the field who both sided with the suggestion of the defendant on actual publication numbers but neither went further as to how many might have seen the remarks through other means. Tugendhat J decided that the number of followers was irrelevant given the sensationalist nature of the remarks and the fact that the remarks could have been searched and republished, and not just by the defendant's followers. Tugendhat J also stated that the court was entitled to infer that publication in the United Kingdom had been far greater than the estimated figures for those who had received direct tweets from the defendant, and that even if the publication in the particular jurisdiction could only be described as insignificant, there remained the possibility and real risk of wider publication. In this instance Bean J awarded Cairns damages of £90,000 (approximately £3,750 per word tweeted).

3.11.2 The approach of the Defamation Act 2013 to actions against persons not domiciled in the UK or a Member State, etc.

Section 9 of the Defamation Act 2013 was introduced to address the issue of 'libel tourism' (a term used to apply where cases with a tenuous link to England and Wales are brought in this jurisdiction). Section 9(1) focuses the provision on cases where an action is brought against a person who is not domiciled in the UK, an EU Member State or a State that is a party to the Lugano Convention. This is in order to avoid conflict with European jurisdictional rules (in particular the Brussels Regulation on jurisdictional matters discussed above).

Section 9(2) provides that a court does not have jurisdiction to hear and determine an action to which the section applies unless it is satisfied that, of all the places in

96 [2012] EWHC 756 (QB).

82   *Civil claims*

which the statement complained of has been published, England and Wales is the most appropriate place in which to bring an action in respect of the statement. This means that in cases where a statement has been published in the UK and also abroad, the court will be required to consider the overall global picture to consider where it would be most appropriate for a claim to be heard. It is intended that this provision will overcome courts readily accepting jurisdiction simply because a claimant frames their claim so as to focus on damage that has occurred within the UK. This would mean that, for example, unlike *Shevill*, if a statement was published 100,000 times in Australia and only 5,000 times in England, that would be a good basis on which to conclude that the most appropriate jurisdiction in which to bring an action in respect of the statement was Australia rather than England. There will however be a range of factors which the court may wish to take into account, including, for example, the amount of damage to the claimant's reputation in this jurisdiction compared with elsewhere, the extent to which the publication was targeted at a readership in this jurisdiction compared with elsewhere, and whether there is reason to think that the claimant would not receive a fair hearing elsewhere.

A UK court can decline jurisdiction if it determines that there is a more appropriate forum. Unless the claimant is able to serve the claim from within the jurisdiction, the leave of the court will need to be sought to serve it outside of the jurisdiction; leave will be granted if the service is authorized by the rule of the court and the jurisdiction is the proper place to bring the claim.

There will of course be situations where slightly different statements are published in different jurisdictions. Section 9(3) of the Defamation Act 2013 makes provision for this and provides that the references in section 9(2) to the statement complained of include references to any statement which conveys the same, or substantially the same, imputation as the statement complained of. This addresses the situation where a statement is published in a number of countries but is not exactly the same in all of them, and will ensure that a court is not impeded in deciding whether England and Wales is the most appropriate place to bring the claim by arguments that statements elsewhere should be regarded as different publications even when they are substantially the same. It is the intention that this new rule will be capable of being applied within the existing procedural framework for defamation claims.

3.12 Self-regulation by social media sites

3.12.1 *Site terms*

Most of the main social media sites operate user content policies, sometimes referred to as site terms, community standards, terms of use, user charters or codes of behaviour, which set out site standards in relation to how users must conduct themselves when using the site's services. They also generally offer ways in which to report offensive or bullying content whether through an email link or a 'report' button. As a result of a consideration of a complaint made to them, social media providers may consider that the activity complained of breaches their policies and may block access to posts or, in extreme cases, close down accounts permanently or for a limited period of time.

The following sections detail the terms used by some of the main sites and the main rules to consider when seeking to have content removed from a site by appealing to that site directly. Often this is a cheaper and quicker option than litigation for users who merely want the content removed as quickly as possible to prevent any further distress or harm to reputation and avoid the unpredictable nature of litigation.

3.12.2 *Facebook*

Clause 5 of Facebook's Statement of Rights and Responsibilities[97] state that users will not 'post content or take any action on Facebook that infringes or violates someone else's rights or otherwise violates the law'.

3.12.2.1 *Groups*

For businesses, 'Group pages' may cause them concern if they are set up against a company by a disgruntled ex-employee, angry consumer or other acquaintance. Facebook's page terms [https://www.facebook.com/page_guidelines.php] state: 'Only authorized representatives may administer a Page for a brand, entity (place or organization), or public figure.' If the individual running the page is identified as a party not meeting those criteria, then the company could apply for Facebook to consider closing the page or consider deleting some of its content. In determining if they will take any action, Facebook will take into account that individuals have a right to express a range of opinions about other individuals or a business, which they enjoy as part of their freedom of expression. However, companies should check if the page administrator is moderating comments unfairly and blocking individuals from the group, thereby denying all stakeholders the opportunity to correct or clarify statements that are misleading or untrue, which can all be raised in support of any argument advanced to Facebook as to why a page should be closed down or certain comments on the page be removed.

3.12.3 *Twitter*

Twitter's 'Rules of Twitter'[98] note that their goal is to provide a service that allows users to discover and receive content from sources that interest them as well as to share content with others. Twitter state that they 'respect the ownership of the content that users share and each user is responsible for the content he or she provides. Because of these principles, we do not actively monitor and will not censor user content, except in limited circumstances.'[99] These limited circumstances include:

- Impersonation of others through the Twitter service in a manner that does or is intended to mislead, confuse, or deceive others.
- Trademark infringement.
- Private information posted about other people's private and confidential information, such as credit card numbers, street address or Social Security/National Identity numbers, without their express authorization and permission.

---

97 Facebook's Community Standards can be accessed at: https://www.facebook.com/legal/terms.
98 http://support.twitter.com/entries/18311.
99 Ibid.

84 *Civil claims*

- Violence and threats.
- Copyright infringement.
- Unlawful use, i.e. illegal activities.
- Misuse of Twitter badges, i.e. verified official accounts of famous brands or persons.
- Abuse and spam.

Twitter also state via their website that they may not comply with a takedown request for a variety of reasons. For example, they do not comply with requests that fail to identify content on Twitter.[100] The number of takedown requests and the reasons why content has or has not been blocked can be accessed via Twitter's website, which publishes quarterly tables concerning takedown requests, broken down country by country.[101]

3.12.4 *Practical considerations for businesses and organizations*

Before a business decides if it wants to initiate a mechanism to seek the removal of material from a social media site (whether via contacting the website or through the courts), it should carefully consider the PR impact of its actions (e.g. will it appear that a business is trying to hide legitimate concerns from employees or a genuine complaint from a customer?).

In particular, it is necessary to consider how to deal with customers who use a business's social-media platform to air genuine complaints. Businesses may decide in such circumstances that it is preferable to deal with the complaint 'head on' by engaging with the poster directly. However, this is not without risks, especially if the dialogue passing between the parties becomes blurred between the personal and private. To minimize such risk, businesses should consider who will be in charge of replying to such postings (e.g. PR teams or the marketing department) and what the agreed bounds of replies should be. It is all too easy in social media to post a throwaway comment in response to a complaint that can escalate into a PR disaster. The following real life example serves as a useful cautionary tale for businesses. After paying £360 for hair extensions and a cut and blow dry, a customer was unhappy with the result and complained on the salon's Facebook page. The hairdresser replied on the business's Facebook web page describing the customer as a 'whining, whingeing old bag' and 'a prize ★★★★', and added: 'Kindly ★★★★ off.'[102] After she complained on Facebook about these posts, the hairdresser went online again and posted further content. He posted: 'Too busy and too fabulous to deal with your neurotic projections Mrs! Maybe you should see a shrink for your histrionic personality disorder? You want to engage me? I will SUE for slander. You are a whining, winging [*sic*] old

---

100 See https://transparency.twitter.com/removal-requests/2013/jul-dec.
101 The tables can be accessed via https://transparency.twitter.com/removal-requests/2013/jul-dec.
102 L. Edmonds (2014) '"Kindly f★★★ off, you are a PRIZE ★★★★! Go see your psych manager SLAG!" Astonishing foul-mouthed rant of hairdresser to customer who posted negative review on Facebook after botched extensions' [http://www.dailymail.co.uk/news/article-2599680/Kindly-f-PRIZE-Go-psych-manager-SLAG-Astonishing-foul-mouthed-rant-hairdresser-customer-posted-negative-review-Facebook-botched-extensions.html; accessed 8 April 2014].

bag, END OF!' Although starting out as a war of words via social media, the matter escalated when the customer reported the abusive content to the police. A spokesman for Wiltshire Police said that the incident had been reported to them and logged as 'anti-social behaviour'. The hairdresser subsequently deleted the business page for the salon from the social networking website and apologised to the customer. The example also demonstrates that responding to customer complaints online may escalate from a civil claim, potentially into a criminal matter if the communication had been abusive enough to warrant prosecution under the Communications Act 2003 (see Chapter 4, 'Communications Act 2003').

In light of the foregoing, a business should:

- Consider the PR impact in advance; and
- Ensure the relevant employees are versed in what to do when they receive a complaint. And also know how to escalate the matter to a higher level if the complaint warrants it, e.g. the Costa Concordia Disaster resulted in social media backlash by going silent online, demonstrating the importance of social media management.[103]

3.12.5 *Self-help measures for ISPs*

Practical measures that internet service providers (ISPs) can take to try and minimize their liability for internet defamation include the following:

- Reserve the right to remove material in any circumstances:

  - In subscriber contracts with businesses;
  - In subscriber contracts with consumers.[104]

- Put in place detailed procedures for dealing with defamation-related complaints such as:

  - setting response times for examining complaints;
  - removing material if necessary;
  - maintaining records of complaints received and the action taken (sites could also consider publishing transparency reports, e.g. Twitter publishes quarterly Reports for Information Requests, Content Removal Requests and Copyright Infringement;[105]
  - adopting clear standards in relation to the limits of acceptable content, e.g. Facebook's Community Standards;
  - placing disclaimers on websites;
  - taking out insurance.[106]

---

103 See http://adage.com/article/digitalnext/post-disaster-retreat-social-media-backfires-carnival /232723/.

104 Businesses should note that regard must be had to the application of consumer protection rules such as those contained in the Unfair Contract Terms Act 1977 and the Unfair Terms in Consumer Contracts Regulations 1994 (SI 1994/3159).

105 Reports for Information Requests, Content Removal Requests and Copyright Infringement can all be accessed via the hub website [https://transparency.twitter.com/].

106 See Chapter 16: Insurance.

86 *Civil claims*

3.13 Defences

3.13.1 *Truth*

3.13.1.1 *A new statutory defence of truth*

Section 2 of the Defamation Act 2013 established a new statutory defence of truth (s 2(1) DA 2013), which abolishes the common law defence of justification (s 2(4) DA 3013). Section 2 is 'broadly to reflect the current law while simplifying and clarifying certain elements'.[107] This means that where a defendant wishes to rely on the new statutory defence, the court would be required to apply the words used in the statute, not the current case law. In cases where uncertainty arises, the current case law would constitute a helpful but not binding guide to interpreting how the new statutory defence should be applied.

The common law defence of justification had been heavily criticised, as the burden of proving the truth of the statement rested with the defendant and it was suggested by certain groups such as the Libel Reform Group that the burden of proof should be reversed. However, section 2(1) of the Defamation Act 2013 leaves the common law position intact in this regard. The core features of the defence are set out in subsection 1, which provides that 'it is a defence to an action for defamation for the defendant to show that the imputation conveyed by the statement complained of is substantially true'.

The explanatory notes to the Act state that this subsection reflects the current law as established in the case of *Chase v News Group Newspapers Ltd*,[108] where the Court of Appeal indicated that in order for the defence of justification to be available 'the defendant does not have to prove that every word he or she published was true. He or she has to establish the 'essential' or 'substantial' truth of the sting of the libel'. Provided that the requirements and safeguards of the 1995 Act and CPR Part 33 are observed, a defendant may now in theory adduce hearsay evidence of whatever degree in an attempt to prove the truth of the particulars of justification, which may prove especially significant in the context of social media. A discussion of the role of hearsay can be found in Chapter 12: Evidence and Procedure.

3.13.1.2 *The 'repetition rule'*

It should be noted that the explanatory notes to the Bill also state that there is a long-standing common law rule that it is no defence to an action for defamation for the defendant to prove that he or she was only repeating what someone else had said (known as the 'repetition rule'). Subsection (1) focuses on the imputation conveyed by the statement in order to incorporate this rule. Users of social media should be aware of this when reposting the views of others.

In any case where the defence of truth is raised, there will be two issues:

- what imputation (or imputations) are actually conveyed by the statement; and
- whether the imputation (or imputations) conveyed are substantially true. The defence will apply where the imputation is one of fact.

107 Explanatory Notes to clause 2 of the Bill at [13].
108 [2002] EWCA Civ 1772 at para 34.

Subsections (2) and (3) replace section 5 of the 1952 Act (the only significant element of the defence of justification that is currently in statute). Their effect is that where the statement complained of contains two or more distinct imputations, the defence does not fail if, having regard to the imputations which are shown to be substantially true, those which are not shown to be substantially true do not seriously harm the claimant's reputation. These provisions are intended to have the same effect as those in section 5 of the 1952 Act, but are expressed in more modern terminology. The phrase 'materially injure' used in the 1952 Act is replaced by 'seriously harm' to ensure consistency with the test in section 1 of the Act.

In *Cairns v Modi*,[109] former New Zealand cricket captain Chris Cairns won a defamation claim against former Indian Premier League (IPL) chairman Lalit Modi for defamatory tweets in the first case of its kind in the UK. Mr Modi had tweeted that Mr Cairns had been removed from the list of players eligible and available to play in the IPL 'due to his past record of match fixing'. The tweet was removed within 16 hours of being posted. However, the words were repeated in a cricket magazine published by Cricinfo UK. It was estimated that approximately 65 people saw the tweet and around 1,000 people read the publication. Cairns sued Modi for defamation and Modi relied on the old defence of justification (i.e. that his comments were true). Bean J rejected this argument stating that Modi had 'singularly failed to provide any reliable evidence to support such a claim'. Bean J awarded Cairns damages of £90,000 (approximately £3,750 per word tweeted).

3.13.2 *Honest opinion*

3.13.2.1 *New statutory defence of honest opinion*

Section 3 of the Defamation Act 2013 establishes a new defence of 'honest opinion' and replaces the common law defence of 'fair comment', referred to by the Supreme Court in *Spiller v Joseph*[110] as *honest comment*. The section broadly reflects the current law while simplifying and clarifying certain elements, but does not include the current requirement for the opinion to be on a matter of public interest.

3.13.2.2 *Conditions for defence to apply*

For the defence to apply, the defendant must show that three conditions are met:

- that the statement complained of was a statement of opinion (s 3(2) DA 2013);
- that the statement complained of indicated, whether in general or specific terms, the basis of the opinion (s 3(3) DA 2013); and
- that an honest person could have held the opinion on the basis of:
    - any fact which existed at the time the statement complained of was published (s 3(4)(a) DA 2013); or
    - anything asserted to be a fact in a privileged statement published before the statement complained of (s 3(4)(b) DA 2013).

---

109 [2012] EWHC 756 (QB).
110 [2010] UKSC 53.

88 *Civil claims*

Section 3(2) is intended to reflect the current law and embraces the requirement established in *Cheng v Tse Wai Chun Paul*[111] that the statement must be recognizable as comment as distinct from an imputation of fact. It is implicit in condition 1 that the assessment is on the basis of how the ordinary person would understand it. As an inference of fact is a form of opinion, this would be encompassed by the defence.

Section 3(3) reflects the test approved by the Supreme Court in *Joseph v Spiller*[112] that 'the comment must explicitly or implicitly indicate, at least in general terms, the facts on which it is based'.[113] The Bill states that the reforms are intended to retain the broad principles of the current common law defence as to the necessary basis for the opinion expressed but avoid the complexities that have arisen in case law, in particular over the extent to which the opinion must be based on facts that are sufficiently true and the extent to which the statement must explicitly or implicitly indicate the facts on which the opinion is based.[114] These are areas where the common law has become increasingly complicated and technical, and where case law has sometimes struggled to articulate with clarity how the law should apply in particular circumstances. For example, the facts that may need to be demonstrated in relation to an article expressing an opinion on a political issue, comments made on a social network, a view about a contractual dispute, or a review of a restaurant or play will differ substantially. Care should therefore be taken when considering the application of the defence and the facts upon which the opinion is based, especially when it comes to social media where gossip or hearsay may be re-tweeted or posted on a social networking site wall without much (or indeed any[115]) thought.

Section 3(4) is an objective test and consists of two elements, and it is enough for one to be satisfied. The first is whether an honest person could have held the opinion on the basis of any fact that existed at the time the statement was published (in ss (4)(a)). The subsection refers to 'any fact', so that any relevant fact or facts will be enough. The existing case law on the sufficiency of the factual basis is covered by the requirement that 'an honest person' must have been able to hold the opinion. If the fact was not a sufficient basis for the opinion, an honest person would not have been able to hold it. The second element of condition 3 (in ss (4)(b)) is whether an honest person could have formed the opinion on the basis of anything asserted to be a fact in a 'privileged statement' that was published before the statement complained of. For this purpose, a statement is a 'privileged statement' if the person responsible for its publication would have one of the defences listed in subsection (7) if an action was brought in respect of that statement. The defences listed are the defence of absolute privilege under section 14 of the 1996 Act; the defence of qualified privilege under section 15 of that Act; and the defences in sections 4 and 6 of the Act relating to publication on a matter of public interest and peer-reviewed statements in a scientific or academic journal.

---

111 (2000) 10 BHRC 525.
112 [2010] UKSC 53.
113 [2010] UKSC 53 at [105].
114 Explanatory Notes to clause 2 of the Bill at para 22.
115 For a discussion of the conversational nature of speech, see Chapters 1, 2, and 4.

3.13.2.3 *Defeating the defence*

Subsection (5) provides for the defence to be defeated if the claimant shows that the defendant did not hold the opinion. This is a subjective test. This reflects the current law whereby the defence of fair comment will fail if the claimant can show that the statement was actuated by malice. Presumably, this will apply to situations of 'fraping' where it can be established that another had accessed the user's account without permission.

3.13.2.3.1 THE DEFENDANT IS NOT THE AUTHOR OF THE STATEMENT

Subsection (6) makes provision for situations where the defendant is not the author of the statement (for example, where an action is brought against a newspaper editor in respect of a comment piece rather than against the person who wrote it). In these circumstances, the defence is defeated if the claimant can show that the defendant knew or ought to have known that the author did not hold the opinion. This may apply in relation to tweets posted on newspaper twitter feeds and social networking site pages.

3.13.2.4 *Repeal of Section 6*

Subsection (8) repeals section 6 of the 1952 Act. Section 6 provides that in an action for libel or slander in respect of words consisting partly of allegations of fact and partly of expression of opinion, a defence of fair comment shall not fail by reason only that the truth of every allegation of fact is not proved if the expression of opinion is fair comment having regard to such of the facts alleged or referred to in the words complained of as are proved. This provision is no longer necessary in light of the new approach set out in subsection (4). A defendant will be able to show that conditions 1, 2, and 3 are met without needing to prove the truth of every single allegation of fact relevant to the statement complained of.

3.13.3 **Publication on matters of public interest**

3.13.3.1 *Creation of a new defence for matters of public interest*

Section 4 of the Defamation Act 2013 creates a new defence to an action for defamation of publication on a matter of public interest. It is based on the existing common law defence established in *Reynolds v Times Newspapers*[116] and it is expected the courts would take the existing case law into consideration where appropriate.[117]

Section 4(1) of the Defamation Act 2013 provides for the defence to be available in circumstances where the defendant can show that:

- the statement complained of was, or formed part of a statement on a matter of public interest (s 4(1)(a) DA 2013); and
- that he reasonably believed that publishing the statement complained of was in the public interest (s 4(1)(b) DA 2013).

---

116 [2001] 2 AC 127.
117 Explanatory Notes to clause 2 of the Bill at para [35].

90 *Civil claims*

The provision reflects the fact that the common law test contained both a subjective element – what the defendant believed was in the public interest at the time of publication – and an objective element – whether the belief was a reasonable one for the defendant to hold in all the circumstances. In relation to the first limb of this test, the section does not attempt to define what is meant by 'the public interest'. However, this is a concept that is well-established in the English common law. It is made clear that the defence applies if the statement complained of 'was, *or formed part of*, a statement on a matter of public interest' to ensure that either the words complained of may be on a matter of public interest, or that a holistic view may be taken of the statement in the wider context of the document, article, etc., in which it is contained in order to decide if overall this is on a matter of public interest. Subsection (2) requires the court, subject to subsections (3) and (4), to have regard to all the circumstances of the case in determining whether the defendant has shown the matters set out in subsection (1).

3.13.3.2 *Reportage*

Subsection (3) is intended to encapsulate the core of the common law doctrine of 'reportage' (which has been described by the courts as 'a convenient word to describe the neutral reporting of attributed allegations rather than their adoption by the newspaper'[118]). In instances where this doctrine applies, the defendant does not need to have verified the information reported before publication because the way that the report is presented gives a balanced picture. In determining whether for the purposes of the section it was reasonable for the defendant to believe that publishing the statement was in the public interest, the court should disregard any failure on the part of a defendant to take steps to verify the truth of the imputation conveyed by the publication (which would include any failure of the defendant to seek the claimant's views on the statement). This means that a defendant newspaper, for example, would not be prejudiced for a failure to verify where subsection (3) applies.

3.13.3.3 *Role of editorial judgment*

Subsection (4) requires the court, in considering whether the defendant's belief was reasonable, to make such allowance for editorial judgment as it considers appropriate. This expressly recognizes the discretion given to editors in judgments such as that of *Flood*, but is not limited to editors in the media context.

Subsection (5) makes clear for the avoidance of doubt that the defence provided by this section may be relied on irrespective of whether the statement complained of is one of fact or opinion.

3.13.4 **The new defence for website operators**

3.13.4.1 *Section 5 of the Defamation Act 2013*

Section 5 of the Defamation Act 2013, which came into force on 1 January 2014, provides that where an action is brought against an operator of a website (for example,

---

118 Per Simon Brown in *Al-Fagih* [2001] EWCA Civ 1634.

an operator of an online forum, blog site or any site that encourages user-generated content) in respect of a statement posted on that operator's website, it will be a defence for the operator to show that it did not post that statement itself (s 5(2) DA 2013). It should also be noted that the introduction of the defence does not affect any of the pre-existing common law or statutory defences available to website operators.[119]

3.13.4.1.1 AN OPERATOR OF A SITE WHO DID NOT POST THE STATEMENT

As noted above, an operator of a website can avail themselves of the section 5(2) defence if they can demonstrate they did not post the statement complained of. Where the actual poster of an offending statement is 'identifiable', section 5 of the Defamation Act 2013 provides a complete defence for website operators. In the social media context, this raises the question of whether social networking sites are websites for the purposes of the application of the defence.

It could be suggested that the law applies to such sites, as to access such micro sites or blogs, one still has to direct the user to a particular URL.

3.13.4.1.2 AN OPERATOR

A further definitional issue posed by section 5 is determining who falls into the definition of an operator. Generally, the individual or entity that exerts day-to-day control over its management will be an operator. For simple sites or interest pages, this definition poses little difficulty. However, with regard to social networking sites and social media sites, there may be more than one operator of a website, group page, blog, community interest page or microsite. In relation to blogs or interest pages, the degree of control in relation to content could be the determining factor as to who is the operator (e.g. the ability to delete, amend or clarify). However, in relation to social networking sites the task may not be so easy, as although individuals have the power to remove content form the page or feed, SNSs often retain editorial discretion though their terms and conditions. During the Bill's parliamentary debates, it was felt that defining the notion of an operator too rigidly would be unhelpful, as technological innovations would mean that any such definition would age quickly and lose relevance.[120] It was also suggested that 'website' should be replaced with 'electronic platform'.[121] However, it was felt that this could be equally problematic.[122]

3.13.4.1.3 TO POST

Notably, section 5 refers to 'posting' rather than 'publication'. The rest of the Act refers to 'publication'. It is suggested that the reason for the use of the word 'post' is to distinguish how a statement becomes available to the public from how it may later be disseminated.

---

119 Section 1 Defamation Act 1996, Regulation 19 of the Electronic Commerce (EC Directive) Regulations 2002. These provisions are discussed in depth below under 'Other Defences'.
120 *Hansard*, HC Debate 21 June 2012, Col 120.
121 *Hansard*, HL Grand Committee, 19 December 2012, Col GC 656.
122 *Hansard*, HL Grand Committee, 15 January 2013, Col GC 190.

92 *Civil claims*

3.13.4.2 *Defeating the defence*

Even if a site can prove that it falls within the definition of a website operator, and did not post the content complained of, the defence is not an absolute one.

Section 5(3) provides that the defence will not be available if the claimant can show that:

* It was not possible for the claimant to identify the person who posted the statement (s 5(3)(a)).
* The claimant gave the operator a notice of complaint in relation to the statement (s 5(3)(b)).
* And the operator failed to respond to the notice of complaint in accordance with any provision contained in the regulations (s 5(3)(c)).

Section 5(4) clarifies the meaning of 'identify' contained in section 5(3)(a) by stating that it is only possible for the claimant to 'identify' a perspective defendant if the claimant has enough information to enable it to bring proceedings against that person.

If it is possible for the claimant to identify the individual who posted the statement and does not need the help of the website operator in assisting with identifying that individual, then the operator will have still have a defence unless the claimant can demonstrate malice on the website operator's behalf.

In relation to social networking sites, this potentially demonstrates the importance of being able to identify the account holder operating the account or page. Indeed, many of the problems associated with social networking sites is the ability for posters to post or upload defamatory or hurtful content without disclosing their real identity. It may also encourage website operators to encourage SNS users to link their real names to their accounts. However, as is explored in detail in Chapter 13: Data Protection and Privacy, recommendations from Europe suggest that such measures may affect individuals' right to privacy should they wish to use a different name in order to protect their privacy rights. Once again these considerations highlight the key importance of balancing individuals' right to freedom of expression, the right to protect reputation, and the right to have a reasonable expectation of privacy when engaging with online mediums. How this balances with the Joint Committee's recommendation that a move away from anonymity is desirable remains to be seen in light of the significant reforms underfoot at European level in relation to privacy rights.

3.13.4.3 *Service of a claim via a social networking site*

3.13.4.3.1 AVAILABILITY OF SECTION 5(4) IMMUNITY

Section 5(4) states that the immunity available to website operators will only apply if the claimant has sufficient information to bring proceedings against the poster complained of. But what of cases where it is possible to identify the individual but not their address for service of the claim form? In England and Wales, the Civil Procedure Rules 1998 provide that the court may allow service by an alternative method or at an alternative place of the claim form (under CPR 6.15) and other documents (under CPR 6.27). CPR 6.27 states that CPR 6.15 applies to any document in the proceedings as it applies to a claim form. The claimant needs to show that there is a 'good reason' for alternative service (e.g. inability to trace an address). It should be noted that any application must state why the applicant thinks the document is likely to reach (or, as the case may be, have reached) the relevant party if served by the alternative method or at the alternative place proposed.

In terms of how the defence will work in practice, the claimant's requisite knowledge will be judged at the time they contact the operator, as it is unlikely prior to this time that they would have sufficient information to pursue a claim against the poster. This view was adopted by Lord Ahmad, during the parliamentary debates;[123] after this time, the availability of the defence will be judged in accordance with the E-Commerce Regulations.

3.13.4.3.2 SERVICE OF A CLAIM VIA FACEBOOK (UNITED KINGDOM)

In *AKO Capital LLP & Another v TSF Derivatives & Others*,[124] Teare LJ granted permission to one of the parties to the case to serve a claim by Facebook. Permission has previously been granted in a small number of county court claims for service and the High Court has allowed service of an injunction by Twitter (where the defendant was only known by his Twitter name).

In *AKO*, AKO Capital LLP and AKO Capital Master Fund Limited sought reimbursement of alleged over-charged commission from its broker TFS Derivatives (TFS). TFS disputed the claim and took the position that if TFS was held to be liable, then some of the damages should be recoverable from an ex-employee of AKO and an ex-employee of TFS.

As noted above, Rule 6.3 of the CPR sets out the general methods for service of a claim. Rule 6.15 of the CPR gives the court power to permit service by an alternative method if it considers there to be good reason to do so. In *AKO*, an interim application had been made under rule 6.15 of the CPR by TFS for permission to serve the claim on one of the ex-employees via Facebook, as TFS was unsure whether one of the ex-employees it sought to join to the claim lived at his last known address.

Teare LJ allowed service by Facebook, as he was satisfied that TFS had shown that the Facebook account belonged to the relevant defendant by demonstrating that:

- he was 'friends' with a number of other TFS colleagues, and;
- that the account was active and in frequent use by showing that the defendant had accepted 'friend requests' recently.

3.13.4.3.3 EXAMPLES FROM OTHER JURISDICTIONS

In New Zealand[125] and Australia,[126] the Courts have permitted service in civil actions via Facebook and Twitter.

---

123 *Hansard*, HL Grand Committee, 15 January 2013, Col GC 193.

124 *AKO Capital LLP & another v TFS Derivatives & others* (February 2012).

125 On 16 March 2009, in the Wellington High Court, Justice David Gendall permitted alternative service via the social-networking site Facebook in *Axe Market Gardens v Craig Axe*, claim number CIV: 2008-485-2676.

126 *MKM Capital Property Limited v Carmela Rita Corbo and Gordon Kinsley Maxwell Poyser (a bankrupt) case* (No SC 608 of 2008).

94 *Civil claims*

In *MKM Capital Property Ltd v Carmela Rita Corbo and Gordon Kinsley Maxwell Poyser*,[127] the Australian Court permitted service via Facebook where the claimants had already been granted a default judgment but had experienced difficulties serving it against the defendants. In an effort to resolve the matters, the claimants looked the defendants up on Facebook, discovered that their profiles displayed both defendants' dates of birth, email addresses, and friends' lists. The profiles also showed that the defendants were 'friends' with each other on Facebook, providing an extra link to identify the individuals as the same individuals who were the subject matter of the default judgment. The claimant put these records before the Australian Capital Territory Supreme Court, stating that service via 'private message' on Facebook could guarantee with sufficient certainty that the defendants would have knowledge of the default judgment. The courts were satisfied that it was reasonable to expect that the defendants would read the message and that the judgment would be brought to their attention. With permission of the court, the default judgment was also served on both defendants at their last known address and at the email addresses specified in their Facebook profiles.

The *MKM* decision was closely followed in March 2009 by *Axe Market Gardens v Craig Axe*,[128] a New Zealand case before the Wellington High Court. In *Axe*, the claimant was experiencing difficulties serving proceedings on the defendant and therefore applied to the court to serve via Facebook, submitting that the defendant was known to be living in England but his exact whereabouts was uncertain. However, the defendant had accessed the money that he had stolen via the internet while in England, was known to have corresponded by email, and had a Facebook site. The court gave the claimant permission for alternative service via Facebook. Unfortunately, no substantive reasons were given for the judgments in either the New Zealand or Australian cases.

The trend in New Zealand and Australia has started to be felt in the UK, notably recently in the unreported case of *Blaney's Blarney*.[129] Donal Blaney, who ran a blog called 'Blaney's Blarney', was being impersonated on Twitter by someone using the Twitter username '@BlaneysBlarney' together with a photograph of Mr Blaney and a link to Mr Blaney's blog, which, when viewed together, gave the impression that the account may be an official account of the claimant Mr Donal Blaney. Injunctive relief was sought by the claimant against the unknown defendant requiring him to cease posting, to preserve the account and passwords, and to identify himself to Mr Blaney's solicitors. Because the defendant was anonymous and there was no easy means of identifying him, Mr Justice Lewison, sitting in the Chancery Division, allowed alternative service of the order, via Twitter, directly on the defendant. This is an interesting point to note for claimants, especially in light of section 5 as usually Norwich Pharmacal proceedings will be issued against the website in question (to obtain the registration data), the approach adopted in *Applause Store Productions Limited and another v Raphael*.[130]

In the Californian case of *Krinsky v Doe*,[131] it was established that the requirements to issue a subpoena commanding an ISP to identify a poster are that a motion to

---

127 Ibid.
128 *Axe Market Gardens v Craig Axe*, claim number CIV: 2008-485-2676.
129 Unreported, 2009.
130 [2008] EWHC 1781 (QB).
131 159 Cal App. 4th 1154, 1172 (2008).

Defamation 95

quash has been filed, the plaintiff must give notice to the poster and establish a prima facie case of defamation before the poster's identity will be released.

3.13.4.3.4 FALSE REGISTRATION DETAILS

If false details have been registered, dual Norwich Pharmacal orders may be sought against the website and, subsequently, against the internet service provider (ISP); however, this use may not be as effective as serving directly or pursuing section 5. The disadvantage of perusing a Norwich Pharmacal order, aside from the length of time and costs associated with it, is that it can only be used on service providers with the jurisdiction of the courts in the United Kingdom. Twitter, whose servers are based in California, is out of reach of the coercive powers of the English courts. Although the US courts give similar relief against service providers, using that would have required Mr Blaney to commence proceedings for disclosure in California. It is noted that website operators have an incentive to comply if they wish to avail themselves of the section 5 defence.

Serving the defendant directly (by traditional methods or, in this case, using Twitter) provides a claimant with a quicker and cheaper option than any pre-action disclosure order. It should also be noted that choosing an alternative method of service does not preclude a claimant from seeking a Norwich Pharmacal order at a later date.

It is acknowledged that the time-scales for complying with the section 5 notice will make this process more accessible to wider members of the public. However, the possibility of alternative service remains an important avenue for claimants who are unable to seek cooperation from website and social networking sites.

3.14 The Defamation (Operators of Websites) Regulations 2013

3.14.1 *Defamation (Operators of Websites) Regulations 2013*

The Defamation (Operators of Websites) Regulations 2013 (the Regulations)[132] came into effect on 1 January 2014 and provide the detail as to the operation of the section 5 website operators' defence. Compliance with the Regulations is not mandatory. However, to benefit from the section 5 defence, a website operator must comply with the strict procedures set out in the Regulations.[133]

The Regulations set out the detail to be included by a complainant in a valid Notice of Complaint (at Regulation 2, which supplements section 5(6) of the Defamation Act 2013). If a Notice of Complaint fails to set out all necessary information, the website operator must merely notify the claimant within 48 hours that the notice is insufficient (Regulation 4). The operator is not required to specify how the Notice of Complaint is deficient. By requiring a certain degree of detail to be provided by the

---

132 The Defamation (Operators of Websites) Regulations 2013 No 3028.

133 Regulation 3 of the Defamation Regulation 2013 and the Schedule to the Regulations, provide for the steps that a website operator must take on receiving a valid notice of complaint in order to benefit from the defence provided by s 5 of the Act.

96 *Civil claims*

complainant before a website operator is obliged to act, these provisions are intended to prevent frivolous and ungrounded claims creating a 'cooling effect' whereby operators remove posts at the first sign of complaint.

Unlike the requirement for the claimant to demonstrate that the material complained of is (prima facie) 'unlawful' to defeat the Regulation 19 defence, these requirements of section 5 do not set a legal threshold. The complainant need not be correct either in law or in fact, for example in identifying words as facts rather than comments or as defamatory as opposed to mere abuse; he simply needs to 'tick the boxes'.

3.14.2 *Procedure*

The Regulations set out the procedure to be complied with by website operators on receipt of a valid Notice of Complaint in order to satisfy section 5(3) of the Defamation Act 2013 and benefit from the website operators' defence. In brief, the website operator must contact the poster within 48 hours of receipt of a valid Notice of Complaint. The website operator must send a copy of the Notice of Complaint to the poster of the statement complained of and require a response from the poster as to whether the poster:

- consents to the material being removed from the website; and
- consents to identification details being provided to the claimant. The deadline for the poster's response is 5 days from notification.

If it cannot contact the poster, the operator must remove the relevant statement from the website within 48 hours of receiving the valid Notice of Complaint, and notify the complainant that it has done so. If the poster is contacted but fails to respond within the 5-day time limit, or consents to removal, the operator must remove the offending statement within 48 hours of this point, and notify the complainant accordingly. If the poster responds by stating that he does not wish the statement to be removed, the operator must inform the complainant within 48 hours. The poster may or may not consent to his details being forwarded to the complainant, in which case the operator must either provide these details to the complainant, if consent is given, or, if consent is refused, notify the complainant that the poster has refused to supply them.

Section 5(11) provides that the defence will be defeated if the claimant shows that the website operator has acted with malice in relation to the posting of the statement concerned.

3.14.3 *Editorial control*

It is possible that an ISP or other intermediary that decides to exert some kind of editorial control over the statements made by its users could be deemed to have posted the material for the purposes of section 5 of the Defamation Act 2013, thereby losing the benefit of the defence. Section 5(12) of the Act provides that the defence will not be defeated where the website merely moderates content. However, editorial control on the part of the website operator beyond mere 'moderation' is likely to invalidate the website operators' defence.

3.14.4 *Moderated sites*

Section 5(12) of the Regulations provides that just because a site moderates the content published on a website does not in and of itself defeat the defence. Disappointingly, 'moderate' is not defined in the Regulations and refers to moderating in general rather than the content that has been complained of. The difficulty with the concept of moderation is that moderation implies that there is some degree of editorial control exerted by the website operator. As the Bill was debated in the Lords, Lord Ahmad stated that the reason why section 5 was included was to provide a defence over content for which they had no editorial control.[134] As noted above, social networking sites often retain editorial discretion though their terms and conditions, although reserving such a right is not the same thing as exercising it. Practically speaking, it is unlikely that Facebook or Twitter, for example, would be able to moderate content on a large scale and even if they were to do so, they would be unlikely to exercise such discretion narrowly, as it may interfere with a poster's right to freedom of expression (Article 10 ECHR[135]).

In the Committee debates, Robert Fello MP moved an amendment to clause 5 which would have expressly recognized that moderation would not attract liability if it had taken place after publication and had not significantly increased the defamatory nature of the publication, extent of publication of the words or removed them from a relevant defence.[136] However, the amendment was removed. The reason for this was that an operator who moderated a statement in a way which changed its meaning so as to make the statement defamatory or increased the seriousness of the defamation, should make them a person who had posted a statement for the purposes of section 5(2) of the Act. It was felt that the offer of protection to an operator who had increased the defamatory nature of a statement, but not significantly so, would offer them a level of protection that was not warranted or just.

3.15 Other defences

3.15.1 *Introduction*

Although as long as the strict requirements are complied with, an operator will avoid liability regardless of whether the poster is identifiable to the claimant, some operators may prefer to rely on previously available defences to defamation actions, rather than invest resources in internal processes to ensure compliance with the Regulations.

3.15.2 *Section 1 of the Defamation Act 1996*

Section 1 of the Defamation Act 1996, which remains in force, provides a defence where the site operator demonstrates that:

- he was not the author, editor or publisher of the statement complained of;[137]
- he took reasonable care in relation to its publication and did not know; and

---

134 Lord Ahmad, *Hansard*, HL Grand Committee, 15 January 2013, Col GC 190.
135 See Chapter 2: Human Rights.
136 *Hansard*, HC Debate, 19 June 2012, Cols 83–86.
137 See s 1(3) Defamation Act 1996 for the definition of an author, editor or publisher.

98 *Civil claims*

- had no reason to believe that what he did caused or contributed to the publication of a defamatory statement.

Under section 1(3) of the Defamation Act 1996, a person is not considered the author, editor or publisher (in the electronic context) if he is involved 'in processing, making of copies of, distributing or selling any electronic medium in or on which the statement is recorded, or in operating or providing any equipment, system or service by means of which the statement is retrieved, copied, distributed or made available in electronic form (s 1(3)(c) Defamation Act 1996); and as the operator of or provider of access to a communications system by means of which the statement is transmitted, or made available, by a person over whom he has no effective control (s 1(3)(e) Defamation Act 1996)'.

3.15.3 *Regulation 19 of the Electronic Commerce (EC Directive) Regulations 2002*

Regulation 19 of the Electronic Commerce (EC Directive) Regulations 2002[138] also provides a defence under which 'hosting intermediaries' shall not be liable if they do not have actual knowledge of unlawful activity.

3.16 Offers of Amends

3.16.1 *Background to the Defamation Act 1996 reforms*

The Offer of Amends regime remains unchanged by the Defamation Act 2013. The background to the Offer of Amends is to be found in Chapter VII of the Report of Sir Brian Neill's Committee held in July 1991 on Practice and Procedure in Defamation. The regime was intended to replace the 'Offer of Amends' procedure in section 4 of the Defamation Act 1952, which had hardly ever been used because it was so complex and onerous on the defendant that it had little practical application.[139] However, the Defamation Act 1996 has made the procedure more accessible to defendants and is increasingly being used as a way to settle matters. It is especially popular with the media and professional writers. This is not to suggest, however, that the defendant has gained significant ground against the claimant; indeed, as a mechanism of just redress, one of the key developments of the 1996 Act is that the claimant is open to recover damages.

3.16.1.1 *General*

Defamation is a tort of strict liability[140] and the absence of intent to cause offence or negligently making statements in relation to the claimant will not in itself create a defence for the defendant facing an allegation of defamation. However, a defendant

---

138 Implementing the EU's Electronic Commerce Directive 2000 (2000/31/EC).
139 Defamation Act 1952; Law of Libel Amendment Act 1888.
140 See Paul Mitchell (2005). *The Making of the Modern Law of Defamation*. Oxford: Hart Publishing, Chapter 5.

who has honestly and mistakenly made an innocent error can create undue hardships for themselves, especially if the claimant chooses to seize upon the comments for financial gain.[141] The Defamation Act 1996 introduced a defence whereby a defendant can choose to remove themselves from the claim at an earlier stage than would be usual by offering to make appropriate amends for their behaviour.[142]

It is up to the claimant to choose to accept this offer and if they decide to do so, the defendant must make appropriate amends and the claim will be at an end. However, if the claimant decides that they do not wish to accept the offer, the claim continues, but the defendant will have created for themselves a defence by virtue of making the offer unless it can be shown that the defendant made those statements knowing or having reason to believe that false and defamatory statements were being made against the claimant.[143]

However, doing so has certain statutory consequences. One of these is that, if the offer is accepted by the aggrieved party but the parties do not agree the amount to be paid by way of compensation, the compensation is determined by a judge, not a jury, 'on the same principles as damages in defamation proceedings'.[144] It should further be noted that if an Offer of Amends is made, and relied on as a defence, then no other defence may be relied on in the alternative.[145]

The reader may ask is this in essence a 'defence', but to view the Offer of Amends procedure in such terms would be to narrowly interpret its purpose; rather, it is an exercise in damage control, a measure taken to offer redress to the claimant which the offending statements caused and for the defendant it limits the impact of their errant, albeit innocently or incorrectly levied remarks.

While on first sight this may appear an unattractive proposition for defendants, as making the amends will involve the payment of damages and an apology, it does mean that claimants will be inclined to take such offers seriously and accept them, thereby bringing a satisfactory resolution for both parties if drafted carefully with consideration to the varying concerns of the parties involved. In *Cleese v Clarke* as quoted in *Nail v News Group Newspapers Limited*,[146] the purpose and justification of the Offer of Amends procedure was explained as follows and bears repetition so that the reader can grasp the rational of the mechanism in the 1996 Act:

> The offer of amends regime provides, as it was supposed to, a process of conciliation. It is fundamentally important that when an offer has been made, and accepted, any Claimant knows from that point on that he has effectively 'won'. He is to receive compensation and an apology or correction. In any proceedings which have to take place to resolve outstanding issues, there is unlikely to be any attack upon his character. The very adoption of the procedure has therefore a major deflationary effect upon the appropriate level of compensation. This is for two reasons. From the Defendant's perspective he is behaving reasonably. He

---

141 See *Abu v MGN Limited* [2003] EMLR 432 at [8].
142 See ss 2–4 of the Defamation Act 1996.
143 See s 4(2) of the Defamation Act 1996 and CPR PD 53 para 2.11.
144 *Nail v News Group Newspapers Limited, Rebekah Wade, Jules Stenson, Geraint Jones, Harper Collins Publications Ltd* [2004] EWCA Civ 1708 at [1]; see s 3(5) of the Defamation Act 1996.
145 See section 4(4) of the Defamation Act 1996.
146 [2005] 1 All ER 1040.

100 *Civil claims*

puts his hands up, and accepts that he has to make amends for his wrongdoing. As to the Claimant the stress of litigation has from that moment at least been significantly reduced.

Whereas juries used to compensate for the impact of the libel 'down to the moment of the verdict, once an offer of amends has been accepted the impact of the libel upon the Claimant's feelings will have greatly diminished and, as soon as the apology is published, it is also hoped that reputation will be to a large extent restored. It is naturally true that if a Defendant or his lawyers thereafter should behave irresponsibly, or try to drag in material to 'justify by the back door', that will be an aggravating factor. On the whole, however, once a Defendant has decided to go down this route, it would make sense to adopt a conciliatory approach and work towards genuine compromise over matters such as the terms of an apology or the level of compensation.[147]

Eady J in *Abu v MGN*[148] stated that there should be nothing in any sense 'rough and ready' about the assessment of the claimant's reputation under the Offer of Amends procedure because it would clearly be inappropriate to deprive either party of a proper analysis of its case. In response to a submission that Parliament cannot have intended that, the defence based on a rejected Offer of Amends should be unanswerable, and, if it were, the statutory mechanism would promote irresponsible journalism.[149]

The Neill Committee expressed the view that a judge fixing compensation under their proposals would clearly take into account such mitigating factors as the defendant's willingness to restore the plaintiff's reputation fully and promptly, achieving a relatively quick and cheap vindication for claimants and discourage claims for unreasonable sums in damages. In *Milne v Express Newspapers (No 1)*,[150] May LJ stated:

> We see the main parliamentary intention as promoting machinery to enable defamation proceedings to be compromised at an early stage without the expense of a jury trial. If there is no issue as to the defamatory meaning of the statement published, an offer to make amends tenders to the Claimant appropriate vindication and proper compensation. The Defendant does not get out cheaply. If compensation is not agreed, it is determined by the court on the same principles as damages in defamation proceedings. As Eady J said in Abu v MGN Ltd, the procedure is not to be confused with summary disposal under sections 8–10 of the 1996 Act. There is no artificial cap on the level of compensation.[151]

3.16.1.2 *The offer*

The offer, in essentials, is an offer of settlement even though as noted above it is variously described as a 'defence' and is made in an attempt to bring an end to matters. It should be noted that the offer need not be drafted on precise terms; indeed, this is

---

147 *Cleese v Clark* [2003] EWHC 137 (QB) at [35] to [37].
148 [2003] 1 WLR 2001.
149 Clearly, the legislation does not apply only to journalists, as was acknowledged by Eady J at [46].
150 [2004] EWCA Civ 664.
151 [2004] EWCA Civ 664 at [45].

not a requirement of the relevant statutory provision, and parties can utilize the assistance of the court in drawing up the terms on which to settle. Section 2(4) of the Defamation Act 1996 sets out the requirements of the offer as follows:

An offer to make amends under this section is an offer –

- to make a suitable correction of the statement complained of and a sufficient apology to the aggrieved party (s 2 (4)(a)),
- to publish the correction and apology in a manner that is reasonable and practicable in the circumstances (s 2 (4)(b)), and
- to pay to the aggrieved party such compensation (if any), and such costs, as may be agreed or determined to be payable (s 2 (4)(c)).

The fact that the offer is accompanied by an offer to take specific steps does not affect the fact that an offer to make amends under this section is an offer to do all the things mentioned in paragraphs (a) to (c). As such the main ingredients of the offer are that:

- The offer must be in writing.
- It must be expressed as an offer of amends under section 2 of the Defamation Act 1996.[152]
- It must be made before service of the defence and can be made before proceedings are issued.

As mentioned above, there is no requirement to draw out the exact terms of the offer. However, while these act as the skeleton of the offer, for some cases it may be more appropriate to flesh out an offer in defined terms. If acting on behalf of the defendant it will be especially important to control the way in which matters are concluded. It is acknowledged, however, that drafting in such a manner may bring up a risk that the offer is too rigid to be appealing to the claimant and may not be viewed favourably when a court is looking to award damages.[153]

While for both parties the procedure offers a way to offer to the claimant all the benefits of settlement via proceedings, it differs greatly in one key respect, which is that it does not specifically include an injunction against the defendant repeating what they have said. There may be other factors that the claimant wishes to consider for bringing a claim, such as the recovery of costs; for claims made against individuals of moderate means, the injunction may have been the only reason for pursuing the claim in the first instance. While it could be suggested that the very gesture of making an Offer of Amends is indicative that the defendant will not repeat the defamatory

---

152 For the avoidance of doubt, it is suggested that the letter should be marked clearly in bold typeface 'Offer of Amends' to refute any suggestion on behalf of the claimant that the letter was not an offer and will assist in avoiding lengthy arguments of construction and the professional costs potentially run up in association with this. Care must be taken when making an offer of amends to ensure that it includes the elements provided for under the Act. A failure to specify the publications covered by the offer or to confirm that the defendant will pay the costs of the claimant might give rise to doubt as to whether the defendant intends to make a statutory offer of amends. See *SD Marine Ltd v Powell* [2006] EWHC 3095 (QB).

153 It should be noted that even if unattractive, the offer will still operate as a defence albeit a less effectual one than a well-pitched and gauged offer.

102   Civil claims

statement, this may prove little comfort to the claimant. It is therefore suggested that in order to make the offer more attractive to a claimant, the defendant could decide if it is tactically advantageous to them to proactively offer up, if appropriate, an undertaking not to repeat the statements made. In offering an undertaking, defendants should only do so from the date of acceptance of the Offer of Amends, not from the date the defamatory statement was made so as to avoid the undertaking having been unwittingly infringed in the interim period. It should also be noted that if the court is called to look to the terms of the offer, it has a general power to grant an injunction.[154] Defendants may prefer to offer an undertaking which will be a private matter between the parties, thus avoiding the publicity of an injunction even if its precise terms are not known to the public. This may be especially valuable to the press, public bodies, and high-profile clients.

3.16.1.3 *Timing of the offer*

Although the statute does not provide a time limit for acceptance, an offer must be accepted or rejected within a reasonable period of time.[155] In terms of making an offer, it can be made at any time but cannot be made after a defence has been served.[156] The advantage of making one is that that it may help avoid proceedings being issued at all, thus bringing the matter to an expedient end and avoiding unnecessary costs in a manner that is compatible with the court's 'Overriding Objective' contained in Rule 1.1 of the Civil Procedure Rules 1998 (CPR).

It is also significant to note that the offer may be withdrawn before it is accepted and an offer which has been withdrawn and subsequently re-put to a claimant will be treated as a new offer.[157] This will not however provide a mechanism by which a defendant can serve a defence and then 'revive' his old offer in a move to circumvent section 2(5) of the Defamation Act 1996.

3.16.1.4 *Qualified offers*

A qualified offer differs from the unqualified offer outlined above. Rather, it is an offer to make amends in relation to a *specific* defamatory meaning. Breaking down the whole publication, this means that part of the statement is accepted by the defendant as having conveyed a defamatory meaning.[158]

It should be noted that where a person wishes to make such a qualified offer in relation to a particular element of their statement only, the defendant must state that this is a qualified offer and sets out the defamatory meaning in relation to which it is made.

3.16.1.5 *Disagreements as to meaning and interpretation*

It is inevitable that on occasion parties will disagree as to what on its face a publication may have been taken to mean. In *English & Scottish Cooperative Investment*

---

154 Section 37 Supreme Court Act 1981 (White Book Volume 2, at 9A-118).
155 See *Tesco Stores Ltd v Guardian News & Media Ltd* [2009] EMLR 5.
156 Section 2(5) of the Defamation Act 1996.
157 Section 2(6) of the Defamation Act 1996.
158 Section 2(2) of the Defamation Act 1996.

Mortgage and Investment Society Limited v Odhams Press Limited,[159] allegations were made that the claimant's accounts contained 'false' entries. However, the intention was to imply that the accounts were incorrect, not false, which with it brought an inference that they were somehow fraudulent or dishonest rather than containing innocent errors. In this case, it was open to the defendant to qualify their statement by saying that they did not wish to imply fraud or dishonesty through the use of the word 'false'.

If a statement has two interpretations, one being more serious than the other, it is open to the defendant under sections 2–4 of the 1996 Act to offer to correct, apologise, and pay for the less serious allegation made.[160] It should be noted that in these circumstances were the claimant to accept the offer, damages would be agreed or in the alternative considered by a judge and compensation awarded to reflect the less serious element of the allegation specified in the defendant's written offer. If the claimant decides not to accept this qualified offer, then there is a risk that the claimant will lose their action if the defendant invokes the offer as their defence under section 2 of the Defamation Act 1996 and the jury determines that the statements made bore the lesser defamatory meaning (or a meaning that was not more defamatory than the publisher's). It is a shield raised against the sword of litigation.

However, this is not to suggest that it will always be worth the defendant taking this gamble; indeed, if the matter does proceed to trial the jury may feel that the statements had a *greater* defamatory meaning than the lesser meaning accepted.

3.16.1.6 *Consecutive or multiple allegations – part offers*

It is entirely possible that in the course of a publication a defendant may make several statements against the claimant, and it is only one or part of them that proves to be false or defamatory in its nature. In such circumstances, a defendant may offer to apologise or offer amends for *some* but not *all* of the imputations made. For example, in *Jones v Pollard*,[161] the defendant alleged that the claimant had been involved in pimping and blackmail. It transpired that the blackmail allegations were false. Using the mechanism provided by the Defamation Act 1996, it is open to the defendant under section 2(2) to apologise generally, or in these circumstances to make an amends in relation to a specific aspect of the statements made, which it is accepted by the defendant that the meaning of the statement conveys. It should be noted that the elements of the statutory offer will only relate to the *particular* meaning that is the subject of the offer.

There is, however, a grey area in terms of what will constitute 'meaning', as the Defamation Act 1996 refers to 'meaning' in the singular and as such it may preclude a defendant from making the offer in relation to more than one element of the meaning. The difficulties presented by qualified offers means that when drafting they should be approached with caution and it should be considered if they are the most appropriate way of dealing with the matters in hand. In terms of considering these conceptual difficulties, the judgment of *Warren v Random House Group Limited*[162]

---

159 [1941] KB 440.
160 Section 2(2) and s 2(5) of the Defamation Act 1996.
161 [1997] EMLR 233.
162 [2007] EWCH 2856 (QB), [2009] QB 600, [2008] 2 WLR 1033.

104   *Civil claims*

proves useful. Gray J suggested that the word *statement* in section 2(2) of the
Defamation Act 1996 refers to the statement complained of, which may not be the
same thing as the publication as a whole.[163] It was suggested that the defendant may
make his offer in relation to an element of his overall statement or may choose to
select a lower defamatory meaning than the claimant had contended for. However, a
defendant cannot make an Offer of Amends while maintaining that the allegations
complained of are not defamatory[164] or are true. In *Warren*, the court stated that this
would be tantamount to 'justification by the back door',[165] as an Offer of Amends has
to contain an acceptance that the original statement refers to and is defamatory of the
claimant.[166]

3.16.1.7 *Withdrawal or substitution of the Offer of Amends*

Under section 2(6) of the Defamation Act 1996, it is open to a defendant to withdraw
an Offer of Amends at any time before it is accepted. In *Warren*, however, the
defendant had made an Offer of Amends that was accepted, but then sought permission to substitute a defence of justification for the Offer of Amends. The court refused
permission to do so, since under the Act the claimant had a statutory right to enforce
the offer once it had been accepted. The court also held that preventing the defendant
from withdrawing the offer was not contrary to his right of freedom of expression
enshrined in Article 10 or Article 6 (the Right to a Fair Trial) of the European
Convention on Human Rights (ECHR). Indeed, the court stated that the Offer of
Amends regime promoted freedom of speech rather than curtailed it. The defendant
had an unfettered right of access to the courts in circumstances where it had made an
Offer of Amends with its eyes open, thereby unequivocally waiving its rights under
Article 6 ECHR.[167]

3.16.1.8 *Acceptance of the offer*

Where the claimant decides to accept the offer,[168] the person bringing the claim 'may
not bring or continue defamation proceedings in respect of the publication concerned

---

163 Gray J's analysis on this point was affirmed by the Court of Appeal; there was no appeal on this point
     in the case.
164 See Report of the Neil Committee 'The new "offer of amends" defence which we are putting forward
     in this Section is aimed at the situation where the plaintiff has admittedly been wronged and the
     defendant is willing to do whatever is reasonable to restore his damaged reputation. It would not be
     appropriate, therefore, where the defendant wishes to maintain or revive his attack on the plaintiff's
     character. We have in mind, accordingly, that in order to take advantage of this new defence the
     relevant defendant would be obliged to foreswear any such attack. In other words, defendants would
     not be allowed to put forward an "offer of amends" while seeking to rely, in mitigation of damages,
     upon any of those matters which would require to be pleaded having a tendency to show that the
     plaintiff is not entitled to an unblemished character' (at [27]).
165 [2003] EMLR 432 at [18].
166 See *Club La Costa (UK) Ltd v Gebhard* [2008] EWHC 2552 (QB); *The Times*, 10 December 2008.
167 A discussion of the effect of the Human Rights Act upon defamation claims can be found in Chapter 2:
     Human Rights.
168 Acceptance will generally only be effective if it is communicated to the defendant. For the avoidance
     of doubt between the parties, it is preferable that such assent is manifested in writing.

against the person making the offer'[169] and the claim will become stayed. This applies to both general and qualified offers.

It should be noted that this does not necessarily mean that the claimant assents to the precise terms of the offer. Indeed, the Defamation Act 1996 sets out the procedure to be adopted when there are disagreements as to the contents of the apology and amounts paid by way of compensation and costs. These are set out in section 3(4)–(6) of the Act. If, however, the parties do agree to the terms of the offer, it is open to them to apply to the court for a confirmatory consent order and if appropriate apply for permission to read a statement of apology in open court.[170] The appropriate procedure where an Offer of Amends is accepted is set out in Part 53, Practice Direction 3 of the CPR.

3.16.2 *Multiple defendants – publication by more than one party*

Where there are multiple defendants, acceptance of an offer in relation to one particular defendant will not extinguish a claimant's rights against the remaining persons in respect of that same publication.[171] Where such an individual makes such a an offer and it has been accepted, then the person who has made such payment or settlement can under section 1(4) of the Civil Liability Contribution Act 1978 recover all or some of the sums paid by him from another person who is liable in relation to the same publication. The maximum extent of this liability will be to the value of the offer or that awarded by the judge.[172] As Eady J explained in *Muhamed Veliu v Xhevdet Mazrekaj, Skender Bucpapaj*:[173] 'the provision clearly contemplates the possibility of one Defendant falling within the statutory regime and another outside it. Its overall effect would appear to be at least to limit, by imposing a cap upon, the extent of the liability of that Defendant who falls within the protection of the offer of amends regime'.[174]

Conversely, as noted in *Veliu*, it is clear that a defendant who has not made an Offer of Amends is not entitled to the benefits that flow specifically from the statutory procedure. This is not because the defendant who makes an offer is entitled to a 'reward' as such (although the outcome may lead to similar consequences) but rather

---

169 Section 3(2) of the Defamation Act 1996.
170 Section 3(1)–(3) of the Defamation Act 1996.
171 See *London Association for the Protection of Trade v Greenlands Ltd* [1913] 3 KB 507 and s 3(7) of the Defamation Act 1996. However, note s 3(8) the Act, which states as follows: '(8) In England and Wales or Northern Ireland, for the purposes of the Civil Liability (Contribution) Act 1978 –

    (a) the amount of compensation paid under the offer shall be treated as paid in bona fide settlement or compromise of the claim; and

    (b) where another person is liable in respect of the same damage (whether jointly or otherwise), the person whose offer to make amends was accepted is not required to pay by virtue of any contribution under section 1 of that Act a greater amount than the amount of the compensation payable in pursuance of the offer.'

172 Section 3(8)(b) of the Defamation Act 1996.
173 [2006] EWHC 1710 (QB) 2006 WL 1981690.
174 [2006] EWHC 1710 (QB) 2006 WL 1981690 at [15].

106 *Civil claims*

because of the effects that such offers have, to a greater or lesser extent, by way of mitigation.[175]

By way of illustration, this would seem to embrace the possibility in an appropriate case of the following scenario (where Defendant 1 has made an offer of amends and Defendant 2 has not):

(i) Notational starting point	£100,000
(ii) Offer of Amends discount (taking into account aggravation and mitigation for using the statutory procedure)	40%
(iii) Maximum liability for Defendant 1	£60,000
(iv) Overall compensation (including aggravation)	£110,000
(v) Maximum liability for Defendant 2	£110,000

Depending on the presence of mitigating or aggravating conduct in a case, the overall compensation could be larger or smaller than the notional starting point.[176]

3.16.3 *Effective offers: practical considerations*

While setting out the terms of the offer to the claimant may bring an end to matters, it may also raise further issues and heated discussions between the parties as to the terms of settlement, as the claimant may see the offer as a 'starting point'. Below are some of the points that will require careful consideration when formulating an offer.[177] When reading the following subsections, the reader should bear in mind that in making an Offer of Amends, 'a Defendant in those circumstances is effectively laying down arms and inviting meaningful negotiation over compensation and restoration of reputation'.[178]

3.16.3.1 *A suitable correction and sufficient apology*

What will constitute an effective offer will be on all fours with the facts of the matter in question. With qualified offers, defendants should proceed with extreme caution in relation to ensuring that the offer relates to the specific meaning which is the subject of the offer and not use the offer procedure as a way to reaffirm the truth of the rest of the publication, thereby potentially fanning the flames of the claimant's sense of injustice.

---

175 [2006] EWHC 1710 (QB) 2006 WL 1981690 at [18]. See also reasons identified by the Court of Appeal in *Nail v News Group Newspapers Ltd* [2005] 1 All ER 1040 at [19] and [22]. Note the proposed restriction upon how defendants were to mitigate did not find its way into the 1996 statutory enactment.

176 *Muhamed Veliu v Xhevdet Mazrekaj, Skender Bucpapaj* [2006] EWHC 1710 (QB) 2006 WL 1981690 at [27].

177 For guidance generally on offers of amends, see *Cleese v Clark* [2003] EWHC 137(QB) and *Abu v MGN* [2002] EWHC 2345 (QB) and the Court of Appeal guidance in *Nail v News Group Newspapers & Harper Collins* [2004] EWCA Civ 1708.

178 *Muhamed Veliu v Xhevdet Mazrekaj, Skender Bucpapaj* [2006] EWHC 1710 (QB) 2006 WL 1981690 at [19].

As a tactical consideration for the defendant where the form of the apology is not agreed, defendants should look to offer a form of wording put to the claimant for acceptance. This is because it is possible for the defendant to publish a correction or apology which is most appropriate on the facts.[179] If an agreement cannot be reached, it is always open to the parties to follow the procedure outlined in section 2(4) of the Defamation Act 1996:

> If the parties do not agree on the steps to be taken by way of correction, apology and publication, the party who made the offer may take such steps as he thinks appropriate, and may in particular:

- make the correction and apology by a statement in open court in terms approved by the court (s 2(4)(a) DA 1996); and
- give an undertaking to the court as to the manner of their publication (s 2(4) (b) DA 1996).

It is suggested, however, that the form of apology needs to be considered very carefully in order to make it attractive to both parties and as such should not be unduly restrictive or weighted in the defendant's favour. The apology should seek to make amends as a genuine reconciliation in the spirit which the legislation was intended. Even if not in the spirit of reconciliation, an aggrieved defendant should be aware that the judge in assessing damages will consider the offer and counter proposals made by the claimant.[180] It is for this reason that the apology must be both practical and realistic in order to avoid any finding by the court that the nature of the apology was so wholly inadequate that the claimant acted reasonably in refusal and potentially viewed as a mitigating factor in the claimant's favour on the issue of damages. If the converse is considered and a defendant makes a 'claimant friendly' offer, it may act in the defendant's favour on issues of reasonableness and quantum.

In *Cairns v Modi*,[181] former New Zealand cricket captain Chris Cairns won a defamation claim against former Indian Premier League (IPL) chairman Lalit Modi for defamatory tweets in the first case of its kind in the UK. Mr Modi had tweeted that Mr Cairns had been removed from the list of players eligible and available to play in the IPL 'due to his past record of match fixing'. The tweet was removed within 16 hours of being posted. However, the words were also repeated in a cricket magazine published by Cricinfo UK. It was estimated that approximately 65 people saw the tweet and around 1,000 people read the publication. Cairns sued Modi for defamation and Modi relied on the defence of justification, i.e. that his comments were true.

The court stated that, although only a small number of people would have read Modi's original message on Twitter, as a consequence of modern technology and communication systems, allegations such as the ones concerning Cairns had the capacity to 'percolate' more widely and more quickly than ever before. The

---

179 For the avoidance of doubt, in the event that the wording of the apology cannot be agreed, the defendant should expressly reserve their right to final approval of the apology.
180 Section 3(1)–(5) of the Defamation Act 1996.
181 [2012] EWHC 756 (QB).

108   *Civil claims*

'percolation' phenomenon was a legitimate factor to be taken into account in the assessment of damages.[182]

3.16.4 *Apologies*

In terms of framing an apology relating to comments made online, defendants need to be receptive to the fact that they need to offer a suitable correction and sufficient apology addressing each element of the tweet that was defamatory in turn, the content, timing of delivery, and form to be agreed between the parties. As such, an effective apology will to an extent be driven by the channel though which the offending content was initially published.

Taking the example of Twitter, if the defendant has as of yet taken no course of action in relation to the tweet, it should be deleted, this information communicated to the claimant, and the defendant should resist any suggestion by the claimant that the apology should be tweeted. This is because 140 characters is insufficient to capture a well-crafted apology and since section 2(4)(b) of the Defamation Act 1996 requires that the defendant should publish a correction and apology in a manner that is reasonable and practicable in the circumstances, in order to avoid causing the claimant any further reputational damage, the defendant should not tweet the apology thereby refreshing the claimant's grievances in the minds of a potentially significant number of followers or those minded to perform searches for the tweet through internet search engines. This will be most especially the case in respect of journalists, high-profile figures, and matters of significant public interest or debate.

In determining what course of action to take, it should be noted if the defendant has already apologised online or deleted their tweets. The reason for this is that if they have taken such measures, this should be outlined in the offer as a step already taken on behalf of the defendant and the claimant should be asked if these actions are deemed sufficient. Wherever possible, copies of such screen dumps showing 'dead links' or 'link not found' search result pages should be provided to the claimant.

3.16.5 *Publication problems presented by social media*

Offers of Amends should be made in relation to *all* publications for which the defendant may be made liable; this is especially important in relation to micro-blogs such as Twitter, social networking sites such as Facebook, and other internet site operators.[183]

3.16.5.1 *Re-tweets*

Another potential problem posed by social media platforms, especially Twitter, is the role of re-tweets (forwarding another person's tweet), which, as noted under the provisions of the Defamation Act 2013, will not necessarily avoid liability from prosecution. Leading on from the example of McAlpine above, QI star Alan Davies asked

---

182 See *Slipper v BBC* [1991] 1 QB 283 and *Ley v Hamilton* (1935) 153 LT 384 considered at [26]–[27].
183 *Green v Times Newspapers* (Unreported) (17 January 2001).

Defamation 109

his 440,000 followers on 3 November: 'Any clues as to who this Tory paedophile is . . .?', before re-tweeting a response naming Lord McAlpine. In terms of limiting the damages that such re-tweets can cause, a defendant should remind the claimant that he has or has arranged for a number of his followers, especially those with the highest number of followers themselves, and any who had re-tweeted, 'Favourited' or commented to remove any associated content.

3.16.5.1.1 CLARIFICATIONS AS TO THIRD-PARTY COMMENTARY

In the *McAlpine* example explored above in relation to 'defamatory meaning', Sally Bercow, the wife of the Speaker of the House of Commons, apologised for her part in falsely identifying the peer as a paedophile but said her actions were not libelous. She tweeted: 'Had letter from Lord McA. His lawyers ambulance chasers tbh #bigbullies. My tweet not libelous but I don't have money to contest a multi-millionaire. Lord McA falsely accused but not by me. I never said Lord McAlpine paedophile.' The risk presented here is that the defendant may inadvertently be appearing on the face of the apology to be clarifying their statement but not actually apologizing for it,[184] which is a significant danger posed by postings made in the 'tweet of the moment'. Wherever possible defendants should be advised to stop posting or engaging with dialogue about the matter or even consider shutting down their account permanently or temporarily as a 'black out period'.

If a defendant has already apologised online, then they should offer the claimant an arrangement that a number of their followers, especially those with the most number of followers themselves and any who had re-tweeted or commented to the original tweet, to re-tweet his apology and clarification so as to ensure that this was seen and received, at the very least by all those who may have seen the original tweet.

3.16.5.2 *@replies: other users*

By way of example, a tweet that begins with another user's username and is in reply to one of their tweets, such as '@NeonGolden I can't believe you thought that movie was cheesy!', appears on the sender's profile page. For recipients, it will appear in the recipient's Mentions and Interactions tabs. Like Mentions, @replies will also appear in the recipient's Home timeline if they are following the sender. Anyone following the sender and the recipient of an @reply will see it in their 'Home' timeline. The tweets will never appear on anyone's profile page, unless they wrote/sent the message.[185]

Another avenue that can potentially result in liability is where comments are directed '@' a particular account user. In this case, the intention would not be for the comment to be circulated widely but nevertheless it will leave a digital trace and is not private in nature. While it is a matter of common sense that if a statement is directed '@' someone and is of a defamatory nature it may result in liability. An issue that is yet to come before the courts and has therefore not received a great deal of judicial consideration, is where the comment is '@' a particular account holder, but

---

184 For the avoidance of doubt, this is not a matter in which an offer of amends policy was made; it is merely used for illustrative purposes.

185 Source: https://support.twitter.com/articles/119138-types-of-tweets-and-where-they-appear#.

110 *Civil claims*

the offending content is made in relation to a third party who subsequently becomes aware of it. According to Twitter's own help guide,

> if you are not the sender or recipient of an @reply, you may still see an @reply to someone else in your timeline. Users will see @replies in their home timeline if they are following both the sender and recipient of the update. Otherwise, they won't see the @reply unless they visit the sender's Profile page. If you send a reply to someone, it does not show on their profile page. Only replies that person has sent will show on their profile.[186]

If a defamatory comment is made, it may mean that the offending tweet is neither seen nor circulated widely. The initial tweet will not be a public tweet, but potentially seen by the defendant's entire following. This will be especially significant for high-profile account users and media outlets that may have extremely large numbers of followers and where claimants argue that damages should be higher to reflect the potential audience who may have seen the offending comments. It can further be argued that the offending content was only intended for the specific recipient or a small number of recipients and that only those individuals who are followers of both the person the tweet is directed to and the defendant's Twitter followers will have seen the tweet.

If the content of a comment made by a third party in itself is defamatory, then the defendant should remind the claimant that the comments of the other party are a matter for the claimant to take up with that person or body. The defendant should also consider if the subsequent comment was more aggravating than this initial statement and assess if this is an issue to be raised on the point of damages. What will be interesting to view in the future is if the '@response' will be considered to be a separate publication with distinct liability or if it will form part of the initial course of action to which the claimant can be joined.

Problems will remain, however, in terms of searches revealed by Google searches and cache results and as such the scope of the audience cannot be determined in precise terms. Defendants should look at ways to delete this content or have the offending content removed. Once this has occurred, and ideally before the Offer of Amends is drafted, this should be communicated to the claimant.

It could also be open to the defendant to invite the claimant to avail themselves of their 'right to be forgotten', discussed in depth in Chapter 14, if they persist in claiming that the continued existence of Google cache results is causing distress (*Google Spain SL (1) and Google Inc (2) v Agencia Española de Protección de Datos (AEPD) (1) and Costeja González (2)* (Case C-131/12)).

3.16.6 *Additional incentives to accept the offer*

3.16.6.1 *Proof of deletion*

It is open to the defendant to provide to the claimant copies of Google Search screen dumps which show that the tweet Google cached has now been removed so that the

186 Ibid.

tweet does not feature in search results when a keyword search is performed (the keyword search covering the contents of the tweet, the name of the claimant, and the name of the defendant). The defendant can offer these pro active measures to the claimant, as a step beyond the requirements of section 2(4) Deformation Act 1996 as a genuine attempt to remove the offending content and serve the defendant as a useful negotiation chip on the question of damages.

The defendant may also wish to consider offering to give an undertaking not to repeat, publish or encourage another to so repeat or publish the allegations of which the complaint is made.

3.16.6.2 *Undertakings*

As mentioned above, the giving of an undertaking can perform the role that an injunction would have offered had the matter successfully progressed via litigation and allay a claimant's concerns about re-publication. In relation to the giving of an undertaking in the social media context, it is wise to express this in the offer as not beginning until the date of the acceptance of the offer to avoid any liability arising out of tweets or re-tweets made in the interim period.[187] The defendant should also expressly draw out that they will not accept liability or offer an undertaking in relation to re-tweets, other users or @replies.

3.16.6.3 *Hiring a social media expert*

Measures could also be taken such as hiring a social media expert IT consultant to carry out the task of removing the offending content, and produce a letter to the claimant to the effect that such actions have been performed.

3.16.6.4 *Facebook wall posts and statuses*

The same rationale as explained in the above section on Twitter may also be of application in relation to posts on Facebook made on a particular 'wall' or in the alternative compromise a status. In terms of statuses, defendants should check to see if their settings were set as 'friends only', 'me only', 'custom' or 'public' and if they have been set to a private or bespoke setting and consider if this point should be raised in the offer.

3.16.7 **Damages**

3.16.7.1 *Introduction*

As it was put by Sir Thomas Bingham, the Master of the Rolls, in *John v MGN Ltd*:[188]

---

187 Of course it is open to the claimant to counter that they wish this date to be as of the date of the letter or if appropriate from the last date on which the offending content was posted or removed. The decision to do so will depend on the contents of the defamatory publication and the size and profile of the audience.

188 [1997] QB 586 at [607E–F].

112 *Civil claims*

The successful plaintiff in a defamation action is entitled to recover, as general compensatory damages, such sum as will compensate him for the wrong he has suffered. That sum must compensate him for the damage to his reputation; vindicate his good name; and take account of the distress, hurt and humiliation which the defamatory publication has caused.

Section 3(1) of the Defamation Act 1996 outlines that in the absence of an agreement, damages will be determined by the court on ordinary principles:

> In doing so the Court will take account of any steps taken in fulfilment of the offer and (so far as not agreed between the parties) of the suitability of the correction, the sufficiency of the apology and whether the manner of their publication was reasonable in the circumstances, and may reduce or increase the amount of compensation accordingly.

At first, the formulation whereby compensation is defined not directly in terms of damages but as being analogous to damages in defamation proceedings may seem unnecessarily complicated and meandering. The rationale behind this was simply that the draftsman was catering for the situation where, as contemplated, such a hearing might take place before a judge without a libel action ever having been started. Practice Direction 53 of the Civil Procedure Rules 1998 at para 3.2 makes different provision for applications under section 3 of the 1996 Act according to whether proceedings are in existence or not.[189]

However, it is not the case that damages will be awarded in every case, referring back to the wording of section 2(4)(c) the offer involves an agreement to 'pay to the aggrieved party such compensation (if any)'. As outlined above,[190] and as stated in section 3(5), the effect of mitigation can be favourable to the defendant when it comes to the issue of the court assessing damages. In *Cairns v Modi*,[191] the Lord Chief Justice, Lord Judge stated that:

> The process of assessing damages is not quasi-scientific, and there is rarely a single 'right' answer. Nevertheless, it is virtually self-evident that in most cases publication of a defamatory statement to one person will cause infinitely less damage than publication to the world at large, and that publication on a single occasion is likely to cause less damage than repeated publication and consequent publicity on social media. By the same token, rapid publication of the withdrawal of a defamatory statement, accompanied by an apology, together with an admission of its falsity given as wide publicity as the original libel diminishes its impact more effectively than an apology extracted after endless vacillation while the libel remains in the public domain, unregretted and insidiously achieving greater credibility.[192]

---

189 [1996] EMLR 439 at [12].
190 See *Lord McAlpine of West Green v Bercow* [2013] EWHC 1342 (QB); *Muhamed Veliu v Xhevdet Mazrekaj, Skender Bucpapaj* [2006] EWHC 1710 (QB) 2006 WL 1981690.
191 [2012] EWHC 756 (QB).
192 [2012] EWHC 756 (QB) at [24].

Defamation 113

It should be noted that the court will not always follow these general observations. In *Kiam v Neil*,[193] substantial damages were awarded despite the fact that a prompt apology was made and placed more prominently than the libellous content when it was initially published.[194] However, the conduct of the parties will still remain an important consideration in assessing damages, which is an especially important consideration given that the case will be decided on the same principles as damages in defamation proceedings.

In terms of assessing the sums which may be reasonable on the facts of the case, *Abu v MGN Limited*[195] offers the following guidance:

- The Defendant needs to be able to assess the gravity of the impact of the libel upon the complainant's reputation and feelings, and this will generally have to be done in the light of the particulars of claim and/or letter before action.[196]
- The offer is to be construed as relating to the complaint *as notified*.[197]
- Damages will be determined on the same basis as in libel proceedings, taking into account mitigation, aggravation, and causation of loss.
- Since damages are 'at large', the court is entitled to take the broad circumstances of the matter into account, insofar as they emerge from the evidence, including the conduct, position, and standing of the claimant.[198]
- Insofar as the words complained of in a libel action put the claimant in a generally bad light, a judge or jury is entitled to reflect that in awarding damages for the specific allegation complained of.[199]
- Although relatively rare, it may be necessary for there to be some disclosure of documents, particularly with regard to certain heads of damage (e.g. lost employment opportunities).[200]

3.16.7.2 *Stalemate situations: disagreement as to damages and apologies*

Troubles can arise if the parties do not agree one of the elements of the offer, as then the matter is referred to be decided by a judge alone in a 'mini-trial'.[201] This can result, however, in considerable satellite litigation, particularly on the assessment of damages, for as we have noted above, these damages must be assessed on 'the same principles as damages in defamation proceedings'.[202]

---

193 [1996] EMLR 439.
194 It could be argued that in light of *Muhamed Veliu v Xhevdet Mazrekaj, Skender Bucpapaj* at [27] there is scope to argue for significant reductions (see *Lord McAlpine of West Green v Bercow* [2013] EWHC 1342 (QB)).
195 [2003] EMLR 432.
196 [2003] EMLR 432 at [8].
197 [2003] EMLR 432 at [9]. It was noted in the judgment that such an approach would also accord with the modern 'cards on the table' approach to litigation generally and, more specifically, with the thinking behind the Defamation Pre-Action Protocol.
198 See generally, Patrick Milmo, W.V.H. Rogers, Richard Parkes, Clive Walker and Godwin Busuttil (eds) (2008) *Gatley on Libel and Slander* (11th edn). London: Sweet & Maxwell, para 9.2.
199 [2003] EMLR 432 at [16].
200 [2003] EMLR 432 at [21]
201 Section 3 of the Defamation Act 1996.
202 Section 2(5) of the Defamation Act 1996.

114   *Civil claims*

3.16.7.3 *The court's case management powers*

As noted in *Cleese v Clarke*,[203] the Offer of Amends procedure is a genuine attempt at reconciliation and as such the courts will use their case management powers in order to avoid lengthy and protracted negotiations on costs points ensuing. Indeed, this is reflected in the fact that Part 53 of Practice Direction 3 of the CPR requires an application by the court to be made under the Part 8 procedure.[204] However, as noted previously in the chapter, the offer may throw up new points of dispute between the parties and issues may become protracted. In *Cleese*,[205] Eady J suggested that in assessing damages the following considerations will apply:

- Timing, scope, and effectiveness of apology.
- Attempts by the parties to bring about constructive resolution to the matter.
- Avoidance of unnecessary costs due to protracted negotiations.
- Pointless point-scoring on behalf of the parties that is not in the spirit of the Offer of Amends procedure.
- Have any sums been paid by way of compensation?[206]
- The mindset of the claimant reading the defamatory content must be considered and the defendant must take their claimant 'as they find them'.
- If practical, round the table meetings should take place so as to encourage a frank exchange of views and the 'placing of cards on the table'.
- Protracted correspondence between solicitors should be avoided.
- Depending on which party was responsible, any delay in the negotiations would tend to increase or reduce the relevant award.

The points raised in *Cleese* are reflected in *Nail v News Group Newspapers*,[207] where Eady J observed at first instance: 'once the Defendant has decided to go down this route, it would make sense to adopt a conciliatory approach and work towards genuine compromise over matters such as the terms of the apology or the level of compensation'.[208] Even in cases of delay and grudging offers, discounts can be fairly substantial[209] – where clearly there was no spirit of conciliation or cooperation Eady J gave a discount of 40% in *Campbell-James v Guardian Media Group*.[210] However, in *Cairns v Modi*, while the overall award of damages totalled some £75,000, the court awarded £15,000 of this specifically to reflect the conduct of the parties in the proceedings. As such, it is a very real and serious consideration when it comes to the court's assessment of damages.[211]

---

203 *Cleese v Clark* [2003] EWHC 137.
204 CRP Part 8 – Alternative procedure for claims.
205 *Cleese v Clark* [2003] EWHC 137.
206 Without prejudice offers shouldn't be brought to the attention of the court but amounts already paid can be.
207 [2005] EMLR 12.
208 [2004] EMLR 19 at para 35.
209 See *Norman Angel v Stainton & Repaircraft* [2006] EWHC 637 (QB) 28/3/06.
210 [2005] EMLR 24.
211 [2012] EWHC 756 (QB) at [42].

Defamation 115

In some ways it is regrettable that the upper limit for general damages was not fixed (say at £10,000[212]) with the onus on the claimant to justify a claim for any additional amount – perhaps linked with making a 'claimant-friendly' apology and correction element or the offer of an undertaking to discourage satellite disputes on damages. One lacuna in the defence is that the claimant cannot get an injunction preventing repetition of the libel. An added encouragement to protract proceedings is the introduction of the rather vague 'contextual evidence' principle permitted by the Court of Appeal decision in *Burstein v Times Newspapers*,[213] allowing in effect the use of evidence that could not support a full justification defence to allow a reduction in damages – which may encourage defendants to pursue more satellite litigation to get even the discounted damages reduced further.

3.16.7.4 *Qualified offers*

In relation to qualified offers, damages should be made in relation to the part of the defamatory publication in relation to which the Offer of Amends is made.[214] Clearly, this will involve considerations as to the likelihood of success if other avenues of defences are considered, such as justification. If justification is pleaded instead the relevant background facts that are true can be evidenced and may assist in reducing damages significantly. Indeed, the court may find that an award of damages is inappropriate; however, taking such a course of action may present real risks to the defendant and as such the position should be considered carefully before proceeding.

3.16.7.5 *Costs and damages in lieu of a specific agreement*

As noted above, if the parties have not arrived at an agreement, then damages will be determined on the same principles as in court proceedings. It is suggested that a claimant who accepts an offer will be entitled to all of his costs subject to an assessment of reasonableness.

In order to prevent any confusion, if costs have not been agreed or a sum put forward, the letter should be marked 'without prejudice save as to costs', as the costs in determining such matters could far outweigh the initial sums involved. In determining what figure to accept or offer, the parties should be encouraged to look realistically at what sum the court is likely to award and not discount an offer that is approaching a desired figure if the risk would not be justified on the facts. However, defendants must err on the side of caution in such circumstances and ensure that the sum put forward represents a realistic sum; indeed, it should always be borne in mind that in making an offer a defendant has accepted all or some liability in relation to their statement and the offer of damages needs to be framed accordingly. Unrealistic offers will simply fan flames and result in matters potentially becoming hotly contested. In terms of driving up costs, this should be avoided if possible in order to end matters as constructively and economically as possible. The time spent in determining the form

---

212 As in the summary procedure in ss 8–10 of the Defamation Act 1996; see *Ferguson v Associated Newspapers*, Gray J, 15/3/02 Westlaw 1654855.
213 [2001] 1 WLR 579 and see *Turner v News Group Newspapers Ltd* [2006] 1 WLR 3469.
214 For a discussion of mitigation considerations, see *Abu v MGN* [2002] EWHC 2345 (QB), [2013] EWHC 515 (QB), 2013 WL 617648, and the Report of the Neill Committee at [27].

116 *Civil claims*

of the offer and the costs to be awarded will also need to be considered. It would seem that if a claimant rejects an offer of a sum as to costs and upon determination by a costs judge they do better, then the question arises of whether they should be able to recover these sum of bringing the matter to determination.[215]

3.16.8 *Non-acceptance*

Situations may arise where the claimant does not accept the offer that has been put forward by the defendant. In these circumstances, the claim will progress in the normal way. However, by using the mechanism, the Offer of Amends will act as an absolute defence to the proceedings unless the claimant can show that the defendant should not be allowed to rely upon it. A situation where this will arise is where the defendant did in fact know that the statements they were making were untrue and were defamatory to the claimant. In order to bar the defendant from relying upon their offer, the claimant will need to meet this burden of proof to demonstrate why this is the case and the matter will be decided by a jury unless determined summarily.

3.16.9 *Disqualification*

3.16.9.1 *When offers will be disqualified*

The test for disqualification of an offer of amends put forward by a defendant is contained in section 4(3) of the Defamation Act 1996 and provides that the defence will not be available if the person by whom the offer was made knew or had reason to believe that the statement complained of:

- referred to the aggrieved party or was likely to be understood as referring to him (s 4(3)(a) Defamation Act 1996); and
- was both false and defamatory of that party (s 4(3)(b) Defamation Act 1996).

However, it shall be presumed until the contrary is shown that he did not know and had no reason to believe that was the case. The Offer of Amends procedure is only a defence in the sense that the claimant cannot proceed to a full trial unless he can demonstrate that the defendant knew or had reason to believe that the statement referred to the aggrieved party, or was likely to be understood as referring to him, and was both false and defamatory of the claimant.[216]

From a reading of this section, it can be seen that the test for 'disqualification' has three elements that must be proved that the defendant was aware of:

- Identification of the aggrieved party.
- A defamatory meaning in the statement.
- The statement was false.

---

215 See *Calderbank v Calderbank* [1976] 3 All ER 333.

216 This has been interpreted favourably to defendants in the sense that actual as opposed to constructive knowledge is required of these elements – actual knowledge, including recklessness as defined by Lord Diplock in *Horrocks v Lowe* [1975] AC 135. Reason to believe was not to be equated with reason to suspect or with constructive knowledge – see *Milne v Express Newspapers* [2005] 1 All ER 1021.

Although the elements can be broken down into three parts, the test is not discrete and all three must be considered together. Essentially, the question that must be considered is whether the defendant knew or had reason to believe that the allegation was false or defamatory in relation to the claimant.[217]

3.16.9.2 *Knowledge*

In terms of knowledge, if the defendant knew that the statements made were false and defamatory and published anyway, then at the heart of what is being suggested by the claimant is that the defendant made these allegations in malice. In determining if the statements were made in malice, the court will have regard to the defendant's motivation, conduct, and the information available to them at the time of the publication of the defamatory statement. It is these factors that will go towards determining if an inference of 'guilty knowledge' can be drawn.

3.16.9.3 *Reason to believe*

If the defendant had reason to believe that the statements they made in the publication were false or defamatory, then it is possible for a defendant to be disqualified from relying on the defence. The advantage to the claimant is that this will be easier to prove than actual knowledge, as discussed above. The cases in this area will be most likely to turn upon the issue of what information was available to the defendant at the time of publication.

In terms of what this will mean, it has been suggested that the assessment could encompass an objective test, although the *Neill Committee* stated that in determining the reckless actions of a defendant, the test is more akin to indifference as to the truth or falsity of the statement.

It is not open to defendants to make themselves wilfully ignorant of obvious facts. This was confirmed in *Sarah Thornton v Telegraph Media Group Ltd*.[218] Tugendhat LJ stated that the failure to check an allegation that is so serious that a check is to be expected is consistent with knowledge that the allegation in question is false and that a person need not check that which they already know a fact check would reveal.[219] However, lack of care will not alone suffice; there must also be some demonstration of bad faith on behalf of the defendant.

In considering how courts may interpret section 4(3), the case of *Milne v Express Newspapers*[220] is worth considering in the context of its judicial history. In *Milne*, it was suggested that the words 'reason to believe' in section 4(3) of the Defamation Act 1996 were not to be equated with reason to suspect or with constructive knowledge on the part of the person offering to make amends.[221] The facts of the case were that the claimant sought permission to appeal against two decisions[222] in their

---

217 See the opening to this chapter, which outlines the availability of the procedure as available to defendants who have made a honest mistake.
218 [2011] EWHC 1884 (QB); 2011 WL 2747828.
219 [2011] EWHC 1884 (QB); 2011 WL 2747828 at [120].
220 [2004] EWCA Civ 664; 2004 WL 1074477.
221 Note, the provision imported the concept of recklessness enunciated in *Horrocks v Lowe* [1975] AC 175.
222 [2002] EWHC 2564, [2003] 1 WLR 927, [2003] CLY 961, and [2003] EWHC 1843.

118   *Civil claims*

defamation action against the defendant newspaper, which had published an article written by a journalist that contained words which the parties accepted conveyed the meaning that the claimant had been suspected of giving false evidence to an inquiry by the Parliamentary Standards Commissioner.

The defendant had made an unqualified offer to make amends, put forward proposals for putting the offer into action, and gave reasons for doing so. The claimant rejected the offer and as such the defendant sought to invoke the offer as a defence. In response, the claimant submitted that the defendant had 'reason to believe that the statement complained of was false'. The defendant applied to strike out the part of the reply that relied on section 4(3).

In the first judgment, the court determined that claimants would only be able to challenge a section 4 defence where the defendant had chosen to ignore or shut his mind to information that should have led him to believe that the allegation was false. The judge held the claimant's submissions were therefore insufficient to rebut section 4 and struck out the relevant paragraphs. The case progressed to a second appeal, where the court upheld the defendant's contentions and refused the claimant permission to amend his reply and ordered that judgment should be entered for the defendant. The claimant submitted that the judge had misconstrued section 4(3) as importing a wholly subjective recklessness or 'bad faith' test of the kind required for proof of malice in defamation proceedings.

The case proceeded to the Court of Appeal where it was heard before May, Tuckey, and Laws LJJ who dismissed the appeal but allowed the second application. First, the judge's interpretation of section 4(3) of the 1996 Act in his first judgment was entirely correct for the reasons that he gave. The words 'reason to believe' in section 4(3) imported the concept of recklessness enunciated in *Horrocks v Lowe*.[223] The court stated that the reason for adopting this approach was that where a claimant established malice on the part of a person who published a defamatory statement, he would have the basis for a claim of aggravated, and possibly exemplary, damages. Malice apart, compensation could be fully assessed and awarded under section 3(5) of the Defamation Act 1996. There would be little point therefore in relying on section 4(3) unless the requirement there was to establish malice. The court, however, did recognize that some claimants might prefer a jury trial could not alone have been the parliamentary purpose. The phrase 'had reason to believe' required an inquiry into what facts were in a person's head and not into what facts ought to have been in his head. Reason to believe was not to be equated with reason to suspect or with constructive knowledge.[224]

Second, the court found that the second judge was right to refuse permission to amend the reply. The claimant's attempt to elevate the proposed amended particulars to a case under section 4(3) fit to go to a jury. The reason for this was that the claimant's central submission relied on far too brittle a chain of inferred or imputed reasoning on the part of the journalist who had written the piece. Finally, as noted in the Neill Report, the court stated that what was required to be proved was not an *inference* but a *reckless indifference* as to the truth.

223 [1975] AC 135.
224 Horrocks applied.

Defamation 119

3.16.9.4 *The interrelationship with other defences*

If a defendant chooses to rely on his offer as his substantive defence, he will not be able to rely on other defences.[225] Tactically, a defendant who has made an offer that has not been accepted by the claimant still has the option open to withdraw the offer and choose to rely upon another defence. However, if this tack is taken it may weaken the defence subsequently pleaded. For example, if a defendant subsequently claims the statement is true (under s 2 of the Defamation Act 2013), the conciliatory act of putting forward an Offer of Amends may weaken the claim significantly. However, there may be circumstances where the withdrawal of the offer is on justifiable grounds, such as where new evidence in the defendant's favour comes to light. Defendants should still refer the Offer of Amends in these circumstances as mitigation when the court considers the prospect of the claimant's damages; however, if the defence of justification is pleaded, for the reasons outlined above, this may have little effect.

3.16.9.5 *Claimant refuses to acccpt a qualified offer*

The Offer of Amends for qualified offers will only relate to that part of the defamatory statement to which it is given.[226] However, as with unqualified offer, the defendant cannot rely on other defences in relation to which the defamatory meaning to which the Offer of Amends is made. However, they can rely on other defences in relation to the rest of the content of the statement to which the offer is not addressed.[227] For the sake of ease, the potential outcomes of the various ways that the court may find in relation to the offer are set out below.

Claimant's course of action	Outcome
1 The claimant fails to prove that the offer should be disqualified in relation to the statement to which the qualified offer is made.[i] The defendant fails to successfully defend other contested defamatory meanings that do not form the subject matter of the offer.	The claimant is entitled to damages on the points that are contested but not recover damages in relation to the statement that was subject to the offer of amends.
2 The claimant fails to make a submission on disqualification. The defendant is successful in submitting a full defence to the other contested defamatory meaning.	The claimant will not recover any damages and loses the action.
3 The claimant successfully submits a valid case to disqualify the defendant's offer. The defendant fails to put up a valid defence to the other defamatory meanings.	The claimant will be entitled to damages in respect of all of the meanings which form the subject matter of the defamatory statement.

(continued)

---

225 Section 4(4) of the Defamation Act 1996.
226 Section 4(2) of the Defamation Act 1996.
227 Section 4(4) of the Defamation Act 1996.

120 *Civil claims*

Claimant's course of action	Outcome
4 The claimant successfully proves that the offer should be disqualified in relation to the statement to which the qualified offer is made. The defendant successfully establishes a defence in relation to the contested defamatory content.[ii]	The claimant will be entitled to damages in relation to the content that forms the subject matter of the offer. This will be subject to mitigation.

[i] See s 4(2) of the Defamation Act 1996.
[ii] Ibid.

3.16.10 *Rejection of the offer by the claimant*

An Offer of Amends differs from more traditional offers such as Part 36 offers in that there is no time limit in which the claimant must accept the offer. However, as is the case with general contractual principles, the rejection of the offer amounts to a termination, which will mean that it cannot subsequently be accepted. The rejection need not be formally brought to the defendant's attention; indeed, it may be that the claimant rejects an offer by their conduct.[228] An example of this could be pursuing a case after an offer has been made.

In *Rigg v Associated Newspapers*,[229] the defendant appealed against a decision to allow disclosure of documents to Rigg pursuant to Part 31 r.31.14 of the CPR. The facts of the case were that a journalist employed by Associated Newspapers interviewed the claimant and had published a newspaper article about her. The claimant felt that statements had been credited to her that she did not make, that the article contained deliberate falsehoods, and that the publication had been published maliciously.

Associated Newspapers made an Offer of Amends to the claimant but maintained that the article had not contained deliberate falsehoods and claimed that this assertion could be supported by the journalist's contemporaneous notes of the interview. The defendant was only prepared to allow the claimant access to the notes after the Offer of Amends had been accepted by the claimant. Gray LJ allowed the appeal holding that an order for disclosure could not be made pursuant to Part 31 r.31.14 of the CPR since the notes had not been 'mentioned' in the newspaper's defence as required by r.31.14 since there was no direct and specific reference in the defence to the notes as required by *Quilter v Heatly*,[230] nor was there any direct allusion to the notes as suggested in *Dubai Bank Ltd v Galadari*.[231] However, Gray J stated that the court would exercise its discretion to make an order for disclosure under Part 31 r.31.12 of the CPR.[232]

The court restated that under section 3 and section 4 of the Defamation Act 1996, where an Offer of Amends was made but not accepted, the fact of the offer would be

228 See *Hyde v Wrench* (1840) 3 Beav 334.
229 [2003] EWHC 710.
230 (1883) 23 Ch D.
231 (No 3) [1990] 1 WLR 731.
232 Note CPR 3.1 the court has wide-ranging general powers as part of the Overriding Objective.

a defence unless the party making it knew or had reason to believe that the statement complained of was both false and defamatory. As such, the contemporaneous notes were relevant to the issues pleaded and were at the heart as to the whether the claimant would decide to accept the Offer of Amends. The court clearly stated, however, that this was not to suggest that the court would rule for such disclosure on a routine or wide-scale basis, in the case of applications for disclosure by claimants faced with a decision whether or not to accept an Offer of Amends.[233] The rationale of this is that it would go against the reason why the mechanism was introduced to the 1996 Act, namely to dispose of cases expediently.

Because an Offer of Amends is made before proceedings are issued, that is also to say, before disclosure has occurred, the claimant may not be in the best position to determine the strength of their case. This will especially be problematic for claimants who may have accepted the offer had they been in receipt of such information.

In terms of the impact that this will have on costs, in *Roache v News Group Newspapers*[234] the court ordered that where claimants have allowed matters to run and created unnecessary costs, they will themselves be liable for such sums.

3.16.11 *Considerations for claimants*

In terms of deciding whether or not to accept or reject an offer, claimants will need to bear in mind the following considerations:

General offers

- The claimant bears a positive burden to prove that the offer should be disqualified.
- There may be significant delays brought about by adopting this process.
- The defendant may withdraw the offer and seek to rely on a different defence.
- The court may take into account the defendant's state of mind at the time of publication in cases which resolve solely on points in relation to whether an Offer of Amends should have been accepted by the claimant.
- Claimants lay themselves open to the risk that they may get nothing if they fail to prove that the offer should have been disqualified.
- In the situation in the bullet point above, the claimant may end up bearing the defendant's costs, which may be significant if the matter was protracted and hotly contested.
- Juries can now make reference to quantum decisions in personal injury cases and as such there is a risk that the claimant will not recover more than that which would be awarded by a judge, which historically has been perceived as a major advantage of trial by jury.
- The Jury may perceive that the claimant should have accepted the offer and this may be reflected in the ultimate sums awarded to complainants.

---

233 Note that upon this issue, *Abu v MGN Limited* [2002] EWHC 2345 was applied.
234 [1998] EMLR 161.

122   *Civil claims*

- If the claimant rejects the offer, under the normal contractual principles as outlined above the offer terminates and unless a fresh offer is issued, it will not be possible for the claimant to subsequently accept it if they later realize the weakness of their case.

Qualified offers

- If the offer applies to one of a myriad of allegations and the Claimant accepts the Offer they will lose their vindication in respect of the other claims as the public may assume that the other matters contained in the statement are globally true.
- Claimants must look at their case critically and assess what the strength of those matters not forming the subject matter of the offer have.
- The process of vindication may prove to be a long and uneven path. Claimants must bear in mind what effect this may have on them in the interim period and what value the vindication will have to them when it eventually comes (if at all).

3.16.12 *Considerations for defendants*

In terms of deciding whether or not to make an offer, claimants will need to bear in mind the following considerations:

General offers

- In making the offer, claimants are incentivised to accept for the reasons outlined at 3.16.1.
- If the claimant accepts the offer, the defendant will be liable for damages and costs that they would not have been liable for if at trial outcome they defeated the claimant's submissions.
- Damages can still be substantial even when taking into account the fact that the offer was made.[235]
- If the defendant invokes the offer as his sole defence and the risk of disqualification of the offer is great, he can admit liability and pay a sum in damages.[236]
- The offer may weaken any subsequent defences put forward by the defendant if they choose to defend the matter on a different ground.

Qualified offers

- The defendant runs the risk of forfeiting a partial justification in mitigation if the article does not bear the meaning in question.

---

235 *Kaim v Neill* [1996] EMLR 493.
236 See CPR Part 36. The defendant can offer a sum and if refused draw this to the court's later attention. Note: This cannot however be drawn to the jury's attention who are more likely to be persuaded to reduce the quantum of damages.

- The defendant can avoid potential liability for any other defamatory meanings in the document.
- If the offer is rejected, it is open to the defendant to make an open offer in correspondence while relying on other defences in relation to other defamatory meanings within the statement which did not form the subject matter of the offer.

3.17 Part 36 offer

Part 36 of the CPR enables either party to a defamation action to make a formal offer to settle (Part 36 offer). If a defendant makes a Part 36 offer of damages, it must be made by way of a payment into court. A Part 36 offer from either party remains open for acceptance for 21 days, after which time it can only be accepted if the parties agree on liability for costs or the court gives permission.

Failure to beat a Part 36 offer usually results in costs having to be paid by the loser from the last date on which he could have accepted the Part 36 offer. In *Jones v Associated Newspapers Limited*,[237] the claimant made a Part 36 offer to settle his claim in return for damages of £4,999, an apology, and an undertaking not to repeat the words complained of. The defendant did not accept the offer and maintained a defence of justification. At trial the jury found in the claimant's favour and awarded him £5,000 in damages. The claimant contended that the jury verdict in his favour meant that he had beaten his Part 36 offer and therefore that, further to CPR 36.14, he ought to have his costs incurred, since the offer had expired assessed on the indemnity basis and that he ought to receive interest on those costs at the base rate plus 4%.

Eady J stated that the claimant had not beaten his Part 36 offer, for although the claimant had achieved a greater financial amount, he had not secured more from the jury verdict than he would have achieved if his Part 36 offer had been accepted.

In terms of the apology, the apology sought in the Part 36 offer had been complete ('no truth at all in the allegation') and at trial the claimant had admitted that he had been rude to the security guard (although considerably less so than as alleged in the article). Moreover, Eady J indicated that even if the Part 36 offer had been beaten by the claimant, while he would have awarded costs to be assessed on the indemnity basis, he would not have awarded enhanced interest on those costs because the claimant had been funded by a Conditional Fee Arrangement and therefore had not personally been out of pocket from funding his litigation. The court noted that if it had been awarded, the interest would have been paid to his lawyers.

3.18 Summary judgment

Section 12 of the Defamation Act 2013 gives the courts, for the first time, the power to order summary judgment in defamation generally in favour of a claimant to be published. This can be contrasted with the similar provision in the Defamation Act 1966, which limited the power to summary disposal proceedings where the parties were unable to agree the terms of an apology or correction.

237 [2007] EWHC 1489 (QB); [2008] 1 All ER 240; [2008] EMLR 6 Court Queen's Bench Division.

Part 3
Criminal liability

Part 3.1

Communications-based offences

4 Communications Act 2003

4.1 Introduction

The Communications Act 2003 (CA 2003) gave effect to the Government's proposals for the reform of the regulatory framework for the communications sector, as set out in the Communications White Paper, *A New Future for Communications*.[1] The Communications Act 2003 is mainly concerned with broadcasting law and the functions of OFCOM; however, section 127 CA 2003 deals with messages of an offensive, obscene or menacing character which are sent via a public electronic communications network. It is for this reason that it has been applied to offensive communications sent via social media sites. Over that past two years, there have been a number of prosecutions brought under section 127 CA 2003 in relation to postings made on social networking sites that have attracted significant publicity mainly due to the severity of the punishments received for offenders who were posting comments 'as a joke'.

In relation to users' understanding of what may constitute criminal activity, it has been a consistent theme that although the posters who have been prosecuted may have few friends on Facebook or followers on Twitter, their posts in many cases were returned on search result engines and thereby brought to the attention of a much wider audience than they might have intended. One of the issues presented by social media is that once the message is posted, the original recipients of the message may copy, re-post, re-tweet or save a copy, thereby bringing the message to a much wider audience even if the author subsequently decided to delete their own post. Another issue presented by such postings is that when search results are returned without their context, it also has the potential to cause significant harm, as those who are interested in the subject are the most likely to make the searches; such examples may include racist statements (*DPP v Collins*[2]) and incitement to commit criminal acts (*DPP v Sutcliffe-Keenan; DPP v Blackshaw*[3]), which may not have been the intention of the user when they posted them. This has resulted in different penalties being applied in different cases and confusion as to when prosecutions will be pursued by the CPS. This chapter will consider cases in which the court has explored how to approach applying the Communications Act 2003 to social

---

1 *A New Future for Communications* (Cm 5010) – published on 12 December 2000.
2 [2006] UKHL 40.
3 [2011] EWCA Crim 2312.

130 *Communications-based offences*

media prosecutions and the response of the CPS that resulted in policy changes in this area.

4.2 Section 127 Communications Act 2003

Section 127(1) CA 2003, which has been most commonly used to pursue social media prosecutions, makes provisions in relation to the improper use of a public electronic communications network. A person is guilty of an offence if they:

- send by means of a public electronic communications network a message or other matter that is grossly offensive or of an indecent, obscene or menacing character (s 127(1)(a)); or
- cause any such message or matter to be so sent (s 127(1)(b)).

Under subsection 2, a person is guilty of an offence if, for the purpose of causing annoyance, inconvenience or needless anxiety to another, they:

- send by means of a public electronic communications network, a message that he knows to be false (s 127(2)(a));
- cause such a message to be sent (s 127(2)(b)); or
- persistently makes use of a public electronic communications network (s 127(2) (c)).

If found guilty under section 127, the individual may be liable, on summary conviction, to imprisonment for a term not exceeding six months or to a fine not exceeding level 5 on the standard scale, or to both (s 127(3)).

The position is similar in other jurisdictions. For example, in India, section 66A(a) of the Information Technology Act 2000 (IT Act (India) 2000) makes it clear that any person who sends, by means of a computer resource or a communication device, any text, audio or video that is offensive or has a menacing character, or is false and has been transmitted for the purpose of causing annoyance, inconvenience, danger, obstruction, insult, hatred or ill will, can be imprisoned for a term that may extend to three years, as well as a monetary fine.

4.2.1 *Background to the Communications Act 2003*

To understand how the elements of the offence developed, it is useful to consider its genealogy. The section can be traced back to section 10(2)(a) of the Post Office (Amendment) Act 1935, which made it an offence to send any message by telephone that is grossly offensive or of an indecent, obscene or menacing character. That subsection was reproduced with no change save of punctuation in section 66(a) of the Post Office Act 1953.

It was again reproduced in section 78 of the Post Office Act 1969, save that 'by means of a public telecommunication service' was substituted for 'by telephone' and 'any message' was changed to 'a message or other matter'. Section 78 was elaborated but substantially repeated in section 49(1)(a) of the British Telecommunications Act 1981 and was re-enacted (save for the substitution of 'system' for 'service') in section 43(1)(a) of the Telecommunications Act 1984 (TA 1984). Section 43(1)(a)

Communications Act 2003   131

was in the same terms as section 127(1)(a) of the 2003 Act, save that it referred to 'a public telecommunication system' and not (as in s 127(1)(a)) to a 'public electronic communications network'. Sections 11(1)(b) of the Post Office Act 1953 and 85(3) of the Postal Services Act 2000 made it an offence to send certain proscribed articles by post.

Section 127 CA 2003 replaced section 43 Telecommunications Act 1984. Section 127 CA 2003 essentially repeats the Telecommunications Act 1984 wholesale, and is almost a word for word repetition of these earlier Acts. The 1984 Act was notable for changing the scope to apply to any 'public telecommunication system' (a necessity following the deregulation of the State monopoly telephone network in 1981[4]). The explanatory notes[5] to the Communications Act 2003 do not offer any clarification as to why the amendment was made. According to Lord Bingham in *DPP v Collins*,[6] the purpose of the legislation which culminated in section 127(1)(a) CA 2003 was to prohibit the use of a service provided and funded by the public for the benefit of the public for the transmission of communications which contravene the basic standards of society; however, its modern application is clearly much wider and covers social networking sites.

4.2.2 *The meaning of 'gross offence'*

In the UK, a person charged under section 127 CA 2003 must be shown to have intended that or be aware that the message was grossly offensive, indecent or menacing, which can be inferred from the terms of the message or from the defendant's knowledge of the likely recipient. It is important to note that knowledge of the recipient's likely reaction is only relevant when making inferences about the defendant's intention, and not as to whether the message itself was grossly offensive.[7] The offence is committed by sending the message. There is no requirement that any person sees the message or be offended by it.

As noted in the genealogy of the Communications Act 2003 and the obiter comments of Lord Bingham in *Collins*, it is not clear on a black letter reading of the law and its preceding acts if the CA 2003 is applicable to social media sites. Social media sites are not public service providers funded by the *public* (*Collins*) and are not the subject of broadcasting law, to which the majority of the CA 2003 is related. However, this has not prevented it being applied to communications sent via sites provided by private companies.[8] Doubts have also been expressed as to whether creating a web page or social network group constitutes 'sending' a message;[9] there are a number of examples where section 127 has been used against internet

---

4   It would appear that this phrase was taken from EC telecoms law, and causes problems of its own, debated in *DPP v Chambers* (discussed below).

5   These notes refer to the Communications Act 2003 (c. 21), which received Royal Assent on 17 July 2003.

6   [2006] UKHL 40 at [7] and [8].

7   See D. Ormerod, 'Telecommunications: sending grossly offensive message by means of public electronic communications network' [2007] Crim LR 98.

8   These issues were explored in *DPP v Chambers*, discussed below.

9   See Policy Memorandum on the Offensive Behaviour at Football and Threatening Communications (Scotland) Bill (2011) at [34].

132 *Communications-based offences*

communications (which will be considered below). It is therefore necessary to explore when and how the offence is committed and whether it has been done knowingly.

4.2.2.1 *Actus reus*

In *DPP v Collins*, Lord Bingham stated that it was plain from the terms of section 127(1)(a), as of its predecessor sections, that the proscribed act, the *actus reus* of the offence, is the sending of a message of the proscribed character by the defined means. The offence is complete when the message is sent. Thus it can make no difference that the message is never received, for example because a recorded message is erased before anyone listens to it. Nor did the Lords consider that the criminality of a defendant's conduct depend on whether a message is received by A, who for any reason is deeply offended, or B, who is not. On such an approach, criminal liability would turn on an unforeseeable contingency. This is clearly problematic in the social media context, as there is a lack of control once a posting is made. As noted in Chapter 1, which explores how social networking sites work, postings will be saved on the profile on which 'User A' posts them (i.e. 'User B's' profile) and on the social networking site (SNS) server. The information may also be stored on A's computer if he used the World Wide Web to make the posting. Analysis of a computer's hard-drive may sometimes reveal the contents of SNS communications, but normally that information would have to be acquired by either accessing the profile itself online, or seeking the information from the relevant SNSs who stored it on their server. Even if the poster subsequently deletes the post, if *Collins* is applied, the offence has already been committed regardless of whether the individual subsequently regrets their actions and deletes the posting. However, as seen throughout the rest of this chapter, and in other chapters in Part 3 of this Handbook, after implementation of the CPS's issuing of the interim guidelines (considered below) for prosecution cases involving a social media element, such factors are taken into account on sentencing and in determining if the Director for Public Prosecutions will proceed with bringing the matter for prosecution at all.

4.2.2.2 *Mens rea*

In contrast with its predecessor subsections, which require proof of an unlawful purpose and a degree of knowledge, section 127(1)(a) provides no explicit guidance on the state of mind that must be proved against a defendant to establish an offence against the subsection. This inevitably raises the question as to what, if anything, must be proved beyond an intention to send the message in question? In *DPP v Collins*, Counsel for the DPP, relied by analogy on section 6 (4) of the Public Order Act 1986, suggesting that the defendant must intend his words to be grossly offensive to those to whom they relate, or be aware that they may be taken to be so.[10] However, this still does not provide a definitive answer as to when an individual may take gross offence and how the statute is to be interpreted.

---

10 For further discussion in the context of the facts of *DPP v Collins* [2006] UKHL 40, see his Lordship's comments at para [10] of the judgment.

Even though the case of *Collins* did not concern a posting made via social media, it is worth exploration to understand how it has been subsequently applied to the medium. Mr Collins made a number of racist phone calls to the offices of his local Member of Parliament. In determining if an offence had been committed under section 127(1)(a) CA 2003, the House of Lords considered the standards of an open and just multiracial society, taking into account the context of the words and all relevant circumstances. This involved an exploration by the court of what constituted *reasonably enlightened* contemporary standards applied to the particular message sent, in its particular context, to determine whether its content was liable to cause gross offence to those to whom it related, or to be aware that it may be taken to do so. In determining if offence would be caused, Lord Bingham noted that usages and sensitivities change over time and should be taken into account. He sated in the judgment: 'there can be no yardstick of gross offensiveness otherwise than by the application of reasonably enlightened, but not perfectionist, contemporary standards to the particular message sent in its particular context. The test is whether a message is couched in terms liable to cause gross offence to those to whom it relates.'[11]

In *Collins*, the issue of whether offence was meant to be caused and how to prove the intent element of the offence caused their Lordships to consider cases concerning statutory interpretation for cases where the mental element of the offence is not provided for in the statute.

Sweet v Parsley,[12] the leading case on statutory interpretation, was considered by the Lords in *Collins* by Lord Reid. His Lordship considered that the court's duty was to consider the words of the Act, if they showed a clear intention to create an absolute offence that is an end of the matter, but that such cases are very rare. More frequently, he noted that the words of the section that creates a particular offence make it clear that *mens rea* is required in one form or another. However, in a large number of cases there is no clear indication either way. Lord Reid noted that in such cases there is a longstanding presumption that Parliament did not intend to make criminals of persons who were in no way blameworthy in what they did. That means that whenever a section is silent as to *mens rea*, as is the Communication Act 2003, there is a presumption that, in order to give effect to the will of Parliament, we must read in words appropriate to require *mens rea*.

Lord Bingham considered that the views of Lord Reid in *Sweet v Parsley* failed to be considered in the present case, as Parliament could not have intended to criminalise the conduct of a person using language that is, for reasons unknown to him, grossly offensive to those to whom it relates, or which may even be thought, however wrongly, to represent a polite or acceptable usage. On the other hand, he considered that a culpable state of mind would ordinarily be found where a message was couched in terms showing an intention to insult those to whom the message relates or giving rise to the inference that a risk of doing so must have been recognized by the sender. The court considered that the same would be true where facts known to the sender of a message about an intended recipient render the message peculiarly offensive to that recipient, or likely to be so, whether or not the message in fact reaches the recipient.[13]

11 [2006] UKHL 40 at [9].
12 [1970] AC 132 at [148].
13 [2006] UKHL 40 at [10].

134 *Communications-based offences*

Collins, a case post-dating the Human Rights Act 1998, also involved considering an individual's Convention rights under Article 10 (freedom of expression). The court stressed that individuals are entitled to express their views strongly and that the proper question for determining if section 127(1)(a) CA 2003 had been infringed was whether the language used went beyond what could be considered as tolerable in society. Considering when interference may be justified and the margin of appreciation, it is significant to note that there is nothing in the case reports in this area to suggest that grounds for a right not to be offended exists.

Connolly v DPP,[14] although prosecuted under the Malicious Communications Act 1988, is worth considering in this regard. Under section 1(1) of the Act (specifically ss 1(1)(b) and 1(4)), it is an offence to send an electronic communication which conveys a message that is grossly offensive to another person where the message is sent with the purpose of causing distress or anxiety to that person. The appellant, a committed Christian, sent photographs of aborted foetuses to three pharmacies that sold the morning-after pill. The appeal was based on her original defence, that the images were neither indecent nor grossly offensive, and that she had not sent them with the purpose of causing distress or anxiety to the recipients. While based on specific circumstances, Dyson LJ's judgment in this case contains a valuable discussion of the qualifications on the right to freedom of expression under Article 10 of the European Convention of Human Rights (ECHR). He held that the relevant 'rights of others' under Article 10(2) ECHR included the right not to receive grossly offensive material intended to distress and that this right subsisted in the workplace as well as in the home.

Ashworth[15] suggests that the legislation culminating in section 127(1)(a) CA 2003 was 'to protect people against . . . messages . . . they might find seriously objectionable'.[16] However, this assumes that the aim of the Communications Act 2003 is to create a right for individuals to be protected from the mischief targeted. It must therefore be borne in mind that *Collins* concerned racist speech, which constituted speech that was 'seriously objectionable', not just offensive. There are already identifiable rights consistent with free-speech principles that prohibit racist speech, such as the right to human dignity or equal respect regardless of race.[17] Regrettably, the House of Lords did not elaborate upon the role of the rights of others further.

4.2.2.3 *DPP v Chambers*

In *DPP v Chambers*,[18] one of the first substantive social media prosecutions to reach an appeal court that fully explored Convention rights, Paul Chambers was prosecuted under the Communications Act 2003 for sending the following tweet: 'Crap! Robin Hood airport is closed. You've got a week and a bit to get your s**t together otherwise I'm blowing the airport sky high!!' Mr Chambers subsequently appealed to the Crown

---

14 [2008] 1 WLR 276.
15 Ashworth, 'Case comment: malicious communication: defendant anti-abortionist – sending photographs of aborted foetuses' [2007] Crim LR 729, 731.
16 *DPP v Collins* [2006] UKHL 40; [2006] 1 WLR 2223 at [7].
17 For case examples, see E. Barendt (2005). *Freedom of Speech*. Oxford: Oxford University Press, p. 15.
18 [2012] EWHC 2157; 2012 WL 2923016.

Court against his conviction. The appeal was dismissed with Judge Jacqueline Davies stating that the tweet was: 'menacing in its content and obviously so. It could not be more clear. Any ordinary person reading this would see it in that way and be alarmed.' However, Robin Hood Airport had classified the threat as non-credible on the basis that 'there was no evidence at this stage to suggest that this is anything other than a foolish comment posted as a joke for only his close friends to see'. Following an appeal to the High Court in February 2012, the judges who heard the case were unable to reach agreement on the correct interpretation of section 127 and the case was referred for a second appeal. On 27 July 2012, Chambers' conviction was quashed. The approved judgment stated that the appeal against conviction would be allowed on the basis that the 'tweet' could not be usefully taken further.[19]

Building upon the judgment of *Collins*, the court took the view that English law (prior to the Communications Act 2003) had long been tolerant of satirical and even distasteful opinions about matters of both a serious and trivial nature. The court also noted that the 2003 Act predated the advent of Twitter and that the statutory reference to 'menacing' was itself based on the wording of the previous Act of 1935. The Lord Chief Justice, Lord Judge expressed the view that, 'the 2003 Act did not create interference with the . . . essential freedoms of speech and expression'.[20] With regard to whether the message was menacing, the court was clearly impatient of the magistrates' and Crown Court's views:

> if the person or persons who receive or read [a message], or may reasonably be expected to receive, or read it, would brush it aside as a silly joke, or a joke in bad taste, or empty bombastic or ridiculous banter, then it would be a contradiction in terms to describe it as a message of a menacing character. In short, a message which does not create fear or apprehension in those to whom it is communicated, or who may reasonably be expected to see it, falls outside this provision, for the very simple reason that the message lacks menace.[21]

4.2.2.4 *Woods*

The judgment in *Chambers* was in many respects a victory for common sense and the protection of an individual's freedom of expression. However, despite the clear guidance of the courts in *Chambers* and the central importance of balancing Convention rights, it was not followed in a number of subsequent cases, especially those heard before magistrates' courts, which are still required to consider Convention rights. In terms of the application of the law in the context of social media, the case of Matthew Woods serves as a useful example of how the law was ill adapted and applied in an *ad hoc* manner prior to the CPS issuing interim guidelines on how to prosecute cases involving a social media aspect (the guidelines are considered in full below). It also demonstrates the lack of application of Strasbourg jurisprudence, which courts are required to consider by virtue of the 'interpretative obligation' contained in section 3 of the Human Rights Act 1998.[22]

---

19 [2012] EWHC 2157; 2012 WL 2923016 at [38].
20 [2012] EWHC 2157; 2012 WL 2923016 at [28].
21 [2012] EWHC 2157; 2012 WL 2923016 at [30].
22 For a discussion of human rights law and the interpretative obligation, see Chapter 2: Human rights.

136 *Communications-based offences*

Matthew Woods, an unemployed 19-year-old from Chorley, Lancashire, was jailed for the maximum penalty of 12 weeks for his Facebook 'joke' which he made after having some drinks at a friend's house. The joke was about April Jones, the missing 5-year-old schoolgirl from Machynlleth, Wales and there was an additional joke about Madeleine McCann, the 3-year-old who went missing during a family holiday in Portugal in 2007. Among Woods' comments were: 'Who in their right mind would abduct a ginger kid?' In another he said: 'I woke up this morning in the back of a transit van with two beautiful little girls, I found April in a hopeless place.' He also wrote: 'Could have just started the greatest Facebook argument EVER. April fools, who wants Maddie? I love April Jones.' He also posted comments of a more sexually explicit nature.

As a result of the public reaction to his posts, Woods was arrested for his own safety after 50 people descended on his home. He pleaded guilty at Chorley Magistrates' Court to sending by means of a public electronic communications network a message or other matter that is grossly offensive contrary to the Communications Act 2003. Martina Jay, acting on behalf of the prosecution stated: 'He started this idea when he was at a friend's house, saw a joke on Sickipedia [an online database devoted to sick jokes] and changed it slightly.' The court was told Woods' Facebook page was available to a large number of people. The CPS confirmed it had reviewed the case file and was content with the prosecution going ahead.

In *Woods*, Bill Hudson, the magistrate handing down the sentence, rationalised the severity of the approach taken by the court by stating that: 'the reason for the sentence is the seriousness of the offence, the public outrage that has been caused and we felt there was no other sentence this court could have passed which conveys to you the abhorrence that many in society feel this crime should receive.'

In *Chambers*, however, the court stated that the intention of the Act was not to create interference with the essential freedoms of speech and expression enshrined in Article 10 of the European Convention on Human Rights (which the courts were required to have regard to as required by section 3 of the Human Rights Act 1998). Lord Judge, LCJ, commented:

> The 2003 Act did not create some newly minted interference with the first of President Roosevelt's essential freedoms – freedom of speech and expression. Satirical, or iconoclastic, or rude comment, the expression of unpopular or unfashionable opinion about serious or trivial matters, banter or humour, even if distasteful to some or painful to those subjected to it should and no doubt will continue at their customary level, quite undiminished by this legislation.[23]

It would appear from a reading of the case transcripts that the prevalent judicial attitudes arise from a desire to restrict the scope of free speech to speech that is civil or palatable (termed 'pro-civility'[24]) and was clearly a reference point used by the

---

23 [2006] UKHL 40 at [28].

24 Geddis, 'Free speech martyrs or unreasonable threats to social peace?' [2004] Public Law 853, 855. See also examples of this attitude in *Percy v DPP* [2001] EWHC Admin 1125; [2002] ACD 24; *Connolly v DPP* [2007] EWHC 237 (Admin) (below at fn 74); *Novartis Pharmaceuticals UK Ltd v Stop Huntingdon Animal Cruelty* [2009] EWHC 2716 (QB); [2010] HRLR 8 (below at fn127).

magistrate in *Woods*. In cases such as *Collins*, censorship in the context of (racist) hate speech, where despite unpopularity or otherwise, the speech is outlawed,[25] repression may be acceptable when that suppression is based on the 'rights of others' because it accords with the principles underlying free speech.[26] However, pro-civility cannot be an acceptable starting point to determine criminal liability in *every* case of distasteful speech that does not necessarily amount to hate speech and may merely be distasteful rather than grossly offensive (whatever that may mean, given the varying approaches taken in the case law).

In *Woods*, the lack of control that Matthew Woods was subsequently able to exert over his comments was not fully taken into account by the court on sentencing, which instead chose to focus its attention on the reaction of those who read the posts (which is the point at which the offence is committed). The prosecution did tell the court that Woods had made the posts 'in a bid to make people think his account had been hacked. He said it got out of hand', which may suggest why in mitigation David Edwards, defending Woods, noted that 'in one moment of drunken stupidity placed himself as public enemy number two – behind only the person who carried out this crime'.

This ability to *control* the intended audience, an area in *Woods* that was not given sufficient attention, is why such emphasis was placed by the court on the fact that his Facebook page was available to a large number of people. Moreover, it wasn't explained if this large group was in fact Woods' Facebook 'friends' or if the post was 'public'. No analysis was given to Woods' understanding of how to adapt his privacy settings on the site to limit audience (indeed, Woods' prosecution came before Facebook introduced a 'guided tour' to privacy on the site) and if Woods actually intended a large proportion of people to see the posts. This is significant because as noted above under the Act, those who are grossly offended by the message or posts in question need not be the intended recipients (see also *DPP v Collins* above). It also raised the issue of how sophisticated an account holder's knowledge is of the regulatory landscape of sites, since messages are sent as an extension of the organization and fulfilment of their social lives, which may be *perceived* by them as 'private'.

In *DPP v Chambers*, the court addressed this point, stating that it was immaterial that the appellant may have intended only that his message should be read by a limited class of people, that is, his followers, who, knowing him, would be neither fearful nor apprehensive when they read it. In their judgment, whether one read the 'tweet' at a time when it was read as 'newspaper content' rather than 'message', at the time when it was posted it was indeed 'a message' sent by an electronic communications service for the purposes of section 127(1).[27]

---

25 See POA, Pt III and in particular s 18; see also Crime and Disorder Act 1998, ss 28(1)(b) and 31(1)(c) in relation to s 5 POA. See also article 17 ECHR, discussed in *Norwood v UK* (2005) 40 EHRR SE11. *Glimmerveen and Hagenbeek v Netherlands* (1982) 4 EHRR 260; *DPP v Collins* [2006] UKHL 40; [2006] 1 WLR 2223. In international law, see article 4 of the Convention on the Elimination of all Forms of Racial Discrimination 660 UNTS 195, entered into force 4 January 1969; article 20(2) of the International Covenant on Civil and Political Rights 993 UNTS 3, entered into force 3 January 1976.

26 Foster, 'Free speech, insulting words or behaviour and art. 10 of the European Convention on Human Rights' (2004) 9(1) Cov LJ 68, 71; F.F. Schauer (1982). *Free Speech: A Philosophical Enquiry.* Cambridge: Cambridge University Press, pp. 3–15.

27 [2006] UKHL 40 at [24–25].

138 Communications-based offences

Although the current wording of the statute and the views of their Lordships in *Collins* confirm that the offence is committed when the message is sent, the application of communications law to social media is not simply a one-dimensional question of ignorance of the law.

4.2.2.5 Tom Daley

The case of *Woods* is interesting to compare with a series of tweets that the DPP investigated in relation to Olympic diving champion Tom Daley. This investigation also pre-dated the guidelines of the Director of Public Prosecutions (DPP) in relation to prosecuting cases involving a social media aspect (considered below). Asked to consider whether to prosecute Daniel Thomas, who had made trollish and homophobic tweets about Tom Daley,[28] the DPP indicated via their blog[29] that section 127 CA 2003 should not be seen as a carte blanche provision for prosecuting content which, however upsetting to some, would normally fall with guarantees of freedom of expression in a democratic society. The DPP stated: 'There is no doubt that the message posted by Mr Thomas was offensive and would be regarded as such by reasonable members of society.' But the question for the CPS is not whether it was offensive, but whether it was so grossly offensive that criminal charges should be brought. The distinction is an important one and not easily made. Context and circumstances are highly relevant and as the European Court of Human Rights observed in the case of *Handyside v UK* (1976),[30] the right to freedom of expression includes the right to say things or express opinions 'that offend, shock or disturb the state or any sector of the population'.[31]

In coming to that decision, the DPP took into account the context and circumstances in the case and the following facts and matters:

- However misguided, Mr Thomas intended the message to be humorous.
- However naïve, Mr Thomas did not intend the message to go beyond his followers, who were mainly friends and family.
- Mr Thomas took reasonably swift action to remove the message.
- Mr Thomas has expressed remorse and was, for a period, suspended by his football club.
- Neither Mr Daley nor Mr Waterfield were the intended recipients of the message and neither knew of its existence until it was brought to their attention following reports in the media.

The DPP was of the opinion that the content was, in essence, a one-off offensive tweet, intended for family and friends, which had made its way into the public domain and wider consumption than originally contemplated. It was not intended to reach

---

28 See http://www.guardian.co.uk/technology/2012/sep/20/footballer-tom-daley-tweet.
29 See http://blog.cps.gov.uk/2012/09/dpp-statement-on-tom-daley-case-and-social-media-prosecutions. html.
30 For a discussion of *Handyside*, see also Chapter 2: Human Rights.
31 See http://blog.cps.gov.uk/2012/09/dpp-statement-on-tom-daley-case-and-social-media-prosecutions. html.

Mr Daley or Mr Waterfield, it was not part of a campaign, it was not intended to incite others, and Mr Thomas removed it reasonably swiftly and has expressed remorse. Against that background, it was concluded that on a full analysis of the context and circumstances in which this single message was sent, it was not so grossly offensive that criminal charges need to be brought. The case can presumably be distinguished from Woods, as in Woods there was a series of postings and they contained sexually explicit content relating to the sensitive issues surrounding a potential child abduction (at the time of posting, April Jones was still missing and it was not known under what circumstances she had disappeared).

It was partly as a result of the mixture of decisions arrived at by prosecutors that the DPP recognized the inherent difficulties in prosecuting cases involving a social media element and stated that in order to ensure that CPS decision-making in these difficult cases is clear and consistent, the CPS would need to issue guidelines on social media cases for prosecutors. The guidelines would assist those tasked with whether criminal charges should be brought in the cases that arise for their consideration.

4.3 CPS interim guidance

4.3.1 *The Interim Guidelines*

On 19 December 2012, the DPP issued Interim Guidelines on Prosecuting Cases Involving Communications Sent via Social Media (the **Guidelines**).[32] The Guidelines are designed to give clear advice to prosecutors who have been asked either for a charging decision or for early advice to the police, as well as in reviewing those cases which have been charged by the police. The DPP has at the same time issued a consultation in respect of the interim guidelines, with responses due by 13 March 2013. The Interim Guidelines applied with immediate effect but will be reviewed at the end of the consultation period in light of the responses received after which final guidelines will be published. As part of that process, the CPS intend to hold a series of round table meetings with campaigners, media lawyers, academics, social media experts, and law enforcement bodies to ensure that the Guidelines are as fully informed as possible.

The Guidelines are primarily concerned with offences that may be committed by reason of the nature or content of a communication sent via social media. However, the Guidance states that where social media is simply used to facilitate some other substantive offence, prosecutors should proceed under the legislation governing the substantive offence in question (e.g. contempt of court, harassment, public disorder).[33]

4.3.2 *The General Principles*

The Guidelines[34] suggest consideration of the following general principles. Prosecutors may only start a prosecution if a case satisfies the test set out in the Code for Crown

32 Interim Guidelines on Prosecuting Cases Involving Communications Sent Via Social Media, issued by the Director of Public Prosecutions on 19 December 2012 [http://www.cps.gov.uk/consultations/social_media_consultation_index.html].

33 Ibid., para 3.

34 Interim Guidelines on Prosecuting Cases Involving Communications Sent Via Social Media.

140 *Communications-based offences*

Prosecutors.[35] This test has two stages, which are detailed at para 12 of the CPS Interim Guidelines. The first is the requirement of evidential sufficiency:

> (12) Evidential sufficiency to provide a realistic prospect of conviction which includes a consideration of:
>
> 1. Credible threats;[36]
> 2. Targeted campaigns against specific individuals;[37]
> 3. Communications which may amount to a breach of a court order;[38]
> 4. Communications which do not fall into any of the categories above and fall to be considered separately because they may be considered grossly offensive, indecent, obscene or false.

As far as the evidential stage is concerned, according to the CPS,[39] a prosecutor must be satisfied that there is sufficient evidence to provide a realistic prospect of conviction. This means that:

- an objective, impartial and reasonable jury (or bench of magistrates or judge sitting alone);
- properly directed and acting in accordance with the law;
- is more likely than not to convict.

This is an objective test based upon the prosecutor's assessment of the evidence (including any information that he or she has about the defence). A case that does not pass the evidential stage must not proceed, no matter how serious or sensitive it may be. It has never been the rule that a prosecution will automatically take place once the evidential stage is satisfied. In every case where there is sufficient evidence to justify a prosecution, prosecutors must go on to consider whether a prosecution is required in the public interest.

The CPS expressly states in the Guidelines that every case must be considered on its own individual facts and merits. In the majority of cases, prosecutors should only decide whether to prosecute after the investigation has been completed. However, the CPS indicate in the guidance[40] there will be cases occasionally where it is clear, prior to the collection and consideration of all the likely evidence, that the public interest does not require a prosecution. In these cases, prosecutors may decide that the case should not proceed further.

---

35 The Code for Crown Prosecutors, January 2013 [https://www.cps.gov.uk/publications/docs/code_2013_accessible_english.pdf].
36 The CPS offer examples of violence to the person or damage to property.
37 The CPS indicate in the guidance that this may include matters which may constitute harassment or stalking within the meaning of the Protection from Harassment Act 1997 or which may constitute other offences, such as blackmail.
38 This can include offences under the Contempt of Court Act 1981 or s 5 of the Sexual Offences (Amendment) Act 1992. All such cases should be referred to the Attorney General, and via the Principal Legal Advisor's team where necessary.
39 Interim Guidelines on Prosecuting Cases Involving Communications Sent Via Social Media at [6–10].
40 Ibid. at [10].

4.3.3 *Cases that fall within paragraphs 12(1), 12(2) or 12(3)*

The CPS suggest that as a general approach, cases falling within paragraphs 12(1), 12(2) or 12(3) above should be prosecuted robustly where they satisfy the test set out in the Code for Crown Prosecutors. Having identified which of the categories set out in paragraph 12 of the Interim Guidelines the communication and the course of conduct in question falls into, prosecutors should follow the approach set out under the relevant heading below.

4.3.3.1 *Credible threats*[41]

Communications which may constitute credible threats of violence to the person may fall to be considered under section 16 of the Offences Against the Person Act 1861 if the threat is a threat to kill within the meaning of that provision. Other credible threats of violence to the person may fall to be considered under section 4 of the Protection from Harassment Act 1997 if they amount to a course of conduct within the meaning of that provision and there is sufficient evidence to establish the necessary state of knowledge.

Credible threats of violence to the person or damage to property may also fall to be considered under section 127 of the Communications Act 2003, which prohibits the sending of messages of a 'menacing character' by means of a public telecommunications network. However, before proceeding with a prosecution under section 127, the CPS suggests that prosecutors heed the judgment of the Lord Chief Justice in *DPP v Chambers*, in particular that: 'a message which does not create fear or apprehension in those to whom it is communicated, or may reasonably be expected to see it, falls outside s 127(i), for the simple reason that the message lacks menace'.[42] As a general rule, the CPS states that threats which are not credible should not be prosecuted, unless they form part of a campaign of harassment specifically targeting an individual within the meaning of the Protection from Harassment Act 1997.[43]

4.3.3.2 *Aggravating factors*

Where there is evidence of discrimination, prosecutors should pay particular regard to the provisions of sections 28–32 of the Crime and Disorder Act 1998 and section 145 of the Criminal Justice Act 2003 (increase in sentences for racial and religious aggravation) and section 146 of the Criminal Justice Act 2003 (increase in sentences for aggravation related to disability, sexual orientation or transgender identity).

4.3.3.3 *Communications targeting specific individuals*[44]

If communications sent via social media target a specific individual or individuals, they will fall to be considered under the Protection from Harassment Act 1997 where they amount to a course of conduct within the meaning of section 7 of that Act. In such

---

41 Ibid. at [15].
42 [2012] EWH2 2157 (Admin), para 30.
43 The Protection from Harassment Act 1997 is considered in Chapter 9.
44 Interim Guidelines on Prosecuting Cases Involving Communications Sent Via Social Media at [19].

142   *Communications-based offences*

cases, prosecutors should follow the CPS Legal Guidance on Stalking and Harassment,[45] which addresses behaviour which is repeated and unwanted by the victim and which causes the victim to have a negative reaction in terms of alarm or distress.

Where communications target a specific individual and the offence of blackmail is made out, prosecutors should seek to prosecute the substantive offence. Again, where there is evidence of discrimination, prosecutors should pay particular regard to the provisions of sections 28–32 of the Crime and Disorder Act 1998 and sections 145–146 of the Criminal Justice Act 2003.

4.3.3.4 *Breach of court orders*[46]

Court orders can apply to those communicating via social media in the same way as they apply to others. Accordingly, any communication via social media that may breach a court order falls to be considered under the relevant legislation, including the Contempt of Court Act 1981 and section 5 of the Sexual Offences (Amendment) Act 1992, which makes it an offence to publish material that may lead to the identification of a victim of a sexual offence.

A recent example of this arose after Sheffield United Striker Ched Evans was convicted of the rape of a 19-year-old woman.[47] North Wales Police investigated claims that the victim had been named and subjected to abuse on Twitter after the trial. As of 6 October 2012, North Wales Police had arrested 23 people on suspicion of offences relating to the naming of the victim. Sheffield United academy and reserve team player Connor Brown was suspended by his club after allegedly making offensive comments about the victim on Twitter, although he did not give her name. On 5 November 2012, nine people who had named the victim on Twitter and Facebook were each told to pay her £624 after admitting the offence at Prestatyn Magistrates' Court. The CPS suggest that in such cases, prosecutors should follow the CPS's legal guidance on Contempt of Court and Reporting Restrictions[48] and observe the requirements for contempt cases to be referred to the Attorney General and via the Principal Legal Advisors Team where necessary.

4.3.3.5 *Cases that fall within paragraph 12(4)*

The CPS suggest communications which do not fit into any of the categories outlined at 12(1)–(3) fall to be considered either under section 1 of the Malicious Communications Act 1988 (MCA 1988) or under section 127 of the Communications Act 2003. These provisions refer to communications that are grossly offensive, indecent, obscene, menacing or false (but as a general rule, menacing communications should be dealt with under the section above on credible threats).

---

45 A copy of the guidance is available at https://www.cps.gov.uk/legal/s_to_u/stalking_and_harassment/.

46 Interim Guidelines on Prosecuting Cases Involving Communications Sent Via Social Media at [22].

47 *R v Evans and McDonald* involved the prosecution of two footballers, Ched Evans and Clayton McDonald, who were jointly accused of the rape of a woman. On 20 April 2012, Evans was convicted and sentenced to five years' imprisonment. McDonald was acquitted.

48 Reporting restrictions in the Criminal Courts, published by the Judicial Studies Board, the Newspaper Society, the Society of Editors, and Times Newspapers Ltd, October 2009.

4.3.3.6 *The high threshold*[49]

Since both section 1 MCA 1988 and section 127 CA 2003 engage Article 10 of the European Convention on Human Rights, prosecutors are reminded that these provisions must be interpreted consistently with the free speech principles in Article 10, which provide that: 'Everyone has the right to freedom of expression. This right shall include the freedom to hold opinions and to receive and impart information and ideas without interference by public authority and regardless of frontiers.'

As the European Court of Human Rights made clear[50] in *Sunday Times v UK (no. 2)*,[51] Article 10 protects not only speech that is well-received and popular, but also speech that is offensive, shocking or disturbing: 'Freedom of expression constitutes one of the essential foundations of a democratic society . . . it is applicable not only to "information" or "ideas" that are favourably received or regarded as inoffensive or as a matter of indifference, but also as to those that offend, shock or disturb.'

As noted in Chapter 2: Human Rights, freedom of expression and the right to receive and impart information are not absolute rights. They may be restricted but only where a restriction can be shown to be both 'necessary' and 'proportionate'. These exceptions, however, must be narrowly interpreted and the necessity for any restrictions convincingly established.[52] The common law takes a similar approach.[53]

4.3.3.7 *Summary*

If the guidelines above are applied, a prosecution is unlikely to be deemed necessary and proportionate by the CPS where:

- The individual has taken swift action to remove the communication or expressed genuine remorse.
- Swift and effective action has been taken by others, for example, service providers, to remove the communication or block access to it.
- The communication was not intended for or obviously likely to reach a wide audience, particularly where the intended audience did not include the victim or target of the communication.
- The content of the communication did not obviously go beyond what could conceivably be tolerable or acceptable in an open and diverse society that upholds and respects freedom of expression.

It is suggested that the inclusion of the catch-all provision 'communications which do not fall into any of the categories above and fall to be considered separately because they may be considered grossly offensive, indecent, obscene or false' retains the lack of clarity in the law which is precisely the mischief which needs to be addressed. While it is acknowledged that there must be some room for manoeuvre in

---

49 Interim Guidelines on Prosecuting Cases Involving Communications Sent Via Social Media at [30].
50 The application of human rights law to social media related prosecutions is considered in depth in Chapter 2: Human Rights.
51 [1992] 14 EHRR 123.
52 See *Sunday Times v UK (no. 2)* [1992] 14 EHRR 123 at [50].
53 *DPP v Chambers* [2012] EWHC 2157.

144　*Communications-based offences*

determining when it may be appropriate to bring prosecutions and that it has been suggested that cases such as *Chambers* have fleshed out the requirements of this section, other cases such as *Woods*, delivered post *Chambers*, highlight that prosecutions may still be brought even when the level of offence, while perhaps distasteful in the extreme, should not engage the criminal law. As such, it is necessary to look to the European Courts and consider a refined model, based upon that EU and UK case analysis that could be adopted.

4.3.3.8 *Children and young people*

According to the CPS Interim Guidelines, the age and maturity of suspects should be given significant weight, particularly if they are under the age of 18. Children may not appreciate the potential harm and seriousness of their communications and a prosecution is rarely likely to be in the public interest. A good contrast to this is provided by the example of the 'Diouf Tweets'.[54] In *Diouf*, a young Leeds United fan became embroiled in a Twitter race row after making himself up to look like El Hadji Diouf. The 10-year-old became embroiled in an online race row after he blacked up to pose with his hero. The child then posted a series of pictures on his Twitter account provoking a backlash from users who said he was racist.

The fan met his favourite player outside Elland Road ahead of his team's home game against Bolton Wanderers on New Year's Day. He said Diouf and other Leeds players found the 'costume' – a blacked-up face and head, Leeds kit and white mohican – funny. As well as Diouf, the child also posed with Leeds United captain Lee Peltier and players Ryan Hall and Sam Byram. The child also said midfielder Paul Green said to him: 'How cool do you look?' The fan also posted pictures of him with Leeds United manager Neil Warnock, who he said found it funny, and posed with police officers outside the ground.

Ahead of the game he tweeted: 'Theres only 2 El-Hadji Dioufs . . . this is how I've come dressed today.' After the pictures were posted, Twitter users took to the social networking site accusing the child of racism. One user called @JacobKing7 wrote: 'This is a touching photo mixed with a touch of racism' and @greatbearbert wrote: 'Wrong on so many levels!' Some questioned why a child was allowed to wear black make-up in the first place, with others saying the picture made them uncomfortable. However, many people defended the child. Norwich City footballer Robert Snodgrass wrote: 'Can't a kid dress up as one of his favourite players these days without people moaning. We were kids once.'

The primary school child said he did not realize it would be offensive and did it as a tribute to his footballing hero. The boy's father was forced to take to his son's Twitter account to defend him from accusations of racism.

Although the issue was not pursued by the authorities, it did create a great deal of press and the 'real time issue' was compounded and carried on by the use of Twitter. The example also highlights the very great differences of opinion as to what amounts to racist content and gross offence, with player, police, and fan opinion at variance. Although in this example the issue did not escalate, there is no

---

54 See http://www.lawinsport.com/blog/laura-scaife/item/off-the-field-and-on-to-the-feed-tackling-racism-online-part-2.

guarantee that in the future this will always be the case, and as such there needs to be some sort of guidance for users as to when a joke may potentially become a criminal offence.[55]

4.3.4 *Interrelationship with the Human Rights Act and speech value*

4.3.4.1 *Introduction*

Much of the content posted on social networking sites is of low value and as such has not created a significant body of Strasbourg jurisprudence to guide prosecutors as to whether criminal prosecution is appropriate in a given case, as the cases are not cases specifically concerned with matters of 'public importance'. The reason for this is that the majority of case law decided under Article 10 of the ECHR has focused on 'high-value' speech that has contributed to discussions of matters that are in the public interest.

4.3.4.2 *Speech value and the European Court of Human Rights*

In determining the weight attached to the speech, the Strasbourg and the domestic courts have put varying categories of speech on a scale. At the pinnacle is political speech (*Campbell v MGN*[56]). Political speech is followed by artistic speech (*Muller v Switzerland*[57], *Otto Preminger v Austria*[58]) and then commercial expression (*Markt Intern v Germany*[59]). Towards the lower end of the spectrum comes celebrity gossip (*Campbell v MGN*[60]), beneath it pornography (*Belfast City Council v Miss Behavin' Ltd*[61]), then gratuitous personal attacks (*Gorelishvili v Georgia*[62]) and hate speech (*Lehideux and Isornia v France*[63], *Norwood v United Kingdom*[64]), the latter of which attracts little, if any, protection.

The court will also consider if the author has had an opportunity to prepare the content which they have written when considering if it is of high or low value and if there has been a 'possibility of reformulating, perfecting or retracting' the contents of a statement before it is placed into the public domain (*Fuentes Bobo v Spain*[65]). While this approach may afford some protection to communications that relate to politics or public affairs, it is unlikely to capture much of the everyday commentary posted online and as such these lower forms of speech will attract little protection. While

---

55 The culpability of minors online will be discussed in a future piece, as it is beyond the scope of this chapter, as it raises specific issues that require detailed analysis.
56 [2004] UKHL 22 at [148].
57 (1991) 13 EHRR 212.
58 (1995) 19 EHRR 34.
59 (1989) 12 EHRR 161.
60 [2004] UKHL 22 at [149].
61 [2007] UKHL 19 at [38].
62 (2009) 48 EHRR 36 at [40].
63 (1998) 5 BHRC 540 at [53].
64 (2004) 40 EHRR SE 111.
65 (2001) 31 EHRR 50 at [46].

146 *Communications-based offences*

lower-level, more informal postings akin to everyday conversations, unlike their higher-value counterparts, may not have been professionally produced, aimed at a wide audience, well resourced and researched in advance, it is suggested that they should attract some form of defence or mitigation. The findings of Lord Judge in chambers did do much to expand upon the value of freedom of expression but there is no guarantee that this approach will be adopted in future – it certainly wasn't in *Woods*. This is not to suggest that that such communications should not be allowed to be made unrestrained; indeed, the test put forward by David Allen allows for adequate safeguards in relation to the complainant's rights. However, by having regard to these considerations when formulating a judgment, the courts should be able to deliver sanctions that are appropriate in the case before them with a greater degree of uniformity and in the spirit of Article 10.

The Guidelines remind prosecutors that under the Malicious Communication Act 1988 and Communications Act 2003, the law only applies to communications of a *grossly* offensive nature. Reiterating the findings of the court in *DPP v Chambers*, the CPS state that this meant that a communication has to be more than simply offensive to be contrary to the criminal law. Just because the content expressed in the communication is in bad taste, controversial or unpopular, and may cause offence to individuals or a specific community, this is not in itself sufficient reason to engage the criminal law. As Lord Bingham made clear in *DPP v Collins*, there can be no yardstick of gross offensiveness, 'otherwise than by the application of reasonably enlightened, but not perfectionist, contemporary standards to the particular message sent in its particular context'.[66]

4.3.4.3 *Context and intent*

Context is important and prosecutors should have regard to the fact that the context in which interactive social media dialogue takes place is quite different to the context in which other communications take place. Access is ubiquitous and instantaneous. As Eady J stated in the civil case of *Smith v ADVFN*[67] in relation to comments on an internet bulletin board: '[they are] like contributions to a casual conversation (the analogy sometimes being drawn with people chatting in a bar) which people simply note before moving on; they are often uninhibited, casual and ill thought out; those who participate know this and expect a certain amount of repartee or "give and take".[68] Banter, jokes, and offensive comments are commonplace and often spontaneous, and communications intended for a few may reach millions of people.

The question the Director of Public Prosecutions (DPP) must answer is where to draw the line and to consider if a review of the entire area of communications-based offences is required in order to avoid an attack on free speech, by design or accident. It is suggested that the courts need to give consideration to the level of responsibility that can be expected of the author when they reach a larger audience than was necessarily intended. For less sophisticated users like Matthew Woods who post foolish things in jest while drunk without regard to consequence or those who post in haste

---

66 [2006] UKHL 40 at [9].
67 [2008] 1797 (QB) *Smith v ADFN* is also considered in Chapter 2: Human Rights.
68 [2008] EWHC 1797 (QB) at [14].

as a reflex response to a situation (e.g. a bad day at work), their level of culpability, and the sanctions which may follow, require careful consideration. It is suggested that the courts, like their Strasbourg counterparts, need to demonstrate a willingness to take into account the experience of the speaker; for example, an established broadcaster will be held to a higher standard than a member of the public (*R (Gaunt) v Office of Communications*[69]), something that is not considered in the draft CPS guidelines.

This is not to advocate that inexperience can act as a defence to making offensive statements where the intervention of the law should be considered. Rather, it is a case of a careful analysis guided by jurisprudence of where to draw the line. In order to balance the rights of others, special attention should be given to the expectations of the intended audience and also the likely attention that the comment by the very nature of the topic discussed will attract. The public should not be prevented from discussing matters of interest or expressing opinions which if shared in a bistro or pub would pass by without much further thought, regardless of the level of taste (or lack thereof).

4.3.5 *Cases decided after the implementation of the Guidelines*

4.3.5.1 *Isabella Sorley and John Nimmo*[70]

In July 2013, Caroline Criado-Perez, the writer and feminist campaigner behind the push to feature the image of Jane Austen on banknotes, received threats via Twitter to rape and kill her. Mr Nimmo had also targeted Stella Creasy, Labour MP for Walthamstow, with the message 'The things I cud do to u (smiley face)' and called her 'Dumb blond . . .' followed by an offensive word.

Isabella Sorley and John Nimmo pleaded guilty to sending by means of a public electronic communications network messages that were menacing in character, contrary to section 127(1)(a) CA 2003. It was established that Mr Nimmo had sent 20 tweets to one of the women and four tweets to the other, using six separate Twitter accounts. Ms Sorley was arrested on 22 October at home after officers identified her as responsible for setting up three anonymous Twitter accounts and sending six tweets to one of the women, all sent on 30 July.

Baljit Ubhey, Chief Crown Prosecutor for CPS London, said that the CPS had reviewed the case in accordance with the Code for Crown Prosecutors and guidelines issued by the Director of Public Prosecutions on prosecuting cases involving communications sent via social media and had decided to proceed with prosecution. The CPS noted that that there was insufficient evidence to support a prosecution in respect of one suspect, whom it was alleged also sent offensive messages to Ms Criado-Perez, and advised the police that no further action should be taken as the

---

69 [2011] EWCA Civ 692 at [43].

70 (Unreported) Westminster Magistrates Court 24 January 2014; J. Cockerell (2014). 'Twitter "trolls" Isabella Sorley and John Nimmo jailed for abusing feminist campaigner Caroline Criado-Perez', *The Independent*, 24 January [http://www.independent.co.uk/news/uk/crime/twitter-trolls-isabella-sorley-and-john-nimmo-jailed-for-abusing-feminist-campaigner-caroline-criadoperez-9083829.html].

148 *Communications-based offences*

high threshold for prosecution had not been met. However, an exploration of the threshold was disappointingly not explored in the CPS's statement, or the reasons why it had not been met.

In respect of one other suspect, who allegedly sent offensive messages to Stella Creasy MP, the CPS determined that although there was sufficient evidence that an offence had been committed under section 127 of the Communications Act 2003, it would not be in the public interest to prosecute. The CPS said that they had applied the DPP's guidelines and had paid particular regard to the young age and personal circumstances of the suspect when determining if it was in the pubic interest to pursue a prosecution.

Interestingly and once again demonstrating the close link with human rights, Baljit Ubhey reminded individuals that as criminal proceedings against both defendants would then be commenced, they had a right to a fair trial.[71] The CPS emphasised that it is extremely important that there should be no reporting, commentary or sharing of information online that could in any way prejudice the proceedings. In light of this statement, individuals who chose to ignore the CPS's stance would leave themselves open to liability under the Contempt of Court Act 1981. Issues in relation to the Contempt of Court Act 1981 with regard to postings on social networking sites are considered in Chapter 11: Contempt of Court.

4.3.5.2 *Issues of anonymity*

This case is not just interesting in terms of how prosecutions are being approached post CPS Guidelines but also because of its potential privacy implications, as the postings were made from anonymous accounts. BBC *Newsnight* producer Mike Deri Smith uncovered the identity of John Nimmo after monitoring the rape and death threats sent on Twitter over the summer. He found that one anonymous person was using multiple accounts to send abusive tweets and spoke to the individual privately over the course of a few hours. After gaining his confidence, he eventually gave up his Playstation user name, which enabled *Newsnight* to trace him to a Facebook account that identified him as John Nimmo of South Shields. *Newsnight* then handed the material to Northumbria Police. Scotland Yard said the evidence demonstrated Nimmo 'acted to cover his identity, anonymously sending messages that were deliberately designed to cause fear and apprehension'. It added that Sorley's actions were 'deliberate, planned and deliberately worded to create fear and a credible menace'.

In evidential terms, the identity of Nimmo was pieced together through the use of private messaging, which raises privacy implications, as Nimmo in his private messages may have thought that they were protected by a reasonable expectation of privacy since they were not posted directly on his Twitter feed.

Although arguably the right outcome was achieved in *Nimmo*, the residual issues concerning criminal procedure and privacy implications highlight the inherent weakness in the current models adopted by the CPS and the need for much clearer guidance as to how content sources online can be evidenced in criminal proceedings

---

71 For a discussion of the interaction, see Article 6 ECHR, Right to a Fair Trial (see Chapter 2: Human Rights).

Communications Act 2003   149

and how they can be used to identity defendants without infringing their privacy rights.

4.3.5.3 *Private entrapment*

As seen in *Nimmo*, private individuals can become involved in the investigation process when tracking down offenders and provides them with a unique opportunity to investigate or expose criminal conduct.[72] *Nimmo* represents just one example of such detection. Vincent Collymore was convicted of assault after being detected through Facebook by the victim who knew only Collymore's nickname and some nightclubs he frequented.[73] In another example, members of the 'Parson Cross Crew' gang in Sheffield were convicted of firearms offences after a member of the public found their pictures posing with the weapons on social networking sites[74] and exposed them anonymously by setting up a Facebook page entitled 'The Parson Cross Crew Named and Shamed'.[75]

4.3.5.3.1 COMPARISON WITH THE USA

In the USA, individuals have set up fake profiles to assist in the law enforcement process (e.g. posing as children in sex offender investigations). The fake account holder does not 'initiate contact with the [target]; all communications begins with the offender [*sic*]' and they never 'instigate lewd conversations or talks of sexual meetings'.[76] If the content of the postings or communications cross an agreed-upon threshold such as attempting to meet, 'Perverted Justice' alerts law enforcement agents.

Social media has made this type of public involvement in criminal investigations far easier and more risk-free. It often involves no more than simply pressing the 'report abuse' button on the social networking site,[77] a process that has been criticised for not always resulting in the reporting of criminal activity to police.[78]

There are, however, clear dangers. Individuals can 'take the law into their own hands' and do so with relative impunity by setting up fake profiles on social networking sites. Vigilantism on social networking sites could be a sinister phenomenon with

---

72 See http://www.lawtimesnews.com/200911025723/Headline-News/Social-media-tripping-up-litigants [accessed 26 April 2012] and http://www.journal-news.net/page/content.detail/id/525232.html [accessed 26 April 2012].

73 See http://www.portsmouth.co.uk/newshome/Victim-tracked-his-attacker-down.5714581.jp [accessed 26 April 2012].

74 Seehttp://www.telegraph.co.uk/news/uknews/6149807/Armed-gang-jailed-after-being-named-and-shamed-on-Facebook.html [accessed 26 April 2012].

75 Majid Khan was also subjected to this pro active 'policing' by members of the public when it was reported to the police that his public profile contained pictures of him posing with firearms; see http://news.sky.com/skynews/Home/UK-News/Facebook-Photo-Shoot-Majid-Khan-Jailed-For-For-Five-Years-For-Posing-With-Gun-On-Facebook [accessed 26 April 2012].

76 See http://www.officer.com/publication/article.jsp?pubId=1&id=35694 [accessed 26 April 2012].

77 See, for example, https://www.facebook.com/clickceop?sk=app_132438026779126 [accessed 26 April 2012].

78 See http://www.smh.com.au/technology/facebook-failed-to-tell-police-about-paedophile-porn-ring-20100826-13ual.html [accessed 26 April 2012].

150   *Communications-based offences*

people's reputations very easily destroyed by malicious or misguided posts. Such activity could lead to liability for defamation, or if performed with relevant *mens rea*, criminal liability under the Computer Misuse Act 1990, or for other serious crimes such as blackmail.

4.3.5.3.2 ADMISSIBILITY OF EVIDENCE

In addition to the privacy and human rights concerns that such behaviour raises, there is an additional danger that the value of such evidence may be compromised if law enforcement agencies seek to rely on it at trial. Unlike the police, who require authorization under the Regulation of Investigatory Powers Act 2000, the private sleuth is unregulated in what he or she says, is not investigating with a view to gathering admissible evidence, and is untrained and unaware of the limits of engagement.[79]

Hofmeyr[80] notes that the courts accept that the absence of State involvement in private entrapment means that the rule of law and fundamental rights are not undermined. This leads to a greater judicial reluctance to exercise the abuse of process jurisdiction,[81] and is therefore forced back on an application under section 78 of the Police and Criminal Evidence Act 1984 (PACE 1984).

Section 78 PACE 1984 states that unfair evidence may be excluded in any proceedings as the court may refuse to allow evidence on which the prosecution proposes to rely if it appears to the court that, having regard to all the circumstances, including the circumstances in which the evidence was obtained, the admission of the evidence would have such an adverse effect on the fairness of the proceedings that the court ought not to admit it (s 78 (1)). Nothing in section 78 shall prejudice any rule of law requiring a court to exclude evidence (s 78(2)).

Although section 78 has a potentially wide scope, its application has been rare and this has been the case also for applications concerning information obtained via private entrapment. In *Smurthwaite*,[82] it was put to the court that police officers incited the accused to organize the murder of his wife, and that they had acted as agent provocateurs. The exclusionary rule was applied narrowly. The court delivered six points on which discretion with regards to entrapment, and a conclusion on admissibility should be based upon:

- Whether the undercover officer was acting as an agent provocateur in the sense that he was enticing the accused to commit an offence he would not otherwise have committed;
- The nature of any entrapment;
- Whether the evidence consists of admissions to a completed offence or relates to the actual commission of an offence;
- How active or passive the officer's role was in obtaining the evidence;

---

79 The potential dangers are evidenced in the following transcript from a UK-based investigation [http://www.answers.uk.com/services/chatscript.htm; accessed 26 April 2012].
80 K. Hofmeyr, 'The problem of private entrapment' [2006] Crim LR 319; forming part of a discussion of the *Loosley Judgment* [2001] UKHL 53, *Attorney General's Reference (No. 3 of 2000)*, which dealt with entrapment and the rule of law.
81 Sang [1980] AC 402.
82 *Smurthwaite* [1994] 1 All ER 898.

Communications Act 2003 151

- Whether there is an unassailable record of what occurred or whether it is strongly corroborated;
- Whether the officer abused his (undercover) role to ask questions which ought properly to have been asked as a police officer in accordance with the PACE Codes.

These guidelines were applied narrowly in *Shannon*, with Choo[83] observing that the Court of Appeal suggested that a section 78 application 'would principally turn'[84] upon whether there was actual instigation or incitement to commit the crime. The judgment also stressed that 'the principal focus of the judge's attention must be upon the procedural fairness of the proceedings, [and] the nature and reliability of the prosecution evidence'.[85] Emphasis on reliability was endorsed by the House of Lords in *Looseley*, being expressly cited by Lords Hoffmann[86] and Hutton.[87] Ormerod,[88] along with other commentators,[89] suggests that a defendant facing private entrapment evidence from social networking sites would face greater difficulty in excluding it than police evidence. Where social media evidence is produced, it will normally include a complete record of the dialogue, and Ormerod envisages that the 'courts would be very reluctant to exclude evidence, particularly of serious crimes such as child pornography and sexual offences, unless the investigator has offered overbearing inducements'.[90]

Although Hofmeyr suggested that a stay ought not to apply in private entrapment cases, defence advocates may decide to draw on the abuse of process jurisprudence in order to inform their section 78 PACE arguments. It has been suggested by Ormerod that emphasis would be placed on considerations such as private investigations undermining the 'integrity of the criminal justice system',[91] as well as those listed by Lord Nicholls (for example, whether the police presented the defendant with an 'unexceptional opportunity'[92]) in *Smurthwaite*, rather than simply on an after-the-event assessment of reliability.

---

83 Andrew Choo (2009) *Evidence.* Oxford: Oxford University Press, p. 193.

84 Shannon [2001] 1 WLR 51 at [21] and see also [43].

85 Shannon [2001] 1 WLR 51 at [38] and see also [39].

86 *Attorney General's Reference (No. 3 of 2000)* [2001] UKHL 53 at [43].

87 *Attorney General's Reference (No. 3 of 2000)* [2001] UKHL 53 at [103]. Lord Nicholls, however, seemed to have a different interpretation: 'Most recently in *R v Shannon* [2001] 1 WLR 51, 68, para 39, Potter LJ, as I read his judgment, accepted that evidence may properly be excluded when the behaviour of the police or prosecuting authority has been such as to justify a stay on grounds of abuse of process.' At [12]. It is also of note that Shannon's complaint to the European Court of Human Rights was declared inadmissible.

88 D. Ormerod and M. O'Floinn, 'Social networking sites, RIPA and criminal investigations' [2011] Crim LR, Issue 10.

89 See, for example, D. Sleight, 'Entrapment' (2010) 107(25) LSG 22.

90 D. Ormerod and M. O'Floinn, 'Social networking sites, RIPA and criminal investigations' [2011] Crim LR, Issue 10.

91 *Attorney General's Reference (No. 3 of 2000)* [2001] UKHL 53 at [36], per Lord Hoffman.

92 *Attorney General's Reference (No. 3 of 2000)* [2001] UKHL 53 at [23], per Lord Nicholls.

4.3.6 Summary diagrams of CPS Guidelines

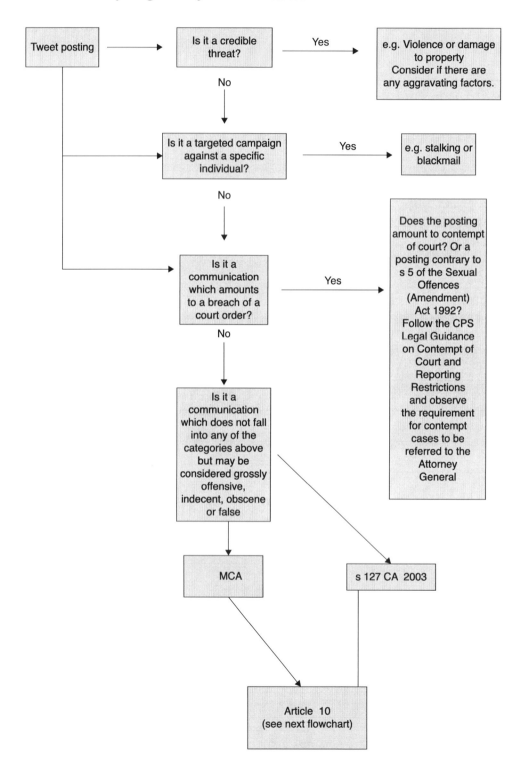

4.3.7 *Refining the CPS model*

4.3.7.1 *A two-tier approach*

In proposing a solution to the problems with the current system that recent cases have highlighted, the Crown Prosecution Service has responded by stating that:

> if the fundamental right to free speech is to be respected, the threshold for criminal prosecution has to be a high one and a prosecution has to be required in the public interest . . . the emerging thinking is that it might be sensible to divide and separate cases where there's a campaign of harassment, [or] cases where there's a credible and general threat, and prosecute in those sorts of cases and put in another category communications which are, as it were, merely offensive or grossly offensive.

However, the CPS have acknowledged that this 'doesn't mean the second category are ring-fenced from prosecution, but it does I think enable us to think of that group in a slightly different way'. In determining which grouping those charged with communications-based offences fall into, it is suggested that the word 'menacing' must be taken to mean more than the words used in section 127(2) – 'annoyance, inconvenience or needless anxiety' – and encompass the common usage definition as 'as threatening harm' (support for this can be found in the judgments of *R v Lawrence, R v Pomroy*[93] and *Treacy v DPP*[94]).

If a two-tier approach is to be considered, then there needs to be some sort of threshold test to ensure that section 127(1) CA 2003 is applied only to comments of a very serious nature. As discussed above, there is no requirement for there to be any recipient of a message, thus consideration needs to be given as to what objective standards may apply. In this regard, the case law relating to blackmail may offer valuable insight:

4.3.7.2 *The Theft Act 1988*

Under section 21(1) of the Theft Act 1968, the word 'menaces' appears, though it is not defined. However, in *Thorne v Motor Trade Association,*[95] it was determined that the word 'menace' should be liberally construed and not limited to threats of violence, but include threats of any action detrimental to or unpleasant to the person addressed. It may also include a warning that in certain events such action is intended.

In *R v Clear,*[96] it was suggested that in order to constitute 'menaces' the threats or conduct of the defendant must be of such a nature and extent that the mind of an ordinary person of normal stability and courage might be influenced or made apprehensive so as to accede unwillingly to the demand. Case law suggests that the term

---

93 (1971) 57 Cr App Rep 64, CA.
94 [1971] AC 537 at 565, 55 Cr App Rep 113 at [146], HL.
95 [1937] AC 797.
96 [1968] 1 QB 670, 52 Cr App Rep 58, CA.

154 *Communications-based offences*

'an ordinary person of normal stability and courage' in this context should be interpreted literally (see *R v Tomlinson,* [97] *R v Boyle, R v Merchant*[98]).

In *Garwood,* however, the court did acknowledge that there are two occasions where the judge may need to spell out the meaning of 'menaces':

- where, on the facts known to the defendant, his threats might have affected the mind of an ordinary person of normal stability, although they did not affect the addressee, the jury should be told that they would amount to menaces; and
- where, although they would not have affected the mind of a person of normal stability, the threats affected the mind of the victim and if the defendant was aware of the likely effect of his actions on the victim, e.g. because he knew of some unusual susceptibility on the victim's part (supporting *DPP v Collins* and suggested as a preferred response to the Ched Evans tweets).

In terms of the formulation of this new test, in his article 'The "Twitter Joke Trial" returns to the High Court', David Allen[99] suggests that the following should apply:

Actus reus

i   a person sends a message or other matter;
ii by means of a public electronic communications network;
iii which is a threat of such a nature and extent that the mind of an ordinary person of normal stability and courage might be influenced or made apprehensive; and:

Mens rea

iv The person sending the message or other matter intends to threaten the person to whom the message or other matter is intended to or is likely to be conveyed.

For cases that fall into the lower category of culpability, the communications-based offences guidelines as they presently stand already require the court to give consideration to such ancillary orders. As such, the regulation and sanction of comments made via social media channels for matters not caught within the higher tier could encompass other forms of orders as set out in the Magistrates' Court Sentencing Guidelines, with examples including Anti-Social Behaviour Orders.[100]
In *Daley,* the CPS stated:

> this is not just a matter for prosecutors. Social media is a new and emerging phenomenon raising difficult issues of principle, which have to be confronted not

---

97 [1895] 1 QB 706 at [710], CCR, per Wills J.
98 [1914] 3 KB 339, CCA.
99 D. Allen (2012). 'The "Twitter Joke Trial" returns to the High Court: Lord Chief Justice to preside over latest appeal in Chambers v Director of Public Prosecutions', *New Statesman,* 22 June [http://www.newstatesman.com/blogs/david-allen-green/2012/06/twitter-joke-trial-david-allen-green].
100 A copy of the magistrates' guidelines is available at: http://www.northants.police.uk/files/linked/WCU/Magistrate%20Sentencing%20Guidelines.pdf.

only by prosecutors but also by others including the police, the courts and service providers. The fact that offensive remarks may not warrant a full criminal prosecution does not necessarily mean that no action should be taken. In my view, the time has come for an informed debate about the boundaries of free speech in an age of social media.[101]

What is clear is that the CPS will need to carefully consider how to afford the correct weight to an individual's right to freedom of expression and address the potential risk that by self-regulating, the private body will be able to decide what standards they feel apply in relation to taking decisions over content. While the immediate danger may appear that the regulators will not do enough to police their sites, there is a converse risk that if the platform providers or search engines are quick to respond to complaints, this may create a feeling among users that too little weight is being afforded to the protection of an individual's expression and simply moderate site content because there has been an open objection to it. This risk could be avoided by a requirement that a court order be obtained to establish some element of illegality or evidence of harm. However, by doing so, the benchmark of demonstrating that harm had been caused could be set too high for most complainants to make use of it given factors such as the resources required to fund such an order.

4.3.8 *The role of platform providers*

4.3.8.1 *Leveson*

During the course of the Leveson Inquiry, a number of website operators and micro site platforms were called to give evidence, most notably Twitter, Google, and Facebook. A number of questions were raised in relation to the activities of the sites. Twitter in particular became a focus of interest to the Leveson Inquiry because of the role played by users in identifying individuals who had been the subject of privacy injunctions. Twitter allows members to operate anonymously, or under a pseudonym,[102] and it is also possible that Twitter as the operator may itself not know the real identity of any member.[103] However, Twitter told the Inquiry that its rules forbid members from using the service for any unlawful purpose,[104] and any material that is found by the company to contravene that policy can be taken down or removed.[105]

4.3.8.2 *Public electronic communications network*

While a review of the present legal position relating to communications-based offences has been put forward by the UK regulator, social media channel representatives have also been invited to consult on the proposed changes as the CPS considers if such

---

101 See http://blog.cps.gov.uk/2012/09/dpp-statement-on-tom-daley-case-and-social-media-prosecutions. html.
102 Colin Crowell, http://www.levesoninquiry.org.uk/wp-content/uploads/2012/02/Transcript-of-Morning-Hearing-7-February-2012.pdf, p. 94, lines 6–7.
103 Ibid., p. 98, lines 22–23.
104 Ibid., p. 96, lines 22–25.
105 Ibid., p. 98, lines 6–9.

156 *Communications-based offences*

mediums should be asked to enforce swifter moderation and removal of offensive content.

In *DPP v Chambers*, a ground-breaking element of the Court of Appeal's analysis came from their finding that the internet itself constitutes a public network, which may have far-reaching applications for the future of what may be caught within the scope of potential prosecutions. In her judgment in the Crown Court, Judge Davies addressed this issue when rejecting a submission that there was 'no case' for the appellant to answer. She said:

> the 'Twitter' website although privately owned cannot, as we understand it, operate save through the internet, which is plainly a public electronic network provided for the public and paid for by the public through the various service providers we are all familiar with . . . The internet is widely available to the public and funded by the public and without it facilities such as 'Twitter' would not exist. The fact that it is a private company in our view is irrelevant; the mechanism by which it was sent was a public electronic network and within the statutory definition . . . 'Twitter', as we all know is widely used by individuals and organizations to disseminate and receive information. In our judgment, it is inconceivable that grossly offensive, indecent, obscene or menacing messages sent in this way would not be potentially unlawful.[106]

In defining the internet thus, the Court stated that the internet 'is plainly a public electronic communications network provided for the public and paid for by the public through the various service providers we are all familiar with', and that 'potential recipients of the message were the public as a whole, consisting of all sections of society'.[107]

Judge Davies' reasoning, with which the court agreed, derived from an analysis of the internet's network infrastructure as a series of links. These links cover networks of networks and services linking individuals, service providers, network providers, platform providers, and content providers.

However, if, as the court did in *Chambers*, these groupings of networks are considered as a single entity, then it has the potential to cast a net over networks previously considered 'private' or 'bespoke'. Such examples could include networks unavailable *to* the public that are nevertheless able to connect *with* the public as well as their supporting platforms and applications (e.g. Facebook and Twitter). However, the definition of a 'public electronic communications network' is derived from an EU concept developed for the purposes of regulation. The European Framework for Electronic Communications is designed around the distinction between public and private networks and services. The former attracts comprehensive regulation which non-public networks are not required to conform to, such as rights and obligations to negotiate interconnection with other public network providers. The similar term 'public communications network' entails further requirements to ensure the availability of the public network, such as taking necessary measures to maintain the perpetual effective functioning of the network and disaster plans for system breakdowns.

---

106 Reproduced [2006] UKHL 40 at [23].
107 [2006] UKHL 40 at [24].

Stringent guidelines also apply with regard to the protection of consumers, including the obligation to publish quality of service information if instructed to do so by Ofcom and offering contracts with specified minimum terms to end-users. Most significantly in terms of the future regulation of social media sites and the role of platform providers, there are additional requirements with regards to data retention and lawful intercept requirements, such as the relevant government authorities requiring operators of public networks to retain communications data relating to the traffic passing over its network and information about subscribers to be made available to authorities on request. A public network provider may also be instructed to maintain the capability to intercept communications over its network at the direction of the government.

By describing and defining the internet as a 'public electronic communications network', the judgment appears to cast a net over a wide range of network and service providers within the scope of EU and UK communications law. It leaves open the possibility, for example, that Twitter could be bound by the above regulatory requirements, which could potentially place significant burdens on the operators of such sites in the future. While these points have faint echoes of the Chinese model, the potential implications of the judgment of the divisional court on the future landscape of policing the online environment remains to be seen, as they have not as of yet received positive or negative judicial treatment.

Twitter, for example, already has a policy in relation to illegal content. Under point 8 of its terms, 'Restrictions on Content and Use of the Services',[108] Twitter states that it operates its site in a way that satisfies applicable laws and regulations. While the immediate danger may appear that the regulators will not do enough to police their sites, there is a converse risk that if the platform providers or search engines are quick to respond to complaints, this may create a feeling among users that too little weight is being afforded to the protection of an individual's expression and simply moderate site content because there has been an open objection to it. This has become a frequent criticism in relation to the Google judgment, conferring the 'right to be forgotten' (discussed in depth in Chapter 14: Data Protection). Search engines currently have the sole discretion to decide whether to accept an individual's claim of a right to be forgotten. This right, established in the Court of Justice of European Union's ruling in Case C-131/12 (*Google Spain SL, Google Inc. v Agencia Española de Protección de Datos*), which allows individuals to have inadequate, irrelevant or excessive information pertaining to themselves removed from online search results. This risk could be avoided in relation to criminal proceedings by a requirement that a court order be obtained to establish some element of illegality or evidence of harm when applying to a social media site to have content removed.

4.3.8.3 *France: #unbonjuif*

The issue of social networking providers' role as judge and jury and the censorship issues this raises is highlighted in the example that follows. The Union of French Jewish Students (UEJF) pursued a claim against Twitter for nearly $50 million after it refused to turn over the names of people who had tweeted racist and anti-Semitic

---

108 See http://twitter.com/tos.

158 *Communications-based offences*

remarks, as ruled by a French court. The case revolved around two hashtags — #unbonjuif (translation: 'a good Jew') and #UnJuifMort (translation: 'a dead Jew'), which became the third-most popular on the site in October. French Twitter presence is growing steadily, with 5.5 million users, according to French data analysts. comScore. Around 500 million tweets are sent each day across the world. Twitter is based in the United States and used the First Amendment to the United States Constitution as an argument against releasing names.

In October 2012, Twitter agreed to remove the offensive hashtags. But its lawyer, Alexandra Neri, told the court that users' details would not be handed over. She said Twitter's data on users was collected and stocked in California and therefore French law could not be applied. She said the only way the site could be forced to hand over details would be if the French justice system appealed to American judges to push for the data. Twitter stated: 'we're not fleeing our responsibility. Our concern is not to violate American law in cooperating with the French justice system. Our data is stored in the US, so we must obey the rule of law in that country,' she said, adding that Twitter had no obligation to hand over data in France.[109]

The Parisian Circuit Court ruled against Twitter. The UEJF considered that the fine was not enough, with its President Jonathon Hayoun stating: '[Twitter] is making itself an accomplice and offering a highway for racists and anti-Semites'. The debate came after a spate of offensive hash tags became among the most popular ones used in France in recent months. These included #SiMonFilsEstGay (translation: 'If my son was gay') – in which users speculated on the worst things they would inflict on a gay relative – #SiMaFilleRameneUnNoir (translation: 'If my daughter brings home a black man'), and #SiJetaisNazi (translation: 'If I were a Nazi').

The ongoing row over offensive tweets has highlighted the gap between the American right to freedom of expression enjoyed by the San Francisco-based site, which is not responsible for content, and European laws on hate speech. Fleur Pellerin, Minister for the Digital Economy in France, stated that because Twitter was opening an office in France and seeking to establish itself in Europe, 'it's in their interest to adapt to the legal, philosophical and ethical culture of the countries in which they're seeking to develop'. She said the French Government was in 'permanent' discussion with Twitter, which was receptive to its ideas. 'They know that they have to adapt to other cultures, legal [systems] and to appreciate the fundamental freedoms of the countries where they operate and I think they're open to discussion.'[110]

Twitter's contractual position with its users, however, remains that it does not moderate content. However, it does have a procedure to flag up potential child abuse, which will be instantly removed and it can also suspend accounts considered illegal or in breach of its rules. French anti-racist associations have demanded Twitter extend its policy to allow users to flag up and seek removal of any tweets considered to be an apology for crimes against humanity or incitement to racial hatred.

---

109 A. Chrisafis (2013) 'Twitter under fire in France over offensive hashtags', *The Guardian*, 9 January [http://www.theguardian.com/technology/2013/jan/09/twitter-france-offensive-hashtags].
110 Ibid.

4.3.8.4 *Germany: Besseres-Hannover- @hannoverticker*

Twitter adopted a similar approach to #unbonjuif in Besseres-Hannover. However, the German example is also interesting in terms of the statements made by Twitter in relation to free speech. Twitter blocked the account of a neo-Nazi group accused of inciting hatred towards foreigners. The San Francisco-based company said it had used a device developed earlier this year to monitor content. 'We announced the ability to withhold content back in Jan,' Twitter's lawyer, Alex Macgillivray, tweeted. 'We're using it now for the first time re: a group deemed illegal in Germany.'

The move came after an investigation into about 20 members of the neo-Nazi group in Lower Saxony, northern Germany, after they were charged with inciting racial hatred and forming a criminal organization. The group was banned last month by the State's interior ministry. In particular, the group, which is estimated to have around 40 active members, stands accused of being behind a threatening video that was sent to the social affairs minister of Lower Saxony, Aygül Özkan.

Mr Macgillivray posted a link to the letter the firm received from German police requesting Twitter to close the account immediately and without opening a replacement account. In a further tweet he wrote that the company aimed to comply with the law as well as retaining its status as a platform for free speech, and 'Never want to withhold content; good to have tools to do it narrowly & transparently'.[111]

Besseres-Hannover had been watched by the authorities for four years after drawing attention to itself through various anti-foreigner campaigns. Its account, @hannoverticker now carries the notice 'withheld'. Dirk Hensen, a Twitter spokesman, said the contents of Besseres-Hannover tweets were still available outside Germany because the German police did not have the jurisdiction to request bans overseas. The group's website has also been blocked.

4.3.8.5 *Facebook Community Standards*

Facebook, under its Community Standards,[112] offers the following terms in relation to offensive speech:

> Ads, or categories of ads, that receive a significant amount of negative user feedback, or are otherwise deemed to violate our community standards, are prohibited and may be removed. In all cases, Facebook reserves the right in its sole discretion to determine whether particular content is in violation of our community standards.

In relation to hate speech, there are additional rules:

> Ads may not contain 'hate speech,' whether directed at an individual or a group, based on membership within certain categories. These categories include, but are not limited to, race, sex, creed, national origin, religious affiliation, marital status, sexual orientation, gender identity, or language.[113]

---

111 'Twitter blocks neo-Nazi account to users in Germany' [http://www.bbc.co.uk/news/technology-19988662], 18 October 2012.

112 See https://www.facebook.com/communitystandards [accessed 15 April 2013].

113 See http://www.facebook.com/ad_guidelines.phpaccessed [accessed 15 April 2013].

160 *Communications-based offences*

The community standards clarify this by stating:

> Facebook does not permit hate speech, but distinguishes between serious and humorous speech. While we encourage you to challenge ideas, institutions, events, and practices, we do not permit individuals or groups to attack others based on their race, ethnicity, national origin, religion, sex, gender, sexual orientation, disability or medical condition.

Interestingly, however, the Community Standards balance the rights of others to their freedom of expression by stating that:

> If you see something on Facebook that you believe violates our terms, you should report it to us. Please keep in mind that reporting a piece of content does not guarantee that it will be removed from the site. Because of the diversity of our community, it's possible that something could be disagreeable or disturbing to you without meeting the criteria for being removed or blocked. For this reason, we also offer personal controls over what you see, such as the ability to hide or quietly cut ties with people, Pages, or applications that offend you.[114]

4.3.9 *Censorship and monitoring*

4.3.9.1 *Interrelationship with human rights*

As noted in Chapter 2: Human Rights, freedom of expression is a protected category and interference with it is only legally acceptable in limited circumstances and for legitimate means. However, even if this delicate balancing act is achieved, it is questionable if any computer system could technically effectively filter tweets for hate speech. Even when tweets are detected, they must be considered by legal specialists before a decision can be taken. In applying this human element, however, there is a danger that this in itself constitutes an interference with freedom of expression and that the legal personality in the best placed position to determine if a claim should be brought remains that person who objects to it. The issues raised in relation to censorship are best examined by reference to legal models outside of the EU or America to see how censorship is approached and if any commonalities with the EU and US models exist.

4.3.9.2 *China*

In China,[115] it has been suggested that government authorities and internet companies such as Sina Corp have historically monitored and censored what people say online,

---

114 See https://www.facebook.com/communitystandards [accessed 15 April 2013].

115 A full discussion of the law in China is beyond the scope of this Handbook. An excellent discussion of the application of Chinese law to the internet is provided by Anne S.Y. Cheung, in her article 'The business of governance: China's legislation on content regulation in cyberspace', *Journal of International Law and Politics*, 38(1/2): 1–37.

but the government has now passed these measures into law.[116] In June 2012, China's State Council Information Office posted a Chinese-language draft of its revised internet law. The draft was entitled 'Methods for Governance of Internet Information Services' and is broader in scope than the existing legal position. The law's preamble now lists 'protecting national safety and public interest' as one of its objectives, and adds that which 'incites illegal gatherings' to the category of illegal speech.

The regulations recently introduced came against a backdrop of control over postings about politically sensitive topics like human rights and elite politics, and popular foreign sites Facebook, Twitter, and Google-owned YouTube are blocked or are subject to censorship. The government began forcing users of Sina's wildly successful Weibo micro-blogging platform to register their real names. The restrictions also came after a series of corruption scandals among lower-level officials exposed by internet users.

The current law already assigns criminal liability to any service providers, broadly defined, who disseminate speech fitting any one of nine categories of harm,[117] which includes information that:

- is contrary to the basic principles that are laid down in the Constitution, laws or administration regulations;
- is seditious to the ruling regime of the State or the system of socialism;
- subverts State power or sabotages the unity of the State;
- incites ethnic hostility or racial discrimination, or disrupts racial unity;
- spreads rumours or disrupts social order;
- propagates feudal superstitions; disseminates obscenity, pornography or gambling; incites violence, murder or terror; instigates others to commit offences;
- publicly insults or defames others;
- harms the reputation or interests of the State; or
- has content prohibited by laws or administrative regulations.

The new rules state that: 'service providers are required to instantly stop the transmission of illegal information once it is spotted and take relevant measures, including removing the information and saving records, before reporting to supervisory authorities'.

The rules will see tighter regulatory control sanctioning the deletion of posts or pages that are deemed to contain 'illegal' information, requiring service providers to hand over such information to the authorities.

4.3.9.3 *Real-name requirement*

The new regulations, announced by the official Xinhua news agency, also require internet users to register with their real names when signing up with network providers.

---

116 A copy of the draft Regulations is currently only available in Chinese [http://www.scio.gov.cn/zxbd/zcfg/201206/t1169111.htm].

117 For an overview of the regulatory bodies, the relevant statutes, and classification of information, see generally H.L. Fu and Richard Cullen (1996) *Media Law in the PRC*. Hong Kong: Asia Law & Practice Publishing.

162 *Communications-based offences*

Strictly speaking, the real-name requirement extends to all 'those who provide service allowing internet users to publish information to the public'. This could include social networks, sites that allow comments on their articles, or any platform that allows for user-generated content to be made publicly available.

The draft law may also make life harder for internet platforms in other ways. It requires more forms, more approvals, and more registrations. The draft law requires that sites store as few as six and as many as twelve months' worth of their activity in daily logs available for inspection, whereas current law requires 60 days' worth. It also explicitly assigns personal liability to offenders in a way the current law does not.

The Chinese Government says that introducing additional rules will assist in the prevention of the dissemination of malicious and anonymous accusations online, the spreading of pornography, and publication of unfounded rumours. Li Fei, deputy head of China's Parliament's Legislative Affairs Committee, said the new rules did not mean people needed to worry about being unable to report corruption online and that 'when people exercise their rights, including the right to use the internet, they must do so in accordance with the law and constitution, and not harm the legal rights of the state, society . . . or other citizens'.

4.3.9.4 *South Korea*

The position in China can be contrasted with that in South Korea. South Korea's online 'real-name' statute – Article 44-5 of the Act on Promotion of Information and Communications Network Utilization and Data Protection, etc. (ICN Act 2007) – was enacted in 2007 in response to such things as posted internet comments describing fictitious sex scandals and plastic surgery operations concerning celebrities, and a number of suicides of celebrities. It required large-scale portal sites with more than 100,000 visitors on average a day to record the real name identities of visitors posting comments, usually via the poster's resident registration number (RRN). A series of security breaches resulting in leaks of personal data concerning millions of South Koreans from those websites that were required to adopt real-name policy also occurred over the last couple of years.

In August 2012, South Korea's Constitutional Court unanimously held that the 'real-name' statute was unconstitutional because the public gains achieved had not been substantial enough to justify restrictions on individuals' rights to free speech.[118] The case decided by the court was brought by individuals who were required to provide their real names in order to make postings and also by an online internet publisher required by the law to verify the names of those posting.

The court ruled, in part, that the confirmation of identity requirement is unconstitutional since:

- Other less restrictive means were available to identify those that violated the rights of others;
- Little evidence existed establishing that the RNN led to a substantial reduction in the quantity of illegal information online; and
- There was a substantial risk that personal information of users could be misused.

118 Case No. 2010 HunMa 47.

Legislative reform has occurred in parallel. Under Korea's new Personal Information Protection Act of 2011, unique identifiers including the RRN may not be processed without consent and explicit legislative approval. Alternative means of identification other than the RRN must now be provided by processors where individuals are subscribing to web-based services. It should be noted that the vast majority of sites have chosen to maintain, voluntarily, the real-name verification system. A key point to note is that although restrictions are being applied to the content uploaded on sites and the platform providers having to comply more with the authorities, the impact is still upon the individual, being required to confirm their identity, etc. It could be suggested that in order to circumvent jurisdiction arguments and complex referring of claims though several countries, the most effective way to deal with the sites in the future could be to require individuals to use their real name on the site.

4.3.10 *Summary*

What is the balance that should be struck between free speech and the application of the criminal law?
Is it the business of the police and prosecutors to protect the sensibilities of individuals or groups against what many people would consider to be bad taste? Simply because the view expressed is controversial or unpopular and may cause offence is not in itself enough for criminal charges.

Section 127 of the Communications Act 2003 is concerned with 'improper use of public communications networks' and makes it an offence if a person 'sends by means of a public electronic communications network a message or other matter that is grossly offensive or of an indecent, obscene or menacing character'. It is also an offence if a person 'for the purpose of causing annoyance, inconvenience or needless anxiety to another, he . . . sends . . . a message that he knows to be false'.

When considering whether a prosecution is in the public interest, should one or more of the following make a prosecution more likely?

- the message is part of a campaign of harassment against an individual or group;
- the message is a threat against the life or well-being of the recipient and/or a member of the recipient's family or other loved ones (should recipient be 'individual'?);
- the message, on an objective consideration, is malicious;
- the message is an incitement to hatred on grounds of race, religion, disability or sexual orientation (and ethnic or national origin?);
- the message causes considerable distress to the recipient and/or their family or loved ones;
- are there any other relevant considerations?

When considering whether a prosecution is in the public interest, should one or more of the following make a prosecution less likely?

164   *Communications-based offences*

- the message is a one-off incident;
- the message is intended to be humorous;
- the message is not directed at a specific individual (or group?);
- the message was not intended to become public or become known to the individual who is the subject of the message;
- the sender of the message has expressed genuine remorse;
- the individual (or individual's family), subject to the message, is not distressed by the message;
- are there any other relevant considerations?

5 Malicious Communications Act 1988

5.1 Background

The Malicious Communications Act 1988 (MCA) describes its purpose and scope in the following terms: 'An act to make provision for the punishment of persons who send or deliver letters or other articles for the purpose of causing distress or anxiety.' The Act pre-dates the internet, although it was updated in 2001 to apply to 'electronic communications' – 'oral or otherwise'.[1]

5.2 Section 1 of the Malicious Communications Act 1988

Section 1 MCA 1988 deals with the sending to another of an electronic communication which is indecent or grossly offensive, or which conveys a threat, or which is false, provided there is an intention to cause distress or anxiety to the recipient. A full consideration of the meaning of gross offence is explored in Chapter 4: Communications Act 2003.

The offence is one of sending, delivering or transmitting, so there is no legal requirement for the communication to reach the intended recipient. The terms of section 1 were considered in *Connolly* and 'indecent or grossly offensive' were said to be ordinary English words.

A person who is found guilty of an offence under section 1 of the Act can receive a maximum prison sentence of six months, a fine of £5,000 or both (s 1 2A(4) MCA 1988).

There is a limited amount of case law available in relation to the Malicious Communications Act 1988, as the majority of prosecutions have been pursued under the Communications Act 2003 (CA). In November 2012, however, an unnamed man was arrested for posting a photo of a poppy being burned, accompanied by a crudely worded (and crudely spelled) caption, which was reported to be: 'How about that you squadey c★★★★'.[2] In July 2011, a blogger accepted a caution for alleging that a contestant on *Britain's Got Talent* had been groomed for success on the show by Simon Cowell.[3] However, it is suggested that the *Britain's Got Talent* case was pursued under the wrong legislation, as the blog was intended for a wide audience rather that directed towards a particular individual (the Act contains the wording 'sent to another

---

1 See section 1(2A)(a) inserted by the Criminal Justice and Police Act 2001.
2 See http://www.theguardian.com/uk/2012/nov/12/teenager-arrested-burning-poppy-facebook.
3 See http://www.theguardian.com/tv-and-radio/2011/jul/03/britains-got-talent-blogger-cautioned.

166   *Communications-based offences*

. . . intended to cause distress to the recipient'). As the matter was settled by the blogger accepting a caution, there was no opportunity to explore if the caution interfered with the blogger's freedom of expression and there is no indication that weight was given to this when the police decided to pursue the matter.

5.3 Distinguishing the Malicious Communications Act 1988 from the Communications Act 2003 – 'sent to another person'

5.3.1 *Comparison with the Communications Act 2003*

Although the MCA 1988 and CA 2003 are often considered interchangeably, the 1988 Act is intended to apply only to one-to-one exchanges rather than broadcasting to a large audience. Indeed, section 1(1) explicitly states that the communication must be sent to another person. In the social media context, this may include:

* Private messaging
* Direct posts on another person's wall
* Posts @ a particular account holder on Twitter

In *Collins*, Bingham LJ observed that the existence of the MCA 1988 was 'not to protect people against receipt of unsolicited messages which they may find seriously objectionable', but rather 'to prohibit the use of a service provided and funded by the public for the benefit of the public for the transmission of communications which contravene the basic standards of our society'.[4]

5.3.2 *Tagging and open posts/tweets*

The MCA 1988 would not, it seems, apply to Paul Chambers, who directed his tweet to an indiscriminate audience, though it was caught by the CA 2003. What has not yet been determined is if posts made on a defendant's own wall which copy in another account holder could classify as a malicious communication directed towards a particular person (e.g. tagging someone in a Facebook status), although presumably depending on the content of the post, tagging would be sufficient to establish that the content was directed towards a particular person. At the time of writing, no such case has been brought before the courts. There is also a possibility that for sustained or prolonged campaigns of tagging, a prosecution could also be pursued under legislation designed to protect individuals from harassment, such as the Protection from Harassment Act 1997.

---

4   [2006] UKHL 40 at [7].

6 Serious Crime Act 2007

6.1 Background

The Serious Crime Act 2007 (SCA 2007) received royal assent on 30 October 2007. One of its objectives was to 'create offences in respect of the encouragement or assistance of crime'.[1] Part 2 of the SCA 2007 covers acts that encourage or assist an offence.

6.2 House of Commons Justice Committee White Paper

The House of Commons Justice Committee in their September 2013 paper, 'Post-legislative scrutiny of Part 2 (Encouraging or assisting crime) of the Serious Crime Act 2007' noted that:

> following the riots in August 2011, the crimes of assisting and encouraging have proved to be significant. The fact that some defendants who placed messages on social media encouraging riot and other offences were convicted of the encouraging offence, and received sentences of four years' imprisonment, shows that these offences can have a very significant role to play in the criminal justice system.[2]

In *R v Blackshaw*,[3] the Court of Appeal confirmed that the Serious Crime Act 2007 would apply to social media platforms, stating that:

> modern technology has done away with the need for such direct personal communication. It can all be done through Facebook or other social media. In other words, the abuse of modern technology for criminal purposes extends to and includes incitement of very many people by a single step. Indeed it is a sinister feature of these cases that modern technology almost certainly assisted rioters in other places to organize the rapid movement and congregation of disorderly groups in new and unpoliced areas.[4]

---

1 Serious Crime Act 2007, Introductory Text.
2 House of Commons Justice Committee in their 2014 paper, 'Post-legislative scrutiny of Part 2 (Encouraging or assisting crime) of the Serious Crime Act 2007' HC 639 at [21].
3 [2011] EWCA Crim 2312.
4 [2011] EWCA Crim 2312 at [73].

168 *Communications-based offences*

6.3 Sections 44 and 46 of the Serious Crime Act 2007

6.3.1 *Section 44: Intentionally encouraging or assisting an offence*

A person commits an offence if:

- They commit an act capable of encouraging or assisting the commission of an offence (s 44(1)(a)); and
- Intend to encourage or assist its commission (s 44(1)(b)).

However, that person will not be taken to have intended to encourage or assist the commission of an offence merely because such encouragement or assistance was a foreseeable consequence of his act (s 44(2)).

6.3.2 *Section 46: Encouraging or assisting offences believing one or more will be committed*

A person commits an offence if:

- they commit an act capable of encouraging or assisting the commission of one or more of a number of offences (s 46(1)(a)); and
- they believe
  - that one or more of those offences will be committed (but has no belief as to which (s 46(1)(b)(i)); and
  - that his act will encourage or assist the commission of one or more of them (s 46(1)(b)(ii)).

6.3.3 *Section 19: Serious Crime Prevention Orders*

Section 19 SCA 2007 provides for the making of a serious crime prevention order (SCPO). A serious crime prevention order can be made:

- On application to the High Court (s 1 SCA 2007); or
- Following conviction for a 'serious crime' in the Crown Court.

The defendant must have been convicted of a 'serious crime' as defined in section 2(2) and schedule 1 to the Serious Crime Act 2007. The order is also subject to safeguards under sections 6–15.

The court can make an order if satisfied there are 'reasonable grounds to believe that the order would protect the public by preventing, restricting or disrupting involvement by the defendant in serious crime in England and Wales'. The order must be in addition to and not a substitute for sentence for the offence. Orders are made on the application of the DPP (or Directors of RCPO and SFO). The order can contain such prohibitions, restrictions or requirements and such other terms as the court considers appropriate for the purposes above.

Application may also be made to the High Court for a Serious Crime Prevention Order under section 1 SCA 2007 in the case of a person who has *not* been convicted

Serious Crime Act 2007 169

of an offence but who has been 'involved in serious crime'. The Attorney General must be consulted before any application is made to the High Court.

The leading authorities are *R v Batcherlor*[5] and *R v Hancox.*[6] In *Hancox*, the court said that there must be reasonable grounds for believing that an order will protect the public by preventing, restricting or disrupting involvement by the defendant in serious crimes, as required by section 19(2) of the Act. That means that there has to be reasonable grounds to believe that there is a real or significant risk, not a bare possibility, that the offender will commit further serious offences. In addition, the court underlined the importance of proportionality and referred to Article 8 of the European Convention on Human Rights. The court said that an order should not be imposed because it was thought that a defendant deserved it; an order was not designed to punish but rather was preventive in character.

6.4 Case Law

6.4.1 *Recent development of a body of case law*

Although the court has confirmed its application to social media, the body of case law involving a social media element that is prosecuted under the statute is in its infancy. However, the 2011 UK riots resulted in a number of social media related prosecutions; the limited case law available is worth exploration to understand the reasoning of the courts and consider how such cases will be approached now that the CPS Guidelines are in effect.

6.4.2 *R v Blackshaw*

During the time of the August 2011 riots in London and other cities across the UK, Blackshaw created a Facebook event entitled 'Smash down in Northwich Town'. The offence or offences which the defendant believed would be committed as a result of his posting were stated by the court to include riot, burglary, and criminal damage. It is important to emphasise that the defendant admitted and was convicted of doing an act capable of encouraging the commission of riot, burglary and criminal damage, and doing so believing that what he did would encourage or assist the commission of one or more of the offences, and that one or more of the offences would in fact be committed.[7]

At 10.30 am on 8 August 2011, he used Facebook to set up and plan a public event called 'Smash down in Northwich Town'. It would start behind the premises of McDonalds at 1 pm the next day. The riots were in full flow and the appellant was aware of this. The purpose of his website, according to the court, was to cause criminal damage and rioting in the centre of Northwich, and the event called for participants to meet in a restaurant in Northwich at lunchtime on 9 August. The website was aimed at his close associates, who he referred to as the 'Mob Hill Massive', and his friends, but he also opened it to public view and included in the website

5 [2010] EWCA Crim 1025.
6 Ibid.
7 [2011] EWCA Crim 2312 at [54].

170   *Communications-based offences*

references to on-going rioting in London, Birmingham, and Liverpool. He posted a message of encouragement on the website that read 'we'll need to get on this, kicking off all over'.

Following his arrest at 11 am on 9 August, the appellant admitted that he had watched media coverage of the riots on the television and that he set up the website. He agreed that the event would be carried out, and that he would have attended himself if he had had enough alcohol. He said that it was not something that he would have done sober, and claimed that he had set the site up for a 'laugh and to meet people to drink with', but in later discussions he agreed that what he had done was stupid and that the effect of his actions was to encourage rioting and looting. He accepted responsibility for his actions. The defendant's later guilty plea made clear that he had not set up the website as a joke. He believed that the offences he was inciting would happen.

The offence or offences that he believed would be committed were riot, burglary, and criminal damage. It is important to emphasise that the applicant admitted and was convicted of doing an act capable of encouraging the commission of riot, burglary and criminal damage, and doing so believing that what he did would encourage or assist the commission of one or more of the offences, and that one or more of the offences would in fact be committed, rather than a joke. He was sentenced to four years' imprisonment.[8]

In his sentencing remarks, the judge made clear that the sentence had to be a deterrent sentence to demonstrate that this conduct would not be tolerated. He took account of the early guilty plea. The court noted that the appellant had sought to take advantage of the public disorder and criminality occurring elsewhere and to transfer it to the peaceful streets of Northwich. If such disorder had arisen, he might become personally involved in the troubles. In short, he had sought to organize criminality that had revolted many right-thinking members of the community, who had expressed their revulsion by contributing to the detection of the offence, enabling the police to give warnings against any attendance. The appellant had sought to create public disorder and mayhem in Northwich. The court therefore stated that a custodial sentence was inevitable. Taking account of the appellant's plea, but as a deterrent to others, a sentence of four years' detention was deemed appropriate. On appeal, Blackshaw argued that the sentence was manifestly excessive as:

- Insufficient credit was given for the early guilty plea;
- Disproportionate weight had been attached to the necessity to impose a deterrent sentence;
- That the judge failed to give adequate weight to the fact that this was a single stupid act;
- No one had been contacted outside the entry on Facebook;
- There was nothing persistent about his conduct;
- The defendant had not taken any further steps to incite any criminal activity.

According to the written grounds of appeal, the judge had failed to 'distinguish between tangible acts of criminality and incitement which, in actual fact, leads to

8 Ibid.

nothing'. Disproportionate weight to the necessity to deter others had been given by the judge to what was a spontaneous but monumentally foolish act.

6.4.3 *R v Perry John Sutcliffe-Keenan*[9]

On 9 August 2011, the defendant used Facebook to construct a web page called 'The Warrington Riots'. On this web page he included a photograph of police officers in riot equipment in a 'stand-off position' with a group of rioters. He also included a photograph of himself and others in a pose described by police as 'gangster like'. He sent invitations on his Facebook to 400 contacts. They were invited to meet at a Carvery in Warrington at 7 pm on 10 August. In addition to his own Facebook contacts, the website was also made available for general public viewing. Through the website 47 people confirmed that they would go to the meeting. In the meantime, the police received communications from local residents who had seen and were concerned by what they read on the web page and they closed the site down in the early hours of 9 August and nobody attended the proposed meeting. The applicant was arrested at 11 am on 9 August 2011. He gave two 'no comment' interviews.

6.4.3.1 *Attempts by the defendant to mitigate actions*

At the hearing, the appellant pleaded guilty. After he entered his plea, it was said on his behalf that he went back to the Facebook site and cancelled the event. It was further said that he woke up at around 10 am and received a telephone call from a friend who had seen the entry on Facebook and asked him about it. This had prompted the appellant to go to the Facebook site and cancel the event, posting a remark to the effect that it was a joke.

The court responded by stating that the prosecution could not gainsay the appellant's assertion that he brought about closure of the event before the police arranged for the Facebook site to be closed down. After discussion, the Recorder said that he would deal with the appellant on the basis that he had retracted the entry as he had changed his mind. The issue that the discussion did not address was the reason for the change of mind, which would have indicated the defendant's intent and if there was a degree of remorse for his actions. It was said on his behalf that the appellant decided to cancel the event after his friend had 'asked him about the Facebook entry'. It was not suggested, however, that he had done so out of an overwhelming sense of regret or concern about the possible consequences of his entry. Nevertheless, it was argued that the appellant had attempted to mitigate his crime by 'putting things right'. The court determined that the circumstances in which the appellant cancelled the event was important to any mitigation that might be available. At that stage, the evidence on the point was incomplete. In an endeavour to establish the facts, further evidence was asked to be provided by the prosecution. Submissions were invited by the court as to whether the evidence should be admitted in the interests of justice under section 23 of the Criminal Appeal Act 1968. The appellant was also given the opportunity to give evidence. He declined the opportunity and the matter was heard on written submission.

9 [2011] EWCA Crim 2312.

172   *Communications-based offences*

Although forensic analysis of the appellant's computer equipment established that the posting on Facebook which cancelled the event stated 'only jokin f★★★ hell', the court stated that the inference was that the event was cancelled as he had received an intimation that the police were searching for him, rather than out of genuine remorse.

Similar to *Woods*, according to the pre-sentence report, the defendant did not remember much about the offence as he had been drinking during the afternoon and evening, and when he was contacted by a friend he had been unable to recall what he had done. However, this did not reduce his sentence, demonstrating that a variety of factors such as the severity of the potential consequences of the postings will be taken into account even if the posting is a poor attempt at a joke while drunk.

In relation to sentencing, the judge identified the relevant features of the case, including the fact that no less than 47 people had agreed to attend the meeting. The appellant had placed considerable strain on police resources in Warrington and caused real panic in the town, where a number of people anticipated scenes of riot similar to those that had been occurring throughout the country. The judge took the view that the case was more serious than that of Blackshaw, but he gave credit to the appellant for having changed his mind. Again the sentence had to be a deterrent sentence and a sentence of four years' imprisonment was imposed.

On appeal, it was argued that:

- The judge had placed too much emphasis on the potential for harm rather than the actual harm which had followed; and
- Insufficient attention had been given to the fact that the appellant thought better of his actions and closed down the site before any harm could be done.

The Court stated that the closing of the site was directly connected to the information that the police were looking for him, showing a lack of genuine remorse.

6.4.4 *R v Pelle*

The *Pelle* case[10] occurred during the London 2011 riots and involved the misuse of Facebook to entice those minded to engage in public disorder to assemble in just such numbers as would achieve their object and frustrate the forces of law and order in seeking to prevent them from doing so.

Pelle, aged 18 at the time of posting, had a Facebook account with 2,000 friends. On three occasions between 6 and 10 August 2011, Mr Pelle published three postings via the social media site which formed the subject matter of the proceedings:

- 'Kill one black youth; we'll kill a million Fedz: riot till we own the cities.'
- 'Notts riot: who's on it?'
- 'Rioting tonight; anyone want something from Flannels?'

Pelle also posted a profile picture of boxes of Vans, Lacoste, Fred Perry, and Adidas trainers intending people to believe he had looted them. Pelle later claimed and the court accepted that he had purchased them legitimately.

---

10 *R v Ahmad Pelle*, Nottingham Crown Court, 25 August 2011 (unreported).

6.4.4.1 *Intent*

On arrest, Pelle suggested that the postings were all a joke, although under interview he conceded the following points, which were drawn out by the court as matters that informed the intent behind the postings on Facebook:

- Pelle wanted the riots to continue as a demonstration by black youths against authority, government, and police so 'the police can't do nothing to us no more';
- He wanted to follow 'Shank' so that youth would take over the streets so that government, police, and society could do nothing; that is a recipe for anarchy;
- He wanted to encourage continued rioting in the major cities of this country and blowing up police stations and government property and shutting them down; and
- He thought his posts might have encouraged people to do what they wanted to do anyway.

The court noted that a number of comments made by other account holders in response to Pelle's initial posts noted that they thought he was a 'stupid idiot'. However, despite the fact that many users held this view, the court were of the opinion that the problem was that others may have taken the defendant's comments seriously. It should be noted that the Serious Crime Act 2007 relates to encouraging or intending to incite others to commit an offence, and as such unlike the Communications Act 2003 and Malicious Communications Act 1998 the offence is not complete by the mere act of posting; the intent behind the posting must also therefore be given careful consideration, which is a strong feature of each of the cases considered in Part 3 of the Handbook. The appeal court noted that the cases of R v *Blackshaw* and *R v Sutcliffe-Keenan* involved inviting individuals to join in riots not inciting contacts to join in violent disorder as Pelle had done, which may suggest why the Court of Appeal did not agree with the submissions of Blackshaw and Sutcliffe-Keenan's solicitors when appealing the length of sentence imposed upon the defendants. Clearly, cases will have to be considered very carefully upon their factual matrix when determining if prosecutors wish to proceed with prosecutions, and in relation to drafting submissions seeking a reduced sentence.

When dealing with the appeals of Blackshaw and Sutcliffe-Keenan, the Court of Appeals judgments contained a clear consciousness that no actual harm in the streets of Northwich and Warrington actually occurred. However, the Court of Appeal was minded to state that it would not be accurate to suggest that neither crime had any adverse consequences. The court stated that 'a number of decent citizens were appalled by what they had read, and given the widespread rioting throughout the country, which at that time was spiralling out of control, we have no doubt that some, at least, of them were put in fear'. The reference by the court to the offensive content of the post, suggests that there is an overlap with the CA 2003 and MCA 1988 as sections 44 and 46 SCA 2007 do not make reference to how the comments are received by a group of recipients or a specific intended recipient.

174 *Communications-based offences*

6.4.5 *R v Bentley*[11]

While the cases discussed so far in this chapter indicate a level of consistency in the approach taken by prosecutors, the case of *R v Bentley* demonstrates the difficulty in determining the poster's intent. Bentley created a Facebook event page called 'Wakey Riots' during the 2011 riots. The event was received by more than 700 people, of whom 62 replied they would not come, 16 said they could, five were 'maybes', and 691 did not reply.

Bentley's messages, such as LMFAO – which means 'Laughing My F****** Arse Off' – were alleged by authorities to have incited criminality. Bentley was arrested under the SCA 2007 and the case was heard before the Leeds Crown Court. The case was thrown out after a one-hour 'trial' that followed a previous Crown Court plea, a directions hearing, and two magistrates' court appearances. Judge Collier, the Recorder of Leeds, said there was not enough evidence to disprove Miss Bentley's claim that it was a joke, adding: 'That's been her account from the start.' The judge expressed bemusement that police had not asked Miss Bentley about the letters LMFAO.

Miss Bentley admitted she did not know most of the people to whom she sent the message. The alarm was raised when one of Miss Bentley's Facebook Friends, Joe Wingfield, aged 16, accessed his Facebook account via his iPhone and told his brother Richard who was a policeman. Earlier, Miss Bentley's friends had warned her she was getting herself into trouble. Natalie Salmon wrote: 'Hollie, this is stupid. Why are you even making this event? You might think it's funny but it's not. All you are doing is causing trouble and not just for yourself but everybody else. If I was you I would just delete this.'

Unlike the previous cases in this chapter, Miss Bentley left the page up, but the judge rejected the Crown's argument that similar previous cases that resulted in jail terms would have been equally difficult to prove. The judge maintained those cases were different because the defendants pleaded guilty and could not accept LMFAO referred to Miss Bentley 'sitting in her bedroom, creating this, and laughing inwardly about Wakefield being burned to the ground'. *Bentley* is difficult to resolve with *Sutcliffe-Keenan* and *Blackshaw*, since in those cases the posters subsequently removed the postings made via the sites, meant the postings as a joke, and did express remorse. It would appear that significant weight was afforded in *Bentley* to the fact that Bentley persistently held that the event was made as a joke, although this emphasis is difficult to accept given that Sutcliffe-Keenan and Blackshaw both also posted the content allegedly 'for a joke'. The case is easier to distinguish from *Pelle*, where the defendant admitted that he wanted to incite criminal activity. What the case does highlight is that greater consistency as to the reasons for pursuing prosecutions and throwing cases out needs to be explored by prosecutors.

11 Leeds Crown Court, 29 November 2011 (unreported).

7 Crime and Disorder Act 1998

7.1 Background

In relation to social media cases, the Crime and Disorder Act 1998 (CDA 1998) has been used to prosecute cases involving social media that have a racially aggravating element. The preamble to the CDA 1998 notes, so far as is relevant to communications-based offences, that it is 'an act to make provision for preventing crime and disorder; to create certain racially-aggravated offences'.

7.2 Section 31 Crime and Disorder Act 1998

Subsection 31(1)(c) CDA 1998 provides that it is an offence to commit racially aggravated disorderly behaviour with intent to cause harassment, alarm or distress. A person guilty of an offence falling within subsection 31(1)(c) CDA 1998 is liable on summary conviction to a fine not exceeding level 4 on the standard scale (s 31(5)).

7.3 Case law

7.3.1 *R v Cryer*

In *R v Cryer*,[1] Joshua Cryer sent racially abusive messages on Twitter to the ex-footballer, Stan Collymore.

7.3.1.1 *Aggravating factors*

Prosecuting, Veronica Jordan said Cryer was 'showing off' and boasted to friends that he had 'found a new hobby'. She said: 'It was not impulsive. He has done this up to seven times over a period of days which did not indicate the hallmarks of impulsive behaviour' and he 'was intending to insult and abuse'.[2]

---

1 Newcastle Magistrates' Court, 21 March 2012 (unreported).
2 'Stan Collymore Twitter race abuser Joshua Cryer sentenced', *BBC News*, 21 March 2012 [http://www.bbc.co.uk/news/uk-england-tyne-17462619].

176 *Communications-based offences*

7.3.1.2 *Mitigation*

In mitigation, it was submitted by Mr Cyer's defence representative, that 'He [Cryer] is not somebody I would regard as being a dyed-in-the-wool racist. The reason he contacted Collymore in the first place was he is a fan of his.'

7.3.1.3 *Sentencing*

Passing sentence, Judge Earl said: 'I don't doubt you are not an inherently racist person, but you did act in an intentionally racist way. I find it difficult to fathom what on Earth you thought you were doing. It was stupid and you ought to have known better.'[3] Mr Cryer was sentenced to two years' community service and ordered to pay £150 costs.

The penalties under the Communications Act 2003 and the Crime and Disorder Act 1998 differ considerably. A person guilty of an offence falling within subsection 31(1)(c) CDA 1998 is liable on summary conviction to a fine not exceeding level 4 on the standard scale, whereas under section 5 of the Communications Act 2003, a person guilty of an offence under section 127(1) is liable under section 127(3), on summary conviction, to imprisonment for a term not exceeding six months or to a fine not exceeding level 5 on the standard scale, or both. Disappointingly, the CPS's Interim Guidelines do not address when it would be more appropriate to proceed with a particular statute, which may result in differing penalties depending upon which act the prosecutor chooses to pursue proceedings. This point was also noted in the joined appeal hearings of *Blackshaw* and *Sutcliffe-Keenan*[4] against the length of their sentence compared with the sentence arrived at in *R v Pelle*[5] for similar offences.

---

3 Ibid.
4 [2011] EWCA Crim 2312.
5 *R v Ahmad Pelle*, Nottingham Crown Court, 25 August 2011 (unreported).

8 Public Order Act 1986

8.1 Introduction

The Public Order Act 1986 (POA 1986) received royal assent on 7 November 1986. The Act was adopted to abolish the common law offences of riot, rout, unlawful assembly, and affray and certain statutory offences relating to public order; to create new offences relating to public order; to control public processions and assemblies; to control the stirring up of racial hatred; and to provide for the exclusion of certain offenders from sporting events.

8.2 Case law

8.2.1 *R v Stacey*[1]

On 19 March 2012, Liam Stacey pleaded guilty at Swansea Magistrates' Court to an offence contrary to section 31(1)(b) of the Public Order Act 1986, in relation to offences committed in connection with football.[2] By his plea he admitted that he used threatening, abusive or insulting words with intent to cause harassment, alarm or distress to users of the Twitter Internet Messaging Service. He also accepted that his offence was racially aggravated.

As well as posting this message on his own account, the appellant linked the message to a site called 'Ha Ha'. That meant that what he had written was capable of being read not just by those persons who followed the appellant's Twitter account but by any other user of Twitter.

The appellant's message provoked very strong responses. The first response was from a person who wrote: 'You my friend are a grade A c★★t heartless bastard.' The court was told that it was not disputed that this response came from a black man. The appellant replied: 'I am not your friend, you w★g c★★t, go pick some cotton.'

---

1 *R v Stacey*, Swansea Crown Court (unreported); *R v Stacey*, Appeal No: A20120033 30 March 2011.
2 Sections 30–37 repealed with saving by the Football Supporters Act 1989 (c. 37, SIF 45A), s 27(5); subject to amendment (27 September 1999) (EW) by 1999 c. 21, ss 6(1), 6(2)(a–b), 7(1), 8(1), 8(2), 8(4), 8(5); subject to amendment (1 April 2001) by 1999, c. 22, ss 90, 106, 108, schedule 13, para 134, schedule 15 Pt. V(7); SI 2001/916, article 2 (with transitional provisions and savings in schedule 2, para 2); subject to amendment (25 August 2000) by 2000, c. 6, ss 165(1), 168(1), schedule 9, para 101; subject to amendment (28 August 2000) by 2000, c. 25, ss 1(2), 1(3), schedule 2, paras 3–7, schedule 3; SI 2000/2125, Article 2.

178　*Communications-based offences*

8.2.1.1 *Continuing availability of the posts*

The court noted that the exchange continued to be available, to all persons using Twitter. Many further messages were posted aimed at the appellant. The appellant received messages which were extremely critical of him and written in abusive language. However, this did not cause him to desist. Over the course of the next hour or thereabouts, he posted at least eight messages which were extremely abusive and insulting. All the messages were available to be read by persons who could access Twitter. Two of these messages were expressly racial; not only were the messages expressly racial but were couched in terms that can only be regarded as extremely offensive. One read, 'You are a silly c★★t, you mothers a w★g and your dad is a rapist bonjour you c★★t.' A second read, 'Go suck a n★★★★er dick you f★★★ing aids-ridden c★★t.'[3]

8.2.1.2 *Role of remorse*

The court noted in the appeal that there came a point in time when the appellant began to realize the enormity of his behaviour. That occurred when one of his friends sent him a message urgently querying what he was doing. He then apologised online for what he had done.

However, the appellant's behaviour still provoked a number of complaints to the police. A complaint was made to the Northumbrian Police Force and we are told that other forces were also contacted by members of the public who were outraged by the appellant's behaviour. The appellant was traced quite quickly. On Sunday 18 March, two police officers attended at his address in Swansea; they arrested him and cautioned him and he immediately admitted that he had posted racist comments on Twitter. He told the officers that he was drunk at the time, that he didn't mean it, and that he was sorry for his actions. The defendant admitted in his plea that he used threatening, abusive or insulting words with intent to cause harassment, alarm or distress to users of the Twitter Internet Messaging Service. He also accepted that his offence was racially aggravated.

8.2.1.3 *Factors put forward in mitigation*

- The offence was completely out of character for the appellant.
- The appellant had no previous convictions.
- The appellant pleaded guilty at the first available opportunity, having earlier admitted his offence to the police officers who interviewed him.
- The case attracted a great deal of publicity. The appellant has been the subject of harsh comment in some quarters and he has become a figure of some notoriety. It was submitted that this was a significant punishment in itself.
- The appellant was genuinely remorseful.

Unlike in *R v Blackshaw* and *R v Sutcliffe-Keenan*, the court accepted that the points raised in mitigation had a degree of validity, demonstrating that each case must be

---

3　The original tweets have been redacted due to their content. The original tweets featured the full words.

tried on its facts. In this case, the sentence was not reduced but that does not necessarily mean that the court would not do so in the future. The court noted that there were at the time no appropriate sentencing guidelines to refer to and that the case was one of the first of its kind. As a body of case law in relation to social media develops within the structure determined by the CPS Interim Guidelines, it is envisaged that the approach adopted by the courts will achieve greater clarity for lower courts attempting to apply the guidelines.

8.2.1.4 *Effect of Alcohol*

As is consistent with judgments such as *R v Blackshaw*, *R v Sutcliffe-Keenan*, and *R v Woods*, it was stated by the court that the offence could not be excused in any way by the fact the appellant had consumed a great deal of alcohol.

8.3 The CPS Interim Guidelines on cases involving social media

The CPS Interim Guidelines[4] note that some cases falling within paragraph 12 of the Guidelines may fall to be considered under public order legislation, such as Part 1 of the Public Order Act 1986.[5] Particular care should be taken in dealing with social media cases in this way because public order legislation is primarily concerned with words spoken or actions carried out in the presence or hearing of the person being targeted (i.e. where there is physical proximity between the speaker and the listener) and there are restrictions on prosecuting words or conduct by a person in a dwelling.

   In *Redmond-Bate v DPP*,[6] Sedley LJ emphasized that under the POA 1986 the mere fact that words were irritating, contentious, unwelcome, and provocative was not enough to justify the invocation of the criminal law unless they tended to provoke violence. In a similar vein in *Dehal v CPS*,[7] Moses J, referring to section 4A of the POA 1986, held that: 'the criminal law should not be invoked unless and until it is established that the conduct which is the subject of the charge amounts to such a threat to public order as to require the invocation of the criminal as opposed to the civil law'.[8]

8.4 Role of Part III of the Act

In some cases, prosecutors may be satisfied that the incitement provisions in Part III of the Public Order Act 1986 are relevant and should be used (Part III of the Act deals with racial hatred). Such cases must be referred to the Special Crime and Counter Terrorism Division (SCCTD) and require the consent of the Attorney General to proceed.

---

4 Interim Guidelines on Prosecuting Cases Involving Communications Sent Via Social Media, Issued by the Director of Public Prosecutions on 19 December 2012 [http://www.cps.gov.uk/consultations/social_media_consultation_index.html]. Considered in depth in Chapter 4: Communications Act 2003.
5 Ibid. at para 42.
6 Divisional Court, 23 July 1999.
7 [2005] EWHC 2154 (Admin).
8 [2005] EWHC 2154 (Admin) at [5].

9 Protection from Harassment Act 1997

9.1 Introduction

The Protection from Harassment Act (PHA 1997) came into force on 21 March 1997 and makes provision for protecting persons from harassment and similar conduct.

9.2 Sections 1 and 4 of the Protection from Harassment Act 1997

The Protection from Harassment Act 1997 prescribes that any two 'acts' which form a course of harassing conduct can be charged as a crime. Section 1 PHA 1997 prohibits harassment and provides that a person must not pursue a course of conduct which:

- amounts to harassment of another (s 1(a)); and
- they know or ought to know amounts to harassment of the other (s 1(b)).

9.2.1 *Conduct amounting to harassment*

For the purposes of this section, the person whose course of conduct is in question ought to know that it amounts to harassment of another if a reasonable person in possession of the same information would think the course of conduct amounted to harassment of the other (s 1(2)).

Section 1(1) does not apply to a course of conduct if it can be shown that:

- it was pursued for the purpose of preventing or detecting crime (s 1(3)(a));
- it was pursued under any enactment or rule of law or to comply with any condition or requirement imposed by any person under any enactment (s 1(3)(b)); or
- in the particular circumstances the pursuit of the course of conduct was reasonable (s 1(3)(c)).

9.2.2 *Sentencing*

Section 2 PHA 1997 provides that a person who pursues a course of conduct in breach of section 1 is guilty of an offence. If found guilty, that person is liable on summary conviction to imprisonment for a term not exceeding six months, or a fine not exceeding level 5 on the standard scale, or both.

9.3 Section 4

Section 4 PHA 1997 makes it an offence to put people in fear of violence. A person whose course of conduct causes another to fear, on at least two occasions, that violence will be used against them is guilty of an offence if he knows or ought to know that his course of conduct will cause the other so to fear on each of those occasions (s 4(1)).

A person is guilty of an offence under section 4(1) if the person, as a result of their conduct, ought to know that it will cause another to fear that violence will be used against them on any occasion if a reasonable person in possession of the same inform-ation would think the course of conduct would cause the other so to fear on that occasion. Section 4(3) contains a defence for persons charged under the section if they can show that:

- their course of conduct was pursued for the purpose of preventing or detecting crime (s 4(3)(a));
- their course of conduct was pursued under any enactment or rule of law or to comply with any condition or requirement imposed by any person under any enactment (s 4(3)(b)); or
- it was reasonable for the protection of himself or another or for the protection of his or another's property (s 4(3)(c)).

If found guilty, a person guilty of an offence under this section is liable:

- on conviction on indictment, to imprisonment for a term not exceeding five years, or a fine, or both (s 4(4)(a)); or
- on summary conviction, to imprisonment for a term not exceeding six months, or a fine not exceeding the statutory maximum, or both (s 4(4)(b)).

If the jury find the defendant not guilty of the offence charged, they may find him guilty of an offence under section 2 (s 4(5)). The Crown Court has the same powers and duties in relation to a person who is by virtue of section 4(5) convicted before it of an offence under section 2 as a magistrates' court would have on convicting him of the offence.

9.4 Restraining orders

The CPS's Stalking and Harassment Guidelines[1] state that if a restraining order is granted, the order should be drafted to meet the particular risks presented in each case and should not be a repetition of routine clauses. In relation to social media, suggested conditions can include:

---

1 https://www.cps.gov.uk/legal/s_to_u/stalking_and_harassment/.

182 *Communications-based offences*

- not to telephone, fax, communicate by letter, text, electronic mail or internet with the victim and others as appropriate, or to send or solicit any correspondence whatsoever;
- not to display any material relating to the victim on social networking sites including YouTube, Facebook, and Twitter;
- not to retain, record or research by any means, private, confidential or personal facts, or information relating to the victim and others as appropriate; or
- not to use a different name or to change names without immediately notifying the court and/or the police.

9.5 Home Office Review of 'The Protection from Harassment Act 1997: Improving Protection for Victims of Stalking'

In their July 2013 paper, summarizing the Responses and Conclusions[2] to the Home Offices 'Review of the Protection from Harassment Act 1997: Improving Protection for Victims of Stalking',[3] the Home Office noted, specifically in relation to social media, that respondents had made a wide range of suggestions to protect victims more effectively, including:

- introducing a requirement for social media providers to control and monitor their sites;
- ensuring internet service providers and social media cooperate with the police during investigations of allegations of harassment and stalking.

A number of respondents raised concerns relating to cyber-stalking. For the most part, social network site operators adopt sensible and responsible positions on illegal, inappropriate, and offensive content hosted on their sites in the terms and conditions they require for use of their services. Internet service providers and social media also already have a legal obligation to cooperate with the police during investigations of allegations of harassment and stalking.[4]

The outcome of the review noted that the Home Office would continue to work with internet service providers and social media to identify effective practices to improve the response to online harassment and stalking.[5]

---

2 Review of the Protection from Harassment Act 1997: Improving Protection for Victims of Stalking, July 2013.
3 Review of the Protection from Harassment Act 1997: Improving Protection for Victims of Stalking, Summary of Consultation Responses and Conclusions, July 2013.
4 Ibid. at p. 17.
5 Ibid. at p. 18.

10 Computer Misuse Act 1990

10.1 Introduction

The Computer Misuse Act 1990 (CMA 1990) was enacted to make provision for securing computer material against unauthorized access or modification, and for connected purposes. The case law explored so far in the Handbook has been in relation to communications-based offences which offend or shock; however, the Computer Misuse Act 1990 has application to social media due to computer hacking of the social networking site's systems. The main provisions of CMA 1990 which apply to social media prosecutions are sections 1 and 3 of the Act.

10.2 Section 1 of the Computer Misuse Act 1990

Under section 1 CMA 1990, it is an offence to gain unauthorized access to computer material. A person is guilty of an offence if:

- he causes a computer to perform any function with intent to secure access to any program or data held in any computer, or to enable any such access to be secured (s 1(a));
- the access he intends to secure, or to enable to be secured, is unauthorized (s 1(b)); and
- he knows at the time when he causes the computer to perform the function that that is the case (s 1(c)).

Section 1(2) deals with the issue of intent. The intent a person has to have to commit an offence under this section need not be directed at:

- any particular program or data (s 2(a));
- a program or data of any particular kind (s 2(b)); or
- a program or data held in any particular computer (s 2(c)).

10.2.1 *Sentencing*

If found guilty of the offence, a person situated in England and Wales is liable to imprisonment for a term not exceeding 12 months or to a fine not exceeding the statutory maximum or to both (s 1(3)(a)). For a person in Scotland, the term of imprisonment is a term not exceeding six months or a fine not exceeding the statutory

184 *Communications-based offences*

maximum or both (s 1(3)(b)). On conviction on indictment, the guilty party will be liable to imprisonment for a term not exceeding two years or to a fine or to both (s 1(3)(c)).

10.3 Section 3 of the Computer Misuse Act 1990

Section 3 CMA 1990 relates to unauthorized acts with intent to impair, or with recklessness as to impairing, operation of a computer. A person is guilty of an offence under section 3 if:

- he does any unauthorized act in relation to a computer (s 3(1)(a));
- at the time when he does the act he knows that it is unauthorized (s 3(1)(b)); and
- either subsection (2) or subsection (3) of the Act applies.

Section 3(2) applies if the person intends by doing the act to:

- impair the operation of any computer (s 3(2)(a));
- prevent or hinder access to any program or data held in any computer (s 3(2)(b));
- impair the operation of any such program or the reliability of any such data (s 3(2)(c)); or
- enable any of the things mentioned in paragraphs (a) to (c) above to be done (s 3(2)(d)).

Section 3(3) applies if the person is reckless as to whether the act will do any of the things mentioned in section 3(2)(a)–(d) above. The intention element referred to in section 3(2) above, or the recklessness element referred to in subsection 3(3) above, does not need to relate to:

- any particular computer (s 3(4)(a));
- any particular program or data (s 3(4)(b)); or
- a program or data of any particular kind (s 3(4)(c)).

In this section, a reference to doing an act includes a reference to causing an act to be done (s 3(5)(a)), can include a series of acts (s 3(5)(b)), or impairing, preventing or hindering something includes a reference to doing so temporarily (s 3(5)(c)).

10.3.1 *Sentencing*

If found guilty of an offence under section 3 in England and Wales, a person is liable to imprisonment for a term not exceeding 12 months or to a fine not exceeding the statutory maximum or to both (s 3(6)(a)). In Scotland, the position is slightly different, as the maximum sentence is six months or a fine not exceeding the statutory maximum or both. If the offence is indictable, the maximum term is ten years or a fine or both.

10.4 Case law

10.4.1 *R v Gareth Crosskey*

In *R v Gareth Crosskey*,[1] a 19-year-old hacked into the Facebook account of Justin Bieber's former girlfriend Selena Gomez by posing as the actress' step-father/manager to persuade Facebook staff to change the password to the account. After accessing and copying her private emails, he contacted celebrity magazines offering to reveal information about her.

Mr Crosskey was charged under section 1 CMA 1990 as he had caused a computer to perform a function to secure unauthorized access to a program/data relating to a client held in a computer belonging to Facebook.

Mr Crosskey was also charged under section 3 CMA 1990 for committing unauthorized acts with intent to impair operation of or prevent/hinder access to a computer knowing that it was unauthorized either intending by doing the act or being reckless as to whether the act would enable the operation of a computer to be impaired, access to a program or data held in a computer to be prevented or hindered, or the operation of a program or the reliability of data held in a computer to be impaired. The attack cost the company $200,000, and resulted in an investigation by the FBI and British law enforcement. Judge Alistair McCreath said his actions had 'real consequences and very serious potential consequences' that could have been 'utterly disastrous' for Facebook. 'He acted with determination, undoubted ingenuity and it was sophisticated, it was calculating,' prosecutor Sandip Patel told a London court. He also said Crosskey stole 'invaluable' intellectual property and that the attack represented 'the most extensive and grave incident of social media hacking to be brought before the British courts'. Mr Crosskey was sentenced to eight months in prison for hacking the Facebook server.

Alison Saunders, Chief Crown Prosecutor for the CPS, noted in relation to the relationship between the criminal law and data protection that 'this was the most extensive and flagrant incidence of social media hacking to be brought before British courts. Fortunately, this did not involve any personal user data being compromised'.[2]

10.4.2 *R v Glenn Mangham*

10.4.2.1 *Accessing servers and restricted areas on SNS servers*

In *R v Glenn Mangham*,[3] a software development student from York repeatedly hacked into Facebook and extracted internal material in spring 2011 using the

---

1 Southwark Crown Court, 16 May 2012 (unreported).
2 See CPS Blog post 'Facebook hacker committed serious offence' [http://blog.cps.gov.uk/2012/02/facebook-hacker-committed-serious-offence.html], posted 17 February 2012. For a discussion of the potential privacy impacts of hacking, see Chapter 13: Data Protection.
3 Southwark Crown Court, 17 February 2012 (unreported); *R v Glenn Mangham*, Court of Appeal Criminal Division [2012] EWCA Crim 973.

186 *Communications-based offences*

account of a Facebook employee who was on holiday. His targets included Facebook Puzzle and Mailman servers and a restricted area of the Facebook Phabricator server. Mangham was charged with committing offences contrary to sections 1 and 3 CMA 1990 and also section 3A of the Act which makes it an offence to make, supply or obtain articles for use in offence under section 1 or 3.

In addition to these sentences, the judge imposed a serious crime prevention order under the Serious Crime Act 2007.[4] The duration of that order was 5 years, beginning with the date of release from either prison or sentencing. Unfortunately, that meant that the start date was unclear. Pursuant to the order the applicant could own and use only one personal computer with internet access. He also had to give notification to the authorities about the use of a computer in the course of employment and was forbidden from using encryption software and from using data wiping software on his personal computer. He was also prevented from deleting any log or history of use and was not permitted to allow another person to use his personal computer. In addition, the court imposed a restriction on the email accounts which he was able to employ (he could only have two email accounts and they had to be with UK-based service providers).

10.4.2.2 *Mitigating factors*

On sentencing, the judge took into account:

- that the applicant was of good character;
- that he was relatively young in years but possibly emotionally younger; and
- that he had a psychological and a personal make-up which had led to the behaviour.

The judge also acknowledged that the defendant:

- had never intended to pass any information that he had obtained to anyone else and in fact never did so; and
- had never intended to make any financial gain for himself.

10.4.2.3 *Aggravating factors*

In terms of the impact of the offending, the judge explained that:

- In the court's view, this was not harmless experimentation;
- The defendant had accessed the very heart of an international business of a massive size;
- The defendant had acquired fundamental knowledge of its internal systems; and
- The defendant had put the entire operation of that business at potential risk.

---

4 See Chapter 6: Serious Crime Act 2007.

The trial judge characterised the behaviour as persistent and sophisticated.[5] Mangham appealed the decision and the case was put before the Court of Appeal on 4 April 2012.[6]

10.4.2.4 *Challenges presented by sentencing*

The Court of Appeal acknowledged that the trial judge had faced a difficult sentencing exercise. He had taken into account all the aggravating and mitigating factors. He rightly highlighted the persistence, sophistication, and deliberateness with which the applicant mounted his attack. Having heard the applicant give evidence, the judge was entitled to conclude that his motive was not to inform Facebook of the defects in their system, by contrast with what he had done with Yahoo, but more to prove that he could beat the Facebook system. The judge also alluded to the strong personal mitigation in relation to the applicant.

However, the Court of Appeal concluded that the balance of the aggravating and mitigating factors was such that the more appropriate sentence would have been 6 months' imprisonment, reduced to 4 months in the light of the applicant's plea and personal mitigation. In particular, the court underlined the points which the judge made at the very outset of his sentencing remarks that the information hacked had not been passed on to anyone and that there was no financial gain involved. The judge was correct, in their view, to identify the damage to Facebook, but it may be that they gave too much emphasis to the potential damage. Facebook acknowledged that although the applicant's activity resulted in the compromise of sensitive and confidential corporate information, all the compromised material was swiftly recovered and Facebook did not suffer any financial loss, apart from the costs of investigation. Moreover, in the appeal court's view, the serious crime prevention order could not be upheld. The trial judge had assessed the applicant as posing a future risk, contrary to the assessment of the probation officer. While the trial judge was entitled to do that, the court was not persuaded that the proportionality of the order was properly assessed in all the circumstances of the applicant's case. The court therefore substituted 4 months for the 8 months on each of the counts and the serious crime prevention order was quashed.[7]

---

5 Reproduced in the Court of Appeals decision [2012] EWCA Crim 973 at [11].
6 Court of Appeal Criminal Division [2012] EWCA Crim 973.
7 The application in relation to the order was made pursuant to the Serious Crime Act 2007: Appeals under Section 24 Order 2008, 2008 SI 1863.

Part 3.2
Criminal law: procedure

11 Contempt of Court Act 1981

11.1 Introduction

The Contempt of Court Act came into force on 27 July 1981. The principal focus of the 1981 Act is on publications that may have an adverse effect on legal proceedings.

11.2 Challenges presented by social media

The creation of the internet has brought about a huge change in the way in which people communicate. Enormous volumes of material can now be stored, communicated, and redistributed to a mass audience. This creates problems for the law of contempt. Historically, newspapers would fade from memory to become 'tomorrow's chip paper'. Now, information on the internet is potentially available forever once it has been posted, and can be found by anyone using a simple search. Social media in particular, which has a viral quality, means that individuals can communicate information to very large volumes of people in a short space of time. Inevitably, this also raises the question of whether individuals understand that when tweeting or posting content which forms the subject matter of proceedings that they may be committing contempt, or if they simply view their behaviour as expressing their opinion on topical matters or issues that have affected them privately. The distinction between public and private content is unclear.[1]

To date, there have been few contempt cases involving publications on the internet, so the law on the issue is sometimes unclear. However, over that past two years there has been an increase in the number of contempt cases via social networking sites in the press, suggesting that the issue will become more important in the future and the law will need to be equipped to deal with online publications.

The Law Commission's White Paper, 'Contempt of Court: Summary for non-specialists',[2] noted that some cases coming before the court (discussed below) involving new media – Twitter, internet blogs, and so on – pose a challenge to the current law on contempt of court, which dates from a time before the internet was widely used. The Commission commented on a number of areas in which social media has impacted upon contempt proceedings, or has the potential to do so in the future.

---

1 A discussion of privacy rights and freedom of expression can be found in Chapter 2: Human Rights, Chapter 4: Communications Act 2003, and Chapter 13: Data Protection and Privacy.
2 'Contempt of Court: Summary for non-specialists', Law Commission Consultation Paper No. 209.

192 *Criminal law: procedure*

The Law Commission's investigation, based on a consultation paper published in November 2012, took note of the fact that the Contempt of Court Act 1981 pre-dated the widespread use of the internet. The report recommended the creation of a new criminal offence of conducting prohibited research by jurors. The aim was to clarify and make more consistent the law on the boundaries of prohibited conduct and increase the legitimacy of the offence, which would become a statutory one, subject to a criminal procedure and sentencing regime in place of the current civil process in the Divisional Court. It would be triable on indictment and receive a maximum sentence of two years' imprisonment or unlimited fine. The report also recommended a limited exception on the current blanket prohibition (under section 8 of the 1981 Act) on jurors subsequently revealing their deliberations, to permit them to reveal miscarriages of justice to the competent authorities, or to participate in carefully controlled research into how juries operate. These findings of the Commission, insofar as they relate to social media, are explored throughout this chapter.

11.3 What is contempt of court?

Contempt of court is the area of law that deals with behaviour that might affect court proceedings. It takes many different forms, ranging from disrupting court hearings to disobeying court orders, to publishing prejudicial information that might make the trial unfair.

The definition of 'the strict liability rule' in section 1 of the 1981 Act is narrowly focused. Its scope relates only to such conduct as tends to interfere with the course of justice 'in particular legal proceedings'.

Section 2 then confines the operation of that rule to a publication when 'the proceedings in question' are active, creating the risk of impediment or prejudice to 'the proceedings in question'. There are therefore at least three exclusions from the rule, though the effect of the exclusion is not the same in all cases.

- Conduct tending to interfere with the justice system in general but not with any particular proceedings is outside the ambit of section 1.[3]
- Conduct during and related to one set of proceedings but likely to prejudice or impede a future set of proceedings is not caught. (They may fall within the common law liability for intentional prejudice, or within an order under section 4(2).)
- A publication might not in itself be likely to cause 'serious' prejudice but may form part of a wave of publicity that has that cumulative effect. Section 2(2) would seem to exclude such a publication from liability.

Section 2(2) contains a double hurdle. It must first be shown that the possible impediment or prejudice must be 'serious', and secondly that the risk of its occurring must be 'substantial'.

---

3 Where this conduct takes the form of a publication impugning the courts or a judge, it is known as scandalizing the court. A discussion of this offence is beyond the scope of the Handbook; see 'Contempt of Court: Scandalising the Court', Law Commission Consultation Paper No. 207 (2012) for further exploration of this offence.

Section 4 makes provisions in relation to contemporary reports of proceedings. In any such proceedings the court may, where it appears to be necessary for avoiding a substantial risk of *prejudice* to the administration of justice in those proceedings, or in any other proceedings pending or imminent, order that the publication of any report of the proceedings, or any part of the proceedings, be postponed for such period as the court thinks necessary for that purpose.

Section 5 relates to discussion of public affairs and states that a publication made as or as part of a discussion in good faith of public affairs or other matters of general public interest is not to be treated as a contempt of court under the strict liability rule if the risk of *impediment or prejudice* to particular legal proceedings is merely incidental to the discussion.

11.4 The meaning of 'communication'

In relation to social media, the Law Commission state that contempt can be committed via social networking sites as the definition of communication is widely drafted. The laws relating to contempt would therefore cover almost all of the new media. The Commission states that Facebook postings, tweets, Flickr photographs, videos on YouTube, and words, videos, music or pictures on any other website[4] would fall within the category of communication.

11.5 The meaning of a publication

The strict liability contempt by publication contained in section 1 of the Contempt of Court Act 1981 only applies to publications. The Act defines publication to include speech, writing, programmes (and other similar broadcasts), and any other form of communication. These publications must be 'addressed to the public at large or any section of the public'. The Law Commission states that 'speech' has an obvious meaning, but does state in relation to social media that 'speech' would also include things said on YouTube films.[5]

'Writing' has been defined in law as 'reproducing words in a visible form'. Case law from a different area of criminal law concluded that something on the internet can be considered to have been 'written', as what was on the computer screen was 'in writing'. Presumably, this would also extend to content that could be accessed via Smartphone or tablets, which have internet connectivity and can access social networking sites and web pages. Further on in the report in relation to juror deliberations, 'mobile phones, laptops, iPads, iPods, Kindles'[6] are given as examples of such devices. This view can be supported by cases such as *Attorney General v Kasim Davey and Joseph Beard*,[7] where contempt was committed by the juror using a Smartphone to post about the trial he was selected to serve on via Facebook.

---

4 'Contempt of Court: Summary for non-specialists', Law Commission Consultation Paper No. 209 at para [92].
5 Ibid. at para [89].
6 Ibid. at para [147].
7 [2012] 1 WLR 991 at [6].

194 *Criminal law: procedure*

11.6 Requirement to be 'addressed to the public'

Another issue raised by social media is if the communication in question is addressed to the public or a large section of it. The Law Commission acknowledges that there is no clear rule on what this means, but a court would examine:

- How many people the publication was addressed to;
- Who those people were; and
- Why the publication was aimed at them.

A private communication that is only sent to one person (for example, an email from one person to another) could not be a publication addressed to the public. By extension, this analysis would likely apply to private messages sent via social networking sites to another individual but not if that message was communicated via private messaging to a number of people, such as a group with many members.

According to the Law Commission, it is not clear whether the courts would treat social networking sites, such as Facebook and Twitter, as publications to the public or a section of the public. They have suggested that factors such as whether the user had turned on their privacy settings so their posting or tweet could only be viewed by a limited number of people[8] would be taken into account when reaching a decision.

11.7 Section 8 Contempt of Court Act 1981: contempt by jurors

11.7.1 *Law Commission's White Paper*

The Law Commission's White Paper noted that there may be worries that section 8 of the Contempt of Court Act 1981 (CCA 1981) is being breached more often than it used to be. The internet and social media may make it easier for friends, families, and others to speak with jurors to find out information about their jury service. Similarly, it is easier for jurors to contact other people in the trial (such as the defendant) and communicate with them.[9]

11.7.2 *Section 8 of the Contempt of Court Act 1981*

Section 8 of the CCA 1981 makes it an offence to obtain or to reveal any 'statements made, opinions expressed, arguments advanced or votes cast by members of a jury in the course of their deliberations'. There are some exceptions to this, which means that revealing deliberations to a court will not be considered contempt in certain circumstances. The maximum punishment for contempt under section 8 is a fine or up to two years in prison (s 14(1) CCA 1981).

---

8 'Contempt of Court: Summary for non-specialists', Law Commission Consultation Paper No. 209 at para [96].
9 Ibid. at para [179].

Contempt of Court Act 1981 195

11.7.3 *Impact of social media upon juror deliberations*

The impact of social media upon juror deliberations has been considered in a number of cases, although prosecutions have been few. The case of *Attorney General v Fraill and Stewart*[10] was singled out by the Law Commission in their report as a case demonstrating the risks social media present to the administration of justice. The case involved misconduct by a juror, Joanne Fraill, and one of the defendants, Jamie Stewart (tried alongside Mr Gary Knox), during the course of a very substantial trial at the Crown Court in Manchester sitting at Minshull Street before His Honour Judge Lakin and a jury in the summer of 2010. Two previous attempts to conclude a trial had failed and in each case the jury was discharged. The third trial began in late May 2010. On 21 May, Joanne Fraill was empanelled as a juror. On 3 August, the majority verdict direction was given in relation to the matter being tried by the Manchester Crown Court.

While they were continuing in retirement, on 4 August, it became apparent to Judge Lakin that an unknown juror had been in Facebook contact with Jamie Stewart, commenting to the effect that she was pleased that Stewart had been acquitted because she was 'with her the whole of the way'. Ms Fraill suggested that it was a pity that Stewart had not been in court when the verdicts involving Knox were announced because she would have been able to see 'the look of delight' on Mr Knox's face. The trail judge was ignorant of the identity of the juror who had been in communication with Stewart. The judge adjourned the jury deliberations for the day after he decided that he should inquire of each juror individually whether there had been any contact with any defendants. In order to establish if any contact had been made, the judge put the following to the jury:

> I have to ask you a question and it is this. Have you at any stage during the period from the retirement of the jury until today contacted or attempted to contact any other person, including any other juror, defendant or former defendant, i.e. a defendant acquitted of allegations made against them, by way of Facebook or email, about either your views of the evidence, your views of the jury verdict so far delivered and any reactions to such verdicts, or any other such matters. In short, I have evidence to suggest that Facebook contact has been made with Stewart. Have you made any such contact?[11]

As a result of the judge's enquiries, the extent of the contact between Fraill and Stewart was investigated. After Stewart had been acquitted on all the counts affecting her, Fraill made her first contact. According to Stewart's unchallenged evidence, confirming her account in interview, Ms Fraill sent an e-mail message to her Facebook account saying 'you should know me, I cried with you enough'.

---

10 *Attorney General v Joanne Fraill and Jamie Stewart* [2011] EWCA Crim 1570.

11 Reproduced at para 13 of the contempt proceedings, *Attorney General v Joanne Fraill and Jamie Stewart* [2011] EWCA Crim 1570.

196   *Criminal law: procedure*

11.7.4 *Jurors conducting their own research on the internet and deliberate disobedience of jury directions*

In *Fraill*, the court referred to *Attorney General v Dallas*,[12] a case where a juror had conducted her own research on the internet. Lord Judge CJ set out four elements that would ordinarily establish the two elements of contempt in cases where there had been deliberate disobedience to a judge's direction or order:

- The juror knew that the judge had directed that the jury should not do a certain act.
- The juror appreciated that that was an order.
- The juror deliberately disobeyed the order.
- By doing so the juror risked prejudicing the due administration of justice.[13]

As a result of the application of *Dallas* to the facts, Fraill was sentenced to eight months in prison, while Stewart was sentenced to a suspended prison sentence. The difference in sentence was because of the different circumstances of Stewart and Fraill (for example, Stewart had a very young child).

11.8 Law Commission's Report and *Your Guide to the Jury Service*

The Law Commission's Report noted that when a person receives their jury summons, they also get a booklet from the court service entitled *Your Guide to the Jury Service*. The booklet is designed to explain to jurors their obligations when sitting on a trial. In the context of social media, the guide explains to jurors that during the trial, they must not 'discuss the evidence with anyone outside your jury either face to face, over the telephone or over the internet via social networking sites such as Facebook, Twitter or Myspace'. It also says that if a juror is 'unsure or uneasy about anything', they can write a note to the judge. The content of the booklet and its relationship to social media was discussed in *AG v Kasim Davey and Joseph Beard*,[14] noting that page 5 of the booklet contains information concerning the use of social networking sites and the judge's directions. The fact that the booklet has been mentioned in relation to contempt proceedings reinforces the importance of the guidance.

11.9 Video: the role of a juror

The guidance booklet is not the only material provided to jurors. In general, on arrival at court on the first day of jury service, jurors will be shown a video[15] that provides a brief description of the court process, as well as the role and responsibilities of jurors in criminal proceedings. The video explains that 'it is vital' that jurors 'are not influenced by any outside factors', so they must not discuss the case with family or friends. Jurors are also told explicitly not 'to post details about any aspect of . . . jury service'.

---

12 [2012] 1 WLR 991.
13 [2012] 1 WLR 991 at [38].
14 *AG v Kasim Davey and Joseph Beard* [2013] EWHC 2317 (Admin) at [11].
15 The video can be viewed at http://www.youtube.com/watch?v=JP7slp-X9Pc&feature=relmfu.

In *AG v Kasim Davey and Joseph Beard*,[16] the court noted that Mr Davey had been shown the video and had disobeyed it by posting information pertaining to the trial on which he had been asked to sit via Facebook. Significantly, this included revealing their deliberations on social networking sites.

Jurors are warned that they 'may also be in contempt of court' if they 'use the internet to research details about any cases' they 'hear, along with any other cases listed for trial at the court'. Presumably, this would therefore include searching for social networking profiles or accounts belonging to those connected with the proceedings.

11.10 Court staff warning

In order to reinforce the message, aside from the video, court staff also warn jurors. The warning that court staff read to jurors now explicitly addresses statements made in relation to social media. The warning is as follows:

> The judge will tell you that you DO NOT discuss the evidence with anyone outside of your jury either face to face, over the telephone or over the internet via social networking sites such as Facebook, Twitter, or Myspace. If you do this, you risk disclosing information, which is confidential to the jury. Each juror owes a duty of confidentiality to the other jurors, to the parties and to the court. Jurors can only discuss the evidence when all 12 jurors are in the jury deliberating room at the conclusion of the evidence in the trial.[17]

Although the examples of Facebook, Twitter, and Myspace are given in the warning, the Law Commission highlight elsewhere in the report that this will also apply to YouTube, and therefore presumably other sites which are of a similar nature to well-established, widely used and accessed sites like Facebook and Twitter.

11.11 The courts' approach to dealing with technology

Although there are increasing policies and warnings in place in relation to jurors' use of social media, different courts have different systems for dealing with jurors' electronic devices that can connect to the internet, such as mobile phones, laptops, iPads, iPods, and Kindles. In some courts, jurors are permitted to keep these devices with them in the area where they have lunch and sit during breaks in the trial. However, the devices must be switched off in court, and are removed when jurors are reaching a verdict in the case in the jury room. In other courts, jurors' devices are removed from them for the whole time that they are at court. And in other courts, jurors can keep their devices even when reaching a verdict in the jury room.[18]

Clearly, there is a risk that if jurors are allowed access to their mobile phone in break-out areas, that they may be tempted to post comments on a particular aspect of

---

16 *AG v Kasim Davey and Joseph Beard* [2013] EWHC 2317 (Admin) at [12].
17 Reproduced in the Law Commission's paper *Contempt of Court Summary for Non-Specialists*, Law Commission Consultation Paper No. 209 at para [146]; and *Your Guide to Jury Service* at page [5] accessible via https://www.gov.uk/jury-service/overview.
18 Reproduced in 'Contempt of Court: Summary for non-specialists', Law Commission Consultation Paper No. 209 at paras [147–148].

198 *Criminal law: procedure*

the trial which they have just heard. The nature of some trials, such as celebrity trials (e.g. News Corporation 'phone hacking' trials and the prosecutions arising out of Operation Yewtree) can be difficult to resist posting about. Courts must draw a line between ensuring justice and also preventing jurors from having access to their personal devices. Courts have attempted to minimize the risk of jurors having access to their smart devices in different ways. By way of example, it was noted in *AG v Kasim Davey and Joseph Beard*[19] that in the jury lounge and foyer of Wood Green Crown Court that six identical notices were prominently displayed warning that contempt of court was punishable with a fine or imprisonment. That meant that certain conduct was prohibited:

> You must not use social networking sites to post details about any aspect of your jury service or about the discussion and decisions made by you and your fellow jurors whilst in deliberation. You may also be in Contempt of Court if you use the internet to research details about any cases you hear along with any other cases listed for trial at the Court.[20]

Although the notices were prominently displayed, they were still ignored by the jurors in this case and so the sensitivity of the trial and the potential for interference with justice as well as the cost of a re-trial if the trial is compromised must be weighted against limiting jurors' access to Smartphones.

11.12 Jurors' ability to recall directions

11.12.1 *Role of jurors, their duties, their intention, and their ability to recall directions for the court*

Although from the foregoing it is clear that in relation to social media the directions given to jurors are clear, there has been some discussion in relation to whether jurors understand the severity of commenting on cases via social media sites and that such behaviour may amount to contempt of court. There is little case law which explores the issue. However, *Attorney General v Kasim Davey and Joseph Beard*[21] is worthy of exploration as the judgment went into significant detail concerning the role of jurors, their duties, their intention, and their ability to recall directions for the court. The case against Mr Davey concerned a juror dropped from the trial of a sex offender following the discovery that he had posted a Facebook message stating: 'Woooow I wasn't expecting to be in a jury Deciding a paedophile's fate, I've always wanted to F★★k up a paedophile & now I'm within the law!' Mr Davey had a Facebook account in the name of 'Alex BawseBeats Jones'. At the end of the first day on his way home on the bus, he posted a message to the account, using his Smartphone. He had about 400 Facebook friends; two of those friends had approved of his comment by using a smiley – a thumbs up sign.

---

19 *AG v Kasim Davey and Joseph Beard* [2013] EWHC 2317 (Admin).
20 *AG v Kasim Davey and Joseph Beard* [2013] EWHC 2317 (Admin) at para [13].
21 *AG v Kasim Davey and Joseph Beard* [2013] EWHC 2317 (Admin).

The following day, on 4 December 2012, he sat again on the jury. On the night of 4/5 December, a Facebook friend sent an e-mail to the Crown Court at Wood Green which began: 'I have reason to believe someone who has been selected for jury service at your court has been posting about the case on the social networking site Facebook.' The email went on to set out what had been posted and gave the name of the person who had posted it as Mr Davey. When challenged by the judge, Mr Davey initially denied being responsible, although he subsequently admitted to the police that he had posted the message. At trial, he apologised and said that he had not intended to cause problems and the post was simply the result of 'spontaneous surprise' at the type of case he found himself on, the Saville investigation being a prominent news story at the time. A number of reasons were submitted by Mr Davey's representatives as to why he had made the posting and the sophistication (or lack thereof) when doing so. Let us explore each of the points put forward by the defendant and the response of the Court to understand how contempt law has begun to be applied in cases involving a social media aspect.

11.12.2 *Submissions in defence*

The submissions were as follows:

- He could not remember what the jury manager had said;
- He did not take that to be a direction or order, but something that was helpful to him;
- He could not recall the video;
- He could not recall the notices in the jury lounge or what the judge had said; he did not know whether that was because he had forgotten it or because he did not take it in at the time;
- He thought the posting might make him seem interesting and more exciting and would reflect well on him, so people who were his Facebook friends might notice him and want to talk to him;
- He thought that by indicating hostility to paedophiles this would reflect well on him;
- The words he used were intended to attract attention. He accepted that he was inviting people to respond, but he was not intending to start a discussion;
- He did not know that he was breaching any order made by the judge;
- He knew he was not meant to discuss the case, but he did not think that by making the posting he was discussing the case and breaching the order of the judge; and
- He thought the judge had only said they should not use the internet to research the case.

11.12.3 *Submissions in relation to creating a real risk of interference or prejudice to the administration of justice*

It was also submitted that Mr Davey was not in breach of his duties as a juror so as to create a real risk of interference or prejudice to the administration of justice, because:

200 *Criminal law: procedure*

- He had remained true to his oath;
- He was exhibiting a prejudice which many had when required to serve as a juror, but it was clear that like others with similar prejudices he would put those aside and try the case on the evidence;
- There was nothing to show that his prejudice would play any part in his determination of the verdict;
- The posting on its face did no more than state that he had a serious dislike for those who committed sexual crimes against children and that if the case was proved, the defendant would receive his punishment;
- He never intended the posting to be taken seriously.

The court did not accept the submissions, noting that that there were two distinct bases on which Mr Davey carried out an act calculated to interfere with the proper administration of justice and which he intended would interfere with the proper administration of justice. The court stated that however immature Mr Davey was at the time, he knew that as a juror he had a duty to act fairly towards the defendant in the trial and to consider the case on the evidence. Not only had he taken an oath to that effect, but he asserted in his evidence that he understood he had to consider the evidence fairly and give a verdict he honestly believed was right on the evidence. However, after hearing evidence for a day, he posted his message to be read by his 400 Facebook friends. The court stated that it was clear from his interview and his evidence that he knew that he was not meant to discuss the case with anyone other than other jurors. He also knew that he was not meant to use the internet in relation to the case, as he told the police this in his interview.

The message made clear that he would use his prejudices in deciding the case; it was suggested that the choice of the term 'fuck up' underlined his deliberate disregard of the duties he had undertaken as a juror. The court rejected his assertion that it was not meant seriously. By the deliberate choice of language he was making clear not only his interference with the administration of justice by disregarding his duties to act as a juror, but his plain intention to do so.

11.12.4 *Role of jury booklet, the video, the speech by the jury manager, and the warning signs as directions which jurors must follow*

The court also rejected the contention that the jury booklet, the video, the speech by the jury manager, and the warning signs are not directions that a juror must follow. They are provided to jurors under the authority of the court and are intended to make clear to jurors and to remind jurors during the trial of their obligations and what will constitute an interference with the administration of justice. The court also rejected the contention that the directions infringed Articles 8 and 10 of the European Convention on Human Rights; the directions were plainly within Articles 8.2 and 10.2.

In *Fraill* (the facts of the case are set out above), juror Joanne Fraill set up a Facebook account in the name of Jo Smilie. She submitted a Friend Request to Jamie Stewart, the defendant, at 6.30 pm. Stewart responded, and saw that the Jo Smilie account named Joanne Fraill as a friend and showed a photograph of Fraill. Stewart immediately recognized this as a photograph of one of the jurors who had recently acquitted her, and realized that the message had come from the juror. Stewart then entered into a conversation with Fraill using the Facebook instant messaging service. Stewart was thus aware that she was communicating with a juror. The conversation took place between 6.31 and 7.07 pm. As seen in *Davey*,[22] even if an individual is posting via a fake account or pseudonym, they can still be found guilty of contempt.

11.13 Injunctions and protected proceedings

11.13.1 *Attorney General v Harkins and Liddle*[23]

In *AG v Harkins and Liddle*, the Attorney General launched an investigation after photographs purporting to show killer Jon Venables were allegedly posted on the internet. Venables and Thompson became notorious in 1993 when they abducted a toddler named James Bulger and tortured him before leaving him for dead. Venables and Thompson were released on parole in 2001, when they were both 18 and were granted almost unprecedented injunctions preventing the publication of their new identities (see *Venables v News Group Newspapers Ltd* 2001 WL 14890). The images in the *Harkins and Liddle* contempt proceedings were uploaded to Twitter on the twentieth anniversary of the murder, allegedly showing Jon Venables attending a birthday party. The picture was re-published by more than 100 Twitter users and could have been viewed by thousands.

In order to understand the context of the prosecution for the tweets which were made via social media, it is necessary to say something of *Venables v News Group Newspapers*,[24] the case in which the worldwide injunction was granted in favour of Venables and Thompson. The injunction was granted as the court determined on the facts presented before it that there was a real possibility that the pair would be in danger of revenge attacks if their identities were disclosed such as to make the instant case an exceptional one. As such, the court was under a positive duty to operate to protect individuals from the criminal acts of others. It was for this reason that in such exceptional cases, the court had jurisdiction to widen the scope of the protection of confidentiality of information, even to the extent of placing restrictions on the press, where if no restrictions were imposed there was a likelihood that the person seeking confidentiality would suffer serious physical injury or even death and no other means of protection was available. She cited Lord Goff's dicta in *A-G v Guardian*,[25] at paragraph 128, stating that a stranger can be restrained from disclosing certain information where it is known to be confidential.[26]

For the foregoing reasons, on 8 January 2001, prior to the release of Thompson and Venables on licence under new identities, the then President of the Family Division Dame Elizabeth Butler-Sloss granted an injunction binding on the whole world preventing the publication of their new identities. The terms of the injunction,

---

22 *AG v Kasim Davey and Joseph Beard* [2012] 1 WLR 991.
23 [2013] EWHC 1455 (Admin).
24 [2001] Fam 430.
25 *Attorney General v Guardian Newspapers Ltd ('Spycatcher')* [1990] 1 AC 109.
26 *Venables* [2001] 2 WLR 1038 at [1065].

202 *Criminal law: procedure*

so far as material to the context of contempt proceedings, were to prevent not only the defendants to that particular case, but significantly, the entire world from publishing or causing to be published in any newspaper, or broadcasting in any sound or television broadcast or by means of any cable or satellite programme or public computer network, any depiction, image in any form, photograph, film or voice recording made or taken on or after 18 February 1993 which purported to be of Venables or Thompson (excluding police photographs of Thompson taken on 18 February 1993 and Venables taken on 20 February 1993) or any description which purported to be of their physical appearance, voices or accents. There were modifications and qualifications to the order at a later date to which it is unnecessary to refer for the purposes of this chapter.

It is against this context that in February 2014, the Attorney General pursued the prosecution of two posters in particular, Dean Liddle and Neil Harkins, for contravention of the *contra mundum* injunction. The pair were charged with contempt following the publication of photos purporting to represent the two killers of James Bulger in breach of the longstanding worldwide injunction. The two had posted on Twitter and Facebook respectively. Both received suspended sentences of nine months, with the court warning that there was little chance of an offender avoiding a substantial and immediate custodial sentence in the event of any future similar publication.

In relation to the prosecution of Neil Harkins, the facts were as follows. On 14 February 2013, Mr Harkins used his Facebook profile to post photographs of persons said to be Venables and Thompson. His Facebook profile indicated that he had 141 friends. The images purporting to be of Venables and Thompson were alleged to have been from the early 1990s and late 2000s. Underneath, Harkins wrote: 'interesting that this photograph is not allowed to be shown and there is an investigation on how it got out. What is more interesting is why he got released and protected in the first place.' Harkins also posted some time after the initial post, but on the same day (14 February 2013): 'Can't imagine what the poor kid went through. What is wrong is the fact he got released and then got done for downloading child pornography and yet he is still protected. What is wrong with the system?' The second post referred to a story, widely published in the British press, that Venables had been recalled to prison in 2010 for accessing images of child abuse.

Although Mr Harkins only had 141 'friends' on Facebook, the court considered it was plain from the evidence it heard in the contempt proceedings, that the placing of this remark on his Facebook profile resulted in it being shared with over 20,000 other people. It was impossible to say how many people did see the post, but the number was, in the opinion of the court, very significant.

On the following day, 15 February, the publication on the Facebook page was notified to the police. About a fortnight later on 28 February 2013, the Treasury Solicitor wrote on behalf of the Attorney General to Mr Harkins informing him that the material he had posted via his Facebook account (the photograph) was prohibited, and that the Attorney General was considering bringing proceedings against Mr Harkins for contempt of court. The letter also asked Mr Harkins to remove the photograph from his social media account.

After receiving the letter, Mr Harkins sent an email to the Treasury Solicitor on 1 March 2013 stating that he had removed the photograph purporting to be of

Venables from his Facebook page. A few days later on 5 March 2013, Mr Harkins wrote a long letter explaining his actions post receipt of the Treasury Solicitor's letter and the steps he had taken to mitigate his actions and the reasons why he had made the postings in the first place. He stated that he posted the images and comment in response to a news article that appeared when he logged in. He mentioned that Thompson and Venables had been returned to prison and there had been speculation about the identity. He continued:

> The article showed the images that I posted which I know are some of many which are widely accessible on the internet. I believed at the time that the images I posted were not within any legal constraints as they were freely accessible on the internet. I was also under the impression that the legal restrictions applied to images published in the media. However having received a copy of the injunction which you enclosed, I realize that is not the case.

It is interesting to compare the case of *Harkins* with that of Dean Liddle, who was also prosecuted for publishing photographs of Venables and Thompson via a social media account. In *Liddle* on 14 February 2014, Dean Liddle tweeted via his Twitter account 'OpinionatedDad' photographs purporting to identify Venables and Thompson as adults. The account had 915 followers and was accessible to the general public. Liddle stated that he had picked up the images for tweeting from photographs widely accessible elsewhere on the internet. The case can be distinguished from Harkins because the photographs purporting to identify Venables and Thompson were removed by Liddle about an hour after they were originally posted. It appeared from subsequent postings on his Twitter account he had removed them because other account holders had pointed out that the images were not those of Venables.

Another interesting distinction from Harkins identified by the court was that Liddle must have appreciated that what he was doing must have been wrong because he knew of the injunction, as one of his tweets stated: 'I heard about it [the injunction] for a while, but posted it as people are talking about being prosecuted for putting it and I don't think it's right.' The court also referred to a further tweet made just after the deletion of the photos which stated: 'So I get a huge fine. Great. They will get £2 a week off me and the evil men who murdered a child will be known publicly – #worthit.'

This matter came to the attention of the Attorney General on 14 February 2013. The Attorney General asked the Metropolitan Police to make inquiries as to who operated the account 'OpinionatedDad', which established that the owner was Dean Liddle.

The Treasury Solicitor wrote in terms similar to the letter to Neil Harkins to Mr Liddle on 5 March 2014. Upon receipt of the letter, Mr Liddle took to Twitter to post the following: 'Just been served with court papers for posting picture of sick child killers Venables and Thompson. What a joke.' And 'love them to take me to court. I'll tell them exactly why I posted pictures of sick child killers.'

It would appear that on the following day, on 6 March, Mr Liddle had the opportunity to reflect upon his actions. He telephoned the Treasury Solicitor to acknowledge receipt of the letter and to express his apologies. He indicated that he now had understood what an injunction was and he realized it was a serious issue. He followed

204 *Criminal law: procedure*

the telephone call up a few days later with an email to the Treasury Solicitor that stated:

> I would like to offer, firstly, my sincerest apology. It was a mistake on my part and one which I vow never to commit again. I must also add however when I posted these photographs on Twitter I had already noticed the exact photo hundreds of times that day on Twitter so was thinking it was still something which was already out in the public, visible to all. Still, I was aware there was a ruling for there not to be printed or posted on line but still did so. My biggest error was in not fully understanding the implication of what an injunction was, what it covered and what breaking the injunction actually meant. I don't want to play dumb here, but I genuinely did not fully understand how serious this situation was. I am now fully aware of the injunctions and why they need to be upheld.

11.13.1.1 *Sentencing*

As the cases were joined, the matter of sentencing was taken together, rather than considered in respect of each defendant. The court took into account that both defendants admitted that they had committed a serious contempt of court when determining the penalty that the court must impose. The court noted that the maximum penalty that it could impose was a two-year prison sentence or an unlimited fine. A fine was not considered appropriate on the facts due to each of the defendant's financial circumstances. However, the court did state that in any event a fine would not be appropriate due to the gravity of the offending. The court therefore went on to consider the facts surrounding the publications, which would be taken into account on sentencing. The points highlighted below by the court may provide a useful benchmark for assessing the types of concerns that are likely to be within the court's consideration in future cases. However, they are not exhaustive and each case will be, to a large extent, influenced by the content posted and the nature of the posting (e.g. if it is a matter of significant public interest, if there are injunctions in place, etc.).

11.13.1.2 *Aggravating factors*

The following features of the case were noted as aggravating factors:

*   The potential consequences, not only to Venables and Thompson but to persons who might be mistakenly identified as them and therefore subject to the serious risk of vigilante attack resulting in serious injury or worse.
*   It was plain that they knew of the prohibition contained in the injunction though they may not have known the full extent of the consequences of what they were doing.
*   They became part of a determined internet campaign on the twentieth anniversary of the death of James Bulger. They freely joined in that campaign.

From the viewpoint of the court, their conduct had to be judged on the basis that they knew that what they were doing was wrong and it was no excuse that others were doing it.

11.13.1.3 *Mitigating factors*

The court also referred to a number of factors in mitigation:

- Both removed the offending pictures;
- The pictures were removed quickly (in the case against *Liddle*);
- Both apologized;
- Both recognized the gravity of their actions and conducted themselves accordingly during the course of the contempt proceedings;
- The admission of contempt was promptly and fulsomely made.[27]

11.13.2 *Attorney General v Baines*[28]

On 27 November 2013, James Baines became the third individual to receive a suspended prison sentence for purporting to identify one of the killers of James Bulger in photographs posted via his Twitter account. He was further ordered to pay £3,000 in costs. The breach was accompanied by a Twitter post clearly demonstrating awareness of the prohibition on identification, stating: 'it's on BBC news about the jon venables pic on twitter saying its been removed eerrm no it hasn't'. The following month he posted on Facebook that he had complete contempt for the police if they were to take action against him.

During the day of 14 February, the respondent continued to maintain his stance of disregarding the statements that had been made that he was wrong, and went so far as to point out that he was doing so with the objective of causing harm. For example, on one occasion he said that he would 'smash this rats head in for what he done'. At 6.41 pm, he sent another Twitter message as follows: 'didn't no that its been on the news anyone who shares the picture will be prosecuted an can go to jail'. Thereafter, he continued to maintain his defiant stance. On 24 February (ten days later), he re-tweeted the same pictures. It is a matter of considerable concern that on 15 March, or thereabouts, he posted on his Facebook account, where he had 627 'friends', statements to the effect that he had complete contempt for the police if they were to take action against him.

On 15 May 2013, the Attorney General had identified him as the owner of the Twitter account and wrote to Mr Baines. Following his receipt of the Attorney General's letter, the respondent said that he would not be paying a fine because 'its that are doing me and they will get the money so looks like jail for me fucking scumbag country'. On 19 May 2013, the office of the Treasury Solicitor telephoned the respondent. He lied in saying that the account was not his. Later he posted a message on the Facebook account of an organization called 'MWI Fightback', which, we are told, appears to be either a right-wing political body or a right-wing racist body. The message was to this effect: 'People are getting punished for posting the pictures of them two scumbags. I know little Jamie's family personally. So whatever I get I'll take it like a man.'

---

27 [2013] EWHC 1455 (Admin) at [27].
28 *Attorney General v James Baines* [2013] EWHC 4326 (Admin).

206   *Criminal law: procedure*

11.13.2.1 *Aggravating factors*

When the contempt proceedings were brought before the court, a number of aggravating features were noted:[29]

* The respondent acted in flagrant breach of the court's injunction.
* He knew of the injunction, but engaged as part of a determined campaign.
* Within the shortest possible time he knew of the consequences, yet he displayed an attitude to this court, to Her Majesty's Attorney General, to the police, and to other authorities of complete contempt for them.
* Those who had suggested that he was in breach of the order were subjected to unpleasant abuse.
* The purpose of his postings was to harm Venables.

11.13.2.2 *Mitigating factors*

In mitigation, two factors were put forward:[30]

* Acceptance, albeit at a late stage, that he had known all along what he had done was wrong.
* Eventually accepted the merits of the Attorney General's case against him

The court noted that the mitigating factors were limited and the admission could have been made at least a month earlier.

The approach adopted in the above cases is interesting to compare with *Venables v News Group Newspapers*,[31] the case which granted the *contra mundum* (against the world) injunction. As noted above, although the issue of publication of the pair's identity via online channels was considered, the issues that could be presented by online platforms was not explored in any depth. Although social media use had not yet exploded (indeed Twitter wasn't even available until 2006), the internet was becoming available to an increasing number of people. For this reason, to the limited extent that the judgment considered online channels, it only focused on the possibility of the press publishing information originating online and to curb its further publication in traditional media outlets rather than the role that the public could play in generating news topics and their discussions of them. It has to be recalled when considering this judgment, that the internet at this time was not a medium though which self publishing, except through a few blogs and online communities, was widespread or facilitated though micro-blogging sites, which can generate large volumes of information and cause topics to 'trend' very quickly. Also, Smartphones with internet connectivity were not widely available and the technology supporting them was in its infancy with networks such as 3G simply unavailable or cost prohibitive to the general public.

In terms of the issues presented by social media, perhaps one of the more interesting aspects that required more analysis is to be found at paragraph D 1 (v)(i)

---

29 [2013] EWHC 4326 (Admin) at [18].
30 [2013] EWHC 4326 (Admin) at [19].
31 2001 WL 14890.

Contempt of Court Act 1981   207

of the judgment concerning the jurisdictional application of the injunction. In this paragraph, Dame Butler-Sloss stated that injunctions may not be fully effective to protect Thompson and Venables from acts committed outside England and Wales resulting from information about them being placed on the internet. It was felt, however, that it could prevent wider circulation of that information through the newspapers or television and radio. It was for this reason that Dame Butler-Sloss added an additional proviso that 'would protect the special quality of the new identity, appearance, and addresses of the claimants or information leading to that identification, even after that information had entered the public domain to the extent that it had been published on the internet or elsewhere such as outside the UK'.[32]

However, what the judgment did not address was what liability the internet publishers themselves could face in light of this. In the 2010 case of *Jon Venables, Robert Thompson v News Group Papers Limited and others*,[33] the issue of the injunction was revisited after a challenge by News Group Newspapers to prohibit permanently the publication of information that would lead to the identification of Venables or Thompson despite it arising from proceedings in open court following Venables' conviction for child pornography charges. Bean J said that the fundamental duty of the State to ensure that suspects, defendants, and prisoners were protected from violence and not subjected to retribution or punishment except in accordance with the sentence of a court applied just as much to unpopular defendants as to anyone else. Perhaps an interesting aspect to note in the case is that at paragraph 38 of the judgment it is acknowledged that Venables' legal representative had submitted that a permanent injunction was necessary because of the continuing public animosity towards him and the risks he faced, and presented evidence of a large number of social networking sites in which contributors actively canvassed vigilante action to bring about his death. The issue arising out of private individuals and social media postings was rather disappointingly not analysed by the court, with the firm focus in the proceedings once again as seen in the 2001 judgment being on the role of the press.

The Venables case is an interesting look at how contempt might be applied in relation to matters that cause significant public outcry. In the so-called 'super injunction' cases, which centred in part around the anonymized injunction obtained by Ryan Giggs in *CTB v News Group Newspapers*,[34] no prosecutions were brought against the individuals responsible for breaking the injunction. It is suggested that the Attorney General's Office has chosen to take a different response in the present case because the extremely sensitive and emotive content was quickly removed. Moreover, the Venables tweet was re-posted approximately 100 times, whereas in the super injunction there were record visits to Twitter in the UK, with one in every 200 visits being made that day to its website to view the super injunction account.

It could be argued that the possibility of locating the thousands of individuals who infringed the injunction and locating the source of the initial tweets would therefore

32 Ibid.
33 2010 WL 3017988.
34 [2011] EWHC 1232.

208   *Criminal law: procedure*

have been a logistical impossibility when measured against the time and resources that could be allocated to address the issue. Moreover, the right to privacy in relation to footballers' pastimes and their public image is not necessarily of such great need of protection as the potential risks posed to the preservation of human life and the ramifications which could arise out of the misidentification of individuals convicted or accused of grievous crimes. It may be that as case law grows in this area, the balance of an individual's human rights such as Article 8 (the right to privacy) and Article 10 (the right to freedom of expression) will become more refined as they have in relation to matters prosecuted under the Communications Act 2003. However, it is likely that these considerations will be pondered by the Attorney General in determining whether or not to bring a prosecution and not where the balance in favour of prosecution lies. As the reader will recall from the start of this chapter, the offence of contempt is one of strict liability (see section 1 Contempt of Court Act 1981). The balancing exercise may also prove useful when deciding sentencing, or at least in the infancy of this area of law offer a framework from which to base any future sentencing guidelines which may be adopted.

11.14 Protected proceedings

11.14.1 *Children and Young Persons Act 1933*

Offences on Twitter can also be committed in relation to minors. Specifically, there have been a number of tweets on the internet which have been suggested to have been made contrary to section 39 of the Children and Young Persons Act 1933 (CYPA 1933). Section 39 CYPA 1933 provides that it is an offence to reveal the name, address or school, or include any particulars calculated to lead to the identification, of any child or young person concerned in the proceedings, either as being the person or in respect of whom the proceedings are taken, or as being a witness therein. Section 33(1)(b) states that it is also an offence to publish in any newspaper as being or including a picture of any child or young person so concerned in the proceedings except in so far (if at all) as may be permitted by the direction of the court.

11.14.2 *Publications by private individuals*

It should be noted that this section of the Act refers to publication by a newspaper and does not refer to private individuals. However, Peaches Geldof tweeted the names of two mothers whose children were involved in a high-profile sex trial of the musician and former member of the rock band *Lostprophets*, Ian Watkins, risking the identification of the children involved (who as the victims of sex offences are entitled to lifelong anonymity). This, despite a well-publicised warning by the South Wales Police as to the potential criminal liability of doing so hours earlier.

Despite these stark warnings of the consequences of posting inappropriate content on social media, many users continued to tweet the name of the girl abducted by teacher Jeremy Forrest, despite widely publicised warnings that to do so was in contempt of court, the girl's identity being protected under both the Children and Young Persons Act 1933 and as a victim of a sexual offence.

11.15 Injunctions granted in relation to social media specifically

11.15.1 *W v M*

In May 2011, in the judgment of *W v M*,[35] the English courts granted the first injunction specifically banning the publication of any information relating to the identity of a woman (protected by the Court of Protection) on any 'social network or media including Twitter or Facebook'.

The order prohibited, pursuant to rule 92(2) of the Court of Protection Rules 2007, the publishing or broadcasting, in any newspaper, magazine, public computer network, internet site, social network or media including Twitter or Facebook, sound or television broadcast or cable or satellite programme service, of any information (including any photograph) that is likely to lead to the identification of:

- M;
- Any person as being

  - a party or former party to these proceedings;
  - a witness in these proceedings (as defined in paragraph 3(8) of this Order), other than an expert witness instructed in the case;
  - a current or past treating healthcare professional or member of M's care team referred to in proceedings in relation to M's care and/or treatment listed in Schedule 2 to this order;

- the Care Home as being the place where M is residing;
- any address or location as being an address or location referred to in the proceedings, save that the location may be stated to be the 'North of England'.

11.15.2 *Court of Protection Rules 2007*

11.15.2.1 *Rule 92(2) Court of Protection Rules 2007*

Rule 92(2) provides that, where the court makes an order under paragraph (1), it may in the same order or by a subsequent order:

(a) impose restrictions on the publication of the identity of—

  (i)   any party;
  (ii) P (whether or not a party);
  (iii) any witness; or
  (iv) any other person;

(b) prohibit the publication of any information that may lead to any such person being identified;

(c) prohibit the further publication of any information relating to the proceedings from such date as the court may specify; or

(d) impose such other restrictions on the publication of information relating to the proceedings as the court may specify.

---

35 *W v M* [2011] EWHC 1197 (COP).

210   *Criminal law: procedure*

11.15.2.2 *Legal basis for reporting restrictions*

11.15.2.2.1 BALANCING CONVENTION RIGHTS

The legal test for making reporting restriction orders in the Court of Protection involves the balancing of rights under Article 8 (respect for private and family life) and Article 10 (freedom of expression).[36] According to Practice Direction 13A, neither of these articles takes precedence over the other.

When conducting the balancing exercise, the courts consider the four propositions identified by Lord Steyn in *Re S*:[37]

> First, neither article has as such precedence over the other. Secondly, where the values under the two articles are in conflict, an intense focus on the comparative importance of the specific rights being claimed in the individual case is necessary. Thirdly, the justifications for interfering with or restricting each right must be taken into account. Finally, the proportionality test must be applied to each. For convenience I will call this the ultimate balancing test.[38]

When considering Article 8, the court noted that the rights of family members, in addition to those of the protected party, must also be considered as part of the balancing exercise undertaken looking at the nature and strength of the evidence of the risk of harm.

Article 10 on the facts required a consideration of the public interest in the general issues in an application for an order that may lead to the shortening of a life, as opposed to the identity and personal circumstances of the protected person. However, the court must bear in mind that it is in the public interest for the practices and procedures of the Court of Protection to be understood.

11.15.2.2.2 INTERRELATIONSHIP WITH ARTICLE 6 ECHR

It should be noted as it was in *W v M*, that other convention rights may be engaged such as those used in Article 6; for example, if there is a suggestion that publication of information relating to the proceedings or the media seeking to contact family members may affect the capacity of a party to participate in the proceedings.

11.15.2.2.3 COMPARISON WITH SUPER INJUNCTIONS

The court noted that although the case had parallels with the so-called super injunction cases in terms of the consideration of the Convention rights which required balancing, the balancing exercise would be invariably different in the Court of Protection because of the circumstances of those whom the court is seeking to protect.

---

36 See Chapter 2: Human Rights for a full consideration of Convention rights and case law concerning privacy and freedom of expression.
37 *Re S (A Child) (Identification: Restriction on Publication)* [2004] UKHL 47 is considered in detail in Chapter 2: Human Rights.
38 *Re S (A Child) (Identification: Restriction on Publication)* [2004] UKHL 47 at para 17.

11.16 Future advisory notes from the Attorney General

On 4 December 2013, it was announced via the gov.uk website[39] that the Attorney General would be issuing future advisory notes to help prevent social media users from committing a contempt of court. The advisories will be published on the Attorney General's Office (AGO) section of the gov.uk website and also through the AGO's twitter feed, @AGO_UK.

11.17 Incorporated Council of Law Reporting (ICLR) blog post on 'The internet, social media and contempt of court: some recent developments'

On 24 December 2013, the ICLR published a blog exploring recent cases of contempt involving social media and the need for further clarification in the law.[40] The post noted that in relation to contempt of court, the risks involved concern the way criminal trials are reported and commented upon and the way this can prejudice the outcome. First, in relation to comments on trials which are pending or in progress, the Attorney General, Dominic Grieve MP, announced on 4 December that in future guidance would be issued, in the form of tweets linking back to fuller details on a website, warning of the risks of contempt being committed by publication of details in specific cases. This marked a change in policy, since previously 'advisories' were only issued to print and broadcast media outlets on a 'not for publication' basis. The new warning system is intended 'to make sure that a fair trial takes place and warn people that comment on a particular case needs to comply with the Contempt of Court Act 1981'.

---

39 https://www.gov.uk/government/news/attorney-general-to-warn-facebook-and-twitter-users-about-contempt-of-court.

40 See http://www.iclr.co.uk/internet-social-media-contempt-court-recent-developments/.

12 Evidence and procedure

12.1 Introduction

Due to the increasing availability of social networking material, the potential for law enforcement agencies to gather such information as part of an investigation is significant. Social media can provide easily accessible up-to-date information about individuals, making sites a highly desirable source of evidence. Although such information is widely discoverable and largely admissible, it can have a disproportionate impact in proceedings if careful consideration is not given to the provenance of such information and the correct weight that should be afforded to it. In criminal proceedings where such information is put before juries, in its raw form such information can have a powerful impact upon the outcome of proceedings if the process is not managed correctly by the court.

As we saw in Chapter 11 on contempt of court, content posted via the medium may in and of itself constitute an offence. However, data gathered from social media sites can also be used to attack credibility. This chapter will consider the use of SNS evidence and the evidential rules that it may engage.

12.2 The use of evidence from social networking sites in criminal proceedings

12.2.1 *Types of proceedings to which SNS evidence has had application*

The use of evidence from social networking sites in criminal proceedings has increased significantly in recent years. There are various ways in which it has impacted upon the criminal law, such as SNS content being exhibited as evidence and the posting or content itself constituting criminal activity. Social media postings in many cases may offer evidence relevant directly or circumstantially to an issue[1] or assist in the investigation of all manner of crimes.[2]

---

1 *Haque and Nuth* [2009] EWCA Crim 1453 where evidence was used as admission.
2 *Southam* [2009] EWCA Crim 2335.

12.2.2 *Types of data exhibited*

The ways in which SNS content is being exhibited in proceedings include:

- Using photographs, text, and 'wall postings' to challenge identification[3]
- Using photographs, text, and posts to suggest inappropriate links between parties[4]
- To challenge witness credibility[5]
- To prove gang membership[6]

12.2.3 *Activity on social networking sites that may amount to criminal activity*

Activity on social networking sites that may amount to criminal activity include:

- Harassment[7]
- Fraud[8]
- Threats to kill, etc.[9]
- Empowering or helping anyone to cheat at gambling[10]

12.2.4 *Interrelationship with Article 6 of the Human Rights Act 1998*

The use of such exhibits does however raise a number of issues which way interfere with Article 6 of the ECHR:[11]

- Authenticity of post
- Proving authorship
- Confessions
- Bad character
- Invasion of privacy through monitoring
- Using fake profiles to 'spy' on individuals or 'trap' them

---

3 *Haque and Nuth* [2009] EWCA Crim 1453 and *McCullough* [2011] EWCA Crim 1413.

4 *Locke v Stuart & AXA* [2011] EWHC 399 (QB).

5 *Walker* [2011] EWCA Crim 141 and, *Delaney* [2010] EWCA Crim 105.

6 As in *H (Buick Wildcat)* [2008] EWCA Crim 3321 and *Bucknor* [2010] EWCA Crim 1152.

7 See http://www.guardian.co.uk/uk/2009/aug/21/facebook-bullying-sentence-teenage-girl [accessed 22 August 2011].

8 *Locke v Stuart & AXA* [2011] EWHC 399 (QB).

9 *Rizwan* [2003] EWCA Crim 3067 (threats made via email) and *Hothi* [2011] EWCA 1039.

10 Section 42 of the Gambling Act 2005. In the USA, in response to the speech delivered at the recent Europol press conference on the global scale of match-fixing (Europol Conference on Match Fixing, 4 February 2013, The Hague, The Netherlands), the MLS (Major League Soccer) in particular has taken a proactive stance to the problem and have already put in place measures and controls such as having a 'soccer security agent' in Las Vegas to monitor gambling activity and hiring a director of security to include the use of social media [http://www.philly.com/philly/blogs/thegoalkeeper/Major-League-Soccer-North-American-Soccer-League-and-United-Soccer-Leagues-respond-to-global-match-fixing-scandals.html?ref=twitter.com].

11 See Chaper 2: Human Rights for an exploration of Article 6 of the ECHR, the right to a fair trial.

214 *Criminal law: procedure*

12.2.5 *Comparison with United States*

12.2.5.1 *Federal Rule of Evidence 401*

Federal Rule of Evidence 401 states that evidence is relevant if it has any tendency to make a fact more or less probable than it would be without the evidence, and if the fact is of consequence in determining the action.

12.2.5.2 *Establishing admissibility*

For admission in court, a party must show that the information is *relevant* and *authentic*. The party intending to adduce the evidence must also:

- Address issues of unfair prejudice;
- Demonstrate the probative value;
- Address hearsay (show an exception or non-hearsay use of the electronically stored information); and
- Demonstrate that the social media postings adduced conform to the original writing (the best evidence rule).

In *Quagliarello v Dewees*,[12] the court held that the defendants could show up to three pictures of the plaintiff from a social media website if she testified on direct examination regarding her emotional distress after the incident alleged in the lawsuit. The plaintiff then would have the opportunity to rebut the photographic evidence on redirect by introducing up to three additional social media photographs from the same time period.

12.3 Investigating known suspects

Even without going undercover by setting up fake profiles, social networking sites represent the possibility to track and locate suspects[13] and to alert the public and seek assistance in searching for or identifying wanted criminals.[14] For these reasons, the potential use which social media can be put to in relation to law enforcement is being quickly realized.[15] If law enforcement authorities have a suspected offender or are targeting a particular group of users as part of an investigation, then social media postings may be investigated as part of that process (e.g. those who associated with the recent Facebook page entitled 'Hunt and Kill Neil Lennon').[16] However, the use of such mediums comes with responsibility and must always be considered in light of Article 6 ECHR.

---

12 2011 US Dist LEXIS 86914, at *9–10 (ED Pa Aug 4, 2011).

13 See investigations and arrests of Craig Lynch [http://news.bbc.co.uk/1/hi/england/suffolk/8456182. stm; accessed 2 August 2011] and Pasquale Manfredi [http://news.bbc.co.uk/1/hi/world/europe/ 8570796.stm; accessed 2 August 2011].

14 See http://edition.cnn.com/2009/TECH/01/14/nz.facebook.arrest/index.html [accessed 2 August 2011].

15 See http://www.eff.org/files/filenode/social_network/20100303_crim_socialnetworking.pdf at p. 32.

16 See N. Haralambous and M. Johnson, 'Facebook – friend or foe?' (2010) 174(31) CL & J 469 for discussion of potential criminal liability of the poster and host. On the latter, see recent decision of the ECJ in *L'Oréal v eBay* (Case c-324/09) (12 July 2011) at [121]–[122].

Evidence and procedure 215

12.4 Identifying suspects

12.4.1 *Use of SNS data*

Social media profiles represent a rich source of materials from which individuals can be identified (e.g. name, area, gender, and many photographs). Although many photographs will record happy events like attending parties or holidays, snaps may also include criminal behaviour such as posing with knives, guns, gang insignia, etc.,[17] or posing with looted goods, which was a common occurrence during the UK riots in 2011.

However, such images may not be so clear-cut. In *R v Mach*,[18] *Mach* was convicted of inflicting grievous bodily harm on an individual who had been dancing with his girlfriend. The victim did not know who his attacker was, but Mach's girlfriend sent the victim an apologetic text message. The victim them went though her Facebook page[19] and found photographs of Mach who he recognized as his attacker; the attacker was listed as one of her 'friends'. Mach was subsequently arrested and identified in a video identity parade.[20]

In relation to witnesses, researching photos of suspects is becoming increasingly commonplace.[21] However, this creates a risk that the witness' initial SNS identification can affect subsequent formal identifications.[22] In *McCullough*,[23] the defendant was charged with robbery. Evidence was adduced that McCullough was in the vicinity where the incident had occurred.[24] McCullough's involvement in the crime depended upon the evidence of a witness, who we shall refer to as W. W had searched the defendant's Facebook account after a friend told him it 'sounded like something . . . [M] would do'.[25] W subsequently identified M in a video identification procedure. It was argued by the defence that the Facebook identification was 'unsatisfactory and unreliable' and contaminated the subsequent procedure.[26] In response, it was argued that the Facebook identification was no different to a street identification. However, when social media sites are searched, that search will be directed towards a particular account against a particular individual. The prosecution in *McCullough* stated that W 'looked at a photograph of the appellant and also photographs of other individuals and groups of people'.[27] This does not accord with the street analogy, as W directed his search

---

17 See http://www.telegraph.co.uk/news/uknews/6149807/Armed-gang-jailed-after-being-named-and-shamed-on-Facebook.html [accessed 26 April 2012].

18 *Mach*, Southwark CC (Mr Recorder Layton QC), September 2009 (unreported).

19 For a discussion of the admissibility of evidence disclosed by private sleuthing, see Chapter 4: Communications Act 2003.

20 Interestingly, since the girlfriend could not be found to give evidence, her text messages to V were admitted under s 114 Criminal Justice Act 2003.

21 See, for example, the convictions of Alex James Kalloghlian [http://www.westmercia.police.uk/news/news-articles/attacker-jailed-after-victim-traced-him-on-facebook.html; accessed 26 April 2012] and Ashleigh Holliman [http://news.sky.com/home/uk-news/article/15458212; accessed 26 April 2012].

22 *H* [2009] EWCA Crim 1453 at [34] and [37] and *McCullough* [2011] EWCA Crim 1413 at [9].

23 *McCullough* [2011] EWCA Crim 1413.

24 CCTV footage captured images of McCullough with R, who admitted theft. R claimed McCullough was not involved in the subsequent robbery, which took place elsewhere.

25 *McCullough* [2011] EWCA Crim 1413 at [6].

26 *McCullough* [2011] EWCA Crim 1413 at [9].

27 *McCullough* [2011] EWCA Crim 1413 at [6].

216 *Criminal law: procedure*

towards a particular account. In contrast, W would not confine his search to a particular house address on a street, yet a particular social media page is to all intents and purposes a specific address (albeit a cyber address in the form of a URL).

A further issue in *McCullough* was that W would not reveal anything about the tipoff that the offender might be McCullough or the Facebook account which was used to access M's account. No printout of the information was provided.[28] As discussed later in this chapter, this can create issues in relation to establishing provenance and authenticity of postings. In *McCullough*, it appears the only safeguard was that W noted his initial description of the suspect, but the initial description did not even match the clothes *McCullough* was wearing on the day, while also neglecting to mention substantial scarring across his face.[29] These are factors that must be specifically pointed out to the jury in a *Turnbull* direction.[30]

12.4.2 *Safeguards for authorities seeking to adduce such evidence*

It is suggested that in light of the *McCullough* judgment there needs to be more safeguards in place when authorities intend to adduce such evidence. Such checks could include:

- investigating officers ensuring descriptions from eyewitnesses are taken as soon after the crime as possible;
- warning against private SNS identifications; and
- if a suspect is brought to the attention of a witness, that witness ought to contact the police for the arrangement of a more formal identification process.

The risks of misidentification occurred in *Jenkins*;[31] a witness initially identified 'SPJ', having seen a photo of him on Bebo, but subsequently claimed this identification was flawed, and that the true perpetrator was 'JJJ'.

12.4.3 *Risk of vigilantism*

The court heard in *Jenkins* that a great deal of discussion took place among the deceased's family as to who had been responsible for her death. That resulted in the witness going to another individual's house who was connected to the matter. The witness was told that SPJ was the suspect. He was asked by members of the family to look up the Bebo page where a photograph, which included one of SPJ, appeared. Having been told that this was the suspect, he said he recognized him and went to the police station. He informed the police that he was 100% sure that the person in the photograph, SPJ, was his mother's assailant. The appellant was over 30 years of age at this time, while SPJ was between 14 and 15 years old.[32]

---

28 *McCullough* [2011] EWCA Crim 1413 at [8].
29 *McCullough* [2011] EWCA Crim 1413 at [10].
30 *Turnbull* [1977] 1 QB 224 at [228].
31 [2011] HCJAC 86.
32 [2011] HCJAC 86 at [22].

The police, in the *Kalloghlian* investigation, which concerned an assault, recognized the tensions raised by Facebook identification, noting:

> [w]e don't normally advocate people using Facebook in this way in order to trace offenders because it can undermine our own identification procedures. However in these circumstances had it not been for Facebook we may not have been able to identify him so effectively. Facebook can be a blessing or a blight but in this case Kalloghlian was completely tripped up by it.[33]

Authentication will represent an important aspect where social media evidence is adduced.

Once the hurdles concerning authenticity have been overcome, images must be of sufficient quality for identification purposes, as emphasised in *Attorney General's Reference (No. 2 of 2002)*;[34] where the images are of poor quality, convictions will be quashed as occurred in *Jabar*.[35] It is suggested that if such evidence will be adduced, the jury must be given an explicit warning about the dangers of mistaken identification.[36]

12.5 Bad character

12.5.1 *Defendants*

12.5.1.1 *Admissibility of bad character evidence*

The admissibility of bad character evidence is set out in sections 98–113 of the Criminal Justice Act 2003 (CJA 2003), which applies to all criminal proceedings begun on or after 4 April 2005.[37] The common law rules governing the admissibility of bad character evidence have been abolished (s 99 (1) CJA 2003) with the exception of the following, which are expressly preserved:

- Any rule of law under which in criminal proceedings evidence of reputation is admissible for the purpose of proving good character, but only so far as it allows the court to treat such evidence as proving the matter concerned (s 9(2) and s 118(1) CJA 2003);
- Evidence or cross examination about the complainant's sexual history in trials for sexual offences continues to be restricted by section 41 Youth Justice and Criminal Evidence Act 1999 in addition to section 112(3)(b) CJA 2003 where the behaviour is also 'bad character' evidence. This means that in a trial for a sexual offence, to adduce evidence of a complainant's previous sexual behaviour that is also 'bad character' evidence, both tests will have to be satisfied.

---

33 See http://www.westmercia.police.uk/news/news-articles/attacker-jailed-after-victim-traced-him-on-facebook.html [accessed 26 April 2012].
34 *Attorney General's Reference (No. 2 of 2002)* [2003] 1 Cr App R 21 (p. 321), Rose LJ at [19].
35 See *Jabar* [2010] EWCA Crim 130.
36 *Ali* [2008] EWCA Crim 1522.
37 Section 141 Criminal Justice Act 2003.

218   *Criminal law: procedure*

12.5.1.2 *Definition of bad character*

'Bad character' in criminal proceedings means 'evidence of or a disposition towards misconduct' (s 99 CJA 2003). Misconduct means the commission of an offence or other 'reprehensible conduct' (s 112 CJA 2003). This definition applies to both defendants and non-defendants. The definition is wide enough to apply to conduct arising out of a conviction, or conduct where there has been an acquittal (*R v Z*[38]). It will also apply to a person who has been charged with another offence, where a trial is pending and the use of the evidence relating to that charge in current proceedings.

12.5.1.2.1 MEANING OF 'REPREHENSIBLE CONDUCT'

According to the CPS Guidelines, 'reprehensible conduct' should be looked at objectively taking account of whether the public would regard such conduct as reprehensible, such as racism, bullying, a bad disciplinary record at work for misconduct, a parent who has had a child taken into care and, of course, minor pilfering from employers. Conduct that should not be regarded as reprehensible could include consensual sexual activity between adults of the same sex. The term 'reprehensible conduct' will avoid arguments about whether or not conduct alleged against a person amounted to an offence where this has not resulted in a charge or conviction.[39]

12.5.1.3 *Admissibility*

There is a two-stage test for admissibility:

Stage 1
The evidence must be admissible through one or more of the seven gateways set out in section 101 CJA 2003:

(a) all parties to the proceedings agree to the evidence being admissible;
(b) the evidence is adduced by the defendant himself or is given in answer to a question asked by him in cross examination and intended to elicit it;
(c) it is important explanatory evidence;
(d) it is relevant to an important matter in issue between the defendant and the prosecution, which includes:

 • whether the defendant has a propensity to commit offences of the kind with which he is charged, except where such propensity makes it no more likely that he is guilty of the offence (s 103(1)(a) CJA 2003);
 • whether the defendant has a propensity to be untruthful, except where it is not suggested that the defendant's case is untruthful in any respect (s 102(1)(b) CJA 2003);

---

38 [2000] 2 AC 483.
39 See http://www.cps.gov.uk/legal/a_to_c/bad_character_evidence/.

Evidence and procedure 219

(e) it has substantial probative value in relation to an important matter in issue between the defendant and a co-defendant;
(f) it is evidence to correct a false impression given by the defendant; or
(g) the defendant has made an attack on another person's character.

Stage 2

The evidence is admissible if it falls within section 101(1)(a), (b), (c), (e) and (f) CJA 2003. Where the evidence falls with section 101(1)(d) or (g) it is admissible unless, on application by a defendant, it has such an adverse effect on the fairness of the proceedings that the court ought not to admit it.

12.5.1.4 *Exclusion of bad character evidence*

12.5.1.4.1 EXCLUSION

The court cannot exclude evidence of bad character of its own motion after the prosecution has served notice that it intends to adduce evidence of bad character.

12.5.1.4.2 SEEKING TO EXCLUDE EVIDENCE

The defence can apply to have the evidence excluded under section 101(3) CJA 2003 where it is admissible under subsection (d) and subsection (g) (where the evidence is relevant to an issue in the case between the prosecution and the defendant or has become admissible because of the defendant's attack on another person).

In these two circumstances, the court *must* not admit such evidence if it appears that its admission would have such an adverse effect on the fairness of the proceedings that it ought not to admit it. In applying the test, the court is directed to take account, in particular, of the amount of time that has elapsed since the previous events and the current charge. This is a stricter test than under section 78 of the Police and Criminal Evidence Act 1984 (PACE 1984), which states that the court *may* refuse to admit the evidence, whereas section 101(3) CJA 2003 states that the court *must not* admit the evidence if it would have such an adverse effect on the fairness of the proceedings.

12.5.1.4.3 EXCLUSION OF EVIDENCE ADMISSIBLE AT
THE BEHEST OF A CO-DEFENDANT

The court has no power to exclude evidence of bad character which is admissible at the behest of a co-defendant once it has passed the test in section 101(1)(e) CJA 2003. In particular, there is no power under section 101(3) CJA 2003 or under section 78 PACE 1984.[40]

---

40 *R v Musone* [2007] EWCA Crim 1237.

220   *Criminal law: procedure*

12.5.1.5 *Powers of the court*

12.5.1.5.1 THE COURT'S POWER TO EXCLUDE EVIDENCE

The power of the court to exclude evidence under section 78 PACE 1984 is preserved by section 112(3)(c) CJA 2003, which provides that 'nothing in this Chapter affects the exclusion of evidence on the grounds other than the fact that it is evidence of a person's bad character'.

In practice, section 78 PACE 1984 will have a very limited application:

- It cannot apply where the defendant has agreed its admissibility or where the defendant has adduced the evidence himself (s 101(1)(a) and s 101(1)(b));
- It may apply to circumstances set out in subsection (1)(c) and (1)(f), although as the definition of important explanatory evidence in subsection (1)(c) and evidence in subsection (1)(f) can only be given to the extent that it is necessary to correct the false impression, then it is likely only to apply in rare or extreme cases.

12.5.1.5.2 POWER OF COURT TO DISCHARGE

Where the evidence of bad character is admitted under section 101 paragraphs (c) to (g) and proves to be so contaminated that any resulting conviction would be unsafe, the court may direct an acquittal or discharge the jury at any time after the close of the prosecution case (s 107 CJA 2003).

Key points include:

- Evidence is contaminated where it is false or misleading in any respect or is different from what it would otherwise have been, e.g. it has been affected by an agreement with other witnesses or by hearing the views or evidence of other witnesses.
- The power to discharge applies only in the Crown Court to a jury trial (s 107(1)) or to a hearing pursuant to section 4A Criminal Procedure (Insanity) Act 1964 to determine whether the defendant did the act or made the omission charged (s 107(1)(b)).
- Section 107 supplements the common law power of the judge to withdraw a case from the jury at any time after the close of the prosecution case, such as no case to answer. It confers a duty on the judge to stop the case if the contamination is such that considering the importance of the evidence to the case, a conviction would be unsafe (s 107(1)(b)). The case should not be stopped if a direction to the jury along the lines in *R v H*[41] would be sufficient to deal with any potential difficulties.
- If the case is stopped, the judge may consider that there is still sufficient uncontaminated evidence against the defendant to merit a retrial or that the prosecution case has been so weakened that the defendant should be acquitted (s 107(1)(b)(ii)). If the judge orders acquittal, the defendant will be acquitted of any other offence for which he could have been convicted if the judge is satisfied

41 [1995] 2 AC 596.

that the contamination would affect a conviction for that offence in the same way
(s 107(2)).

12.5.1.6 *Defendants: SNS activity as bad character*

12.5.1.6.1 PREVIOUS CONVICTIONS

Express reference to a person's convictions and cautions may appear on social
networking sites if they post about it themselves or if another account holder does so
(e.g. a status update after attendance at a magistrates' court). According to Ormerod,
attempts to adduce such material as evidence would engage the bad character
provisions.[42]

12.5.1.6.2 EXAMPLES THAT THE CROWN MAY WISH TO ADDUCE

The Crown may choose to rely on social media postings that comprise other reprehensible conduct not formally recorded in the way that previous convictions are; the
Crown would already have a record of this.

12.5.1.6.2.1 *Propensity*   Examples that the Crown may wish to adduce include:

- Evidence of propensity to offend in a particular manner (for example, images of
  D posing at the scene of a crime or discussion of gang-related activity);
- Evidence to rebut coincidence of a criminal lifestyle.

Although there is limited case law in this area, decided cases offer some useful illus-
trations as to how social media postings have been used by the Crown. In *R v A*,[43]
evidence that the defendant had used social networking sites to gather stories of incest
from female victims was admitted as relevant at D's trial for committing incest.

12.5.1.6.2.2 *Rebutting false impressions created by defendants*   Evidence may also be
adduced to rebut situations where the defendant has created a false impression about
themselves (under s 101(1)(f)). Postings may also be used to attack the defendant's
character where they have attacked the character of another.

However, the use of such information must be approached with caution. As noted
throughout this Handbook, postings on social media sites may be explicit, crude,
fanciful, and exaggerated. Ormerod notes that postings in their 'raw form' may have
a disproportionate impact upon jurors. It is suggested that there needs to be careful
consideration as to how much material is admitted and in what format. The issue
may form the subject matter of pre-trial directions.[44]

---

42 D. Ormerod and M. O' Floinn, 'Social Networking Sites, RIPA and Criminal Investigations' [2011]
    Crim LR, Issue 10, 2011 at [669–770].
43 *A* [2009] EWCA Crim 513.
44 There is also the problem of distinguishing bravado and fantasy from reality.

222 *Criminal law: procedure*

12.5.2 *Co-defendants*

12.5.2.1 *Adducing evidence under section 101(1)(e)*

Social media evidence can also be adduced by co-defendants under section 101(1)(e). In *Bailey*, a defendant used social media to search for evidence against a co-accused.[45]

12.5.2.2 *Publicly available information*

There is limited case law in this area. However, in *Delaney* (where the defendant was charged with wounding),[46] a central issue was whether the defendant was the aggressor or had acted in self-defence. The defendant was allowed to adduce evidence about the complainant from his Facebook page, in which the complainant had publicly shared information that he would 'be most likely to be arrested' for assault and that if the defendant was not convicted, the complainant would deal with the matter himself. Additional statements from the complainant's page were also admitted.[47]

12.5.2.3 *Fabrications, spiteful postings, and exaggeration*

Cases will rarely be clear-cut. If such information is adduced, it should be approached with caution to ensure that it is genuine, is not boastful or exaggerated, and is not an elaborate fabrication designed to exculpate another from liability or information that is compiled out of revenge or spite.

12.5.3 *Confessions*

Individuals often use social media to share some of the most intimate aspects of their lives.[48] As noted during the riots in the UK in 2011, individuals may use social media to brag directly about their exploits or make less explicit – but no less incriminating – statements.[49] Subject to section 76 (for the Crown) or section 76A PACE 1984 (for a co-defendant), such 'confessions' will be admissible (under s 128(2) CJA 2003).

If the 'confession' has been unprompted, it is unlikely that a challenge under section 76 could be substantiated by suggesting that the information is unreliable, or given under oppression.[50] That is not the case if the 'confession' resulted from

---

45 See, for example, *Bailey* [2008] EWCA Crim 817 at [46]–[49].
46 *R v Delaney* [2010] EWCA Crim 105.
47 The trial judge excluded a photograph of V adopting a 'boxing stance, naked to the waist' as more prejudicial than probative.
48 See J. Grimmelmann, 'Saving Facebook' (2009) 94 Iowa LR 1137; S. Friewald, 'A Comment on James Grimmelmann's Saving Facebook' (2009) 5 Iowa LR Bulletin, 5.
49 See, for example, *People v Valdez* (16 December 2011) Case No. G041904 (California Court of Appeals) WL 6275691.
50 An interesting 'reliability' argument against the admissibility of a confession could, however, cite sociological research indicating that many SNS users deceive and maintain fake personas through their SNS profiles. Care must be taken when relying on such general assumptions. It will be dependent on numerous factors, such as the age of the user, and even the form of social networking site used, with some being used for professional networking. In relation to levels of deception on LinkedIn, see J. Guillory and J.T. Hancock, 'The Effect of LinkedIn on Deception in Resumes' (2012) 15(3). *Cyberpsychology, Behavior, and Social Networking* 135.

Evidence and procedure   223

responses to a series of previous posts, particularly if those posts derive from under-cover police officers (or indeed private individuals, discussed in Chapter 4: Communications Act 2003 in relation to *R v Nimmo*[51]). In such circumstances where such evidence is adduced, a challenge may be made under section 76(2)(b) PACE 1984, as the circumstances may have caused the defendant to make an unreliable statement.

12.5.4 *Bad character of non-defendants*

12.5.4.1 *Definition of non-defendants*

'Non-defendants' are not defined in the Criminal Justice Act 2003 but the term should include victims, whether or not they give evidence, the deceased in cases of homicide, witnesses, police officers who have been involved in the case, third parties who are not witnesses in the case, and defence witnesses.

12.5.4.2 *Protection of feelings and reputation*

The provision was intended to protect the feelings and reputations of witnesses, etc., as well as preventing the trial being distracted by satellite issues.[52] Since its introduction, the section has been interpreted by courts in a manner that is consistent with that purpose, as was seen in the cases of *Miller, Braithwaite* and *Brewster*.[53]

12.5.4.3 *Admissibility*

Evidence of bad character of non-defendants is admissible only through one of the three gateways in section 100 CJA 2003:

- It is important explanatory evidence; that is, without it, the court or jury would find it impossible or difficult to properly understand other evidence in the case; *and* its value for understanding the case as a whole is substantial (s 100(2) CJA 2003).
- It has substantial probative value in relation to a matter that is *both* an issue in the proceedings *and* is of substantial importance in the context of the case as a whole. In assessing this value, the court must have regard to the following factors:

  - The nature and number of the events, or other things, to which the evidence relates;
  - When those things or events are alleged to have happened or existed;
  - The nature and extent of the similarities and the dissimilarities between each of the alleged instances of misconduct where the evidence is evidence of a person's misconduct and it is suggested the evidence has probative value by reason of similarity between that misconduct and other alleged misconduct;

---

51 Westminster Magistrates' Court, 24 January 2014 (unexplored) is explored in depth in Chapter 4: Communications Act 2003.
52 See *Miller* [2010] EWCA Crim 1153 and *Carr* [2008] EWCA Crim 1283.
53 *Miller* [2010] EWCA Crim 1153, *Braithwaite* [2010] EWCA Crim 1082 and *Brewster* [2010] EWCA Crim 1194.

224 *Criminal law: procedure*

- ○ The extent to which the evidence shows or tends to show that the same person was responsible each time where the evidence is evidence of a person's misconduct and it is suggested that that person is also responsible for the misconduct charged and the identity of the person responsible for the misconduct charged is disputed;
- ○ Any other factors the court considers relevant.

- All parties to the proceedings agree to the evidence being admissible. Prosecutors should only agree to admitting evidence of the bad character of a prosecution witness when one or both of the other gateways are satisfied or it is in the interests of justice to do so.

12.5.4.4 *Malicious motives or willingness to give false evidence*

In *Mateza*, social media materials were used to demonstrate malicious motives or willingness to give false evidence.[54] Such evidence may potentially be used to show false complaints in sexual cases; such postings may be admissible where they reveal inconsistencies or a motive for lying. However, care must be exercised in such circumstances that the material in question is not merely being used to attack the witness's character without any probative value being established.[55] However, the case of *Miller*[56] confirms that if the evidence adduced against a non-defendant is evidence of mere allegation, it will rarely be admissible unless it can be proved.

12.5.5 **Witness testimony**

12.5.5.1 *Witness's previous statements*

Earlier SNS postings consistent with a witness's testimony may be admissible under section 120 CJA 2003. By way of example, a witness may testify as to the truth of his social media postings (s 120(4) CJA 2003)[57] and that they constitute evidence of a complaint of the crime now prosecuted (s 120(7) CJA 2003).

If such evidence is adduced under section 120 CJA 2003, the SNS posts are evidence of their truth. However, there may be other circumstances in which section 120 CJA 2003 may apply, such as adducing such evidence to show that a witness has fabricated their account of events (s 120(2))[58] or to have made a statement he cannot now be expected to recollect (s 120(6)).[59]

---

54 See *Mateza* [2011] EWCA Crim 2587.
55 A useful discussion of the probative value of Facebook postings was considered in the American case of *Rice v Reliastar Life Insurance Co.*
56 *Miller* [2010] EWCA Crim 1153. See also *Braithwaite* [2010] EWCA Crim 1082.
57 See *AA* [2007] EWCA Crim 1779. The jury needs to be warned that this is not independent evidence: *H* [2011] EWCA Crim 2344.
58 See *Athwal* [2009] EWCA Crim 789. For critique, see R. Munday (2010). 'Athwal and all that: previous statements, narrative, and the taxonomy of hearsay', *The Journal of Criminal Law*, 74(5): 415.
59 See *Chinn* [2012] EWCA Crim 501.

12.5.5.2 *Previous inconsistent statements*

Under section 119 CJA 2003, previous inconsistent statements from social networking sites can be put to a witness. The conditions to do so are that:

- the witness admits having made them and they are inconsistent with his present testimony (s 119(1)(a) CJA 2003); or
- the witness is hostile and his previous statements have been proved under section 3 Criminal Procedure Act 1865 (CPA 1865) or his previous statements are relative to the subject matter of the indictment (s 4 or 5 CPA 1865) (s 119(1)(b) CJA 2003).[60]

As with previous consistent statements, the SNS messages then become admitted as evidence of the truth of their contents. If the preliminary hurdle of authentication discussed above can be overcome, sections 119 and 120 CJA 2003 will allow for a great deal of SNS evidence to be put to a witness and adduced as evidence of its truth.

12.5.6 *Compelling a suspect to reveal his SNS password*

In some circumstances, the police may deem it necessary to seek access to an individual's social media account. In order to gain access to the account, the police may require the individual to supply their account password and login details to them. In such situations, the individual who has been asked for that data may object and the police may need to compel them to provide such data to them.

Section 49 RIPA 2000 contains a specific power to compel certain passwords. Compelling reasons would need to exist for such a power to be exercised. In any case, it is likely that section 49 would only apply if the information contained on a SNS profile is 'protected information'. The definition of 'protected information' contained in section 56 RIPA 2000 includes 'electronic data which, without the key to the data . . . cannot, or *cannot readily*, be accessed'. Examples could include private messages between two users on social networking sites, but would be unlikely to include postings made on walls or Twitter feeds, which are widely accessible to the public via other means. Moreover, such information would also be sorted on the site's server[61] and could be accessed by applying to the site for disclosure where legal proceedings are anticipated. Ormerod[62] also notes that 'further challenges would be likely to arise based on the privilege against self incrimination and the right to silence which lie at the heart of the fair procedure guarantees of Article 6'.[63]

---

60 For further difficulties, see Ormerod's comment on *Billingham* [2009] Crim LR 529.
61 See Chapter 1: Introduction to Social Media and the Law, *How Social Networking Sites Work*.
62 D. Ormerod and M. O' Floinn, 'Social Networking Sites, RIPA and Criminal Investigations' [2011] Crim LR, Issue 10, 2011 at [783].
63 *Greater Manchester Police v Andrews* [2011] EWHC 1966.

226   *Criminal law: procedure*

12.5.7 *Authentication issues*

12.5.7.1 *Definition of a document*

Printouts of SNS electronic communications are documents,[64] and likely to contain statements which may be adduced as evidence in criminal trials. If conviction depends on the authenticity of the SNS printouts, the jury must be satisfied beyond reasonable doubt.[65]

12.5.7.2 *Guidance on authentication for judges*

There is little practical guidance for judges on authentication. Under section 133 CJA 2003, statements in documents can be adduced by 'producing either (a) the document, or (b) . . . a copy of the document or of the material part of it, *authenticated in whatever way the court may approve*'. The drafting of this section leaves a wide discretion for judges in terms of assessing authentication.[66] As the rules are wide, it is useful to consider the position in the USA where there have been a number of cases concerning the authentication of the provenance of social media postings adduced as evidence. Rule 901 of the US Federal Rules of Evidence (FRE) states that in order to 'satisfy the requirement of authenticating or identifying an item of evidence, the proponent must produce evidence sufficient to support a finding that the matter in question is what its proponent claims'.

Authentication of SNS evidence has arisen in numerous US cases, and similar challenges are arising in English courts.[67] Frequent challenges to SNS evidence include:

- that exhibits proffered accurately represent what appeared on the SNS;
- that the evidence can be shown to have originated from the alleged source, as opposed to a hacker or someone with access to the SNS account; and
- when authentication arises as an issue, of what must the judge be satisfied to admit the evidence before the jury?

12.5.7.3 *Proof of authorship*

One of the main issues concerning authentication is not that that the post is indeed in original form, but that the defendant denies authoring it. Factors such as testimony of a witness with knowledge[68] or distinctive characteristics within the communication[69]

---

64 Section 134(1) of the Criminal Justice Act 2003 defines document as 'anything in which information of any description is recorded'.

65 R. Pattenden (2008) 'Authenticating "things" in English law: principles for adducing tangible evidence in common law jury trials', *International Journal of Evidence and Proof*, 12: 288, 292–293.

66 *Saward* [2005] EWCA Crim 3183 at [44].

67 See, for example, *Bucknor* [2010] EWCA Crim 1152 and *Bailey* [2008] EWCA Crim 817 at [46]–[49] in the context of 'chat-room' communications.

68 *State v Bell*, 2009-Ohio–2335 (18 May 2009) at [31] (involving chat room conversations).

69 *In re. F.P.* 878 A. 2d 91 (Pa Super, 2005); *Tienda* No. PD–0312–11 (2012); *Manuel II* No. 12–09–00454-CR, WL 3837561 (2011). For an interesting decision regarding the reliability of photos on Facebook (although in the context of a probation revocation hearing), see *Altajir* SC 18706 (Conn Supreme Court 2012).

have been deemed to suffice. However, in some US cases, courts have required more compelling evidence that the posting can be traced to the alleged author,[70] such as in *Williams*[71] and *Eleck*,[72] where testimony from witnesses who participated in the disputed communications was held to be insufficient proof of authorship. Surprisingly, this was despite the courts' acceptance that the messages originated from the profiles of the alleged authors. In both cases, the courts expressed concern about exclusivity of access to the profile, commenting on the (in)security of SNS platforms.

12.5.7.3.1 THRESHOLD FOR ADMISSIBILITY

If authentication thresholds are set too high, any person can simply claim their account was hacked, rendering potentially reliable evidence inadmissible. If evidence cannot be gathered from a social network provider (and possibly the relevant internet access provider (IAP)), or admission by the author who posted the material, or some highly distinctive feature showing that only s/he could have written it, SNS evidence would then be inadmissible.

12.5.7.3.2 CLAIMS THAT ACCOUNTS HAVE BEEN HACKED

In *Eleck*, the court also commented on the 'general lack of security of the medium'.[73] There have been reports of Facebook accounts being hacked,[74] often for distinct fraudulent purposes,[75] and unauthorised access can also occur when an individual leaves their profile 'logged in' on a device. The case of *Clevenstine*[76] considers some of the potential pitfalls that onerous authentication requirements may cause. In *Clevenstine*, MySpace evidence was authenticated by testimony of participants in the communications, the defendant's wife who found the information, hard-drive analysis, and expert evidence from a MySpace official.

12.5.7.3.3 COOPERATION OF SITES TO AUTHENTICATE EVIDENCE

In terms of seeking the cooperation of sites to authenticate evidence, it should be borne in mind that some sites contain terms and conditions as part of their site use which address the subject. Facebook, for instance, states that it 'does not provide expert testimony support [because] Facebook records are self-authenticating pursuant to [US] law'.[77]

---

70 See, for example, *Griffin v State of Maryland* 419 Md 343, 19 A 3d 415 (2011).

71 *Williams* 456 Mass 857, 926 NE 2d 1162 (2010).

72 *Eleck* 130 Conn App 632, 32 A 3d 818 (2011).

73 The court in *Griffin* 419 Md 343, 19 A 3d 415 (2011) at 357–358 was equally concerned about this.

74 See http://countermeasures.trendmicro.eu/over-10000-facebook-account-details-hacked-and-published/; [accessed 26 April 2012].

75 See http://mashable.com/2010/04/23/hacker-facebook/ [accessed 26 April 2012].

76 *People v Clevenstine* 68 AD 3d 1448, 891 NYS 2d 511 (2009).

77 See https://www.facebook.com/safety/groups/law/guidelines/ [accessed 26 April 2012].

228 *Criminal law: procedure*

12.5.7.3.4 CLAIMS THAT ANOTHER PERSON HAS ACCESSED A USER'S ACCOUNT

If a person contends that another person must have used their account inappropriately, this could be disproved by tracing usage to an individual's computer through his/her IP address, which would still require cooperation from the relevant social networking site and internet access provider.[78]

12.5.7.3.5 ESTABLISHING AUTHENTICITY IN ORDER TO ADMIT EVIDENCE

There is no clear consensus in UK law as to what a judge must be satisfied of for social media evidence to be admitted. In *Robson*,[79] Shaw J decided the question of authenticity of a video on the balance of probabilities, which he equated with prima facie evidence of authenticity. Then in *Murphy*,[80] the Northern Ireland Court of Appeal also sought to apply a prima facie standard, and referred to the decision in *Robson*.

12.5.7.3.5.1 *Suggested test* In *Quinn*, the court appeared to follow that interpretation of *Murphy*, stating that '[t]he test of whether the video is prima facie authentic is no more than a test of potential relevance'.[81] Pattenden suggests that a test could be approached by the court as follows:

- the disputed SNS evidence must have logical relevance, and this is satisfied when it is:

  - possibly authentic and
  - bears on the probabilities of a 'contested issue'; and

- the disputed SNS evidence must be legally relevant, and this is satisfied if there is 'some admissible evidence of provenance, continuity (if relevant) and integrity'.[82]

As noted above in relation to UK cases, issues surrounding authentication need careful consideration.

12.5.7.3.5.2 *Comparison with tests applied in the USA* In the UK there is little assistance in case law that assists in exploring how information is authenticated. In *United States v O'Keefe*,[83] the court noted that '[a] piece of paper or electronically stored information, without any indication of its creator, source, or custodian may not be authenticated under Federal Rule of Evidence 901'. According to *Arkfield*,[84] the

---

78 *Applause Store Productions Ltd v Raphael* [2008] EWHC 1781 (QB).
79 *Robson* [1972] 1 WLR 651.
80 *Murphy* [1990] NI 306.
81 *Quinn* [2011] NICA 19 at [13].
82 R. Pattenden (2008) 'Authenticating "things" in English law: principles for adducing tangible evidence in common law jury trials', *International Journal of Evidence and Proof*, 12: 272, 280–281.
83 537 F Supp 2d 14, 20 (DDC 2008).
84 Michael R. Arkfeld, *Arkfeld on Electronic Discovery and Evidence* § 8.11(C), at 8–63 (3rd edn).

Evidence and procedure 229

authentication of electronically stored information involves the following questions, at a minimum:

- How was the evidence collected?
- Where was the evidence collected?
- What types of evidence were collected?
- Who handled the evidence before it was collected?
- When was the evidence collected?

12.5.7.3.5.3 *Need to consider social media evidence in its context* The challenge for courts and litigators is how to apply this to the social media context. In *People v Valdez*,[85] a police expert printed copies of the defendant's profile on a social media website that contained photographs and biographical information about the defendant. The expert went on to explain that although the profile is accessible to the public, only the individual who created the profile, or one who has access to that person's login ID and password, has the ability to upload or manipulate content on the page. As a result, the court held that a reasonable consideration of fact could conclude from the information posted –including personal photographs, communications, and other details – that the social media profile belonged to the defendant.

Ultimately, authentication ought not to be overly taxing in terms of the standards to be attained. Ormerod suggests that a judge could be satisfied of authentication, sufficient to leave the evidence to the jury; for example, on testimony from a witness that she had a pre-existing SNS 'friendship' with an individual and had received/seen the relevant communication from that individual. If the circumstantial evidence is weak, then it should be approached with caution, with the case of *Bucknor*[86] confirming this. In the American case of *Griffin*,[87] the need to establish with the purported creator of SNS posts that they own the profile and uploaded the relevant information was suggested as a method of authenticating the postings.

12.5.8 *Excluding social media evidence*

12.5.8.1 *Introduction*

Defendants may seek to exclude social media evidence in proceedings through a number of different routes, in addition to those already described above.

12.5.8.2 *Hearsay*

12.5.8.2.1 CHALLENGING SOCIAL MEDIA EVIDENCE

Social media evidence may be challenged on admissibility, as it may constitute hearsay evidence. The rules relating to hearsay, contained in the Criminal Justice Act 2003, render inadmissible any evidence which:

---

85 201 Cal App 4th 1429, 1434–37 (Cal App 4th Dist 2011) (section on authentication not published).
86 *Bucknor* [2010] EWCA Crim 1152.
87 *Griffin v State of Maryland* 419 Md 343, 19 A 3d 415 (2011).

230   *Criminal law: procedure*

- constitutes a representation of fact or opinion made otherwise than in the course of the present proceedings;
- is being relied on at trial for the truth of some representation; provided also
- it was one of the purposes of the maker of the representation that someone believe or act upon the truth of the representation for which it is now relied on.

If the above is applied, social media postings would fall outside of the rule;[88] indeed, times, dates, and IP addresses of users will all be admissible if relevant.[89] Overcoming the basic authentication test is all that is required, the computers involved in generating the data appearing on sites will be presumed to be operating properly,[90] and section 129(1) does not require that the setting information for them be proved accurate.[91] Moreover, images which are sought to be adduced, unless for the text or dialogue in them, do not infringe the hearsay rule in the same way that CCTV footage does not.[92]

12.5.8.2.2 POSTINGS AND CHAT DIALOGUE AS 'STATEMENTS'

In relation to postings and chat dialogue, such communications constitute 'statements' for the purposes of section 115 CJA 2003. However, they will not be classified as hearsay because the statements will not be relied on for the truth of any 'matter stated'. Statements which have not been deemed to constitute hearsay include statements relied on to demonstrate simply that a user is capable of understanding English, or has knowledge of a particular fact,[93] or has knowledge of how to use an SNS account, and that a person 'X' is 'friends' with user 'Y'.[94]

Not all postings will be so clear-cut. In *Twist*,[95] Hughes LJ offered the example of texting a defendant with the statement 'will you have any crack tomorrow', where the defendant has been charged with possession with intent to supply drugs, has received SNS messages from X stating 'need more cheap drugs like last time', that will be a statement.[96] However, it won't be relied on for the truth of the express matter stated

---

88 See J.C. Smith, 'The Admissibility of Statements by Computer' [1981] Crim LR 387.

89 C. Tapper, 'Electronic Evidence and the Criminal Justice Act 2003' [2004] CTLR 161.

90 Section 129(2) reiterates the presumption of regularity.

91 R. Pattenden, 'Machinespeak' [2010] Crim LR 623. Arguably, Pattenden is too restrictive in limiting s 129(1) to information that 'has been in a person's mind' (at [632]). The reason why, for example, the breath used in an intoximeter test does not need to be proved under s 129(1) is because the accuracy of the printout does not depend on the breath, but on the calibration of the machine and setting information.

92 See *Taylor v Chief Constable of Cheshire* [1986] 1 WLR 1479.

93 For example, in *Toissant-Collins* [2009] EWCA Crim 316, a letter sent to D reporting that a fellow gang member X had been killed by V showed D's knowledge of that fact and was circumstantial evidence of his being motivated by revenge.

94 On hearsay issues based on witnesses' ability to identify by names provided by others, see *Phillips* [2010] EWCA Crim 378. An example of this reported to us by a judge from Snaresbrook Crown Court was of a victim of a street robbery who overheard a member of the group address the group leader by a 'street name', Y. The victim searched that name on Facebook and found the group all pictured. Coupled with other evidence there was a successful conviction. No hearsay issues arose.

95 [2011] EWCA Crim 1143.

96 Hughes LJ in *Twist* [2011] EWCA Crim 1143 at [15], however, suggests that questions are not 'statements'. For critique, see D. Ormerod [2011] Crim LR 793.

Evidence and procedure 231

(X needs cheap drugs), it will be relied on for the truth of the implied matter (that X knows D to be a dealer).[97] It might not be hearsay since it was not X's purpose to cause D to believe the matter stated for which the representation is relied on at trial (that D sells drugs); that was already a matter of mutual knowledge.[98]

12.5.8.2.3 POSITION IN THE UNITED STATES

In the US, so far as is relevant to social media, the hearsay rule states that '[a] statement is not hearsay if . . . [t]he statement is offered against a party and is the party's own statement, in either an individual or representative capacity'. In *People v Oyerinde*,[99] a case concerning first-degree murder and carjacking, the court held that the defendant's Facebook messages were not hearsay, but rather a party admission, because he sent them to another person. The judge applied the test as it would be applied to any other out-of-court statement and determined that such messages were not hearsay. The same court also admitted Facebook messages sent to the defendant and another individual under the 'state of mind' exception. In *Miles v Raycom Media Inc*,[100] it was held that a Facebook page containing unsworn statements made by third parties that were offered to prove the truth of the matter asserted constituted inadmissible hearsay (under Federal Rule of Evidence 801).

12.5.8.2.4 RELEVANCE TO PROCEEDINGS

As suggested in relation to the admission of bad character evidence in the UK, there is a risk that social media postings may be used for purely prejudicial reasons which are largely irrelevant to the litigation in question, such evidence would be distinguishable from cases such as A[101] (discussed above) in which there was real value as it went to the nature of the offence in question – incest. In such cases, the US courts have weighted the probative value of the evidence against the potential prejudice that it may cause. In *Rice v Reliastar Life Insurance Co*,[102] a civil suit concerning a police shooting, the plaintiff included in the complaint a screen shot of the officer's social media page. The image, which was captured a week after the shooting, contained a photo of Clint Eastwood in wild west gunslinger attire with the caption, 'How I feel most of the time!!!!' The court struck out paragraphs of the complaint related to the screen shot and the image itself, stating that they were 'merely argumentative and prejudicial' and did not 'add to the substantive allegations of the complaint'.

---

97 If X merely believes that D is a dealer, the evidence is irrelevant according to *Kearley* [1992] 2 AC 228.
98 *Twist* [2011] EWCA Crim 1143 and *Mateza* [2011] EWCA Crim 2587.
99 2011 Mich App LEXIS 2104, at *26–27 (Mich Ct App Nov 29, 2011).
100 2010 US Dist LEXIS 122712, at *7–9, n. 1 (SD Miss Nov 18, 2010).
101 *A* [2009] EWCA Crim 513.
102 2011 US Dist LEXIS 32831 (MD La Mar 29, 2011).

Part 4
Commercial law

13 Data protection and privacy

13.1 Application to social media

13.1.1 *General*

Information is one of the most valuable and most controversial tools of modern life. Governmental and non-governmental bodies now hold vast quantities of information about individuals that has been derived from those individuals' uses of such technologies. The regulation of who holds this information, how they hold it, and in what circumstances they use it and/or pass it on to others, has been the subject of detailed legislation and guidance over many years. The 2014 Annual Report of the UK Information Commissioner's Office (ICO) recorded that the ICO responded to a record number of data protection and freedom of information complaints in the previous year. In a press release concerning the Annual Report, the ICO referred to Facebook and Google's right to be forgotten as signs that organizations' use of data is getting ever more complicated.[1]

As noted in the introductory chapter, the use of the internet and micro sites has led to an exponential increase in the volume of data being processed by businesses and websites. Consumers have become increasingly willing to share details in order to facilitate purchases, play online games, and connect with friends and colleagues. Information can be accessed or shared practically and conveniently by the click of a mouse or Smartphone. Social media are a tool for expression and communication between individuals but also a means of mass communication.

Data gathered via such channels will inevitably contain personal data about individuals (e.g. email addresses, names, gender, age, residential address) that may be required to fulfil the service provided by the site provider or as requested by the site provider as a prerequisite to using their site (e.g. Facebook and Twitter). Individuals may also choose to upload personal information to their social media profiles; for example, Facebook pages may contain photographs, Twitter may detail an individual's day-to-day expressive activities, and LinkedIn profiles may contain details of employment history. The medium could be described as having an almost seductive quality, one that entices individuals (and indeed businesses) to share their data, resulting in a change in attitude to the sharing of personal data online.

---

1 'Data use is getting more complicated: the public need someone they can trust to watch over their information', ICO news release, 15 July 2014 [http://ico.org.uk/news/latest_news/2014/data-use-is-getting-more-complicated-15072014].

236 *Commercial law*

A report conducted by the Special Eurobarometer on behalf of the European Union[2] found that in relation to attitudes towards data protection in the technological age, 74% of Europeans see disclosing personal information as an increasing part of modern life. The most important reason for disclosure is to access an online service, for both social networking and sharing site users (61%) and online shoppers (79%). Over half of internet users are informed about the data collection conditions and the further uses of their data when joining a social networking site or registering for a service online (54%). Just over a quarter of social network users (26%) and even fewer online shoppers (18%) feel in complete control of their data.

13.1.2 *Issues raised by social media*

Two of the most controversial issues relating to social media websites and their data processing activities, are how such data is being processed and how privacy rights are being respected.[3] These concerns raise issues in relation to many activities in individuals' everyday lives and expressive activities, with examples including:

- Employers using social networking site content to monitor employees or vet prospective job applicants;[4]
- Universities monitoring applicants;
- Using social networking site content as evidence in civil and criminal proceedings.[5]

Although the Committee of Ministers of the Council of Europe have noted that social networking sites can assist with the furtherance of individuals' enjoyment of their rights of expression, there is also a risk that inaccurate, misleading or private information may be shared online without individuals' consent.[6] It was noted by the committee that social networking sites had raised particular difficulties in this regard. In particular, the right to freedom of expression and information, as well as the right to private life[7] and human dignity may be threatened on social networking services, which can shelter discriminatory practices. It was suggested that these threats arise for various reasons, including:

- a lack of legal and procedural safeguards surrounding processes that can lead to the exclusion of users;

---

2 Special Eurobarometer 359, Attitudes on Data Protection and Electronic Identity in the European Union, June 2011.

3 See, for example, P. Rioth (2010) 'Data protection meets Web 2.0: two ships passing in the night', *UNSW Law Journal*, 33: 532–561.

4 I. Byrnside (2008) 'Six degrees of separation: the legal ramifications of employers using social networking sites to research applicants', *Vanderbilt Journal of Entertainment and Technology Law*, 2: 445–477; A.R. Levinson (2009) 'Industrial justice: privacy protection for the employed', *Cornell Journal of Law and Pubic Policy*, 18: 609–688.

5 *Locke v Stuart &AXA* [2011] EWHC 399 (QB).

6 Recommendation CM/Rec (2012) 4 of the Committee of Ministers to Member States on the protection of human rights with regard to social networking services (Adopted by the Committee of Ministers on 4 April 2012 at the 1139th meeting of the Ministers' Deputies).

7 See Chapter 2 for a full consideration of human rights law and its applicability to social media.

Data protection and privacy 237

- inadequate protection of children and young people against harmful content or behaviours, a lack of respect for others' rights;
- the inability to control privacy settings, a lack of user-friendly terms and conditions concerning privacy; and
- a lack of transparency about the purposes for which personal data are collected and processed.

13.1.3 *Committee of Ministers for the Council of Europe*

The Committee of Ministers for the Council of Europe has suggested that the processing activities involved in social media has given such site operators 'great potential to promote the exercise and enjoyment of human rights and fundamental freedoms, in particular the freedom to express, to create and to exchange content and ideas, and the freedom of assembly'.[8] However, although social networking services can assist the wider public to receive and impart information, the vast development of micro sites in particular (e.g. Facebook offers apps, games, shops outlets) has raised and continues to raise new challenges in relation to the protection of personal data, one such example being targeted advertising based on online behaviour (a very valuable source of data for micro sites such as Facebook when they seek to target their adverts on the page to a particular user[9]).

In their opinion on social media, the Article 29 Working Party stated that the large amount of data shared with such sites uploaded in posts and combined with data outlining the user's actions and interactions with other people, can create a rich profile of that person's interests and activities.[10] It is for this reason that personal data published on such sites can be used by third parties for 'a wide variety of purposes, including commercial purposes, and may pose major risks such as identity theft, financial loss, loss of business or employment opportunities and physical harm'.[11]

13.1.4 *Application to businesses*

The Data Protection Act 1998 (DPA 1998), which presently governs the regulation of data in the UK, can be a difficult piece of legislation to negotiate as a business or individual, but data protection is simple in concept and does not need to be complicated or difficult in practice. This chapter looks at the main compliance issues and possible pitfalls that may be relevant to social media. The chapter also considers how the law may change in the future as a result of draft regulations and directives being considered and refined at an EU-wide level.

The issues surrounding data protection and privacy relating to their impact upon private individuals has pervaded much of the academic commentary in the area. For businesses, the main concern is how to look at those privacy aspects and adopt

---

8 Recommendation CM/Rec (2012) 4 of the Committee of Ministers to Member States on the protection of human rights with regard to social networking services (adopted by the Committee of Ministers on 4 April 2012 at the 1139th meeting of the Ministers' Deputies), para 1.
9 For the issues raised in relation to trading standards, see Chapter 14.
10 http://ec.europa.eu/justice/policies/privacy/docs/wpdocs/2009/wp163_en.pdf.
11 Ibid.

238   *Commercial law*

practices and policies that meet the demands of the law and respect data subject rights. For businesses, this chapter will consider how the Act impacts upon their use of social media as part of their marketing activities and customer engagement. The focus will be on those aspects of the DPA 1998 that influence directly how businesses deal with individuals; some aspects of the Act are not touched on at all. However, the chapter will help you understand the main areas of risk when you are handling information about individuals gathered via social media and the steps you may have to take in order to deal with that data in a manner which is legally compliant.

13.2 What is privacy and why is it protected?

13.2.1 *Social media and data protection in the context of privacy*

In order to explore the types of privacy issues that social media raises, it is useful to consider what the concept of 'data protection' actually is and how it has become manifested within special legal regulation.

13.2.2 *Application of privacy and individuals' right of protection*

Data protection applies to individuals and their rights (which may on occasion be qualified) that relate to the use and disposal of their data in connection with their personality. In recent years, these rights have become increasingly important as technology has enabled the collecting, storing and conciliation of large pools of data. The aim of data protection law is the protection of privacy in relation to data; however, this says little about what privacy is and why it needs protection.

13.2.3 *Defining 'privacy': a brief history*

Various definitions have been proposed for 'privacy'. According to Schoeman,[12] it has been regarded as a claim, entitlement or right of an individual to determine what information about himself (or herself) may be communicated to others; the measure of control an individual has over information about himself, intimacies of personal identity, or who has sensory access to him; and a state or condition of limited access to a person, information about him, intimacies of personal identity. However, this definition does not connect the impact of technology upon privacy rights. Surprisingly, given that it was written over 100 years ago, Warren and Brandeis, in their famous article published in the *Harvard Law Review* in 1890,[13] connected the need to recognize the right to privacy in common law with the effects of the new inventions of the age and the spreading of 'business methods' unknown up to that point. It is a theme that echoes through the ages and is still applicable today. Contemporary developments

---

12 F.D. Schoeman (1984) *Philosophical Dimensions of Privacy: An Anthology*. Cambridge: Cambridge University Press; F.D. Schoeman (1984) *Privacy: Philosophical Dimensions of the Literature*. Cambridge: Cambridge University Press.

13 S.D. Warren and L.D. Brandeis (1890) 'The right to privacy', *Harvard Law Review*, 4(5): 193–220.

for Warren and Brandeis included photography (latterly debated in relation to privacy rights and CCTV; see *Peck v United Kingdom*[14]) and the press. According to Warren and Brandeis, newspapers invaded privacy in an negative way as '[g]ossip is no longer the resource of the idle and the vicious, but has become a trade, which is pursued with industry as well as effrontery'.[15] Given the increasing use of Facebook and Twitter postings on newspaper articles in relation to celebrities and those caught up in criminal proceedings or political scandals, one wonders if little has changed, save for the medium by which such gossip and information is communicated and the viral qualities of these new platforms, facilitated by developments in technology, compared with traditional print media.

Warren and Brandeis noted that in relation to instantaneous photography, such advancement in technology made it possible to take a picture of someone against his or her will, whereas previously it had been necessary to sit for one portrait for lengthy periods of time. Warren and Brandeis stated that, 'the law of contract or of trust might afford the prudent man sufficient safeguards against the improper circulation of his portrait',[16] whereas instantaneous photography meant that protection, in a legal sense of misuse of that image, could not so easily be afforded. In their exposition, Warren and Brandeis reviewed the contemporaneous practices of common law courts of justice, and concluded that the rights protected were 'not rights arising from contract or from special trust, but are rights as against the world'[17] (i.e. they perceived them as absolute rights), but 'the principle which has been applied to protect these rights is in reality not the principle of private property, unless that word be used in an extended and unusual sense'.[18] They proposed that a solution would be to interpret a 'right to privacy' in a manner that would complement the right used by judges in relation 'to a casual letter or an entry in a diary and to the most valuable poem or essay, to a botch or daub and to a masterpiece'.[19] However, they noted that this was only one aspect of the right and that 'the law has no new principle to formulate when it extends this protection to the personal appearance, sayings, acts, and to the personal relation, domestic or otherwise'.[20] Warren and Brandeis supported the need for the acknowledgement of the 'right to privacy' with the change in the structure of publicity and the appearance of new technologies of the age. The protection of the individual gained a new background replacing proprietary rights: privacy means the protection not only of privacy, but the protection of autonomy in its wide sense, including not only the protection of proprietary autonomy. The right is lost only when the author himself communicates his production to the public, in other words, publishes it;[21] in the modern context, this may be through publishing a thought on Twitter. Remarkably

---

14 (2003) 36 EHRR 41; [2003] EMLR 287.
15 S.D. Warren and L.D. Brandeis (1890) 'The right to privacy', *Harvard Law Review*, 4(5): 193–220 at [196].
16 Ibid. at [196].
17 Ibid. at [213].
18 Ibid. at [213].
19 Ibid. at [199].
20 Ibid. at [213].
21 Ibid. at [199–200]; see also *Duke of Queensberry v Shebbeare*, 2 Eden, 3 329 (1758); *Bartlett v Crittenden*, 5 McLean, 32, 4I (1849).

240 *Commercial law*

since it was written in 1890, there is much to be garnered from the importance of the law of contract and the emerging right of privacy, which remains applicable in the social media context (e.g. site terms and conditions and privacy policies).

13.2.4 *Defining 'privacy' in the modern sphere*

In terms of how we view privacy in modern terms, 'data protection' appeared in Europe as an answer to the dangers of electronic data processing, which were becoming widespread via the time of the so-called electronic revolution, which began in the 1970s. This resulted in the first generation of data protection laws, developed in response to computer systems and the ability to create mass databases from which it was possible to collate and match data through the use of indexing and search engines performed on the basis of keyword searches. At the same time, the appearance of international computer networks opened the road for globalization of data processing as well. The content of the legal protection provided by it has changed significantly since its appearance several times, and is still changing presently as technological advances become increasingly sophisticated.

In the modern age while following on from early definitions, data protection is a tool of privacy protection, and as such is aimed necessarily at the individual; the object of data security is data itself. This may be interpreted as the protection of the integrity and confidentiality of data, irrespective of the information content and legal qualification of data.[22]

13.2.5 *Interrelationship with data security*

Data security is served by technical and organizational measures, which may be stipulated both by legal and extra-legal norms. Data security regulations are applied by several legal norms, including the legal formulation of data security regulations concerning qualified data (secrets of State and intelligence). The interrelationship between data protection and data security is complex, although there are certain key features that assist with understanding the nature of the connectivity of security and privacy. Throughout the development of data protection laws, post 1970, although to a variable extent, legislation has usually contained data security rules serving data protection (which give specifications of the technical, organizational or other measures that are to be followed by the addressee of the norm when treating personal data). Such measures indicate that with regard to personal data, data security is one of the objectives of data protection regulation.

A new development among the tools of privacy protection is the increasing role of data security technologies; this has been especially marked over the past few years, which has seen increased focus on users' sophistication with the development of computer technology.

---

22 I. Székely (1994) 'Az adatvédelem és az információszabadság filozófiai, jogi, szociológiai és informatikai aspektusai. Budapest. Kézirat (kandidátusi értekezés)' ['. . . data protection is the protection of data subjects, data security is the protection of data']. The two notions are present in a similar sense in the practice of the Hungarian data protection commissioner (ABI): ABI 1999, 350.

Data protection and privacy   241

The effective protection of privacy in an open network environment might be provided primarily by technological tools (for example, with so-called 'strong' encryption). These tools do not offer legal protection, but in several cases they become objects of legal regulation themselves – exactly because their use has become widespread in the protection of privacy, or because of the consequences of such use. (The use of 'strong' encryption, for example, might hinder legitimate data collection carried out in relation to protecting one's privacy[23] for reasons of national security or criminal investigation. In such cases, the legislator might have to intervene in order to strike a balance between the interests of national security on the one hand, and the protection of privacy on the other.) Such regulation cannot be considered as legal regulation of data protection, although it is relevant regarding privacy, since it can hinder or facilitate the use of technologies enhancing privacy.

Apart from technologies that enhance the protection of *data*, there are some that serve specifically the function of *privacy* protection: these are commonly referred to as privacy enhancing technologies (PETs). Privacy enhancing technologies may enhance data security as well, but the aim of these solutions is not a general protection of data content, but the protection of privacy using technological and organizational solutions. The notion of privacy enhancing technology follows the privacy orientated definition of Burkert, who understood security as the 'technical and organizational concepts that aim at protecting personal identity'.[24]

The legal framework of the technological protection of privacy is frequently influenced by legal regulation of tools and methods that cannot be considered exclusively privacy enhancing technologies. For example, 'strong' encryption, which might be used for encrypting any data content that can be used by data controllers in order to ensure the safety of data held on their servers (e.g. requiring data to be kept in encrypted form, with password protection in non-standard English of a minimum number of characters, containing a mixture of numbers and letters or case sensitivity).

13.3 History of data protection legislation

13.3.1 *Introduction*

As discussed above, the period before the appearance of data protection was one not yet characterized by the widespread availability of devices that possessed the capability for storing and processing data. Primitive computer systems and electronic filing meant that there was a very small likelihood that somebody would make links between personal data, process that data, and create a personality profile that would expose an individual to privacy breaches or security risks, as such activities required large investments of time and sophisticated technology, which was very expensive compared with the value to be gained from accessing such data. As technology became accessible on

---

23 For example, see the UK Government's 'be cyber streetwise' publicity campaign [https://www.cyber-streetwise.com/], UK Home Office; 'New campaign urges people to be "Cyber Streetwise" ' [https://www.gov.uk/government/news/new-campaign-urges-people-to-be-cyber-streetwise], Home Office, Cabinet Office and Department for Business, Innovation and Skills; 'Keeping the UK safe in cyber space' [https://www.gov.uk/government/policies/keeping-the-uk-safe-in-cyberspace], Office of Cyber Security and Information Assurance.

24 H. Burkert (1997) 'Privacy-enhancing technologies: typology, critique, vision' at [215].

242   *Commercial law*

a wider scale, privacy concerns increased and with it an increase in discussion as to how to protect individuals' privacy rights.

13.3.2 *The Younger Committee Report*

In 1972, the UK Government set up the Younger Committee, which was tasked with a broad remit to consider whether legislation was needed to protect individuals and organizations from intrusions into their personal privacy. The Younger Committee Report[25] concluded that the general public's principal concern was that the government might have the ability to construct a central computer databank containing their information. The report recommended ten principles for the use of computers for the processing of personal data – the forerunners of the present 'data protection principles'.

In response to the Younger Commission's Report, the government produced a White Paper,[26] which concluded that 'the time has come when those who use computers to handle personal information, however responsible they are, can no longer remain the sole judges of whether their own systems adequately safeguard privacy'.[27]

The report contained a specific commitment to legislation that would set up mechanics to review the situation and to ensure that computer-assisted technologies for processing data operated with appropriate safeguards. The perceived function of the legislation contemplated was to define the standards and criteria and establish a permanent statutory body to oversee the use of computers in both the public and private sectors and operated with the appropriate safeguards.

13.3.3 *The Lindop Report*

Three years after the publication of its White Paper, the government commissioned the Lindop Report,[28] which looked in more detail at the practical aspects of data protection and the mechanics of how it could be implemented. One of the Lindop Report's key recommendations was that a Data Protection Authority should be created and that Codes of Practice for the processing of data should be drafted and adopted by different sectors.

13.3.4 *The OECD Guidelines*

A key development in terms of the recognition of the global nature of data transfers came in 1980, when the Organization for Economic Co-operation and Development (OECD) adopted guidelines on the Protection of Privacy and Trans-border Flows of Personal Data. This was followed in 1981 by the Council of Europe Data Protection

---

25 Younger Committee (Report of the Committee on Privacy), Cmnd 5012 (1972). London: HMSO.
26 Younger Committee (Report of the Committee on Privacy), Cmnd 5012 (1972); White Paper, Cmnd 5353 (1975).
27 White Paper, Cmnd 5353 (1975).
28 Report of the Committee on Data Protection, Cmnd 7341 (1978).

Convention, which was based in part on the recommendations of the Younger Committee, establishing an agreement covering the automatic handling of personal information and broad guidelines for the safeguarding and control of information stored and processed on computers. It also provided guarantees in relation to the collection and processing of personal data, and made unlawful the processing of sensitive personal data (relating to issues such as race, politics, health, religion, sexual life, and criminal record) in the absence of proper legal safeguards. The Convention also enshrined the individual's right to know that information is stored about him, and the right to have it corrected where necessary.

As noted of importance in the OECD guidelines, the Convention dealt with cross-border transfers for information and stated that only countries with data protection laws equivalent to those set out in the Convention could ratify the Convention. This meant that data could be transferred freely between ratifying countries, but could only be transferred to other countries under restrictions.

13.3.5 *The Data Protection Act 1984*

There was significant debate in the UK about the Convention as the government was concerned that it might impact upon business activity and commerce and wanted to ensure that the UK met international standards to enable data to be transferred. In 1982, a Bill was introduced, which after passing through Parliament became the Data Protection Act 1984. The 1984 Act contained the provisions of the Younger Report as reflected in the Council of Europe Convention.

The 1984 Act established new rights for individuals to know if an organization was processing personal data about them and the right to have a copy of the information and as recommended in the Lindop Report, it established the office of Data Protection Registrar who had powers to enforce the regime. For the first time, individuals had the possibility of complaining to the Registrar and then to the newly established Data Protection Tribunal should their complaint proceed.

13.3.6 *The 1995 EU Directive*

The UK was not alone in introducing legislation. As a result of the Council of Europe Directive, there were vast differences in scope and content, which meant that the position across Europe lacked the uniformity necessary to harmonize the protection of data. In 1990, the European Commission addressed this by producing a draft directive aimed at harmonizing laws across the EU and assisting the free movement of data within the EU. Due to the complexity of the subject matter, the Directive was debated at length and was not approved in final form until 1995 (officially Directive 95/46/EC on the protection of individuals with regard to the processing of personal data and on the free movement of such data). Member States were given three years to implement it; in the UK, the Directive was implemented by means of the Data Protection Act 1998.

13.3.7 *Article 29 Working Party and Europe*

In recognition of the economic and social importance of social networking and associated websites, the European Commission has launched a number of initiatives and

244 *Commercial law*

consultations to address some of the negative issues associated with this sector, such as risks for children online. In October 2007, the European Network and Information Security Agency (ENISA) published a position paper, Security Issues and Recommendations for Online Social Networks,[29] aimed at regulators and providers of social networks and which explored the following areas for reform:

- Government Policy Recommendations

    o Encourage Awareness-raising and Educational Campaigns
    o Review and Reinterpret Regulatory Framework
    o Increase Transparency of Data Handling Practices
    o Discourage the Banning of SNSs in Schools

- Provider and Corporate Policy Recommendations

    o Promote Stronger Authentication and Access-control where Appropriate
    o Implement Countermeasures against Corporate Espionage using SNSs
    o Maximise Possibilities for Reporting and Detecting Abuse
    o Set Appropriate Defaults
    o Providers should offer Convenient Means to Delete Data Completely

- Technical Recommendations

    o Encourage the Use of Reputation Techniques
    o Build in Automated Filters
    o Require the Consent of the Data Subject to Include Profile Tags or e-Mail Address Tags in Images
    o Restrict Spidering and Bulk Downloads
    o Provide more Privacy Control over Search Results
    o Recommendations for Addressing SNS Spam
    o Recommendations for Addressing SNS Phishing

- Research and Standardization Recommendations

    o Promote and Research Image Anonymization Techniques and Best Practices
    o Promote Portable Networks
    o Research into Emerging Trends in SNSs

In February 2008, the Commission proposed a Safer Internet Programme for 2009–2013. Also in 2008, the Commission formed the Social Networking Task Force with Europe's major social networks, researchers and child welfare organizations. The focus for this group was the development of voluntary guidelines for the use of social networking sites (SNSs) by children. The Commission's objective has been one of self-regulation in this sector.

---

29 ENISA Position Paper No. 1, 'Security Issues and Recommendations for Online Social Networks', October 2007.

13.3.8 *The Rome Memorandum*

In March 2008, the Berlin International Working Group on Data Protection in Telecommunications adopted a memorandum[30] that analyzed the risks for privacy and security posed by social networks and provided guidelines for regulators, providers and users (Rome Memorandum). The Rome Memorandum recommended the following:

- More transparency and open information for users:
  - Information must be tailored to the specific needs of the targeted audience (especially for minors) to allow them to make informed decisions;
  - Information of users should also refer to third party data.

- To provide privacy policies.
- To introduce the creation and use of pseudonymous profiles as an option.
- To live up to promises made to users to foster and maintain user trust through clear and unambiguous information about how their information will be treated by the service provider, specifically when it comes to sharing personal data with third parties.
- To introduce privacy-friendly default settings to improve user control over use of profile data:
  - *Within the community*, e.g. allow restriction of visibility of entire profiles, and of data contained in profiles, as well as restriction of visibility in community search functions. Tagging of photos (i.e. the addition of links to an existing user profile or the naming of depicted persons) should be bound to the data subject's prior consent.
  - *Create means allowing for user control over third party use of profile data* – vital in particular to address risks of ID theft.
  - *Allow for user control over secondary use of profile and traffic data*, e.g. for marketing purposes, as a minimum: opt-out for general profile data, opt-in for sensitive profile data (e.g. political opinion, sexual orientation) and traffic data.
  - *Comply with user rights recognized in national, regional and international privacy frameworks*, including the right of data subjects to have data – which may well be entire profiles – erased in a timely manner.
  - *Address the issues that may arise in cases of a takeover or merger of a social network service company* – introduce guarantees for users that new owner will maintain present privacy (and security) standard.

- To adopt appropriate complaint handling mechanisms, where they do not already exist, for users of social networks, but also with respect to third party personal data.

---

30 Report and Guidance on Privacy in Social Network Services, International Working Group on Data Protection in Telecommunications 43rd meeting, 3–4 March 2008, Rome (Italy) [http://www.datens-chutz-berlin.de/attachments/461/WP_social_network_services.pdf].

246   *Commercial law*

- To improve and maintain security of information system by using recognized best practices in planning, developing, and running social network service applications, including independent certification.
- To devise and/or further improve measures against illegal activities, such as spamming and ID theft.
- To offer encrypted connections for maintaining user profiles, including secured log-in.
- That social network providers acting in different countries or even globally should respect the privacy standards of the countries where they operate their services.

13.3.8.1 *Children and minors*

An issue that has gown in prevalence as a result of the use of social networking is the effect it has on children and the need to protect their privacy. There have been many reports in the UK and USA in relation to young teenagers and even children as young as eight years of age committing suicide as a result of online bullying or as a result of embarrassing information about them being shared online within their friendship or school networks. There is also a risk that children do not understand the permanency of their postings and how it may affect their future employability or access to university.

The Working Party believes that a multi-pronged strategy would be appropriate to address the protection of children's data in the SNS context. Such a strategy could include:

- Awareness-raising initiatives via schools, the inclusion of the basic principle of data protection in educational curricula, the creation of ad hoc educational tools, and the collaboration of national competent bodies.
- The implementation of PETs, for example, privacy-friendly default settings, pop-up warning boxes at appropriate steps, age verification software, etc.
- Self-regulation by SNS providers to encourage the adoption of codes of practice that should be equipped with effective enforcement measures.

The Working Party recommends that, if these steps are not successful, ad hoc legislative measures to discourage unfair and/or deceptive practices in the SNS context should be adopted.

13.3.9 *Facebook's audit*

Perhaps in terms of social media, one of the most useful resources available to those interested in understanding how sites may be regulated was its audit. Facebook was audited by the Irish Data Protection Commissioner[31] as a result of a number of complaints raised by data subjects concerning the protection of their data on the site. Facebook in Europe is based in Ireland, which is why the audit was conducted by the Irish regulator.

---

31 Facebook Ireland Limited Report of re-audit: Data Protection Commissioner, 21 September 2012.

Data protection and privacy 247

In December 2011, the Commissioner had published the results of a detailed audit of Facebook. The audit contained a list of detailed time lines, best practice recommendations and provided for a review of the implementation of those recommendations, with a formal review in 2012. The 2012 report summarized the outcome of that review in terms of the following areas, which were highlighted as being of concern from a data protection perspective:[32]

- Privacy policies
- Advertising
- Access requests retention
- Cookies and plug-ins
- Third party apps
- Disclosure of content to third parties
- Facial recognition and tags
- Data security
- Deletion of accounts
- Friend finders
- Posting on other users' and groups' profile pages
- Facebook credits
- Profiles of individuals using the site under an alias name
- Reporting abusive content and behaviours
- Compliance systems put in place by the site
- Site governance

The list detailed above and the content of the report was by no means an exhaustive restatement of all of the issues raised in relation to social networking sites and privacy concerns. Clearly, as the site develops increasingly sophisticated platform developments, new concerns may arise. In respect of the site as it was at 2012, a number of complaints have been raised by pressure groups, such as *Europe Against Facebook*, which are still outstanding.[33] It is clear that on-going cooperation between the Commissioner and Facebook will be necessary in order to bring forward new innovations in relation to data security.[34]

The Irish Commissioner noted that Facebook took a constructive approach to the audit and that most of the areas recommended made by the Irish Commissioner's Office had been implemented by Facebook. The Commissioner noted that significant changes had been made in relation to transparency of site terms for users, better control over privacy settings, clearer retention periods for the deletion of data and/or an enhanced ability for users to delete content, improved access to the users' own data, and Facebook increasing its capacity to ensure that it is complying with Irish and EU data protection requirements.

The investigation into the operation of the site has meant that Facebook has had to make a number of changes to the site in order to comply with the privacy principles

---

32 Ibid. Chapter 2 deals with each of these concerns in detail.
33 See http://www.europe-v-facebook.org/EN/en/html.
34 See Executive Summary, Facebook Ireland Limited Report of re-audit: Data Protection Commissioner, 21 September 2012.

248　*Commercial law*

brought to its attention by the Irish Commissioner. Significantly, the controversial site feature of face recognition has had to be turned off for users in the EU (Facebook Ireland is responsible for all Facebook activities outside of the USA and Canada). Users must also now be given the right to delete their accounts, in order to comply with the fifth principle that data must not be kept for longer than is necessary.

However, in relation to new end user education, social plug-ins, impression data for EU users, fully verified account deletion, and minimizing the potential for ad targeting based on words and terms that could be classified as sensitive personal data, full implementation has not yet been achieved, but is planned to be achieved.

Facebook has not just faced questions from the Irish Commissioner. On 24 January 2014, the Chamber Court of Berlin[35] rejected Facebook's appeal of an earlier judgment by the Regional Court of Berlin in cases brought by a German consumer rights organization. In particular, the court:

- Requested that Facebook do not operate its 'Find a Friend' functionality in a way that violates the German Unfair Competition Act 2004;
- Requested that Facebook do not use certain provisions in its terms and conditions, and privacy notices concerning advertisements, licensing, personal data relating to third parties and personal data collected through other websites; and
- Insisted that Facebook provide users with more information about how their address data will be used by the 'Find a Friend' functionality.

This approach may also represent a new development in the data protection context because under German Law, one of the conditions for consumer rights organizations to be able to commence legal proceedings is that there is a violation of the Unfair Competition Act 2004. Recognizing data protection law violations as violations of the Unfair Competition Act 2004 may make it easier for consumer rights organizations to bring privacy-oriented cases.

13.3.10　*The Data Protection Act 1998*

The Data Protection Directive (95/46/EC) (the Directive) introduced an extensive data protection regime, imposing broad obligations on those who collect personal data[36] as well as conferring broad rights on individuals about whom data are collected (data subjects – see definition below). The Directive was implemented in the UK through the Data Protection Act 1998, replacing the UK's Data Protection Act 1984 in its entirety. The 1998 Act is considered in depth throughout this chapter.

13.3.11　*Draft European General Data Protection Regulation*

In recent years there has been an increasing awareness that a high level of data protection is essential to foster people's trust in online services and in the digital economy

---

35 Landgericht Berlin Im Namen des Volkes Geschäftsnummer: 16 O 551 /10 Urteil verkündet am: 06.03.2012.
36 Defined below.

in general. Privacy concerns are among the top reasons for people not buying goods and services online. With the technology sector directly contributing to 20% of overall productivity growth in Europe and 40% of overall investment aimed at the sector, individual trust in online services is vital for stimulating economic growth in the EU. On 25 January 2012, the European Commission unveiled a draft European General Data Protection Regulation[37] that will supersede the Data Protection Directive after noting that as a result of modern technology, with EU Commissioner Vivian Reading specifically noting social media as a key example, the 1995 Directive was unable to meet the increasing demands placed upon privacy protection in the digital age.[38]

The European Commission plans to unify data protection within the European Union with a single law, the General Data Protection Regulation (DPR). The current EU Data Protection Directive 95/46/EC does not consider important aspects like globalisation and technological developments like social networks and cloud computing sufficiently, and the Commission determined that new guidelines for data protection and privacy were required.

A proposal for a regulation was released on 25 January 2012. Subsequently, numerous amendments have been proposed in the European Parliament and the Council of Ministers. The EU's European Council aims for adoption in late 2014 (which at the time of writing is now delayed) and the regulation is presently planned to take effect after a transition period of two years. The key changes relate to:

- Strengthening the 'right to be forgotten' to help people better manage data protection risks online. When individuals no longer want their data to be processed and there are no legitimate grounds for retaining it, the data will be deleted. The rules are about empowering people, not about erasing past events or restricting the freedom of the press.
- Guaranteeing easy access to one's own data.
- Establishing a right for individuals to freely transfer personal data from one service provider to another (data portability).
- Ensuring that consent must be given explicitly by individuals when it is required for certain types of data processing.
- Increasing the responsibility and accountability of those processing data by introducing data protection officers for companies with over 250 employees, and the principles of 'privacy by default' and 'privacy by design' to ensure that individuals are informed in an easily understandable way about how their data will be processed.

Article 3 of the Regulation deals with territorial scope and makes significant changes. The Regulation will apply to the processing of personal data of data subjects in the EU, regardless of where the data controller or data processor is located, where the

---

37 Proposal for a Regulation of the European Parliament and of the Council on the Protection of Individuals with Regard to the Processing of Personal Data and on the Free Movement of such Data, Brussels, 25.1.2012, COM (2012) Final 2012/0011 (COD), European Council.

38 On 25 January 2012, the European Commission issued a consultation paper entitled 'Safeguarding Privacy in a Connected World' [http://ec.europa.eu/justice/data-protection/document/review2012/com_2012_9_en.pdf].

250   *Commercial law*

processing is related to offering EU data subjects goods or services (irrespective of whether payment is required) or monitoring them. The Regulation indicates that 'monitoring' data subjects will involve tracking individuals, regardless of the origins of the data, or collecting data about individuals with the intention to use data processing techniques to 'profile' them for analyzing or predicting their personal preferences, behaviours, and attitudes. Therefore, the same rules will apply to organizations located outside Europe if they process personal data of EU individuals, including for these monitoring purposes.

At the time of writing, the current planned date for full implementation is late 2016 but this could slip. It is worth emphasising that it is not yet clear whether the draft Regulation will be adopted exactly in its current form or, if amendments are made, what form these are likely to take. In terms of what business can do to 'future proof', taking an audit of current compliance against the DPA 1998 would be a good start. Business should also monitor developments in the progress of the draft Regulation and once there is more clarity as to obligations and timetable, revisit their data protection measures as necessary.

13.3.12 *Leveson*

During the course of the Leveson Inquiry,[39] a number of website operators and micro site platforms were called to give evidence, most notably Twitter, Google, and Facebook. A number of questions were raised in relation to the activities of the sites.

Twitter in particular came into focus and was of interest to the Inquiry because of the role played by users in identifying individuals who had been the subject of privacy injunctions. Twitter allows members to operate anonymously, or under a pseudonym,[40] and it is also possible that the company itself may not know the real identity of any member.[41] However, Twitter told the Inquiry that its rules forbid members from using the service for any unlawful purpose,[42] and any material that is found by the company to contravene that policy can be taken down or removed.[43]

13.4 The Data Protection Act 1998

13.4.1 *Framework created by the Data Protection Act 1998*

The Data Protection Act 1998 (DPA 1998) creates a framework within which all processing of personal data must be carried out. The scope of these defined terms is such that any UK-established entity or individual obtaining personal information is likely to have to operate within the DPA framework. The DPA 1998 applies to data controllers[44] established in the UK, where personal data is processed in the context of

---

39 Lord Justice Leveson, *Report into the Culture Practices and Ethics of the Press*, 29 November 2012. London: Department for Culture, Media and Sport. HC 8708-i-iii, 2012–13.
40 Colin   Crowell,   http://www.levesoninquiry.org.uk/wp-content/uploads/2012/02/Transcript-of-Morning-Hearing-7-February-2012.pdf, p. 94, lines 6–7.
41 Ibid., p. 98, lines 22–23.
42 Ibid., p. 96, lines 22–25.
43 Ibid., p. 98, lines 6–9.
44 See definition below.

Data protection and privacy   251

that establishment.[45] Establishment is widely defined and captures entities which operate online, such as social media sites. The obligations of the DPA 1998 will apply wherever processing takes place. Although on first reading the application of the DPA 1998 may appear complex, conceptually data protection is simple, it is about treating information about individuals with proper respect. The 1995 Directive stated the objective clearly in Article 1: 'In accordance with this directive, Member States shall protect the fundamental rights and freedoms of natural persons, and in particular their right to privacy with respect to the processing of personal data.' In order to achieve this general objective, the law prescribes certain standards and rules. These deal with the collection and use of information, the quality and security of information, and the rights of individuals with respect to information about themselves.

At this stage, we need to understand the significance of three of the definitions in the Act: data, personal data, and processing. These are interlinked; taken together, they define the scope of the Act.

13.4.2 *Application to social networking sites*

In the legal sense, as far as data protection is concerned, social networks are information society services.[46] An information society service is defined as 'any service normally provided for remuneration at a distance, by means of electronic equipment for the processing (including digital compression) and storage of data, at the individual request of a recipient of the service'.[47] The DPA 1998 therefore applies to sites that are established or have servers in the UK, where the data is processed.[48]

13.4.3 *The Rome Memorandum 2008*

In March 2008, the Berlin International Working Group on Data Protection in the telecommunications field adopted a memorandum that analyzes the risks for privacy and security posed by social networks and provides guidelines for regulators, providers, and users (The 'Rome Memorandum'[49]). The Rome Memorandum details a number of risks associated with the use of social network services.

One key concern of the working group was that the notion of 'oblivion' does not exist on the internet. Once published, content that has been uploaded to the internet may in theory remain accessible forever; this may be the case even though the data subject has deleted the content form the 'original' site, as there may be copies with third parties (including archive services and the 'cache' function provided by a well-known search engine provider). Additionally, some service providers refuse to speedily

---

45 See s 5 DPA 1998.

46 As defined in Article 1, para 2 of Directive 98/34/EC as amended by Directive 98/48/EC. The issues presented in relation to locating social media within existing legal definitions is explored in depth in Chapter 1.

47 Article 1, para 2 of Directive 98/34/EC as amended by Directive 98/48/EC.

48 See Transfers of Data Outside of the EEA for a consideration of the application of the DPA 1998 to sites established within and outside the EEA.

49 Report and Guidance on Privacy in Social Network Services, 'Rome Memorandum', 43rd Meeting, 3–4 March 2008, Rome (Italy).

252 *Commercial law*

comply (or even to comply at all) with user requests to have data, and especially complete profiles, deleted.[50]

It was also noted that there is a misleading notion of 'community' on social media. Many service providers claim that they are bringing communication structures from the 'real' world into cyberspace. A common claim is that it is safe, for example, to publish (personal) data on those platforms, as it would just resemble sharing information with friends face-to-face. However, a closer look at some features in some services reveals that this parallel has some weaknesses, including that the notion of 'friends' in cyberspace may in many cases substantially differ from the more traditional idea of friendship, and that a community may be very big. If users are not openly informed about how their profile information is shared and what they can do to control how it is shared, they may by the notion of 'community' as set out above be lured into thoughtlessly sharing their personal data which they would not have otherwise done. The very name of some of these platforms (e.g. 'MySpace') creates the illusion of intimacy on the web.

The committee also noted that although sites may not charge subscription fees to use their platforms, social network users may in fact 'pay' through secondary use of their personal profile data by the service providers, such as for (targeted) marketing.

The growing need to refinance services and to make profits may further spur the collection, processing, and use of user data, when they are the only real asset of social network providers. Social network sites are not public utilities, although the term 'social' may suggest otherwise. At the same time, Web 2.0 as a whole is 'growing up', and there is a shift from start-ups sometimes run by groups of students with less financial interests to major international players entering the market. As for many providers of social networks, user profile data and the number of unique users (combined with frequency of use) are the only real assets these companies have, which may create additional risks for the disproportionate collection, processing, and use of users' personal data.

Users may also give away more personal information than they are aware they are doing. For example, photos may become universal biometric identifiers within a network and even across networks. Face recognition software has been dramatically improved over the past years, and will continue to reap even 'better' results in the future. Once a name can be attached to a picture, this can also endanger the privacy and security of other, possibly pseudonymous or even anonymous user profiles (e.g. dating profiles, which normally have a picture and profile information, but not the real name of the data subject published). Additionally, the European Network and Information Security Agency points to an emerging technology called 'content based image retrieval' (CBIR), which creates additional possibilities for locating users by matching identifying features of a location (e.g. a painting in a room, or a building depicted) to location data in a database. Furthermore, 'social graph' functionalities popular with many social network services do reveal data about the relationships between different users. A further issue relates to traffic data, as social network service providers are technically capable of recording every single move a user makes on their site – eventually sharing personal (traffic) data (including users' IP addresses, which

---

50 See Chapter 3: Defamation and E-Commerce Directives takedown procedure.

can in some cases also resemble location data) with third parties (e.g. for advertising or even targeted advertising).

In many jurisdictions, this data will also have to be disclosed to law enforcement and/or (national) secret services upon request, including maybe also foreign entities under existing rules on international cooperation. The dangers of such identifying data in criminal proceedings and its admissibility are discussed in depth in Chapter 12: Evidence and Procedure.

Perhaps one of the most potent risks presented by social media noted in the report is the potential for the misuse of profile data by third parties. Depending on available privacy (default) settings and whether and how users use them, as well as on the technical security of a social network service, profile information, including pictures (which may depict the data subject, but also other people) may be made available to – in the worst case – the entire user community. At the same time, very little protection exists at present against copying any kind of data from profiles, and using them for building personal profiles and/or re-publishing them outside of the social network service.

13.4.4 *Scope of DPA 1998 and definitions*

The DPA 1998 is based on a number of key definitions that can be found in the Glossary annexed to the Act. The DPA 1998 only regulates the use of 'personal data' by 'data controllers'.

13.4.4.1 *Data controllers and data processors*

Throughout this chapter, the terms data controller and data subject are used, both of which are defined in the DPA 1998. These concepts are important as they determine:

- Who is responsible for compliance with data protection rules;
- How data subjects can exercise their rights;
- How effective data protection authorities can operate.

13.4.4.2 *Data controller*

13.4.4.2.1 DEFINITION OF DATA CONTROLLER AND OBLIGATIONS

All of the obligations under the Act fall on the data controller. Online entities are subject to the same notification requirements as offline businesses and should register with the information commissioner[51] if they are an entity with a UK trading establishment. Holding the position of data controller can be a consequence of a party's chosen role or imposed by legislation. A data controller is the person who either alone or jointly or in common with other persons, determines the purposes for, and the manner in which any personal data is or is not to be processed (s 1 DPA 1998). In relation to any contact information, or other personal data that the site operator

---

51 Registrations can be completed via http://www.ico.org.uk/for_organizations/data_protection/registration/data-protection-registration.

254 *Commercial law*

processes about its own users or subscribers, it will clearly be a data controller and will need to comply with the DPA 1998.

For any personal data that is posted on a site by third party subscribers, the issue is less clear-cut. In *The Law Society and Others v Rick Kordowski (Solicitors from Hell)*,[52] Mr Kordowski set up and ran a website on which members of the public were invited to 'name and shame "Solicitors from Hell"'. He moderated posts and charged a fee for adding or removing them. Mr Justice Tugendhat had no hesitation in accepting that Mr Kordowski was a data controller under DPA 1998 and this was not disputed by any party. It was clear in the circumstances that Mr Kordowski decided the purposes and manner in which the personal data was processed.

In other cases, the forum might be provided free of charge or the person or organization running the site might take much less of a role in moderating content. For example, members of many large social networking sites are able to add posts directly to the site without first having them checked by a site moderator. However, even if the content is not moderated before posting, this does not necessarily mean that the person or organization running the site isn't a data controller. If the site only allows posts subject to terms and conditions which cover acceptable content, and if it can remove posts which breach its policies on such matters, then it will still, to some extent, be determining the purposes and manner in which personal data is processed. It will therefore be a data controller.

It is the opinion of the Article 29 Working Party[53] that in relation to social media sites, the site operator will be the data controller, regardless if a different entity is acting as the website host. In this scenario, the host will be the data processor.[54] In effect, the data controller is the party that decides what to do with personal data and how that activity is to be carried out. These decisions can be made with, or at the same time as, another data controller in respect of the same personal data. Data controllers do not need to hold the data or process it. It is sufficient to instruct a third party how to process the personal data to be deemed a data controller. It is control rather than possession of personal data that is the determining factor for the purpose of the application of the DPA 1998. Therefore, where another party processes information on behalf of the data controller, the controller is required to ensure that the processor has implemented the necessary security measures in relation to such data.

Data controllers must ensure that any processing of personal data for which they are responsible complies with the DPA 1998. Failure to do so risks enforcement action, even prosecution, and compensation claims from individuals. It should be noted that significantly, data processing that is undertaken by a website operator who is located outside of the European Economic Area (EEA) but whose server is located or whose site is hosted in the UK, will be subject to the DPA 1998.

The Article 29 Working Party published an opinion on how the operation of social networking sites can meet the requirements of EU data protection and concluded that the Directive generally applies to the processing of personal data by SNSs, even

---

52 [2011] EWHC 3185 (QB).

53 http://ec.europa.eu/justice/policies/privacy/docs/wpdocs/2009/wp163_en.pdf.

54 And an appropriate contact should be entered into between the parties to hold the Data Processor to standards equivalent to the DPA 1998.

when their headquarters are outside the EEA. The Working Party points to its earlier opinion on search engines,[55] where it explained how the place where a company is established, and where the equipment it uses for the provision of its service is situated, determines if the Directive (and the rules subsequently triggered by the processing of internet protocol (IP) addresses and the use of cookies) applies.

The Working Party states that both SNS providers and providers of individual applications on social networking sites are data controllers under the Directive. While SNS users' use of social media sites will generally be covered by the household exemption under Article 3(2) of the Directive, the Working Party opines that not all activities of an SNS user are necessarily covered by that exemption. In those cases, users might be considered to have taken on some of the responsibilities of a data controller, and the user needs the consent of the persons concerned or some other legitimate basis provided in the Directive. The opinion lists a number of activities where this may be the case, including where:

- The activities of the SNS user extend beyond a purely personal or household activity, for example, when the SNS is used as a collaboration platform for an association or a company.
- Access to profile information extends beyond self-selected contacts, such as when access to a profile is provided to all members within the SNS, or the data is indexable by search engines, or if a user takes an informed decision to extend access beyond self-selected 'friends' (for example, by making his profile information available to all members of a specific network).

The application of the household exemption is also constrained by the need to guarantee the rights of third parties, particularly with regard to sensitive data. The Working Party clarifies that social networking sites fall outside of the scope of the definition of electronic-communication service. Therefore, the Data Retention Directive (2006/24/EC) does not apply to social networking sites.[56]

13.4.4.2.2 REGISTRATION REQUIREMENTS

By virtue of section 4(4) DPA 1998, and subject to section 27(1), it is the duty of a data controller to comply with the data protection in relation to all personal data with respect to which he is the data controller. Further, section 17(1) provides that 'personal data shall not be processed unless an entry in respect of the data controller is included in the register maintained by the Commissioner under section 19 . . .'.

Data controllers are obliged to comply with the Data Protection Principles and, unless exempt, have an entry on the Information Commissioner's Register of data controllers. Data controllers are exempt from notification, but not compliance with the Principles, if their processing is limited to the following purposes:

55 EC Article 29 Working Party opinion on data protection issues related to search engines, 4 April 2008.
56 This distinction is explored in Chapter 1: Introduction to Social Media and the Law: *The Legal Classification of Social Networking Sites*. See also 'retention of data' dealt with at page [285] of this chapter.

256   *Commercial law*

- staff administration (including payroll);
- advertising, marketing and public relations (in connection with their own business activity);
- accounts and records;
- some not-for-profit organizations;
- organizations that process personal data only for maintaining a public register;
- organizations that do not process personal information on computer.

It should be noted that a data controller that fails to notify the Information Commissioner of its processing commits a criminal offence (s 17 DPA 1998).

13.4.4.3 *Processors*

To qualify as a data processor, a party must be a separate legal entity from the data controller, and process personal data on the data controller's behalf. Data processors are not directly subject to the Act. However, most data processors, if not all, will be data controllers in their own right for the processing they do for their own administrative purposes, such as employee administration or sales.

In 2003, in the case of *Bodil Lindqvist v Kammaraklagaren*,[57] the ECJ held that the act of identifying a natural person on an internet site by name or other personal identifiers constitutes 'processing' of personal data within the meaning of Article 3(1) of the Directive. The Court also found that such processing is not covered by the exception in Article 3(2) of the Directive. The Court concluded that the exception related only to activities which are carried out in the course of private or family life of individuals and that this is clearly not the case where personal data is made accessible on the internet to an indefinite number of people.

13.4.4.4 *ICO guidance on identifying data controllers and data processors*

On 28 May 2014, the ICO published new guidance in relation to identifying data controllers and data processors.[58] The ICO notes that the guidance was in response to the increasing complexity of information systems and business models, which has resulted in a number of organizations working together in an initiative that involves processing personal data. The guidance seeks to address the increasing difficulty organizations can face in determining whether they or the organizations they are working with have data protection responsibility.

13.4.4.5 *Contracts*

The relationship between a controller and a processor must be governed by a contract 'which is made or evidenced in writing'. The requirement could therefore be satisfied

---

57 Case C-101/01 [2003] ECR I-12971.
58 'Data controllers and data processors: what the difference is and what the governance implications are', Information Commissioner's Office, 28 May 2014.

Data protection and privacy 257

by an oral agreement that is recorded in writing. Most controllers comply with the provision by entering into standard terms, to give certainty that obligations equivalent to Principle 7 is being complied with. Controllers must ensure that the processor only acts on the instructions of the controller, there is no requirement that they should be in writing or detailed. Note that the Article 29 Working Party is inclined toward a more restrictive view (Working Party Paper on Controllers and Processors discussed below).

Data controllers must also ensure that processors provide sufficient guarantees about their security measures to protect the processing and take reasonable steps to check that those security measures are being put into practice. Data processors are also required to take the same security measures that the data controller would have to take if it were processing the data itself.

13.4.4.6 *Data Protection Regulation*

Article 73 of the DPR is significant as it deals with joint liability for processors. The Article states that a person (data subject) will have the right to claim compensation from a data controller or a data processor if they suffer damage as a result of unlawful processing. Where more than one controller or processor is involved in the processing, they will be jointly and severally liable for the entire amount of the damage unless they have an appropriate written agreement determining their responsibilities (pursuant to Article 24). It will therefore be important for outsourcing contracts under which data processing activities are delegated to a processor to clearly set out each party's responsibilities and liabilities. The same will apply for plug-ins and apps provided via social networking sites (considered later in this chapter).

Where several organizations jointly determine the purposes and means of the processing of personal data, they must under Article 24 of the DPR now make the 'essence of the arrangement' available for data subjects, so that it is clear what their respective roles and responsibilities are.

13.4.4.7 *Article 29 Working Party standard clauses*

On 21 March 2014, the Article 29 Working Party adopted a working document on standard contractual clauses for the transfer of personal data from data processors established in the EU to data sub-processors established in third countries. The contractual clauses contained in this working document have not been adopted by the European Commission and do not have the status of an official set of model clauses, nor a finalised set of ad hoc clauses.

The issue of overseas transfers is dealt with in depth later in this chapter.

13.4.5 *The eight principles of data protection*

At the heart of the DPA 1998 is a set of eight principles known as the Data Protection Principles (contained in Schedule 1 DPA 1998). They deal with the collection, use, quality, and security of personal data and with data subjects' rights and are summarized below:

258 *Commercial law*

- Fairly and lawfully processed;[59]
- Processed for specified purposes;[60]
- Adequate, relevant and not excessive;[61]
- Accurate and, where necessary, kept up to date;[62]
- Not kept for longer than is necessary;[63]
- Processed in line with the rights of the individual;[64]
- Kept secure;[65] and
- Not transferred to countries outside the European Economic Area unless the information is adequately protected.[66]

The DPA 1998 places a duty on all data controllers, enforceable by the Information Commissioner, to comply with the eight data protection principles when processing personal data. The principles are the foundation on which the rest of the data protection edifice is built. Almost everything else prescribed in the Act is related in one way or another to compliance with the principles.

13.4.6 *The meaning of processing*

The DPA 1998 applies to the 'processing' of 'personal data'. Processing is widely defined as activities that encompass recording, holding, using, disclosing or erasing data.[67] This means that practically any business operating in the UK that holds information about individuals, whether employees, customers or anyone else, is affected by the Act. The DPA 1998 is not intended to prevent the processing of personal data, but to ensure that it is done fairly and without adversely affecting the rights of data subjects. In the Information Commissioner's view, personal data is being processed where information is collected and analyzed with the intention of distinguishing one individual from another and to take a particular action in respect of an individual. This can take place even if no obvious identifiers, such as names or addresses, are held.

13.4.7 *The meaning of a data subject*

The information must be classed both as 'data' and as 'personal data' before any of the provisions of the DPA 1998 apply. A data subject is defined as any individual about whom personal data is processed. Typically, data subjects include individuals on contact lists or marketing databases, employees, contractors, consultants, suppliers, and customers (including those dealing with companies through the internet).

---

59 Schedule 1, Data Protection Act 1998, Part 1, Principle 1.
60 Ibid., Principle 2.
61 Ibid., Principle 3.
62 Ibid., Principle 4.
63 Ibid., Principle 5.
64 Ibid., Principle 6.
65 Ibid., Principle 7.
66 Ibid., Principle 8.
67 Section 1(1) DPA 1998.

13.4.8 *The meaning of personal data*

The DPA 1998 applies only to personal data. Section 1(1) DPA states that 'personal data' means data that relates to a living individual who can be identified:

- from the data; or
- from the data and other information which is in the possession of, or is likely to come into the possession of, the data controller, and includes any expression of opinion about the individual;
- and any indication of the intentions of the data controller or any other person in respect of the individual.

Data is defined as information which is being processed by means of equipment that operates automatically in response to instructions given for that purpose, or is recorded with the intention that it should be processed by means of such equipment.[68] Data covered by the DPA 1998 falls into four categories:

- Automatically processed data.
- Data forming part of a relevant filing system.
- Data forming part of an accessible record.
- Data recorded by a public authority.

As well as names and addresses, emails are covered (as well as their subject headings); such data in emails may be caught where it:

- Identifies a living individual.
- Is held in live computer systems.
- Is held in back-up systems.
- Has been deleted but is capable of retrieval.

In *Lindqvist*,[69] the Court of Justice of the European Union held that identification of persons on a website by their name, or by other characteristics which amount to personal data would constitute processing for the purposes of the European Directive which the DPA 1998 is based upon. The Information Commissioner has issued guidance[70] on the meaning of 'personal data' which draws heavily on an opinion of the Article 29 Working Party (a European group set up to look at the operation of the Directive).

In the case of *Durant v Financial Services Authority*,[71] the Court of Appeal narrowly interpreted the meaning of personal data. Mr Durant had requested information from the Financial Services Authority by way of a subject access request (made under

---

68 Ibid.

69 Case C-101/01 [2003] ECR I-12971.

70 Determining what is personal data, Information Commissioners Office, 2012 [http://ico.org.uk/for_organizations/guidance_index/~/media/documents/library/Data_Protection/Detailed_specialist_guides/PERSONAL_DATA_FLOWCHART_V1_WITH_PREFACE001.ashx].

71 [2003] EWCA Civ 1746.

260 *Commercial law*

s 7 DPA 1998) against Barclays Bank. The Court of Appeal held that this did not amount to his personal data, as it related to the complaint itself. Auld LJ established two points for determining whether information is personal data:

- whether the information is biographical in a significant sense; and
- whether the information has the putative data subject as its focus.

This judgment was followed in 2007 by an Article 29 Working Party opinion on the concept of personal data (WP 136) (WPO), which identified three central concepts of how data may relate to an individual in a way that makes it personal data. These fell into the following categories:

- Purpose;
- Content; and
- Result.

Although the opinion is not binding, it offered a wider interpretation of the meaning of 'personal data' than *Durant* and should therefore be considered when determining if information is personal data. The status of the opinion was lent weight by the publication by the Information Commissioner's Office (ICO) of its own technical guidance note.[72] The note seeks to reconcile the Option with *Durant* and assist those charged with determining what is and what is not personal data with a reference point where it is not obvious whether data falls within the definition contained in the DPA 1998.

The approach taken in the ICO's guidance note was confirmed in a High Court decision addressing the nature of personal data, albeit in the context of the Freedom of Information Act 2000 (FOIA 2000). In *R (Kelway) v The Upper Tribunal (Administrative Appeals Chamber) and Northumbria Police and R (Kelway) v Independent Police Complaints Commission*,[73] it was held by the court that although *Durant* remains the lead authority on the interpretation of the meaning of personal data, it has to be viewed in the light of its factual scenario and as such is one of a number of tests that may be applied in determining whether information is personal data. The court held that the opinion of the Working Party and the ICO's guidance must also be considered along with *Durant*, when determining if information constitutes personal data. This was followed in 2014 by the Court of Appeal decision in *Edem v The Information Commissioner & Anor*,[74] another case dealing with the data protection exemption contained in the FOIA 2000. In particular, the court found that a first-tier tribunal (determining whether the names of FSA employees were personal data) had been wrong solely to follow the approach taken in *Durant*. Instead, the court specifically referred to the ICO technical guidance note.

---

72 ICO Guidance Note, 'Determining what is personal data' [http://ico.org.uk/for_organizations/guid-ance_index/~/media/documents/library/Data_Protection/Detailed_specialist_guides/PERSONAL_DATA_FLOWCHART_V1_WITH_PREFACE001.ashx].
73 [2013] EWHC 2575 (Admin), 20 August 2013.
74 [2014] EWCA Civ 92 (7 February 2014).

The following diagram may be used to determine if the information concerned is personal data and could be used alongside the Working Party opinion and the ICO guidance note when formulating a view as to whether information constitutes personal data.

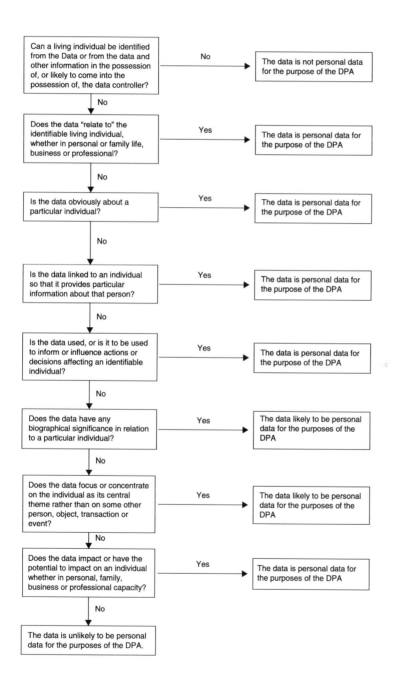

262 *Commercial law*

13.4.8.1 *Sensitive personal data: additional rules*

There are additional rules in relation to the processing of sensitive personal data. Sensitive personal data includes data relating to race, political opinions, health, sexual life, religious and other similar beliefs, trade union membership, and criminal records.[75]

Sensitive personal data will only be processed fairly and lawfully as required by the first data protection principle if at least one of a number of additional conditions is satisfied, which include measures such as ensuring that the individual has given his explicit consent to the processing (this need not necessarily be in writing). The conditions for processing are explored in more detail in the following sections of this chapter. The Information Commissioner has indicated that explicit consent requires the consent of the data subject to be absolutely clear and should, where appropriate, cover the detail and purposes of the processing, the type of data to be processed, and any special aspects of the processing, such as disclosures of the data.[76] Opt-in consent is required in the case of sensitive personal data (that is, positive, prior consent) and opt-out consent will not be sufficient.

Sensitive personal data may only be published on the internet with the explicit consent of the data subject or if the data subject has made the data manifestly public himself.[77] It should be noted that in some EU Member States, images of data subjects are considered a special category of personal data since they may be used to distinguish between racial/ethnic origins or may be used to deduce religious beliefs or health data. The Working Party in general does not consider images on the internet to be sensitive data,[78] unless the images are clearly used to reveal sensitive data about individuals. However, the Working Party is of the opinion that in relation to minors, social media sites should take appropriate action to limit the risks.

The Article 29 Working Party suggest that as data controllers, social networking sites may not process any sensitive data about SNS members or non-members without their explicit consent[79] and if a site includes in the profile form of users any questions relating to sensitive data, the site must make it clear that answering such questions is voluntary.

13.4.8.2 *IP addresses*

Each computer or other device connected to the internet has its own IP (internet protocol) address so that it can identify and communicate with other computers/devices. Whenever an individual uses that computer and/or device, it either uses the same address each time (a static IP address) or with a different number (dynamic IP address). Some internet service providers (ISPs) allocate dynamic addresses as a matter of course, others use static addresses.

---

75 Section 2 DPA 1998.

76 http://www.ico.org.uk/for_organizations/data_protection/the_guide/conditions_for_ processing.

77 Member States may lay down exemptions from this rule; see Article 8.2(a) second sentence and Article 8.4 of the Data Protection Directive.

78 Article 29 Data Protection Working Party, Opinion 5/2009 on online social networking at para 3.4.

79 Both members and non-members of social networking sites have the rights of data subjects if applicable, according to the provisions of Article 10–14 of the Data Protection Directive.

Data protection and privacy 263

As soon as a user visits a website, the IP address is available to the site – websites commonly keep records. The site user's ISP also keeps a record of internet activity, even if the IP address with which it provides the user is dynamic. Only limited information is freely available about IP addresses – as they are allocated in batches, they usually reveal a user's ISP and geographic location (e.g. a city but not a street address or postcode). An IP address by itself is not personal data under the DPA 1998,[80] as it is focused on a computer and not an individual. There is no English case law to back this up, but the reasoning was applied by the Hong Kong Privacy Commissioner in a complaint about Yahoo's disclosure of information about a journalist to Chinese authorities.[81] An IP address can become personal data when combined with other information or when used to build the profile of an individual (i.e. when combined with enough data to identify the person in question), even if that individual's name is unknown.

Most websites don't profile their visitors using IP addresses; they are typically only interested in information such as counting visitors, countries of origin and choice of ISP, or working organization (if a batch of IP addresses is for one organization). However, problems arise if the site intends to advertise and market products.

By way of example, visiting a website may involve a user, during the course of their browsing session clicking an advert; on their next visit, the same user is shown similar adverts – this mechanism fails with dynamic IP addresses and most websites use cookies[82] to track users for personalised marketing purposes in preference to IP addresses. The file created by the cookie can be used to identify an individual and allows the operator of the site to develop a detailed profile of that person's activity at its site.

13.4.9 *Conditions for processing*

Once it has been established whether the DPA 1998 applies to the data in question, there are technical requirements contained within the Act that must be taken care of in order for processing of personal data to be lawful. These are referred to as the conditions for processing.

The DPA 1998 requires that personal data should be processed in accordance with privacy notices provided to data subjects, not used for different unspecified purposes and processed subject to appropriate security.

13.4.9.1 *General rules for conditions for processing*

Principle 1 of the DPA 1998, referred to above, imposes a general requirement to process fairly and lawfully, but also imposes specific conditions. It makes it an explicit requirement that processing is not allowed unless one or more of the following

---

80 Note that 'personal data' means data which relate to a living individual who can be identified (s 1(1) DPA 1998).

81 The Disclosure of Email Subscribers' Personal Data by Email Service Provider to PRC Law Enforcement Agency, case number 200603619, Report R07-3619, issued 14 March 2007.

82 A cookie is a small text file sent from a website to a visitor's computer.

264 Commercial law

conditions contained in Schedule 2 DPA 1998 is satisfied. Schedule 2 provides that personal data may be processed:

- with the consent of the data subject;
- to establish or perform a contract with the data subject;
- to comply with a legal obligation;
- to protect the vital interests of the data subject;
- for the exercise of certain functions of a public interest nature;
- for the legitimate interests of the data controller unless outweighed by the interests of the data subject.

13.4.9.2 *Additional rules for sensitive personal data*

Schedule 3 DPA 1998 lists additional conditions for processing sensitive data. Such data may be processed:

- with the explicit consent of the data subject;
- to perform any right or obligation under employment law;
- to protect the vital interests of the data subject or another person;
- for the legitimate activities of certain not-for-profit bodies;
- where the data have been made public by the data subject;
- in connection with legal proceedings;
- for the exercise of certain functions of a public interest nature;
- for medical purposes;
- for equal opportunity ethnic monitoring.

13.4.9.2.1 EXTENSION OF CONDITIONS

The list of conditions in Schedule 3 has been extended by two statutory instruments to include circumstances prescribed in those instruments:

- for the prevention or detection of any unlawful act;
- for protecting the public against dishonesty or malpractice;
- for publication in the public interest;
- for providing counselling, advice or any other service;
- for carrying on insurance business;
- for equal opportunity monitoring other than ethnic monitoring;
- by political parties for legitimate political activities;
- for research;
- for any lawful functions of a constable;
- by elected representatives;
- in the form of disclosures to elected representatives.

13.4.10 *The rights of data subjects*

Regardless of the informality of the medium, the rights of data subjects pervade. The following categories indicate a list, which is by no means exhaustive, of the rights individuals have in relation to their data:

Data protection and privacy 265

- The right of access (s 7 DPA 1998);
- The right to establish the existence of personal data (s 7(1)(a) DPA 1998);
- Rights in relation to automated decision-making and the rationale behind the decision-making process (s 7(1)(d) DPA 1998);
- The right to prevent processing which is likely to cause damage or distress (s 18 DPA 1998);
- The right to prevent processing for the purposes of direct marketing activity (s 11 DPA 1998);
- The right to prevent automated decision-making (s 12 DPA 1998);
- The right to compensation (s 13 DPA 1998);
- The right to have inaccurate data amended (s 14 DPA 1998)
- The right to rectification, blocking erasure or destruction of data (s 14 DPA 1998);
- The right to complain to the Information Commissioner (s 15 DPA 1998);
- The right to take a matter to court (s 15 DPA 1998).

13.4.11 *Consent*

13.4.11.1 *Meaning of consent*

Consent is not defined in the DPA 1998. However, article 2(h) of the Directive says that 'the Data Subject's consent' shall mean 'any freely given, specific and informed indication of his wishes by which the Data Subject signifies his agreement to personal data relating to him being processed'. As article 2(h) covers all consent, it is a useful standard as the threshold for the consent that must be obtained.

Organizations should keep clear records of what an individual has consented to, and when and how this consent was obtained, so that they can demonstrate compliance in the event of a complaint.

The key points are that for consent to be valid, it must be:

- Freely given – the individual must have a genuine choice over whether or not to consent to marketing. Organizations should not coerce or unduly incentivise people to consent, or penalise anyone who refuses. Consent cannot be a condition of subscribing to a service or completing a transaction.
- Specific – in the context of direct marketing, consent must be specific to the type of marketing communication in question (e.g. automated call or text message) and the organization sending it. (Discussed further below.)
- Informed – the person must understand what they are consenting to.

Organizations must make sure they clearly and prominently explain exactly what the person is agreeing to, if this is not obvious. For example, site policies should refer the site user to its terms and conditions and privacy policy and detail how their information will be used, especially if the consent sought is not always obvious; this may especially be the case in respect of data that is passed outside of the company or its group or perhaps sold on in the future as a marketing list.

Consent should cover all processing activities carried out for the same purpose or purposes. If the data subject's consent is to be given following an electronic request, the request must be clear, concise, and not unnecessarily disruptive to the use of the

266 *Commercial law*

service for which it is provided. The data controller bears the burden of proof to illustrate that it has obtained the data subject's consent.

13.4.11.1.1 THE DRAFT DATA PROTECTION REGULATION

Article 7 of the Draft Data Protection Regulation requires that processing will be legal and lawful only where consent is freely given, specific, and informed. Under the regulation, as a general rule consent should not be implied but requires either a clear statement or affirmative action from the data subject. Silence or inactivity should therefore not constitute consent.

Although it is not mandatory in the UK to obtain the consent of data subjects before processing personal data, it is often the simplest way to legitimise processing. Under the current Draft Data Protection Regulation, consent will have to be explicit in all circumstances, regardless of circumstances. Article 7(a) of the Directive[83] requires that 'the Data Subject has given his explicit consent'. When processing sensitive personal data held under article 8,[84] the Directive requires that 'the Data Subject has given his explicit consent to the processing of data'. If data is transferred to an overseas jurisdiction which does not provide a comparable level of protection of personal data as detailed in article 26(1)(a),[85] then the controller must ensure that 'the Data Subject has given his consent unambiguously to the proposed transfer'. Since consent must be specific and informed, it will be necessary to set out the purposes for which information is to be used where these are not obvious. This would tend to be supported by the opinion of the Working Party who have explored what is meant by valid consent and in one paper have suggested that it may mean a voluntary choice 'by an individual in possession of all of his facilities, taken in the absence of coercion of any kind, be it social, financial, psychological or other'.[86]

This will raise the bar of consent as the burden of proof will lie with data controllers to demonstrate compliance through a clear statement or affirmative action from the data subject. The current planned date for full implementation is late 2016 but this could slip. We would also emphasise that it is not yet clear whether the draft Regulation will be adopted exactly in its current form or, if amendments are made, what form these are likely to take.

13.4.11.2 *Further consents for new processing activities*

However consent is obtained, it will be specific to the purpose(s) disclosed to the individual concerned. This will mean that further consent will be required for new processing activities which fall outside the scope of the purposes for which the original consent was given. This may include unauthorized transfers to third parties, as well as to new uses of the data by the original Data Controller e.g. marketing activity, customer profiling etc.

---

83 Effected in UK law by Sched 2 para 1 DPA 1998.
84 Effected in UK law by Sched 3 para 1 DPA 1998.
85 Effected in UK law by Sched 4 para 1 DPA 1998.
86 WP29 131.

Data protection and privacy 267

13.4.11.3 *Cookies*

13.4.11.3.1 CITIZEN'S RIGHTS DIRECTIVE

Consent is central to the rules on direct marketing. Organizations will generally need an individual's consent before they can send marketing texts, emails or faxes, make calls to a number registered with the Telephone Preference Service, or make any automated marketing calls under the Privacy and Electronic Communications Regulations 2003. They will also usually need consent to pass customer details on to another organization. If they cannot demonstrate that they had valid consent, they may be subject to enforcement action.

In November 2009, the Citizen's Rights Directive[87] introduced a new regime in relation to the requirements which online providers must meet in relation to using cookies.[88] Sites were able to rely on users 'opting-out'[89] of the regime that was previously in force; however, the new regime requires that sites obtain informed consent from site users. The changes to the law have been implemented through the Privacy and Electronic Communications (EC Directive) (Amendment) Regulations 2011 (SI 2011/1208) (2011 Regulations).[90] Under the new regime, the use of cookies is only allowed if the user concerned:

* Has been provided with clear and comprehensive information about the purposes for which the cookie is stored and accessed.[91]
* Has given his or her consent.[92]

13.4.11.3.2 RESPONSIBILITY FOR COMPLIANCE

One of the issues raised by the use of cookies is who has responsibility for compliance. The 2011 Regulations do not define who should be responsible for complying with the requirement to provide information about cookies and obtain consent. Where a person operates an online service and any use of cookies will be for their purposes, it is clear that that person will be responsible for complying with this Regulation.

---

87 Directive 2009/136/EC of the European Parliament and of the Council of 25 November 2009 amending Directive 2002/22/EC on universal service and users' rights relating to electronic communications networks and services, Directive 2002/58/EC concerning the processing of personal data and the protection of privacy in the electronic communications sector, and Regulation (EC) No. 2006/2004 on cooperation between national authorities responsible for the enforcement of consumer protection laws.
88 A discussion of the law in relation to cookies is beyond the scope of this chapter; useful resources in relation to the law and cookies can be found in the Information Commissioner's Guidance note on the rules on use of cookies and similar technologies, May 2012.
89 Regime that was previously in force to a requirement for informed consent (Article 5(3), revised E-Privacy Directive), Directive 2002/58/EC of the European Parliament and of the Council of 12 July 2002 concerning the processing of personal data and the protection of privacy in the electronic communications sector (Directive on privacy and electronic communications).
90 Which amend the Privacy and Electronic Communications Regulations 2003 (SI 2003/2426) (2003 Regulations).
91 Regulation 6(1) revised 2003 Regulations.
92 Regulation 6(2) revised 2003 Regulations.

268 *Commercial law*

The person setting the cookie is therefore primarily responsible for compliance with the requirements of the law. It is also important to remember that users are likely to address any concerns or complaints they have to the person they can identify or have the relationship with – the company running the website. It is therefore in both parties' interests to work together.

Third parties setting cookies, or providing a product that requires the setting of cookies, may wish to consider putting a contractual obligation into agreements with web publishers to satisfy themselves that appropriate steps will be taken to provide information about the cookies and obtain consent.

If the website needs the cookie in order to function (i.e. remember a user's preferences, name, group, etc.), then it may fall within a category of cookies called 'strictly necessary'. Consent is not needed for such a cookie. However, if there is anything additional like analytics, then consent will need to be obtained, because that cookie isn't strictly necessary. As the circumstances are rare where a site only uses a strictly necessary cookie, sites should exercise great caution when considering relying on this exemption.

13.4.11.3.3 GETTING CONSENT IN PRACTICE

Which method will be appropriate to get consent for cookies will depend in the first instance on what the cookies you use are doing and to some extent on the relationship you have with users:

- Pop ups and similar techniques.
- Terms and conditions: it is not uncommon for consent to be gained online using the terms of use or terms and conditions to which the user agrees when they register or sign up.
- Privacy and cookies policy.

The key point is not who obtains the consent but that valid, well-informed consent is obtained.

13.4.12 *Accuracy of data*

13.4.12.1 *Principle 4 of the DPA 1998*

Principle 4 of the DPA 1998 requires that personal data shall be accurate and, where necessary, kept up to date. Schedule 1, Part II, 7 of the DPA 1998 states that the fourth principle is not to be regarded as being contravened by reason of any inaccuracy in personal data which accurately record information obtained by the data controller from the data subject or a third party in a case where:

- the purpose or purposes for which the data were obtained and further processed;
- the data controller has taken reasonable steps to ensure the accuracy of the data; and
- if a subject has informed the data controller that they think the data is inaccurate, the data shall indicate this. Schedule 1, Part IV, 70(2) states that for the purposes

Data protection and privacy 269

of this Act data are inaccurate if they are incorrect or misleading as to any matter of fact.

13.4.12.2 *Online forums*

Where a data controller runs an online forum, it has a responsibility to take reasonable steps to check the accuracy of any personal data that is posted on its site by third parties and is presented as a 'matter of fact'. Expressions of opinion will not qualify as matters of fact. So, for example, a post which records someone's age or date of birth may be 'incorrect or misleading as to any matter of fact', but a post that gives an opinion on how old someone looks cannot be. What are considered to be 'reasonable steps' for the person or organization running the site to take will depend on the nature of the site and how active a role the data controller takes in selecting, allowing or moderating content. There may also be a higher expectation where children are the primary users of the site.

13.4.12.2.1 INFORMATION COMMISSIONER'S VIEW ON REASONABLE STEPS

The Information Commissioner's Office (ICO) has stated that its expectation of 'reasonable steps' would, however, vary depending on the individual circumstances of the case. For example, in a situation where the vast majority of the site content is posted directly by third parties, the volume of third party posts is significant, site content is not moderated in advance, and the site relies upon users complying with user policies and reporting problems to the site operator, the ICO would not consider that taking 'reasonable steps' requires the operator to check every individual post for accuracy. The ICO recommends 'reasonable steps' for a data controller running this type of social networking site to include the following:

- Having clear and prominent policies for users about acceptable and non-acceptable posts.
- Having clear and easy to find procedures in place for data subjects to dispute the accuracy of posts and ask for them to be removed.
- Responding to disputes about accuracy quickly, and having procedures to remove or suspend access to content, at least until such time as a dispute has been settled.

13.4.12.2.2 MECHANISMS TO DEAL WITH INACCURATE DATA

A person or organization running such a site may also wish to set up a mechanism that allows it to add a note to a post indicating that the data subject disputes its factual accuracy. In practice, however, it will probably be more practical for the site to simply remove or suspend access to the disputed post in this type of situation.

13.4.12.2.3 USE OF SITE POLICES AND COMMUNITY STANDARDS

The ICO also expects a person or organization running a social networking site or online forum to have policies in place that are sufficient to deal with:

270 *Commercial law*

- Complaints from people who believe that their personal data may have been processed unfairly or unlawfully because they have been the subject of derogatory, threatening or abusive online postings by third parties;
- Disputes between individuals about the factual accuracy of posts; and
- Complaints about how the person or organization running the site processes any personal data (such as contact details) given to it by its users or subscribers.

13.4.12.2.4 ADVICE FOR INDIVIDUALS OBJECTING TO INACCURATE DATA

The ICO has stated that it will advise members of the public who approach it about any type of unfair or inaccurate posting about them to do one or more of the following in the first instance:

- Follow the website's procedure for dealing with inaccurate, unfair or derogatory postings;
- Contact the website administrator;
- Take the matter up directly with the organization or individual who has posted the personal data, if they feel this would be appropriate; and
- If it is alleged that a posting is libellous, threatening or constitutes harassment, then consider taking legal advice or contacting the police.

The ICO has stated that it will not consider complaints made against individuals who have posted personal data while acting in a personal capacity, no matter how unfair, derogatory or distressing the posts may be. This is because where an individual is posting for the purposes of their personal, family household or recreational purposes, the section 36 exemption will apply. The ICO will consider complaints about posts made by businesses, organizations or individuals acting for non-domestic purposes in the normal way, using a proportionate approach.

13.4.12.2.5 MODERATING SITE CONTENT

In its paper of April 2011 entitled 'Line to take – Dealing with complaints about information published online',[93] the ICO stated that it did not believe that it was the purpose of the DPA 1998 to regulate individuals' freedom of expression.[94] This is the case even though some individuals may use this right of free speech to post offensive, inaccurate or libellous statements about other individuals or organizations. The individual's right to express such views comes from Article 10 ECHR and is reflected in the drafting of the exemption contained in section 36 (and s 32), the so-called 'domestic purposes exemption'. It should also be noted that because it is a public organization, the ICO itself must consider section 36 and interpret it in a manner that is compatible with the Convention right enshrined by Article 10 ECHR.

---

93 http://www.ico.org.uk/about_us/how_we_comply/disclosure_log/~/media/documents/disclosure_log/ IRQ0417298b.ashx.
94 See Chapter 2: Human Rights for an exploration of the issues surrounding freedom of expression.

13.4.12.2.6 THE 'DOMESTIC PURPOSES' EXEMPTION

13.4.12.2.6.1 *Section 36 DPA 1998*   It should be noted in the first instance that when individuals publish information online for domestic purposes (see below), in the opinion of the ICO, the Data Protection Principles do not apply to their actions. This is the case where individuals group together to process personal data (e.g. individuals running a blog together). There is an exemption in the DPA 1998, which states that when personal data is processed by an individual for their own personal purposes, the data protection principles do not apply. This exemption is often referred to as the 'domestic purposes' exemption. Section 36 states that 'personal data processed by an individual only for the purposes of that individual's personal, family, or household affairs (including recreational purposes) are exempt from the data protection principles and the provisions of Parts II and III'. The exemption is worthy of consideration because although much of the literature and research produced by the ICO is in relation to blogs, the content discussed in the research papers concerning the categories of speech will also have application to postings made by social media sites.

13.4.12.2.6.2 *When does the DPA 1998 apply?*[95]   The ICO suggests that the following activities constitute acts by individuals expressing their personal views:

- Posting personal data on a social networking site to keep in contact with friends.
- Publishing a blog about your daily activities or keeping an online diary.
- Using an online forum to 'rant' about your neighbour or a political figure.
- Posting a comment about a tradesman on a 'ratings' site.
- Leaving your personal review of a product on an e-commerce site.
- Taking part in a local newspaper's discussion forum.

Section 36 can't be used by organizations which process personal data. This means that organizations that use social media or other online forums have responsibilities under the DPA 1998:

- If they post personal data on their own or a third party's website;
- If they download and use personal data from a third party website;
- If they run a website which allows third parties to add comments or posts about living individuals, and they are a data controller for the website content.

The section 36 exemption also doesn't apply to processing by individuals for non-domestic purposes. This means that if an individual, such as a sole trader, is using social media to process personal data for business purposes, then they will also have responsibilities under the DPA 1998.

---

95 Social Networking and Online Forums – When does the DPA Apply? Version: 1.1 20140226 [http://ico.org.uk/for_organizations/data_protection/topic_guides/~/media/documents/library/Data_Protection/Detailed_specialist_guides/social-networking-and-online-forums-dpa-guidance.ashx].

272 *Commercial law*

The section 36 exemption is based on the purposes for which the personal data is being processed, not on the nature or content of the data itself. It applies whenever someone uses an online forum purely in a personal capacity for their own domestic or recreational purposes. It doesn't apply when an organization or an individual uses an online forum for corporate, business or non-domestic purposes.

13.4.12.2.6.3 *Organizations*   Organizations such as businesses, charities, and political parties increasingly use social networking sites or other online forums for their ordinary corporate or organizational purposes. Examples of this include:

- A business promoting its services by posting customers' reviews of a product.
- A police force posting pictures of suspects with details of their alleged crimes.
- A political party carrying out membership recruitment.
- A school asking its alumni to provide their details for a planned reunion.

The domestic purposes exemption cannot apply to the processing of personal data done by organizations through social networking sites. This is still the case even if an organization gets a member of its staff to do the processing for it through their personal networking page. This is because the employee is acting on behalf of the organization and the processing is for the organization's corporate or organizational purposes, not for the purposes of the employee's personal, family or household affairs. The ICO would consider it poor practice for an organization to encourage or allow employees to use their own personal networking pages for corporate purposes.

13.4.12.2.6.4 *Groups of individuals*   The section 36 exemption refers to an individual processing personal data for domestic purposes. Sometimes online forums can be used or set up by a group of individuals and the question is then asked whether the domestic purposes exemption can apply in these circumstances. The ICO view is that the key issue here remains the purpose behind the processing. If processing personal data for non-domestic purposes, then they will be subject to the requirements of the DPA 1998 regardless of whether they are acting as a sole individual, as part of a group of separate individuals, or on behalf of a group (such as a club or society) with its own separate legal identity.

In this circumstance, although the capacity in which the users are acting may affect who is identified as the data controller, and whether more than one data controller exists, it doesn't alter the basic premise that you can't rely on the exemption at section 36 of the DPA 1998 if the purpose behind your processing is not your own personal, family or household affairs.

This does not mean, however, that the status of the group can never be relevant to this issue. In general, the more formal and the more distinct the group is from its individual members, the less likely it is that the domestic purposes exemption will apply. This is because a more formal group (such as a club or society) that exists independently of its individual members, and whose membership can change over time, is more likely to process personal data for its own distinct purposes rather than for the domestic purposes of its individual members.

Data protection and privacy 273

13.4.12.2.7 EXAMPLES

13.4.12.2.7.1 *Groups of individuals*   As the distinction is not always an easy one to draw in practice, the application of the exemption is best explored by reference to worked examples.

> ## Example 1
>
> *A group of friends who met on holiday set up a social networking page to share their photographs and arrange a further trip for the following year.*

According to the ICO,[96] the purpose of the processing is clearly for the individuals' recreational purposes. In this situation, the domestic purposes exemption applies. It doesn't make any difference that more than one individual is processing personal data on the same subject. The following questions may help a group of individuals to decide whether the exemption applies to them or not, but they should not be treated as an exhaustive list:

- Is the site or networking page commercial? Does it generate income through advertising or subscriptions? Has it been set up to pursue a professional or commercial objective?
- Is the personal data being processed for the distinct, collective purposes of the group, rather than for the personal, family or household purposes of its individual members?
- Is the personal data clearly being posted on behalf of an organization?
- Is the group separately legally constituted in some way?
- Is the personal data being posted on behalf of a group that is distinct from its members?
- Would the group continue to exist if its membership changed?
- Does it have its own set of rules that exist separately from its members?

If the answer to any of the questions above is 'yes', then it is unlikely that the processing is being carried out by an individual for his or her domestic purposes and it is therefore unlikely that the section 36 exemption applies.

13.4.12.2.7.2 *Individuals*   The section 36 exemption only applies when an individual is processing personal data for their own personal, family or household affairs (including recreational purposes). This means that even when the processing is clearly done by an individual rather than a group or organization, if the purpose of the processing is non-domestic then the exemption won't apply.

96 Ibid.

274   *Commercial law*

Example 1[97]

A sole trader sets up a website to promote their nail bar and tanning salon and, with permission, includes reviews from named satisfied customers. The purpose behind this processing of personal data is clearly commercial rather than domestic and the section 36 exemption won't apply.

Example 2[98]

A private individual decides to sell off some unwanted gifts using an online auction site. They process the personal data of prospective buyers who 'message' them through the auction site. Although the seller might make some money from the sale, we would distinguish the selling of personal possessions from the running of a business, and would accept that this processing is purely for domestic purposes.

Example 3[99]

A seller runs a business buying goods wholesale and selling them on via an online auction site. They retain details of their previous and regular customers for marketing and delivery purposes. Here, the seller is clearly operating a business and processing the personal data in pursuit of a commercial (rather than a domestic) objective. The section 36 exemption will not apply.

13.4.12.2.7.3 *Personal views, journalists, and expressions of opinion*   The domestic purposes exemption doesn't necessarily apply whenever a personal view is expressed. For example, online versions of daily newspapers often include an 'opinion' section where a journalist gives their personal view on a matter of media interest. What is important here is that although the opinion given is a personal opinion, it isn't being given for a domestic or recreational purpose. The journalist is providing personal comment for the editorial purposes of the newspaper.

Although the domestic purpose exemption won't apply in this circumstance, there is another exemption (at s 32 DPA 1998) which may apply to personal data that is processed for the special purpose of journalism, art and literature. Section 32 DPA 1998 may apply if a data controller posted personal data on an online forum:

- For one of the special purposes of journalism, art and literature;
- In the reasonable belief that publication would be in the public interest; and
- In the reasonable belief that compliance with the provision of the DPA 1998 in question would be incompatible with the special purposes.

---

97 Ibid.
98 Ibid.
99 Ibid.

13.4.12.2.8 EXAMPLES

Example 1[100]

A company has a website and decides that it will improve customer relations and awareness of its products if it sets up a social networking account and asks its senior staff to post messages commenting on the latest developments within the industry. Some of these messages comment on the actions of high-profile business leaders within the industry. In this situation, although senior staff may express a mixture of corporate and personal views, the messages aren't being posted for recreational or domestic purposes. They are part of the company's marketing strategy and are being posted for corporate purposes. The senior staff members are posting as part of their job and section 36 does not apply.

Example 2

An employee of the same company has a keen personal interest in the industry in which he works. He isn't asked to post messages on behalf of the company but he follows the managing director's posts from his home computer and Smartphone. He has strong views on the actions of a particular figure within the industry, and posts a comment in response to one of his managing director's messages on this subject. Here, the employee is acting purely in a personal capacity. Although the subject matter is related to his work, he hasn't been asked to post messages on behalf of the company and he is acting out of his own personal and recreational interest. Therefore, section 36 applies.

13.4.12.2.9 USING SOCIAL MEDIA FOR BOTH DOMESTIC AND NON-DOMESTIC PURPOSES

The examples given above all consider situations where there is one clear purpose for using an online forum. In reality, some users of social media do so for mixed purposes. For example, many people in the public eye have social media accounts that they use both for personal, family, and recreational purposes and to promote their business interests by raising their public profile. The ICO recognizes that this is a difficult area.[101] The ICO suggests that one straightforward solution for people in this situation is to keep their personal and non-personal affairs apart by having separate online profiles for their work and personal lives; this is also beneficial as any goodwill attributed to the account may remain with the individual rather than the company. In *Flexman v BG Group (unreported)*, Flexman, a human resources executive for BG Group, resigned in June 2011 after putting his CV online and advertising his interest in other 'career opportunities' through his LinkedIn profile. Flexman was ordered to

100 Ibid.
101 Ibid.

276 *Commercial law*

remove his CV from the profile after a 'complaint' about his profile and was called to a disciplinary hearing for 'inappropriate use of social media'.[102]

The ICO has stated that it appreciates that not everyone will want to do this and it will be a matter of personal choice for the individual.[103] Ultimately, however, if an individual chooses to use social networking sites for mixed purposes, then they need to make sure that any posts that aren't made for purely domestic or recreational purposes comply with the DPA 1998.

13.4.12.2.10 QUALITY OF DATA

The ICO notes that data should be fit for the purpose for which it is to be used (Data Protection Principles 3, 4, and 5). The ICO states that those running sites should always seek to get good quality information in the first place. How they then approach maintaining accuracy, relevance, keeping information up to date and other data quality matters will 'depend on the circumstances'.[104]

In the case of obtaining information about data subjects from third party sources, sites need to take reasonable steps to ensure the accuracy of the data. One way to do this is to check with the data subject at a suitable opportunity. Indeed, asking data subjects to check the accuracy of their information from time to time will help to ensure that information is kept up to date. The frequency with which such checks need to be made will depend on the volatility of the data.

13.4.12.3 *The right to prevent processing likely to cause damage or distress*

13.4.12.3.1 SECTION 10 DPA 1998

The right to prevent processing which is likely to cause damage or distress is enacted in the UK through section 10 DPA 1998. Section 10(1) provides that an individual may at any time by notice in writing to a data controller ask it to cease processing because:

- the processing of those data or their processing for that purpose or in that manner is causing or is likely to cause substantial damage or substantial distress to him or to another (s 10(1)(a)); and
- that damage or distress is or would be unwarranted (s 10(1)(b)).

However, this right is subject to section 10(2), which qualifies 10(1). Processing may be justified by the data controller, thereby displacing 10(1) if:

---

102 For further exploration of employees, goodwill and social media, see L. Scaife (2012) 'Social media – time for a firm wide policy?', *Lexology*, 11 April 2012 [http://www.lexology.com/library/detail. aspx?g=5c1f9b6c-b252-4de4-9fa8-3774841237f7].

103 Social Networking and Online Forums – When does the DPA Apply? Version: 1.1 20140226 [http:// ico.org.uk/for_organizations/data_protection/topic_guides/~/media/documents/library/Data_Protection/ Detailed_specialist_guides/social-networking-and-online-forums-dpa-guidance.ashx].

104 Ibid.

Data protection and privacy 277

- for the performance of a contract to which the data subject is a party, or
- for the taking of steps at the request of the data subject with a view to entering into a contract.

Section 10(3) requires the data controller to provide to the data subject within 21 days of receiving a notice under section 10(1) a written notice stating:

- that he has complied or intends to comply with the data subject notice; or
- his reasons for regarding the data subject notice as to any extent unjustified and the extent (if any) to which he has complied or intends to comply with it.

Significantly, section 10(4) provides that if a court is satisfied, on the application of any person who has given notice under subsection (1) which appears to the court to be justified (or to be justified to any extent), the data controller in question has failed to comply with the notice, the court may order him to take such steps for complying with the notice (or for complying with it to that extent) as the court thinks fit.

13.4.12.3.2 APPLICATION TO SOCIAL NETWORKING SITES

In relation to the removal of website content from social networking sites, these provisions may act as a useful additional incentive to seek the removal of offending posts and could be coupled with a request under the e-commerce directives for the removal of site content which is distressing, untruthful or libellous.[105] Sites should also consider the interrelationship of this provision with rights in relation to inaccurate data[106] when considering how to write to a social networking site when seeing the removal of distressing or inaccurate content. Given that section 10 does not need to be exhausted and does not affect other rights (s 10(5), above) it is also important to consider tactically how to approach the use of the rights and at what stage the complainant of the site content may wish to make use of them. Website operators should be aware that there are a variety of rights available to data subjects and should consider how they intend to comply with the provisions of the act and avoid liability for a failure to comply with their obligations in relation to data subjects. However, these considerations have to be viewed in light of the recent views of the Information Commissioner, on content that has been generated via social networking sites.

13.4.12.4 *Rectification, erasure blocking, and destruction*

As noted in the Irish Information Commissioner's audit of Facebook (discussed earlier in this chapter), one of the key rights that users require in relation to data is its rectification, blocking, and deletion. This right is given effect through section 14 DPA 1998. Section 14 provides that:

---

105 See Chapter 3: Defamation for a full exploration of the takedown notice provisions contained in the e-commerce directives.
106 See s 10 DPA 1998.

278   *Commercial law*

- If the requirements mentioned in paragraph 7 of Part II of Schedule 1 have been complied with, the court may, instead of making an order under subsection (1), make an order requiring the data to be supplemented by such statement of the true facts relating to the matters dealt with by the data as the court may approve (s 10(10)(a)); and
- If all or any of those requirements have not been complied with, the court may, instead of making an order under that subsection, make such order as it thinks fit for securing compliance with those requirements with or without a further order requiring the data to be supplemented by such a statement as is mentioned in paragraph (a) (s 10(10)(b)).

Section 14(3) provides that where the court makes an order under section 14(1) or where it is satisfied that the data complained of has been removed, blocked or rectified, then the court may require the data controller to notify third parties of that rectification, destruction or deletion.

Section 14(4) DPA 1998 relates to damages suffered as a result of any contravention to compensation under section 13 of the Act. If the court is satisfied that there is a substantial risk of further contravention, the court can also order the rectification, destruction or deletion of the data.

13.4.12.4.1 RECTIFICATION RIGHTS

Section 3 of the DPR makes provision in relation to rectification. Article 16 of the Act confers upon the data subject a right to obtain from the controller the rectification of personal data relating to them that is inaccurate. The data subject shall have the right to obtain completion of incomplete personal data, including by way of supplementing a corrective statement.

Supplementing section 14(3) DPA 1998, Article 13 of the Act requires that the data controller shall communicate any rectification carried out in accordance with Article 16 to each recipient to whom the data has been disclosed, unless this proves impossible or involves a disproportionate effort. The logistics of such communications sites such as Twitter is one such example; however, for smaller sites such communication may be justified.

13.4.12.5 *Erasure and the right to be forgotten*

Article 17 of the DPR confers rights in relation to the erasure of data and the right to be forgotten. Arguably, this is the most potent concept to come out of the paper, safeguarding privacy in a connected world,[107] placing an onus on data controllers to prove they need to keep the collected data and strengthening individuals' right to have information deleted.

Personal data communicated by a user when he registers with a social networking site should be deleted as soon as either the user or the SNS provider decides to delete

---

107 On 25 January 2012, the European Commission issued a consultation paper entitled 'Safeguarding Privacy in a Connected World' [http://ec.europa.eu/justice/data-protection/document/review2012/com_2012_9_en.pdf].

Data protection and privacy 279

the account. According to Article 6 para 1(e) of the Data Protection Regulation, data must be 'kept in a form which permits identification of Data Subjects for no longer than is necessary for the purposes for which the data were collected or for which they are further processed'.

Article 17(1) of the DPR provides that the data subject shall have the right to obtain from the controller the erasure of personal data relating to them and the abstention from further dissemination of such data, especially in relation to personal data made available by the data subject while he or she was a child, where one of the following grounds applies:

- The data are no longer necessary in relation to the purposes for which they were collected or otherwise processed (Article 17(1)(a) DPR);
- The data subject withdraws consent on which the processing is based according to point (a) of Article 6(1), or when the storage period consented to has expired, and where there is no other legal ground for the processing of the data (Article 17(1)(b) DPR);
- The data subject objects to the processing of personal data pursuant to Article 19 DPR (Article 17(1)(c) DPR);
- The processing of the data does not comply with this Regulation for other reasons (Article 17(1)(d) DPR).

If the personal data has been made public, then in accordance with Article 17(2) DPR the data controller shall be required to take reasonable steps including technical measures, in relation to data for the publication of which the controller is responsible, to inform third parties which are processing such data, that a data subject requests them to erase any links to, or copy or replication of that personal data. If the data controller has authorized a third party publication of personal data, the data controller shall be considered responsible for that publication. Sites should therefore take care to ensure that organizational measures and contracts are in place with any third parties who assist with the platform management of the site to avoid unwanted risk exposure to liability.

Article 17(3) DPR provides that the data controller shall carry out the erasure without delay, except to the extent that the retention of the personal data is necessary:

- For exercising the right of freedom of expression in accordance with Article 80;
- For reasons of public interest in the area of public health in accordance with Article 81;
- For historical, statistical, and scientific research purposes in accordance with Article 83;
- For compliance with a legal obligation to retain the personal data by Union or Member State law to which the controller is subject.[108] Member State laws shall

---

108 Regulation of Investigatory Powers Act 2000; Anti-Terrorism, Crime and Security Act 2001; Privacy and Electronic Communications (EC Directive) Regulations 2003 (SI 2003/2426); The Regulation of Investigatory Powers (Acquisition and Disclosure of Communications Data: Code of Practice) Order 2007 (SI 2007/2197); The Data Retention (EC Directive) Regulations 2009 (SI 2009/859); Data Protection Directive 95/46/EC; Privacy and Electronic Communications Directive 2002/58/EC.

280 *Commercial law*

meet an objective of public interest, respect the essence of the right to the protection of personal data, and be proportionate to the legitimate aim pursued;

- In the cases referred to in Article 17(4).

Article 17(4) of the DPR provides that instead of erasure, the controller shall restrict processing of personal data where:

- Their accuracy is contested by the data subject, for a period enabling the controller to verify the accuracy of the data;
- The controller no longer needs the personal data for the accomplishment of its task but they have to be maintained for purposes of proof;
- The processing is unlawful and the data subject opposes their erasure and requests the restriction of their use instead;
- The data subject requests to transmit the personal data into another automated processing system in accordance with Article 18(2) DPR.

13.4.12.5.1 *GOOGLE SPAIN & GOOGLE*

The judgment of *Google Spain & Google*,[109] of which an opinion of the ECJ has been sought, raises very interesting points about both data protection rules on the one hand, in particular the so-called 'right to be forgotten' and its application to search engines, and the territorial scope of EU data protection rules on the other, in particular their application to internet companies based outside the EU.

The case started with a number of complaints from Spanish residents to the Spanish Data Protection Agency (AEPD) about information concerning events several years previous that could be found upon 'Googling' their name. The AEPD upheld the complaints and issued a decision calling on Google Spain and Google to take the necessary measures to withdraw the data from their index and to render future access to the information impossible via their search engine. Google and Google Spain have appealed against that decision before the Spanish courts.

In the national proceedings, two issues have arisen upon which a ruling from the ECJ has been sought. The first concerns the territorial scope of EU data protection law. Google maintains that as the search engine is run by Google, based in California, it is subject only to US data protection legislation. It argues that Google Spain is only responsible for selling advertising on Google and has no role in the operation of the search engine itself. The AEPD points out that Google indexes Spanish websites using crawlers and robots and uses a Spanish domain name. Moreover, the centre of gravity of the litigation lies in Spain, concerning as it does information published on a Spanish website, in Spanish, about Spanish residents.

The second issue concerns whether Google can be considered to be the 'controller' of personal data and be required to remove that information when that data has been lawfully published on another website and is kept on the page from which it originates.

---

109 Case C-131/12.

13.4.12.5.2 RULING OF CJEU

The Court of Justice of the European Union (CJEU) ruled on 13 May 2014[110] that by searching automatically, constantly, and systematically for information published on the internet, the operator of a search engine 'collects' data within the meaning of the Directive. The Court considers, furthermore, that the operator, within the framework of its indexing programmes, 'retrieves', 'records', and 'organizes' the data in question, which it then 'stores' on its servers and, as the case may be, 'discloses' and 'makes available' to its users in the form of lists of results. Those operations, which are referred to expressly and unconditionally in the Directive, must be classified as 'processing', regardless of the fact that the operator of the search engine carries them out without distinction in respect of information other than the personal data. The Court also pointed out that the operations referred to by the Directive must be classified as processing even where they exclusively concern material that has already been published as it stands in the media. A general derogation from the application of the Directive in such a case would have the consequence of largely depriving the Directive of its effect.

The Court also held that the operator of the search engine is the 'controller' in respect of that processing, within the meaning of the Directive, given that it is the operator that determines the purposes and means of the processing. The Court observed in this regard that, in as much as the activity of a search engine is additional to that of publishers of websites and is liable to affect significantly the fundamental rights to privacy and to the protection of personal data, the operator of the search engine must ensure, within the framework of its responsibilities, powers, and capabilities, that its activity complies with the Directive's requirements. This is the only way that the guarantees laid down by the Directive will be able to have full effect and that effective and complete protection of data subjects (in particular of their privacy) may actually be achieved.

As regards the Directive's territorial scope, the Court observed that Google Spain is a subsidiary of Google Inc on Spanish territory and, therefore, an 'establishment' within the meaning of the Directive. The Court stated:

> The Court rejects the argument that the processing of personal data by Google Search is not carried out in the context of the activities of that establishment in Spain. The Court held, in this regard, that where such data are processed for the purposes of a search engine operated by an undertaking which, although it has its seat in a non-Member State, has an establishment in a Member State, the processing is carried out 'in the context of the activities' of that establishment, within the meaning of the directive, if the establishment is intended to promote and sell, in the Member State in question, advertising space offered by the search engine in order to make the service offered by the engine profitable.

> As far as the extent of the responsibility of the operator of the search engine, the Court held that the operator is, in certain circumstances, obliged to remove links

---

110 Judgment in Case C-131/12 *Google Spain SL, Google Inc v Agencia Española de Protección de Datos, Mario Costeja González* [http://curia.europa.eu/jcms/upload/docs/application/pdf/2014-05/cp140070en.pdf].

282   *Commercial law*

to web pages that are published by third parties and contain information relating to a person from the list of results displayed following a search made on the basis of that person's name. The Court made it clear that such an obligation may also exist in a case where that name or information is not erased beforehand or simultaneously from those web pages, and even, as the case may be, when its publication in itself on those pages is lawful.[111]

The Court pointed out in this context that processing of personal data carried out by such an operator enables any internet user, when he makes a search on the basis of an individual's name, to obtain, through the list of results, a structured overview of the information relating to that individual on the internet. The Court observed also that this information potentially concerns a vast number of aspects of his private life and that, without the search engine, the information could not have been interconnected or could have been only with great difficulty. Internet users may thereby establish a more or less detailed profile of the person searched against. Furthermore, the effect of the interference with the person's rights is heightened on account of the important roles played by the internet and search engines in modern society, which render the information contained in such lists of results ubiquitous. In the light of its potential seriousness, such interference cannot, according to the Court, be justified by merely the economic interest that the operator of the engine has in the data processing.

However, in as much as the removal of links from the list of results could, depending on the information at issue, have effects upon the legitimate interest of internet users potentially interested in having access to that information, the Court held that a fair balance should be sought in particular between that interest and the data subject's fundamental rights, in particular the right to privacy and the right to protection of personal data. The Court observed in this regard that, while it is true that the data subject's rights also override, as a general rule, the interest of internet users, this balance may however depend, in specific cases, on the nature of the information in question and its sensitivity for the data subject's private life and on the interest of the public in having that information, an interest which may vary, in particular, according to the role played by the data subject in public life.

Finally, in response to the question of whether the Directive enables the data subject to request that links to web pages be removed from such a list of results on the grounds that he wishes the information appearing on those pages relating to him personally to be 'forgotten' after a certain time, the Court held:

> if it is found, following a request by the data subject, that the inclusion of those links in the list is, at this point in time, incompatible with the Directive, the links and information in the list of results must be erased. The Court observes in this regard that even initially lawful processing of accurate data may, in the course of time, become incompatible with the Directive where, having regard to all the circumstances of the case, the data appear to be inadequate, irrelevant or no longer relevant, or excessive in relation to the purposes for which they were

111 Ibid.

processed and in the light of the time that has elapsed. The Court adds that, when appraising such a request made by the data subject in order to oppose the processing carried out by the operator of a search engine, it should in particular be examined whether the data subject has a right that the information in question relating to him personally should, at this point in time, no longer be linked to his name by a list of results that is displayed following a search made on the basis of his name. If that is the case, the links to web pages containing that information must be removed from that list of results, unless there are particular reasons, such as the role played by the data subject in public life, justifying a preponderant interest of the public in having access to the information when such a search is made.

The Court pointed out that the data subject may address such a request directly to the operator of the search engine (the controller), which must then duly examine its merits. Where the controller does not grant the request, the data subject may bring the matter before the supervisory authority or the judicial authority so that it carries out the necessary checks and orders the controller to take specific measures accordingly.

13.4.12.5.3 THE UK ICO'S KEY POINTS ON GOOGLE SPAIN

On 20 May 2014, the ICO published an overview of what it perceived to be the key points of the Court of Justice of the European Union judgment regarding Google and the removal of search results, highlighting the following points:

- In operating their search service, Google is processing personal data and is acting as a data controller under the terms of the European Data Protection Directive.
- Google is established in Spain in terms of its search engine service under the terms of the Directive. Spanish data protection law therefore applies to Google.
- Search providers can be required to remove links to web pages that contain personal information published by third parties, from the list of results displayed, following a search on the person's name, where the processing of the personal data does not comply with the relevant provisions of the Directive.
- A search provider can be required to consider removal regardless of the legal status of the personal information in the third party web pages.
- The Court highlights the significance of interference to personal data rights that can be caused by the availability of the links associated with a name.
- The Court observed that the data subject's rights also override, as a general rule, the legitimate interest of internet users to access information.
- A balance will have to be struck between these interests. It will depend, in specific cases, on the nature of the information in question and its sensitivity for the individual's private life. It will also depend on the interest in communicating the information to the public, an interest which may vary, according to the role played by the data subject in public life.
- The Court observed that lawful processing of personal data might, in the course of time, become incompatible with the Directive.

284   *Commercial law*

Requests to remove links should be directed to the search provider as data controller. Where the controller does not grant the request, the data subject may bring the matter before the data protection supervisory authority or the courts.[112]

13.4.12.5.4 THE ICO'S VIEWS ON THE RIGHT TO BE FORGOTTEN

On 20 May 2014, the ICO published via its blog its views on the Google Spain judgment.[113] The ICO stated that although it has been suggested that there are much wider implications of the judgment for freedom of expression in general, 'it is important to keep the implications in proportion and recognize that there is no absolute right to have links removed. Also, the original publication and the search engine are considered separately: the public record of a newspaper may not be deleted even if the link to it from a search website is removed'.

The ICO stated via the blog that they recognized that there will be 'difficult judgments to make on whether links should be removed'. It is also important to remember that the exemption for journalism, art and literature under section 32 of the Data Protection Act can be applied by media organizations, bloggers and other publishers of information, depending on the circumstances.

The Deputy Commissioner and Director of Data Protection, David Smith stated in the blog that there will need to be consultation with national regulators and the Working Party to consider the implications of the judgment; in the meantime, they expect search providers to start the process of considering what solutions are needed to deal with requests to remove links. The ICO has stated that it recognizes that 'the challenge is logistical and technical. Any solutions should enable appropriate consideration to be given to each case, and should reflect a judgment that upholds the data protection rights of individuals'.

13.4.12.6 *Steps for seeking the removal of data online*

For individuals seeking the removal of data online, it is important to think about what precisely is being sought and on what grounds the information can be removed. As a practical matter, it is also vital, if users wish to have their request considered as efficiently as possible, that they follow the online instructions for filling out the forms seeking removal carefully. In particular, users should:

- Provide the URL for each link appearing in a Google search for their name that they request to be removed.
- If it is not obvious, an explanation as to why the linked page is about the user (or, if the user is submitting the form on behalf of someone else, why it is about that person). As a matter of ensuring that requests are dealt with promptly, it would

---

112 'ICO overview of key points of the Court of Justice of European Union judgment regarding Google and the removal of search results', ICO Blog, 20 May 2014 [http://iconewsblog.files.wordpress.com/2014/05/key-points-of-cjeu-case.pdf].

113 D. Smith (2014) 'Four things we've learned from the EU Google judgment', 20 May [http://iconewsblog.wordpress.com/2014/05/20/four-things-weve-learned-from-the-eu-google-judgment/; accessed 28 May 2014].

be a good idea to offer an explanation in any event, even if the meaning is obvious, as search engine providers are likely to receive large volumes of requests. Providing such information may help with facilitating the removal of the information expediently.

- Explain to the search engine why the individual considers that the information published via the URL in the search results is 'irrelevant, outdated, or otherwise inappropriate' (these words are taken from the *Google Spain* judgment and are therefore a useful benchmark when drafting a request).

Practical tips

- Use every opportunity to check that a data subject's contact details are correct (address, telephone number, email address).
- Set a schedule for checking other elements of the information held about a data subject according to the likelihood of frequent change.
- Check that adequate consents have been obtained from data subjects, including adopting consent mechanisms that can provide a consent audit trail.
- Adopt transparent terms and conditions that allow users to understand their privacy rights.

13.4.12.7 *Retention of personal data*

13.4.12.7.1 DATA RETENTION

Social networking sites fall outside the scope of the definition of electronic communications services provided in Article 2 letter (c) of the Framework Directive (2002/21/EC).[114] SNS providers may offer additional services that fall under the scope of an electronic communications service, such as a publicly accessible email service, which are subject to the provisions of the E-Privacy Directive and the Data Retention Directive (2006/24/EC). The Data Retention Directive requires communications service providers to retain customers' communications data for between six months and two years.

13.4.12.7.2 MONITORING AND TERRORISM

As noted above, Article 17(3)(d) of the DPR provides for compliance with a legal obligation to retain the personal data by Union or Member State law to which the controller is subject. In terms of monitoring and surveillance, Member State laws must meet an objective of public interest, respect the essence of the right to the protection of personal data, and be proportionate to the legitimate aim pursued

---

114 This distinction is explored in Chapter 1: Introduction to Social Media and the Law: *The Legal Classification of Social Networking Sites.*

286　*Commercial law*

(Article 17(3)(d) DPR).[115] An exploration of the use of social media by terrorist organizations and its role in counter-terrorism can be found in Chapter 2.

13.4.12.7.3 OPINION OF CJEU

On 8 April 2014, the CJEU held that the Data Retention Directive is incompatible with the fundamental privacy rights of data subjects. According to the CJEU, the Directive required the retention of data of a precise nature that related to the private lives about whom it was retained and allowed competent national authorities access to that data. As a result, the CJEU was of the opinion that the Directive interferes with individuals' right to privacy and the protection of their personal data. After analysing the Directive, the CJEU concluded that by adopting the Directive, the CJEU had exceeded the limited imposed by the principles of proportionality.[116]

13.4.12.7.4 APPLICATION TO SOCIAL MEDIA

Some social networking sites also retain identification data of users who were banned from the service, to ensure that they cannot register again. In that case, these users must be informed that such processing is taking place. In addition, the only information that may be retained is identification information, and not the reasons why these persons were banned. This information should not be retained for more than one year.

13.4.12.7.5 ICO'S PERSONAL DATA ONLINE CODE OF PRACTICE

According to the ICO's Personal Data Online Code of Practice,[117] personal data communicated by a user when they register with a social networking site should be deleted as soon as either the user or the SNS provider decides to delete the account. Similarly, information deleted by a user when updating their account should not be retained. Social networking sites should notify users before taking these steps with the means they have at their disposal to inform users about these retention periods. For security and legal reasons, in specific cases, it could be justifiable to store updated or deleted data and accounts for a defined period of time in order to help prevent malicious operations resulting from identity theft and other offences or crimes.

It is advised that site operators should review when a user does not use the service for a defined period of time and in that event, the profile in question should be set to inactive, i.e. no longer visible to other users or the outside world, and after another period of time the data in the abandoned account should be deleted. Social networking sites should notify users before taking these steps with whatever means they have at their disposal.

115　For examples of the use of social media in criminal evidence at terrorist trials, see *R v Ahma (Bilal Zaheer)* 2012 WL 5995906.

116　For a consideration of proportionality principles and their interaction with human rights, see Chapter 2.

117　Information Commissioner's Office Personal Data Online Code of Practice, July 2010 [http://ico.org.uk/~/media/documents/library/Data_Protection/Detailed_specialist_guides/personal_information_online_cop.pdf].

13.4.12.7.6 INVITATIONS TO THIRD PARTIES

Section 11 DPA 1998 refers to direct marketing as 'the communication (by whatever means) of any advertising or marketing material which is directed to particular individuals'.

The Privacy and Electronic Communications (EC Directive) Regulations 2003 (PECR) provide rules about sending marketing and advertising by electronic means, such as by telephone, fax, email, text and picture or video message, or by using an automated calling system. The PECR also include other rules relating to cookies, telephone directories, traffic data, location data, and security breaches.

Some social networking sites allow their users to send invitations to third parties. The prohibition on the use of electronic mail for the purposes of direct marketing does not apply to personal communications.

In order to comply with the exception for personal communications, social networking sites must comply with the following criteria:

- No incentive is given to either sender or recipient;
- The provider does not select the recipients of the message;
- The identity of the sending user must be clearly mentioned;
- The sending user must know the full content of the message that will be sent on his behalf.

13.4.12.8 *Data transfers by third parties*

13.4.12.8.1 BACKGROUND DATA TRANSFERS BY THIRD PARTIES

It is becoming increasingly common for social networks to allow third parties to operate apps and 'plug-ins' via their platforms[118] (e.g. *Candycrush* and *Farmville* being notable examples on Facebook). A plug-in (or plugin, extension, add-on/addon) is a software component that adds a specific feature to an existing software application. When an application supports plug-ins, it enables customization.

In order to develop the app or to facilitate the user's engagement with it, personal data may need to be shared with the entity running the app. In its opinion on social networks, the Article 29 Working Party stated that application providers may also be data controllers, if they develop applications which run in addition to the ones from the social networking site and users decide to use such an application.[119]

However, because of the fluidity of the app that is running through an existing platform, it has not always been the case that there has been sufficient notice to users or privacy disclaimers in relation to how and when their data is transferred and to whom. It has also been unclear as to what the data being collected by the developer is being used for, and if those uses go beyond that which is required in order to facilitate the

---

118 For research into this area, see Y. Hashemi (2009) 'Facebook's privacy policy and its third party partnerships: lucrativity and liability', *Boston University Journal of Science and Technology Law*, 15: 140–161.

119 Opinion 5/2009 at para 3.1 [http://ec.europa.eu/justice/policies/privacy/docs/wpdocs/2009/wp163_en.pdf].

288   *Commercial law*

user's enjoyment and engagement with the facilities provide by the app; indeed, data may be put to wider purposes than the user has knowledge.

The Article 29 Working Party also considered the interplay between apps and data privacy and highlighted the risk posed by them.[120] Such measures include the social networking site having the means to ensure that third party applications comply with the Data Protection and Privacy Directives. This implies, in particular, that they provide clear and specific information to users about the processing of their personal data and they only have access to necessary personal data. Therefore, layered access should be offered to third party developers by the social networking site so they can opt for a mode of access that is intrinsically more limited. Social networking sites should ensure furthermore that users may easily report concerns about applications.

13.4.12.8.2 APPS

13.4.12.8.2.1 *Background*   The Data Protection Act 1998 exists to protect individuals' privacy. Just as with any other business or project, you need to comply with the DPA 1998 when developing a mobile app. A typical mobile ecosystem contains many different components, including mobile devices themselves, their operating systems, and apps provided through an app store. In many ways, these are simply developments of earlier concepts that have been used on less portable computer hardware for years. However, the mobile environment has some particular features that make privacy a pressing concern:

- Mobile devices such as Smartphones and tablets are portable, personal, frequently used, and commonly always on.
- A mobile device typically has direct access to many different sensors and data, such as a microphone, camera and GPS receiver, together with the user's combined data, including email, SMS messages, and contacts.
- There are many different app configurations, and it is not necessarily obvious how an app deals with personal information behind its user interface.
- Mobile devices often have small screens, typically with touch-based interfaces. This can make it more challenging for apps to effectively communicate with app users.
- Consumers' expectations of convenience can make it undesirable to present a user with a large privacy policy, or a large number of prompts, or both.

Additionally, an organization based outside of the UK that develops apps for the UK market should consider that its users in the UK will clearly expect any apps they use to respect their privacy according to the DPA 1998.

13.4.12.8.2.2 *Who will control the personal data?*   It is vital to know where and how data will flow when an app is used, and who is in control of the data throughout the life cycle of the app. If an organization decides how personal data is dealt with, this means that they will be a data controller in respect of that personal data. For instance,

120 Opinion 5/2009 [http://ec.europa.eu/justice/policies/privacy/docs/wpdocs/2009/wp163_en.pdf].

if they are distributing an app whose code purely runs on the mobile device and does not collect or transfer data elsewhere, then they are unlikely to be a data controller with regard to that app.

If the app sends a user's personal data elsewhere for processing, data controllers should also be clear and transparent about where this is and who will be in control of the transferred data. Data controllers should remember that apps are often designed much like web pages, whether the content comes from the device itself or from an internet-accessible resource and should not let the 'app' appearance get in the way of clarity and transparency as to where and how personal data is being processed.

The following table details some examples of different situations and who would qualify as a data controller:

Table 13.1

Example scenario	Who is the data controller?
Social media connected app where the app allows users to share information with each other, including suggesting friends based on contacts stored on the users' devices. This is achieved by designing an app to communicate with a central server under the business's control. The business does not use third party advertising, instead providing advertising itself.	The business will be the data controller for any personal data received by the central server.
Social media (cloud hosted). This is the same as the mechanism of the above app, except that the central server is hosted on infrastructure belonging to a cloud provider.	The business will be the data controller for any personal data received by the central server. The cloud provider is a 'data processor'.
Advertisement-funded game where the app is a free-to-download game, which funds itself by including adverts provided by a third party ad network. The ad network may use personal data to deliver advertising based on previous browsing interests (online behavioural advertising).	The ad network is a data controller, but as the developer the business will likely have a duty to inform users of what personal data will be collected, how it will be used, by whom, and what control users can exercise.
Review apps. The app is designed solely to submit user reviews to a third party reviews website not under the business's control.	The organization responsible for the reviews site is a data controller for any personal data submitted to it. As a developer, the developer is not a data controller, but should nevertheless explain clearly what happens to the data that the app submits.

13.4.12.8.2.3 *Outsourcing* Even though it is possible to contract out tasks such as website hosting, the responsibility for data protection always rests with the data controller. If an organization is a data controller, it should therefore take care when appointing a service provider. This process should be managed via entering into a written contract, or evidenced in written form. The requirements for such contracts and issues raised by outsourcing to contractors located outside of the EEA are explored in detail in this chapter; the reader should refer to these sections when considering how to approach outsourcing.

290 *Commercial law*

13.4.12.8.2.4 *What data will the app collect?* The ICO has stated that organizations should only collect and process the minimum data necessary for the tasks that they want your app to perform. Collecting data just in case it may be needed in future is bad practice, even when the user has consented to provide that information. App owners should also consider if it is in their best interest to hold data that is not needed, as this will help in reducing the risk that data may be lost or mishandled. Data controllers could also set aside time in the design stage to consider the data types your app might access, collect or transmit and think about how these could affect a user of the app. Data controllers should also be aware that personal data must not be kept for longer than is necessary for the task at hand and retention periods for the personal data held should be put in place.

For each data type collected, it is prudent to record how important it is to the overall purpose of the app, and what justification exists for collecting it. Data controllers should also record where that data may be transmitted. For each identified data type, you should also consider the potential impact on the app user if that data were to be misused. In order to do this, data controllers will need to assess how many times or how frequently data will be processed and how long it needs to be stored. Data controllers should also consider the accuracy and how easy it might be to identify a particular individual or device from that data and aim to use the least privacy-intrusive data possible.

13.4.12.8.2.5 *Subject access* As a data controller, you will have a legal responsibility to respond to a user if they make a written request for a copy of their personal data that you hold. This is called a 'subject access request' and includes requests made by email or through social media. The ICO's Subject Access Code of Practice provides more detail. In order to reduce the number of formal subject access requests you receive, you might consider providing users with routine access to their personal data, perhaps through an online service.

It is important to draw a distinction when considering certain platforms between the social networking site itself (e.g. Facebook) and individuals who develop software which runs through the platform (e.g. online games such as *Farmville*). Facebook addresses this point in their legal terms[121] by stating that developers/operators of applications and websites will adhere to clause 5 of their terms 'Protecting Other People's Rights' by obtaining user consent and making it clear that it is the operator/developer and not Facebook who is collecting their information, display a prominent privacy policy, not post users' identification documents or sensitive financial information on Facebook, or tag users or send email invitations to non-users without their consent.

It is suggested that social networking sites that allow third party operators and developers to run apps via their site will need to put in place stringent terms to deal with the collection of data and will need to ensure that those using the site adhere to the eight principles of the DPA 1998. It is suggested that disclaiming responsibility for such applications will not be sufficient to satisfy the Information Commissioner that a social networking site took appropriate steps to manage the processing of

---

121 https://www.facebook.com/legal/terms.

Data protection and privacy 291

such personal data. Such steps could include terms which state that developers and operators only request data which is necessary to operate the application, have a privacy policy that tells users what user data will be gathered and how it will be used, and include the privacy policy URL in the developer's application. Developers could also be required to not use, display, share, or transfer a user's data in a manner inconsistent with their privacy policy. Developers could also be required to delete all data received from the social networking site concerning a user if the user asks them to do so, and will provide a mechanism for users to make such a request.

Social networking sites could also require that operators and developers are not allowed to include data received from the site concerning a user in any advertising creative, directly or indirectly transfer any data received from the social networking sites to (or use such data in connection with) any ad network, ad exchange, data broker, or other advertising related toolset, even if a user consents to that transfer or use.

The measures suggested are not exhaustive. Other steps could include:

- not allowing developers to sell data which they have captured;
- requiring developers to delete user data if it is used in a way that the social networking site determines is inconsistent with users' expectations;
- reserving the right to limit access to data;
- allowing individuals to remove or disconnect from the application; and
- providing individuals with contact details for the operator/developer so that they can contact them if there is any allegation of infringement or violation of their rights.

13.4.12.9 *Mobility and geolocation*

Several mobile-only and predominantly mobile accessed social networks have emerged, all with unique features that would potentially attract users. Increasingly, features such as 'checking in' at a location or 'posted from e.g. Brent, London' are featuring on social network posts revealing the location of the user.

Location-based social networks allow members to share their location through GPS, Bluetooth, email or text messaging. The member of the network may also add comments about restaurants, allow friends to know where they are going, share information, or find friends that are a few blocks away or even in the café across the road. Some of the well-known location based mobile social networks include BrightKite Aka-Aki, and Mobiluck.[122] The mobile social network sites may be clustered in six main categories based on their dominant features. These are:

---

122 See Chapter 1 for an explanation of these platforms.

292   *Commercial law*

Table 13.2

e group texter	This service focuses on sending short, text-based messages to a group of people at once.
The radar	The radar knows where the user and his/her friends are. These sites support location-based services by keeping track of where the user's contacts are. Most of these sites allow the user to check if there is anyone close to a particular venue or location, while some of them actively alert him/her if any of his/her contacts are within a certain distance.
The Geotagger	These sites allow users to tag locations with images and information that appear on a world map. The user may tag favourite places for shopping, dining or any other activity and share these tags with their friends and the network.
The dating service	These sites are identical to their online counterparts. Users create a profile and they are matched with other users. Some also use radar features to alert the user if an interesting (according to the profile) person is nearby, e.g. Plenty of Fish and Tinder.
The social networker	These sites aim to be as similar as possible to online social networking platforms. Some of the well-known social networking sites such as Facebook and Twitter have also a mobile version.
The Media share	These sites share media files with groups of people. There are also location-based social networks that are not targeting mobile devices only, such as picasa and flickr.

Location data, insofar as they provide key information about an individual (in short, who is where), quickly came to be viewed as a potential source of revenue. Firms have developed a wide variety of services drawing on such data. The first such services offered information to individuals on, for example, the nearest chemist or restaurant to their position. Next, services based on the one-off use of location data (providing information at a given moment in time) were supplemented by services based on continuous use of the data (navigational assistance). This first stage has now given way to a second stage, with the development of services that are no longer based on locating people at their own request (users wishing to avail themselves of a service), but on their being located (at the request of a third party). Tracking and search services have developed whereby individuals can be located via their mobile phones even if they are not using them, but provided they are switched on. The key issue for the processing of location data has thus moved on from being a question of storage (essentially, on what conditions should location data be stored by electronic communications operators?) to being a question of use (how can we ensure that data are used for supplying value-added services in accordance with the principles applicable to the processing of personal data?).

Location data, that is data which indicate the current location of a data subject (usually gathered via mobile phones) relating to a subscriber or user of a public electronic communications network, may only be processed if the subscriber or user cannot be identified from that data or, if they can be (and only to the extent it is necessary for the provision of a *value-added service*), with the informed consent of the relevant user or subscriber. Recital 18 of the Regulations give 'advice on least expensive tariff packages, route guidance, traffic information, weather forecasts and tourist information' as examples of such value-added services. The information may

Data protection and privacy 293

also be used by the communications provider in question, the third party provider of the value-added service or a person acting on behalf of either of these (i.e. outsourcing of aspects of the communication provider's services to third parties, acting as the communications provider's data processor is permitted).

Guidance issued by the ICO[123] in this area states that that ultimate responsibility for compliance with the regulations in this area lies with the communications provider. This means that communications providers must ensure that Principle 7 of the DPA 1998 (data security) should be complied with. This will invariably mean that if aspects of location trafficking is outsourced to a third party, that this is done though a data processing agreement which contains clauses ensuring that any data processor only processes such data in accordance with a standard equivalent to the requirements imposed upon data controllers under the DPA 1998.

Although consent is a key concept within the current legal regime, as noted above, consent is not defined in the DPA 1998, which has created a lack of clarity as to what exactly it means to secure consent from a customer in respect of a location-based service. It is perhaps unsurprising therefore that confusion arises as to the exact nature of the consent that is required at law in order to process geolocation data. What sort of information should the data subject be provided in order to ensure that any ensuing consent is 'informed'? Does the consent need to be secured and renewed with each use of the relevant location-based service? Section 14, para 4(b) of the E-Privacy Regulations, which deals with the issue of location data, states that: 'a user or subscriber who has given his consent to the processing of data . . . shall . . . in respect of each connection to the public electronic communications network in question or each transmission of a communication, be given the opportunity to withdraw such consent, using a simple means and free of charge'.

Section 14 would on a cold reading seem to suggest that users must be given an opportunity to withdraw their consent to the processing of their location data each time they connect to their mobile phone network. However, the E-Privacy Directive (2002/58/EC), which the Regulations implement, suggests that subscribers should be able to withdraw their consent 'for each connection to the network' (i.e. they should be able to effectively switch on and off their consent in respect of each use of their mobile phone). The Commissioner has indicated that, in the case of a corporate subscriber, a person making decisions on behalf of the company is likely to be able to give consent, unless the communications provider has reasonable grounds to believe otherwise.

As the privacy regulations are not prescriptive as to how service providers should obtain this consent, the UK Information Commissioner has suggested that subscribers and/or users should be given sufficient clear information in order to have a broad appreciation of how the data are going to be used, who they might be disclosed to and the consequences of giving consent to such use. This guidance implies that a blanket statement buried in a site's terms and conditions would not be sufficient to obtain the specific informed consent necessary for each value-added service requested and to market their own electronic communications services.

---

123 Guide to the Privacy and Electronic Communications Regulations [http://ico.org.uk/for_organizations/privacy_and_electronic_communications/~/media/documents/library/Privacy_and_electronic/Practical_application/the-guide-to-privacy-and-electronic-communications.pdf].

294 *Commercial law*

The Information Commissioner also suggests the communications provider should make the user or subscriber aware that they can opt out. The user or subscriber should also be provided with an opportunity to withdraw their consent on the occasion of each connection to the network or on each transmission of a communication (Regulation 14(4)(b), Privacy Regulations).

In practical terms, systems can theoretically be put in place to ensure that app users remain anonymous and their sensor data is sent to the servers encrypted. Furthermore, the transmission can in theory also be limited to a particular area and is only activated in critical situations for a defined time period and only with the explicit consent of the user. Consequently, the users decide for themselves whether at all, when and which data they want to make available.

In November 2005, the EU's Article 29 Working Party published an opinion on the protection of individuals in relation to the processing of location data in which it highlighted a number of issues resulting from the increase in the use of location data over the last 20 years.[124]

13.4.13 *Direct marketing*

13.4.13.1 *Value of social media*

Most sites rely on advertising in order to generate revenue. The global market for advertising on social media sites was estimated to be US$2.6 billion in 2009.[125]

Section 11 DPA 1998 provides that an individual is entitled (at any time by notice in writing to a data controller) to require the data controller at the end of such period as is reasonable in the circumstances to cease, or not to begin, processing for the purposes of direct marketing personal data in respect of which he is the data subject.

13.4.13.2 *Types of marketing conducted via social media*

Direct marketing is an essential part of the SNS business model; different marketing models can be used by social networking sites. Nevertheless, marketing using users' personal data should comply with the relevant provisions of both the DPA 1998 and the ePrivacy Directive.

- *Contextual marketing* is tailored to the content that is viewed or accessed by the user.
- *Segmented marketing* consists in serving advertisements to targeted groups of users; a user is placed in a group according to the information he has directly communicated to the social network.
- *Behavioural marketing* selects the advertisements based on the observation and analysis of users' activity over time. These techniques may be subject to different legal requirements, depending on the applicable legal grounds and the characteristics of the user.

---

124 'Working Party 29 Opinion on the use of location data with a view to providing value added services', 2130/05/EN, WP 115, November 2005 [http://ec.europa.eu/justice/policies/privacy/docs/wpdocs/2005/wp115_en.pdf].

125 Deborah Aho Williamson (2008) 'Social networking ad spending', *eMarketer*, 13 May.

In a blog post in August 2014, the ICO's head of enforcement highlighted the need for effective powers to regulate spam advertising. The blog post drew upon text messages and emails, noting that in 2013/2014 the ICO received 120,000 concerns regarding unsolicited calls and 30,000 concerns regarding texts. It was noted that the concerns had been voiced via newspapers, social media and by the public.[126]

13.4.13.3 *Section 11(3) DPA 1998*

Section 11(3) DPA 1998 defines direct marketing as the communication by whatever means of any advertising or marketing material which is directed to a particular individual. If the court is satisfied, on the successful application by a person under section 11(1), the court may, if the data controller fails to comply with a notice supplied by a data subject under section 11(1), require them to take such steps to comply with that notice.

All *data controllers* (i.e. direct marketers in this context) must comply with the eight data protection principles listed in Schedule 1 to the DPA 1998 (the Principles) when processing personal data.

13.4.14 *Fair processing and consent*

13.4.14.1 *Information that must be provided to data subjects*

The DPA 1998 requires organizations to process personal data in accordance with the eight data protection principles. Principle 1, which is most relevant to sites, requires organizations to process personal data fairly and lawfully. In order for processing to be fair, individuals must given certain 'fair processing information'. This means that they must be told:

- ○ that the organization is processing their personal data;
- ○ what the organization will use their personal data for; and
- ○ any additional information which is necessary to make the processing fair.

- • If the organization collects personal data directly from the individuals, the organization must provide them with the fair processing information when it first processes (i.e. collects or uses) their personal data.
- • If the organization doesn't collect the personal data directly from the individual, the organization must provide the fair processing information as soon as is reasonably practicable. However, it is not required to provide the fair processing information if to do so would involve 'disproportionate effort'. This is dependent on the facts, including:

  - ○ the amount of time, effort, and cost in providing the fair processing information balanced against
  - ○ the prejudicial or effectively prejudicial effect on the individual.

---

126 E. Eckersley (2014) 'An effective regulator needs effective powers', 12 August [http://iconewsblog. wordpress.com/2014/08/12/an-effective-regulator-needs-effective-powers].

296   *Commercial law*

- When processing personal data, the organization must also satisfy at least one lawful condition set out in the DPA 1998. The conditions relevant to the proposed products are either that:

  ○ the individual has consented to the processing; or
  ○ the processing is necessary for the purposes of the organization's legitimate interests or those of the organizations it discloses the personal data to. The processing must not be unwarranted by reason of prejudice to the rights and freedoms of the individual.

Each of these conditions is of equal status. In other words, the organization does not need individuals' consent to process their personal data where it complies with the legitimate interests condition.

Guidance from the Information Commissioner's Office states that privacy terms should be clear and genuinely informative and emphasize that policies should provide individuals with a real understanding of what will happen to their information once they hand it over and where and to whom it may be transferred. Best practice is to adopt an independent policy that details privacy terms rather than deal with privacy rights as part of the company's terms and conditions.

In addition, the ICO Guidelines make it clear that organizations should not provide unnecessary information in the policy – the emphasis must be on giving clear, understandable and genuine information on what will happen to an individual's data.

13.4.14.2 *European data regulators place spotlight on using legitimate interests as a ground for data processing*

Many UK data controllers have asked for clarification of the Data Protection Act's sixth condition for processing personal data: 'where processing is necessary for the purpose of legitimate interests pursued by the data controller or by a third party to whom the data are disclosed'. The circumstances under which it would be appropriate to use this or another condition for processing, most notably in the form of consent, has often been the subject of debate, particularly where new forms of advertising are concerned.

The Article 29 Working Party has now addressed this issue. In its latest opinion, the Working Party explains its approach towards considering the legitimate interests of the data controller[127] when disclosing personal information to a third party. A legitimate interest balancing test is explained in the opinion, accompanied by useful reference examples.

The ICO suggest in their 2014 Guidance Note on *Big data and data protection* (accessible via the ICO's website) that there is also a difference between using personal data when the purpose of the processing fits with the reason that people use the service and one where the data is being used for a purpose that is not intrinsic to the delivery of the service. A retailer using loyalty card data for market research is an example of the former. A social media company making its data available for market research is an example of the latter. This does not mean that the latter is necessarily

---

127 Opinion 06/2014 on the notion of legitimate interests of the data controller under Article 7 of Directive 95/46/EC, 844/14/EN WP 21, adopted on 9 April 2014.

Data protection and privacy 297

unfair; this depends on what people are told when they join and use the social media service. The ICO emphasise therefore that it is important to make people aware of what is going to happen to their data if they choose to use the service.

The ICO suggest that a key factor in deciding whether a new purpose is incompatible with the original purpose is whether it is fair. In particular, this means considering how the new purpose affects the privacy of the individuals concerned and whether it is within their reasonable expectations that their data could be used in this way. If, for example, information that people have put on social media is going to be used to assess their health risks or their credit worthiness, or to market certain products to them, then unless they are informed of this and asked to give their consent, it is unlikely to be either fair or compatible. Where the new purpose would be otherwise unexpected, and it involves making decisions about them as individuals, then in most cases the organisation concerned will need to seek specific consent, in addition to establishing whether the new purpose is incompatible with the original reason for processing the data.

13.4.14.3 *Privacy and Electronic Communications Regulations*

13.4.14.3.1 BACKGROUND TO THE REGULATIONS

The Privacy and Electronic Communications (EC Directive) Regulations 2003 (PECR) of 11 December 2003 (the Privacy Regulations) as amended by the Privacy and Electronic Communications (EC Directive) (Amendment) Regulations 2011. The PECR were designed to complement the DPA 1998, and set out more detailed privacy rules in relation to the developing area of electronic communications. However, organizations must also still comply with the DPA if they are processing personal data.

Regulation 4 of PECR specifically states that, 'nothing in these Regulations shall relieve a person of his obligations under the Data Protection Act 1998 in relation to the processing of personal data'. There is some overlap with the DPA 1998, and they use some of the same concepts and definitions – including the definition of direct marketing.

If an organization is sending unsolicited direct marketing by electronic means, or employing someone else to do so on its behalf, it must comply with PECR. This includes telephone calls (both live and automated), faxes, emails, text messages and other forms of electronic message. Essentially, to market by SMS or e-mail, organizations will generally need prior permission from individuals, but not businesses.

13.4.14.3.2 THE SOFT OPT-IN

Regulation 22 provides a slightly different regime for existing customers. If the individual is an existing customer, organizations may be able to market similar products without prior express consent. This rule is called the 'soft opt-in' and is covered by Regulation 22. This means organizations can send marketing texts or emails if:

- they have obtained the relevant contact details in the course of a sale (or negotiations for a sale) of a product or service to that person;
- they are only marketing their own similar products or services; and

298 *Commercial law*

- they gave the person a simple opportunity to refuse or opt out of the marketing, both when first collecting the details and in every message after that.

The test of whether a product or service is 'similar' is whether the customer would reasonably expect messages about the product or service in question.

The soft-opt in does not apply to third party marketing. Opt-in consent must be obtained for such marketing. If organizations wish to share data with third parties, then consent will need to be sought. This could be achieved by setting out the third party uses of data in the privacy policy and seeking active opt-in consent though the use of tick boxes when the customer signs up for the scheme.

13.4.14.3.3 USE OF PRE-TICKED BOXES

The Data Protection EU Working Party makes it clear that in its opinion a pre-ticked box is not sufficient to meet the requirements for valid, unambiguous consent.[128] The Working Party Opinion does not have the legal status of domestic legislation but it would likely be referred to by the ICO in the event of a complaint in assessing an organization's compliance with the DPA 1998.

Although the law is not prescriptive about how consent must be communicated, 'specific' is generally taken to imply the need for some positive action. Passive behaviour, like the failure to respond to a communication or to tick a box, will only be taken as valid for compliance purposes in very specific circumstances. The ICO Marketing Code of Practice[129] states that while some organizations provide pre-ticked opt-in boxes and rely on the user to 'un-tick' if they wish to withhold consent, in the ICO's opinion this is more akin to an opt-out as it assumes consent unless the user clicks the box. A pre-ticked box will therefore not automatically be sufficient to demonstrate consent, as it will be harder to show that the presence of the tick represents a positive, informed choice. Although the Code does not have the status of law, the ICO would refer to it in the event of an investigation when assessing compliance.

In the unreported County Court John Lewis spamming case brought under PECR,[130] John Lewis were ordered to pay damages for sending 'spam' emails. Mr Mansfield began receiving the promotional emails after registering his details with John Lewis' website which opted-him-in for marketing using a pre-ticked consent box. Mr Mansfield argued it was for John Lewis to prove he consented and after a short hearing the judge ruled in his favour. Mr Mansfield states that John Lewis argued 'that because I had not opted-out of receiving their emails, I had automatically opted-in'. At a hearing, a judge ruled the company acted unlawfully as it could not prove that the claimant had agreed to receive the emails or was one of their customers. The incident is at the time of writing the first occasion an individual has won damages following a ruling on the legislation. The case highlights the risks of using pre-ticked boxes to evidence consent.

---

128 http://ec.europa.eu/justice/policies/privacy/docs/wpdocs/2011/wp187_en.pdf.
129 ICO, Direct Marketing Code of Practice [http://ico.org.uk/for_organizations/sector_guides/~/media/documents/library/Privacy_and_electronic/Practical_application/direct-marketing-guidance.pdf].
130 *Mansfield v John Lewis* (Unreported), May 2014.

Data protection and privacy 299

13.4.14.4 *The Data Protection Directive*

13.4.14.4.1 RECITAL 57 OF THE DPR

Recital 57 of the DPR states that where personal data are processed for the purposes of direct marketing, the data subject should have the right to object to such processing free of charge and in a manner that can be easily and effectively invoked.[131]

13.4.14.4.2 ARTICLE 19(2) OF THE DPR

Article 19(2) of the DPR provides that where personal data are processed for direct marketing purposes, the data subject shall have the right to object free of charge to the processing of their personal data for such marketing. This right shall be explicitly offered to the data subject in an intelligible manner and shall be clearly distinguishable from other information.

13.4.14.5 *Personal messages*

Some social networking sites allow their users to send invitations to third parties. The prohibition on the use of electronic mail for the purposes of direct marketing does not apply to personal communications. In order to comply with the exception for personal communications, a social networking site must comply with the following criteria:

- No incentive is given to either sender or recipient;
- The provider does not select the recipients of the message;
- The identity of the sending user must be clearly mentioned;
- The sending user must know the full content of the message that will be sent on his behalf.[132]

For a discussion of the law relating to advertisements on social media sites, see Chapter 14: Trading and advertising standards.

13.4.15 **Compensation**

13.4.15.1 *Section 13 DPA 1998*

If a data subject suffers loss as a result of the actions of a data controller in relation to their data, then under section 13(1) DPA 1998 the data subject may be entitled to compensation from the data controller. Individuals are also generally entitled to compensation from data controllers if they suffer distress that causes damage.

It is a defence under section 13(3) of the Act for a data controller to show that they have taken such care as in all the circumstances was reasonably required to comply with the requirement concerned.

---

131 http://www.europarl.europa.eu/document/activities/cont/201305/20130508ATT65776/ 20130508ATT65776EN.pdffrectification.
132 Article 29 Data Protection Working Party, Opinion 5/2009 on online social networking at para 3.8.

300 *Commercial law*

In *Halliday v Creation Consumer Finance Ltd (CCF)*,[133] the court said that the DPA 1998 does not oblige businesses to pay individuals compensation for distress that causes damage where the distress caused is not attributable to a breach of the Act. Halliday had previously won an order from a district court against Creation Consumer Finance Limited (CCF), in which the finance company was ordered to pay £1,500 in compensation and legal costs to settle claims that it had breached Halliday's rights under the Act. CCF was also ordered to end a credit agreement that had been in place with Halliday, delete all of the consumer's personal data from its systems, and provide Halliday with a list of organizations it had passed his details onto and ensure that those bodies deleted the information.

However, CCF paid the £1,500 it owed Halliday into a closed bank account. The company pursued the bank to have the money returned and then sought to recover the money from Halliday. During this process Halliday noticed that CCF had entered incorrect information about him in their systems that showed that he was £1,500 in arrears. Halliday also found out that the information had been shared with credit reference agency Equifax.

Halliday claimed that CCF had breached the terms of the district court order and that he had been 'highly distressed' about that fact and 'especially when coupled with the court's seeming inability to protect its process from abuse', according to the Court of Appeal's judgment. He said that CCF should have to pay between £6,000 and £18,000 to compensate him for the distress it had caused.

The Court of Appeal said that Halliday could not claim compensation for distress that was not caused by the actual data protection breach itself: in order to be eligible to claim compensation for distress that causes damage under the DPA 1998, 'it is clear that the claimant has to be an individual, that he has to have suffered distress, and that the distress has to have been caused by contravention by a Data Controller of any of the requirements of the Act', Lady Justice Arden said in the Court of Appeal's ruling.

> In other words, this is a remedy which is not for distress at large but only for contravention of the data processing requirements. It also has to be distress suffered by the complainant and therefore would not include distress suffered by family members unless it was also suffered by him. When I say that it has to be caused by breach of the requirements of the Act, the distress which I accept Mr Halliday would have felt at the non-compliance of the order is not, at least directly, relevant because that is not distress by reason of the contravention by a Data Controller of the requirements of this Act. If the sole cause of the distress had been non-compliance with a court order, then that would have lain outside the Act unless it could be shown that it was in substance about the non-compliance with the Data Protection Act.[134]

The court said that Halliday's distress had not been directly related to CCF's data protection breach and that therefore the finance company should only have to pay £750 in substantial damages and a further £1 in nominal damages in way of compensation over the case. Lady Justice Arden said that the breach 'did not lead to a loss of creditor reputation' for Halliday and that there was 'no proof of any fraudulent or malicious intent on the part of CCF'. The breach was caused by a single error only by CCF.

---

133 *Halliday v Creation Consumer Finance Ltd* [2013] EWCA Civ 333, 15 March 2013.
134 Ibid. at [20].

Data protection and privacy 301

13.4.15.2 *Recital 118 and Article 79 DPR*

Recital 118 of the DPR states that any damage which a person may suffer as a result of unlawful processing should be compensated by the controller or processor, who may be exempted from liability if they prove that they are not responsible for the damage, in particular where he establishes fault on the part of the data subject or in case of force majeure.

Article 79 of the DPR provides that one of the following sanctions must be imposed for breach of the Regulation:

- a written warning (for first and unintentional breaches);
- regular audits;
- a fine up to €100 million or up to 5% of the annual worldwide turnover in case of an enterprise, whichever is greater (up from 2% in the Commission's proposal).

Imposing one of these sanctions is mandatory but there is a list of mitigating factors to take into account when assessing which sanction to apply. These include the nature, gravity and duration of the incompliance, repetitive breaches, the degree of cooperation with the supervisory authority to remedy the infringement and mitigate its effects, and the specific categories of personal data affected by the breach. If the controller or the processor is in possession of a valid 'European Data Protection Seal', a fine shall only be imposed in cases of intentional or negligent incompliance.

13.4.16 **The right to object to profiling**

13.4.16.1 *Social media sites' use of profiling*

Increasingly, social media is providing SNS providers with vast amounts of data from which an individual's interests and preferences can be identified.[135] For advertisers, such data can be used to profile users to create a portrait of potential customer bases and help them to make decisions regarding their service. The use of behavioural advertising is seen as a 'commercial pot of gold' in the advertising and marketing industry.[136] The potential earnings are significant; it is estimated that British Telecom (BT) alone could have earned £87 million per year from a deal with Phorm.[137] ISPs have begun to link up with advertisement delivery providers to try to capture the potential of the information flows to and from their subscribers. Customers can be broken down into groups of customers sharing similar goals and characteristics, for example:

- Demographics – their age, gender, income, etc.
- Psychographics – their personality type, preferences, etc.
- Behaviour – their similar likes and dislikes, sports, hobbies, etc.

Big data often involves bringing together data from different sources. Currently it appears that big data analytics mainly uses structured data, e.g. in tables with defined fields, but

---

135 The types of data that can be gathered is explored in Chapter 1: Introduction to social media and the Law.
136 L. Edwards and C. Waedle (eds) (2009) *Law and the Internet*, 3rd edn. Oxford: Hart Publishing at p. 531.
137 Paul Ohm, *University of Illinois Law Review* 1417 (2009) at 1434.

302 *Commercial law*

it can also include unstructured data. For example, it is possible to obtain a feed of all the data coming from a social media source such as Twitter. This is often used for 'sentiment analysis', i.e. to analyse what people are saying about products or organisations. A retailer might combine this data with their own in-house data collected from point-of-sale terminals and loyalty cards, to produce rich and detailed information for marketing. From an IT perspective, combining data from different sources in this way presents particular challenges. Technologies have been developed for big data that do not require all of the data to be put into a single database structure before it can be analysed. When contemplating they creation of such databases, companies should be mindful to ensure that they are complying with the 8 principles of the DPA 1998.

The ICO's 2014 Guidance Note on Big data and data protection (accessible via the ICO's website) notes that big data analytics often repurposes data that was obtained for a different purpose and in some cases by another organisation. Companies such as DataSift take data from Twitter, Facebook and other social media and make it available for analysis for marketing and other purposes. Social media data can also be used to assess individuals' credit worthiness (according to Deville, Joe. Leaky data: how Wonga makes lending decisions. Charisma, May 2013 http://www.charisma-network. net/finance/leaky-data-how-wonga-makeslending- Decisions). In many cases the data that is being used for the analytics has been generated automatically, by interactive technology, rather than being consciously provided by individuals. For example, mobile phone presence data is used to analyse the footfall in retail centres.

Profiling necessarily entails a risk that the profile generated, based on mathematical models, will not be accurate. Indeed, profiles will almost certainly be inaccurate if more than one user browses online from the same computer; the predictive profile created will be a 'mixed profile' based on the combined browsing habits of all of the computer's users. Such inaccurate profiling has the potential to harm users. According to the Electronic Privacy Information Centre (EPIC), 'opaque industry practices result in consumers remaining largely unaware of the monitoring of their online behaviour, the security of this information and the extent to which this information is kept confidential'.[138]

Users may be irritated by the constant display of irrelevant advertisements on their computer screen. Alternatively, the advertising displayed may infer something about the user that is incorrect, thus leading to user embarrassment. It can also reveal sensitive information about the individual about, for instance, political affiliations or sexual orientation, which he or she may not want to disclose. For example, in the USA the store Target profiled customers in order to send coupons to pregnant women and parents. A teenager who had used a family computer was sent coupons based on her internet browsing habits (e.g. searches about pregnancy), thereby revealing that she was pregnant to her parents who were not aware of their daughter's condition.[139]

In the specific context of social media, a good exploration of the issues involved in providing information to online users in a user-friendly way, can be found in *Bilton's*

---

138 Quoted by T.M. Lenard and P.H. Rubin (2009) 'In Defense of Data: Information and the Costs of Privacy', pp. 40 and 41. Washington, DC: Technology Policy Institute [http://www.techpolicyinstitute. org/files/in defenseöf data.pdf].

139 http://www.forbes.com/sites/kashmirhill/2012/02/16/how-target-figured-out-a-teen-girl-was-pregnant-before-her-father-did/.

Data protection and privacy 303

article in the *New York Times* analysing Facebook's privacy policy, and highlighting that it was 5,830 words long and contained 170 options for users.[140] There is a risk therefore that although the uses for which data is being put is disclosed to users, it is done in a way that makes it inaccessible to them. If a user is profiled, there is a risk that this profile will be disclosed without his or her informed consent or marketing materials sent without the user's consent, such as in the 'Target' pregnancy product discount coupons matter discussed above.

Anecdotal evidence suggests that such breaches are prevalent.[141] Other notable examples include the hacking of the European Union's emissions trading system database and the subsequent sale of the data contained therein on the black market.[142]

13.4.16.2 *Data Protection Directive's approach to profiling under DPR*

Article 20 of the DPR deals with matters relating to profiling. Subsection 1 of Article 20 provides that every natural person shall have the right not to be subject to a measure which produces legal effects concerning this natural person or significantly affects this natural person, and which is based solely on automated processing intended to evaluate certain personal aspects relating to this natural person or to analyse or predict in particular the natural person's performance at work, economic situation, location, health, personal preferences, reliability or behaviour. Article 20(2) DPR provides that, subject to the other provisions of this Regulation, a person may be subjected to a measure of the kind referred to in Article 20(1) DPR only if the processing:

- is carried out in the course of the entering into, or performance of, a contract, where the request for the entering into or the performance of the contract, lodged by the data subject, has been satisfied or where suitable measures to safeguard the data subject's legitimate interests have been adduced, such as the right to obtain human intervention; or
- is expressly authorized by a Union or Member State law which also lays down suitable measures to safeguard the data subject's legitimate interests; or
- is based on the data subject's consent, subject to the conditions laid down in Article 7 and to suitable safeguards.

Article 20(3) DPR provides that automated processing of personal data intended to evaluate certain personal aspects relating to a natural person shall not be based solely on the special categories of personal data referred to in Article 9.

In the cases referred to in paragraph 2, the information to be provided by the data controller under Article 14 DPR, shall include information as to the existence of

---

140 Nick Bilton (2010) 'Price of Facebook privacy? Start clicking', *New York Times*, 12 May http://www.nytimes.com/2010/05/13/technology/personaltech/13basics.html?_r=1.

141 M. Hammock and P.H. Rubin (2011) 'Applications want to be free: privacy against information', *Competition Policy International*, p. 3 [http://papers.ssrn.com/sol3/papers.cfm?abstract_id=1781906].

142 S. Carney (2011) 'EU carbon market suffers further setback', *Wall Street Journal*, 28 January [http://online.wsj.com/article/SB10001424052748703956604576109272255053468.html; accessed 23 March 2014].

304   *Commercial law*

processing for a measure of the kind referred to in paragraph 1 and the envisaged effects of such processing on the data subject.

13.4.16.3 *Practical tips in relation to marketing*

> **Practical tips**
>
> The following measures should be considered when conducting such data capturing exercises (in addition to complying with the Cookies Regulations discussed above):
>
> - Create transparency and consumer control.
>   - Provide consumer-friendly and prominent notices regarding online behavioural advertising practices.
>   - Provide an easily accessible way for consumers to choose whether to have their information collected for those purposes (this is especially important in relation to sensitive personal data which will require express consents).
> - Provide for reasonable security for any data they collect for behavioural advertising.
> - Retain data only if it is needed to fulfil a legitimate business or law enforcement need.
> - If you need to alter the way in which you use data, get consent by:
>   - Prominently displaying changes to privacy policies which are drawn to the readers' attention in a consumer-friendly way.
>   - Keep an audit trail of any promises that it makes regarding how the site handles or protects consumer data so you can recall what policy was in effect and for which dates; and
>   - If there is a material change in the data gathered or the uses to which it is being put, obtain express consent from affected customers before using data, even if you have previously collected it.
> - Get consent to use sensitive data.
> - Entities should collect sensitive data for behavioural advertising only after they obtain affirmative express consent from the consumers to receive this advertising.

13.4.16.4 *Interrelationship with the criminal law*

13.4.16.4.1 ARTICLE 15(1) OF THE E-PRIVACY DIRECTIVE

While profiling represents issues in relation to the extent that individuals consent to marketing activity, as noted in Chapter 2: Human rights and Part 2 of this Handbook, it may subsequently be disclosed to law enforcement authorities. In Szoka and Thierer, note that social media data and profiling which occurs in relation to that data

Data protection and privacy 305

may give governments access to a 'honey pot' of surveillance data that might be associated with individual users.[143] In order to understand how such data may be accessible to law enforcement agencies, it is necessary to consider Article 15(1) of the E-Privacy Directive. Article 15(1) provides that Member States may enact restrictions to the scope of the obligation to guarantee the confidentiality of communications when they 'constitute a necessary, appropriate and proportionate[144] measure within a democratic society to safeguard national security (i.e. State security), defence, public security, and the prevention, investigation, detection and prosecution of criminal offences or of unauthorized use of the electronic communication system, as referred to in Article 13(1) of Directive 95/46/EC'.

Controversially, Article 15(1) is phrased in a narrower manner than Article 13(1) of Directive 95/46,[145] which allows Member States to introduce exceptions to the principles contained therein for the purpose of 'the protection of the rights and freedoms of others, the Court has concluded that it does not preclude the possibility of Member States laying down an obligation to disclose personal data in the context of civil proceedings'.[146]

13.4.16.4.2 REPORT OF THE INCEPTION OF COMMUNICATIONS COMMISSIONER

The Report of the Inception of Communications Commissioner which was laid before both Houses of Parliament on 8 April 2014[147] makes clear the Commissioner is of the view that RIPA 2002 is fit for purpose despite advancements in communications technology. RIPA 2000 is considered in depth in Chapter 2: Human Rights.

13.4.17 *The right to access data*

13.4.17.1 *Sections 7 and 8 of the DPA 1998*

A data subject has a right, on making a request to the data controller, to be informed whether personal data of which he is the data subject is being processed by or on behalf of that data controller (sections 7 and 8 DPA 1998). If so, the data subject also has a right to:

- A description of the personal data held, the purposes for which it is being processed and the recipients or classes of recipients to whom the data may be disclosed.
- Any information available to the data controller as to the source of the data (subject to certain stated confidentiality and related protections for individual sources).

---

143 B. Szoka and A. Thierer (2008) 'Online advertising & user privacy: principles to guide the debate', *Progress Snapshot*, 4(19): 3 [http://papers.ssrn.com/sol3/papers.cfm?abstract_id=1348600; accessed 28 March 2014].

144 Proportionality and the margin of appreciation is discussed in depth in Chapter 2: Human Rights.

145 Directive 95/46 article 13(1) allows Member States to introduce exceptions to the principles contained therein for the purpose of 'the protection of the rights and freedoms of others'.

146 Nor does it compel Member States to set forth such an obligation. See *Productores de Musica de España (Promusicae) v Telefónica de España SAU* (C-275/06) [2006] ECR I-271; [2008] 2 CMLR 17.

147 Report of the Inception of Communications Commissioner 2013 (HC 1184).

306 *Commercial law*

- The DPA 1998 provides that, in order to meet these obligations, a copy of the data in permanent form must be provided (in hard copy, on disk, and so on).

13.4.17.2 *Opinion of the Article 29 Working Party*

The Working Party demands that SNS providers should respect the rights of the individuals whose personal data is processed on social networking sites according to the provisions laid out in Articles 12 and 14 of the Directive. It states that:

- Both members and non-members of social networking sites have the rights of data subjects specified in the Directive, including the right, on making a request to the data controller, to be informed whether personal data of which he is the data subject is being processed by or on behalf of that data controller (Article 12).
- Both members and non-members should have access to an easy-to-use complaint handling-procedure set up by the social networking site.
- Users should, in general, be allowed to adopt a pseudonym.

For a subject access request (SAR) to be valid, it should be made in writing. Platforms should note the following points when considering the validity of a request:

- A request sent by email or fax is as valid as one sent in hard copy.
- Social networking sites do not need to respond to a request made verbally but, depending on the circumstances, it might be reasonable to do so (as long as the social networking site is satisfied about the person's identity), and it is good practice to at least explain to the individual how to make a valid request, rather than ignoring them.
- If a disabled person finds it impossible or unreasonably difficult to make a subject access request in writing, the social networking site may have to make a reasonable adjustment for them under the Equality Act 2010 (in Northern Ireland this falls under the Disability Discrimination Act 1995). This could include treating a verbal request for information as though it were a valid subject access request. The social networking site might also have to respond in a particular format that is accessible to the disabled person, such as Braille, large print, email or audio formats. If an individual thinks the social networking site has failed to make a reasonable adjustment, they may make a claim under the Equality Act (or Disability Discrimination Act 1995 in Northern Ireland). Information about making a claim is available from the Equality and Human Rights Commission or from the Equality Commission for Northern Ireland.
- If a request does not mention the Act specifically or even say that it is a subject access request, it is nevertheless valid and should be treated as such if it is clear that the individual is asking for their own personal data.
- A request is valid even if the individual has not sent it directly to the person who normally deals with such requests – so it is important to ensure that the social networking site and its employees can recognize a subject access request and treat it appropriately.

13.4.17.3 The ICO's Code on Subject Access Requests

The ICO's Code on Subject Access Requests states that:

> SARs might also be received via your organization's Facebook page or Twitter account (if it has one), other social media sites to which the organization subscribes, and possibly via third party websites. Although you may not insist on the use of a particular means of delivery for a SAR, if you have a preference (e.g., by email to a particular mailbox) it is good practice to clearly indicate what it is. This should encourage requesters to submit SARs by the means you find most convenient, but you must still respond to SARs which are sent to you by other means.[148]

This means that in theory, data subjects may make a SAR using any Facebook page or Twitter account your organization has, other social media sites to which it subscribes, or possibly via third party websites. This might not be the most effective way of delivering the request in a form the social networking site will be able to process quickly and easily, but there is nothing to prevent it in principle.

Sites should therefore assess the potential for SARs to be received via social media channels and ensure that they take reasonable and proportionate steps to respond effectively to requests received in this way. What is reasonable and proportionate would depend on the facts of the case. However, the ICO notes that: 'The Information Commissioner has discretion as to whether to take enforcement action and would not take it where it is clearly unreasonable.'[149]

The ICO has also indicated that sites are entitled to satisfy themselves of the identity of the person making the request. Because the requester must provide evidence of their identity and because the site might require them to pay a fee, they will often have to supplement a SAR sent by social media with other forms of communication. The ICO has also stated that sites may decline to use social media to supply information in response to a SAR if technological constraints make it impractical, or if information security considerations make it inappropriate to do so. In these circumstances, sites should ask for an alternative delivery address for the response.

One of the challenges posed by social media is the fact that it has a snowball factor. As noted in a recent European Commission factsheet,[150] an Austrian law student requested all the information that a social networking site kept about him on his profile. The social network sent him 1,224 pages of information. This included photos, messages and postings on his page dating back several years, some of which he thought he had deleted. He realized that the site was collecting much more information about him than he thought and that information he had deleted – and for which the networking site had no need – was still being stored. The DPA 1998 specifies that a subject access request relates to the data held at the time the request was received, 'however, in many cases, routine use of the data may result in it being amended or even deleted while you

---

148 http://www.ico.org.uk/about_us/consultations/~/media/documents/library/Corporate/ Research_and_reports/draft_subject_access_cop_for_consultation.ashx.

149 http://www.ico.org.uk/~/media/documents/library/Data_Protection/Detailed_specialist_guides/subject-access-code-of-practice.PDF, p. 10.

150 How will the data protection reform affect social networks? European Commission 2012 [http://ec.europa.eu/justice/data-protection/document/review2012/factsheets/3_en.pdf].

308 *Commercial law*

are dealing with the request. So it would be reasonable for you to supply information you hold when you send out a response, even if this is different to that held when you received the request'. This would be necessary to deal with the fact that data held may alter if contained on a social media platform or uploaded by another user.

13.4.17.4 *Subject access requests made via social networking sites*

13.4.17.4.1 APPLICATION OF EXISTING LAW

The usual rules apply when giving access to personal information linked to identifiers, such as information filed under a customer's name and address or a patient's NHS number, regardless of whether the individual accesses the service online or in more traditional ways. Where individuals access services online, it is good practice to also allow them online access to their personal data. Although this may not always be possible, in many cases it will be. The use of metadata, or other flagging, can help to determine the data that can be released automatically in response to a request and that which needs prior assessment by the data controller.

13.4.17.4.2 NON-OBVIOUS IDENTIFIERS

Although the collection and use of non-obvious identifiers can constitute the processing of personal data, there are significant practical difficulties in granting subject access to information of this sort.

There will be many cases where an organization only holds non-obvious identifiers and either has no interest in, or no certainty of, the 'real world' identity of an individual. While these identifiers may be personal data, there is a major privacy risk inherent in granting subject access to information that is only logged against a non-obvious identifier such as an IP address or cookie, rather than against other information more clearly related to a particular individual. The problem arises because the information held is linked to the device used to go online, rather than directly to the person using it. In reality, this means that the organization holding the information may not be able to determine with any degree of certainty whether the information requested is exclusively about the person making the subject access request, or about a group of people using the same device to go online. In many cases, it is difficult to envisage what practical measures the organization holding the information could take to satisfy itself on this point.

Where a reliable link between the subject access applicant and the information held cannot be established, and where, therefore, there is an obvious privacy risk to third parties, the Information Commissioner would not necessarily seek to enforce the right of subject access unless there is a genuine risk to an individual's privacy if they fail to do so. However, this information still needs to be carefully protected because of the risk that otherwise someone may, with greater or lesser certainty, be able to infer something about a particular person – for example, if it was published and combined with information held by other organizations. Where an organization does hold details of the 'real world' personal identity of the subject access applicant, and can be satisfied with a reasonable degree of certainty that the applicant in question is responsible for the activity to which the requested information relates, the Information Commissioner would expect subject access to be given. This may be the case where an individual has provided their 'real world' personal details in order to register for an online service.

Data protection and privacy 309

13.4.17.5 *Exemptions*

The subject access right set out in sections 7 and 8 DPA 1998 is subject to certain exemptions specified in Schedule 7. These include, for example, the disclosure of confidential references, examination marks, and examination scripts.

There are exemptions from these 'non-disclosure' obligations. The exemptions do not impose an obligation on data controllers to disclose personal data, but they may permit the data controller on occasion to disclose personal data in a way which would otherwise be illegal. These exemptions tend to be particularly useful where disclosures are required for litigation or in the event of regulatory investigations.

The principal exemption from the non-disclosure requirement is contained in section 35 DPA 1998. Section 35 permits disclosures that are required by or under any enactment, by any rule of law or by the order of a court. Personal data are also exempt from the non-disclosure provisions where the disclosure is necessary (a) for the purpose of, or in connection with, any legal proceedings (including prospective legal proceedings), or (b) for the purpose of obtaining legal advice or as is otherwise necessary for the purposes of establishing, exercising or defending legal rights.

When unsure if an exemption applies, the data controller can ask the person requesting disclosure of information (e.g. the Police) to obtain a court order or otherwise demonstrate why a disclosure is legally required. The ICO has produced guidance on applying these exemptions, which can be accessed via its website.

In addition, the following exemptions from prohibitions on disclosure may apply:

- *Crime and taxation*: Under section 29(3) DPA 1998, personal data processed for (a) the prevention or detection of crime, (b) the apprehension or prosecution of offenders, or (c) the assessment or collection of any tax or duty or of any imposition of a similar nature, are exempt from the non-disclosure obligations in any case to the extent to which the application of those obligations would be likely to prejudice any of these crime prevention and taxation purposes. A similar exemption applies to personal data processed for the purposes of discharging statutory functions (e.g. the Police or the courts).
- *Journalism, literature and art*: Under section 32 DPA 1998, personal data that are processed only for the 'special purposes' (journalism, artistic and literary purposes) are exempt from the data protection principles, except the seventh data protection principle (the obligation to implement appropriate security of personal data) if (a) the processing is undertaken with a view to the publication of journalistic, literary or artistic material, (b) the data controller reasonably believes that publication would be in the public interest, and (c) the data controller reasonably believes that, in all the circumstances, compliance with relevant data protection obligations (non-disclosure of information) is incompatible with those journalistic, literary or artistic purposes.
- *Publicly available information*: Under section 34 DPA 1998, personal data are exempt from the non-disclosure provisions, if the data consist of information which the data controller is obliged by or under any enactment (other than an enactment contained in the Freedom of Information Act 2000) to make available to the public, whether by publishing it, by making it available for inspection, or otherwise and whether gratuitously or on payment of a fee.

310   *Commercial law*

13.4.17.6 *Disproportionate effort*

The DPA 1998 does not permit data controllers to exclude information from their response to a SAR certain information merely because it is difficult to access. The Act deals with the situation where supplying information in permanent form to the requester is impossible or would involve disproportionate effort. But it does not place any express limits on your duty to search for and retrieve the information they want.

Section 8(2) provides that data controllers must comply with their obligation to provide information in intelligible form by supplying the data subject with a copy of the information in permanent form, unless the supply of such a copy is not possible or would involve 'disproportionate effort'. The so-called 'disproportionate effort' exception is in section 8(2) DPA 1998. It has caused considerable confusion. The Act does not define 'disproportionate effort' but it is clear that there is some (albeit limited) scope for assessing whether complying with a request by supplying a copy of the information requested in permanent form would result in so much work or expense as to outweigh the requester's right of access to their personal data.

In addition, even if the data controller considers that they do not have to supply a copy of the information in permanent form, the requester still has the right:

* to be informed whether you are processing their personal data; and
* if so, to be given a description of:
  - the personal data in question;
  - the purpose of the processing; and
  - the recipients or classes of recipients; and
* to be given information about the source of the personal data.

13.4.17.7 *Dealing with repeated or unreasonable requests*

The DPA 1998 does not limit the number of SARs an individual can make to any organization. However, it does allow some discretion when dealing with requests that are made at unreasonable intervals. The Act states that data controllers are not obliged to comply with an identical or similar request to one which they have already dealt with, unless a reasonable interval has elapsed between the first request and any subsequent ones.

The Act offers some assistance in deciding whether requests are made at reasonable intervals and suggests consideration of the following:

* The nature of the data – this could include considering whether it is particularly sensitive.
* The purposes of the processing – this could include whether the processing is likely to cause detriment (harm) to the requester.
* How often the data is altered – if information is unlikely to have changed between requests, you may decide that you need not respond to the same request twice.[151]

---

151 http://ico.org.uk/for_organizations/data_protection/the_guide/principle_6/~/media/documents/library/ Data_Protection/Detailed_specialist_guides/subject-access-code-of-practice.PDF, Chapter 8, p. 39.

Data protection and privacy 311

Section 8(6) DPA 1998 states that the 'information to be supplied pursuant to a request . . . must be supplied by reference to the data in question at the time when the request is received'. If there has been a previous request or requests, and the information has been added to or amended since then, when answering a SAR data controllers should note that they are required to provide a full response to the request, not merely supply information that is new or has been amended since the last request.

The ICO's Code of Practice states that the ICO accepts that in practice data controllers may attempt to negotiate with the requester to get them to restrict the scope of their SAR to the new or updated information; but if they insist upon a full response, then the data controller would need to supply all the information.

13.4.17.8 *DPR*

Article 15 of the DPR, which concerns the right of access for the data subject, provides at subsection 1 that the data subject shall have the right to obtain from the controller at any time, on request, confirmation as to whether or not personal data relating to the data subject are being processed. Where such personal data are being processed, the data controller shall provide the following information:

- The purposes of the processing;
- The categories of personal data concerned;
- The recipients or categories of recipients to whom the personal data are to be or have been disclosed, in particular to recipients in third countries;
- The period for which the personal data will be stored;
- The existence of the right to request from the controller rectification or erasure of personal data concerning the data subject or to object to the processing of such personal data;
- The right to lodge a complaint to the supervisory authority and to the contact details of the supervisory authority;
- Communication of the personal data undergoing processing and of any available information as to their source;
- The significance and envisaged consequences of such processing, at least in the case of measures referred to in Article 20.

Subsection 2 confers upon the data subject a right to obtain from the data controller communication of the personal data undergoing processing. Where the data subject makes the request in electronic form, the information shall be provided in electronic form, unless otherwise requested by the data subject.

In relation to time scales for responses, 'although the DPA gives the Data Controller up to 40 days to comply with a request, it is good practice to give access sooner than this, or in real time, where the technology allows this'.[152]

---

152 Personal Information Online Code of Practice, p. 32 [http://www.ico.org.uk/~/media/documents/library/data_protection/detailed_specialist_guides/personal_information_online_cop.ashx].

312   *Commercial law*

13.4.18 *Jurisdiction*

13.4.18.1 *Applicability of DPA 1998 to establishments located overseas*

The Internet has disrupted traditional notions of applicable law and jurisdiction. Individuals and companies can now become subject to the law of a foreign country even without a physical presence. Under Article 4(1)(a) of the European Data Protection Directive (DPD), European law applies where 'the processing [of personal data] is carried out in the context of the activities of an establishment of the controller on the territory of the Member State'. Alternatively, under Article 4(1)(c) of the DPD, European law applies even in the absence of a European establishment, if – for the processing of personal data – the controller 'makes use of equipment . . . situated on the territory of that Member State'.

The DPA 1998 says organizations established in the UK, or non-European[153] ones using equipment in the UK, must comply with UK law regardless of where the personal data originates. The recitals to the DPA 1998 state in relation to establishments the test is not one of legal formalism but purposive, i.e. what processing is actually taking place. However, when collecting, storing, using or distributing personal data across international borders, organizations in the UK and elsewhere could be required to comply with several different sets of rules. The Berlin International Working Group on Data Protection in Telecommunications[154] suggests that user information should specifically comprise information about the jurisdiction under which the service provider operates, about users' rights (e.g. to access, correction and deletion) with respect to their own personal data, and the business model applied for financing the service.

There have been some cases in European law reports that have dealt with the applicability of European data protection based on arguments centring on lack of jurisdiction to regulate a particular provider's activity. One case involved the on-going dispute between Facebook and the data protection authority for the German state of Schleswig-Holstein. A German court overturned an order by the Schleswig-Holstein Data Protection Authority[155] requiring German companies to deactivate their Facebook fan pages, holding that German companies had no effective control over the data hosted by Facebook, whose European base is in Ireland.

The question which is consistently raised in relation to jurisdiction is whether the processing of personal data takes place 'in the context of the activities of an establishment' in a Member State; and – if the answer to this question is negative – whether they 'make use of equipment' situated in the EU. In Europe, the test has been applied broadly with the dropping of a cookie on an EU user's web browser 'use of equipment' in the EU; however, there have been concerns that 'jurisdictional overextension' could result in 'undesirable consequences, such as a possible universal application of EU law'.[156]

---

153 Section 70 DPA 1998 states that 'EEA State' means a State that is a contracting party to the Agreement on the European Economic Area signed at Oporto on 2 May 1992 as adjusted by the Protocol signed at Brussels on 17 March 1993.

154 http://www.datenschutz-berlin.de/content/europa-international/international-working-group-on-data-protection-in-telecommunications-iwgdpt.

155 ULD to website owners: 'Deactivate Facebook web analytics', Press release dated 19 August 2011 [https://www.datenschutzzentrum.de/presse/20110819-facebook-en.htm].

156 Working Party Article 29 Opinion 8/2010 on applicable law, 0836-02/10/EN WP 179, adopted on 16 December 2010 [http://ec.europa.eu/justice/policies/privacy/docs/wpdocs/2010/wp179_en.pdf].

Data protection and privacy 313

In its 2010 opinion on applicable law, the Article 29 Working Party proposed that in any future legislation, relevant targeting of individuals would be taken into account in relation to controllers not established in the EU. This approach is reflected in the European Commission Proposal for the GDPR. Under Article 3(2) of the GDPR, the application of European law would extend to the processing of personal data by a controller not established in the EU, where 'the processing activities are related to: (a) the offering of goods or services to such data subjects in the Union; or (b) the monitoring of their behaviour'. Critics argue that this extension of extraterritorial application constitutes a dramatic shift from a 'country of origin' to a 'country of destination' approach and portends general application of the GDPR to the entire internet.[157]

In *Google v Spain*,[158] the referring court asked the Grand Chamber whether Article 4(1)(a) of Directive 95/46 should be interpreted as meaning that processing of personal data is carried out in the context of the activities of an establishment of the controller on the territory of a Member State, within the meaning of that provision, when one or more of the following three conditions are met:

- the operator of a search engine sets up in a Member State a branch or subsidiary which is intended to promote and sell advertising space offered by that engine and which orientates its activity towards the inhabitants of that Member State; or
- the parent company designates a subsidiary located in that Member State as its representative and controller for two specific filing systems which relate to the data of customers who have contracted for advertising with that undertaking; or
- the branch or subsidiary established in a Member State forwards to the parent company, located outside the European Union, requests and requirements addressed to it both by data subjects and by the authorities with responsibility for ensuring observation of the right to protection of personal data, even where such collaboration is engaged in voluntarily.

The Grand Chamber held that:

Article 4(1)(a) of Directive 95/46 is to be interpreted as meaning that processing of personal data is carried out in the context of the activities of an establishment of the controller on the territory of a Member State, within the meaning of that provision, when the operator of a search engine sets up in a Member State a branch or subsidiary which is intended to promote and sell advertising space offered by that engine and which orientates its activity towards the inhabitants of that Member State.[159]

13.4.18.2 *DPR*

13.4.18.2.1 RECITAL 19 OF THE DPR

Recital 19 of the DPR provides that any processing of personal data in the context of the activities of an establishment of a controller or a processor in the European Union

---

157 Ibid.
158 Case C-131/12 at [45].
159 Case C-131/12 at [100].

314 Commercial law

should be carried out in accordance with this Regulation, regardless of whether the processing itself takes place within the EU or not. Establishment implies the effective and real exercise of activity through stable arrangements. The legal form of such arrangements, whether through a branch or a subsidiary with a legal personality, is not the determining factor in this respect.

13.4.18.2.2 RECITAL 20 OF THE DPR

Importantly, Recital 20 goes on to state that in order to ensure that individuals are not deprived of the protection to which they are entitled under this Regulation, the processing of personal data of data subjects residing in the European Union by a data controller not established in the EU should be subject to this Regulation where the processing activities are related to the offering of goods or services to such data subjects, or to the monitoring of the behaviour of such data subjects.

13.4.18.2.3 RECITAL 27 OF THE DPR

Organizations should note that the location of servers is addressed by Recital 27 of the DPR. Recital 27 provides that the main establishment of a controller in the EU should be determined according to objective criteria and should imply the effective and real exercise of management activities determining the main decisions as to the purposes, conditions, and means of processing through stable arrangements. This criterion should not depend on whether the processing of personal data is actually carried out at that location; the presence and use of technical means and technologies for processing personal data or processing activities do not, in themselves, constitute such main establishment and are therefore not determining criteria for a main establishment. The main establishment of the processor should be the place of its central administration in the EU.

The potential impact that such a shift may have is exemplified in the first instance decision of *Alfacs Vacances SL v Google Spain SL*.[160] This case involved disturbing photographs of corpses burned at an accident on the claimant's campsite in 1978. The accident had not been in any way the fault of the campsite and yet it was still coming back as the 'top search' result on Google for the campsite. The effect on the business owner's livelihood from this extremely damaging unwanted publicity was therefore considerable. Though Alfacs Vacances had sent some notices to Google Inc., the complaint was finally filed exclusively against Google Spain SL, its Spanish subsidiary, whose activity is limited to marketing and advertising services. As the entity actually running the search engine was Google Inc. – an American company – Google Spain SL alleged lack of standing to be sued and the judge dismissed the case. Under the new regime, the ruling may have been considerably different and in the future companies such as Facebook and Google may even be bound by law to wipe all user information from their database, if anyone makes such request.

160 Ruling of 23 February 2012, issued by the Court of First Instance of Amposta.

Data protection and privacy   315

13.4.18.2.4 RECITAL 63 OF THE DPR

Recital 63 of the DPR states that where a controller not established in the EU is processing personal data of data subjects residing in the EU whose processing activities are related to the offering of goods or services to such data subjects, or to the monitoring of their behaviour, the controller should designate a representative, unless the controller is established in a third country ensuring an adequate level of protection, or the controller is a small or medium-sized enterprise or a public authority or body or where the controller is only occasionally offering goods or services to such data subjects. The representative should act on behalf of the controller and may be addressed by any supervisory authority. Recital 64 states that in determining whether a controller is only occasionally offering goods and services to data subjects residing in the EU, it should be ascertained whether it is apparent from the controller's overall activities that the offering of goods and services to such data subjects is ancillary to those main activities. Significantly for social media sites, the DPR makes no exception for user-generated content.[161]

13.4.18.3 *Overseas transfers of data*

13.4.18.3.1 BACKGROUND

A data controller may only transfer personal data outside the EEA to a country whose data protection laws have not been approved by the European Commission,[162] if there is an adequate level of protection for the rights of data subjects. Principle 8 of the DPA 1998 states 'personal data shall not be transferred to a country or territory outside the EEA unless that country or territory ensures an adequate level of protection for the rights and freedoms of data subjects in relation to the processing of personal data'.

Other principles of the DPA 1998 will also usually be relevant to sending personal data overseas. For example, Principle 1 (relating to fair and lawful processing) will in most cases require you to inform individuals about disclosures of their personal data to third parties overseas. Principle 7 (concerning information security) will also be relevant to how the information is sent and the need to have contracts in place when using subcontractors abroad.

The adequacy of the level of protection associated with a particular transfer may be ensured in a number of ways. The data controller may:

*   carry out his own assessment of the adequacy of the protection;
*   use contracts to ensure adequacy;
*   obtain Commission approval for a set of Binding Corporate Rules governing intra-group data transfers; or
*   rely on one of the exceptions to the prohibitions on transfers of personal data outside the EEA.

It is often advanced by search engines and other web-based providers such as social networking sites, that since their servers are situated outside of the EU, they are

---

161 See above in relation to the ICO's position in relation to online postings and s 36 Domestic Purpose Exemption.

162 A list can be found at http://ico.org.uk/for_organizations/data_protection/the_guide/principle_8.

316 *Commercial law*

therefore not subject to the EU data protection regime. The DPA 1998 says that personal data transferred overseas shall enjoy an adequate level of protection.

13.4.18.3.2 ADEQUACY CRITERIA

13.4.18.3.2.1 *General and legal considerations* The Data Protection Act 1998 (Schedule 1, Part II, para 13) provides that, when considering whether there is 'an adequate level of protection' for the purposes of Principle 8, the level of protection must be one which is 'adequate in all the circumstances of the case'. In addition, in assessing adequacy, particular consideration should be given to specific listed criteria. For ease of reference, these criteria may be divided into two groups:

* general adequacy criteria, and
* legal adequacy criteria.

If an assessment of the 'general adequacy criteria' has revealed that, in the particular circumstances of the case, the risk to the rights of data subjects associated with the transfer is low, an exhaustive analysis of the 'legal adequacy criteria' may not be necessary. If a high risk is identified (e.g. if the data is particularly sensitive), then a more comprehensive investigation of the legal adequacy criteria will be required.

13.4.18.3.2.2 *General adequacy criteria*

* The nature of the personal data.
* The purposes for which the data are intended to be processed.
* The period during which the data are intended to be processed.
* The country or territory of origin of the information contained in the data.
* The country or territory of final destination of the information: Transfers may be made in several stages involving transfers to one, then another, and then another country. Where it is known that there will be a further transfer to another country or territory, the level of protection given in the country of final destination will be relevant in assessing the adequacy of the protection associated with the transfer.
* Any security measures taken in respect of the data in the country or territory of destination. Organizations exporting data may be able to ensure that the personal data are protected by means of technical measures (such as encryption or the adoption of information security management practices such as those in ISO17799/ BS7799). In practice, security is often a key factor in the commercial considerations of the parties.

13.4.18.3.2.3 *Legal adequacy criteria* The ICO suggests that it will not always be necessary to carry out a detailed consideration of the legal adequacy criteria where consideration of the general adequacy criteria indicates that the risk to the rights of data subjects associated with the proposed data transfer is low. Where consideration of the general adequacy criteria indicates a higher risk, the legal adequacy criteria come into play. For example, where the exporting data controller is proposing to set up a permanent operation in a third country and anticipates making regular, large-scale transfers to that country.

Data protection and privacy   317

To make a legal adequacy assessment, consider the following:

- The law in force in the country or territory in question.
  - ○ Consider whether the third country:
    - Has a data protection regime in place that meets the standards set out in the Article 29 Working Party document adopted on 24 July 1998 (WP 12).
    - Has any legal framework for the protection of the rights and freedoms of individuals generally.
    - Recognizes the general rule of law and, in particular, the ability of parties to contract and bind themselves under contracts.
- The international obligations of the recipient country or territory.
- Consider whether the third country has:
  - ○ Adopted the OECD Guidelines[163] and put in place appropriate measures to implement the Guidelines.
  - ○ Ratified Convention 108[164] and established appropriate mechanisms for compliance with the Convention.
- The rules or codes of practice that govern the processing of personal data in the third country.
- Whether the recipient country has in place any relevant codes of conduct or other rules (general or sectoral) enforceable in that country or territory (whether generally or by special arrangement in particular cases).

13.4.18.3.2.4 *Model contract clauses as a basis for transferring personal data outside the EEA*

13.4.18.3.2.4.1 Background

The European Commission is empowered to recognize standard contractual clauses (known as model contract clauses) as offering adequate safeguards for the purposes of Article 26(2) of the 95 Directive. The Commission has approved four sets of model contract clauses (listed below).

The Information Commissioner is empowered to authorize transfers of personal data in such a manner 'as to ensure adequate safeguards for the rights and freedoms of data subjects' under paragraph 9, Schedule 4 DPA 1998. Following approval by the Commission, the Information Commissioner has in turn also approved the following sets of model contract clauses.

---

163 OECD Guidelines Governing the Protection of Privacy and Transborder Flows of Personal Data, C(80)58/FINAL, as amended on 11 July 2013 by C(2013) 79.

164 Convention for the Protection of Individuals with regard to Automatic Processing of Personal Data, Strasbourg, 28 January 1981.

318 *Commercial law*

13.4.18.3.2.4.2 Set I: controller–controller
In Commission Decision 2001/497/EC, dated 15 June 2001,[165] the Commission approved model clauses for transfers from data controllers in the EEA to data controllers outside the EEA. These clauses were authorized by the Information Commissioner on 21 December 2001.

13.4.18.3.2.4.3 Set I: controller–processor
In Commission Decision 2002/16/EC, dated 27 December 2001,[166] the Commission approved model clauses for transfers from data controllers in the EEA to data processors outside the EEA. These clauses were authorized by the Information Commissioner on 18 March 2003. It should be noted that this set of clauses is no longer available for new users but continues to have effect in relation to arrangements put in place prior to 15 May 2010.

13.4.18.3.2.4.4 Set II: controller–controller
These clauses were approved by Commission Decision 2004/915/EC, dated 27 December 2004,[167] in which the Commission approved an alternative set of model clauses for transfers from data controllers in the EEA to data controllers outside the EEA and were authorized by the Information Commissioner on 27 May 2005.

13.4.18.3.2.4.5 Set II: controller–processor
These clauses were approved by Commission Decision 2010/87/EU, dated 5 February 2010,[168] in which the Commission approved a new set of model clauses for transfers from data controllers in the EEA to data processors outside the EEA to replace the Set I controller-to-processor clauses and were authorized by the Information Commissioner on 17 May 2010.

13.4.18.3.2.4.6 Status of the clauses
If a business uses the model clauses in their entirety in its contract, it will not have to make its own assessment of the adequacy of protection afforded to the rights of data subjects in connection with transfer of their personal data.

---

165 Commission Decision of 15 June 2001 on standard contractual clauses for the transfer of personal data to third countries, under Directive 95/46/EC, 2001/497/EC [http://eurlex.europa.eu/legal-content/en/ALL/;jsessionid=QssQT1tDCVdVjK9ylXcC6t9l7B1pGtpG1r9gbQ0z8X1mhMlQ5pvc!208781961?uri=CELEX:32001D0497].

166 Commission Decision 2002/16/EC of 27 December 2001 on standard contractual clauses for the transfer of personal data to processors established in third countries, under Directive 95/46/EC (Text with EEA relevance) (notified under document number C(2001) 4540) [http://eur-lex.europa.eu/legal-content/en/ALL/?uri=CELEX:32002D0016].

167 Commission Decision 2004/915/EC of 27 December 2004 amending Decision 2001/497/EC as regards the introduction of an alternative set of standard contractual clauses for the transfer of personal data to third countries (notified under document number C(2004) 5271).

168 Commission Decision 2010/87/EU of 5 February 2010 on standard contractual clauses for the transfer of personal data to processors established in third countries under Directive 95/46/EC of the European Parliament and of the Council (notified under document C(2010) 593).

Data protection and privacy 319

13.4.18.4 *Ensuring adequacy via other means*

You do not necessarily need to use the model contract clauses when entering into an international outsourcing arrangement if you have found an alternative means of complying with, or using an exception to, Principle 8. For example, ensuring compliance with the security requirements of Principle 7 will go some way towards satisfying the adequacy requirements of Principle 8 (given the continuing contractual relationship between you and your processor and your continuing liability for data protection compliance under the Act).

13.4.18.4.1 SAFE HARBOR

13.4.18.4.1.1 *General* The Safe Harbor scheme is recognized by the European Commission as providing adequate protection for the rights of data individuals in connection with the transfer of their personal data to signatories of the scheme in the USA. When a US company signs up to the Safe Harbor arrangement, they agree to:

* follow seven principles of information handling; and
* be held responsible for keeping to those principles by the Federal Trade Commission or other oversight schemes.

It should be noted that Safe Harbor is voluntary and certain types of companies cannot sign up to it. You can view a list of the companies signed up to the Safe Harbor arrangement on the US Department of Commerce website.[169]

In July 2007, the EU and the US signed an agreement to legitimize and regulate the transfer of passenger name record information (PNR) from EU airlines to the US Department of Homeland Security (DHS). This agreement is regarded as providing adequate protection for the personal data in question.

13.4.18.4.1.2 *German commissioners' view on Safe Harbor* On 24 July 2013, the Conference of the German Data Protection Commissioners at both the Federal and State levels issued a press release[170] stating that surveillance activities by foreign intelligence and security agencies threaten international data traffic between Germany and countries outside the EEA.

In their release, the German Commissioners described the supervisory authorities' existing powers with respect to international data transfers (as granted by the Federal Data Protection Act and the European Data Protection Directive) and considered concerns regarding surveillance activities by foreign intelligence agencies, in particular the US National Security Agency ('NSA'). As a result of their report, the German Commissioners have decided:

* to stop issuing approvals for international data transfers until the German Government demonstrates that unlimited access to German citizens' personal data

---

169 http://export.gov/safeharbor/.
170 http://www.bfdi.bund.de/DE/Home/homepage_Kurzmeldungen2013/PMDerDSK_SafeHarbor.html?
nn=408908.

320   *Commercial law*

by foreign national intelligence services comports with the fundamental principles of data protection law (i.e. necessity, proportionality and purpose limitation); and
- to review whether to suspend data transfers carried out pursuant to the Safe Harbor Agreement and EU standard contractual clauses.

13.4.18.4.1.3 *Data subjects' challenge of Facebook's Safe Harbor arrangements*   The German Commissioners are not the only ones to challenge the security provided by Safe Harbor and the nature of the surveillance conducted by the NSA. The Irish High Court granted the activist group Europe v Facebook a judicial review[171] of an earlier decision by the country's Data Protection Commissioner, who refused to launch an investigation into Facebook's alleged transfer of customer data to the NSA.

The review was requested after Edward Snowden's PRISM revelations showed that the NSA was requisitioning large amounts of customer data from US tech firms such as Facebook, Microsoft, Apple, and Google. Europe v Facebook considered this a breach of European data protection law, and specifically of 'Safe Harbor' and complained to data protection officials in Ireland (regarding Facebook and Apple) and Luxembourg.

Although enjoying success with their arguments in Luxembourg and Germany, initially the Irish Data Protection Commissioner rejected Europe v Facebook's investigation request, arguing that there was no evidence of unlawful data transfers, and that being registered for the Safe Harbor scheme means Facebook had 'met their data protection obligations'. However, the Irish High Court has now granted Europe v Facebook its right to appeal, with Europe v Facebook citing the call by the German data protection officials for the Safe Harbor agreement to be suspended and calling for an analysis of the agreement last year by the Article 29 Working Party of EU Data Protection Commissioners, who recommended bringing in a proper certification scheme with third-party audits.[172]

13.4.18.4.1.4 *Practical measures for site providers*   Jurisdictional issues can raise practical compliance difficulties for organizations:

- Sites may not know where information they are responsible for is being processed at any particular time; or
- Sites may not know where people they are collecting information about are situated, what privacy standards they might expect, or what the law in their country says.

Given the practical problems that arise from these territorial issues, a good practice approach is particularly useful.

The principles of the DPA 1998 have international roots and are similar to those found in other countries' laws, within and beyond the EU. Compliance with the principles should generally serve as a reliable foundation for international compliance, despite variations in national laws. However, sites may need to take different, or additional, measures, depending on the people they aim to collect personal data about, the nature of the service they are providing, and the regions at which they are aiming their services.

171 *Max Schrems v Data Protection Commissioner* JR No 765 JR 2013.
172 Opinion 3/2010 on the principle of accountability, 00062/10/EN WP 173 [http://ec.europa.eu/justice/policies/privacy/docs/wpdocs/2010/wp173_en.pdf].

Data protection and privacy 321

In summary, organizations will need to assess if they have:

- incorporated standard and/or model clauses (which are approved by the European Commission as offering adequate safeguards under the DPA) into this agreement or a separate data processing agreement between the parties; and
- procured that any sub-contractor or other third party who will be processing and/or receiving or accessing the personal data in any restricted countries either enters into:
  - a direct data processing agreement with the customer on such terms as may be required by the customer;
  - a data processing agreement with the supplier on terms which are equivalent to those agreed between the customer and the sub-contractor relating to the relevant personal data transfer;
- In the case of the USA, the Safe Harbor scheme is recognized by the European Commission as providing adequate protection for the rights of data individuals in connection with the transfer of their personal data to signatories of the scheme in the USA.

When aiming to collect personal data from people in a particular country or countries, it is good practice to try to understand any relevant cultural values and expectations that could lead to processing of personal data being considered to be inappropriate or intrusive. In practice, this can be difficult, especially if your service is not targeted at a particular group or territory. If in doubt, advice should be sought from experts in the countries you are targeting.

It is good practice to be as open as possible with customers about where any processing of personal data is taking place and the likely consequences of this, if any. Note, however, that the DPA 1998 does not give individuals a right to insist that their personal data is only processed in one country and not in others.

13.4.18.4.1.5 *Practical points to consider when outsourcing services which involve the transfer of personal data overseas* The following list highlights some of the key commercial questions to ask when considering outsourcing aspects of your services overseas. It is by no means exhaustive but should provide a useful guide for the types of issues from a data protection perspective that you should be considering when entering into outsourcing arrangements with overseas providers.

- Can the entity confirm in writing that it will only process data in accordance with your instructions and will maintain an appropriate level of security?
- Can it guarantee the reliability and training of its staff, wherever they are based? Do they have any form of professional accreditation?
- What capacity does it have for recovering from a serious technological or procedural failure?
- What are its arrangements and record regarding complaints and redress – does it offer compensation for the loss or corruption of data entrusted to it?
- If it is an established company, how good is its security track record?
- What assurances can it give that data protection standards will be maintained, even if the data is stored in a country with weak, or no, data protection law, or where there is governmental data interception?

322   *Commercial law*

- Powers are strong and lacking safeguards?
- Are they willing to offer an audit right to your organization?
- Have the parties identified a point of contact for privacy and security matters?
- Does it sub-contract any of your services out to another sub-contractor?

  ○ Are these on the same terms as your own security arrangements with the sub-contractor?
  ○ Do you want to make appointing sub-contractors conditional upon obtaining your consent?

- Can it send you copies of your information regularly, in an agreed format and structure so that you hold useable copies of vital information at all times?
- Do you require indemnity protection from them in the contract to manage your damages in the event of a breach?

  ○ Does it cover losses of data subjects?
  ○ Does it cover business losses such as legal expenses and costs of complying with regulatory investigations and business interruption?

13.4.19 *Breach notification*

13.4.19.1 *Reporting a breach*

Aside from telecoms providers (discussed below) there is no legal obligation on data controllers to report breaches of security that result in loss, release or corruption of personal data. The Information Commissioner believes serious breaches should be brought to the attention of his Office. The nature of the breach or loss can then be considered together with whether the data controller is properly meeting his responsibilities under the DPA 1998.

'Serious breaches' are not defined. However, the following should assist data controllers in considering whether breaches should be reported:

- The potential detriment to data subjects.
- The volume of personal data lost / released / corrupted.
- The sensitivity of the data lost / released / corrupted.

13.4.19.2 *ICO PECR security breach guidance*

On 26 September 2013, the ICO published new breach notification guidance entitled 'Notification of PECR security breaches',[173] which applies to telecom operators, internet service providers ('ISPs') and other public electronic communications service ('ECS') providers (these definitions are discussed in Chapter 1).

Under Regulation 5A of PECR, 'service providers' have a specific obligation to notify the Information Commissioner – and in some cases their own customers –

---

173 Notification of PECR security breaches: Privacy and Electronic Communications Regulations [http://ico.org.uk/~/media/documents/library/Privacy_and_electronic/Practical_application/notification-of-pecr-security-breaches.pdf], 26 September 2013.

about a 'personal data breach'. They are also required to keep a log of those breaches. In essence, a service provider is someone who provides any service allowing members of the public to send electronic messages. It will include telecoms providers and internet service providers. Regulation 5(1) of PECR defines a service provider as 'a provider of a public communications service'. Regulation 2 incorporates further relevant definitions from the Communications Act 2003. A public communications service is defined in section 151 of the Communications Act 2003 as 'any electronic communications service that is provided so as to be available for use by members of the public'. By way of example, the note states that 'a shopping portal or an online newspaper would be a content service, and not an electronic communications service'. The guidance also states that organizations will need to consider a range of factors to determine whether they are service providers with notification obligations under PECR. They suggest that an organization that meets the following criteria is likely to be a service provider:

- it provides a service which transmits electronic signals (and is not purely providing content);
- the service is available to members of the public;
- the service is provided as a primary activity, rather than as a supplementary service such as wi-fi provided in a pub or on a train; and
- if there are multiple organizations involved in providing the service, this organization directs and controls the provision of service to the end user.

Data breach logs also must be maintained and submitted to the ICO on a monthly basis. The ICO provides a template log to help service providers understand what information needs to be submitted to the ICO.

13.4.19.3 *When and how to notify customers*

Service providers caught by the mandatory notification rules must notify affected customers without undue delay – in other words, as soon as they have sufficient information about the breach. If doing so would put a proper investigation of the breach at risk, a service provider can ask the ICO to approve a delay in notification until it has completed its investigation. Organizations do not need to tell subscribers about a breach if they can demonstrate that the data were encrypted.

The means of communication should be prompt and secure. It should be a specific message about the breach, and not be combined with a communication on another topic.

13.4.19.4 *Notifying breaches to subscribers*

13.4.19.4.1 WHEN A NOTIFICATION IS REQUIRED

The ICO website states that providers may also need to tell their subscribers about a breach if the breach is likely to 'adversely affect their personal data or privacy'. The ICO suggests that the following may be indicators that an individual has been adversely affected:

324 *Commercial law*

13.4.19.4.1.1 *Adverse effect* Whether the breach is likely to adversely affect individuals is primarily a decision for the service provider, based on the circumstances of the case. Service providers should consider the following factors:

- the nature and content of the personal data;
- whether it includes sensitive personal data, as defined in the DPA 1998, or other details people might consider intrusive – especially financial information, location data, internet log files, web browsing histories, email data or itemised call lists;
- what harm could be caused to the individual – and in particular whether there is a threat to physical safety or reputation or a risk of identity theft, fraud, financial loss, psychological distress or humiliation;
- who now has access to the data, to the extent this is known.

It should be noted that, although an organization decides not to tell subscribers, the ICO can require them to do so, if the ICO considers the breach is likely to have an adverse effect on users.

13.4.19.4.1.2 *What must be supplied* If an organization decides to tell users about a breach, then they must without unnecessary delay tell them:

- the organization's name and contact details;
- the estimated date of the breach;
- a summary of the incident;
- the nature and content of the personal data;
- the likely effect on the individual;
- any measures taken to address the breach;
- how they can mitigate any possible adverse impact of the breach.

13.4.19.5 *Risks of using automated systems – reputation management*

The time, manpower and cost of notifying data subjects of breaches can be a large cost to businesses be it through covered resources to manage the breach or the cost of setting up dedicated call centres to deal with concerned customers. Indeed, for large organizations this can be especially challenging. While automatic notifications can seem like a good way to battle this resource war, a case study from Twitter serves as a useful example of the dangers of automated messaging. In March 2014, Twitter instructed thousands of users to change passwords due to accounts being 'compromised' – but it has since said the emails were sent by mistake.[174]

The reset notices were sent out to users on 3 March 2014, prompting many to question if the service had been hacked. The social network would not say how many users had been affected, but apologised for the inconvenience. Twitter users, particularly those with high profiles, are frequently targeted. Groups such as the Syrian Electronic Army (SEA) have become adept at tricking users into unwittingly

---

174 'Twitter resets user passwords by accident', 4 March 2014 [http://www.bbc.co.uk/news/technology-26418987; accessed 28 May 2014].

handing over log-in details for social media. The round of emails sent by Twitter came with a warning that: 'Twitter believes that your account may have been compromised by a website or service not associated with Twitter.' It added: 'We've reset your password to prevent accessing your account.' It has since blamed a 'system error' for the notices being sent, although those who received the email will still need to reset their details despite the false alarm. Last year, similar emails were sent out for a real breach. Some 250,000 users' passwords had been stolen, as well as usernames, emails and other data (this is considered in Chapter 16: Insurance).

13.5 Terms and conditions and privacy policies

13.5.1 *Introduction*

Most readers of this book will have been asked to 'Click here to read our privacy notice' as they scroll through a web page to get to the services or to 'Click here to say you have read and understood our privacy policy' before completing an online transaction, not understanding what it's all about or paying much attention to the content of that notice. Those of you who run online businesses may have spent time thinking about protection privacy online and how to draft notices that inform your customers how you are using their information, while trying to consider how you can utilize that data to drive your business forward.

When considering how compliant a social networking site is with the law, the first source often reviewed is the site's terms and conditions, privacy policies, and cookies polices. Some sites refer to these by different names, such as terms of service (Twitter), or adopt in addition to their privacy policies additional terms such as 'Community Standards' (Facebook).

13.5.2 *What is a privacy statement?*

A privacy statement sets out the practices of an organization in relation to how it handles and makes use of a user's personal data. Data may be used for a number of reasons, such as to allow the user to access the site or to fulfil an order. However, it may also be used to market to individuals, identify their preferences or habits and to make additional commercial uses of their data such as selling it to third parties. The transparency and accessibility of privacy terms for site users has been much debated in recent years and questions have been raised as to how much the average user really understands about the uses to which their data is being put. Social networking sites have been criticised in particular for making changes without drawing such changes to account holders' attention, and the Irish Information Commissioner in particular has been critical in relation to the knowledge users have, and if they are able to give informed consent in relation to the data that has been collected about them.

13.5.3 *Incorporation issues*

To ensure that users are legally bound by a site's terms of use, the terms must be agreed by both parties and properly incorporated into a contract between the organization and the user. It is not enough to simply make the terms of use available from

326 *Commercial law*

the site – users must agree that they are bound by them either before or at the same time as using a service or purchasing products.

Privacy policies can be incorporated by reference to them in the terms and conditions for the site or can be incorporated separately (e.g. one tick box for the terms and conditions and one tick box for the privacy policy) to indicate that the privacy policy has been read and its terms accepted by the user.

13.5.4 *Unfair Terms in Consumer Contract Regulations 1999 (Regulations)*

The key test to apply when assessing compliance is that 'a contractual term which has not been individually negotiated shall be regarded as unfair if, contrary to the requirement of good faith, it causes a significant imbalance in the parties' rights and obligations arising under the contract, to the detriment of the consumer' (Regulation 5(1)). In the following paragraphs, a conservative approach is adopted when highlighting possible failure to comply. However, a risk assessment has also been included as to whether the terms in question should be amended or whether the risk of challenge is low.

13.5.5 *Terms of use (terms and conditions)*

13.5.5.1 *Being bound by the terms of use*

Firms should draft contracts in plain and intelligible language and must give consumers a proper opportunity to read all of the terms of the contract.

13.5.5.2 *Unilateral right to vary the terms*

In addition to Regulation 5 (see above), the Regulations include an indicative list of terms that are likely to be unfair. Terms that enable a firm unilaterally to change contract variables are less likely to be unfair if:

- the term enables the firm to change a contract variable only with a valid reason which is specified in the contract; or
- the term permits a change in the rate of interest or other charges for financial services under the contract and there is a valid reason (which is not specified in the contract) for that change and the contract provides for the firm to give the consumer notice at the earliest opportunity thereafter (rather than in advance) and the consumer is free to dissolve the contract immediately; or
- if, in a contract of indeterminate duration, the contract provides for the firm to give the consumer reasonable notice in advance of making the change and the consumer is free to dissolve the contract.

13.5.5.3 *Reserving wide discretion*

One of the key concerns under the Regulations is where the company reserves to itself a wide discretion in how the rights under the terms will be exercised. If throughout

Data protection and privacy 327

their terms of use, reference is made to companies having the ability to exercise their sole discretion, this may be indicative of an imbalance between the rights and obligations of the parties, potentially to the detriment of the customer. If these rights could be subject to a reasonableness qualification or subject to certain express parameters, this would assist in the assessment of fairness.

13.5.5.4 *Technical jargon*

Regulation 7 of the Regulations requires that 'A seller or supplier shall ensure that any written term of a contract is expressed in plain, intelligible language'. For example, it is common to find reference to computer viruses, logic bombs, Trojan horses, worms, harmful components, corrupted data, and other malicious software or harmful data on website terms and conditions, terms that are unlikely to be understood by the average user.

13.5.5.5 *Assessing what data an organization is gathering*

It is a good idea to perform a data audit if you collect data so that you understand what data your organization is collecting and what consent you may need to gather in order to achieve compliance. For example:

Use of data	Do we have consent (Y/N)	Do we want to seek consent?	What should be changed to ensure we are meeting the demands of data protection legislation
Sale, rental, loan of data to third party with consent			
Reputable partners, suppliers, agencies as data processors			
The wider Group and joint venture companies			
Use the wider group may make of shared data			
Other users, may be accessible via search engine listings			
(Other use, etc., etc.)			

When conducting this exercise, it is a good practice for the organization in question to 'put themselves in the shoes' of a user and to consider the following questions as if they were the user:

* Would they understand why the data are being collected?
* Would they understand the implications of this?
* Would they be likely to object or complain?

328   *Commercial law*

13.5.5.6 *Making sure that individuals understand*

The basic legal requirement is to make sure that individuals know who is collecting the data, what they intend to do with that information, and who it may be disclosed to or shared with. The ICO suggests in its Privacy Notices Code of Practice[175] that organizations can go beyond the basic requirements of fair processing and tell individuals:

- If you intend to pass information on, the names of those organizations, and details as to how those organizations may use that information;
- How long your organization or the other organization intends to keep the information;
- Whether replies to questions are mandatory or voluntary;
- If there are any consequences of not providing the information (e.g. missing out on a benefit, discount or offer);
- Whether the information will be transferred overseas;
- Details of any security measures that your organization has in place to keep personal data secure;
- Individuals rights of access or rectification of their data and how they can exercise those rights.

13.5.5.7 *Data utilization and monetization*

Data collected via social media sites is a rich resource for businesses and the site providers themselves; the data gathered has the potential to enable new ways for companies to interact with consumers and increase brand exposure. The development of new technologies such as Facebook Beacon, face recognition and analytics also offer social media sites innovative ways to monetise the rich consumer data collected by the sites, as well as providing an enhanced customer experience through augmented reality and geolocation marketing technologies. However, as with any new product, legal and reputational implications for a company's brand should be considered carefully before crossing the Rubicon and making use of such technologies.

13.5.5.7.1 SELLING A MARKETING LIST

13.5.5.7.1.1 *The requirement to act fairly and lawfully* Organizations must act fairly and lawfully when selling a marketing list. If an organization obtained details from individuals with the intention of selling them on, it must have made it clear that their details would be passed on to third parties for marketing purposes and obtained their consent for this.

13.5.5.7.1.2 *Ways in which marketing lists can be utilized* Marketing lists can be utilized in two main ways – they can be sold or they can be licensed:

- In the case of an outright sale of a database as an asset in its own right, the transfer of personal data from one data controller to another will amount to

---

175 ICO Privacy Notices Code of Practice, December 2010.

Data protection and privacy 329

processing under the DPA 1998 and the buyer will become a data controller in respect of the database.

- Where the database is licensed, the process of making the database available for access by the licensee also involves data being transferred to the licensee, who will become a data controller in respect of that transferred data. A transaction may therefore grind to a halt if either the seller/licensor of the database or the buyer/licensee cannot deal with it without breaching the DPA 1998.

13.5.5.7.1.3 *Informing users about their use of data*   Organizations must act fairly and lawfully when processing personal data, which includes the sale of a marketing list. One aspect of this is that data may only be sold to or licensed for use by a third party where this is consistent with what data subjects were told at the time their data were collected (or which was notified to them subsequently). Another aspect is that the data controller must comply with at least one of the 'fair processing conditions' in the DPA 1998. Only two of these will be relevant in the present case, namely:

- that data subjects have consented; or
- the processing is in the company's 'legitimate interests' and does not prejudice the rights and freedoms of the data subjects (this is a balancing exercise and where the company's and individuals' interests conflict, the interests of data subjects will prevail).

Any buyer of a database will presumably want to use it to send marketing material. Whether they will be able to do so will depend on how the data were collected and what data subjects were told at the time (or subsequently). The general rule is that unsolicited marketing can only be sent to individuals where they have consented. The rules about consent depend on the means of communication. Different rules apply to post, SMS, telephone, etc., and are discussed above in relation to PECR. Organizations selling lists should note that in any sale of a licence agreement, a buyer would require that Endless LLP give a warranty that all necessary consents have been obtained to use the marketing list for the purposes of the acquisition of the license and should consider if they are able to give this assurance and the commercial implications of doing so.

13.5.5.7.1.4 *Case study: Facebook's changes to their privacy policy*   A change to the Facebook Statement of Rights and Responsibilities and their Data Use Policy in August 2013 serves as a useful example of how changes to policies can change the uses which social media sites can make of user data. The changes related to the use of the mobile version of the site and articulate what the social network was *already doing*, in a clearer fashion. One key change in relation to the sharing of data with third parties was as follows (the additions are set in bold and the deletions are struck though for the readers ease of reference):

We only provide data to our advertising partners or customers after we have removed your name or any other personally identifying information from it, or have combined it with other people's data in a way that it no longer personally identifies ~~associated with~~ you.

330 *Commercial law*

This change suggests that data provided to advertisers about users may be stripped of personal identity, but that can none the less be *associated* with that user in a *persistent* manner. At the time of the change, Facebook also allowed advertisers *associate* data they already have about users with data from Facebook:

> We also allow advertisers to reach people on Facebook using the information they already have about you (such as email addresses or whether you have visited their websites previously).

Furthermore, Facebook expanded its claims for automating the tagging of profile pictures based on other data sources:

> We are able to suggest that your friend tag you in a picture by scanning and comparing your friend's pictures to information we've put together from your profile pictures and the other photos in which you've been tagged.

Facebook also made more wide-ranging changes to their policy by adding the following wording to the end of the 'uses of your data' section, which reads that data may be used:

> So we can show you content that you may find interesting, we may use all of the information we receive about you to serve ads that are more relevant to you. For example, this includes:
> – things we infer from your use of Facebook FB −1.05%.

13.5.5.8 *Aggregate data*

Aggregating data that is non-identifiable is outside the scope of the DPA 1998. If the data is aggregated and anonymized, it will no longer be personal data and as such consent to use such data will not need to be sought. However, it is good practice to let individuals know how their data may be used (e.g. for statistical purposes).

Depending on the exact circumstances, however, there could be a residual risk of identification and it is often difficult to create a truly anonymous dataset if underlying information is retained. The recent Article 29 Working Party Opinion recommended regular risk assessments in the light of this residual risk.[176] Organizations should also consider the issues presented by Big Data, discussed elsewhere in this chapter.

13.5.5.9 *Use of 'Like' buttons, 'plug-ins' and 'analytics' by social media sites*

Sites such as Facebook make use of 'Like buttons', which allow users to like posts, e.g. made by their friends, groups they have joined or for posts made on their wider network. However, in 2011 the German data protection authority in Schleswig-Holstein ordered all institutions in the state to shut down their Facebook fan pages and remove plug-ins such as the 'Like' button from their websites.

---

176 Opinion 05/2014 on Anonymisation Techniques, 0829/14/EN WP216, adopted on 10 April 2014 [http://www.cnpd.public.lu/fr/publications/groupe-art29/wp216_en.pdf].

The Unabhängige Landeszentrum für Datenschutz (ULD, or Independent Centre for Privacy Protection in English) said in a statement in August 2011 that Facebook carried out an excessive amount of monitoring on its users without letting them know in reasonable detail how much they were being profiled.[177] It said much of this monitoring, done in the name of web analytics and used to target advertising, they did not consider to be compliant with German state and federal law. The authority ordered that all private and public institutions remove their Facebook fan pages and plug-ins or face formal complaints, prohibition orders and fines. It also recommended that private citizens should not set up Facebook accounts and avoid clicking on 'Like' buttons. The statement issued via their website stated:

'ULD has pointed out informally for some time that many Facebook offerings are in conflict with the law,' ULD commissioner Thilo Weichert said. 'This unfortunately has not prevented website owners from using the respective services and the more so as they are easy to install and free of charge. Web analytics is among those services and especially informative for advertising purposes. It is paid with the data of the users.'

The statement went on to sate that:

'ULD expects from website owners in Schleswig-Holstein to immediately stop the passing on of user data to Facebook in the USA by deactivating the respective services,' the organization wrote. 'If this does not take place by the end of September 2011, ULD will take further steps.'

The ULD said those further steps could include formal complaints for public entities, and a prohibition order and penalty fine for private entities.

'Whoever visits Facebook.com or uses a plug-in must expect that he or she will be tracked by the company for two years,' the authority explained. 'Facebook builds a . . . personalised profile. Such a profiling infringes German and European data-protection law.'

The ULD also complained that user information regarding privacy, as worded in Facebook's terms and conditions, did 'not nearly meet the legal requirements relevant for compliance of legal notice, privacy consent and general terms of use'.

The matter has not however been confined to the state of Schleswig-Holstein. Hamburg also warned the social network in 2011 that its facial recognition feature was in breach of data-protection laws. The UK Information Commissioner's Office has also expressed worries over the privacy implications of that feature.

13.5.5.9.1 LIKE-GATING

Apps like ShortStack, Heyo, TabSite and many more, make use of like-gating (also known as "fan-gating") features. It works by showing different content to fans and

---

177 ULD to website owners: 'Deactivate Facebook web analytics' [https://www.datenschutzzentrum.de/presse/20110819-facebook-en.htm].

332 *Commercial law*

non-fans. On 7 August 2014 Facebook made updates to their API and SDKs, and significantly announced the following:

> You must not incentivize people to use social plugins or to like a Page. This includes offering rewards, or gating apps or app content based on whether or not a person has liked a Page. It remains acceptable to incentivize people to login to your app, checkin at a place or enter a promotion on your app's Page (https:// developers.facebook.com/blog/post/2014/08/07/Graph-API-v2.1/).

Apps already using this functionality will continue to like-gate until November 5 2014. After that, the like-gating functionality of the app will stop working. Like-gating functionality will not work for any new apps created going forward.

Facebook stated that the change was made:

> To ensure quality connections and help businesses reach the people who matter to them, we want people to like Pages because they want to connect and hear from the business, not because of artificial incentives. We believe this update will benefit people and advertisers alike (https://developers.facebook.com/blog/ post/2014/08/07/Graph-API-v2.1/).

Ultimately, Facebook suggest that his will improve the experience for both users (they will see content they actually want to see) and advertisers (targeting by interests is more effective). For an in-depth discussion of the application of advertising law in social media see Chapter 14.

13.5.5.10 *Facebook Beacon*

13.5.5.10.1 OPERATION OF BEACON

Beacon was launched on 6 November 2007 with 44 partner websites. The controversial service, which became the target of a class action lawsuit, was shut down in September 2009.

Beacon was a part of Facebook's advertisement system that sent data from external websites to Facebook, for the purpose of allowing targeted advertisements and allowing users to share their activities with their friends. Some user activities on partner sites were published to a user's News Feed; the program would automatically report the activity and the user's personally identifiable information to Facebook – regardless of whether the user was a Facebook member. If the user was a Facebook member, Facebook would publish the activity on his member profile and broadcast it to everyone in his 'friends' network. To prevent Facebook from posting a particular trigger activity, a member had to affirmatively opt out by clicking an icon in a pop-up window that appeared for about ten seconds after performing the activity.

As a result of the way in which data was being captured and subsequently used and disseminated, a number of privacy concerns were raised over the legality of the operation, as large amounts of information Facebook members allegedly did not intend to share were disseminated by Facebook

Data protection and privacy 333

On 20 November 2007, civic action group MoveOn.org created a Facebook group and online petition demanding that Facebook not publish their activity from other websites without explicit permission from the user to do so. In fewer than ten days, this group gained 50,000 members.

13.5.5.10.2 AMENDMENTS TO FACEBOOK'S PRIVACY POLICY

Facebook amended its privacy statement on 6 December 2007 to include information in relation to Facebook Beacon, which read as follows:

> Facebook Beacon is a means of sharing actions you have taken on third party [web] sites, such as when you make a purchase or post a review, with your friends on Facebook. In order to provide you as a Facebook user with clear disclosure of the activity information being collected on third party sites and potentially shared with your friends on Facebook, we collect certain information from that [web]site and present it to you after you have completed an action on that [web]site. You have the choice to have Facebook discard that information, or to share it with your friends.

Interestingly, the policy went on to state that Facebook Beacon had the ability to track the activity of Facebook users who were not logged in, and even those who did not have a Facebook account:

> Like many other websites that interact with third party [web]sites, we may receive some information even if you are logged out from Facebook, or that pertains to non-Facebook users, from those [web]sites in conjunction with the technical operation of the system. In cases where Facebook receives information on users that are not logged in, or on non-Facebook users we do not attempt to associate it with individual Facebook accounts and will discard it.

13.5.5.10.3 LANE V FACEBOOK, INC.

Matters came to a head as a result of the class action law suit of *Lane v Facebook, Inc.*[178] In August 2008, 19 individuals brought a putative class action lawsuit in the US District Court for the Northern District of California against Facebook and the companies that had participated in Beacon, alleging violations of various federal and state privacy laws. The putative class comprised only those individuals whose personal information had been obtained and disclosed by Beacon during the approximately one-month period in which the program's default setting was 'opt out' rather than 'opt in'. The complaint sought damages and various forms of equitable relief, including an injunction barring the defendants from continuing the program.

The named claimants reached a settlement agreement with the defendants before class certification. Although Facebook promised to discontinue the 'Beacon' program itself, the claimants' legal team conceded at the fairness hearing in the District Court that nothing in the settlement would preclude Facebook from reinstituting the same program with a new name.

---

178 *Megan Marek v Sean Lane*, individually and on behalf of all others similarly situated, *et al.*: on petition for writ of *certiorari* to the United States Court of Appeals for the Ninth Circuit 571 US ___ (2013).

334   *Commercial law*

While Facebook agreed to pay US$9.5 million, the parties allocated that fund in an unusual way. The claimants' legal team was awarded nearly a quarter of the fund in fees and costs, while the named claimants received modest incentive payments. The unnamed class members, by contrast, received no damages from the remaining US$6.5 million. Instead, the parties earmarked that sum for a '*cy pres*' remedy – an 'as near as' form of relief – because distributing the US$6.5 million among the large number of class members would result in too small an award per person to bother. The *cy pres* remedy agreed to by the parties entailed the establishment of a new charitable foundation that would help fund organizations dedicated to educating the public about online privacy. A Facebook representative would be one of the three members of the new foundation's board.

The parties agreed to expand the settlement class barred from future litigation to include not just those individuals injured by Beacon during the brief period in which it was an opt-out program – the class proposed in the original complaint – but also those injured after Facebook had changed the program's default setting to opt in. Facebook thus insulated itself from all class claims arising from the Beacon episode by paying the claimants' legal team and the named claimants some US$3 million and spending US$6.5 million to set up a foundation in which it would play a major role. The District Court approved the settlement as 'fair, reasonable, and adequate'.[179]

Megan Marek was one of four unnamed class members who objected to the settlement. Her challenge focused on a number of disconcerting features of the new foundation: the facts that a senior Facebook employee would serve on its board, that the board would enjoy nearly unfettered discretion in selecting fund recipients, and that the foundation – as a new entity – necessarily lacked a proven track record of promoting the objectives behind the lawsuit. She also criticised the overall settlement amount as too low. The District Court rebuffed these objections, as did a divided panel of the Ninth Circuit on appeal.[180] A petition for rehearing *en banc* was denied, over the dissent of six judges.[181]

13.5.5.10.4 IMPORTANCE OF SYSTEMS TO RECORD WHEN AN INDIVIDUAL HAS OPTED OUT OF TARGETED ADVERTISING

On 29 November 2007, Stefan Berteau, a security researcher for Computer Associates, published a note on his tests of the Beacon system, and found that data was still being collected and sent to Facebook despite users' opt-outs and not being logged into Facebook at the time. This revelation was in direct contradiction to the statements made by Chamath Palihapitiya, Facebook's vice-president of marketing and operations, in an interview with *The New York Times* published the same day:

> Q. If I buy tickets on Fandango, and decline to publish the purchase to my friends on Facebook, does Facebook still receive the information about my purchase?

---

179   Fed Rule Civ Proc 23(e)(2); see *Lane v Facebook, Inc.*, Civ No C 08-3845, 2010 WL 9013059 (ND Cal, Mar 17, 2010).
180   *Lane v Facebook, Inc*, 696 F 3d 811 (2012).
181   *Lane v Facebook, Inc*, 709 F 3d 791 (2013).

A. Absolutely not. One of the things we are still trying to do is dispel a lot of misinformation that is being propagated unnecessarily.[182]

On 30 November 2007, Louise Story of *The New York Times* blogged that not only had she received the impression that Beacon would be an explicit opt-in program, but that Coca-Cola had also had a similar impression, and as a result, had chosen to withdraw their participation in Beacon.[183]

On 5 December 2007, Facebook announced that it would allow people to opt out of Beacon.[184] Founder Mark Zuckerberg apologized for the controversy:

> This has been the philosophy behind our recent changes. Last week we changed Beacon to be an opt-in system, and today we're releasing a privacy control to turn off Beacon completely. You can find it here. If you select that you don't want to share some Beacon actions or if you turn off Beacon, then Facebook won't store those actions even when partners send them to Facebook.[185]

On 12 August 2008, a class action lawsuit was filed against Facebook, Blockbuster Inc., Overstock.com, Fandango, Hotwire.com, GameFly, Zappos.com, and any additional 'John Doe' corporations that activated Facebook Beacon when they released their common member's personal information to their Facebook user friends without their consent through the Facebook Beacon program. The lawsuit alleges the release of the information was a violation of the Video Privacy Protection Act 1988, Electronic Communication Privacy Act 1986, Computer Fraud and Abuse Act 1986, California Consumer Legal Remedies Act 1750, and the California Computer Crime Law.

On 21 September 2009, Facebook announced that it would shut down the service. On 23 October 2009, a class action notice was sent to Facebook users who may have used Beacon. The proposed settlement would require Facebook to pay US$9.5 million into a settlement fund. The named claimants (approximately 20) would be awarded a total of US$41,000, and the claimants' lawyers would receive millions from the settlement fund.

13.6 Guidance for social networking providers

13.6.1 *General recommendations*

Based on the DPA 1998, the ICO's recommendations include the following steps:

- Organizations operating social networking sites should build sites so that individuals can set privacy settings to restrict who will have access to information they post on a site.
- Information solicited from individuals to register with or use the networking service should not be more than is necessary to operate the site (e.g. should not be overly intrusive or facilitate ID theft).

182 Brad Stone (2007) 'Facebook executive discusses Beacon Brouhaha', *Bits (blog)* (*New York Times*, 29 November).
183 Louise Story (2007) 'Coke is holding off on sipping Facebook's Beacon', *Bits (blog)* (*New York Times*, 30 November).
184 Mark Zuckerberg (2007) 'Thoughts on Beacon', Facebook Blog (5 December).
185 Ibid.

336 *Commercial law*

- Individuals should receive a clear privacy notice explaining how their details will be used (in particular, any disclosures of information to third parties using the site or otherwise).
- Individuals should agree to site usage terms and conditions, including undertaking to obtain all necessary consents to the posting of third party information to the site and agreeing to indemnify the website operator in respect of any third party claims arising from breach of that undertaking. Individuals should also agree to keep their passwords secure.
- The website operator should provide a point of contact to discuss any issues arising from use of the site and enable individuals to have access to information that relates to them and amend or delete personal information relating to them as they think appropriate.

13.6.2 *List of recommendations*

13.6.2.1 *Privacy policy/data use policy*

Issue	Conclusion/best practice recommendation
Privacy and data use policy Complexity and accessibility of user controls	• Simpler explanations of its privacy policies • Easier accessibility and prominence of these policies during registration and subsequently • An enhanced ability for users to make their own informed choices based on the available information The relative size of the links to the privacy policy and site statement of rights and responsibilities on the second page of the sign-up process must be aligned with the other information presented on that page.

13.6.2.2 *Advertising*

Issue	Conclusion/best practice recommendation
Advertising Use of user data	There are limits to the extent to which user-generated personal data can be used for targeted advertising. Sites must be transparent with users as to how they are targeted by advertisers. Consider whether data collected via social plug-ins for the purpose of targeted advertising is being used by the social networking site. Consider moving user options to exercise control over social ads to the privacy settings from the account settings to improve accessibility. It should also improve user knowledge of the ability to block or control ads that users do not wish to see again. If considering providing individuals' profile pictures and names to third parties for advertising purposes, users would have to provide their consent. Do not retain ad-click data indefinitely. Draft appropriate polices and obtain necessary consents when conducting targeted advertising utilizing sensitive data.

(continued)

Data protection and privacy 337

If the availability and use of features on site that allow users to filter and block certain types of ads does not appear well known to users, take steps to better educate users about the options which they present to control ad content.

13.6.2.3 _Access requests_

Issue	_Conclusion/best practice recommendation_
Access requests	If identifiable personal data is held in relation to a user or non-user, it must be provided in response to an access request within 40 days, in the absence of a statutory exemption.

13.6.2.4 _Retention_

Issue	_Conclusion/best practice recommendation_
Retention of data	The information provided to users in relation to what happens to deleted or removed content, such as friend requests, pokes, removed groups and tags, and deleted posts and messages should be improved if not already meeting the standards explored in this chapter.
	Users should be provided with an ability to delete friend requests, pokes, tags, posts, and messages and be able to insofar as is reasonably possible delete on a per item basis.
	Users must be provided with a means to exercise more control over their addition to groups.
	Personal data collected must be deleted when the purpose for which it was collected had ceased.
	Provide sufficient information in the Data Use Policy to educate users that login activity from different browsers across different machines and devices is recorded.
	Data held in relation to inactive or de-activated accounts must be subject to a retention policy.

13.6.2.5 _Cookies/social plug-ins_

Issue	_Conclusion/best practice recommendation_
Cookies/social plug-ins	It is not appropriate for sites to hold data collected from social plug-ins other than for a very short period and for very limited purposes.
	Obtain appropriate consents for the use of cookies.

338 *Commercial law*

13.6.2.6 *Third party apps*

Issue	Conclusion/best practice recommendation
Third party apps	The complexity for a user to fully understand in a meaningful way what it means to grant permission to an application to access their information must be addressed. Users must be sufficiently empowered via appropriate information and tools to make a fully informed decision when granting access to their information to third party applications.
	It must be made easier for users to understand that their activation and use of an app will be visible to their friends as a default setting.
	The privacy policy link to the third party app should be given prominence within the application permissions screen and users should be advised to read it before they add an app. This should be supplemented with a means for a member to report a concern in this regard via the permissions screen.
	As the link to the privacy policy of the app developer is the critical foundation for an informed consent, sites should deploy a tool that will check whether privacy policy links are live.
	Ensure that it is not possible for an application to access personal data over and above that to which an individual gives their consent or enabled by the relevant settings.
	Verify that when a friend of a user installing an app had chosen to restrict what such apps can access about them that this cannot be overridden by the app. It should be made easier for users to make informed choices about what apps installed by friends can access personal data about them. The easiest way at present to manage this is to turn off all apps via a user's privacy settings but this also prevents the user from using apps themselves.
	If authorization tokens granted to an application can be transferred between applications to potentially allow a second application to access information which the user had not granted by way of the token granted to the first application, then sites should consider advising application developers of their own responsibility to take appropriate steps to ensure the security of the authorization tokens provided by it. Sites should also consider how they can take appropriate security measures.
	Reliance on developer adherence to best practice is not always sufficient to ensure security of user data. Proactive monitoring and actions against apps that breach platform policies may be useful. However, this is not necessarily sufficient to assure users of the security of their data once they have third party apps enabled. Sites should take additional steps to prevent applications from accessing user information other than where the user has granted an appropriate permission.

Data protection and privacy 339

13.6.2.7 Disclosures to third parties

Issue	Conclusion/best practice recommendation
Disclosures to third parties	The current Single Point of Contact arrangements with law enforcement authorities when making requests for user data should be further strengthened by a requirement for all such requests to be signed-off or validated by a designated officer of a senior rank and for this to be recordable in the request. Standard forms should be used requiring all requesting entities to fully complete the section as to why the requested user data is sought so as to ensure that the site when responding can form a good faith belief that such provision of data is necessary as required by its privacy policy. Sites should also re-examine their privacy policy to ensure that the current information provided is consistent with their actual approach in this area.

13.6.2.8 Facial recognition/tag suggestion

Issue	Conclusion/best practice recommendation
Facial recognition/tag suggest	Sites should ensure the consent collected from users for this feature can be relied upon if the site makes use of such technology.
	Sites should offer the user the ability to delete the user's facial profile, e.g. allowing the user to disable 'tag suggestions'.

13.6.2.9 Data security

Issue	Conclusion/best practice recommendation
Security	Policies and procedures in operation should be formally documented.
	Sites should put in place an appropriate framework to ensure that all access to user data is on a need-to-know basis. Sites should expand their monitoring to ensure that there can be no employee abuse through inappropriate password resets of a user's account.
	Ensure that tools are in place for ensuring that staff are authorized only to access user data on a strictly necessary basis.
	Ensure adequate measures are in place for mitigating against the risk of large-scale harvesting of user data via 'screen scraping' while allowing the service to be effectively provided to legitimate users.

340   *Commercial law*

13.6.2.10 *Deletion of accounts*

Issue	Conclusion/best practice recommendation
Deletion of accounts	Ensure robust processes are in place to irrevocably delete user accounts and data upon request within 40 days of receipt of the request (not applicable to back-up data within this period).

13.6.2.11 *Friend finder*

Issue	Conclusion/best practice recommendation
Friend finder	Aside from the storage of synchronized data for its users, sites should makes no additional use of telephone numbers or other contact details uploaded as part of the synchronization feature unless the user chooses to supply email addresses for friend finder purposes.
Synchronization	Users should be made aware that where they choose to sync their contact information from a mobile device, those contact details are transmitted in plain text and are therefore not secure during transmission.
	Although this is not within the site's control, users should nevertheless be made aware when choosing this option.
	Disabling synchronization does not appear to delete any of the synchronized data. This requires an additional step via the 'remove data' button within the app. Sites should make it clear to users that disabling synching is not sufficient to remove any previously synced data.
	Ensure that passwords provided by users for the upload of contact lists for friend-finding purposes are held securely and destroyed.

13.6.2.12 *Tagging*

Issue	Conclusion/best practice recommendation
Tagging	Allow users to disable tagging of them once they fully understand the potential loss of control and prior notification that comes with it.

13.6.2.13 *Posting on other profiles*

Issue	Conclusion/best practice recommendation
Posting on other profiles	Sites should consider introducing increased functionality to allow a poster to be informed prior to posting how broad an audience will be able to view their post and that they be notified should the setting on that profile be subsequently changed to make a post that was initially restricted available to a broader audience. We recommend the sending of a notification to the poster if any such change, with an ability to immediately delete their post if they are unhappy.

Data protection and privacy 341

13.6.2.14 *Pseudonymous profiles*

Issue	Conclusion/best practice recommendation
Pseudonymous profiles	Ensure there is sufficient justification for child protection and other reasons for the policy of refusing pseudonymous access to its services.

13.6.2.15 *Abuse reporting*

Issue	Conclusion/best practice recommendation
Abuse reporting	Sites should have appropriate and accessible means in place for users and non-users to report abuse on the site. We are also satisfied from our examination of the User Operations area that the site is committed to ensuring it meets its obligations in this respect.

13.6.2.16 *Compliance management/governance*

Issue	Conclusion/best practice recommendation
Compliance management/governance	Compliance requirements for the conduct of direct marketing by electronic communications means should be fully understood by site staff members engaged in marketing.
	Sites should adopt documented procedures to ensure that data protection considerations are taken fully into account when direct marketing is undertaken either by or on behalf of the site and that appropriate training be given to staff and contractors.
	Sites should ensure that data protection law and by extension European data protection laws are fully addressed when sites roll out a new product to its users.

13.7 Practical guidance for individuals

In order to protect themselves, before posting information on social networking sites individuals should:

- Use privacy settings to limit access to information to a restricted group of close contacts.
- Be careful not to post information that can be used for ID theft or which might be compromising (e.g. if seen by an employer or potential employer).
- Obtain consent from other people before uploading pictures of them or posting other personal information about them on the site.
- Keep passwords secure.
- Read updates provided by sites in relation to privacy settings.
- Visit the site's privacy page or FAQs if you have concerns.

14 Trading and advertising standards

14.1 Introduction

Social networking sites are essentially self-promoting, in that users spread the word for the sites. In a world where instant communication prevails, tweets, re-tweets, and viral messages, not to mention video clips, projected via an array of digital platforms are the quickest means of spreading a marketing message. The more quickly social networking sites grow, the more quickly the content uploaded to them spreads. This viral quality is therefore an appealing way for businesses to market their products and services. Social media platforms are sophisticated enough to enable specific targeted advertisements (e.g. on Facebook) or to enable companies to provide adverts and links to existing offerings such as online shops on their website. A tweet, for example, could have the direct link embedded along with an advert highlighting the arrival of the company's latest products or services. It is for these reasons that many advertisers have chosen to conduct consumer promotions involving social media to generate attention to and participation in their promotions. Public image for celebrities, in particular, is a potentially lucrative source of revenue, allowing celebrities to engage directly with their fan base. Getting a re-tweet or a favourite from a celebrity is a modern-day equivalent of an autograph.

14.2 Application to social media context

While *paid-for* space online has been the subject of regulation for a considerable time, the rise in advertisers utilizing *non-paid-for* space online, such as social networking sites, has presented new legal considerations.

The Advertising Standards Authority's remit to deal with such complaints under the CAP Code extends to the areas of non-broadcast advertising, sales promotion, and direct marketing (i.e. 'marketing communications'), which in the digital sphere specifically includes:

- company or trading websites;
- paid-for online advertising, such as pop-ups, banners, and paid listings;
- non-paid-for online marketing communications, including social media user-generated content provided by private individuals, if adopted and incorporated within the company's own marketing communications on its website or in other non-paid-for online space under the organization's control.

Social networking websites generally have terms and conditions in place that govern the use of their sites in relation to the following areas which are subject to legal regulation in the UK:

- Disseminating unsolicited or unauthorized advertising or promotional materials.
- Mass unsolicited messages (i.e. 'spamming').
- Administration and advertisement of promotions on the site.
- Paid-for promotions.
- Multi-level marketing (pyramid schemes).
- Consumer sweepstakes.
- Contests.
- Giveaways.

This chapter will consider the ways in which advertisements and endorsements posted via social media sites have begun to become regulated in the UK.

14.3 Regulatory bodies

While there is no single, comprehensive piece of advertising legislation in the UK, there exists various provisions within statutory enactments that impact on the dissemination of information such as trade descriptions legislation and data protection laws. Advertising is also regulated through a series of voluntary codes and standards which businesses are expected to comply with, such as the British Code of Non-broadcast Advertising, Sales Promotion and Direct Marketing (otherwise known as the CAP Code). Anyone can bring a complaint, so long as it falls under its remit, including businesses who consider that their competitors' marketing communications are non-compliant. The CAP Code is enforced and administered by an independent body called the Advertising Standards Authority (ASA). The Code does not have the force of law but its importance must not be overlooked, as failure to comply can have adverse consequences for an organization.

In addition to UK regulation there exist a number of international standards that may apply to businesses conducting online marketing activity. One such set of guidance is published by the International Chamber of Commerce (ICC), which relates to marketing and advertising through electronic media. The guidelines build on the ICC International Code of Advertising Practice and the ICC International Code of Direct Marketing and are broad in nature, covering email as well as internet advertising and any other form of marketing conducted through electronic media.

It is important for businesses to note that in addition to broad principles and codes relating to advertising, there may be a number of industry specific bodies that regulate marketing campaigns within their specific sector; for example, the Financial Conduct Authority (formerly the Financial Services Authority prior to the changes introduced by the Financial Act 2012) has special rules in relation to promoting financial products and the use of social media.[1]

---

1 These rules are explored in depth in Chapter 15: FCA Regulated Bodies.

344   *Commercial law*

14.4 The Committee of Advertising Practice Code (CAP)

14.4.1 *Application of the Code*

In the UK, the ASA's UK Code of Non-broadcast Advertising, Sales Promotion and Direct Marketing (CAP Code) is a self-regulating non-binding code of conduct designed to encourage appropriate standards in advertising. Under the Code, the ASA has a remit to deal with complaints which fall within the CAP Code and extends to the areas of non-broadcast advertising, sales promotion and direct marketing (i.e. 'marketing communications').

While paid-for space online has been the subject of regulation for a considerable time, the rise in advertisers utilizing non-paid-for space, such as social networking sites, has presented new legal considerations. In December 2010, the Office of Fair Trading (OFT) released a publication stating its view that, 'online advertising and marketing practices that do not disclose they include paid-for promotions are deceptive under fair trading laws. This includes comments about services and products on website blogs and micro blogs such as Twitter'.

14.4.2 *Extension of the remit of the Code to the social media context*

In response to the issue, the CAP explored the issues presented by social media platforms in its paper 'Extending the digital remit of the CAP Code'[2] and extended the scope of its code in relation to advertisements in the digital sphere. The drafting of paras 2.3 to 2.7 is now framed so as to focus specifically upon material that can be properly accepted as constituting an advertisement or other marketing *communication*.[3] To determine if the communication is caught by the new rules, CAP will consider the following factors:

- **Is the communication designed to sell something?**

    o   CAP cautions that a communication may be designed to sell even if does not:
    o   Include a price.
    o   Overtly seek an immediate or short-term financial transaction.
    o   Refer to a transactional facility.

- **Does the 'additional assessment criteria' apply?**

    o   Even if the organization is not intending to sell something, if either of the following apply, the communication is likely to be caught by the rules.
    o   The communication has appeared in the same or very similar form as an advertisement in paid-for third party space.

---

2   Extending the Digital Remit of the CAP Code [http://www.asa.org.uk/Media-Centre/2010/~/media/Files/CAP/Codes/CAP%20Digital%20Remit%20Extension.ashx].
3   Extending the Digital Remit of the CAP Code at para [2.5].

○ The communication includes, or makes easily accessible, an 'invitation to purchase' (defined in section 2(1) Consumer Protection from Unfair Trading Regulations 2008).

14.4.3 *Exceptions*

14.4.3.1 *Editorials and press releases*

The existing exclusions set out in the CAP Code will continue to apply, such as editorials and press releases. Advertisers will however have to take particular care with heritage advertising (old advertisements).

14.4.4 *Heritage advertising*

Heritage advertising must not be part of a current promotional strategy and must be placed in an appropriate context. The ASA reserves the right to take action in respect of advertisements that it has recently adjudicated against. The ASA has not yet indicated what it considers to be 'recent'.

14.4.5 *Sanctions*

If the ASA finds that an advertisement breaches the Code, it may ask the advertiser to withdraw or change it. Although the ASA cannot levy fines, it may instead:

- Name and shame offenders, both on an ASA micro site.
- Remove paid-for search advertisements that link directly to the non-compliant marketing communication on the advertiser's own website or other non-paid-for space online under its control. The cooperation of search engines will be required to implement this.

14.5 Consumer Protection from Unfair Trading Regulations 2008

14.5.1 *Application in social media context*

The Consumer Protection from Unfair Trading Regulations 2008 (CPRs),[4] came into force on 26 May 2008, and implemented the Unfair Commercial Practices Directive (UCPD) into UK law.[5]

The UCPD was aimed at harmonising legislation across the European Community relating to business practices that were unfair to consumers. It was envisaged that creating legislative harmony between Member States would make it easier for traders based in one Member State to market and sell their products to consumers in other

---

4 Statutory Instrument 2008/1277.
5 Directive 2005/29/EC.6.

346   *Commercial law*

Member States and give consumers greater confidence to shop in the UK, and across borders, by providing a high common standard of consumer protection. As the internet becomes one of the main ways in which individuals shop for goods and social media becomes a key way to interact with brands, this objective can be seen as increasing in importance.

The CPRs apply to commercial practices before, during, and after a contract is made. The CPRs contain a general prohibition of unfair commercial practices and, in particular, contain prohibitions of misleading and aggressive commercial practices. Although the task of complying with the regulations may seem onerous, generally speaking, if consumers are treated fairly, then traders are likely to be complying with the CPRs. This means that fair dealing businesses should not have to make major changes to their practices. However, if a trader misleads, behaves aggressively, or otherwise acts unfairly towards consumers, then the trader is likely to be in breach of the CPRs and may face action by enforcement authorities.

Social media, however, can be a grey area when it comes to promotions and marketing activity as customer engagement with brands and advertising becomes increasingly interactive. For instance, bloggers or Twitter account holders may be paid to post about certain products without their followers or readers being aware that the poster is paid to do so by the brand. Heather Clayton, Senior Director of the OFT's consumer group, has stated that: 'the integrity of information published online is crucial so that people can make informed decisions on how to spend their money. We expect online advertising and marketing campaigns to be transparent so consumers can clearly tell when blogs, posts and micro blogs have been published in return for payment or payment in kind. We expect this to include promotions for products and services as well as editorial content.'

As such, the interrelationship between the CPRs and social media needs to be considered. The regulations of relevance are:

*   Using editorial content in the media to promote a product where a trader has paid for the promotion without making that clear in the content or by images or sounds clearly identifiable by the consumer (advertorial) (Schedule 1, para 11, Regulation 3(4)(b));
*   Falsely claiming or creating the impression that the trader is not acting for purposes relating to his trade, business, craft or profession, or falsely representing oneself as a consumer (Schedule 1, para 22, Regulation 3(4)(b));
*   Making persistent and unwanted solicitations by telephone, fax, e-mail or other remote media except in circumstances and to the extent justified to enforce a contractual obligation (which prohibits spam) (Schedule 1, para 26, Regulation 3(4)(b)); and
*   Misleading consumers by act or omission (for example, in relation to any endorsement of the product), where this is likely to have an impact on the consumer's decision-making about the brand, product, or service (Regulation 3(4) and Regulation 6).

It should be noted that the primary legal responsibility for complying with the law lies jointly with the brand owner and any agencies involved with the promotion.

14.5.2 *Enforcement*

Regulation 19 of the CPRs imposes a duty to ensure compliance on every 'enforcement authority', which includes the OFT. In fulfilling its duty, the enforcement authority must consider, whether, in the circumstances, it can use 'established means' to control unfair practices (Regulation 19(4)). For example, ASA has regimes to control misleading advertisements. It should be noted that, this does not give consumers or competitors a right of action for themselves.

14.5.3 *Legislative and Regulatory Reform Act 2006*

The CPRs are supplemented by section 22 of the Legislative and Regulatory Reform Act 2006, which among other things provides that in exercising their regulatory functions, enforcers must have regard to the statutory Regulators' Compliance Code. Section 5 of the Code is of particular importance to advertisers, as it relates to the provision of information and guidance to make it easier for businesses to understand and meet their regulatory obligations.

In terms of ensuring the proportionality of the course of action the enforcement authority adopts, section 8 requires regulators to give businesses the opportunity to try and remedy breaches before formal enforcement action is taken (unless immediate action is required). These enforcement powers are supported by Regulation 23 of the CPRs and section 29 of the Trade Description Act 1986, which introduces a criminal offence of intentionally obstructing, or making false statements to, an officer of an enforcement authority.

14.5.4 *Site terms and conditions*

In addition to the legal regulations governing advertisement, social media platform providers may also regulate the use of their sites by advertisers though contract law. Advertisers should therefore carefully review a platform provider's terms and conditions concerning commercial communications before it embarks upon an advertising campaign. By way of example, in April 2011 Facebook banned Ad.ly, a service that was paying celebrities to endorse products in their Facebook page updates, as it violated section 3.1 of the site's terms of service, which states: 'You will not send or otherwise post unauthorized commercial communications (such as spam) on Facebook.'

14.6 Indirect marketing and falsely holding out as a consumer

There are also risks presented by indirect marketing. These can be avoided, especially in the case of family businesses or sole traders by keeping business and private user activity separate. Essentially, commercial activity on Facebook should take place through a 'Business Page' on the site or run the risk of indirect marketing if the page is run through an individual's 'personal profile' (e.g. selling your status update to an advertiser). The latter activity is prohibited by Facebook's terms and conditions.

348   *Commercial law*

In March 2011, the OFT took action under the Consumer Protection Regulations against *Markco Media*,[6] a group-buying website, which, among other things, had an employee falsely represent himself on Facebook as a consumer. Marko Media were pursued for bait pricing after it heavily promoted a sale of Apple iPhone 4s when it only had eight handsets available. Following extensive promotion of the iPhone sale, including via a press release, a national newspaper interview, and marketing on Facebook and Twitter, almost 15,000 people signed-up and registered with Groupola for the sale. In addition to the main issue, the OFT was also concerned about misleading comments made by one Groupola employee on the company's Facebook page at the time of the sale. The employee represented himself as an ordinary consumer and made positive comments about the company. The company was therefore asked to sign an undertaking that they would not be making statements (including comments on social networking and blogging websites) without clearly and prominently disclosing when the author is an employee or has another relevant relationship with the company. There is no reason to believe that this approach will be departed from in future cases.

14.7 Paid promotions

If a Twitter user is paid by a brand owner or marketing practitioner specifically to use Twitter to promote a brand, product or service, then certain requirements have been imposed by the regulator. In the Snickers 'You're not yourself when you're hungry' campaign,[7] complaints were made to the ASA that the series of character celebrity tweets were misleading. Rio Ferdinand, for example, posted a series of tweets which included the statement, 'You're not you when you're hungry @snickersUk#hungry#spon' and a photograph of himself holding a Snickers chocolate bar. The ASA held that consumers would have understood the series of tweets to amount to marketing communications as the '#spon' tag was used in conjunction with the text '@snickersUk' (which mirror the guidelines adopted in the United States by the US Federal Trade Commission). The use of #ad has also been approved for these purposes. As tweets are limited to 140 characters, the use of the '#ad' or '#spon' hashtag allows maximum room for the message itself, but also makes clear to consumers that the message has been paid for.

The seriousness of ensuring compliance with the regulator's requirements was highlighted in June 2012 when the ASA upheld a complaint against the Nike #makeitcount campaign.[8] Nike sought to defend the claim on the grounds that the footballers as part of their sponsorship deal were required to take part in marketing activities and submit their own ideas for the content of the tweets. However, the ASA rejected this argument as the tweet's final content was agreed with the help of a member of the Nike marketing team.

---

6   www.oft.gov.uk/news-and-updates/press/2011/30-11.

7   http://www.asa.org.uk/ASAaction/Adjudications/2012/3/Mars-Chocolate-UK-Ltd/SHP_ADJ_185389. aspx.

8   http://www.asa.org.uk/ASAaction/Adjudications/2012/6/Nike-%28UK%29-Ltd/SHP_ADJ_183247. aspx.

Similarly, the ASA received a complaint about a tweet by Gemma Collins, on behalf of Toni and Guy,[9] which made reference to her satisfaction with their service and offered consumers a discount. As the tweets appeared to have been written on a spontaneous visit to the salon, and did not contain a clear identifier such as '#ad', the ASA considered that they were not obviously identifiable as marketing communications and the complaint was therefore upheld.

Another complaint was received about a further tweet from Wayne Rooney on behalf of Nike. This tweet stated 'The pitches change. The killer instinct doesn't. Own the turf, anywhere. @NikeFootball #myground pic.twitter.com/22jrPwdgC1'. The complainant again challenged whether the tweet was obviously identifiable as a marketing communication. The ASA considered that the content of the tweet followed by '@NikeFootball' and '#myground' meant the tweet was obviously identifiable as a marketing communication and therefore the complaint was not upheld (Nike (UK) Ltd, 4 September 2013).

Nike (UK) Ltd said the inclusion of the '@NikeFootball' official Nike Football Twitter address would have left consumers in no doubt that the tweet was a Nike marketing communication, because it directly and prominently referenced the Nike brand and its official Twitter address. They believed it was potentially clearer to consumers than if they had included an indicator such as '#ad' or '#spon'. They considered consumers would understand that a tweet by Wayne Rooney would only include the @NikeFootball address if the tweet was a marketing communication for Nike Football. They believed the wording of the tweet as a whole did not misleadingly imply that Wayne Rooney was tweeting as a consumer of Nike products rather than as a Nike-sponsored athlete, and therefore the commercial intent was clear.

Nike said that because the tweet was one of a series of five tweets by Wayne Rooney over four days, as part of their campaign for the FC247 football collection, all of which referenced the @NikeFootball address, consumers would have understood that they were part of a Nike Football ad campaign. They considered that was particularly the case because of the contrast between those tweets and Wayne Rooney's other tweets made around the same time. Notwithstanding that, Nike said they had designed the tweets in such a way that it was clear they were marketing communications whether viewed as a tweet directly from Wayne Rooney or viewed as a re-tweet, which was the case with the tweet viewed by the complainant. Nike considered the use of the @NikeFootball address meant the tweet was identifiable as a marketing communication in all contexts on Twitter. They investigated the ad under CAP Code (Edition 12) rules 2.1, 2.3, and 2.4 (Recognition of marketing communications), but did not find it in breach.

The ASA noted the tweet included the statement 'The pitches change. The killer instinct doesn't. Own the turf, anywhere', followed directly by the @NikeFootball Twitter address, the hashtag 'myground', and a link to a picture. The ASA considered the reference to Nike Football was prominent and clearly linked the tweet with the Nike brand. While it considered that not all Twitter users would be aware of Wayne Rooney's sponsorship deal with Nike or the particular Nike campaign the tweet promoted, in the particular context of a tweet by Wayne Rooney the wording of the

---

9 *Toni and Guy (Lakeside) Ltd*, 11 July 2012.

350   *Commercial law*

initial statement was such that in combination with '@NikeFootball' and '#myground', the overall effect was that the tweet was obviously identifiable as a Nike marketing communication.

14.8 United States of America

14.8.1 *The Federal Trade Commission*

The UK regulator is not the only body to adopt an approach towards the issue of the exploitation of social media platforms for commercial gain. The US Federal Trade Commission (FTC) practice guidance '.com Disclosures', which was originally released in 2000, was updated in 2013 to take into account the expanding use of Smartphones with small screens and the rise of social media marketing, and considers the effect that this may have upon the consumer and their understanding of what is and what is not an advertisement and when disclosures will be required. The new guidance applies to all devices and platforms that consumers may use to view the ad. The new FTC guidance now goes further than its UK counterpart in several respects. For instance, the new guidance states that if an advertisement without a disclosure would be deceptive or unfair, or would otherwise violate a Commission rule, and the disclosure cannot be made clearly and conspicuously on a device or platform, then that device or platform *should not be used*. Moreover, like the original guidance, the updated .com Disclosures calls on advertisers to avoid using hyperlinks for disclosures that involve product cost or certain health and safety issues. The guidelines also call for labelling hyperlinks as specifically as possible, and cautions advertisers to consider how their hyperlinks will function on various programs and devices.

The celebrity or endorser may wonder what this new guidance means in terms of their tweets and how they can comply with the law when dashing off 140 characters of text on a Smartphone to their American audience. In order to address this concern, the FTC offers worked examples in the Appendix to the guide, which are based around the example of a series of mock tweets by 'JuliStarz' for a weight-loss pill somewhat similar to a series of tweets last year by a famous reality TV star and her equally famous siblings.

14.8.2 *The Word of Mouth Marketing Association*

The Word of Mouth Marketing Association (WOMMA) updated its *Social Media Marketing Disclosure Guide*[10] to help marketers comply with the FTC's *Guides Concerning the Use of Endorsements and Testimonials in Advertising*.

WOMMA recommend that for marketers to avoid challenges to their social media marketing practices, they should review the WOMMA guide and consider implementing the best practices and adopting the sample disclosure language in the WOMMA guide, such as:

---

10 The Word of Mouth Marketing Association (WOMMA *Social Media Marketing Disclosure Guide*, August 2012 [http://uk.practicallaw.com/cs/Satellite?blobcol=urldata&blobheader=application%2Fpdf&blobkey=id&blobtable—ungoBlobs&blobwhere=1247495804205&ssbinary=true].

Trading and advertising standards 351

- Instituting a company-wide social media policy and ensuring their advocates, agencies, partners, networks, and vendors have similar policies in place.
- Educating advocates, agencies, partners, networks, and vendors on when and how disclosure is required under the FTC Guides and the marketer's social media policy.
- Monitoring marketing and advertising campaigns to ensure they comply with the FTC Guides.
- Using reasonable efforts to correct any failures to comply with the FTC Guides.
- Educating employees and monitoring their use of social media to ensure that when employees communicate about a marketer's products or services, they appropriately disclose their relationship to the company and do not misrepresent themselves as ordinary customers.

14.8.3 *Space-constrained tweets*

Take the following example:

> JuliStarz tweet: Shooting movie beach scene. Had to lose 30lbs in 6 wks. Thanks Fat-Away Pills for making it easy. Typical loss: 1lb/wk.

In the mock example, the FTC state that the above tweet would require two disclosures:

- that JuliStarz is a paid endorser for Fat-away; and
- the amount of weight that consumers who use Fat-away can generally expect to lose in the depicted circumstances, which is much less than the 30 pounds Juli says she lost in 6 weeks.

The FTC state that in such circumstances, these required disclosures can easily be incorporated into a space-constrained ad. In the example, Juli could have stated that she is a paid endorser by beginning with 'Ad:', which only takes up four characters. In order to understand the key differences, it is necessary to consider some decisions of the UK regulator that help to highlight the more rigorous approach which is to be adopted by the FTC.

14.8.4 *#spon*

While in the #MakeitCountcampaign[11] the use of '#spon' or '#ad' would have been considered sufficient to disclose *paid-for* content, the FTC suggest that consumers might not understand that '#spon' means that the message was sponsored by an advertiser. The test instead which should be applied is if a *significant proportion of reasonable viewers* would understand that the tweet was an advert. If not, then this amounts to a tweet that is deceptive.

---

11 http://www.asa.org.uk/ASAaction/Adjudications/2012/6/Nike-%28UK%29-Ltd/SHP_ADJ_183247. aspx.

352   *Commercial law*

> e.g. JuliStarz: Shooting movie beach scene. Had to lose 30lbs in 6 wks. Thanks Fat-Away Pills for making it easy. Typical loss: 1lb/wk bit.ly/f56 #spon

Moreover, putting #spon directly after the link might confuse consumers and make it less likely that they would understand that it is a disclosure.

14.8.5 *bit.ly*

Providing a link to a site where consumers can find the full details of the product and its disclaimers may also be insufficient. Consumers viewing 'bit.ly/f56', which links to the advertiser's official website for the product, might not realize the nature and relevance of the information that could be found by clicking on it. Moreover, if consumers can buy Fat-Away in brick and mortar stores, at third-party online retailers, or in any way other than by clicking on the link, consumers who do not click on the link would be misled.

> e.g. JuliStarz: Shooting movie beach scene. Had to lose 30lbs in 6 wks. Thanks Fat-Away Pills for making it easy. Typical loss: 1lb/wk bit.ly/f56/disclose[6]

Similarly, consumers viewing 'bit.ly/f56/disclose[6]', which leads to a third-party website with disclosures, would not necessarily understand what they will find at that website, or why they should click on that link.

14.8.6 *Series of related tweets*

> e.g. 6hrs: JuliStarz: Shooting movie beach scene. Had to lose 30lbs in 6 weeks. Thanks Fat-Away pills for making it easy.
> e.g. 4hrs: JuliStarz: I am a paid spokesperson for Fat-Away Pills. Typical weight loss 1lb/wk.

For a series of tweets that have to be 'pieced together' in order to tell the 'advertisement story', the FTC still considers that the stance for space-constrained ads should be taken. The FTC states that putting information in a subsequent message is problematic, because unrelated messages may arrive in the interim. By the time the disclosure arrives, consumers might no longer be reading these messages, or they simply might not realize that those disclosures pertain to the original message. However, the FTC has stated that the need to directly identify something as advertising in its text, could already be covered by the 'promoted' message seen next to sponsored tweets in some cases. However, the example does not say what happens if tweets follow in very quick succession and if in such circumstances the tweets in question will be judged on a case by case basis.

It would be interesting to see how the UK Rio Ferdinand 'You aren't yourself when you're hungry' campaign[12] would have been decided under the FTC guidelines. In this adjudication, Rio Ferdinand (along with Cher Lloyd, Katie Price, and

---

12 *Mars Chocolate UK Ltd*, 7 March 2012, Complaint Ref: A12-185389.

Amir Khan) posted a series of tweets which included the statement 'You're not you when you're hungry @snickersUk#hungry#spon' and a photograph of himself holding a Snickers chocolate bar. Ferdinand had also posted a series of seemingly unrelated posts about knitting and other uncharacteristic sorts of behaviour which were in fact related to the Snickers campaign, acting as a 'build up' to get followers' attention. While the ASA held that consumers would have understood the series of tweets to amount to marketing communications as the '#spon' tag was used in conjunction with the text '@snickersUK', one wonders if the matter would have been adjudicated differently if the UK regulator chooses to move towards a more rigorous approach similar to that of the FTC in the future (as it has been minded to do in the past and upon which its current model until recently mirrored), or what would have happened if an action had been brought by an American consumer. Such considerations in these circumstances may include if each tweet must be considered in turn, judging each as a discrete tweet on the same merits as the requirements highlighted in relation to *space-constrained tweets* (above) or if there would have to be a more encompassing approach, looking at the timing, frequency, and theme of the tweets in order to arrive at an adjudication. These matters, while they may not affect the overall outcome of the case, given the robust approach of the FTC in the examples, must surely however go to the heart of regulatory sanctions and financial penalties levied on offenders.

Furthermore, regulatory infractions are not the only issues for celebrities and advertisers to be alive to. Some of the most potent damage caused to Ferdinand, even though the ASA adjudicated in his favour, came from the damage he caused with his fan base. In many cases, this damage is in terms of current and future unquantifiable loss that the regulators could financially impose. By way of example in the Snickers case, several of Ferdinand's followers complained after his burst of tweets, with one user tweeting: 'Do you really need the money that badly?' and another adding 'I'm not on here to be advertised at.' Given the fine balancing act between fan interaction and commercial exploitation (e.g. revenue and goodwill), celebrities will have to not only comply with the legalities but also demonstrate to fans (existing and potential) that their opinions are valued and that their loyalty is not taken for granted.

14.9 Contractual obligation to promote the company even if the form of the message is not determined by the advertiser

Since some consumers have less experience with advertising hosted on social media sites, and advertising is often difficult to distinguish from genuine user-generated content, marketers should pay particular attention to ensuring their marketing communications are obviously recognizable as such. A useful example in this regard comes from Keith Chegwin's tweets regarding a sales promotion for Publishers Clearing House. The tweet Chegwin posted stated: 'Just a quickie: Log on to pchprizes.co.uk 4 Your chance 2 win £100k plus Win £2,500 a week 4 life. Have a go X'. A member of the public challenged whether the tweet was a marketing communication and should therefore be identified as such. The ASA noted that Keith Chegwin had not been required or invited to tweet on PCH's behalf but they considered that his contractual obligation to promote the company, and this promotion in particular, meant that the tweet constituted part of PCH's promotional activity

354   *Commercial law*

and was therefore advertising. They considered that as the Code required marketing 'must be obviously identifiable as such', an identifier such as '#ad' should have been included in the tweet and concluded in its absence that the tweet breached the Code.[13]

14.10 Links to paid subscriptions

The ASA Council has also been asked to consider various other questions regarding remit and social media.[14] A journalist tweeted about an article that she had written for *The Times* and provided a link to it. If one of her followers subsequently clicked on this link they were taken to an excerpt from the article and a pay wall, where the follower was required to take out a subscription to *The Times* in order to finish reading the article. The Council was asked to decide whether this constituted a marketing communication for the purposes of the Code. Although the Council recognized that both the journalist and the paper could benefit from an increase in the number of people subscribing to the paper, they also considered the fact that the journalist was under no contractual obligation to promote the paper and that the paper had no control over the content of the journalist's tweets. In light of this they decided that the tweet was not a marketing communication for the purposes of the Code and was therefore outside its remit. Further guidance on the use of '#ad' and '#spon' to identify content as a marketing communication can be found on the IAB and ISBA website.[15]

Practical tips

The IAB and ISBA[16] recommend that brand owners and marketing practitioners follow three steps when a payment has been made in order for someone to editorially promote a brand, product or service within social media:

1. Ensure that the author or publisher of the message discloses that payment has been made. This will ensure that it is clear to consumers that it is a marketing communication. See below examples.
2. Ensure that authors adhere to the appropriate terms and conditions of the social media platform or website that they are using in relation to promoting a product or service. This includes search engines likely to index the content.
3. Ensure that the content of the 'marketing communication' adheres to the principles of the CAP Code.

---

13 *Genting Alderney Ltd t/a Publishers Clearing House*, 9 January 2013.
14 Remit: Social Media [http://www.cap.org.uk/Advice-Training-on-the-rules/Advice-Online-Database/Remit-Social-Media.aspx].
15 http://www.iabuk.net/sites/default/files/IAB%20ISBA%20Guidelines%20on%20the%20Payment%20for%20Editorial%20Content%20-%20July%202012.pdf.
16 IAB – ISBA Guidelines on the Payment for Editorial Content to Promote Brands within Social Media, July 2012.

14.11 Clarity of adverts' content

One of the key issues in relation to adverts, especially those involving a promotion, prize or discount, is if the terms of that promotion are clear to members of the public and the importance of providing links to terms and conditions. In relation to social media, this issue is especially important, as the number of characters that can be posted is often limited (e.g. Twitter postings are limited to 140 characters). The difficulty of drafting such campaigns and the perils of tweets that are not carefully reviewed prior to posting was highlighted in *Pet Plan Limited*,[17] which involved a prize promotion on the @PetplanUK Twitter feed. The text stated 'To celebrate #petdentalcare month we are giving away 10 goodie bags filled full of dental treats. Follow and RT to win! #competition'. The complainant challenged whether the promotion breached the Code, because significant conditions, including the closing date, were not made clear contrary to CAP Code 8.17 and 8.28.

Pet Plan said there were no terms and conditions available for the promotion, and that this was an isolated incident and they were committed to being transparent with consumers. They said they had template terms and conditions for use in their promotions and, having received the complaint, they had reiterated internally the need to ensure they were properly implemented when running a prize promotion via social media. They submitted a copy of their template terms and conditions for different social media and said they were updating their website to include them. They also said a link to those terms and conditions would be added to any tweets that included prize draws or competitions.

The ASA upheld the complaint noting that there were no terms and conditions available; in their opinion, all applicable significant conditions for promotions should be communicated before or at the time of entry, and that consumers could enter, by re-tweeting the message, once they had seen the tweet. All applicable significant conditions, such as the closing date and how winners would be selected, should have been made clear before or in the tweet that included details of how to enter, which was also a significant condition. Because that was not the case, and because participants were not able to retain conditions or easily access them throughout the promotion, ASA concluded that the ad breached Rules 8.17 (Significant conditions for promotions) and 8.28 (Prize promotions).

14.12 Endorsements and testimonials by bloggers

14.12.1 *Blurring advertising and blogs – why it pays to know the Ad Rules*

If a company or PR agency uses a blogger to advertise their products, both parties to the arrangement need to be aware that if they fail to disclose a material connection between the blogger and company (e.g. free products or other perks to the blogger), both the blogger and company may become the subject of regulatory action and consumer backlash, who may feel the goodwill they vested in the blogger is diminished if it comes to light that a blog is a glorified advertisement facility for a third party.

---

17 ASA Adjudication on Pet Plan Ltd, *6 September 2012, Complaint Ref: A12-199639.*

356 *Commercial law*

There are no specific rules relating to such platforms. However, as a result of the *Handpicked Media* case,[18] the OFT issued a '*Q and A*' in response to issues put to them by advertisers.[19] In *Handpicked Media,*[20] a network of bloggers and niche websites across a variety of sectors operated by Handpicked Media caused the company to become the subject of enforcement action. The OFT took the clear view that paid-for blogging and promotion should be disclosed to consumers to ensure that they are not misled.

On 13 November 2013, ASA published on its website 'Blurring Advertising and Blogs – Why it pays to know the Ad Rules'.[21] The note reminded bloggers who are paid to write positive reviews or comments about a product or service that they must be up-front with their followers by making clear that it's advertising. Put simply, a blogger who is given money to promote a product or service has to ensure readers are aware the post is an advert. In order to address the issues highlighted in the *Handpicked Media* case, and the points raised by the new application of the CAP Code, in July 2012 the Internet Advertising Bureau in association with the Incorporated Society of British Advertisers issued Guidelines on the Payment for Editorial Content to Promote Brands within Social Media.[22] In the guidelines, they recommended that brand owners and marketing practitioners follow three steps:

- If a payment has been made (either in cash or free products), the author or publisher must disclose this.
- Authors must comply with the terms and conditions of the social media platforms they are using and the search engines likely to index the content.
- The 'marketing communication' must comply with the CAP Code.[23]

14.12.2 *Companies and PR agencies looking to enter into commercial relationships with bloggers*

The ASA stated in the note that all of this applies equally, if not more so, to those companies and PR agencies looking to enter into commercial relationships with bloggers. Under the Advertising Code, although the blogger would be named as part of any ASA investigation into misleading advertising, ultimately the advertiser is responsible for the material posted. By way of example, the ASA state that if a paid-for entry on a blog wasn't disclosed, it would investigate the advertiser and hold them accountable.[24] As well as holding an advertiser to account, if a blogger is unwilling to cooperate, then the ASA can consider a range of sanctions to achieve compliance.

---

18 Press releases 2010, 'OFT secures promotional blogging disclosures 134/10', 13 December 2010.

19 http://www.oft.gov.uk/OFTwork/consumer-enforcement/consumer-enforcement-completed/handpicked_media/q-and-a/.

20 Press releases 2010, 'OFT secures promotional blogging disclosures 134/10', 13 December 2010.

21 http://www.asa.org.uk/News-resources/Media-Centre/2013/Blurring-advertising-and-blogs.aspx.

22 http://www.iabuk.net/sites/default/files/IAB%20ISBA%20Guidelines%20on%20the%20Payment%20for%20Editorial%20Content%20-%20July%202012.pdf.

23 Ibid.

24 http://www.asa.org.uk/News-resources/Media-Centre/2013/Blurring-advertising-and-blogs.aspx.

The ASA stressed that it is perfectly legitimate for a blogger to accept payment in return for promoting something in their blog and that the rules do not prohibit PR companies sending free gifts or samples to bloggers in the hope of receiving a positive review. If, however, they are paid to say something positive, then it becomes an advertisement and they must disclose it.

> ### Practical guidance
>
> How can bloggers make it clear if their blog contains paid-for content? The following steps may help bloggers and PR agencies achieve compliance:
>
> 1. Signposting content as 'ad', 'advertorial' or 'sponsored content' is suggested as the easiest method to make it immediately clear to readers that the content is paid for or sponsored.
> 2. Seek free expert guidance on the rules in this area and how to stick to them by contracting the ASA's Copy Advice Team.[25]

14.12.3 *Commercial considerations and reputation management*

Bloggers can hold great sway and influence among their followers. It's important, therefore, that they treat their followers fairly. The fact is the reputation and trust that bloggers work so hard to foster among their followers can disappear very quickly. Misleading your followers may prove detrimental in terms of advertisement for your blog, especially if it becomes the subject of an ASA investigation.

14.12.4 *Approach taken in US by the Federal Trade Commission*

The FTC revised its guidance relating to the Use of Endorsements and Testimonials in Advertising in 2009.[26] The FTC have now adopted a general principle of liability for communications made through endorsements and testimonials which states that 'advertisers are subject to liability for false or unsubstantiated statements made through endorsements, or for failing to disclose material connections between themselves and their endorsers. Endorsers also may be liable for statements made in the course of their endorsements'.

So far as the guidance relates to social media, the FTC has indicated that:

• Endorsers, along with the sponsoring advertisers, are subject to liability for failing to make material disclosures relating to the endorsement relationship (e.g. gifts, employment, franchises, and/or other connections and circumstances).

---

25 http://www.cap.org.uk/Advice-Training-on-the-rules/Copy-Advice-Team.aspx.
26 Federal Trade Commission, 'Guide Concerning the Use of Endorsements and Testimonials in Advertising', 16 CFR Part 255.

358   *Commercial law*

- The commercial relationship itself may trigger the obligation to disclose endorsement arrangements.
- Advertisers need to take reasonable steps to ensure that material disclosures are made.
- Advertisers cannot rely on the remoteness of the social media endorsers or on the advertiser's lack of control over them to escape liability.
- Advertisers may be technically liable for a remote endorser's failure to disclose. However, liability will be judged on the quality of the advertiser's policies, practices, and policing efforts.

The FTC offer in the guidance the example of a tennis player who has attended 'Clinic X' for treatment on a sports injury, and 'touts the results of her surgery – mentioning the clinic by name – on a social networking site that allows her fans to read in real time what is happening in her life'.[27] The FTC suggest, given the nature of the medium in which her endorsement is disseminated, consumers might not realize that she is a paid endorser. Because that information might affect the weight consumers give to her endorsement, her relationship with the clinic should be disclosed.

In light of the FTC Guides:

- Companies who provide products to a blogger for purposes of a product review should not tell the blogger what to say in the review, or ask to review or retain editorial review rights over the content of the post prior to publication.
- Companies should monitor product reviews made by bloggers to ensure that the claims made are truthful and can be substantiated.

14.13 Summary chart

WHAT YOU CAN DO	*WHAT YOU CANNOT ASSUME*
Establish and distribute both internally and externally to outside media agencies working on your behalf a social media policy that requires endorsers, for example, to: • disclose any incentives they receive to promote your company's products or services; and • agree to include the wording required by ASA.	You should not assume that you are not responsible for the actions of media agencies working on your behalf. Make sure you have systems in place to provide guidance and training to bloggers and agents so that they disclose what is required by ASA and that their statements are truthful. Always remind them to stop and think what they are stating is fair or if it is in any way misleading.
Make sure that you disclose very clearly any material connections between your company and endorser: are they being paid, receiving a free product, or an employee of your company.	Even if the product has little value you still need to think if these provisions apply, consider when disclosing if you have an ongoing relationship with the adviser, and if as a result of that relationship consumers may still feel misled even if the items received are small.

(continued)

27 Ibid. at [Example 3].

WHAT YOU CAN DO	WHAT YOU CANNOT ASSUME
This will also apply to imposing upon you agencies who work on your behalf with such a requirement and could also be dealt with in your social media policy.	
Communicate with your bloggers on a regular basis and make sure that they understand that they cannot make false or misleading statement about products or services.	Don't assume that you can forget about compliance. It may be a good idea to refer bloggers to your social media policy each time you send them a new product so that each party understands its respective obligations and how the relationship will be monitored.
You may wish to ask a member of your in-house PR team to monitor key blogs to see if bloggers are complying with the requirements you have imposed on them. Again, such a right could be put into a social media policy.	
On Twitter, use hashtags such as #paid-ad, #paid or #ad to make required disclosures.	Do not adopt polices and then bury them away where users of the site cannot find them. This is unlikely to be clear to consumers and you may still be considered to have been misleading customers. Always have in mind what the expectation of the average site user is and work towards making the site accessible to that example user. You should not assume that users have a sophisticated knowledge or will go to significant lengths in order to seek out information. It should be reasonably prominent, e.g. in a banner at the bottom of a page.
For blogs and other social networks, post a link on your profile page directing people to a full statement detailing the nature of your relationship and the benefits each party receives under it. You could also require bloggers to put such statements in to their pages by making it a condition of your relationship with them or by detailing it in your social media policy.	

14.14 Advergames

The current CAP Code covers 'advergames' (video games used to promote a product or organization) in paid-for space. CAP has clarified that advergames appearing on an advertiser's own website or in other non-paid-for space online under its control will also be regulated from 1 March 2011. Some companies use advergames as part of their 'cover' (the background image that appears on their group page) on Facebook; these will therefore be caught by the CAP Code.

15 FCA regulated bodies

15.1 Introduction

The Financial Conduct Authority (FCA) is the regulator of the financial services industry in the UK. Its aim is to protect consumers, ensure the financial services industry remains stable, and promote healthy competition between financial services providers. The FCA has rule-making, investigative, and enforcement powers that they use to protect and regulate the financial services industry. Regulated firms need to be alive to the rules that govern the marketing of their services via social networking accounts (which may include YouTube, Facebook, Twitter, etc.).

The law in relation to advertising promotions is dealt with in Chapter 14; however, in relation to bodies regulated by the FCA, there are special rules in relation to financial promotions.

15.2 Financial promotions using new media

15.2.1 Background

The Financial Services Authority (FSA), the predecessor to the FCA, produced an update in July 2010 entitled *Financial Promotions Using New Media*,[1] following a review into the media channels that firms use to communicate financial promotions to customers. In particular, a shift towards the use of 'new media' was noted.

The note sets out guidance for firms' use of social media, referred to as 'new media'. This guidance essentially states that financial promotions rules apply whatever medium is used. According to the guide, new media channels include:

- Social networking websites (Twitter and Facebook)
- Forums
- Blogs
- iPhone applications

---

1 'Financial Promotions Using New Media', *Financial Promotions Industry Update*, No. 5, June 2010.

15.2.2 *What is a financial promotion?*

The term 'financial promotion' is not referred to in the Financial Services and Markets Act 2000 (FSMA 2000) other than in the heading and side note of section 21, but this expression is commonly used to describe the communication of an invitation or inducement to engage in investment activity as outlined in that section. In addition, the term 'financial promotion' is defined and used by the FCA in its handbook of rules and guidance (FCA Handbook). Reference in this note to the term 'communication' should be read as meaning 'financial promotion', unless the context indicates otherwise.

Section 21 FSMA 2000 contains the basic restriction on unauthorized persons (that is, persons not authorized in accordance with section 31 FSMA 2000) communicating financial promotions.[2]

15.2.3 *Relationship with the Financial Promotion Rules*

The guidance notes state that where the Financial Promotions Rules apply, they generally apply in a way that is 'media-neutral'. The rules focus on the content of the financial promotion rather than the medium used to communicate it. For this reason, the FSA stated that applying the rules to financial promotions made using new media no different to financial promotions made using any other medium. As such, the communication rules are contained in the following rules and apply to new media as much as they did to traditional media outlets:

15.2.3.1 *COBS 4: Communicating with clients, including financial promotions*

COBS 4.1	Application
COBS 4.2	Fair, clear and not misleading communications
COBS 4.3	Financial promotions to be identifiable as such
COBS 4.4	Compensation information
COBS 4.5	Communicating with retail clients
COBS 4.6	Past, simulated past and future performance
COBS 4.7	Direct offer financial promotions
COBS 4.8	Cold calls and other promotions that are not in writing
COBS 4.9	Financial promotions with an overseas element
COBS 4.10	Systems and controls and approving and communicating financial promotions
COBS 4.11	Record-keeping: financial promotion
COBS 4.12	Restrictions on the promotion of non-mainstream pooled investments
COBS 4.13	UCITS

---

2 A discussion of the specific law relating to financial promotions is beyond the scope of this volume. However, an excellent discussion of the regulatory landscape affecting financially regulated bodies in the UK can be found in J. Kirk, QC and J. Ross (2013) *Modern Financial Regulation*. London: Jordan Publishing.

362   *Commercial law*

15.2.3.2 *BCOBS 2: Communications with banking customers and financial promotions*

BCOBS 2.1	Purpose and application: Who and what?
BCOBS 2.2	The fair, clear and not misleading rule
BCOBS 2.3	Other general requirements for communications and financial promotions
BCOBS 2.4	Structured deposits, cash deposit ISAs and cash deposit CTFs

15.2.3.3 *ICOBS 2: General matters*

ICOBS 2.2	Communications to clients and financial promotions
ICOBS 2.3	Inducements
ICOBS 2.4	Record-keeping
ICOBS 2.5	Exclusion of liability and reliance on others

15.2.3.4 *MCOB3: Financial promotion of qualifying credit, home reversion plans and regulated sale and rent back agreements*

MCOB 3.1	Application: who?
MCOB 3.2	Application: what?
MCOB 3.3	Application: where?
MCOB 3.4	Purpose
MCOB 3.5	General
MCOB 3.6	Form and content of non-real time qualifying credit promotions
MCOB 3.7	Unsolicited real time financial promotions of qualifying credit, a home reversion plan or a regulated sale and rent back agreement
MCOB 3.8	Form and content of real time qualifying credit promotions
MCOB 3.8A	Form and content of financial promotions of home reversion plans
MCOB 3.8B	Form and content of financial promotions of regulated sale and rent back agreements
MCOB 3.9	Confirmation of compliance: financial promotions of qualifying credit, home reversion plans or regulated sale and rent back agreements
MCOB 3.10	Records: non-real time financial promotions of qualifying credit, a home reversion plan or a regulated sale and rent back agreement
MCOB 3.11	Communication and approval of qualifying credit promotions for an overseas person or an unauthorized person
MCOB 3.12	The internet and other electronic media
MCOB 3 Annex 1	Examples of qualifying credit promotions

15.3 The FSA's 2010 review

15.3.1 *FSA's research of social media sites*

During February 2010, the FSA conducted a review of approximately 30 Twitter and Facebook pages using different search terms within the financial sector. They looked at the pages containing a wide range of promotions, including those from small and larger firms that offered a wide range of products, such as financial advice and investments.

The FSA also visited a variety of forums to gain an insight into the posts and comments made in relation to the posts that were being made.

The FSA also examined discussions on insurance, investments, investment advice, and mortgages available on the forums – of which 20 were randomly selected for review.

15.3.2 *Findings*

The FSA identified good and poor practice during the review among firms who had adopted new media as part of their marketing strategies to communicate financial promotions. It was noted that some promotions lacked risk warnings. Other promotions, while not very specific about products or services, nevertheless went beyond the definition of 'image advertising' (see below). Firms may not have considered these factors to meet the definition of a financial promotion and had not therefore applied the relevant communication rules.

15.4 Non-promotional communications

It should be noted that the FSA's guidance specifically states that their rules cover all communications by regulated firms to clients, not just promotional ones. The rules for non-promotional communications[3] are fairly high-level – the main rule is that communications must be:

- fair
- clear; and
- not misleading.

15.5 Image advertisements

Firms cannot assume that because a communication is made using new media, it is an image advertisement and exempt from the financial promotion rules. An image advertisement only consists of the following:

- The name of the firm;
- A logo or other image associated with the firm;
- A contact point; and
- A reference to the types of regulated activities provided by the firm or to its fees or commissions.

When a communication goes beyond the definition of image advertising in any way, it will need to comply with all of the relevant financial promotions rules. The

---

3 The communication rules including the financial promotion rules are contained in COBS 4, BCOBS 2, ICOBS 2, and MCOB 3.

364   *Commercial law*

treatment of image advertising varies depending on which sourcebook applies. The following chart is designed to assist in determining which sourcebook applies.

Investment products	Image advertising is exempt from most of the detailed financial promotions rules and guidance in COBS 4, but it will still need to comply with the high-level 'fair, clear and not misleading' rule. Image advertising is defined in the Handbook glossary.
Mortgage products	MCOB 3 contains a specific exemption for 'image advertising' or 'brand advertising' set out in MCOB 3.2.5R.
Insurance products	There is no equivalent provision relating to 'image' or 'brand' advertising in ICOBS 2.2 and firms cannot rely on exemptions.

Regulated bodies must ensure that any financial promotion is compliant with all the relevant rules and the systems and controls are in place to deliver this. Firms should be particularly aware of the image rules when using mediums such as YouTube, Facebook or Twitter to upload promotional advertising.

15.6 Stand-alone compliance

It is important to note in relation to social networking promotions that the 2010 guidance specifically states that all promotions must comply with 'stand-alone compliance'.

The term 'stand-alone compliance' means to describe our expectation that every financial promotion must comply with all of the relevant financial promotions rules. It is not acceptable, for example, for firms to omit important risk information just because they intend to give it later in the sales process. As noted in Chapter 14: Trading and Advertising Standards, in *Mars Chocolate UK Limited*,[4] much of the debate with the ASA centred on the fact that there was a series of five tweets, some of which contained marketing communications and some of which did not (cumulatively they were all marketing promotions). The rules in relation to financially regulated bodies are significantly more stringent and care needs to be taken when any promotion is made via social networking sites.

15.7 Requirements for social media postings

All financial promotions must be stand-alone compliant, regardless of their form, content, location or target audience, although these factors will be relevant to firms' assessments of what to include. As ever, it remains the responsibility of firms to assess what information they need to include in a promotion in order to ensure compliance with the rules and guidance.

4 ASA Complaint Ref: A12-185389, decision dated 7 March 2012.

15.8 2014 Guidance?

The 2012 paper, *Journey to the FCA*, acknowledged that many firms support the publishing of details of unsuitable financial promotions, as this helps them understand what is not acceptable. The industry also welcomes firms' right to make representations before the ban is confirmed and the notice is published. They would also like to know more about how exactly this process will work, for example, what the requirements are for social media promotions. The FCA has indicated that it is to publish social media guidance for financial services firms early next year, as the regulator has been in talks with firms over their increased use of social media and how it fits with regulation.

A FCA spokesman said the guidance had not stemmed from any particular concern but was in response to increased questions from firms, as noted in the consultation process forming the *Journey to the FCA* paper. The guidance is due to be published in the first quarter of 2014.[5]

15.9 Penalties for breaching the financial promotions regime

It is a criminal offence for an unauthorized person to communicate a financial promotion in breach of section 21 FSMA 2000. If found in contravention, that person is liable to a fine and/or up to two years' imprisonment (s 25 FSMA 2000). In addition, according to section 30 FSMA 2000, agreements entered into by a person as a customer as a result of an unlawful financial promotion are unenforceable against that customer.

If an unauthorized person has contravened section 21 FSMA 2000, on application by the appropriate regulator (with financial promotions this will be the FCA), the court may under sections 380 and 382(1) FSMA 2000:

- Grant an injunction restraining the contravention.
- Make an order that he and any other person who appears to have been 'knowingly concerned' in the contravention take such steps as the court may direct to remedy it.
- Make an order restraining him from disposing of or otherwise dealing with any of his assets which he is reasonably likely to dispose of or deal with.
- Make an order that he or a person who has been knowingly concerned in the contravention, must restore the other party to its position prior to entering into the agreement and pay such sum as appears to the court to be just.

15.9.1 Disciplinary action

Where an authorized person communicates or approves a financial promotion and it breaches the financial promotion rules (or any other relevant rules in the FCA Handbook[6]), this is not a criminal offence under section 21 FSMA 2000, but instead, the FCA may take disciplinary action.

---

5 This guidance was not published at the time this edition of the book went to press.
6 http://fshandbook.info/FS/html/FCA/.

366   *Commercial law*

15.9.2 *Other penalties*

The communicator of a misleading or inaccurate financial promotion faces reputational damage and potentially:

- A claim for misrepresentation.
- Criminal liability under the insider dealing legislation, section 89 of the Financial Services Act 2012 (misleading statements) or the Theft Act 1968.
- Civil action under the market abuse regime.
- Actions under the Consumer Protection from Unfair Trading Regulations 2008 (see Chapter 14).

15.10 What should firms consider before using new media?

15.10.1 *Checklist of social media issues*

The following table highlights some of the issues that financially regulated bodies will need to be alive to when engaging with 'new media'.

Issue	Suggested solution	In-house measures
New media may date more quickly than traditional media channels.	Regularly review to ensure that information is up-to-date.	Appoint a social media officer or member of the marketing team to review the firm's social media presence at regular intervals and monitor user comments and interactions. Ensure that all posts that are not in agreed form are run past legal and compliance teams.
Consider whether this channel is a suitable method for the type of communication.	For example, Twitter limits the number of characters that can be used, which may be insufficient to provide balanced and sufficient information. Digital marketing executives to liaise with legal team to see if medium is appropriate.	Appoint digital marketing executives to liaise with legal team to see if medium is appropriate. Record decisions made or amendments deemed necessary. Add to social media financial promotions portfolio to ensure that there is an audit trail.
Is risk information displayed prominently and clearly using this media channel?	Can the risk information be displayed prominently and clearly using this media channel?	Digital marketing executives to liaise with legal team to see if medium is appropriate.
Are all existing materials available appropriate and legally compliant?		Review all existing materials to see if they are appropriate. Review archives of promotions made on sites.

Issue	Suggested solution	In-house measures
Does the advert go beyond Image Advertising?	Consider if the promotion contains anything other than: • the name of the firm, • a logo or other image associated with the firm, • a contact point, and • a reference to the types of regulated activities provided by the firm or to its fees or commissions.	If deemed inappropriate, arrange for cache to be removed by Google and delete content. Digital marketing executives to liaise with legal team to see if promotion is legally compliant.

A firm's senior management must make sure they have the systems and controls to ensure their promotions are compliant.

15.10.2 *Use of checklists*

The FCA has stated[7] that there is no harm in a firm using a checklist to ensure it has produced a compliant advert and followed its own systems. Problems may arise where checklists are used in isolation – that is, when all the boxes may have been ticked but no-one at the firm has stood back and determined whether the material actually meets the high-level rules. So, using a checklist alone will not necessarily guarantee compliant promotions; nor will it necessarily be proof of adequate systems and controls.

---

7 http://www.fca.org.uk/firms/being-regulated/financial-promotions/financial-promotion-faq.

16 Insurance

16.1 Purchasing insurance against social media claims

Social media claims or potential claims may arise in almost any context, from branding and advertising issues to defamation and privacy claims, consumer class actions and securities claims. As a result, when considering purchasing or renewing insurance coverage, companies should consider the following areas.

16.2 Common areas of exposure to risk

The most common claims are as follows:

- Employees allege that employer or an employee improperly gained access to a password or social media page.
- Claims of discrimination, e.g. a supervisor only 'friends' certain employees.
- Claims of defamation: disparaging comments made via social media.
- Loss of intellectual property.
- Personal injury: libel or defamation.
- 'Digital wildfire'.
- Spread of inaccurate or intentionally false information.
- Negative and quick-spreading commentary.
- Reputational risk.

16.3 ABI report

The Association of British Insurers' (ABI) report *Identifying the Challenges of a Changing World*[1] is an analysis of the issues facing the UK insurance industry and society, and launches a debate on how insurers can play a key role in finding solutions to the issues that will shape our world in the 2020s and beyond.

The report identified seven over-arching trends most relevant to insurers, including the digital revolution and the impact of social media. The report noted that for insurance customers by 2030, empowerment through technology will be a central fact of life, underpinning the most basic and most sophisticated of daily tasks through the use

---

1 *Identifying the Challenges of a Changing World*, Association of British Insurers, 2013 [https://www.abi. org.uk/~/media/Files/Documents/Publications/Public/JoinTheDebate/Identifying%20the%20Challenges/ Identifying%20the%20challenges%20of%20a%20changing%20world%20Full%20document.ashx].

Insurance 369

of small, portable devices that could easily replace the wristwatch. At the heart of this empowerment will be constant access to information, much of it tailored to the individual's requirements and available through a variety of channels. As a result, customers will view it as the norm to interact publicly (through social media and other online communities) as well as privately with their insurer to provide feedback about their experience and to have complaints resolved swiftly, albeit the personal aspect of the industry will remain important. The report examines the extent to which the insurance industry can play a greater role in meeting the challenges of a changing world. Otto Thoresen, ABI director-general, said: 'The rules of day-to-day life are being rewritten, and insurance has a key role to play in tackling many of the issues that matter for society. Insurance provides cover against risks inherent in all aspects of life.'[2]

The ABI is using the report as a springboard to launch its 'Big Debate' within the industry and among other stakeholders on how to deliver better solutions for customers. The debate will likely focus on regulation, stimulating economic growth and infrastructure investment, welfare reform, paying for life after work, and the acceptable use and security of personal data now available.

16.4 Coverage

16.4.1 *Areas to consider*

Since claims can raise a variety of issues and take different guises (from common law fraud and misrepresentation claims to invasion of privacy and cyber-extortion), looking at an inventory of existing policies with a 'social media' lens can assist in seeing and seeking potential coverage that may come into play. From there it will be possible to consider the types of coverage a business may require in order to protect itself from claims arising in the social media context, to the extent permissible by law.

You may wish to consider a comprehensive general liability policy, which typically provides coverage for bodily injury and property damage, as well as for advertising and personal injury.

However, care should be taken when looking at the wording used in the policy and you should not just assume that such liabilities will be covered. For instance, some definitions of 'property damage' may exclude electronic data, while a coverage endorsement may specifically provide some coverage. 'Personal injury' typically includes publications or utterances that are in violation of an individual's right to privacy, or that are defamatory or disparaging.

How these coverages may apply depends on the language of the policy, the facts and applicable law. In the first instance, it may be helpful to analyze potential 'pockets' for coverage, should a claim be made; or if a defamation claim were to become an employment-related claim, then coverage under an employment practices liability policy should be examined to see if there are any obvious exclusions or subtle restrictions that can be addressed when negotiating the coverage. Policyholders willing to invest in reviewing and comparing choices and policy wording can tailor the coverage to their needs and potential exposures. For example, some technology, media, data privacy breach and professional liability policies provide coverage for first-party loss

2 Ibid.

370   *Commercial law*

(damage suffered directly by the company), including internal hacker attacks or business interruption, or expenses to maintain or resurrect data.

16.4.2 *Publicity coverage*

Many policies also provide 'publicity coverage' to respond to adverse PR, but require policyholders to use the insurance company's in-house public relations department or consultant to minimize any damage to the policyholder's reputation. This coverage is commonly found in policies sold to restaurants and other food establishments and will have application in the social media context where bad reviews can go viral.

In terms of what such coverage should seek to address, this type of coverage may not require actual 'contamination' or 'damage' but merely reports of such damage, true or untrue, in the media or on the internet. This risk is particularly important to recognize in a social media world, where rumours can spread quickly and unchecked.

16.4.3 *Third-party loss*

Businesses should also consider if their policies offer coverage for third-party loss (claims asserted against the company by third parties). Claims may include allegations of violations of privacy rights and individuals' personal data, duties to secure confidential personal information pursuant to statutory enactments, breaches by employees or others, infringement of intellectual property rights, unfair competition, defamation and consumer protection, and deceptive trade practices statutes. The coverage sought may include areas such as regulatory actions, lawsuits and demands including reimbursement of defence costs and indemnification for judgments and settlements.

Looking at coverage with a proactive approach can help negotiate terms that afford your business appropriate protection if and when the claim hits.

16.5 Key coverage enhancements to seek

Policies should cover:

A broad definition of 'claim'	Coverage should apply to the following areas: • demands; • investigations; • complaints; and • civil, criminal, and administrative and regulatory proceedings. However, it should be noted that with a broader definition of 'claim' comes a corresponding obligation to report what may constitute a claim.
A broad definition of 'loss'	'Loss' should encompass a broad range, including statutory fines and penalties (where insurable), as well as defence and investigative costs.

Insurance   371

Narrowed exclusions	Exclusions should be narrow and tailored and contain 'exceptions' where coverage will be provided.
	Exclusions for bad conduct committed by insureds or employees should be triggered only by a final adjudication of the excluded conduct.
	Defence costs should be covered.
	Exclusions should be severable, so that if one aspect of the exclusion 'fails', coverage for other matters is not lost part and parcel.
Defence and settlement flexibility	Consider whether the insurer provides a defence or the insured seeks control over the defence.
	Negotiate 'consent to settle' provisions.

Bibliography

Advertising Standards Authority, *Blurring Advertising and Blogs* [http://www.asa.org.uk/News-resources/Media-Centre/2013/Blurring-advertising-and-blogs.aspx].

Allen, D., 2012, 'The "Twitter Joke Trial" returns to the High Court: Lord Chief Justice to preside over latest appeal in *Chambers v Director of Public Prosecutions*' [http://www.newstatesman.com/blogs/david-allen-green/2012/06/twitter-joke-trial-david-allen-green], 22 June.

Amos, M., 2006, *Human Rights Law*. Oxford: Hart Publishing.

Arkfeld, M.R., 2011, *Arkfeld on Electronic Discovery and Evidence*, § 8.11(C), at 8–63 (3rd ed.). Phoenix, AZ: Law Partner Publishing.

Ashworth, A., 'Case comment: malicious communication: defendant anti-abortionist – sending photographs of aborted fetuses' [2007] Crim LR 729, 731.

Barendt, E., 2005, *Freedom of Speech*. Oxford: Oxford University Press.

Berlin International Working Group on Data Protection in Telecommunications paper on Social Networking Sites [http://www.datenschutz-berlin.de/content/europa-international/international-working-group-on-data-protection-in-telecommunications-iwgdpt].

Bilton, N., 2010, 'Price of Facebook privacy? Start clicking', *New York Times*, 12 May [http://www.nytimes.com/2010/05/13/technology/personaltech/13basics.html?_r=1].

Boyd, D.M. and Ellison, N.B., 2007, 'Social network sites: definition, history, and scholarship', *Journal of Computer-Mediated Communication*, 13(1): 210–230.

Brown, I., 2011, 'Communications data retention in an evolving internet', *International Journal of Law and Information Technology*, 19(2): 95–109.

Burkert, H., 1997, 'Privacy-enhancing technologies: typology, critique, vision', in P.E. Agre and M. Rotenberg (eds), *Technology and Privacy: The New Landscape*. Cambridge, MA: MIT Press.

Byrnside, I., 2008, 'Six degrees of separation: the legal ramifications of employers using social networking sites to research applicants', *Vanderbilt Journal of Entertainment and Technology Law*, 2: 445–477.

CAP Social Media [http://www.cap.org.uk/Advice-Training-on-the-rules/Advice-Online-Database/Remit-Social-Media.aspx].

Carney, S., 2011, 'EU carbon market suffers further setback', *Wall Street Journal*, 28 January [http://online.wsj.com/article/SB10001424052748703956604576109272255053468.html; accessed 23 March 2014].

Casadevall, J., Myjer, E., O'Boyle, M. and Austin, A. (eds), 2012, *Freedom of Expression: Essays in Honor of Nicolas Bratza*. Oisterwijk: Wolf Legal Publishers.

Chrisafis, A., 2013, 'Twitter under fire in France over offensive hashtags', *The Guardian*, 9 January [http://www.theguardian.com/technology/2013/jan/09/twitter-france-offensive-hashtags].

Cockerell, J., 2014, 'Twitter "trolls" Isabella Sorley and John Nimmo jailed for abusing feminist campaigner Caroline Criado-Perez', *The Independent*, 24 January [http://www.independent.co.uk/news/uk/crime/twitter-trolls-isabella-sorley-and-john-nimmo-jailed-for-abusing-feminist-campaigner-caroline-criadoperez-9083829.html].

Bibliography 373

Cotriss, D., 2008, 'Where are they now: TheGlobe.com', *The Industry Standard*, 29 May.

Council of Europe, July 2012, *Factsheet – Hate speech* [http://www.echr.coe.int/Documents/FS_Hate_speech_ENG.pdf].

Cheung, A.S.Y., 2006, 'The business of governance: China's legislation on content regulation in cyberspace', *International Law and Politics*, 38(1): 1–37.

Choo, A., 2009, *Evidence*. Oxford: Oxford University Press.

Committee of Advertising Practice, 2010, *Extending the Digital Remit of the CAP Code* [http://www.cap.org.uk/News-reports/~/media/Files/CAP/Misc/CAP_Digital_Remit_Extension.ashx].

Crowell, C., 2012, http://www.levesoninquiry.org.uk/wp-content/uploads/2012/02/Transcript-of-Morning-Hearing-7-February-2012.pdf.

Crown Prosecution Service, 2012, Interim guidelines on prosecuting cases involving communications sent via social media. Issued by the Director of Public Prosecutions, 19 December 2012.

Cullen, R., 1996, *Media Law in the PRC*. Hong Kong: Asia Law and Practice Publishing.

Dark, C., 2011, 'Social media and social menacing . . .', *Foreign Policy Association*, 20 December [http://foreignpolicyblogs.com/2011/12/20/social-media-and-social-menacing/].

Data Protection Working Party (DPWP), 2009, Published Opinion 5/2009 on online social networking, 12 June.

Data Retention Expert Group (Commission Decision 2008/324/EC) on webmail and web-based messaging: DATRET/EXPGRP (2009) 2 – FINAL – ANNEX, 3 December 2009. Datenschutzkonferenz: Geheimdienste gefährden massiv den Datenverkehr zwischen Deutschland und außereuropäischen Staaten (German Data Protection Commissioner's Opinion on Safe Harbor) [http://www.bfdi.bund.de/DE/Home/homepage_Kurzmeldungen2013/PMDerDSK_SafeHarbor.html?nn=408908].

Edmonds, L., 2014, "Kindly f*** off, you are a PRIZE ****! Go see your psych manager SLAG!" Astonishing foul-mouthed rant of hairdresser to customer who posted negative review on Facebook after botched extensions", *Daily Mail*, 8 April [http://www.dailymail.co.uk/news/article-2599680/Kindly-f-PRIZE-Go-psych-manager-SLAG-Astonishing-foul-mouthed-rant-hairdresser-customer-posted-negative-review-Facebook-botched-extensions.html].

Edwards, L. and Waedle, C. (eds), 2009, *Law and the Internet* (3rd ed.). Oxford: Hart Publishing.

El Akkad, O., 2012, 'Why Twitter's censorship plan is better than you think', *The Globe and Mail*, 31 January [http://www.theglobeandmail.com/technology/digital-culture/social-web/why-twitters-censorship-plan-is-better-than-you-think/article543062/].

Ellison, N., Steinfield, C. and Lampe, C., 2007, 'The benefits of Facebook "friends": social capital and college students' use of online social network sites', *Journal of Computer-Mediated Communication*, 12(4): 1143–1168.

European Commission, 2012, http://ec.europa.eu/justice/data-protection/document/review2012/factsheets/3_en.pdf.

European Court of Human Rights, Research Division, 2011, *Internet: Case-law of the European Court of Human Rights*. Council of Europe/European Court of Human Rights.

Federal Trade Commission, Guides Concerning the Use of Endorsements and Testimonials in Advertising.

Financial Services Authority, 2010, 'Financial promotions using new media', *Financial Promotions Industry Update*, No. 5, June.

Foster, 'Free speech, insulting words or behaviour and art.10 of the European Convention on Human Rights' (2004) 9(1) Cov LJ 68.

Friedman, U., 2011, 'U.S. officials may take action again al-Shabab's Twitter account', *Foreign Policy*, 20 December [http://blog.foreignpolicy.com/posts/2011/12/20/us_officials_may_take_action_again_al_shababs_twitter_account; retrieved 5 April 2012].

Friewald, S., 2009, 'A comment on James Grimmelmann's saving Facebook', *Iowa Law Review Bulletin*, 95: 5–11.

374 *Bibliography*

Geddis, A., 'Free speech martyrs or unreasonable threats to social peace?' [2004] Public Law 853.

General principles on the right to freedom of opinion and expression and the Internet; and Human Rights Council, Resolution 20/8, A/HRC/RES/20/8.

Grimmelmann, J., 2009, 'Saving Facebook', *Iowa Law Review*, 94: 1137–1206.

Guillory, J. and Hancock, J.T., 2012, 'The effect of LinkedIn on deception in resumes', *Cyberpsychology, Behavior, and Social Networking*, 15(3): 135–140.

Hafner, K., 2001, *The Well: A Story of Love, Death and Real Life in the Seminal Online Community*. New York: Carroll & Graf.

Hammock, M. and Rubin, P.H., 2011, 'Applications want to be free: privacy against information', *Competition Policy International*, March [http://techpolicyinstitute.org/files/hammock-rubin_applications want to be free.pdf; accessed 23 March 2014].

Hansard, HC Debate, 21 June 2012, Col 120.

Hansard, Public Bill Committee, 26 June 2012 (Morning), Session 2012–13, Publications on the Internet Defamation Bill, Col 163.

Hansard, HL Grand Committee, 19 December 2012, Col GC 656.

Hansard, HL Grand Committee, 15 January 2013, Col GC 190.

Hansard, HL Grand Committee, 15 January 2013, Col GC 190, Lord Ahmad.

Haralambous, N. and Johnson, M., 2010, 'Facebook – friend or foe?', 174(31) CL & J 469.

Hashemi, Y., 2009, 'Facebook's privacy policy and its third party partnerships: lucrativity and liability', *Boston University Journal of Science and Technology Law*, 15: 140–161.

Hauben, M., Hauben, R. and Truscott, T., 1997, *Netizens: On the History and Impact of Usenet and the Internet*. Los Alamitos, CA: IEEE Computer Society Press.

Hiltz, R. and Turoff, M., 1993, *The Network Nation* (revised edition). Reading, MA: Addison-Wesley.

Hofmeyr, K., 'The problem of private entrapment' [2006] Crim LR 319.

House of Commons, Library Research Papers, The Human Rights Bill [HL], Bill 119 of 1997/98, No: 98/24, February 1998.

Human Rights Committee, General Comment 34: Freedoms of opinion and expression, CCPR/ C/GC/34 (GC 34) 12 September 2011.

Internet Advertising Bureau, 2012, 'Guidelines on the payment for editorial content to promote brands within social media', July [http://www.iabuk.net/sites/default/files/IAB%20ISBA%20 Guidelines%20on%20the%20Payment%20for%20Editorial%20Content%20-%20July%20 2012.pdf].

Intelligence and Security Committee, 2013, *Access to Communications Data by the Intelligence and Security Agencies*, Cm 8514. Norwich: TSO.

Jenkins, B.M., 2011, 'Is Al Qaeda's Internet strategy working?', CT-371, 6 December. Santa Monica, CA: Rand Corporation.

Joint Committee on the Draft Defamation Bill Report Session 2010–2012, HL 203, HC 930-I.

Joint Declaration on Freedom of Expression and the Internet, The United Nations (UN) Special Rapporteur on Freedom of Opinion and Expression, the Organization for Security and Cooperation in Europe (OSCE) Representative on Freedom of the Media, the Organization of American States (OAS) Special Rapporteur on Freedom of Expression and the African Commission on Human and Peoples' Rights (ACHPR) Special Rapporteur on Freedom of Expression and Access to Information, Press Release R50/11.

Kanalley, C., 2010, 'YouTube gives users ability to flag content that promotes terrorism', *The Huffington Post*, 13 December [http://www.huffingtonpost.com/2010/12/13/youtube-terrorism-flag_n_796128.html].

Kazeniac, A., 2009, 'Social networks: Facebook takes over top spot, Twitter climbs' *Blog. compete.com*, 9 February [https://blog.compete.com/2009/02/09/facebook-myspace-twitter-social-network/; retrieved 7 August 2013].

Kjuka, D., 2013, 'How social networks are dealing with terrorists' [ttp://www.rferl.org/content/twitter-facebook-terrorists/24906583.html].

Kohlmann, E. with Lefkowitz, J. and Alkhouri, L., 2011, 'The antisocial network: countering the use of online social networking technologies by foreign terrorist organizations' [http://homeland.house.gov/sites/homeland.house.gov/files/Testimony%20Kohlmann%5B1%5D.pdf].

Knapp, E., 2005, *A Parent's Guide to MySpace*. Bridgend: DayDream Publishers.

La Rue, F., 2011, 'Report of the Special Rapporteur on the promotion and protection of the right to freedom of opinion and expression', A/HRC/17/27, 16 May [http://www2.ohchr.org/english/bodies/hrcouncil/docs/17session/A.HRC.17.27_en.pdf].

Legg, A., 2012, *The Margin of Appreciation in International Human Rights Law*. Oxford Monographs in International Law. Oxford: Oxford University Press.

Leonard, T.M. and Rubin, P.H., 2009, *In Defense of Data*. Washington, DC: Technology Policy Institute [http://www.techpolicyinstitute.org/files/in%20defense%20of%20data.pdf].

Levinson A.R., 2009, 'Industrial justice: privacy protection for the employed', *Cornell Journal of Law and Pubic Policy*, 18: 609–688.

López-Rey, M., 1978, 'Crime and human rights', *Federal Probation*, 43(1): 10–15.

Milmo, P., Rogers, W.V.H., Parkes, R., Walker, C. and Busuttil, G., 2007, *Gatley on Libel and Slander* (10th ed.). London: Sweet & Maxwell.

Ministry of Justice, 2006, *Making Sense of Human Rights: A Short Introduction*, DCA 45/06. London: Ministry of Justice.

Ministry of Justice, 2012, *The Government's Response to the Report of the Joint Committee on the Draft Defamation Bill*, Cm 8295. Norwich: TSO.

Mitchell, P., 2005, *The Making of the Modern Law of Defamation*. Oxford: Hart Publishing.

Munday, R, 2010, 'Athwal and all that: previous statements, narrative, and the taxonomy of hearsay', *Journal of Criminal Law*, 74: 415–433.

Office of Fair Trading, 2010, 'OFT secures promotional blogging disclosures', press release 134/10, 13 December.

O'Flaherty, M., 2012, 'Freedom of Expression: Article 19 of the ICCPR and the Human Rights Committee's General Comment No 34', *Human Rights Law Review*, 12(4): 627–654.

Ohm, P., 2009, 'The rise and fall of invasive ISP surveillance', *University of Illinois Law Review*, 2009: 1417–1496.

Ormerod, D., 'Telecommunications: sending grossly offensive message by means of public electronic communications network' [2007] Crim LR 98.

Ormerod, D. and O' Floinn, M., 'Social networking sites, RIPA and criminal investigations' [2011] 10 Crim LR 766.

Parks, M.R. and Floyd, K., 1996, 'Making friends in cyberspace', *Journal of Computer-Mediated Communication*, 1(4).

Pattenden, R., 2008, 'Authenticating "things" in English law: principles for adducing tangible evidence in common law jury trials', *International Journal of Evidence and Proof*, 12(4): 273–302.

Pattenden, R., 'Machinespeak' [2010] Crim LR 623.

Rioth, P., 2010, 'Data protection meets Web 2.0: two ships passing in the night', *UNSW Law Journal*, 33: 532–561.

Romm-Livermore, C. and Setzekorn, K., 2008, *Social Networking Communities and E-Dating Services: Concepts and Implications*. New York: IGI Global.

Rosenbush, S., 2005, 'News Corp.'s place in MySpace', *Business Week*, 19 July.

Rowbottom, J., 2012, 'To rant, vent and converse: protecting low level digital speech', *Cambridge Law Journal*, 71(2): 355–383.

Scaife, L., 2012, 'Social media – time for a firm wide policy?', *Lexology*, 11 April [http://www.lexology.com/library/detail.aspx?g=5c1f9b6c-b252-4de4-9fa8-3774841237f7].

Scaife, L., 2013, 'The Communications Act 2003: a new approach coming out of the woods?', *Communications Law Journal*, 18(1): 5–10.

376   *Bibliography*

Schauer, F.F., 1982, *Free Speech: A Philosophical Enquiry*. Cambridge: Cambridge University Press.

Schoeman, F.D. (ed.), 1984, *Philosophical Dimensions of Privacy: An Anthology*. Cambridge: Cambridge University Press.

Schoeman, F.D., 1984, *Philosophical Dimensions of Privacy: An Anthology*. Cambridge: Cambridge University Press.

Sleight, D., 'Entrapment' (2010) 107(25) LSG 22.

Smith, J.C., 'The admissibility of statements by computer' [1981] Crim LR 387.

Social Media and Human Rights, Strasbourg February 2012, CommDH (2012)8.

Stone, B., 2007, 'Facebook executive discusses Beacon Brouhaha', Bits (blog), *New York Times*, 29 November [http://bits.blogs.nytimes.com/2007/11/29/facebook-responds-to-beacon-brouhaha/].

Story, L., 2007, 'Coke is holding off on sipping Facebook's Beacon', Bits (blog), *New York Times*, 30 November [http://bits.blogs.nytimes.com/2007/11/30/coke-is-holding-off-on-sipping-facebooks-beacon].

Székely, I., 1994, Az adatvédelem és az információszabadság filozófiai, jogi, szociológiai és informatikai aspektusai. Budapest. Kézirat (kandidátusi értekezés).

Szoka, B. and Thierer, A., 2008, 'Online advertising & user privacy: principles to guide the debate', *Progress Snapshot*, 4(19): 1–6 [http://www.pff.org/issues-pubs/ps/2008/pdf/ps4.19onlinetargeting.pdf].

Tapper, C., 'Electronic evidence and the Criminal Justice Act 2003' [2004] CTLR 161.

Tulkens, F., 2011, 'The paradoxical relationship between criminal law and human rights', *Journal of International Criminal Justice*, 9(3): 577–595.

United Nations Commission on Narcotic Drugs, and Commission on Crime Prevention and Criminal Justice, 2010, 'Drug control, crime prevention and criminal justice: a human rights perspective', Note by the Executive Director. E/CN.7/2010/CRP.6 – E/CN.15/2010/CRP.1, 3 March.

United Nations Human Rights Council, 2012, Summary of the Human Rights Council panel discussion on the promotion and protection of freedom of expression on the Internet. Report of the Office of the United Nations High Commissioner for Human Rights, A/HRC/21/30, 2 July.

United Nations Office on Drugs and Crime, 2013, *Comprehensive Study on Cybercrime*. New York: United Nations.

United Nations Office of the High Commissioner for Human Rights, 2012, Rabat Plan of Action on the prohibition of advocacy of national, racial or religious hatred that constitutes incitement to discrimination, hostility or violence. Conclusions and recommendations emanating from the four regional expert workshops organized by OHCHR, in 2011, and adopted by experts in Rabat, Morocco on 5 October 2012 [http://www.ohchr.org/Documents/Issues/Opinion/SeminarRabat/Rabat_draft_outcome.pdf].

United States Subcommittee on Counterterrorism and Intelligence of the Committee on Homeland Security's Subcommittee on Counterterrorism and Intelligence, 2011, Jihadist Use of Social Media: How To Prevent Terrorism and Preserve Innovation', 112th Congress, First Session, 6 December 6.

Vajic, N. and Voyatis, P., 'The Internet and freedom of expression: a "brave new world" and the ECtHR's evolving case law', in J. Casadevall, E. Myjer, M. O'Boyle and A. Austin (eds), *Freedom of Expression: Essays in Honor of Nicolas Bratza*. Oisterwijk: Wolf Legal Publishers.

Walden, I., 2011, 'Law enforcement access in a cloud environment', School of Law Legal Studies Research Paper Series No. 74/2011. London: Queen Mary, University of London.

Warren, S.D. and Brandeis, L.D., 1890, 'The right to privacy', *Harvard Law Review*, 4(5): 193–220.

Weimann, G., 2006, *Terror on the Internet: The New Arena, the New Challenges*. Washington, DC: US Institute of Peace Press.

Wellman, B., Salaff, J., Dimitrova, D., Garton, L., Gulia, M. and Haythornthwaite, C., 1996, 'Computer networks as social networks: collaborative work, telework, and virtual community', *Annual Review of Sociology*, 22: 213–238.

Williamson, D.A., 2008, 'Social networking ad spending to fall', *eMarketer*, 13 May [http://files.eric.ed.gov/fulltext/EJ903459.pdf].

Word of Mouth Marketing Association (WOMMA), 2012, *Social Media Marketing Disclosure Guide* [http://uk.practicallaw.com/cs/Satellite?blobcol=urldata&blobheader=application%2Fpdf&blobkey=id&blobtable—ungoBlobs&blobwhere=1247495804205&ssbinary=true].

Zuckerberg, M., 2007, 'Thoughts on Beacon', Facebook Blog, 5 December [http://www.facebook.com/notes/facebook/thoughts-on-beacon/7584397130; retrieved 30 October 2009].

Websites

- "Social graph-iti": There's less to Facebook and other social networks than meets the eye', *The Economist* [http://www.economist.com/node/9990635; retrieved 19 January 2008].
- http://www.alexa.com (accessed November 2010).
- Opinion of the European Data Protection Supervisor at [http://www.edps.europa.eu/EDPSWEB/webdav/site/mySite/shared/Documents/EDPS/PressNews/Press/2011/EDPS-2011-06_Data Retention Report_EN.pdf; accessed 2 August 2011].
- http://www.justice.gov/opa/pr/2011/February/11-nsd-238.html.
- http://www.cps.gov.uk/news/press_releases/137_07/.
- 'Boko Haram: Nigerian Islamist leader defends attacks', *BBC News* [http://www.bbc.co.uk/news/world-africa-16510929].
- See http://www.bbc.co.uk/news/uk-20851797. In Western Asia, a number of recent criminal cases related to internet social media content have also been reported [see http://www.bbc.co.uk/news/worldmiddle-east-20587246].
- "Twitter libel" Caerphilly councillor pays rival £3,000' [http://www.bbc.co.uk/news/uk-wales-south-east-wales-12704955], June 2009 (unreported).
- 'Tweet revenge: Tory to sue 10,000 Twitter users who branded him a paedo', *Daily Mirror*, 19 November 2012 [http://www.mirror.co.uk/news/uk-news/lord-mcalpine-to-sue-10000-twitter-1444634].
- http://www.guardian.co.uk/technology/2012/sep/20/footballer-tom-daley-tweet.
- http://blog.cps.gov.uk/2012/09/dpp-statement-on-tom-daley-case-and-social-media-prosecutions.html.
- http://www.lawinsport.com/blog/laura-scaife/item/off-the-field-and-on-to-the-feed-tackling-racism-online-part-2.
- http://www.lawtimesnews.com/200911025723/Headline-News/Social-media-tripping-up-litigants [accessed 26 April 29012].
- http://www.journal-news.net/page/content.detail/id/525232.html [accessed 26 April 2012].
- http://www.telegraph.co.uk/news/uknews/6149807/Armed-gang-jailed-after-being-named-and-shamed-on-Facebook.html [accessed 26 April 2012].
- http://news.sky.com/skynews/Home/UK-News/Facebook-Photo-Shoot-Majid-Khan-Jailed-For-For-Five-Years-For-Posing-With-Gun-On-Facebook [accessed 26 April 2012].
- http://www.theguardian.com/technology/2013/jan/09/twitter-france-offensive-hashtags.
- 'Twitter blocks neo-Nazi account to users in Germany' [http://www.bbc.co.uk/news/technology-19988662 [18 October 2012].
- http://www.westmercia.police.uk/news/news-articles/attacker-jailed-after-victim-traced-him-on-facebook.html [accessed 26 April 2012].
- http://news.sky.com/home/uk-news/article/15458212 [accessed 26 April 2012].

378   *Bibliography*

- http://countermeasures.trendmicro.eu/over-10000-facebook-account-details-hacked-and-published/ [accessed 26 April 2012].
- http://mashable.com/2010/04/23/hacker-facebook/ [accessed 26 April 2012].
- https://www.cyberstreetwise.com/ UK Home Office; 'New campaign urges people to be "Cyber Streetwise".
- http://www.theguardian.com/uk/2012/nov/12/teenager-arrested-burning-poppy-facebook.
- http://www.theguardian.com/tv-and-radio/2011/jul/03/britains-got-talent-blogger-cautioned.
- 'Stan Collymore Twitter race abuser Joshua Cryer sentenced' [http://www.bbc.co.uk/news/uk-england-tyne-17462619], 21 March 2012.
- http://www.independent.co.uk/news/uk/crime/twitter-trolls-isabella-sorley-and-john-nimmo-jailed-for-abusing-feminist-campaigner-caroline-criadoperez-9083829.html.
- Video: 'Your Role as a Juror' [http://www.youtube.com/watch?v=JP7slp-X9Pc&feature=relmfu].
- https://www.gov.uk/government/news/attorney-general-to-warn-facebook-and-twitter-users-about-contempt-of-court.
- Incorporated Council of Law Reporting (ICLR) Blog Post on 'The internet, social media and contempt of court: some recent developments' [http://www.iclr.co.uk/internet-social-media-contempt-court-recent-developments/].
- http://www.guardian.co.uk/uk/2009/aug/21/facebook-bullying-sentence-teenage-girl [accessed 22 August 2011].
- http://www.philly.com/philly/blogs/thegoalkeeper/Major-League-Soccer-North-American-Soccer-League-and-United-Soccer-Leagues-respond-to-global-match-fixing-scandals.html?ref=twitter.com.
- http://news.bbc.co.uk/1/hi/england/suffolk/8456182.stm) and Pasquale Manfredi (http://news.bbc.co.uk/1/hi/world/europe/8570796.stm) [accessed 2 August 2011].
- http://edition.cnn.com/2009/TECH/01/14/nz.facebook.arrest/index.html [accessed 2 August 2011].
- http://www.eff.org/files/filenode/social_network/20100303__crim_socialnetworking.pdf at p.32.
- http://ec.europa.eu/justice/policies/privacy/docs/wpdocs/2009/wp163_en.pdf.
- See http://www.europe-v-facebook.org/EN/en/html.
- http://www.forbes.com/sites/kashmirhill/2012/02/16/how-target-figured-out-a-teen-girl-was-pregnant-before-her-father-did/.
- http://adage.com/article/digitalnext/post-disaster-retreat-social-media-backfires-carnival/232723/.

Twitter

- Terms are accessible via https://support.twitter.com/articles/20169997#.
- Reports for Information Requests, Content Removal Requests and Copyright Infringement can all be accessed via the hub website [https://transparency.twitter.com/].
- Twitter. 'Twitter page of the Taliban' [https://twitter.com/alemarahweb].
- 'Tweets still must flow', Thursday, January 26, 2012 | By Twitter (@twitter) [19:25 UTC] accessible via https://blog.twitter.com/2012/tweets-still-must-flow.
- Twitter's 'Rules of Twitter' [http://support.twitter.com/entries/18311].
- https://support.twitter.com/articles/119138-types-of-tweets-and-where-they-appear#.

Bibliography 379

ICO

- http://www.ico.org.uk/for_organisations/data_protection/registration/data-protection-registration.
- Determining what is personal data, Information Comissioner's Office, 2012 [http://ico.org.uk/for_organisations/guidance_index/~/media/documents/library/Data_Protection/Detailed_specialist_guides/PERSONAL_DATA_FLOWCHART_V1_WITH_PREFACE001.ashx].
- http://www.ico.org.uk/for_organisations/data_protection/the_guide/conditions_for_processing.
- http://ico.org.uk/for_organisations/privacy_and_electronic_communications/the_guide/security_of_services?hidecookiesbanner=true.
- ICO's paper of April 2011 entitled 'Line to take: dealing with complaints about information published online' [http://www.ico.org.uk/about_us/how_we_comply/disclosure_log/~/media/documents/disclosure_log/IRQ0417298b.ashx].
- Social Networking and Online Forums – When does the DPA Apply? Version: 1.1 20140226 [http://ico.org.uk/for_organisations/data_protection/topic_guides/~/media/documents/library/Data_Protection/Detailed_specialist_guides/social-networking-and-online-forums-dpa-guidance.ashx].
- http://www.ico.org.uk/about_us/consultations/~/media/documents/library/Corporate/Research_and_reports/draft_subject_access_cop_for_consultation.ashx.
- Subject Access Code of Practice [http://www.ico.org.uk/~/media/documents/library/Data_Protection/Detailed_specialist_guides/subject-access-code-of-practice.PDF].
- Personal Information Online Code of Practice [http://www.ico.org.uk/~/media/documents/library/data_protection/detailed_specialist_guides/personal_information_online_cop.ashx].

ICO Codes of Practice

- Subject Access Code of Practice, Information Commissioner's Office, February 2014.
- Direct Marketing, Information Commissioner's Office, October 2013 (updated 2014).
- Cookies Guide Marketing, Information Commissioner's Office December, 2013.
- Identifying 'data controllers' and 'data processors' Data Protection Act 1998, on Information Commissioner's Office, 2013/2014.
- Privacy Notices Code of Practice, Information Commissioner's Office, December 2010.

Facebook

- Facebook's Statement of Rights and Responsibilities and Facebook's Community Standards can be accessed via URL: https://www.facebook.com/legal/terms.
- http://www.facebook.com/ad_guidelines.php [accessed 15 April 2014].
- https://www.facebook.com/communitystandards accessed [accessed 15 April 2014].
- https://www.facebook.com/safety/groups/law/guidelines/ [accessed 26 April 2012].
- https://www.facebook.com/legal/terms.

Papers

- UN Congress for Data Security, 6 December 2011.
- Ministry of Justice Draft Defamation Bill: Consultation Paper CP3/11, March 2011.
- A New Future for Communications (Cm 5010) – published on 12 December 2000.
- Policy Memorandum on the Offensive Behaviour at Football and Threatening Communications (Scotland) Bill (2011).

380   *Bibliography*

- House of Commons Justice Committee in their 2014 paper, Post-legislative scrutiny of Part 2 (Encouraging or assisting crime) of the Serious Crime Act 2007 HC 639.
- Report of the Joint Committee in response to Ministry of Justice Draft Defamation Bill: Consultation Paper, HL Paper 203, HC 930-I, 19 October 2013.
- Leveson, Report into the Culture, Practices and Ethics of the Press was published on Thursday 29 November 2012. The Report can be downloaded at http://www.official-documents.gov.uk/document/hc1213/hc07/0780/0780.asp.
- Lord McNally, Vol II, p 438; Q 151 [Christie-Miller]; Law Society, Vol III, p 99.
- A copy of the Magistrates' Guidelines is available at: http://www.northants.police.uk/files/linked/WCU/Magistrate$20Sentencing$20Guidelines.pdf.
- A New Future for Communications (Cm 5010) – published on 12 December 2000.
- Review of the Protection from Harassment Act 1997: Improving Protection for Victims of Stalking, Summary of Consultation Responses and Conclusions, July 2013.
- Contempt of Court Summary for Non-Specialists, Law Commission Consultation Paper No 209.
- Special Eurobarometer 359, Attitudes on Data Protection and Electronic Identity in the European Union, June 2011.
- Recommendation CM/Rec(2012)4 of the Committee of Ministers to Member States on the protection of human rights with regard to social networking services (adopted by the Committee of Ministers on 4 April 2012 at the 1139th meeting of the Ministers' Deputies).
- Younger Committee (Report of the Committee on Privacy) (Cmnd 5012), HMSO, 1972.
- Younger Committee report on Privacy (Cmnd 5012, 1972), White Paper (Cmnd 5353, 1975).
- Lindop Report of the Committee on Data Protection (Cmnd 7341, 1978).
- ENISA Position Paper No. 1 Security Issues and Recommendations for Online Social Networks, October 2007.
- Report and Guidance on Privacy in Social Network Services, International Working Group on Data Protection in Telecommunications 43rd meeting, 3–4 March 2008, Rome (Italy) [http://www.datenschutz-berlin.de/attachments/461/WP_social_network_services.pdf].
- Facebook Ireland Limited Report of re-audit: Data Protection Commissioner, 21 September 2012.
- Opinion of the Article 29 Working Party, Opinion 5/2009 [http://ec.europa.eu/justice/policies/privacy/docs/wpdocs/2009/wp163_en.pdf].
- EC Article 29 Working Party opinion on data protection issues related to search engines, 4 April 2008.
- EC Article 29 Working Party Opinion 3/2010 on the principle of accountability, 00062/10/EN WP 173 [http://ec.europa.eu/justice/policies/privacy/docs/wpdocs/2010/wp173_en.pdf].
- The Disclosure of Email Subscriber's Personal Data by Email Service Provider to PRC Law Enforcement Agency case number 200603619, Report R07-3619, Issue 14, March 2007.
- European Commission issued a consultation paper entitled 'Safeguarding Privacy in a Connected World' [http://ec.europa.eu/justice/data-protection/document/review2012/com_2012_9_en.pdf].
- http://www.europarl.europa.eu/document/activities/cont/201305/20130508ATT65776/20130508A.

Guide

- Your Guide to Jury Service [https://www.gov.uk/jury-service/overview].

Index

A Small World 9
abuse reporting 340
accuracy of data 268–9; online forums 269–76
admissibility of evidence 150–1, 214, 227, 229; bad character evidence 217, 218–19, 223–4
advertising and marketing 336, 342–3; advergames 359; CAP Code 342, 343, 344–5, 359; clarity of adverts' content 355; contractual obligation to promote the company even if the form of the message is not determined by the advertiser 353–4; data utilization and monetization 328–30; direct marketing see direct marketing; endorsements and testimonials by bloggers 355–9; financial promotion using new media 360–2; image advertisements 363–4; indirect marketing 347; links to paid subscriptions 354; paid promotions 348–50; regulatory bodies 343; unfair trading regulations and 345–7; United States of America 350–3
Advertising Standards Authority 342, 343, 364; CAP Code 342, 343, 344–5, 359; endorsements and testimonials by bloggers and 356–7; paid promotions and 348–50
African Commission on Human and Peoples' Rights 36
aggravation: computer misuse 186–7; contempt of court 204, 206; racial 175–6, 177
aggregate data 330
Al-Qaeda 43, 47, 49
Al-Shabaab 44, 45
amends see offers of amends for defamation
anonymity: offensive/obscene/menacing messages and 148–9; pseudonymous profiles 340
anti-Semitism 157–8
anxiety-inducing messages see malicious communications
apologies: for defamation 107, 108

apps: data transfers and 288–91; third party 337–8
Arab Spring 49, 70
archiving: defamation and 75–6
Article 29 Working Party 237, 243–4, 254–5, 257, 262, 305–6, 312
assistance of crime see encouragement or assistance of crime
Association of British Insurers (ABI) 368–9
Australia: service of claim via social networking site 93, 94
authentication issues 226–9
authorship: proof of 226–9

bad character evidence: admissibility 217, 218–19, 223–4; co-defendants 219, 222; confessions 222–3; defendants 217–21; definition of 'bad character' 218; exclusion 219; non-defendants 223–4; powers of court 220–1
Badoo 9
balancing of rights 32–5
behavioural data 7
Belgium 12
Berlin International Working Group on Data Protection in Telecommunications 245, 251; Rome Memorandum 245–6, 251–3
Besseres_Hannover 45, 159
blog sites 8; endorsements and testimonials by bloggers 355–9
Brandeis, L. D. 238–9
Brazil 12
British Code of Non-broadcast Advertising, Sales Promotion and Direct Marketing (CAP Code) 342, 343, 344–5, 359
business networking sites 8

CAP Code 342, 343, 344–5, 359
case management: offer of amends for defamation and 114–15
categories of social media: explanation of specific media platforms 9–12; foreign language social networks 12–14;

382 *Index*

mobile-only social networks 16; types of sites 8–9; vertically organized communities gathered round specific topic 15–16
censorship 37, 160–3
Chambers, Paul 166
character evidence *see* bad character evidence
children and young people: data protection and 246; offensive/obscene/menacing messages and 144–5; revealing identity of children in court proceedings 208–9
China 12, 48; censorship and monitoring 160–2
Cloob 13
co-defendants: bad character evidence 219, 222
communications sector regulation 129; background to CA 2003 130–1; CA 2003 s 127 130–9; CPS interim guidance 139–64; meaning of 'gross offence' 131–9
compensation: data subjects 299–301
compliance management 341
computer misuse 183, 227; aggravation 186–7; case law 185–7; mitigation 186; sentencing 183–4, 187
confessions 222–3
consent: data protection and 265–8, 297–8
consultants: offer of amends for defamation and 111
consumer protection: falsely holding out as a consumer 348; unfair terms in contracts 325; unfair trading regulations 345–7
contempt of court 191; aggravation 204, 206; challenges presented by social media 191–2; Court of Protection Rules 209, 210–11; definition 192–3; future advisory notes from Attorney Generalo 211; Incorporated Council of Law Reporting (ICLR) and 211; injunctions and 201–8, 209–11; by jurors 194–201; meaning of a publication 193; meaning of 'communication' 193; mitigation 205, 206–8; protected proceedings 208–9; requirement to be addressed to the public 194; sentencing 204
contracts: contractual obligation to promote the company even if the form of the message is not determined by the advertiser 353–4; data protection 256–7; incorporation of terms of use 325; *see also* terms of use
cookies 267–8, 337
corporations and companies: defamation and 67–9, 84–5; online forums and 272; relationships with bloggers 356–7
correspondence: privacy right and 28–9
Costolo, Dick 75
Council of Europe 236, 237, 242–3

court orders: breach of 142
courts: dealing with technology 197–8; offer of amends for defamation and 114–15; powers of court regarding bad character evidence 220–1; warnings to jurors by court staff 197
Creasy, Stella 147, 148
Criado-Perez, Caroline 147
Crown Prosecution Service (CPS): Guidelines *see* Interim Guidelines on Prosecuting Cases Involving Communications Sent via Social Media
cyber-stalking 183

damages: for defamation 111–16
data protection 235–6, 240; accuracy of data 268–94; application to businesses 237–8; application to social networking sites 251; Article 29 Working Party 237, 243–4, 254–5, 257, 262, 305–6, 312; breach notification 321–4; Committee of Ministers for the Council of Europe and 236, 237; compensation 299–301; conditions for processing 263–4; consent 265–8, 297–8; contracts 256–7; cookies and 267–8; data controllers 253–6; data processors 253, 256, 258; data security 240–1, 339; data subjects 258, 264–5; data transfers by third parties 287–91; direct marketing and 294–5; erasure/deletion of data 277, 278–85; European Union and 243–4, 248–50, 257; fair processing 295–9; framework created by DPA 1998 250–1; guidance for individuals 341; guidance for social networking providers 335–41; history of data protection legislation 241–50; individual's right of protection 238; IP addresses 262–3; issues raised by social media 236–7; jurisdiction 311–21; meaning of personal data 259–63; mobility and geolocation 291–4; online forums 269–76; principles 257–8; privacy and 238; rectification rights 277–8; registration requirements 255–6; retention of personal data 285–7, 336–7; right to access data *see* subject access requests; right to be forgotten 278, 284; right to object to profiling 301–4; right to prevent processing likely to cause damage or distress 276–7; Rome Memorandum 245–6, 251–3; sensitive personal information 262, 264; terms and conditions and privacy policies 324–34; types of data 7
defamation 22–3, 37; apologies 107, 108; application to social media 53–4; damages

111–16; defences 86–98, 99, 119; definition 58; determining meaning of words 61–4; distinction between libel and slander 59–60; essential ingredients of an action 58–9; jurisdiction 80–2; libel tourism 80–1; limitation period 73; offer of amends *see* offers of amends for defamation; Part 36 offers 123; publication and 63–4, 65, 69–80, 108–10; self-regulation by social media sites and 82–5; single publication rule 73–8; sources of law 54–7; specific considerations for social media 61–4; statements conveying defamatory meaning 60; substantial harm test 64–9; summary judgments 123; technology outstripping the law 55; who can sue 57–8

defences: defamation 86–98, 99, 119

defendants: bad character evidence 217–21

deletion of accounts 339

deletion of data 277, 278–85

Delicious 9

derived data 7

development of social media 3–4; history 4–5; social interaction 5–6

Digg 9

digital media sharing sites 9

direct marketing: s 11(3) DPA and 295; types of marketing conducted via social media 294–5; value of social media 294

directions to jurors 198–9

disabled people 305

disciplinary action: financial services 365

disclosed data 7

distress: data protection and right to prevent processing likely to cause damage or distress 276–7; *see also* malicious communications

documents: authentication issues 226–9

Doostang 9

editorials 345; defamation and editorial judgement and control 90, 96

electronic communications services (ECS) 17–18

Electronic Frontier Foundation 47

Elsbury, Colin 53

emoticons 63

encouragement or assistance of crime 167; attempts to mitigate actions 171–2; believing one or more offences will be committed 168; case law 169–74; House of Commons Justice Committee White Paper 167; intention 168, 173; Serious Crime Prevention Orders 168–9

endorsements and testimonials by bloggers 355–9

entrapment: private 149–51

entrusted data 7

erasure of data 277, 278–85

European Convention on Human Rights 21; applicants 22; balancing of rights 32–5; compatibility of UK legislation with 24; incorporation into UK law 23; respondents 22–3; rights contained within 21, 26–35; rights of particular application to social network sites 26–32

European Framework for Electronic Communications 156

European Network and Information Security Agency (ENISA) 244, 252

European Union 236; data protection and 243–4, 248–50, 257; safe harbor scheme 318–21

evidence 212; admissibility of *see* admissibility of evidence; character *see* bad character evidence; exclusion 219, 220, 229–31; hearsay 229–31; identifying suspects 215–17; investigating known suspects 214; use of evidence from social networking sites in criminal proceedings 212–14; witnesses 224–5

exaggeration 222

exclusion of evidence 219, 220, 229–31

expression, freedom of 30–2; balancing of rights and 32–3; offensive/obscene/ menacing messages and 143, 145–7, 160

fabrication 222

Facebook 9, 155, 239; Beacon 331–4; censorship and monitoring 161; Community Standards 159–60; contempt of court and 202–3; data protection and 246–8, 277; defamation and 61, 83, 84–5, 111; encouragement or assistance of crime and 169–74; Facebook rape (Frape) 72–3; group pages 83; hacking into 185–6; indirect marketing and 347; offensive/ obscene/menacing messages 159–60; privacy policy 329–30, 332; response to terrorism and 47–8; safe harbor scheme and 319; service of claim via 93; settings 111; subject access requests and 290; tagging 166; terms of use 83; use of 'like' buttons 330–1

facial recognition 338

fair processing 295–9

fair trial right 26–7

false impressions: rebuttal of 221

fear of violence 181

Federal Trade Commission (FTC; USA) 350, 357–8

feelings: protection of 223

384 *Index*

Fello, Robert 97
Financial Conduct Authority (FCA) 343, 360
financial services 360; considerations before using social media 366–7; financial promotion using new media 360–2; FSA's 2010 review 363; guidance 365; image advertisements 363–4; non-promotional communications 363; penalties for breaching financial promotions regime 365–6; requirements for social media postings 364; stand-alone compliance 364
Financial Services Authority (FSA) 360, 363
Flickr 9
Floyd, K. 5
foreign language social networks 12–15
foreign nationals: libel tourism 80–1
forums *see* online forums
Foursquare 10
France: offensive/obscene/menacing messages 157–8
Frape 72–3
friend finders 339
Friendster 10

Geni 10
geolocation 291–4
Germany 45; offensive/obscene/menacing messages 160; safe harbor scheme and 319
Goodreads 15
goodwill 68
Google 155; data protection and 280–4; Google Plus 10
government and the state: ECHR cases and 22–3; human rights issues and public authorities 25–6
Greece 12–13
Grieve, Dominic 211
gross offence 131–2, 166; *actus reus* 132; *mens rea* 132–4

hacking *see* computer misuse
harassment 180; conduct amounting to harassment 180; Home Office Review 182; putting people in fear of violence 181; restraining orders 181–2; sentencing 180–1
hate speech *see* offensive/obscene/menacing messages
hearsay evidence 229–31
heritage advertising 345
history of social media 4–5
Hofmeyr, K. 150, 151
Home Office: Review of the Protection from Harassment Act 1997 182
honest opinion: as defence to defamation 87–9

House of Commons: Culture, Media and Sport Committee 55; Justice Committee 167
human rights issues 21; applicants under ECHR 22; background to Human Rights Act 23; balancing of rights 32–5; evidence and 213; fair trial right 26–7; freedom of expression *see* expression, freedom of; Interim Guidelines on Prosecuting Cases Involving Communications Sent via Social Media and 145–7; international jurisprudence and opinion and 35–42; interpretative obligation under Human Rights Act 23–4; limitation periods 26; *locus standi* and 25–6; nature of rights contained within ECHR 21, 26–35; privacy right 27–9; public authorities and 25–6; respondents under ECHR 22–3; rights of particular application to social network sites 26–32
Hungary 13
hyperlinks: defamation and 70–2
Hyves 14

identification of suspects 215–17
image advertisements 363–4
incidental data 7
incitement: public order offences 180
Incorporated Council of Law Reporting (ICLR): contempt of court and 211
indecent messages *see* malicious communications
indirect marketing 347
Information Commissioners Office 18, 235, 262; breach notification and 321, 322–3; erasure of data and 283; location data and 293–4; online forums and 269, 270, 271, 273, 275, 276; retention of data and 286; right to be forgotten and 284; subject access requests and 290, 306–7
information sharing 6–7
information society service (ISS) providers 16–17
information storage 7
injunctions: contempt of court and 201–8, 209–11
Instagram 10
insurance: ABI Report 368–9; common areas of exposure to risk 368; coverage 369–70; key coverage enhancements to seek 370–1; purchasing insurance against social media claims 368
intelligence and security agencies: access to communications data by 19
intention: encouragement or assistance of crime and 168, 173; offensive/obscene/ menacing messages 146–7

Inter-American Commission on Human Rights 36

Interim Guidelines on Prosecuting Cases Involving Communications Sent via Social Media 139; cases decided after implementation of Guidelines 147–51; cases that fall within paras 12(1)–(3) 141–5; general principles 139–40; interrelationships with Human Rights Act 145–7; public order offences 179; refining CPS model 153–5; summary diagrams 152–3

intermediaries: freedom of expression and 37

International Chamber of Commerce (ICC) 343

International Covenant on Civil and Political Rights 1966 (ICCPR) 35–6, 41–2

internet service providers (ISPs): defamation and 54, 69–70, 74, 85

interpretation of legislation: Human Rights Act and 23–4

investigation of suspects 214

IP addresses 262–3

Iran 13

Ireland: Facebook data protection audit 246–8, 277

IWIW 13

Japan 13

jargon 326

Jenkins, Brian 45

Jerrold, Douglas W. 53

jurisdiction: data protection and 311–21; defamation cases 80–2

jurors: contempt of court by 194–201; directions to 198–9

Kaneva 10

Kickstarter 10

Kohlmann, Evan 48

Korea (South): censorship and monitoring 162–3

LaRose, Colleen 49

Last.fm 15

Law Commission: contempt of court and 191–2, 193, 194, 196

legal classifications of social network sites: electronic communications services (ECS) 17–18; information society service (ISS) providers 16–17; Intelligence and Security Committee 19; locating SNS within existing statutory frameworks 16

Leveson Inquiry 155, 250

Li Fei 162

libel *see* defamation

limitation periods: defamation 73; human rights issues and 26

Lindop Report 242

LinkedIn 10

location data 291–4

locus standi: human rights issues and 25–6

LunarStorm 14

McAlpine, Lord 61–2

McCants, William 44, 47, 49

Macgillivray, Alex 159

MacKinnon, Rebecca 47

Magistrates' Court Sentencing Guidelines 154

malicious communications 165–6; distinguishing from Communications Act 2003 166

margin of appreciation 31–2

marketing *see* advertising and marketing

Meetup 10

menacing messages *see* offensive/obscene/ menacing messages

mitigation 171–2; computer misuse 186; contempt of court 205, 206–8; racial aggravation 175–6, 178

Mixi 14

MMPORG sites 9

mobile-only social networks 16, 291–4

moderation 97; online forums 270

monetization of data 328–30

monitoring of communications 160–3

Mubarak, Hosni 49

MySpace 10

Nasza Klasa 14

Neill Report 98, 117, 118

Neri, Alexandra 158

Netherlands 14

Netlog 12

New Zealand: service of claim via social networking site 93, 94

Newsvine 10

Nike 348–50

Nimmo, John 147–8

Odnoklassniki 14

offensive/obscene/menacing messages 129–31, 163–4; aggravating factors 141; anonymity and 148–9; breach of court orders 142; censorship and monitoring 160–3; children and young people and 144–5; context and intent 146–7; CPS Guidelines *see* Interim Guidelines on Prosecuting Cases Involving Communications Sent via Social Media; credible threats 141; freedom of expression and 143, 145–7, 160; meaning

386 *Index*

of 'gross offence' 131–9; private entrapment 149–51; public electronic communications network and 155–7; role of platform providers 155–60; targeting specific individuals 141–2; *see also* malicious communications

offers: amends *see* offers of amends for defamation; Part 36 offers 123

offers of amends for defamation 98–100; acceptance of offer 104–5; additional incentives to accept offer 110–11; apologies 107, 108; consecutive or multiple allegations 103–4; considerations for claimants 121–2; considerations for defendants 122–3; court's case management powers 114–15; damages and 111–16, 115–16; disagreement as to meaning and interpretation 102–3; disqualification of offers 116–20; effective offers 106–8; multiple defendants 105–6; non-acceptance 116; offer 100–2; part offers 103–4; proof of deletion 110–11; qualified offers 102, 115, 119, 122–3; rejection of offer by claimant 120–1; stalemate situations 113; timing of offer 102; undertakings 111; withdrawal or substitution of offer 104

online forums: accuracy of data and 269–76; groups of individuals and 272–3; individuals and 273–4; moderation 270; organizations and 272; personal views, journalists and expression of opinions 274; quality of data 276; use for domestic and non-domestic purposes 275–6

operation of social media: nature of information sharing 6–7; nature of information storing 7

opinion: honest opinion as defence to defamation 87–9; international jurisprudence and opinion on human rights issues 35–42; personal views, journalists and expression of opinions 274

Organization for Economic Co-operation and Development (OECD): guidelines on data protection 242–3

Organization for Security and Cooperation in Europe 36

Orkut 10, 12

Ormerod, D. 18, 221, 225

outsourcing: data protection and 288

overseas establishments: data protection and 311–21

Overton, Iain 61

paid promotions 348–50

paid subscriptions 354

Parks, M. R. 5

Part 36 offers 123

Partyflock 14

passwords: compelling suspect to reveal password 225

PatientsLikeMe 15

Pellerin, Fleur 158

Pengyou QZone 12

personal data 259–63

Pimentel, Jose 49

Pinterest 10

platform providers 155–60

Poland 14

Posterous 11

PR agencies: relationships with bloggers 356–7

press releases 345

pre-ticked boxes 297–8

previous convictions 221

primary publication 69–73

privacy policies and statements 324, 325, 335; *see also* terms of use

privacy right 27–9; definition of 'privacy' 238–40; individual's right of protection 238; privacy enhancing technologies (PETs) 241

private entrapment 149–51

profiling: right to object to 301–4

promotion *see* advertising and marketing

propensity to offend 221

protected proceedings: contempt of court and 208–9

pseudonymous profiles 340

public electronic communications network 155–7

public interest: as defence to defamation 89–90

public order offences 178; case law 177–9; CPS Interim Guidelines 179; incitement 179

publication: defamation and 63–4, 65, 69–80, 108–10; primary 69–73; secondary 69–73, 78–80; single publication rule 73–8; size of audience and 73

publicly available information 222

racial aggravation 175, 177; case law 175–6

real-name requirements 161–2

rectification rights 277–8

Reddit 11

regulation: advertising 343; communications sector *see* communications sector regulation

remedies 22

remorse 178

RenRen 12

repetition rule: defamation and 86–7

reportage: defamation and 90
reputation: bloggers and 357; protection of 223; risks of using automated systems 324
restraining orders 181–2
retention of personal data 285–7, 336–7
Rome Memorandum 245–6, 251–3
Russia 14

safe harbor scheme 318–21
sanctions: CAP Code 345; penalties for breaching financial promotions regime 365–6
Savile, Jimmy 61
Schoeman, F. D. 238
search engines: defamation and 72
Second Life 11
secondary publication 69–73, 78–80
security: data security 240–1, 339
self-regulation: defamation and 82–5
sensitive personal information 262, 264
sentencing: computer misuse 183–4, 187; contempt of court 204; harassment 180–1; racial aggravation and 176
Serious Crime Prevention Orders 168–9
service data 7
service of claim via social networking site 92–5
sexual history: evidence of 217
sharing of information 6–7
Sina Corp 160–1
Sina Weibo 12
single publication rule 73–8
slander *see* defamation
Smith, Mike Deri 148
Snapchat 11
social interaction 5–6
soft opt-in 297
Sorley, Isabella 147–8
sources of law: defamation 54–7
Spain 14; data protection in 280–4
spiteful postings 222
storage of information 7
strict liability 98, 192, 193
StumbleUpon 11
subject access requests 290–1, 336; Data Protection Directive and 310–11; disproportionate effort 309; exemptions 308–9; ICO code on 290, 306–7; non-obvious identifiers and 307–8; opinion of Article 29 Working Party 305–6; repeated or unreasonable requests 309–10; social network sites and 307–8; ss 7 and 8 of DPA 2998 304–5
subscriptions 354
substantial harm test: defamation and 64–9

summary judgments: defamation 123
suspects: compelling suspect to reveal password 225; identification of 215–17; investigation of 214
Sweden 14

tagging 166, 338, 340
Taliban 43, 47
taxonomy of social networking data: diagram of monitoring and engagement 8; types of data processed 7
technical jargon 326
technology: courts dealing with technology 197–8; privacy enhancing technologies (PETs) 241; technology outstripping the law 55
Tencent Weibo 12
terms of use 324, 347; aggregate data 330; assessing what data organization is gathering 326–7; being bound by terms of use 325; data utilization and monetization 328–30; defamation and 82–3; Facebook Beacon 331–4; incorporation into contracts 325; making sure individuals understand 327; reserving wide discretion 326; technical jargon 326; unfair terms 325; unilateral right to vary terms 326; use of 'like' buttons, plug-ins and analytics 330–1
terrorism 42–3; case law 48–9; platform providers' response to 45–8; retention of data and 285–6; social media and 43–4; US Committee on Homeland Security's Subcommittee on Counterterrorism and Intelligence 44–5
testimonials by bloggers 355–9
third parties: apps 337–8; data transfers by 287–91; disclosures to 338; insurance coverage for third party loss 370
threats *see* malicious communications
ticked boxes 297–8
timing of publication 63–4
Travbuddy 15
'trending' topics 62–3
TripAdvisor 15
truth: as defence to defamation 86–7
Tuenti 14
Twitter 155, 156, 166, 239; censorship and monitoring 161; contempt of court and 203–4, 205; defamation and 61, 75–7, 83–4, 108–10; marketing and 348–50, 351–3; offensive/obscene/menacing messages 147–8, 157–8, 159; racial aggravation and 175–6, 177; response to terrorism and 45–7; re-tweeting 75–7, 108–10; terms of use 83–4
Twoo 11

388 *Index*

Ubhey, Baljit 147, 148
Unabhängige Landeszentrum für
  Datenschutz (ULD) 330–1
unfair terms 325
unfair trading regulations 345–7
Union of French Jewish Students (UEJF)
  157–8
United Nations: Comprehensive Study
  on Cybercrime Paper 38–42; Counter-
  Terrorism Committee 43; Human Rights
  Committee (HRC) 35, 36; International
  Covenant on Civil and Political Rights 1966
  (ICCPR) 35–6, 41–2; Special Rapporteur
  on Freedom of Expression 35, 36–7
United States of America 159; authentication
  issues 228–9; Committee on Homeland
  Security's Subcommittee on
  Counterterrorism and Intelligence 44–5;
  defamation in 77–8; endorsements and
  testimonials by bloggers and 357–8;
  evidence in 214; Federal Trade
  Commission 350, 357–8; hearsay evidence
  231; marketing 350–3; private entrapment
  149–50; safe harbor scheme 318–21; service
  of claim via social networking site 94–5
utility of social media 3

vertically organized communities gathered
  round specific topic 15

Viadeo 11
video games: advergames 359
vigilantism 149–50, 216–17
virtual worlds 9
VKontakte 14

Warren, S. D. 238–9
website operators: defence against
  defamation 90–7
Weibo 162
Weimann, Gabriel 43
Weisburd, Aaron 44
Wiser.org 15
witnesses 224–5
Woods, Matthew 136–7, 146
Word of Mouth Marketing Association
  (WOMMA) 350–1
Wordpress 11

Xing 11

Yammer 11
Younger Committee Report 242, 243
YouTube 12; censorship and
  monitoring 161; response to terrorism
  and 47

Zoo 12
Zooppa 15